Mastering

Rational XDE

Mastering™
Rational® XDE

Wendy Boggs

Michael Boggs

SYBEX® San Francisco London

Associate Publisher: Joel Fugazzotto

Acquisitions and Developmental Editor: Tom Cirtin

Production Editor: Mae Lum

Technical Editor: Eric Aker

Copyeditor: Rebecca Rider

Compositor: Maureen Forys, Happenstance Type-O-Rama

Graphic Illustrator: Maureen Forys, Happenstance Type-O-Rama

Proofreaders: Amey Garber, Emily Hsuan, Darcey Maurer, Laurie O'Connell, Nancy Riddiough, Monique van den Berg

Indexer: Lynnzee Elze

Book Designer: Maureen Forys, Happenstance Type-O-Rama

Cover Designer: Design Site

Cover Illustrator: Tania Kac, Design Site

Library of Congress Card Number: 2003101651

ISBN: 0-7821-4205-2

Manufactured in the United States of America

10 9 8 7 6 5 4 3 2 1

For Katherine

Acknowledgments

WE WOULD LIKE TO extend our heartfelt thanks to the many people who were instrumental in putting this book together. Thank you to Tom Cirtin, who helped us develop the concept and content of this book, and to Eric Aker for his technical review. Thanks to the Sybex editorial and production team: Mae Lum, Rebecca Rider, and Maureen Forys. Thanks to the indexer Lynnzee Elze and to the proofreaders: Amey Garber, Emily Hsuan, Darcey Maurer, Laurie O'Connell, Nancy Riddiough, and Monique van den Berg. And, of course, thanks as always to our friends and family for your continual support and encouragement.

Contents at a Glance

Contents

Appendix

Introduction

My, isn't it nice to get out of the Stone Age? Back in the days of the caveman, people had to worry about finding food and getting eaten by dinosaurs. They soon developed a language to communicate with one another. Then, those cavemen figured out how to build simple tools like a rock hammer. Ever since, we have been evolving further; we still need to find food, but with a McDonald's or Carl's Jr. on every street corner, it is a bit easier now. As for the dinosaurs...well, they're extinct and we're not.

In the ever-changing world of software development, we're also coming out of the Stone Age. Back in the early years of software development, we had development languages, but modeling and designing were pretty much left to the individual to figure out. Like the cavemen, we developed some rudimentary tools to help in our daily lives. These initial development tools became more and more refined as the years went on and computers became more powerful. Then came the concepts of object orientation. With these concepts came some tools for modeling, including the Unified Modeling Language (UML). As the concepts of object orientation evolved, more tools were developed to aid people in modeling and designing systems. For many years, Rational Rose was one of the prominent modeling tools that was available.

With the introduction of Rational Rose, modelers could model systems following object-oriented principles and could even generate skeletal code from that model. Users of Rose could even take existing code and reverse engineer the model from that code. As a result of Rose, designers, developers, and architects had the tools they needed to do their job effectively and efficiently. The software development world had changed. We were no longer in the Stone Age but had passed into the Modern Age.

In this modern age, developers and designers had wonderful tools to do their job. But one of the difficulties that still existed was integrating these tools. Designers came up with their models and generated code from it. Developers made changes to the code and had to get it back into the model.

One day, a developer was walking down the street toward a corner carrying his development tool. Coming up to the same corner from a different street was a designer carrying his modeling tool. Unfortunately, the two of them were so engrossed in what they were carrying that they weren't looking at where they were going and WHAM! They ran into each other. Both of them tumbled to the ground and the tools they were carrying got all mixed up. When they stood up and dusted themselves off, the two tools they were carrying were now inextricably linked. "Your development environment is in my modeler!" said the designer. "You've got your modeler in my development environment!" cried the developer. Then, they both noticed that the new tool was quite good and well integrated. They named it XDE, for the Xtremely Determined Engineers who weren't paying attention and ran into each other!

The newest step in tool evolution has now occurred with the release of Rational XDE. *Now the development environment and the modeling tool have become one.* The issues of code and model synchronization are no longer plaguing the people.

Who Should Read This Book

This book is designed for beginning and intermediate users of Rational XDE, as well as those who are just getting interested in it. As we developed this book, we tried to do so from the perspective of someone with experience in object-oriented analysis, design, and development. Readers should be familiar with the Unified Modeling Language (UML) as well as object-oriented development, especially using Java or Microsoft .NET. For those of you without a grounding in the UML, please turn first to the Appendix, "Getting Started with the UML."

This book covers the fundamentals of Rational XDE:

- How to navigate in XDE
- How to create use case diagrams and tie them to requirements repositories
- How to create sequence diagrams
- How to create class diagrams
- How to create statechart diagrams
- How to create Enterprise JavaBeans (EJB)
- How to synchronize the model with Java or .NET code
- How to model databases
- How to create component and deployment diagrams
- How to share your models with other team members
- How to use and create your own patterns
- How to store patterns as Reusable Asset Specifications (RAS)

This book does not need to be read sequentially. Each chapter was designed to give you a detailed understanding of one piece of Rational XDE. We have provided exercises at the end of the chapters to give you some practice using XDE. However, these exercises do build on the exercises from previous chapters.

Although the book explains the fundamentals of XDE and modeling elements, it does not cover every feature of XDE. If you are new to XDE, we recommend that you read the chapters sequentially and complete all of the exercises. The exercises walk you through modeling a sample system. Once again, if you are unfamiliar with the UML, consult the UML primer at the back of the book.

How This Book is Organized

This book is organized into twelve chapters divided into three parts, followed by an appendix, all of which are described in the following sections.

Part I: Liberated Development with Rational XDE

Part I introduces you to Rational XDE and how XDE is used in the software development lifecycle. The exercises in Parts II and III help you continue this learning process. These exercises build a timekeeping system, which is introduced in Chapter 3. So, by the end of Part I, you should understand the functionality of XDE, where it fits in the software development lifecycle, and you should be familiar with the background on which the exercises in Parts II and III are based.

Chapter 1: Introduction to Rational XDE We cover the evolution of modeling tools and the Unified Modeling Language. We discuss the different UML diagrams available in XDE.

Chapter 2: XDE and the Software Development Lifecycle This chapter illustrates how XDE fits in the scheme of things. We look at activities in both the Rational Unified Process and Extreme Programming methodologies.

Chapter 3: Introduction to the Exercises: A Study for Real-World Application Development The remainder of the book includes exercises that help you learn how to use Rational XDE. In this chapter, we introduce the scenario on which these exercises are based; we look at a fictitious hotel chain, StayHere, Inc. StayHere is developing a timekeeping system and wants to use XDE to do so. All exercises are related to the timekeeping system for StayHere.

Part II: Visual Modeling with XDE

Part II details how you use XDE. We cover how to create the various UML diagrams and how to model Java and Microsoft .NET elements. We also discuss database modeling and how to share the model with other developers. When you have read Part II, you should be able to create use case, sequence, class, component, deployment, and freeform diagrams. You should also be able to transform entity classes into database tables and generate the database. Lastly, you should be able to share your model with other team members by reporting and publishing the model to the Web.

Chapter 4: Integrated Use Case Management XDE gives you the ability to create use case diagrams and manage use cases in RequisitePro. We explain how to create use cases and diagrams in XDE. We also discuss the integration to Rational RequisitePro and detail procedures for using it. The exercise in this chapter covers using Rational XDE to create use cases and to manage use case specifications.

Chapter 5: Modeling Java and J2EE Elements in XDE Chapter 5 covers the use of Rational XDE with a Java development environment. We explain how XDE can be used with either the Eclipse Java platform or IBM WebSphere. We also discuss how to create the various UML diagrams and Java elements, and illustrate how to synchronize the code and the model. We also introduce how to use Enterprise JavaBeans (EJB) technology and talk about the strong support that Rational XDE provides to EJB developers.

Chapter 6: Modeling Visual Studio .NET Elements in XDE This chapter covers Rational XDE for .NET. This environment provides Microsoft .NET developers with a cohesive modeling and development tool. We discuss the UML diagrams and constructs that you can create using XDE, and we highlight the code and model synchronization. The exercise in this chapter demonstrates the capabilities of modeling .NET elements for the StayHere timekeeping system.

Chapter 7: Modeling Databases with XDE Databases are an important aspect of most software projects, so XDE allows you to model databases as well as objects. We cover transforming entity classes into database tables, generating databases, and reverse engineering databases. In the exercise, you transform some of the entity objects in the timekeeping project into database tables.

Chapter 8: Publishing and Reporting Models Once you have modeled the application in XDE, you need to share this information with other team members. XDE contains web publishing capability as well as some standard model reports. You can use these features to share information from the XDE model with all members of your team, even those who do not have direct access to XDE.

PART III: PATTERNS

XDE includes a set of Gang-of-Four patterns that we discuss in detail and show you how to use in this part. Also, XDE gives you the ability to create your own patterns and save them so that they can be used by others. By the end of Part III, you should have a general understanding of the Gang-of-Four patterns and how to apply them. Furthermore, you should be able to create your own patterns and save them as Reusable Asset Specifications.

Chapter 9: Using Patterns XDE comes with some standard Gang-of-Four patterns that you can use in your projects. This chapter discusses how to use such patterns in your model, and we also cover binding patterns to your model. In the exercise, we illustrate the use of one of the Gang-of-Four patterns in the timekeeping project.

Chapter 10: Gang-of-Four Patterns Many Gang-of-Four patterns come with XDE. We discuss each pattern that you can use in detail. In this chapter, the exercise is a thought experiment in which we discuss where some of the Gang-of-Four patterns could be used in the timekeeping project.

Chapter 11: Introduction to Reusable Asset Specifications While Chapters 9 and 10 introduce how to use patterns, this chapter shows you how to package patterns so that they can be used by others. This functionality largely applies to patterns you create, so the exercise of saving a pattern as a Reusable Asset Specification is left to Chapter 12.

Chapter 12: Creating Your Own Patterns Chapter 12 discusses how to create your own patterns that you can use in your applications. The exercise covers creating patterns and saving them as Reusable Asset Specifications.

APPENDIX: GETTING STARTED WITH THE UML

The appendix is a UML primer for those who are not familiar with the UML specification. The appendix covers the basics of the different types of UML diagrams, and the notation that is used on each of the diagrams. If you aren't familiar with the UML, the appendix is a good place to start, before you read the remainder of this book.

About the Website

In the book, as we explore the features of XDE, we'll build some XDE models for a sample timekeeping system. On the web page that accompanies this book, you will find XDE models that represent the completion of each exercise. We've also included a link to the Rational website, from which you can find all sorts of information about Rational partners and products, the UML, and object modeling. A link to the Rational Developer Network (RDN) is also provided. RDN is a service for licensed users of Rational products and it includes white papers, patterns, process modules, and more.

Go to the Sybex website (`www.sybex.com`), use the Catalog or Search tool to find this book's web page, and click the Downloads button.

How to Contact the Authors

If you have any questions at all about XDE, or you need further assistance, please feel free to contact us. You can contact Wendy at `wboggs@boggsconsulting.com`, or Mike at `mboggs@boggsconsulting.com`.

Part I

Liberated Development with Rational XDE

In this part:

Chapter 1

Introduction to Rational XDE

RATIONAL HAS DEVELOPED AN exciting new tool designed especially for designers and developers of Java and Microsoft .NET applications. This tool combines the modeling power of Rational Rose with the Integrated Development Environment (IDE) of a programming tool. This chapter introduces you to this new tool—Rational eXtended Development Environment (XDE)—some of its features, and how it can be used in systems design and development.

Featured in this chapter:

- Evolution of XDE
- Introducing visual modeling
- Introducing Java and visual modeling
- Introducing .NET and visual modeling
- Features of Rational XDE
- XDE user interface
- Versions of Rational XDE

In the Beginning...

It is evening. The sky is still and there is a hush across the savannah as the cavemen gather excitedly around the stony wall. A small lizard scurries in and then, as if sensing the tension in the air, hastily scuttles away again. Grunting nervously, the leader of the cavemen reaches for a jagged rock and carefully begins marking the wall's surface. One of the others grunts out a name. Gradually, a stick figure emerges, then an oval. Some in the group yell and point wildly as the leader scratches a thin line between the other symbols. The excitement grows as he inscribes names for these items: "Actor" and "Use Case." It is evening, and a system has been born.

This was the world before XDE.

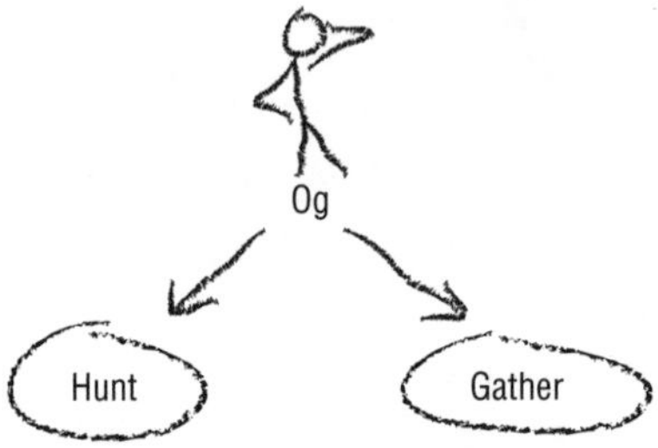

Okay, so maybe it wasn't that bad, but we have evolved a little. Back in the good old days, we would work with a Unified Modeling Language (UML) tool such as Rational Rose to design our system and its architecture. Then we would move all that stuff over to a development environment such as IBM's WebSphere to write the actual code to the design specifications. The UML tool would help a lot in this transition by automatically creating at least some skeletal code from the design. So there we were, switching to a new tool. But then, oops! We would need to change the system design, so we'd have to switch back to the UML tool. We'd work on the design a little, but then we need to switch back to the development tool to code some more. So we'd make the transition again, using the round-trip engineering features of the UML tool. But once again, we'd discover we needed to change the design, so it would be back to the other tool. After a while, we'd make some changes and, gulp! We'd realize that we forgot to synchronize those changes back in the model. So then our model would be out of sync with the code. A few dizzying cycles of this, and an aspirin or two, and we'd probably have gotten a little frustrated.

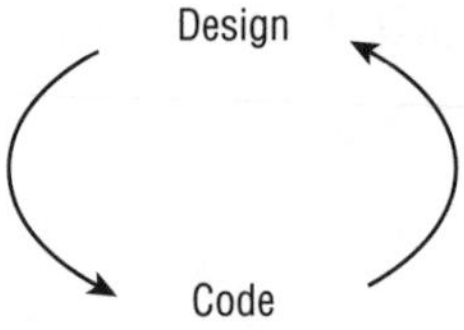

And so it went. We were still able to design and code our system, but the switching back and forth between tools could become a bit of a headache. Once the model and code were out of sync, it became an increasingly difficult task to realign them.

One of the problems was that constantly switching environments led to a shift in focus. We'd take off our designer hats and put on our programming hats to work in WebSphere, and then we'd put our designer hats back on to work in Rose. This type of transition does not always lead to good code. The developers should *always* be thinking about the system design as they're building the code. Chances are, as they are working on code, they'll find areas of the design that could use a little optimization. On the other side, the designers *always* have to keep the code in mind as they are building the system design. On many projects, the developers and designers are actually the same people. Aside from the split personality issues, they have to use multiple tools and switch back and forth between them to accomplish their goals. Rational XDE changes all that.

XDE was specifically designed to break down the "brick wall" barrier between design and coding—to help us keep in mind that they are just different perspectives of the same solution. Just as requirements can't be thrown over the wall to designers, the system design shouldn't be thrown over the wall to the developers. XDE helps us see the system design *and* code as we go along, rather than allowing us to become too focused on one or the other. It combines the design and development environments into a single, comprehensive tool. We will spend a lot of time in this book discussing the two main perspectives of XDE—code and design—and how these integrate into a system.

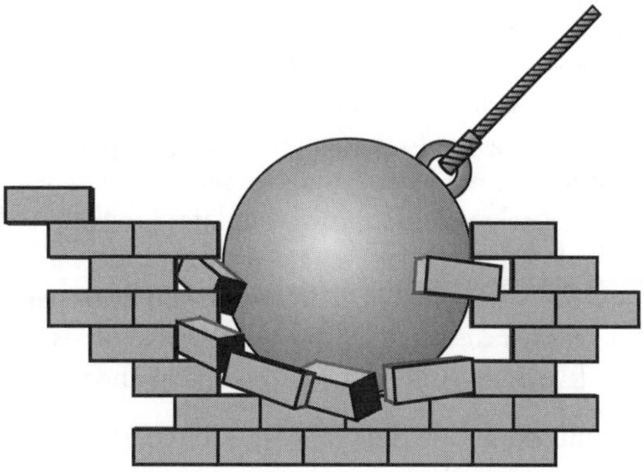

Another challenge the development teams ran into was keeping the code and the design synchronized. Although tools would help with this process, it was still a laborious effort, and in many cases, it caused teams to let the two get out of sync. As a result, the systems became difficult to maintain. Teams didn't have a clear picture of the system design without poring over hundreds or even thousands of lines of code. Frequently, the team undertaking an enhancement to one of these systems would need to reconstruct a goodly portion of the design in order to get their arms around the system and be able to proceed with the changes.

Sometimes the development teams want to rework some code in their systems to bring them into current standards or take advantage of new ideas. This kind of reworking really occurs during the first development of a system. If you are a developer, take a look at some code you wrote early in a project compared to that from a later iteration. Are you still willing to claim authorship of the original code? Or would you rather make some changes to it before showing it to others?

This concept of reworking the code is referred to as *refactoring*. It is often done, but very informally and on an ad-hoc basis. The problem is that some chunks of the system become optimized and standardized, but other chunks go untouched. Different people can refactor different chunks of the system without using a consistent method to do so. This causes many of the true benefits of refactoring—code standardization, optimization, consistency, and readability—to go unfulfilled. As you go through a project, you should always be looking for opportunities to improve the design and code. But if refactoring is such a great thing, why aren't more companies doing it? Some of the reasons we've heard are

- There is barely enough time in the project to finish it, let alone think about making it better.
- Refactoring is perceived to be a manual and difficult process.
- Developers like working on new and exciting things, not on tweaking the things they've already built.

With all these issues floating around, no wonder refactoring isn't done more often! But XDE can help make this task more palatable and even enjoyable. Granted, XDE can't bend the laws of time and space to give you more time on the project, but it can help make some of the more tedious tasks of design and development easier and quicker. For example, XDE can keep the model and code synchronized at all times. You can now invest the time you've been spending doing this tedious task in refactoring. XDE can also decrease the amount of time you need to use patterns. Before XDE, you selected a pattern you wanted, designed it, and coded it. Now you can select the pattern you want, walk through a short wizard, and it is *built for you.* Again, you can now invest the time you save in refactoring—or in going home on time for once! Now that XDE has given you all this extra time to spend refactoring, we're going to sweeten the deal by explaining how you can cut the refactoring work itself in half. Because the model and code are synchronized, you only have to refactor one or the other. Without the synchronization, you would need to refactor both the code and the model, and then manually check to be sure the two are synchronized.

Finally, another problem you encounter when you use separate design and development tools is not being able to easily take advantage of *reuse.* Reusability is the holy grail of object-oriented development, yet few developers really achieve it. Some of the reasons for this are

- Project teams don't have time to look into reusing pieces of other projects.
- Frequently, there is no repository of reusable items that a team can browse. By the time they track down the potentially reusable items, they've lost the time advantage that they would have gained from reuse.
- A project may be perceived as "so different from anything that's been done before that we couldn't possibly reuse anything."

Promoting reuse is one of the major reasons Rational created XDE. It incorporates both design and implementation patterns into a single environment. The tool lets you browse and incorporate elements of multiple models. Rather than have you research patterns in a book, learn how to use the ones you want, and then manually design and code them, you can simply walk through a few wizards to incorporate the patterns into your model and code. Because XDE lets you implement patterns at a granular level, you are working with patterns that can apply in just about any system. Even if the organization's business processes are unique, you can take advantage of reuse as much as possible. We will be focusing a great deal on patterns and refactoring in this book, and we'll show you how XDE can help in both of these areas.

Introducing Visual Modeling

Visual modeling is, as its name suggests, a way to visualize the design and architecture of a software system. The concept has been around for a long time, but the notation has changed. Remember those flowcharts we had to create in college before we wrote the code? (Actually, most of us built the flowcharts *after* we wrote the code, but that's another issue.) Visual modeling is essentially the evolution of that concept. It is a blueprint we create before we code, so that we know the code will have a solid design foundation.

One of the key advantages to visual modeling is that you can use it to make changes to a software system relatively cheaply. Let's go back for a minute to the practice of creating the flowchart after we wrote the code. It was nice to eventually have a documented design, but we lost the ability to really analyze the system architecture before the code was written. Once the code is built, it can be extremely difficult to make changes to the design, especially extensive changes. If we build a visual model, though, we can analyze, tear apart, and restructure the system's architecture before the code is even built. Over the lifetime of a system, this can save thousands or even hundreds of thousands in maintenance costs.

This is especially relevant for large-scale systems. Without a blueprint, there is no guarantee that the code created by different developers will integrate. There is also no guarantee that the same design approach was taken in different parts of the system, or that the code is consistent. The only way for someone to understand the system structure is to go through the code itself, trying to visualize how the system was put together and how it can best be modified.

We wouldn't do this with buildings (imagine someone trying to build a skyscraper with no blueprints), but we've been able to get away with it, at least to a certain extent, in information technology. This is because an information system is somewhat unique—it is possible to go back in and change the architecture of a system that has already been built. It may not be easy, it may not be cheap, but it is possible. This practice has come at a great cost, though, and we in the information technology industry are moving past this informal way of designing applications to a more systematic approach.

A fairly recent development in visual modeling is the creation of the UML, which is used by XDE, and will be used extensively in this book. The UML is a series of diagrams and a set of notation that is used to visually model system design. It was first developed in the mid 1990s, as the three methodologists Grady Booch, Ivar Jacobson, and James Rumbaugh (collectively known as the "three amigos") sought to unify their different modeling approaches. These three experts worked with other methodologists to incorporate best practices from the many different modeling notations available at the time, such as Object-Oriented Software Engineering (OOSE), Booch, and Object Modeling Technology (OMT). UML version 0.9 was released in 1996. In 1997, a consortium of individuals and companies organized by Rational Software responded to a request for proposal by the Object Management Group (OMG) for a common metamodel to describe software-intensive systems.

Over time, the UML has been modified and expanded to incorporate ideas from new techniques and technologies, such as web application development and formal business modeling. However, it has remained independent of any specific tool, programming language, or development methodology. Instead, it is intended to be a general notation that you can use to analyze and design any object-oriented system.

The UML is currently controlled and maintained by the OMG, a vendor-independent standards body. Many companies, both large and small, have worked with the OMG to contribute to the growth and development of the UML. For more information about the OMG, or to download the latest UML specifications, see `www.omg.org`.

The UML contains many different types of diagrams, as shown in Table 1.1. Each of these is intended to give you a slightly different perspective of the system. Use Case diagrams, for example, give you a sense of what the system will do from the customers' point of view. Class diagrams are created from the developers' point of view, and Component diagrams from a system integrator's point of view. Taken together, these diagrams give the team a complete picture of the system and its architecture.

TABLE 1.1: UML DIAGRAMS

DIAGRAM TYPE	PURPOSE
Use Case	Communicates to the customer what functionality (in terms of use cases) is in the project scope, and who the system actors (anyone or anything interacting with the system) are.
Activity	Shows the workflow in a business process; or shows the steps through a use case.
Collaboration	Shows the objects participating in a scenario of a use case, how the objects are related, and the messages sent between the objects.
Sequence	Shows the objects participating in a scenario of a use case, how the objects are related, and the messages sent between the objects. A sequence diagram shows the same information as a collaboration diagram, but in a different format.
Class	Diagrams the classes (or a subset of the classes) in a system, along with their relationships, attributes, and operations. Class diagrams may also show packages of classes or subsystems.
Statechart	Shows the dynamic behavior of an object, including the states in which it may exist, how it transitions between the states, and how it behaves in each of the states.
Component	Shows the physical components that make up the system, and their dependencies.
Deployment	Addresses how the system will be deployed.

With the complete blueprint provided by the UML diagrams, the team can debate and then document the decisions made in the system architecture. More importantly, the diagrams become a repository of information that the team members can use to communicate more effectively with one another. Anyone needing to see information related to the system design can simply examine the UML diagrams.

The UML appears to be rapidly becoming the standard modeling language used in the industry. It has been adopted as a standard by numerous organizations, and more and more tools are being created to support the notation.

What's New in UML 1.4

The most recent version of the UML is version 1.4, which was made public in 2001. Some of the major changes made in this version include the following:

Refinement of component modeling This is to better support the modeling of component-based systems using technologies such as Enterprise JavaBeans (EJB) or COM+.

Refinement of collaborations and collaboration instances The UML specification now includes formal descriptions of collaborations (a set of roles and associations that define the participants needed to accomplish a specific task), interactions (the communications between the participants), instances, and collaboration instance sets. The new UML specification also introduces the concept of a parameterized collaboration, which is a generic way of representing a design pattern. These types of collaborations can be used for documenting design patterns and frameworks.

Refinement of profiles Profiles are used to model a specific implementation of the UML. The UML specification now more clearly defines how the UML can be extended and customized for a specific domain. It requires that profiles extend, rather than modify, the documented UML specifications.

In addition, many other minor changes and refinements were made to the specification. For a complete copy of the UML 1.4 specification, see `www.omg.org`. Work is currently underway to develop version 2.0 of the UML, which will be a major revision of the standard. Visual modeling is becoming increasingly important. In fact, UML 2.0 is designed to pave the way for executable models. See the OMG website for more information.

Introducing Java and Visual Modeling

Due to the richness of the UML and the fact that Java is a pure object-oriented language, the majority of Java constructs can be easily modeled in the UML. UML can be used with *Java 2 Standard Edition (J2SE)* or *Java 2 Enterprise Edition (J2EE)*.

J2SE is an object-oriented language developed in the 1990s. Java is a strongly typed language where object-oriented constructs are strictly enforced. Its structure is similar to C++, but Java does not use pointers. It can be used to create applications, web applets, and other types of systems. J2SE has the capability to create database applications and widely scaled applications, but it lacks a form of support for concurrency and persistence. J2EE is more suited for those types of uses.

At its core, J2EE is a set of classes and interfaces that the developer can build upon to more easily create database and enterprise applications. Servlets and EJBs are the major constructs used in J2EE. They let the developer write thin-client interfaces to processes that run on an application server. EJBs can even automatically handle the persistence of information for a session and have built-in functionality for communicating with other EJBs.

In Chapter 5, "Modeling Java and J2EE Elements in XDE," we will discuss Java modeling and XDE in detail. In this section, we provide a brief mapping of standard J2SE and J2EE elements to the UML.

Java classes Each Java class is represented in the UML as a compartmentalized rectangle as shown here:

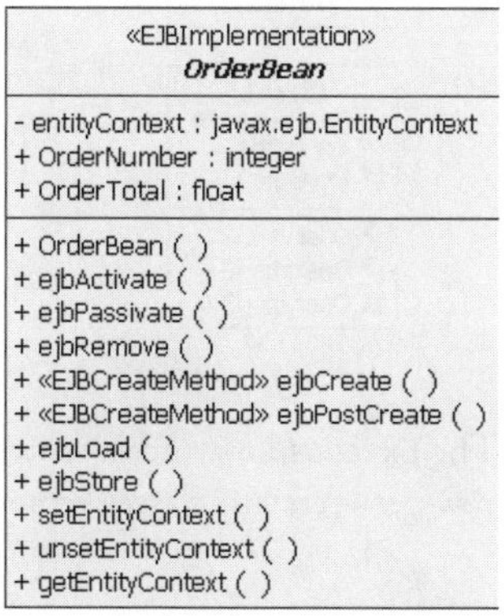

This rectangle can be broken down into the following components:

Class name The top portion of the rectangle shows the *class name*. The class name in the model and the class name in the code should be exactly the same. If the class is abstract, the class name will be italicized.

Stereotype The top portion may also show the *stereotype* of the class. A stereotype is a UML mechanism for describing different types of an element. For example, interfaces and EJB Session Beans are special types of classes, and both can be considered class stereotypes.

Attributes The middle section of the rectangle stores the variables, or *attributes*, of the class. The attribute name is followed by a colon and its data type. Variables can be modeled either in the classes or as a relationship with another class.

Operations The lower section of the rectangle shows the methods, or *operations*, of the class.

PACKAGES

A package in the UML is analogous to a package in Java. In addition, the UML supports the idea of *subsystems*, which are packages of classes that implement one or more interfaces. The UML symbol for a package is shown here:

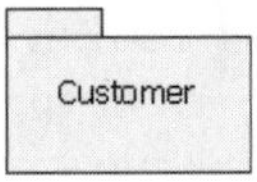

`Interfaces` and `Implements keyword` A Java interface is shown in the UML as a class with a stereotype of <<Interface>>. On a diagram, there are two ways to show that a class realizes an interface: by using a realizes relationship (top) or by using the interface "lollypop" notation (bottom).

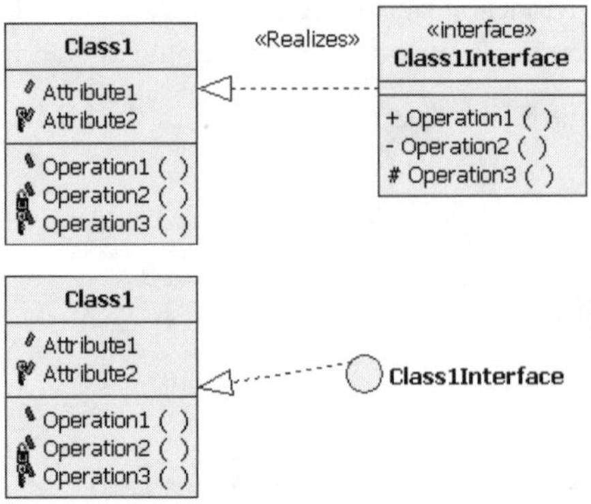

`Extends` keyword The `Extends` keyword is represented in the UML by a *generalization* relationship. This type of arrow between two classes represents an inheritance relationship:

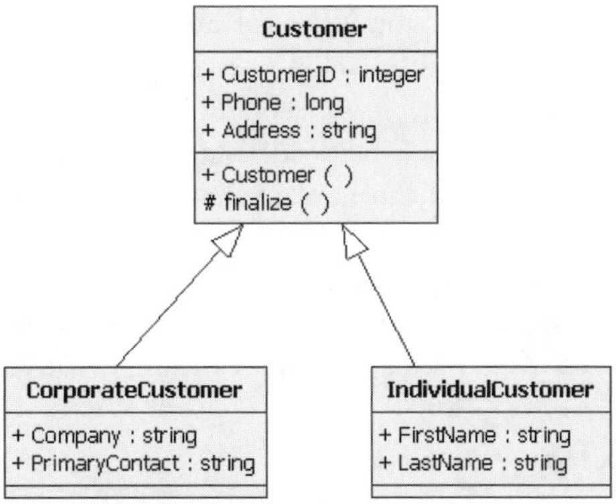

Java is one of the pure object-oriented (OO) languages and is therefore perfectly suited to the UML. In Chapter 5, we'll discuss the use of Java and XDE in greater detail.

Introducing .NET and Visual Modeling

.NET is a new framework used to simplify the design and development of distributed applications. It handles much of the system infrastructure for you, including items such as memory management, thread management, security, and the intricacies of managing distributed components. It can be used to develop many types of applications, such as web-based applications, XML web services, or Windows applications.

The two pieces of the .NET Framework are the *Common Language Runtime (CLR)* and the *.NET Framework class library*. The CLR handles the system at execution time, dealing with issues such as memory management, security, thread management, and type checking. The .NET Framework class library is a framework of classes that the developer uses during the coding process.

The crux of all this is that it allows developers to focus on implementing business functionality, rather than having to worry about infrastructure details. This, in turn, speeds the application development process.

Like Java, .NET classes and constructs can be modeled in XDE using the UML. XDE supports modeling, code generation, and reverse engineering of Visual Basic .NET, ASP .NET, and C# .NET. In Chapter 6, "Modeling Visual Studio .NET Elements in XDE," we'll discuss the use of .NET and XDE in greater detail.

What is Rational XDE?

Pop Quiz!

What is XDE?

(A) eXtensive Documentation Editor?

(B) eX-Director of Enron?

(C) eXpensive Dial-up Entity?

(D) X-ray Detection Emitters?

(E) None of the above!

If you guessed (e), you're right! XDE is Rational's new *eXtended Development Environment*, and it represents a new way to design and develop systems. Rational defines XDE as "a complete visual design and development environment." It is essentially a design tool that is available directly in an IDE. But it is also much more than this. It takes advantage of patterns, lets you work with multiple models, maintains code and model synchronization, and integrates with leading tools for requirements management and version control.

XDE was built from the ground-up for developers, and is primarily a tool for designers and developers. In many organizations, the designers *are* the developers. Rather than switch from a design tool to a development tool and back again, they can simply use XDE.

Features of XDE

In this section, we will take a look at the different features of XDE. The features available vary a little depending upon the version of XDE you have: XDE Modeler, XDE Professional .NET Edition, or XDE Professional Java Platform Edition. See the upcoming "Versions of XDE" section in this chapter for a discussion of which features are available in which version. The following is a summary of the key features of XDE:

Cross-model references Rather than needing to keep the entire design and implementation for a system in a single model, you can create as many different models as you need for different pieces of the system or to represent different perspectives of the system. One model can reference elements contained in a separate model. XDE pulls together information from several different models into a comprehensive picture.

System perspectives To really understand a system, you have to see it from many different perspectives. The customer is concerned with the functionality. The architect is concerned with how the system is decomposed into layers and subsystems, and how those elements relate. A developer is concerned with how the code is structured. A database administrator is concerned with database structure, triggers, and stored procedures. XDE includes the concept of a "perspective" to help you see the system from these different angles. Although you can always switch perspectives to get to the information you need, you can use a perspective to see one aspect of the system.

Reusable Asset Specifications (RAS) Rational has developed an innovative way to create and share reusable components. While many design patterns and code templates exist, the Reusable Asset Specification (RAS) combines these elements. As you complete projects and find reusable assets, you can create your own RAS for those assets and share them with other project teams.

Gang-of-Four (GOF) patterns Some of the most widely used design patterns were developed by Erich Gamma, Richard Helm, Ralph Johnson, and John Vlissides. This group of designers became known as the "Gang of Four." These patterns have been incorporated into many systems and can greatly speed up the development process. XDE has extensive support for the Gang-of-Four patterns, allowing you to incorporate them through the use of wizards.

Ability to build and reuse patterns We spend so much of our time reinventing the wheel, especially in software development. XDE includes a built-in pattern engine and pattern wizards that will let you gather your existing design or code information into a reusable pattern. You can apply patterns, either industry standard or your own, simply by selecting them in XDE.

Patterns are doing for the design world what components have already begun to do for the programming world: they give us the ability to reuse a concept so that building a system becomes more of a process of assembling what's already there than of building things.

Integration with leading IDEs As already mentioned, XDE is an eXtended Development Environment. As such, it integrates seamlessly directly into popular development tools such as IBM WebSphere Studio and Microsoft Visual Studio .NET. The developer can use the modeling tool as a direct part of their development environment. The integration also makes code and model synchronization easier.

Synchronization of code and model Some of the best designers still have the problem of keeping the model and code in sync with one another. One of the unique things about this tool is its ability to *automatically* keep the code and the design synchronized. It makes code generation and reverse engineering a simple, day-to-day operation rather then a complex effort undertaken only when needed. You can work on either the code or the design model, and XDE will automatically update the other.

Assisted modeling In order to help developers get up to speed on the UML, XDE includes wizards written for specific programming languages. It isn't necessary for a developer to be a UML expert to model their system. XDE will present information in familiar terms and assist the developer in the modeling process.

Industry-standard UML modeling at all levels of abstraction As previously mentioned, the UML is the Unified Modeling Language and it is an industry-standard notation for modeling systems. XDE supports UML version 1.4 and lets you create the following types of diagrams in your models: Class, Use Case, Activity, Statechart, Sequence, Component, and Deployment.

Model validation XDE can review your model, looking for compliance to the UML or to language-specific guidelines. This feature helps keep the design and the code consistent as the project goes along, rather than having the team wait until the end, and potentially recode or redesign a portion of the system. Of course, formal code reviews and design reviews are still a good idea.

Free-form modeling Sometimes the UML isn't quite enough to meet a project's needs. XDE gives you the option of creating new diagrams using your own graphics and notation. For example, you can create a network diagram or an overview diagram of the system for upper management.

Web publishing The models you create in XDE wouldn't do a whole lot of good if you were the only person who could view them. XDE provides a method to publish your model to either a public or private website so that you can collaborate with other members of the team. The model helps you communicate with everyone on the team, but not everyone who looks at the model needs to have XDE installed. Anyone with a web browser and access to the website can view the model.

Model reporting XDE can create four standard reports from your models: summary, summary with diagrams, Use Case reports, and Class reports. This helps alleviate some of the mundane work in documenting your design.

Integrated use case management In order for your project to be successful, you must be able to trace requirements to design and code. XDE integrates with RequisitePro, Rational's requirements management tool, allowing you to link use cases in XDE with the details of the use cases in RequisitePro. This helps you ensure that the design and code you're building map back to the user's requirements. It also helps you estimate the impact of a change; if a requirement changes, you can quickly and easily see which areas of the code and design implement that requirement.

Integration with Rational ClearCase No man is an island, and few programmers develop alone. Typically a developer is part of a larger team, where each member needs to see the work that the other members have done. ClearCase is Rational's version control tool that will let someone check out an XDE model or a part of an XDE model, make any needed changes, and deliver the changed model back into a workspace where everyone can see it. ClearCase keeps track of what was changed so that the team can always get back to an earlier version of the model if necessary.

Support for Java and .NET platforms XDE is really an IDE with UML modeling capabilities. XDE can be installed into many development environments, including

- IBM WebSphere Studio Application Developer (version 4.0.3 as of this writing)
- IBM WebSphere Studio Application Developer Integration Edition (version 4.1.1 as of this writing)
- Eclipse Workbench
- Microsoft Visual Studio .NET

Developers can keep working in the IDE that they are already familiar and comfortable with, thus reducing the learning curve and helping to speed development. Please refer to the Rational website, `www.rational.com`, for changes and additions to supported environments.

Database modeling XDE includes a unique data-modeling feature that supports the visualization of a database design using the UML. The whole team can then use XDE to see whatever perspective of the system they need: the design, the code, or the database design.

XDE User Interface

The user interface in XDE is drastically different from the one in Rational Rose or many other UML modeling tools. It was designed to look and feel like the standard IDEs currently available.

Before we get into the details of the user interface, it is important to discuss XDE *perspectives*. A perspective in XDE is simply a different way of looking at the system. For example, a modeling perspective is focused on the design view. A separate Java perspective focuses mainly on the source code. You can use one of XDE's prebuilt perspectives or create one of your own. In the following discussion, keep in mind that the specific windows you see will depend upon which perspective you have open. Figure 1.1 is an overview of the XDE user interface. In this example, we have the *modeling perspective* open.

NOTE *To switch between perspectives in the Java version of XDE, either select Perspective ➢ Open from the menu, or use the Perspectives toolbar. Each time you open a new perspective from Perspective ➢ Open, a toolbar button is automatically added to the Perspectives toolbar.*

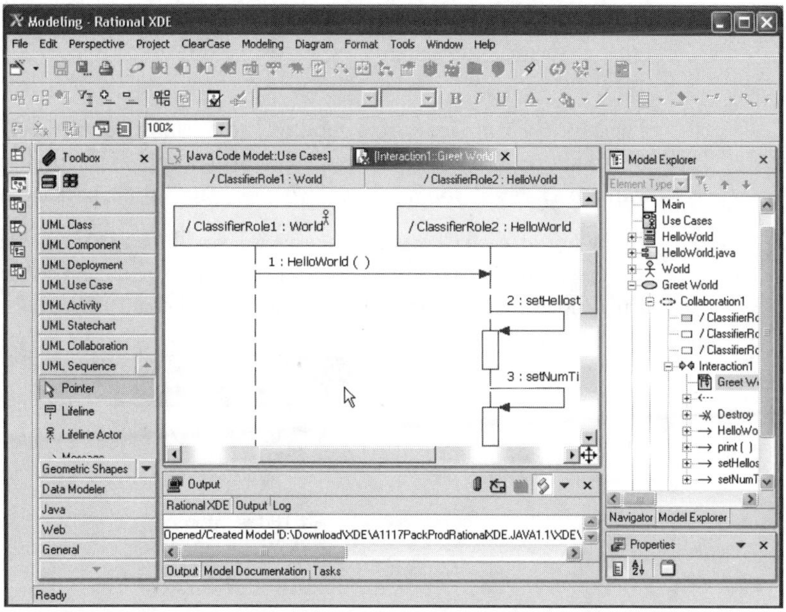

FIGURE 1.1
The XDE user interface

As you can see, the user interface is very different from that of Rose or many other modeling tools. Some of the significant pieces of the user interface include the following:

Diagram window The diagram window is used to display one of the UML diagrams in your model. You can open more than one diagram at once; the title of each diagram is displayed in a tab along the top of the diagram window. The diagram window is also used to view source code.

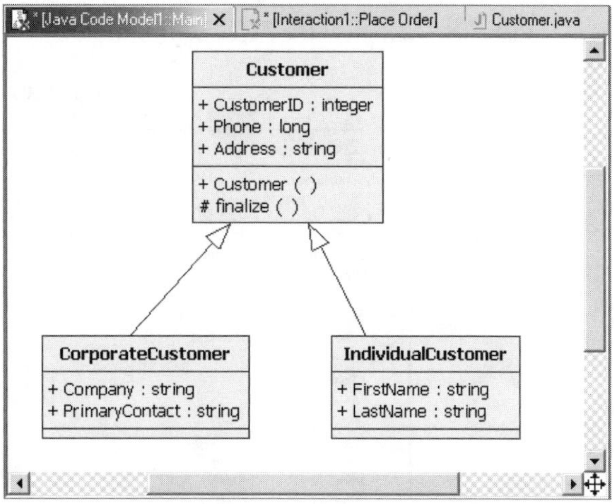

Model Explorer You can use the Model Explorer to quickly view the elements in the model and switch between them. Using the Model Explorer, you can add, delete, or move elements in the model. It is organized as a tree structure, so you can see which elements are contained within which other elements. For example, the attributes and operations of a class appear below the class in the tree structure.

The Model Explorer is also a good way to organize your model. You can create packages, which are similar to directories, and place model elements in the packages. You can even create packages within packages if you need to. If you are using Java, a package here corresponds to a Java package.

To the left of each element in the tree is a small icon that lets you know what type of element it is (use case, class, class diagram, component, relationship, and so on). An asterisk next to the element name shows that the element has some unsaved changes.

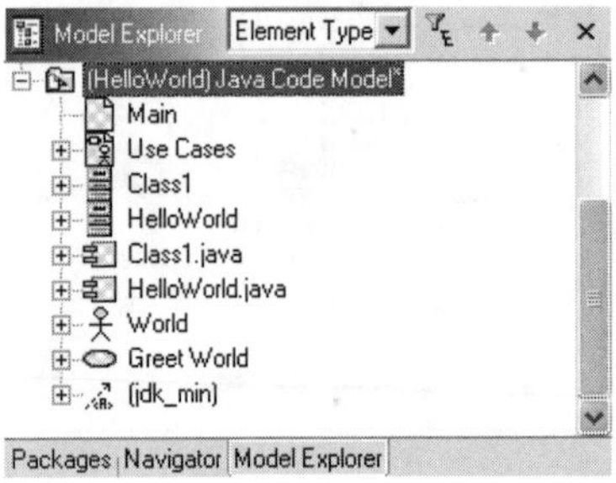

Properties window The Properties window in XDE is very similar to the Properties window in most of the currently available IDEs. It is used to view or edit detailed properties for each of the model elements. For example, you can use it to set whether a class is abstract, or to set the visibility of the class among other properties. In XDE, you can edit the properties of the model, a diagram, a model element, a shape, or a connector. The specific properties available will depend upon the item you have selected. The properties are arranged in logical groupings. If you would rather see them in alphabetic order, press the Alphabetic button.

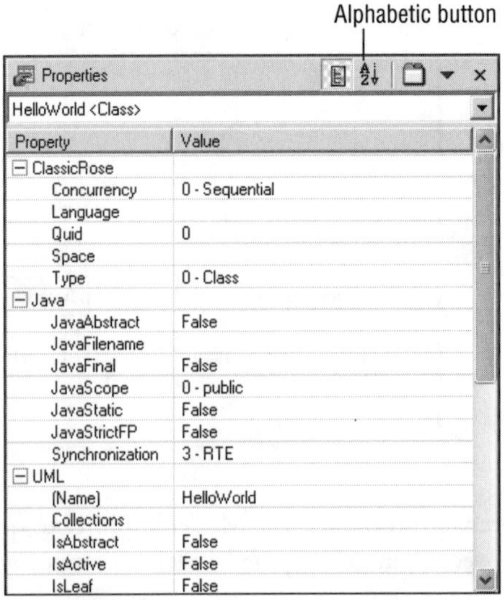

Documentation window You can use the Documentation window to enter comments and notes about the different elements in the model. For example, you may want to briefly describe the purpose of a particular class. The Documentation window provides an area for this. To view or change the documentation for a model element, simply select it in the Model Explorer, and view or edit the text in the Documentation window.

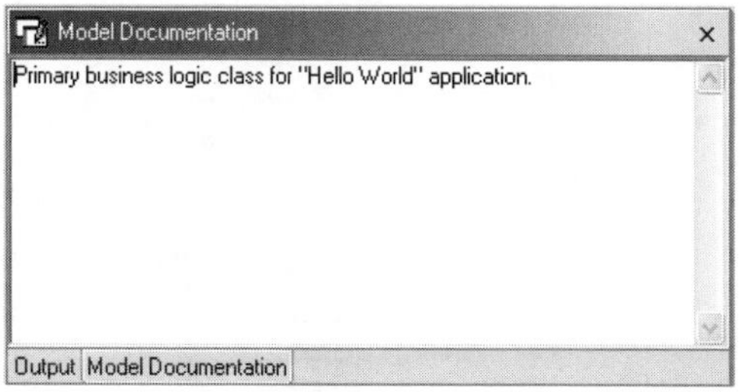

Output window The Output window displays the status of the model. For example, when you open a model, a message is displayed in the Output window.

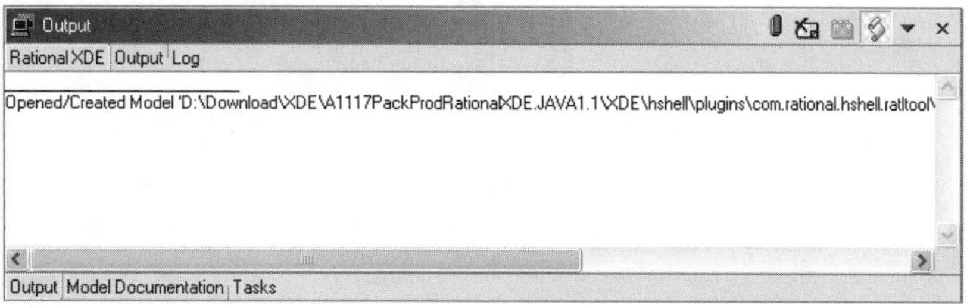

Tasks window The Tasks window displays items that you enter to keep track of your design and development tasks. For example, you can enter the task **Code the Order class**, and mark the task as complete when you are done. You can assign tasks a low or high priority and enter detailed information about each task, such as a description of the task and the file associated with the task.

The Tasks window also displays XDE-generated messages, errors, and warnings. For example, if there is a problem synchronizing the model with the code, XDE will display a detailed error message to you in this window.

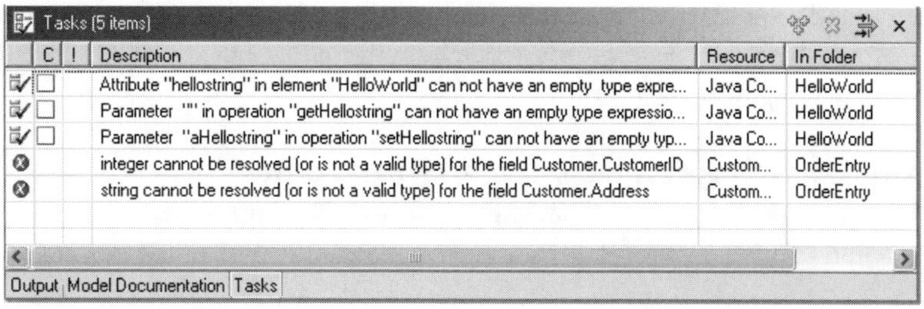

Toolbox The toolbox is used to add elements to a diagram. The specific items shown by default in the toolbox will depend upon the type of diagram you are currently using. However, you can always get to any of the items available in the toolbox.

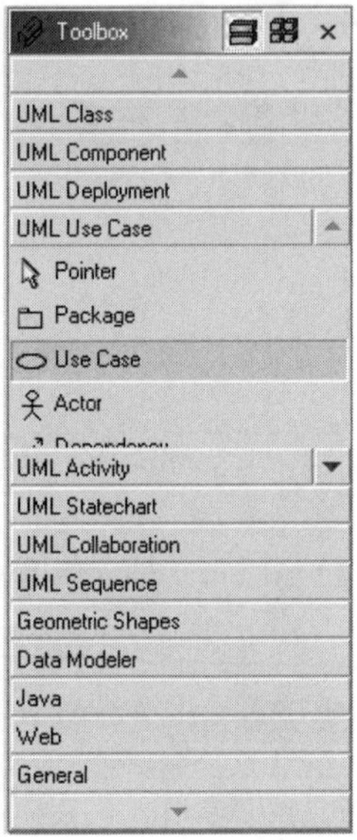

You have the option of customizing the user interface to hide or show these windows. Choose Perspective ➢ Show View, and then select the window you wish to show. To hide an item, simply close the window.

Versions of XDE

Rational XDE has four different versions. Each version has the major features of the product. The differences between them are the programming languages and development environments in which they work.

XDE Modeler

The basic version of XDE is called the XDE Modeler; it can be installed standalone (which uses the Eclipse IDE), installed into an existing IBM WebSphere installation, or installed into Visual Studio .NET. This version allows you to perform all of the modeling and pattern usage tasks described in the previous section, and you can create the UML diagrams mentioned earlier. In addition, you can apply and create patterns in the model using the code templates for the patterns.

You will not be able to generate code from the model, but you will be able to use the model directly in the development environment.

Rational XDE Professional: Java Platform Edition

The Java edition of XDE allows you to perform all of the modeling and pattern usage tasks and integrates with a Java development environment. When installed as a standalone product, XDE

Professional includes a Java platform–integrated development environment. This IDE is based on the IBM Eclipse platform. This environment will let you create J2SE applications. The Eclipse IDE does not include support for J2EE constructs such as servlets and EJBs. Additionally, Eclipse will let you create Java 2 Swing interfaces, but there is not a graphical development environment for these. Swing objects will need to be created manually.

Even with these restrictions, the Eclipse IDE included with XDE Professional is a very powerful tool. You can write, debug, compile, and execute Java applications; you can maintain synchronization of the UML models and the code; you can integrate with a version control tool; and you can implement the code templates through patterns. XDE will even write some standard code for you, such as get and set operations for each attribute in your model. Figure 1.2 shows the XDE Java Eclipse user interface. Note that you can view the code, the design, or both at once using XDE.

FIGURE 1.2
XDE code and design

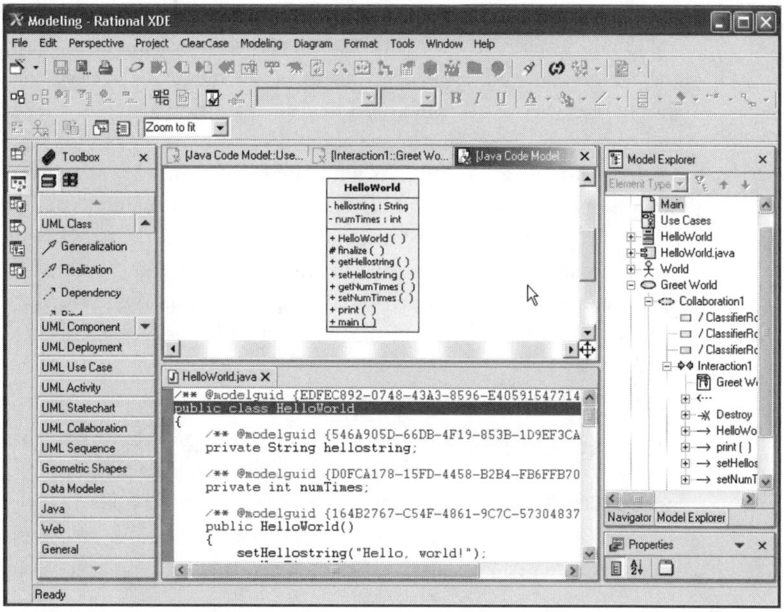

XDE Professional becomes even more impressive if you use IBM WebSphere Studio Application Developer. WebSphere is a J2EE IDE built on the Eclipse platform. XDE directly integrates itself into WebSphere. This gives you a consistent look and feel between the model perspective and development perspective in WebSphere. You can create views that show the code and model on the same screen. You can also set up XDE to automatically synchronize the model and code so that when you add model elements, the skeletal code will be created for them. In addition, WebSphere lets you create J2EE constructs such as EJBs. XDE assists you in this effort through some standard Java code templates. WebSphere also includes a graphical environment for creating Swing constructs. In short, XDE Professional is the tool of choice if you are a WebSphere developer.

RATIONAL XDE PROFESSIONAL: .NET EDITION

The .NET Edition of XDE Professional is designed for use in Microsoft's Visual Studio .NET. Using this version of XDE, you can round-trip engineer Visual C# .NET, ASP .NET, or Visual Basic .NET. As with the Java Platform Edition, the .NET version of XDE is integrated directly into the development environment—in this case, Visual Studio .NET. The menus and features of XDE are available directly in Visual Studio, so developers can continue to use the tools they are used to. Visual modeling simply becomes another part of the IDE, just like the debugger and code editor.

The XDE tool can also help the developer visualize how their application uses the .NET Framework. It can, for example, reverse-engineer an existing .NET application. The developer can then create a class diagram to see how their classes inherit from or depend upon the components in the .NET Framework.

You can switch between design and development views in the model so that you can keep working in whichever environment you are most comfortable. Of course, you can always view the code and the UML design at the same time. You can either manually or automatically synchronize your code and design using XDE's synchronization settings. All you need to do is establish the rules that XDE should use when synchronizing. The .NET Edition also has full support for the XDE pattern engine and code templates. You can use built-in patterns, such as the Gang of Four, or create your own.

If developers aren't familiar with the UML, there is an assisted modeling feature that allows developers to work with the UML and design, but using Visual Studio .NET terminology. This feature helps developers become more familiar with the UML without losing productive time. XDE can also reverse-engineer existing applications and create UML elements, further enhancing the developer's ability to learn the UML as they go. In addition to the UML diagrams, developers can create their own freeform diagrams and add these to the model.

COMPARING XDE VERSIONS AND FEATURES

The majority of XDE's features are available in all versions, but there are some variations. Table 1.2 is an overview of the features available in the current version of XDE. Check Rational's website, `www.rational.com`, for updates to the features and versions.

TABLE 1.2: OVERVIEW OF XDE FEATURES

FEATURE	XDE MODELER	XDE JAVA (ECLIPSE)	XDE JAVA (WEBSPHERE)	XDE .NET
Cross-model references	X	X	X	X
System perspectives	X	X	X	X
Reusable Asset Specifications	X	X	X	X
Gang-of-Four patterns	X	X	X	X
Ability to build and reuse patterns	X	X	X	X
Integration with IBM WebSphere			X	

Continued on next page

TABLE 1.2: OVERVIEW OF XDE FEATURES *(continued)*

FEATURE	XDE MODELER	XDE JAVA (ECLIPSE)	XDE JAVA (WEBSPHERE)	XDE .NET
Integration with Microsoft Visual Studio .NET				X
Integration with Eclipse		X		
Synchronization of code and model		X	X	X
Assisted modeling				X
UML modeling	X	X	X	X
Model validation	X	X	X	X
Freeform modeling	X	X	X	X
Web publishing	X	X	X	X
Model reporting	X	X	X	X
Integrated use case management	X	X	X	X
Integration with Rational ClearCase	X	X	X	X
Database modeling		X	X	X

Differences between Rose and XDE

When XDE was first introduced, many assumed that it was the latest and greatest version of Rose. But the more you work with the tool, the more you will realize that XDE is a unique product designed to meet different needs.

The primary difference between the two is that XDE includes both UML modeling and a development environment. Rose focuses strictly on modeling—and does it quite well—but it does not have a built-in development environment. Some other differences include these:

The pattern engine XDE comes with a pattern engine and wizards for adding a pre-existing design or code pattern to your application. You can also create and reuse your own patterns. XDE has a Reusable Asset Specification (RAS) that is used to document and apply patterns and other reusable assets.

Automatic code and design model synchronization Rose has powerful code generation and reverse-engineering abilities, but Rose requires the user to manually start the process. XDE also includes the option to have the synchronization occur every time the code or model change.

The intended users Rose was created more for the application designers, while XDE is for both designers and developers.

The user interface The XDE interface is consistent with most currently available IDEs, while Rose has its own look and feel.

Multiple models XDE allows you to work with several models at once, while Rose allows only one model at a time to be open. XDE also supports the sharing of elements between models more easily.

If you are currently using Rose, you can import your Rose models directly into XDE. To convert a Rose model to XDE, simply open the Rose model from within XDE. Then, save it into XDE format (`.mdx` file).

To import a Rose model into an existing XDE project, select File ➢ Import. In the Import dialog box, select File System as the import source. Navigate to the directory with the Rose model and click OK. Choose the directory or directories that contain the Rose model files, and select the file(s) you wish to import, as shown here:

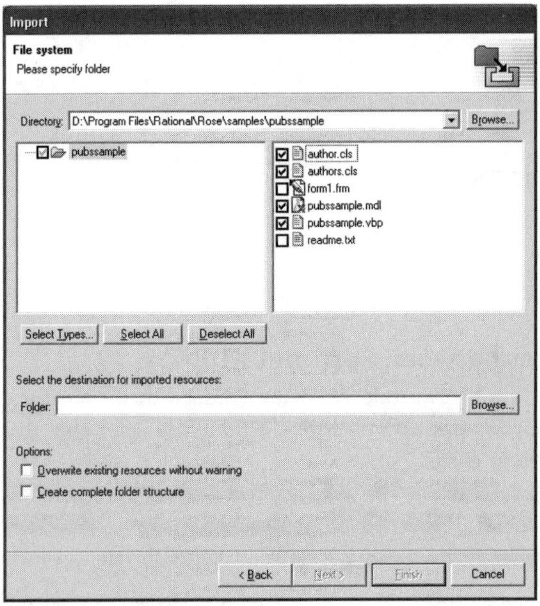

In the area labeled Select the Destination for Imported Resources, choose the XDE project you wish to import the Rose models into. Select Finish to complete the process.

Once the import is complete, be sure to save the XDE model.

Most of the model elements in Rose will be directly imported into XDE. However, there are a few exceptions. For example, collaboration diagrams in the Rose model will not import into XDE. Table 1.3 lists the major areas where there are differences between Rose and XDE, and a translation occurs into the XDE model.

TIP *A more complete table is in the XDE online help.*

TABLE 1.3: DIFFERENCES ENCOUNTERED IN IMPORTING A ROSE MODEL INTO XDE

RATIONAL ROSE MODEL	RATIONAL XDE MODEL
References to external files or URLs	URLs
Static attributes	Class or instance variable
Association class	Class imported but not relationships
Realizes relationship	Dependency with stereotype <<reside>>
Use Case view	Package named Use Case
Logical view	Package named Logical View
Component view	Package named Component View
Deployment diagram	Package named Deployment View, and a deployment diagram named Deployment Diagram in the Deployment View package
Subsystem	Package
State/Activity Model	ActivityGraph if the State/Activity Model contains at least one activity diagram, activity, ObjectFlowState, or partition element. If not, converted to StateMachine.
Link	Not supported
Message	Converted to a Stimulus owned by the InteractionInstance. Stimulus unnamed, but any Action associated with it will have the name of the Message.
Operation	If the Message name corresponds to a valid Operation and Creation is FALSE and Synchronization is not Return, the operation will be converted to a CallAction on the Stimuli. The CallAction will reference the Operation.
Association LinkElement	Not supported
Association NamedDirection	Not supported
Collaboration diagram	Not supported

Summary

In this chapter, we took a quick look at what XDE is, why it was developed, and what it can do. We'll spend the remainder of this book exploring XDE in more detail.

XDE is a design and development tool that integrates directly into the Eclipse, WebSphere, or Visual Studio .NET development environments. It blurs the line between design and development, and therefore, it helps overcome some of the challenges we used to face: designers who didn't think about code, coders who ignored design, and design and code that got out of sync. Using XDE, you can build a design model in UML 1.4, build your code in Java or a .NET language, and work on the design and code simultaneously.

In the next chapter, we'll explore XDE in the context of the *software development life cycle*. XDE does not require you to use a specific methodology, but in Chapter 2 we'll discuss how you can use XDE in the Rational Unified Process (RUP) or in eXtreme Programming (XP).

Chapter 2

XDE in the Software Development Lifecycle

In this chapter, we discuss how you can use XDE within the different phases (analysis, design, development, testing, and deployment) of the software development lifecycle. Specifically, we look at where in the lifecycle it is used, what it is used for, and who uses it. After this discussion, we talk about how to use XDE in a team environment with Rational ClearCase.

There are, of course, other iterative methodologies, but here we focus on two of the most common: the Rational Unified Process (RUP) and eXtreme Programming (XP).

Featured in this chapter:

- XDE and the Rational Unified Process
- XDE and eXtreme Programming
- Configuration management and XDE

XDE and the Rational Unified Process

As a design and development tool, XDE can really be used in a number of different software development lifecycle methodologies. It does, however, work really well with the methodology developed by Rational, the *Rational Unified Process (RUP)*. In this section, we look at where XDE can be used in the context of a RUP project, who uses it, and what they use it for.

Introducing the Rational Unified Process

One of the difficult aspects of software development has always been managing a project to a successful conclusion. It can be easy to forget that information technology is still a relatively young industry, and we're still developing processes and methodologies to help drive projects to completion. There are a number of individuals and companies who have been working on this problem and who have helped the industry come a long way. In addition to creating great design and development tools, Rational created one of these methodologies, the Rational Unified Process. RUP is designed as an iterative and incremental software development process where the project team analyzes, designs, builds, tests, and deploys functionality in small sections. In the traditional waterfall methodology we all know and love (some love more than others), the project team analyzes all the requirements, and then creates a design to meet those requirements. After the design is approved, the team codes and tests the software. Finally, after the software has been built and all testing has been run, the team deploys the software to the end users.

In an iterative and incremental process, the team determines the high-level functionality to be developed, and then plans multiple iterations of analysis, design, development, and testing. If they'd like, they can even include deployment in the iterations, although many projects focus on deployment toward the end. Deployment planning, however, should occur in earlier iterations.

As each iteration is completed, some of the functionality is made ready. Incrementally, each iteration's functionality builds on the last until the project team provides the project's entire functionality.

The Phases of Software Design

RUP is divided into nine disciplines and four phases. RUP defines a *discipline* as "a collection of related activities that are related to a major 'area of concern'." The disciplines in RUP include

- Business modeling
- Requirements
- Analysis & design
- Implementation
- Test
- Deployment
- Configuration & change management
- Project management
- Environment

Each of these disciplines will be detailed later in this chapter. Each is divided into multiple workflows that are further divided into multiple activities. One of the benefits of this approach is that these activities are standardized. When one team member claims to be done with the "Architectural Analysis" activity, everyone else will know what this means.

For the most part, activities from each of these disciplines are used in each of the four phases of the project:

- Inception
- Elaboration
- Construction
- Transition

Figure 2.1 shows an overview of the RUP process, including phases, iterations, and disciplines.

FIGURE 2.1
Rational Unified Process

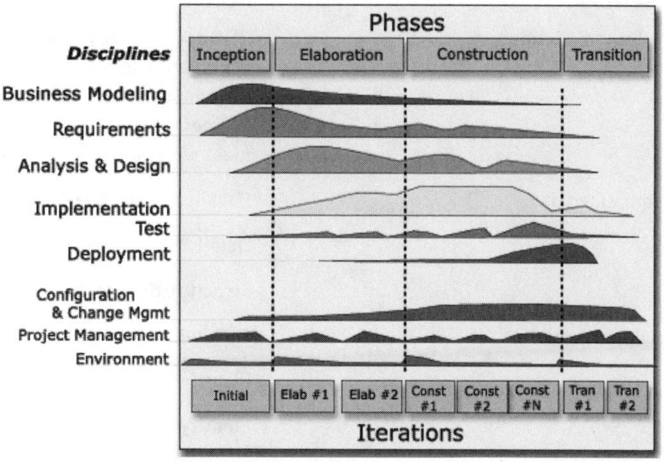

The *Inception phase* begins when a project starts. The first thing the project manager needs to do is create the team and become thoroughly familiar with the project. During Inception, one of the most important activities involves developing the project vision. The *vision* is the written document that expresses the purpose of the project, the needs of the stakeholders, and the features to be implemented. Toward the end of Inception, the project team ensures that all stakeholders agree with this vision. Then, the team divides the remainder of the project into iterations and prepares for the Elaboration phase.

NOTE *In longer, more complex projects, the Inception phase may be divided into multiple iterations as well.*

The *Elaboration phase* is for verifying the architecture and detailing the significant requirements of the project. Up to this point, the project has been conducted in a manner very similar to the traditional process; however, we now depart from this tradition into the world of the iterative process. The team determines the significant functionality and details these requirements into use cases. The architect uses these to create the architecture for this project and to verify that it will work. By the end of Elaboration, the significant requirements should be detailed, the architecture should be tested, and plans for Construction should be developed.

After Elaboration, the project moves into the *Construction phase*. During Construction, the remaining requirements are detailed and the majority of the coding is completed. Construction's end arrives when the coding and initial testing are complete.

The last phase is the *Transition phase,* where the team either puts the software into production or packages it for sale. Creating support and training materials for the end users is also done during this phase. At the end of Transition, the project team has successfully completed the project, and the end users have a product that meets their needs.

Rational XDE can be used during each of these phases and for activities in many of the disciplines of RUP. Table 2.1 lists the disciplines and activities that are supported by XDE.

TABLE 2.1: XDE IN RUP DISCIPLINES AND ACTIVITIES

DISCIPLINE	ACTIVITIES
Business modeling	XDE doesn't really support the business modeling discipline. You can create actors, use cases, and classes in XDE, but it does not include the notation for business actors, business use cases, or business objects. You can also create activity diagrams to document workflow.
Requirements	Find Actors and Use Cases
	Detail a Use Case
	Structure the Use Case Model
Analysis and design	Architectural Analysis
	Identify Design Mechanisms
	Identify Design Elements
	Construct Architectural Proof-of-Concept
	Incorporate Existing Design Elements
	Describe the Run-time Architecture
	Describe Distribution
	Capsule Design
	Use Case Analysis
	Use Case Design
	Subsystem Design
	Class Design
	Design Test Classes and Packages
	Database Design
Implementation	Structure the Implementation Model
	Implement Component
	Fix a Defect
	Implement Test Components and Subsystems
	Perform Unit Tests
	Integrate Subsystem
	Integrate System

Continued on next page

TABLE 2.1: XDE IN RUP DISCIPLINES AND ACTIVITIES *(continued)*

Deployment	Develop Deployment Plan
Configuration and change management	Create Deployment Unit
	Make Changes
	Deliver Changes
	Update Workspace

NOTE *XDE doesn't include the business modeling stereotypes by default, but you can add them yourself. Select the ellipsis "..." button in the Stereotype property for an actor, use case, class, or other element. Type in the new stereotype name and select a file for the stereotype icon.*

THE ROLES IN SOFTWARE DESIGN

A *role* defines a set of responsibilities someone has within a project. For example, someone with the responsibility of gathering detailed requirements from the customer plays the role of a Requirements Specifier. There are a number of roles in RUP; some will use XDE and some will not. Roles are different from *position names*; someone in a position may play multiple roles on a project. For example, someone with the organizational title "Analyst" may play the roles of Requirements Specifier, System Analyst, and Requirements Reviewer. The roles that will use XDE include the following:

Business Process Analyst The Business Process Analyst may use activity diagrams in XDE to document the workflow of a business process. XDE doesn't support full business modeling, but you can create activity diagrams.

System Analyst The System Analyst uses XDE to build the use case diagrams and enter information about use cases, actors, and their relationships. The person in this role is also responsible for tying the use cases in XDE to the requirements in RequisitePro, if RequisitePro is being used. If not, they may still be responsible for manually tracing the requirements in some document to the use cases in XDE.

Software Architect The Software Architect builds and reviews diagrams in XDE, such as class diagrams and component diagrams, that focus on the architecture of the system. The person in this role also decides how the system should be partitioned into architectural layers and subsystems and may create packages in XDE for each of the layers and subsystems. As the project goes along, the Software Architect verifies that the appropriate elements are being placed in each of the layers and may refactor the subsystems.

Capsule Designer In real-time systems, the Capsule Designer deals with concurrency issues and threads of control. The Capsule Designer can use XDE to model the classes and other elements needed to handle concurrency issues in the system.

Designer The Designer is concerned with the system design at a more detailed level than the Software Architect. Designers build and review various types of diagrams, including class diagrams, sequence diagrams, activity diagrams, and statechart diagrams. They also look at the use case diagrams built by the System Analyst, and may provide input into the diagrams built by the Software Architect.

Database Designer Because XDE includes data modeling, Database Designers can work directly in XDE to design the database structure. They also review the class diagrams created by the Designers; these diagrams serve as good input into the database design.

Implementer In RUP, Implementer is the term used for a coder or developer. These team members use XDE to view the design and build the code from it. In many organizations, the Implementer and Designer roles are actually played by the same person.

Integrator An Integrator uses XDE to plan and implement the subsystem and system integration.

Tester The Tester uses XDE to write and execute any testing code, such as unit tests, needed for the system.

Configuration Manager The Configuration Manager configures the link between XDE and ClearCase. If a version control tool other than ClearCase is used, the Configuration Manager establishes policies for version control using XDE and that tool.

Deployment Manager The Deployment Manager builds and reviews deployment diagrams in XDE.

Code Reviewer, Architecture Reviewer, and Design Reviewer All of these roles use XDE to review the current code and design.

Any Role Anyone on the team with access to XDE can look through the diagrams to gain a better understanding of the system and how it is put together. Given appropriate access rights, any member of the team can also check out a piece of the XDE model, make changes, and check it back in again.

The next section discusses each of the disciplines and activities for which you can use Rational XDE. Four of the disciplines (business modeling, test, project management, and environment) do not include activities in which you can use XDE. These activities are oriented toward the infrastructure of the project—setting up tools, defining business processes, managing the project, and conducting tests.

XDE and the Requirements Discipline

The main focus of XDE is on design and implementation, but it's important to tie that design back to the requirements of the system. This gives you two things: you can be sure all the requirements were implemented, and you can be sure that every piece of code is there because the user needed it.

XDE is not a complete requirements tool—Rational RequisitePro serves that purpose. What XDE lets you do is create the use case diagrams to visually display to the team what is included in the system and what is not. It also lets you tie the use cases back to RequisitePro, where you can find more detailed requirements information.

Figure 2.2 is an overview of the requirements discipline in RUP.

FIGURE 2.2
RUP requirements discipline

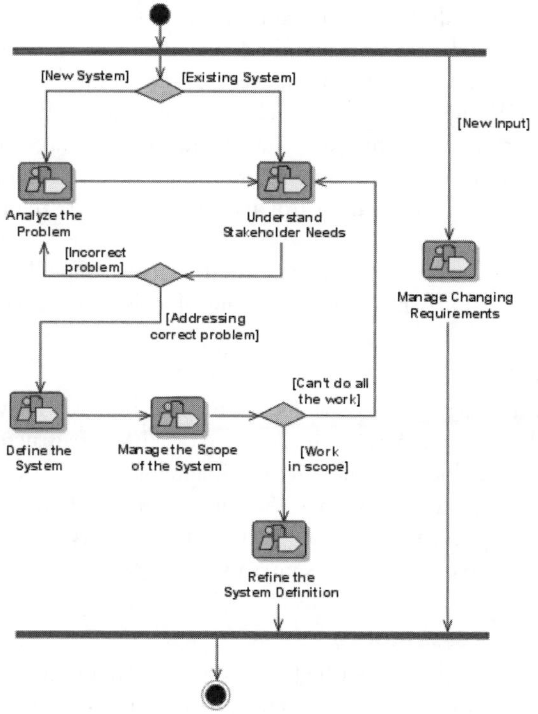

FIND ACTORS AND USE CASES

During the earlier iterations of a project, the team identifies and refines the actors, the use cases, and the relationships between them. The result of this analysis is one or more use case diagrams, each showing a subset of the actors, use cases, and relationships in the system.

As the team identifies actors, they are documented in XDE on a use case diagram. A typical project has at least one use case diagram that exclusively shows actors. On the same diagram or on a new use case diagram, the team can also show any generalization relationships between the actors. As a general rule, we wouldn't recommend showing actors, generalization relationships, use cases, and associations all on the same diagram; it can easily become too cluttered and difficult to read. In XDE, you can also attach a brief description of each actor.

The same process occurs for use cases. The team uses XDE to capture any use cases found, along with their descriptions. The detailed flow of events for each use case can't be entered directly into XDE, but you can attach a Word document or other file that contains the flow of events, or you can use the RequisitePro integration to tie the use cases back to the requirements. The team builds one or more use case diagrams to document the use cases and any includes, extends, or generalization relationships between them.

NOTE *Technically, you can enter the flow of events in the element documentation window in XDE. However, there is limited space in this area and you can't mark requirements for integration into RequisitePro. We recommend documenting the flow of events in a separate document.*

In addition to these diagrams, the team uses XDE to create some use case diagrams that show the relationships between the use cases and the actors.

To organize the model, the team can use XDE to group the use cases and actors into packages. To do this in XDE, right-click the model and select Add UML ➢ Package. Then, in the Explorer window, right-click the elements you want to add to the package and select Cut. Right-click the package and select Paste. Not all systems are complex enough to need packages of use cases and actors, but if you have a large number of use cases (say, more than 30 or so), it can help to organize them.

Finally, the team can generate a use case model survey from XDE using the reporting feature. Refer to Chapter 8, "Publishing and Reporting Models," for a discussion of the available reports.

DETAIL A USE CASE

As we mentioned earlier, most of the documentation for a use case will most likely be placed in a file outside of XDE. However, part of the detailing of a use case may be the creation of an activity diagram to illustrate the flow of events. Activity diagrams can be created in XDE. In XDE, right-click the use case and select Add Diagram ➢ Activity diagram. Add the swimlanes, activities, transitions, and other details to the diagram. Please see Chapter 4, "Integrated Use Case Management," for more information related to creating shapes on activity diagrams.

STRUCTURE THE USE CASE MODEL

After the use cases have been identified, the System Analyst structures the use case model, adding associations between the use cases and actors, between use cases and use cases, and between actors and actors. Also, the Analyst examines the use cases to see if there are any missing use cases or actors. Finally, the Analyst examines the model for redundancies and inaccuracies. When the Analyst is done, the team has a properly structured use case model. But remember that this, like many other things in RUP, is an iterative process. The use case model may be restructured several times before it is finalized.

Chapter 4 details the steps of creating and structuring the use case model with XDE. If the use case specifications are in files, you can link these files to the appropriate use case or actor in your model. If you are using Rational RequisitePro to manage requirements on the project, you can associate the use cases and actors in the model to the specifications and details in RequisitePro. All of this helps you get one complete view of the use cases and their requirements.

XDE can also report information about the use case model. See Chapter 8 for more on these reporting capabilities.

XDE and the Analysis and Design Discipline

As we saw earlier in Table 2.1, XDE is heavily used in analysis and design. In fact, all but three of the RUP activities in this discipline are supported by XDE. In this section, we look at the activities one at a time, and we discuss how XDE is used in each. Figure 2.3 is an overview of the analysis and design discipline.

FIGURE 2.3
RUP analysis and design discipline

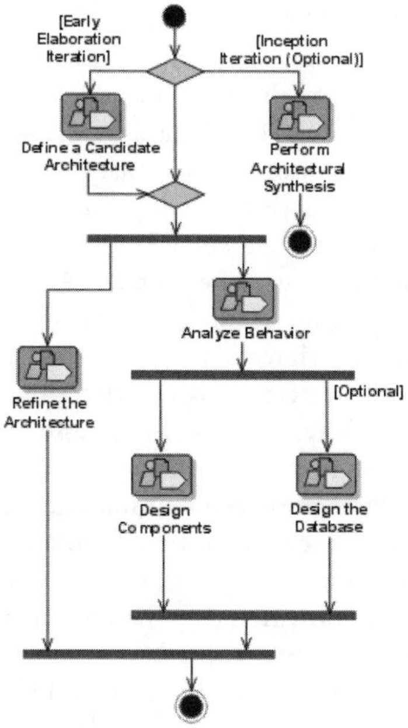

ARCHITECTURAL ANALYSIS

Architectural analysis is the significant task of setting up the architecture of the project. This task is memorialized by a software architecture document, which incorporates several diagrams that illustrate various aspects of the architecture of the system. RUP incorporates the *4+1 views of architecture* in the software architecture document. As you can see in Figure 2.4, the 4+1 views of architecture include the logical view, the implementation view, the process view, the deployment view, and the use case view. A sixth "view," although not part of the 4+1 model, is the data view, which can also be modeled in XDE.

FIGURE 2.4
4+1 views of architecture

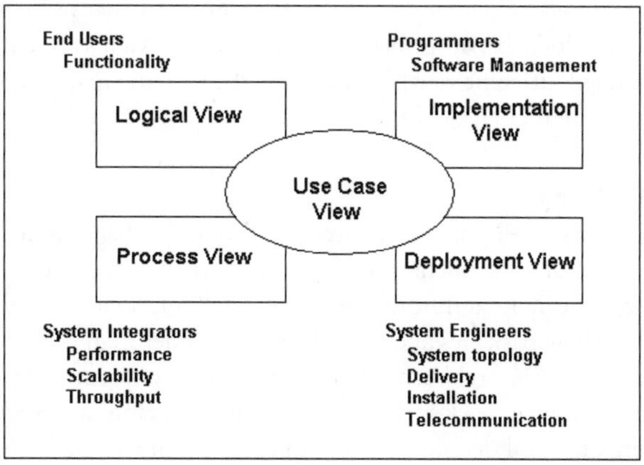

4+1 Views of Architecture: A Brief Overview

The 4+1 model divides the architecture into five perspectives: the use case view, the logical view, the process view, the implementation view, and the deployment view.

The *use case view* shows the architecturally significant use cases—those with some level of architectural risk. Architecturally significant use cases are those that cause architects to worry, lose sleep at night, and make the little hairs on the back of their necks stand on end. Issues such as new technology or system interfaces can contribute to their worry. Basically, architectural significance is a measure of the amount of architectural risk the use case contains. As we discussed earlier in this chapter, the Elaboration phase includes verifying the architecture. This verification is done by the project manager and architect determining the architectural risk and then devising a plan to overcome it. That plan should be discussed in the project's software architecture document.

The *logical view* includes all of the subsystems, packages, classes, interfaces, and logical architectural layers. It is, as its name implies, a logical perspective of the architecture that is not concerned with how these classes and packages might be organized into source code libraries.

A big part of the design effort lies in the logical view. In it, the team determines how to implement the functionality of the system—in other words, what classes, subsystems, interfaces, and other elements the system will need; what information they should contain; what behavior they should exhibit; and what the relationships are between them. Issues such as reuse, flexibility, scalability, and maintenance all come into play here. The team is also defining and/or using patterns, such as the "Gang-of-Four" patterns (see Chapter 10, " Gang-of-Four Patterns"), or higher-level patterns, such as error handling, security, database connectivity, interprocess communication, and so on.

The *implementation view* is concerned with how classes, packages, and other model elements are physically stored. It includes files such as source code files, executable files, DLLs, and so on. The implementation view is also where the team considers the dependencies between the different files. This is particularly important when you are dealing with reuse because the dependencies between the files will let you know what can or cannot be easily reused. This view is documented using one or more component diagrams.

The *process view* focuses on concurrency issues and threads of control within the application. It defines the processes that exist, and the threads of control in each process.

Finally, you use the *deployment view* to model how the system will be deployed onto physical nodes. It is concerned with both the hardware and the software (operating systems, DBMS software, drivers, and so on) required to deploy the system. It includes the hardware nodes, the executable files running on each, and the links between them. The deployment view is documented in a deployment diagram.

By using these different views, you can see the system architecture from different perspectives, and you can make sure that all of the issues related to these different perspectives have been addressed.

Modeling the Views

The various views (4+1) of the architecture should be diagrammed in XDE and included in the software architecture document. For the use case view, include the use case diagram, annotated to show the architecturally significant use cases. The logical view should include package diagrams (class diagrams that show packages and/or subsystems rather than classes) from XDE. The package diagrams should show the architectural layers, the subsystems, and any architecturally significant packages. You can also include class diagrams, activity diagrams, and sequence diagrams if they help to clarify the architectural decisions. The implementation view should include one or more component diagrams that display architecturally significant components and their dependencies. The process view should include a class diagram showing the various threads of execution the system contains. Finally, a deployment diagram consisting of nodes and processes can illustrate the deployment view.

The data view can include an entity-relationship diagram of the database and a series of diagrams (class, activity, or sequence) showing the methods for accessing data in the system. All of these types of diagrams can be created and maintained using Rational XDE. The various diagrams are discussed in Part II, "Visual Modeling with XDE."

While completing the architectural analysis, the team develops initial versions of these 4+1 views to complete an architectural overview. The views can (and will) evolve as the project moves along.

Identify Design Mechanisms

Design mechanisms are those architectural elements that will be used throughout the project. In Elaboration, the architect determines what design mechanisms to use for such characteristics as security, error handling, and concurrency. These mechanisms denote a standard way that each of these characteristics is implemented in the project. All designers and implementers on the project team should follow these mechanisms. One of the main purposes of these mechanisms is to foster consistency across the project team. For example, if the architect devises a standard method to handle security, and all team members use it, the software application is much easier to support and maintain when it is built.

XDE can be used to both document and use the design patterns. The patterns may be developed for a specific project, or they could be applied at an organizational level. Either way, XDE has the ability to store custom patterns and also includes a number of built-in patterns. As an organization develops design and code for these standard mechanisms, the methods to implement them can be abstracted as Reusable Asset Specifications (RAS) in XDE. Please see Chapter 11, "Introduction to Reusable Asset Specifications (RAS)," for further information on RAS.

Construct an Architectural Prototype

After the vision of the project is clearly understood and agreed upon by all stakeholders, Elaboration can begin. One of the most important tasks to complete during Elaboration is to construct an architectural prototype. The architect is primarily responsible for this activity. The *architectural prototype* is what results when some small amount of system functionality is created to test the chosen architecture. This can involve developing a use case to production-level functionality or a very small test to write 10 lines of code to ensure connection to a database. Whatever the architecturally significant aspects of the system are, they should be tested as part of the architectural prototype.

You can use XDE to build this architectural prototype. Once an architecturally significant use case has been identified, use XDE to create activity or sequence diagrams for the use case. You can then create any needed class diagrams, and the skeletal code for Java, J2EE, VB .NET, ASP .NET, or C# .NET can be automatically created. You then go to the coding perspective in XDE and code the significant classes to the level that the architect requires for the prototype.

Describe the Run-time Architecture

The run-time architecture of a system describes the interactions of the various execution threads throughout the system. This is one of the 4+1 views of architecture—the process view. It is important to see how the processes interact in designing the system. For example, the architect may need to investigate using synchronous or asynchronous communication between processes. A diagram of processes also helps to show if the system is adequately threaded.

This process view diagram is created as a class diagram showing the individual threads of execution, as well as associations between them indicating how they communicate with one another. You can create the diagram using Rational XDE. Simply create a class diagram and add a class on it for each threaded process. Add the associations between the processes to illustrate the methods of communication.

DESCRIBE DISTRIBUTION

The distribution of a system is the model of physical deployment. This includes nodes, devices, and connections. *Nodes* are the physical machines on which the various components of the system will execute. *Devices* are components that do not have processing power. *Connectors* are the physical connections between nodes and devices. These connectors can be either physical cables or wireless network connections. The other aspect of distribution involves the mapping of the executable files and processes to the nodes. Consider both hardware configuration and mapping of components to hardware when you plan the system distribution.

Distribution is best depicted through one or more deployment diagrams showing the nodes, devices, connectors, and processes. Optionally, the UML allows for these diagrams to be overlaid with a component diagram to show the dependencies between the software components and the physical machines on which those components execute. You can create these deployment diagrams using XDE. In Java, .NET, or the professional modeler version of XDE, you can include one or more deployment diagrams to illustrate the physical hardware and software distribution of the system.

USE CASE ANALYSIS

Even after the requirements have been documented in use cases, this does not provide enough information to code an application. The use case specifications give you the information to begin the analysis model, but they won't let you know what classes, subsystems, and so on will be needed. Use Case Analysis is an initial step toward this detailed information.

For each use case, this step involves going through a first pass at defining the elements needed to implement the functionality in the use case. You can analyze the objects and messages necessary to execute the behavior by creating one or more sequence diagrams. These are interaction diagrams that show the objects and messages needed to carry out some functionality in the use case. You can also create class diagrams, with analysis-level classes, to further analyze the preliminary "design" of the system.

To create a sequence diagram in XDE, create a collaboration and then create an interaction instance. On the sequence diagram, add the actors that communicate with the use case and create messages to document the behavior from the use case. Create objects to contain the responsibilities represented by the messages.

See Chapter 4 for more information on creating the analysis model.

IDENTIFY DESIGN ELEMENTS

In this step, the Software Architect reviews the preliminary "design" from the Use Case Analysis step. Looking through the sequence diagrams and class diagrams in XDE, they begin to identify some of the design elements that they need.

For example, they look for groups of classes that might be a good candidate to form a subsystem. As subsystems are defined, they also define the interfaces for them, and assign classes to the appropriate subsystems. They look through the analysis classes and refine them as necessary, merging or splitting analysis classes to form some initial design classes. Active classes will also be added to represent the threads of control in the system.

As all of these decisions are being made, they are documented in a class diagram (or more likely several class diagrams) in XDE. In all likelihood, the architect or an Implementer uses XDE to generate code for some of these classes and runs some initial tests to be sure the class design works. With feedback from the testing, the design may be refined.

Incorporate Existing Design Elements

Going through the analysis model is a good way to find some design elements, but we're missing a large piece here. Your organization may already have some elements available: component libraries, code from existing applications, and so on. Before you waste time reinventing the wheel, check to see what is already available.

In XDE, the simplest way to do this is to look through the Reusable Asset Specifications. These will be discussed in more detail in Chapter 11. Briefly, however, a RAS is a design and code pattern that you can simply pull into your application. For example, someone may have already created the design and code needed to extract billing information from your accounting system. Now, if you need that functionality, all you have to do is incorporate the RAS into your project.

Use Case Design

The "design" in the Use Case Analysis activity gives us a rough idea of the objects and messages we need to implement a use case, and the classes and subsystems from the Identify Design Elements and Incorporate Existing Design Elements activities give us a list of some available elements. However, this is not enough to actually build the system; we need more details. We can get these details by refining the sequence diagrams to incorporate implementation details, such as the programming language being used. Class diagrams can also be refined, and the classes migrated from analysis level to design level.

As you refine the sequence diagrams, you associate the objects to classes in the design model (from the Identify Design Mechanisms or Incorporate Existing Design Elements activities), and then you associate the messages to operations. If you need a class that does not exist, create it. Similarly, if an operation does not exist in the class to satisfy the message, create one. When this process is done, you have a design model for the dynamic behavior in the use case. What remains in the design model is the class, subsystem, and database design before the code for the components can be written.

As was the case for the Use Case Analysis activity, the Use Case Design activity can be completed using Rational XDE. Once you have created the initial, analysis-level sequence diagram, either you can create another sequence diagram as a copy, or you can use the original diagram, and then associate the objects to classes. If you haven't created the classes yet, you can do that at the same time. Once you have finished associating objects and classes, you can associate the messages to operations. Again, if the operations have not been included in the model yet, you can create them at this time. At the same time, you can begin to refine your class diagrams to include implementation-specific, design-level detail. Class diagrams are further refined in the Class Design activity, as described next.

CLASS DESIGN

The Use Case Analysis and Use Case Design activities help define which classes will be needed to fulfill the requirements in the use case. However, this is not quite enough detail to warrant coding the components yet. Some details about the classes still need to be discovered, especially in the category of the relationships between the classes. The multiplicity, navigability, and optionality of the associations need to be clarified. Also, some operations may be duplicated between some classes and would best be placed in one or more helper classes. Or the designer may see functionality that could be abstracted between classes and may set up interfaces or generalization relationships. In addition, the operations that have been established from the Use Case Design activity are public operations. Some of the functionality may need to be placed in private or protected operations and used by the public operations. In essence, the Use Case Design activity gives you a class model that works to meet the needs, but the Class Design activity refines that model to be more efficient and take advantage of reusable components better. XDE can assist with all of these activities. You can create the associations, abstract some classes into new ones, create public and private operations, and even use patterns to implement some design concepts.

DATABASE DESIGN

The design of the database comes out of the design of the classes. You can start this activity after you complete the Use Case Analysis effort, and it involves designing the database tables, columns, triggers, and stored procedures for persistent storage. After you determine the classes, you can include the persistent attributes in the data model. The XDE tool has functionality to create the model elements for the tables and columns based on class persistence. XDE can then generate the code necessary to create the database. If you make the database design iterative, you can build the database so that it houses the data for the functionality ready by the end of each iteration and so that it continually evolves into the final database for the final software product.

There have been some good debates (well, okay, they were more like arguments) about when database design should be conducted. Traditionally, database design has occurred as early as possible in the process, and a transition to an iterative approach to database design can be difficult in some organizations. There are three basic options for the timing of the database model and design model: build the database model before the design model, build the design model before the database model, or build the two in parallel. The following are synopses of each approach:

Building the database model before the design model If you use the first approach, the requirements feed into the Database Design activity. The database group builds the data model, and from that the designers identify some entity classes that may be needed. This approach is more often used in situations where you have a legacy database and an application that is being re-engineered, but some organizations prefer to always use it. The advantage is that it gives the database team a model as early as possible, and it can work for teams that are not willing to develop the data model iteratively. A key disadvantage is that it gives the process more of a data-centric, rather than an object-centric, focus. This can lead to poor design decisions and ultimately an application that is harder to maintain. It can also make it harder to trace the design back to requirements (portions of the design will trace back to the data model instead), so it can be harder to verify that all requirements were met.

Building the design model before the database model Using the second approach, the requirements feed into the design model. Some of the classes in the design model will be stereotyped as entity classes, which hold information that should be made persistent. These entity classes and their relationships then become input into the data model. This has the advantage of keeping the process object-centric, and the design model can be easily traced back to the requirements. It allows the functionality and requirements implemented in the design model to drive the data structure, rather than the data structure driving the system design. The disadvantage is that it can be hard for a database group to adjust to an iterative process; the concept of reworking a database design may seem wasteful.

Building the two models in parallel The third option is to have the requirements feed into both the data model and the design model at the same time. The two models are developed in parallel, but each constantly provides input into the other. For example, the design team may identify a new entity class that becomes input into the data model. Alternatively, the database team may find a new data source that changes the database structure and affects the system design. This can be a very good approach because it allows for maximum productivity and coordination of the two efforts. It does, however, require a great deal of coordination effort, which is not feasible in some projects.

We recommend the second or third approaches, but each organization must make its own decision.

Subsystem Design

When you create classes, you group information and related behavior into a class. Subsystems work in much the same manner. You group similar classes into a subsystem and provide a common interface to it. Then, you can create a subsystem realization diagram that shows how the subsystem interface interacts with the classes contained in the subsystem to carry out its responsibilities. Also, you can create a subsystem interaction diagram that shows how the various subsystems interact with the actors to carry out the functionality of the system. XDE can help you build both of these diagrams as sequence diagrams. The purpose of these diagrams is to show the organization of the subsystems and how they work with one another. By designing components as subsystems, you can build components that can be used in multiple systems. For example, a security subsystem could handle all security processing for all applications in your organization. Should you decide to use subsystems in this manner, XDE can help you create Reusable Asset Specifications for these reusable components.

Design Test Classes and Packages

Just as you design your code in XDE, you can design any test classes or packages you might need. A *test class* is simply a class that exists for the sole purpose of testing. Model the test classes and relationships using class diagrams, and model the messages sent between the test classes and other classes using sequence diagrams. The process is essentially the same as designing code: determine what functionality you need to perform the test, decide what classes will be needed to carry out that functionality, assign responsibilities to the classes, and document how the classes interact in a sequence diagram. On the class diagram, document all of the information, behavior, and relationships of the test classes. Typically, these class diagrams are separate from the class diagrams for the application classes.

XDE and the Implementation Discipline

In addition to analysis and design, the other side of XDE's personality is the implementation, or coding, piece. We won't get into the specific details of coding in Java, Visual Basic, ASP, or C# here. Please see Chapter 5, "Modeling Java and J2EE Elements in XDE," and Chapter 6, "Modeling Visual Studio .NET Elements in XDE," for detailed instructions with these languages. Instead, let's look at where in the RUP implementation discipline XDE can be used. XDE is used in the majority of implementation activities; all but three of these activities use XDE.

Figure 2.5 is an overview of the implementation discipline.

STRUCTURE THE IMPLEMENTATION MODEL

This is the process of organizing the source code by identifying the source code components, defining their interfaces, and deciding what classes and other model elements will reside in each component. This step also includes defining other types of components, such as executable files, and examining the dependencies between the components.

You can use XDE to both document this information and implement it. As you build your classes in the design model and then synchronize the design and code, XDE creates the source code components and the dependencies between them. It can also create the executable components in the model.

Toward the beginning of the project, the team should establish rules and naming conventions for the implementation model. For example: what will the directory structure for the code look like? How many executables are being created and what is each one for? What should the rules be for establishing dependencies between the components?

FIGURE 2.5

RUP implementation discipline

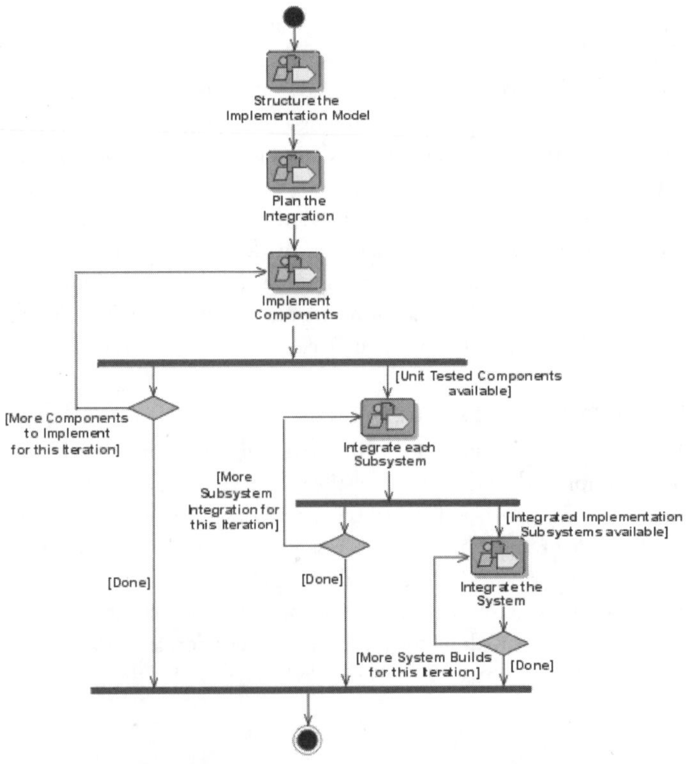

Then, go into XDE and set up the infrastructure. You can create packages for each of the directories in the source code structure. You can also create components on a component diagram for each of the executable files. As new classes are added, and new source code components are automatically being created, don't forget to update the component diagrams.

Implement Component

This is the heart of the implementation discipline: actually writing the code. The difference between traditional approaches and RUP/XDE is that the code is built incrementally, and the team iterates between code and design, with each piece providing input to the other.

Use XDE's code and model synchronization in this step. Work in the modeling perspective and code perspectives as needed to design and build the code. The synchronization feature will help you transition from one to the other and back again as needed.

Fix a Defect

In this activity, the team fixes any problems discovered during a test cycle. Problems could range from minor bug fixes to major changes.

Start by looking through the change request to gain an understanding of the problem. Then, look through any needed diagrams in XDE to determine which classes will be affected by the change.

In the modeling perspective, make any changes needed, and resynchronize the code and model. Update the code as needed, and be sure to synchronize it with the design.

Implement Test Components and Subsystems

Like the application code, test code can be written directly in XDE. Begin with the design artifacts, such as the class diagrams and sequence diagrams, from the Design Test Classes and Packages activity. Working with the design as a guide, switch to the coding perspective and begin the code. If you discover problems with the design, just change the code or switch back to the modeling perspective to change the design.

It can be helpful to isolate the test code into its own subsystem or subsystems. When you prepare to create a build, you don't need to incorporate the test code, so having it isolated can help. Follow the guidelines that were established in the Structure the Implementation Model activity.

Perform Unit Tests

Using XDE, execute the test code you wrote in the Implement Test Components and Subsystems activity. Be sure to record your test results, but this will be done outside of XDE. Within XDE, however, you can record the tasks needed to fix any problems that you discovered.

Integrate Subsystem

As developers complete their work on classes and components, they use XDE to deliver their changes to a central repository. The Integrator can then review the components and their changes, and ensure that the subsystem is ready to be integrated.

The Integrator works directly in XDE to create the subsystem interface, develop subsystem integration tests, and run these tests. The Integrator also uses XDE to write any integration code that may be needed and to record any outstanding tasks for subsystem integration.

Once the subsystems are integrated, deliver them using the Deliver Stream command to a system integration workspace, in preparation for the Integrate System activity.

INTEGRATE SYSTEM

This activity is very similar to the subsystem integration, but this time you're integrating all of the subsystems together into the full system. Use XDE to write integration code, develop and run integration tests, and track any outstanding integration tasks.

XDE and the Deployment Discipline

The deployment discipline in RUP contains more than just the tasks needed to physically deploy the software. It also includes planning for the deployment, creating training and support materials, writing release notes, and managing the acceptance and beta tests. Figure 2.6 is an overview of the deployment discipline.

A large part of developing the Deployment Plan involves deciding on the physical layout of the system. In other words, you need to answer questions such as:

- What hardware will we need to deploy?
- What should the workstation configuration be?
- How will the nodes on the network communicate (LAN, Internet, and so on)?
- What operating system and other software is required on the servers and workstations?

FIGURE 2.6
RUP deployment discipline

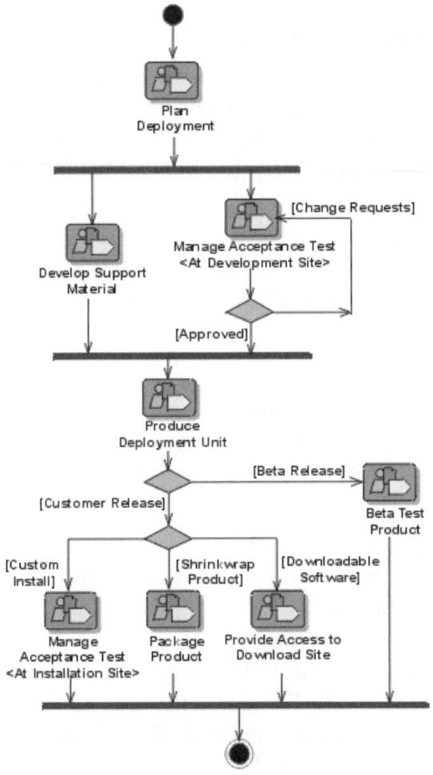

The list goes on, but essentially you are trying to define three things: the hardware needed, the software needed, and the connections between the hardware nodes. At this point in the project, you take into account things such as disaster recovery, load balancing, and network security.

XDE can help you document this effort by providing the capability to build a deployment diagram. The deployment diagram shows the nodes, the connections between them, and the processes running on each.

If you would rather use a more traditional network diagram or another notation used by your organization, XDE will support this effort by allowing you to create a freeform diagram.

XDE and the Configuration and Change Management Discipline

ClearCase is the configuration management tool developed by Rational. By integrating with ClearCase, XDE can provide check in, check out, merge, and other configuration management capabilities.

Figure 2.7 is an overview of the configuration and change management discipline.

Create Deployment Unit

XDE can be used to automatically create the files you'll need for deployment. In Java, these would be the deployment descriptors, EAR files, WAR files, and JAR files. In the .NET languages, these might be EXE files, DLLs, COM objects, and so on. In Java, you can simply right-click an element in the Model Explorer, and select More Java Actions ➢ Deploy. In the .NET languages, the process varies by language; see Chapter 6 for details.

Make Changes

Through its integration with ClearCase, XDE can keep track of what changes were made to each of the source code files and model elements. You can check out a file or model element and make the needed changes, all within the environment of XDE.

See the section "Configuration Management and XDE" later in this chapter for further details.

FIGURE 2.7
RUP configuration and change management discipline

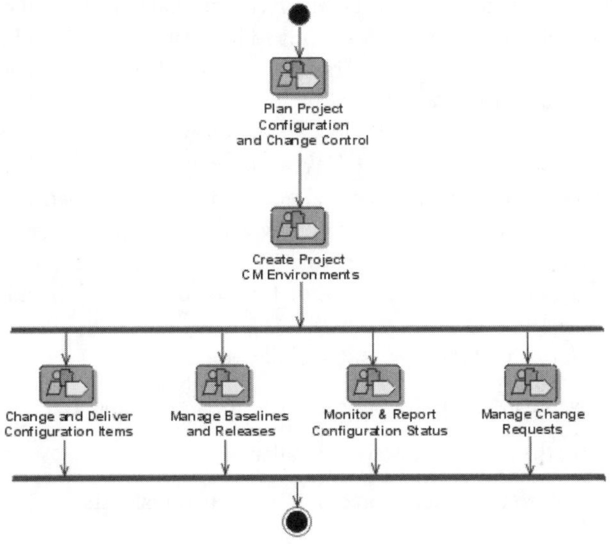

DELIVER CHANGES

Again, through the integration of XDE and ClearCase, you can deliver your changes back in to a central repository. In this way, you're almost continuously integrating the system. Check out the files and make changes. Then, run your unit tests directly in XDE, and select ClearCase ➢ Deliver Stream.

See the section "Configuration Management and XDE" later in this chapter for further details.

UPDATE WORKSPACE

You may or may not need this activity, depending upon your configuration management environment. There are two ways you can look at the team's files: you can use the configuration management tool to create a copy of all the files for you, or you can have a view into a shared repository, in which case you are always seeing the most current versions of the files. ClearCase supports both options.

If you have a dynamic view into the current versions, you do not need to update your own workspace. However, if you have a static view (in other words, a copy of all of the files), you need to periodically recopy the files so that you can see other peoples' changes. ClearCase has a Rebase option that copies all of the files into your private workspace. In XDE, select ClearCase ➢ Rebase Stream. See the section "Configuration Management and XDE" later in this chapter for further details.

XDE and eXtreme Programming

In addition to RUP, one of the iterative methodologies in the industry is known as *eXtreme Programming*, or *XP*. In this section, we introduce you to XP and talk about how XDE can be used in an XP project.

Introducing XP

The eXtreme Programming process is a lightweight methodology for developing software. It relies on certain tenets to achieve project success and efficiency, such as not allowing overtime, having the customer always available, and limiting documentation to only the most essential elements. It is a rapid, iterative process that accepts the fact that requirements will change, and allows for this change in the schedule. It was originally developed by Kent Beck and has been gaining momentum in the industry for some time. XP is particularly effective for projects that have uncertain and frequently changing requirements.

Unfortunately, because XP is less formal, there is sometimes a misconception that XP is simply a return to "cowboy programming." We would like to emphasize that XP was not designed to be a chaotic process; it is a rapid process, but that does not necessarily mean it is chaotic. XP has just enough structure to ensure project quality without the process getting in the way of project success. Quality is key to XP; the use of patterns and standards is central to an XP project. At the same time, though, XP is more relaxed in terms of formal documentation and formal meetings than some other methodologies.

To complete an XP project successfully, you should

- Have small groups of programmers (between 2 and 12)
- Have the customer always be available
- Be able to create automated unit and functional tests

Figure 2.8 shows an overview of the XP process.

FIGURE 2.8
XP process overview

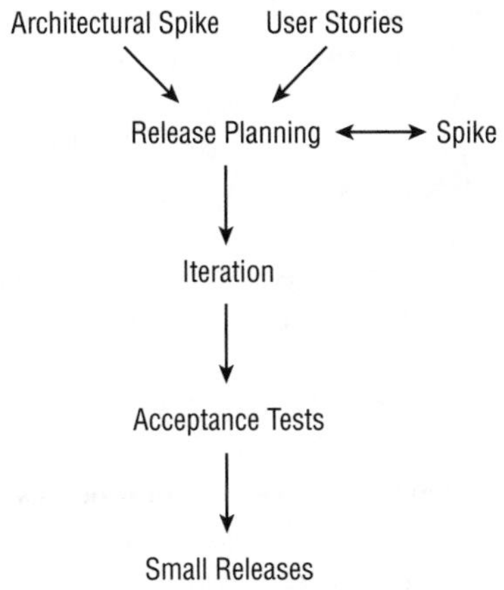

The XP process is largely focused around release planning and iteration planning. Release planning is a little different in XP. The team brings together technical and business staff to talk about the different features (user stories, which we'll discuss shortly) and their priorities. The release plan drives the work to be done in the iterations, and integration tasks are done very frequently.

The process begins with *user stories*. A user story is a short narrative about what the user would like the system to do. They can range anywhere from a few sentences to a page or two, and are similar in purpose to use cases. A big difference between user stories and use cases, however, is that user stories should be very high-level, without a lot of requirements. When it's time for the developers to build a user story, they collect the detailed requirements. Initially, though, the user stories should provide only enough detail for the developers to make a reasonably accurate estimate of how long the story will take to build.

Once the initial user stories are written, the developers get together to plan releases. They go through each user story and estimate how long it will take to build in terms of ideal weeks. An *ideal week* is a week of uninterrupted work time (with no overtime). It does include testing but does not include interruptions, extra work, or tasks unrelated to the project. The customers then decide the priority of each user story. With this prioritized list, the developers decide which stories to include in which releases and when to release them, and they document all of this in a release plan.

An XP project includes frequent releases. The idea is to start getting feedback from the customers as early as possible so that the feedback can be integrated more easily into the rest of the project.

Then the team goes through an iteration planning meeting to plan the coming iteration. An iteration in XP runs from one to three weeks. Any shorter, and they aren't good milestones. Any longer, and you can lose the momentum of the project. In planning, the team never assumes overtime. In fact, "no overtime" is one of the tenets of XP. A group of people stuck with overtime every week is an inefficient group of people. One of the ways XP maintains the momentum of the project is to prevent the team from getting burned out.

In the iteration planning meeting, the customer decides which user stories to implement in the iteration. The stories are then broken down into the programming tasks needed to implement them. The developers sign up to complete tasks, and they estimate how long each task takes. Each task should be between one and three ideal programming days, where an *ideal programming day* is one without interruption or overtime. If tasks are shorter than a day, they should be combined. Any task longer than three days should be split into smaller tasks. The developers also plan some time into the iteration for refactoring the work from previous iterations.

The developers include acceptance testing in each iteration, in order to get customer feedback as soon as possible. The team first translates the user stories into automated acceptance tests. The customer runs the acceptance tests, records the results of the testing, and decides which failed tests should receive the highest priority.

An iteration may also include architectural spikes. A *spike* is a proof-of-concept of a particularly difficult or risky aspect of the architecture. For example, the team may know that they will need to interface with a COBOL legacy system. In this case, to produce a spike, the developer might build a quick interface, just to be sure it can be done. The code from the spike may or may not be kept in the final version of the software, and in most cases, it won't be kept. The purpose of the spike is really just to reduce risk.

XP is based upon the following 28 rules and practices:

- Write user stories.
- Create the schedule with release planning.
- Make frequent small releases.
- Measure project velocity.
- Divide the project into iterations.
- Start each iteration with iteration planning.
- Move people around.
- Start each day with a stand-up meeting.
- Fix XP when it breaks.
- Design for simplicity.
- Choose a system metaphor.
- Use CRC cards for design sessions.
- Create spike solutions to reduce risk.
- Don't add any functionality early.
- Refactor whenever and wherever possible.
- Make sure the customer is always available.
- Write the code to agreed standards.

- Code the unit test first.
- Pair-program all production code.
- Only allow one pair to integrate code at a time.
- Integrate often.
- Use collective code ownership.
- Leave optimization until last.
- Do not allow any overtime.
- Write unit tests for all code.
- Do not release any code until it has passed all unit tests.
- Create tests whenever a bug is found.
- Run acceptance tests often and publish the score.

In the sections that follow, we look specifically at how XDE supports some of these rules and practices.

"So," you may be asking, "which one do I use: a more formal methodology such as RUP (although RUP can be tailored to be less formal), or a less formal process such as XP?"

As with any good question in the software industry, the answer is a resounding "it depends." There are a number of factors to consider in this decision, and discussing all of the pros and cons of both approaches is outside the scope of this book. Briefly, however, we'll discuss a few things you should consider. First, we recommend that you take a look at your organization. In particular, look at the skills of the developers, examine the existing processes (are they formal or informal?), and refamiliarize yourself with the culture of your organization. Also consider how open your organization is to change. If the culture is very structured, transitioning to a less structured process such as XP might be difficult. On the other hand, if your culture is very informal, using the full RUP without customization might be difficult. Either way, consider any cultural changes that may need to take place, and recognize that these changes do not occur overnight.

Also consider the characteristics of your project. XP is best suited for small-to-medium sized projects with no more than 12 developers. It's specialized for projects that have extensive requirements change, and projects in which the customer is available to be a part of the project team. XP requires the use of automated rather than manual testing in a project, so the project team must have an automated testing tool available.

Another consideration is the criticality of the system architecture. RUP takes time up front because you need to carefully design the architecture before building the rest of the system. XP's philosophy is to let the architecture emerge and solidify as the project goes along and both the code and design are refactored. Again, there are pros and cons to both approaches, but if it's important for you to have a solid architecture earlier in the project, RUP may be a better choice. If your design needs to be more fluid, XP could be a good way to go.

Finally, remember that this is not a binding decision. It's very possible to use RUP on one project and XP on another (although you may face training issues and have to maintain more than one methodology). Both RUP and XP can be tailored to meet your organization's needs, and you can change methodologies if your organization's needs change.

This was a very brief introduction into the world of XP. Before embarking on your first XP project, we highly recommend further reading. The website `www.extremeprogramming.org` is a good place to begin. Also, see the "For Further Reading" section at the end of this chapter for more sources.

XDE in an XP Project

Figure 2.9 again shows the XP process, but here we have highlighted the areas supported by XDE.

FIGURE 2.9
XDE in the XP process

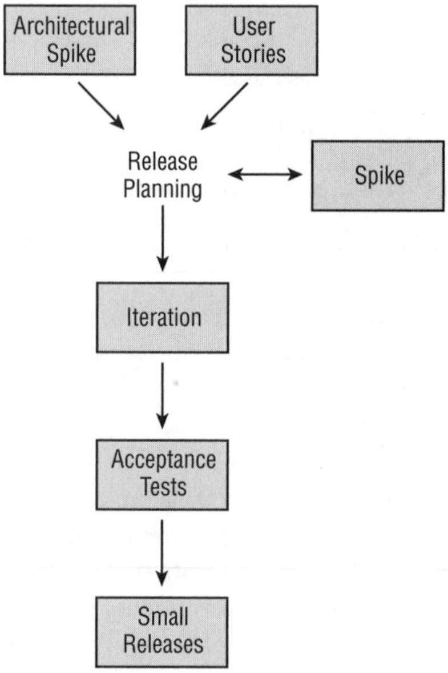

XDE is not, and is not intended to be, a tool to cover the entire lifecycle of a software product. Its focus is on design and development, and, to a certain extent, testing.

A requirements management tool such as RequisitePro can support user stories and requirements. XDE integrates with RequisitePro to tie the use cases in XDE to the use cases and other requirements in RequisitePro. Because XP deals with user stories rather than with use cases, you need to set up a User Story requirement type in RequisitePro. If you are using a requirements management tool other than RequisitePro, you can still set up the traceability between the requirements and the design, but it will be more of a manual process. We recommend that you go through the effort, because we've found that it helps to ensure both that all requirements are handled by the design, and that all of the eventual code comes from a requirement, not from a developer trying out a new component. A final option is to simply attach a Word document or URL containing the user stories and/or requirements directly to an XDE model. To do so, right-click an element in the Model Explorer, and select Add UML ➢ URL. You can use this option to attach either a URL or an external file of any type to the XDE model.

XDE helps support release planning, in that the designers and developers can look at what's already been built to estimate the effort needed to finish the work. Much of the release planning, however, is accomplished through meetings and estimation efforts, and therefore XDE is not directly used in this area of the lifecycle. Tools that might be applicable are project management tools such as Microsoft Project or one of the various estimation tools available on the market.

Architectural spikes, on the other hand, are directly supported by XDE. As mentioned earlier, an architectural spike is essentially a proof-of-concept for an uncertain area of the architecture. The developers can use XDE to design (minimally) and code an architectural proof-of-concept whenever one is needed. See the section "Creating Spike Solutions to Reduce Risk" later in this chapter for more information about architectural spikes and XDE.

An iteration is broken down into the process shown in Figure 2.10. Note that again the areas directly supported by XDE have been highlighted.

FIGURE 2.10
XP iteration

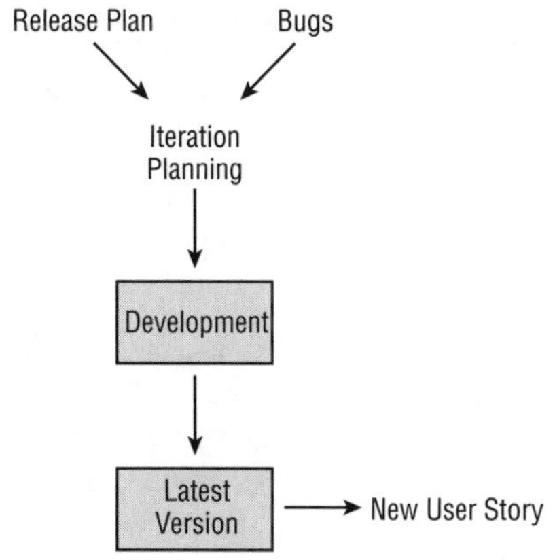

Development is, of course, the main area in which XDE is used in an iteration. Within the Development task in XP are the design, coding, unit testing, and refactoring tasks, all of which are supported by XDE. Using XDE, you can design the system with UML diagrams, code both the system and the unit tests, and refactor the code and design.

Acceptance tests may be supported by XDE, but whether acceptance testing is done with XDE depends on whether the organization would rather use a separate testing tool. The developers can build acceptance tests using XDE and then release these tests to the customer.

Finally, the releases themselves can be created and managed directly in XDE. See the section "Making Frequent Small Releases and Integrating Often" later in this chapter for more information on incremental and full builds in XDE.

In the next section, we briefly discuss the XP rules that are directly supported by XDE.

XDE and XP Rules and Practices

XP includes a standard set of rules and practices that should be followed on all XP projects. These are listed earlier, in the section "Introducing XP." As a design and development tool, XDE directly supports a subset of the XP rules and practices, as explained in the following sections.

Making Frequent Small Releases and Integrating Often

In Java, XDE can build the EJB, JAR, and WAR files you need to deploy your application. In .NET, XDE can build the executable files and other files you need to deploy. Because the process can be set up to run automatically, it's relatively easy to create frequent releases. Of course, the developers still need to go through any errors generated in the build process and correct them before deploying.

You can create either an incremental build or a full build. In most projects, you will create incremental builds frequently—in an XP project, daily, or even several times a day. At more significant milestones, such as the end of an iteration, a full build is more appropriate.

In XDE, you can specify automatic building. In this case, the system is continuously built. Every time someone saves a file, it is integrated into a continuous, incremental "build." This offers you the advantage of finding out as quickly as possible whether there are problems with the code. If you want, you can manually create builds as well. In an XP project, we recommend automatic builds, which more fully support the XP principle of frequent builds. There are a few options you can set:

Automatic builds Select Window ➢ Preferences. In the Workbench area is the Perform Build Automatically on Resource Modification option. If this check box is selected, XDE automatically creates an incremental build every time a file is saved. If not, you need to create builds manually.

Automatic save Select Window ➢ Preferences. In the Workbench area is the Save All Modified Resources Automatically Prior to Manual Build option. If this check box is selected, XDE saves all files that have been modified since the last manual build.

Build order Select Window ➢ Preferences. In the Build Order area, you can set the order in which projects should be compiled and integrated into a build. Leave the Use Defaults check box selected if you want XDE to figure out which projects should be built first. To determine the build order, look over any architectural documentation, particularly items such as component diagrams, which show the dependencies between components. These dependencies directly influence the build order; if A depends on B, you'll need to compile B first.

At the time of this writing, XDE for Java can deploy to the following application servers. Check Rational's website, `www.rational.com`, for updated specifications on supported application servers.

- WebSphere 4.0
- WebLogic 5.1
- WebLogic 6.0
- WebLogic 6.1
- Sun J2EE Reference Implementation
- Web Server (J2EE 1.2)

Starting Each Iteration with Iteration Planning

At the beginning of each iteration, the developers sign up for the tasks they will complete during the iteration. While XDE is not a full scheduling and project management tool (and is not intended to be), the developers can use it to keep track of the tasks they plan to complete, the file(s) affected by each task, and the priority and status of each task.

One of the views available in the Eclipse version of XDE is the Tasks window. Use Perspective ➢ Show View ➢ Tasks to view the Tasks window if it is closed. The developers can add or delete tasks and mark tasks as completed. XDE also automatically generates tasks. For example, if a compilation error is found, a task is created to fix the problem. The Tasks window is shown here:

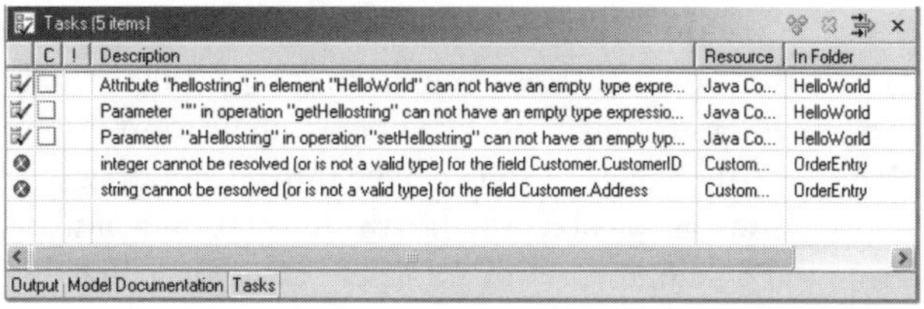

Moving People Around

Have you ever been on a project where one guru seems to know all about the system, but everyone else only knows just pieces and parts? Have you ever been there when the guru's gone? It's not a pleasant place to be.

In XP, all of the developers "move around" the system. In other words, rather than have specific individuals responsible for specific pieces of the code, everyone becomes familiar with all areas of the system. This isn't possible (or at least it isn't practical) if the code resides on individual workstations. That's where XDE can help. Because XDE integrates with ClearCase, any member of the team can check out any piece of the code, make changes, and check it back in again.

If you don't have ClearCase, XDE does provide a history function, where you can see previous versions of a file. However, there isn't any check in/check out functionality directly in XDE. You can also still use your version control software, or even a manual version control process, outside of XDE. In other words, it is still possible to follow the XP rule of moving people around, it's just a little more difficult.

Designing with Simplicity

Quite a few of us in the information technology industry have had the unfortunate experience of working with some code that was over-designed. By that, we mean code that was architected and re-architected and re-architected again until it was so complex that no one could possibly understand it anymore.

Don't get me wrong; there's nothing wrong at all with re-architecting, or refactoring, as long as the process is controlled and serves a purpose. The purpose of this effort should be to make the design simpler, not more complex. Simple designs are easier to understand, document, build, and maintain. They aren't always easy to come up with, though. In fact, you may find that it is actually much easier to create a complex design, which is why refactoring is so critical. As the project goes along, the team makes the design simpler and simpler through refactoring.

One relatively easy way to help ensure a simple design through XDE is through the use of patterns. They can help keep you from accidentally over-designing by providing simple, efficient, tested solutions. XDE comes with a number of patterns, including the Gang of Four, but you can also create your own. See Chapter 10 and Chapter 12, "Creating Your Own Patterns," for more information.

Creating Spike Solutions to Reduce Risk

A *spike solution* is a proof-of-concept of a very risky or uncertain part of the architecture. While we'd love to be able to get the architecture right from the beginning, reality sometimes gets in the way. We may say, "No problem, we can interface with those legacy systems," but when it comes down to it, we may run into trouble.

So, rather than wait to discover a problem until it's too late to do anything about, we create a spike solution early in the project. In this example, making a spike would involve developing a small bit of code, just to prove that the integration can be set up. It won't be a fully functional prototype by any means, and most of the time, the code will be thrown away, but it does help you reduce risk by letting you know as soon as possible whether the integration will work.

As a design and development tool, XDE can be used to directly support this XP discipline. You can design, build, and unit test the spike solution using XDE.

Refactoring Whenever and Wherever Possible

One of the core design principles within XP is to constantly refactor the design. *Refactoring* is simply the process of examining the current design and optimizing it. In XP, optimizing means simplifying—don't create a complex design if a simple one will do.

Refactoring in XDE is a continuous process. A developer may look at the design model and find a way to simplify it. They can change the model and then synchronize it with the code to implement the change, or they can change the code, and then have XDE automatically update the model.

Writing Code to Agreed Standards

Coding standards are certainly nothing new to XP. We've been working with them for years to help others understand and maintain our code. Or at least we should be working with them; sometimes, unfortunately, we find situations in which standards are not consistently followed. XP does insist that coding standards are agreed upon and followed, and XDE can help developers stick to them. To do so, the developers set up a number of preferences in XDE. These are briefly listed here, but the details are language-specific and will be discussed in further detail later in this book. XDE preference settings include

- Code formatting, such as spacing, new lines, and indentation
- Default prefixes and suffixes for naming classes and other model elements
- Valid attribute types
- Semantics for the code
- Commenting styles (including Javadoc in Java)

Another way to enforce standards is through the use of *code templates*. A code template in XDE is, as its name suggests, a piece of code that is automatically created when code is generated. One of the limitations of many modeling tools is that the code generated from the model is fairly skeletal; you get the class name, attributes, operation signatures, and relationships, but you still have to go in and code the operations yourself. This makes sense—after all, unless it has ESP, there's no way for modeling software to predict what you want each operation to do.

In some cases, though, *you* can predict the operation's logic. For example, you know that pretty much every set operation has the same code: `attribute = newvalue`. Modeling tools are already able to automatically code things such as get and set functions for you, but code templates give you the option of automatically generating code for other operations.

A benefit of this is in standards compliance. Say, for example, you create a code template for a `ValidateSecurityRights()` function. Now, you don't need to worry that different developers will use different approaches for checking a user's security rights. XDE will generate the standard function body, which can then be modified if necessary.

Coding the Unit Test First

XP stresses the idea of building unit tests before building the code. This can take a little getting used to, but in our experience, it has proven to be beneficial. The tests help the developers keep in mind why the code is being written in the first place so that when the code is developed, they already know exactly what it needs to do. Because it's not very likely that a developer will make the same mistake when writing a test and when writing code, there's only a small chance of an error being duplicated in both the code and the test. Because the code and the test won't have the same error, the unit test helps you increase the quality of the system.

Unit tests should be automated and run any time the code is changed. This practice helps to integrate regression testing throughout the project. If a change needs to be made to some code, the change is first made to the unit test for that code. So, the developers are working on little bugs and changes as they go along rather than having to deal with huge bugs and changes at the end.

XDE can be used to build unit tests as well as application code. There are testing frameworks for a number of languages out there, but here we take a quick look at a framework called JUnit, developed by Kent Beck and Erich Gamma, which tests Java code.

Using JUnit, you import the JUnit framework. Then you simply create a class (the test class) for each class you want to test (the code class). The test class should be derived from the JUnit class called TestCase. In the test class, you add methods that start with `test`. The test method will test some specific functionality in the code class. Start by putting a minimal amount of testing logic in the test method. For example, just test to be sure objects were instantiated correctly. Then, write the actual code in the code class, and run the test method to make sure everything worked. Refine the code as needed, adjusting the test method and constantly running small tests. By doing so, you can be sure at the end of the day that you have a class that works. The following is a brief example of a code class and its corresponding test class:

```
import junit.framework.*;
public class TestAccount extends TestCase
{
   public TestAddFunds
      {
         Account Checking = new Account();
         Checking.Addfunds(60);
         AssertEquals(60, Checking.balance);
      }
}

public class Account
```

```
{
   private double balance;

   public Account()
   {
      balance = 0;
   }

   public AddFunds(double depositamount)
   {
      balance = balance + depositamount;
   }
}
```

As you can see in this simple example, the TestAccount class exists only for testing purposes. In a real-world situation, this would be the first pass at testing. Once you're satisfied that this functionality works, you would add more functions to the test class and the Account class. By the final release, the Account class should have all of the functionality it needs, including error handling, and the test class should test all of the capabilities of Account.

Of course, you don't have to use a pre-existing test framework. You can always write your test cases from scratch, or from a framework that you or your organization has developed. The benefit of using a pre-existing framework is that it has been tested thoroughly, so you lessen the risk of the test itself causing more problems than the code.

Whatever approach you take, use XDE to build the unit tests before you write the code, and follow the approach described earlier. Build a little bit of functionality, run the unit test, then build a little more functionality and test again, and so on.

USING COLLECTIVE CODE OWNERSHIP

The whole team can always own the code collectively; it's just a matter of letting everyone know that anyone can work on any piece of code. XDE makes this a little bit simpler through its integration with ClearCase, Rational's configuration and change management tool.

With ClearCase, all of the code is stored in one central repository. Developers can check out portions of the code, check them back in, and merge them with other changes. See the following section, "Configuration Management and XDE," for more detailed information.

Configuration Management and XDE

Configuration management can be a part of the project that everyone hates to do but hates even more when it's not done. *Configuration management* is the task of controlling versions of the code and other project artifacts. Whether you are using RUP, XP, or some other methodology, configuration management is a critical piece. Without it, you can't necessarily tell what the most recent version of the code is, what builds you have, what changes you've made, or who else is making the changes.

XDE tries to make the configuration management process as simple as possible by directly integrating with ClearCase, Rational's configuration management tool (see "XDE and ClearCase" later in this section to learn how to use the tool). In the following sections, we'll discuss version control and configuration management at a high level, and then describe how ClearCase can be used to implement version control in XDE.

Overview of Version Control in XDE

Version control in XDE is essentially a matter of dividing the model into more manageable pieces, and then setting up policies and tools to let developers check out the pieces, make changes, and check them back in again. To accomplish this, you first split the XDE model into separate files, also known as *storage units*. Table 2.2 lists the different model elements that can be saved into their own storage unit, and the file extension that will be used.

TABLE 2.2: MODEL ELEMENTS IN STORAGE UNITS

Element	File Extension
Model	`.mdx`
Use Case	`.ucx`
Actor	`.acx`
Package	`.pkx`
Subsystem	`.ssx`
Object	`.obx`
Class	`.clx`
Interface	`.ifx`
Component	`.cmx`
Component Instance	`.cnx`
Diagram	`.dgx`
Interaction	`.inx`
Interaction Instance	`.iix`
Collaboration	`.cbx`
Collaboration Instance	`.cix`
Activity Graph	`.agx`
State Machine	`.smx`
Exception	`.exx`
Enumeration	`.enx`
Signal	`.sgx`
Facade	`.fcx`
Node	`.ndx`
Node Instance	`.nix`

Once you've set up the storage units, they can be added to version control, and checked out, modified, and checked back in. A storage unit that is under version control is referred to as a *controlled unit.* In the remainder of this section, we assume that you are working with controlled units.

You don't have to use Rational ClearCase as your configuration management tool, although it is integrated into XDE and therefore is a little easier. Once you've created the controlled unit files, you can use any version management tool you want to control the files. Just keep in mind that with any tool other than ClearCase, you need to go outside of XDE to check things in or out.

Strategies for Creating Controlled Units

How you separate your model into controlled units affects how easy it is to maintain later. While saving everything as its own controlled unit may sound like a good idea, it does mean that there's more potential for merging and coding issues. Here's a quick example to illustrate.

John checks out class A, which is stored in its own controlled unit. Another class, B, depends on class A. Jim's got class B checked out. As Jim's working on class B, he's testing it with the old version of class A, because John hasn't checked class A back in yet. Class B works fine, so Jim checks it back in. But now when John checks class A back in with the new changes, class B stops working. Jim finds the problem in a testing cycle later, gives up, and goes to get a mocha and some aspirin.

This is a simple example with two developers; imagine if you're working on a team of 20. Or 50. Or 100. The potential for these types of problems increases dramatically based on the number of developers and the amount of coupling between the classes (if the classes are fairly independent, these types of issues won't come up as much). But in the previous example, if class A and class B had been in the same controlled unit, Jim couldn't have changed class B until John was done with class A, assuming that John had the file checked out exclusively.

NOTE *Files do not have to be checked out exclusively; XDE supports two or more developers working on the same controlled unit at the same time. Through its merge feature, the changes made by the developers can be merged. More on this in a bit.*

On the other hand, you could just create one big controlled unit for the whole system. Then, of course, you lose the advantage of having a controlled project at all. In fact, you create more problems than you solve. Now, if John wants to change something, he has to check out the whole controlled unit (the whole system!). Not exactly the most productive approach.

The typical project, of course, lies somewhere between these two extremes. Here are some things to consider when you are partitioning the project:

How many developers are there? The more you have, the more you want to be sure that your controlled units are fairly independent of one another. Tightly coupled controlled units can cause problems such as those in the earlier example.

How independent are the classes? If your classes are tightly coupled, separating each into its own controlled unit is probably a bad idea. Instead, try to identify groups of classes that are relatively independent of other groups. In particular, look at the packages of classes you've set up in your model. These might be good candidates for controlled units.

How independent are the subsystems? Subsystems can be a great way to partition the model. The classes encapsulated within the subsystems are all in the same controlled unit, so a developer can make the changes they need to make to a subsystem without having to check out each class independently. Because subsystems are (or should be) fairly independent of one another, you minimize the types of conflicts we've discussed.

Who owns the code? If you have communal ownership of the code, you do run the risk of two or more people needing to change the same unit at the same time. In this case, you may want to consider using exclusive checkouts when possible. With an *exclusive checkout,* one developer can't check out a file until it has been checked in. In other words, two developers can't change the same code at the same time. Consider this policy carefully before implementing it, though, because it can diminish productivity by making the developers wait for each other.

If, on the other hand, each developer or small group of developers owns some part of the code, you may want to consider partitioning the model along these lines. Each developer can then check out their assigned portions of the code.

NOTE *XDE doesn't include the functionality to set ownership of controlled units. Use the access rights options in ClearCase, or use a manual process to establish ownership.*

How volatile is the code? It might not be a problem to merge the changes made by multiple developers if the code doesn't change that often. Consider grouping less volatile classes together into one or more controlled units and creating additional units for the more volatile pieces.

Where are you in the project schedule? Early on, it can be detrimental to set up too many controlled units. After all, the code structure is pretty likely to change as the project goes along. Wait until the architecture is at least somewhat stable before partitioning your model.

MERGING CHANGES

If two or more developers make changes to the same code at the same time, you need to merge the changes. If the changes were made to different areas of the code, the merge isn't a problem. In this case, both developers' changes are incorporated into the final copy of the code.

The complexity occurs when developers make changes to the same areas of the code. Someone needs to go in and determine which changes should be accepted. XDE has a compare/merge feature that lets you compare and merge two or more XDE models, but a simpler way is to use the integration between ClearCase and XDE to resolve these issues.

When you check in a file, ClearCase automatically detects a merge situation.

XDE and ClearCase

There are a few fundamental things you can do with XDE and ClearCase. The basic steps to get set up are as follows:

1. Connect to ClearCase.
2. Mount a Version Object Base (VOB).
3. Create a view.
4. Add the project to ClearCase.

5. Add files to the source control.
6. Check the files in and out, and merge changes as needed.
7. Deliver and rebase streams when needed.
8. Create builds when needed.

Before you can work with ClearCase and XDE, you must first connect to ClearCase. To do so, select ClearCase ➢ Connect to Rational ClearCase. If you have ClearCase installed, this option establishes a connection between XDE and ClearCase.

The next step is creating and mounting a VOB to store your files.

Mount a What? VOBs and XDE

In ClearCase, *VOB* stands for Versioned Object Base. Essentially, it is just a repository that you can use to manage the files for one or more projects. It's a high-level container on a server or shared location where the projects and files are stored. Mounting a VOB makes it available to the team for use, and unmounting it prevents anyone from checking in, checking out, or performing any other actions on the files in the VOB.

WARNING *Before you can mount a VOB, be sure your ClearCase administrator has set up a VOB storage location and created the VOB. They must also give you access to the VOB.*

Generally, only a configuration management administrator creates, mounts, or unmounts a VOB. Once it has been mounted, the rest of the team uses it. In XDE, you can't create a VOB, but you can mount or unmount a VOB that was already created using ClearCase. In other words, security issues, such as who can mount or unmount a VOB, are handled by ClearCase, not by XDE. Use ClearCase directly to set up users and access rights.

To mount a VOB, follow these steps:

1. Select ClearCase ➢ Mount VOB.
2. In the Mount window, select the VOB to mount, and press OK. The VOB will be made available for use.

ClearCase and ClearQuest

If you are using both Rational ClearCase and Rational ClearQuest, you should know that you need to perform some integration between these tools. ClearQuest tracks bugs and change requests, while ClearCase manages the project files. Once these are integrated, you can say that a file in ClearCase was changed because of a particular bug or change request from ClearQuest. Essentially, the integration lets you track what changed and why.

XDE does integrate with ClearCase, but the integration with ClearQuest is not available. You can still track what changed, by whom, and when, and manually enter comments that explain why the change was made, but you cannot tie the change back to a ClearQuest bug or change request.

Working with Views

A VOB provides a place to store files, but a *view* is what allows users to see the files in the VOB. A view is just a "window" into the VOB. Everyone who wants to use an XDE model under ClearCase control must have a view set up. There are two ways to set up a view:

1. Select ClearCase ➢ Create New View. The View Creation Wizard will appear:

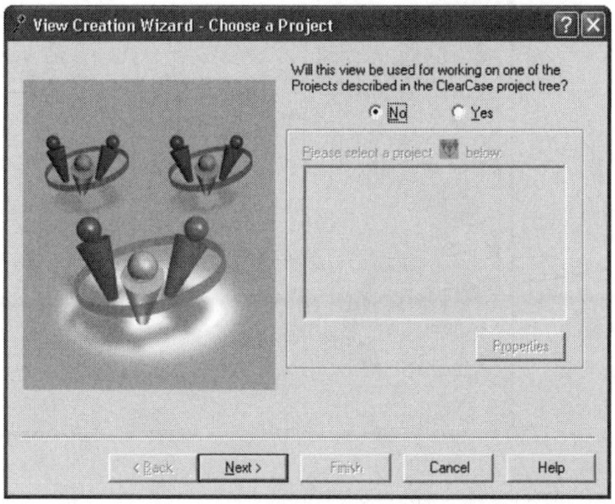

2. Select Yes on this screen and select the project if you are going to be working on a project that has already been set up under ClearCase. The project will use Unified Change Management. Otherwise, select No.
3. Next, select the location for the view. A copy of the most recent files from the VOB will be stored in this view.

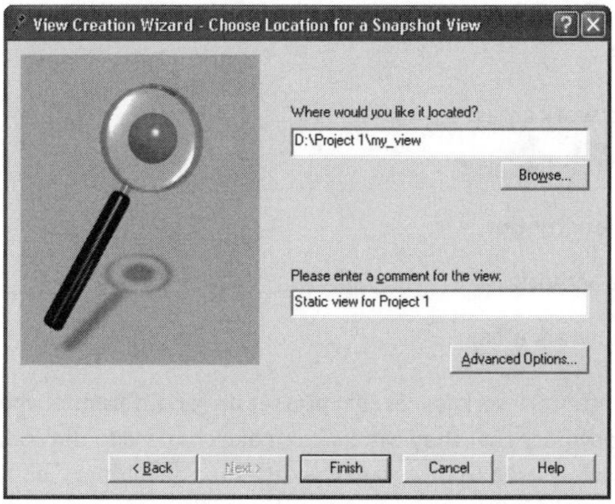

The second way to add a view is through the ClearCase Explorer window. The explorer is just another way to access views and the files contained within them. Figure 2.11 shows the ClearCase Explorer window.

FIGURE 2.11
ClearCase Explorer

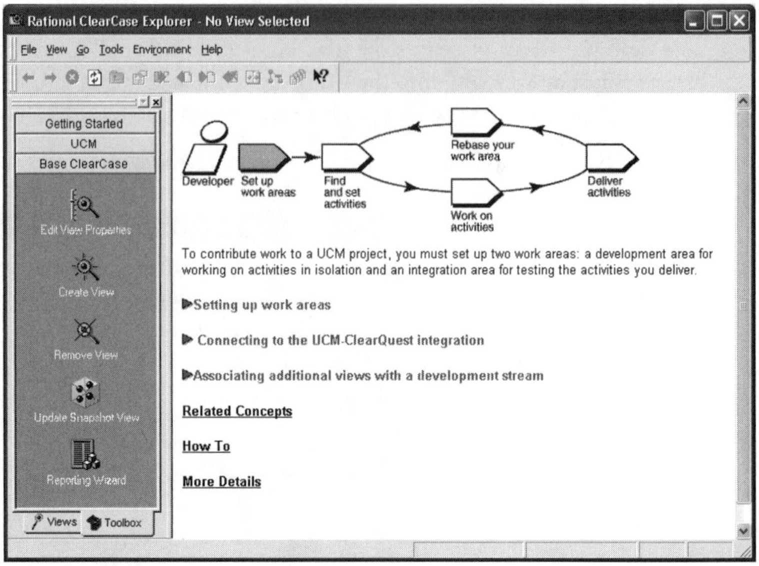

UNIFIED CHANGE MANAGEMENT

Unified Change Management, or UCM, is a configuration management strategy created by Rational. Your ClearCase administrator will have decided whether to set the project up using UCM. UCM helps to ensure that bugs and change requests are managed, that changes to the project artifacts are tied back to the bug or the change request that justified them, and that the configuration management process as a whole is being well managed.

In UCM, the configuration management piece of the software development process is divided into five fundamental steps:

- Set up your work areas.
- Find and set activities.
- Work on the activities.
- Deliver the activities.
- Rebase your work area.

Work areas are different workspaces that you set up for different purposes. Typically, each developer has their own private workspace that they can use to make changes to the code. There is typically also an integration workspace, which is used to integrate the different developers' code together. In a complex project, there might be two types of integration workspaces: a subsystem integration workspace and a system integration workspace. Developers deliver their changes to the subsystem integration workspace. After the subsystems are integrated, they are transferred to the system integration workspace, where the overall system is built.

Continued on next page

UNIFIED CHANGE MANAGEMENT *(continued)*

An *activity* is a series of steps that must be completed to finish a development task. For example, a developer could be assigned the activity "Fix bug #47." The developer may have to change four source code files and make a database change to implement the fix. All of these changes would be tied back to the activity.

Rebasing a work area is the process of copying the most current versions of the project files to a workspace. Developers will want to periodically rebase their workspaces to be sure that they are always working on the most current version of the code.

Like other aspects of the Rational Unified Process, UCM represents an iterative approach. The five steps are repeated as necessary throughout the project; as new bugs or enhancement requests are found, new activities will be created, worked on, and delivered. Developers will rebase their work areas as other developers complete their changes, and new workspaces will need to be created for new developers.

To add a view here, select the Create View button along the left-hand side. The View Creation Wizard will appear, just as it does when you select ClearCase ➢ Create New View from XDE. This wizard is exactly the same as the one started from XDE so you can follow the earlier steps to complete the process.

ADDING A PROJECT OR SOLUTION TO SOURCE CONTROL

Once a VOB has been set up and mounted and you have a view available, you need to create a new project (in XDE for Java) or solution (in XDE for .NET) under source control. (If you already have a project you want to add to source control, you can add it through the Move Project Into ClearCase command, explained at the end of this section.) To create a new project under source control, follow these steps:

1. Select File ➢ New ➢ Project.
2. Select the type of project you want to create and press Next.
3. Enter the project name. Deselect the Use Default Location check box and click Browse to find a location for the new project. In the Browse For Folder window, switch to the location of your ClearCase view. Locate the appropriate directory in this view, and click OK. Click the Finish button. Your new project will be created in the ClearCase view.

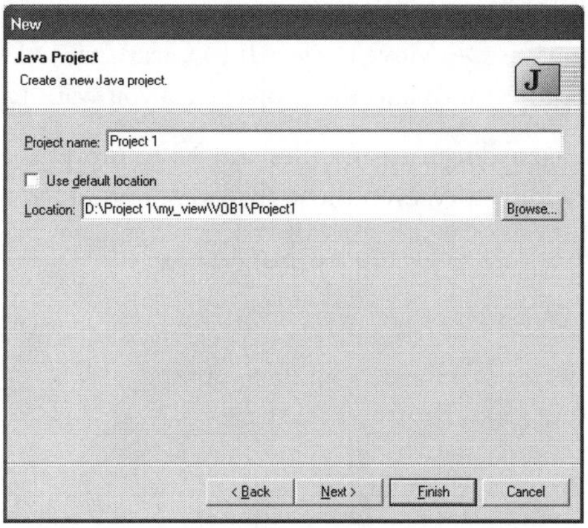

If you are using the Java version of XDE, you will be prompted to add the directory for the new project to source control.

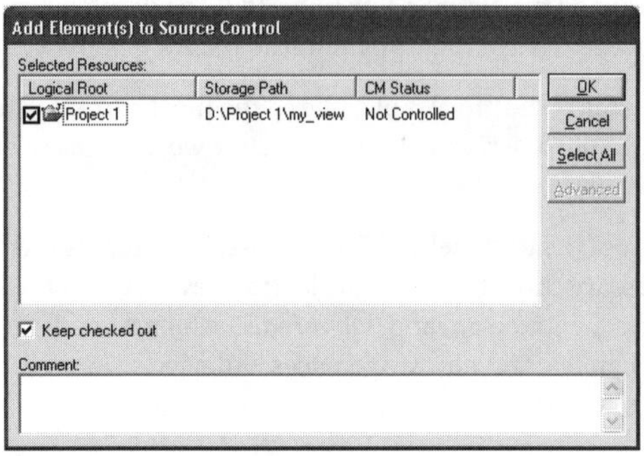

If you are using the .NET version of XDE, select Source Control ➢ Add Solution To Source Control to add the new project to ClearCase.

Now that the project has been added to source control, you will see a small green check mark next to it in the Navigator window.

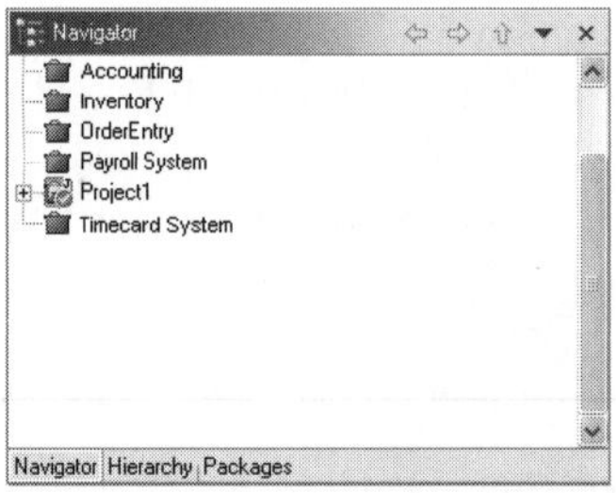

You may have an existing project or two that were never added to source control. To add an existing project:

1. Right-click it in the Navigator.
2. Select ClearCase ➢ Move Project Into ClearCase. XDE prompts you for the view directory to move the project into and the project files you want to add to source control.
3. Select the view directory and files and XDE moves the files. All files in the project are moved to the view directory, even those that were not added to source control.

The next step is to add files to the project.

ADDING FILES TO SOURCE CONTROL

If you've created a model under source control, the elements you create in the model can automatically be added to source control as soon as you create them. This is the simplest approach and can be enabled by setting the ClearCase options in XDE. Select Window ➢ Preferences, and then you can select the ClearCase option.

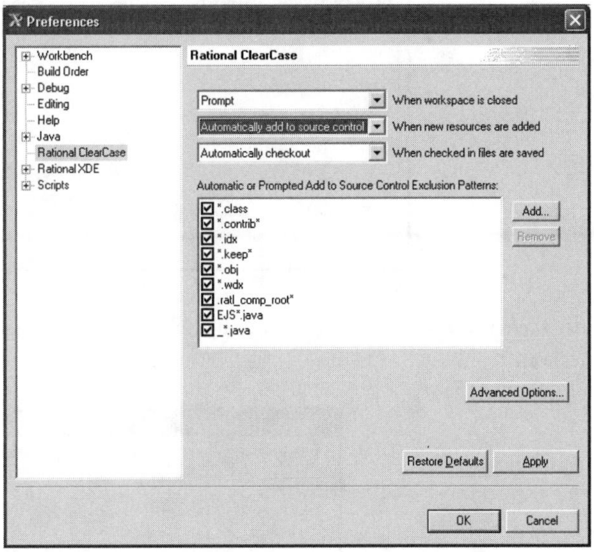

Set the When New Resources Are Added drop-down list box to Automatically Add To Source Control. If you want, you can have XDE prompt you before adding new elements to source control by setting this option to Prompt. The final option is Do Nothing, in which case you have to manually add new elements to source control.

A final option is to exclude certain types of files from being automatically added to version control. Use the lower portion of the ClearCase options screen to select files you want ClearCase to ignore. In the screen shown previously, for example, new classes are not automatically added to source control, and XDE will not prompt you to add new classes.

To manually add an element to source control, right-click it in the Explorer window. From the pop-up menu, select ClearCase ➢ Add To Source Control. Note that before you can add an element to source control, the project it is contained in must be added.

CHECKING IN AND CHECKING OUT

The essence of a configuration management tool is, of course, the ability to check files out, make changes to them, and check them back in. This is a pretty straightforward process in XDE.

Checking Out a File

To check out a file, right-click it and use the ClearCase ➢ Check Out option. You will see the Check Out Element(s) window:

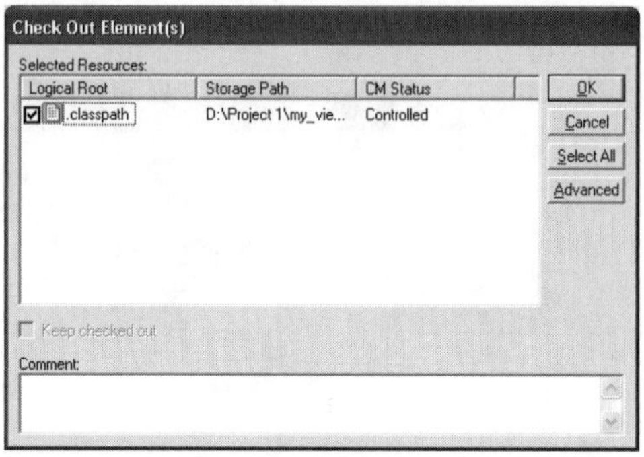

Select the file(s) you want to check out and click OK or select the Advanced button to set the type of checkout:

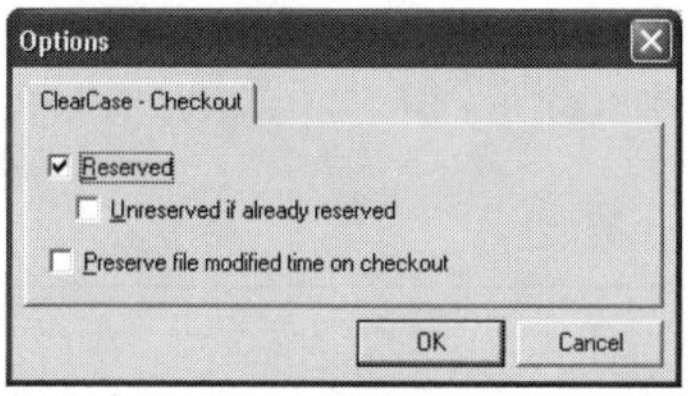

There are a few options here:

- Deselect both the Reserved and Unreserved If Already Reserved check boxes. This gives you an unreserved checkout. Anyone else can also check out the file, and you'll need to merge your changes later.
- Select Reserved, but not Unreserved If Already Reserved. The Reserved option tries to give you an exclusive checkout of the file. If it succeeds in getting you an exclusive checkout, no one else may check out the file until you've checked it back in. If ClearCase can't give you an exclusive checkout (for example, if someone else already has it checked out), the checkout process stops.
- Select both Reserved and Unreserved If Already Reserved. With these options, ClearCase tries to give you an exclusive checkout, but if this isn't possible you'll still be given a nonexclusive checkout.

Once you've made your decision on the type of checkout you need, click OK to complete the checkout process.

TIP *To set the default type of checkout, go to the ClearCase options area of Window ➢ Preferences. Select the Advanced Options button and then the Operations tab. The checkout type you select here will be the default for checkouts in the future.*

Checking In a File

To check in a file, right-click it and select ClearCase ➢ Check In. Select the file(s) to check in and click OK, or select the Advanced button. There are three options in the Advanced window:

Check in even if identical By default, ClearCase will not allow you to check in a file if you haven't changed it (you can right-click and select Undo Checkout in this case). If you want to do a check-in, even if the file hasn't changed, select this option and ClearCase will allow the check-in.

Query for comment on each file If selected, ClearCase prompts you for a comment for each file you want to check in. The comment should briefly explain what was changed and why.

Preserve file modified time on check-in If you have a file already open in an editor and are checking it out, you are prompted to reload the file because it appears to have changed. Selecting this option prevents this prompt from appearing.

MERGING CHANGES

If two or more developers have changed the same file at the same time, the changes need to be merged. ClearCase automatically detects a merge situation, and displays the files in a window in which you can compare and merge them. Figure 2.12 shows a simple example of file differences that might require a merge.

In this example, one line was added to `Account.java`. ClearCase marks lines that were added, removed, or changed, and it uses different icons to let you know what the changes are. Table 2.3 lists the icons and their meanings.

FIGURE 2.12

Compare and merge files.

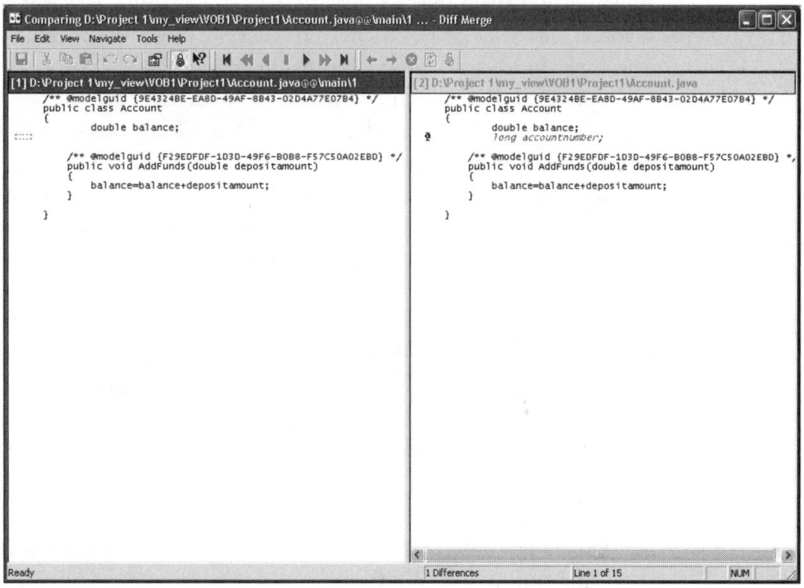

TABLE 2.3: ICONS FOR COMPARING AND MERGING FILES

ICON	MEANING	ICON	MEANING
	Changed		Inserted
	Deleted		InsertMoved
	DeleteMoved		Padding
	Different Object ID		Unchanged

The Diff Merge tool can compare and merge up to 16 versions of a file at a time. One of the *contributors* (file versions) is the base file, against which all of the other contributors are compared. You will see icons such as the ones listed in Table 2.3 next to any lines that were added, removed, or changed.

To merge the files, you must go through each difference, and decide which contributor's code to accept for that difference. Use the Next Difference button in the toolbar to find the differences.

Then, select the number of the contributor whose code should be accepted. For example, in Figure 2.12, shown earlier, we would select contributor 1 if we didn't want to keep the new variable, and contributor 2 if we did want to keep it.

DELIVERING AND REBASING STREAMS

When you and your team are using ClearCase, the changes you make won't be available to others until you deliver them to your development stream. Similarly, you can't see the changes that others have made until they deliver them to the development stream and you rebase the stream. *Rebasing* a stream is the process of retrieving the most recent versions of all of the files in the stream so that you can be sure you're working with the most current files.

To deliver your changes to the stream, select ClearCase ➢ Deliver Stream. To rebase, select ClearCase ➢ Rebase Stream.

Using ClearCase, the team can periodically create builds. A *build* is an operational version of the system, or a subset of the system. For details on creating builds with ClearCase, see the ClearCase documentation. To start the process from XDE, select ClearCase ➢ ClearCase Build.

For Further Reading

Although we address the topics of this chapter as thoroughly as is necessary for you to be able to take full advantage of XDE, there is more you can learn. For more information on the Rational Unified Process, see the following sources:

- `www.rational.com`
- Kruchten, Phillipe. *The Rational Unified Process: An Introduction,* Second Edition (Addison-Wesley, 2000)
- Jacobson, Ivar, et al. *The Unified Software Development Process* (Addison-Wesley, 1999)

For more information on eXtreme Programming, see

- `www.extremeprogramming.org`
- Beck, Kent. *Extreme Programming Explained: Embrace Change* (Addison-Wesley, 1999)
- Beck, Kent and Fowler, Martin. *Planning Extreme Programming* (Addison-Wesley, 2000)
- Jeffries, Ron, et al. *Extreme Programming Installed* (Addison-Wesley, 2000)

For more information on Rational ClearCase, see

- `www.rational.com`
- White, Brian A. and Clemm, Geoffrey M. *Software Configuration Management Strategies and Rational ClearCase: A Practical Introduction* (Addison-Wesley, 2000)

Summary

Even the best of tools may not help an organization reach its full potential. A tool in the context of a well-developed software development lifecycle methodology, however, can make a significant difference for a team. In this chapter, we discussed how XDE can be used in two of the more common iterative methodologies used today: the Rational Unified Process and eXtreme Programming.

In both cases, XDE is mainly used in the analysis, design, and coding steps, and in the testing to some degree. RUP is broken down into four phases and nine disciplines. XDE can be used in all four phases and in five of the nine disciplines. In eXtreme Programming, XDE is used to develop code and architectural spikes, to develop acceptance tests and unit tests, to create and track releases, and to track tasks that need to be done.

Here are some important things to remember from this chapter:

Select a methodology. You don't have to select one of the two discussed here, but do consider some of the items we talked about during your selection process. For example, look at your corporate culture, current skill sets, and existing processes. Then select the methodology that will best fit your organization's needs.

Determine how XDE will be used in your methodology. Identify the steps in which XDE will be used, and be sure everyone on the team knows when and how to use XDE to accomplish their goals.

Set up a ClearCase repository, as well as configuration management policies. Be sure everyone on the team is set up to use ClearCase and is familiar with the policies.

In the remainder of this book, we explore an example of how XDE can be used in a real-world project. The next chapter is an introduction to the problem domain used in the exercises.

Chapter 3

Introduction to the Exercises: A Study for Real-World Application Development

IN THIS CHAPTER, we introduce a hypothetical case study to develop a timekeeping system for an enterprise and to interface this new system with an existing legacy application. We will use this full-scale example in the exercises throughout the remainder of this book.

Although this is a hypothetical example, it includes many of the real-world elements that projects must face: tight deadlines, low budgets, personnel issues, and so on. Please keep these conditions in mind as you work through the exercises in this book. You can use XDE to reduce the time needed to design and code a system, so it can help with the budget, the schedule, and other typical project challenges.

Featured in this chapter:

- Project background
- A new plan: developing a timekeeping system
- Vision statement
- Existing architecture
- Business analysis

Background

Allow us to introduce you to StayHere, Inc.—a small fictional hotel chain with 20 properties across the United States. The company was founded 18 years ago by an innkeeper who started with one small inn. From there, he started to purchase other properties and eventually built the business up to what it is today. StayHere employs approximately 700 people including the corporate office, hotel management, bell staff, restaurant staff, and housekeeping staff.

Not long ago, the Chief Financial Officer (CFO) of the corporation made a presentation to the Board of Directors showing that the recent economic downturn has caused a drop in sales and a concomitant drop in gross and net profit. The corporation has managed to eke out at least a small profit each year up until now. The CFO's grim news showed that for the first time in its history, StayHere would post a loss. The board formed a task force to investigate methods that could improve the situation. The group came back with ideas for comarketing campaigns, promotions, and other strategies designed to influence sales. They also investigated the overhead cost–side of the equation. StayHere had not engaged in any nefarious accounting practices designed to shield the company's real costs, so the data was readily available. The task force concluded that the corporation had bloated its corporate office staff to 100 employees when fewer should be able to accomplish the same tasks. So, each manager in the office was charged with reducing their headcount by 20 percent—not a fun prospect to consider.

The Human Resources (HR) director investigated her staff of 15 and thought about how she could reduce the staff to 9. First, she asked everyone in the department to fill out a short survey indicating roughly how much time they spent on various HR-related tasks. When she tabulated the results, she discovered that the top three time-intensive tasks were

- Handling timesheets
- Handling changes to employee data
- Handling new hires and terminations

She decided to tackle these issues in order of their severity. She began by investigating the timesheet process, which was very time-intensive and manual. She found that StayHere uses a legacy human resources system and that employees at the hotels do not have direct access to it. As a result, timesheets must be delivered from the hotels to the HR staff, who then enter the information into the legacy system so that paychecks will print properly. She figured that optimizing this process would enable her to reduce her staff by at least 20 percent.

A New Plan: Developing a Timekeeping System

Armed with the survey data, the HR director got together with StayHere's CFO and asked if they could start a project to optimize the timekeeping process. He thought that was a great idea and they started the project.

The first question they asked was what the real problem was. Based on results from the HR director's survey data, this problem seemed apparent. After creating a vision statement for the project (see following sidebar), they also investigated the alternatives it mentions.

The remainder of this chapter covers the outcome of the vision discussion and the investigation of the alternatives presented in it. This project will be used throughout the remainder of the book as an exercise to instruct you in the use of the Rational XDE product.

Vision Statement

The following is the vision statement for the StayHere Timekeeping project. This statement briefly overviews the project: it states the problem and then identifies the users and stakeholders and the features of the system. The vision statement should make this project easy to understand for any team member.

Introduction

This vision statement identifies the project stakeholders, the stakeholder needs, and the high-level features of the StayHere Timekeeping system.

References

The following documents are referenced in this vision statement. You can refer to these documents for the project's detailed requirements.

- Software Requirements Specification: Contains detailed functional requirements for the project
- Supplementary Specification: Contains detailed nonfunctional requirements for the project

Problem Statement

Routine personnel time-tracking tasks are severely impacting an already overwhelmed Human Resources department. An estimated 25 percent of the staff's time is currently consumed by administrative tasks associated with timekeeping. These tasks include collecting hard copies of timesheets, reviewing the timesheets for completeness and accuracy, obtaining a manager's approval if needed, and entering time-card data into the legacy payroll system to prepare for a payroll run. In addition, the staff must maintain payroll codes (regular time, overtime, sick leave, and so on), and distribute a list of the codes to all the employees any time the codes are changed.

This, in turn, affects the HR department's ability to provide other services, including payroll reporting and reconciliation; benefits counseling and administration; and hiring, promotion, and firing functions. A successful solution would reduce the time the HR department spends on timekeeping-related tasks by 60 percent or more.

Stakeholders and Users

The stakeholders of this project and their current job responsibilities are as follows:

Stakeholder	Responsibilities
HR Administrator	Maintain employee records.
	Review and enter employee timecard data.
	Maintain and distribute payroll codes.
	Report payroll.
	Reconcile payroll.

Continued on next page

VISION STATEMENT *(continued)*

Stakeholder	Responsibilities
	Administer benefits.
	Counsel employees about their benefits.
	Oversee the hiring process and associated recordkeeping.
	Oversee the promotion process and associated recordkeeping.
	Oversee the firing process and associated recordkeeping.
	Resolve employee grievances.
HR Manager	Manage the HR department.
Employees	Provide information to the HR department related to employee and time information.

Here are the users of the system and their responsibilities in the final system:

User	Responsibilities
HR Administrator	Review and adjust the timecards.
	Maintain payroll codes.
HR Manager	Approve specific types of timecard adjustments.
Employees	Enter timecard data.
Managers	Approve employees' timecards.

KEY STAKEHOLDER NEEDS

Interviews with the stakeholders provided the following list of needs:

Stakeholder	Priority	Need
Employee	High	Timely processing of timecard information so that the payroll process is not delayed
	High	Access to up-to-date payroll codes to reduce errors in timesheets
	Medium	Access to timecard information from previous pay periods
HR Administrator	High	Reduced time spent on timekeeping functions
	High	Consistency in the data between applications
	Medium	Ability to view a summary of employee time data
HR Manager	High	Reduced time spent in the HR department on timekeeping functions

Continued on next page

VISION STATEMENT *(continued)*

FEATURES

The following features were identified as needed for the new system:

- Ability for an employee to submit and view their own timesheet information
- Ability for an employee's manager to approve timesheets for their employees
- Ability for an HR administrator to review a timesheet for accuracy, and make any needed adjustments
- Ability for an HR administrator to maintain payroll codes

The following features are available in the legacy system and will *not* be included in this project:

- Payroll
- Benefits administration
- Employee personal information maintenance (name, address, and so on)

ALTERNATIVES

Four primary alternatives were discussed in relation to this project. A summary of the analysis of each of the alternatives is provided below:

Do nothing This alternative proposes keeping the existing legacy system and current human resources processes.

Advantages	Disadvantages
Reduced training time. Staff is already familiar with current software and processes.	High annual cost
Reduced potential for errors. Staff is already familiar with current software and processes.	Failure to meet the needs identified earlier

Purchase a commercial timekeeping software package This alternative proposes finding commercial software that will meet the needs of the company.

After an initial review of the marketplace, the team identified four packages that provide the types of functionality needed. These fall into two categories: the first category includes packages that provide full human resources management including payroll, benefits administration, employee record maintenance, and timekeeping; the second category includes applications that provide only for timekeeping.

Advantages	Disadvantages
Saves the time that would be required for the Information Technology department to develop an in-house solution	The cost of packages in the first category (complete human resources management) are prohibitively high.
	The timekeeping packages are unable to interface with the existing legacy system unless major modifications are made.
	The packages cannot be customized or modified.

Continued on next page

VISION STATEMENT *(continued)*

Rewrite the legacy system to speed timekeeping functions This alternative proposes that portions of the legacy system be rewritten to optimize timecard processing.

Advantages	Disadvantages
No need to maintain and integrate two systems	The skill set of current IT staff does not support this solution; the existing system was developed in a technology with which most of the current IT staff are not familiar.
	Increases investment in an outdated technology.
	Eliminates the option of providing some of the functionality over the company intranet.
	For security reasons, not all employees currently have access to the legacy system; this would still hold true for the altered system. Therefore the HR department would still need to manually enter timecards.

Develop a separate system for timekeeping functions This alternative proposes building a separate system for timekeeping functions, which would interface with the legacy system.

Advantages	Disadvantages
Ability to interface with the legacy system	Time required for the IT staff to develop a separate application
Customized application to meet the company's needs	

ASSUMPTIONS AND DEPENDENCIES

The following assumptions were made in preparing this vision statement:

- The existing legacy system will continue to be used to run payroll and administer benefits.
- The existing legacy system will continue to maintain an employee's personal information.

Existing Architecture

The current process is supported by a legacy system that was written about 15 years ago by developers who are no longer with the company. There are two people in the IT department who maintain the system; the rest of the IT department is focused on newer technologies. Figure 3.1 is an overview of the high-level network architecture of the legacy system.

FIGURE 3.1
Existing high-level network architecture

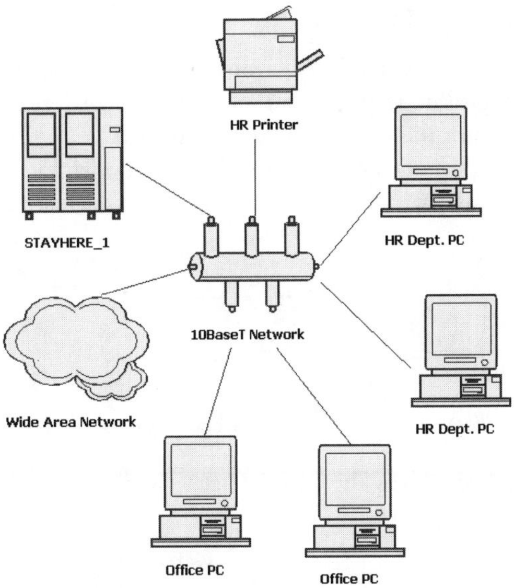

The architecture hasn't really changed much in the last 15 years, but it has been upgraded to run the most current versions of DB2 and COBOL. The mainframe hosts two applications, payroll and accounting. The relationship between these is shown in the deployment diagram in Figure 3.2. The users of the system connect through desktop PCs using terminal emulator software to interact with these applications.

FIGURE 3.2
Existing system deployment diagram

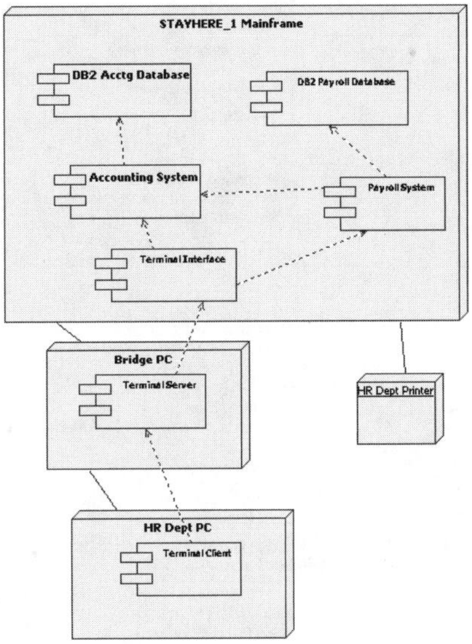

Business Analysis

To focus the problem statement a little bit more, the project manager decided to include some business modeling in the project. In particular, she wanted to analyze the current timekeeping process and discuss ways in which the process could be improved.

To begin, the team put together a business use case model, focusing on the administrative side of the business. The use cases were grouped into packages, which are shown in Figure 3.3.

FIGURE 3.3
Business use case packages

NOTE *If you aren't familiar with business use case or package notation, see this book's appendix, "Getting Started with UML."*

Figures 3.4 through 3.6 show the business actors and use cases within each of the three packages.

FIGURE 3.4
Personnel business use cases

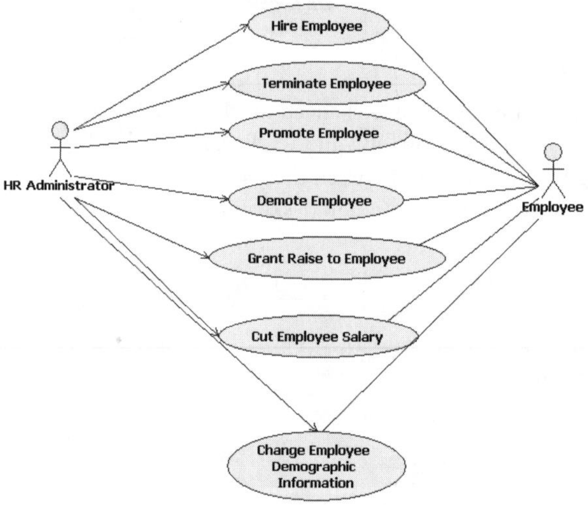

FIGURE 3.5
Payroll business use cases

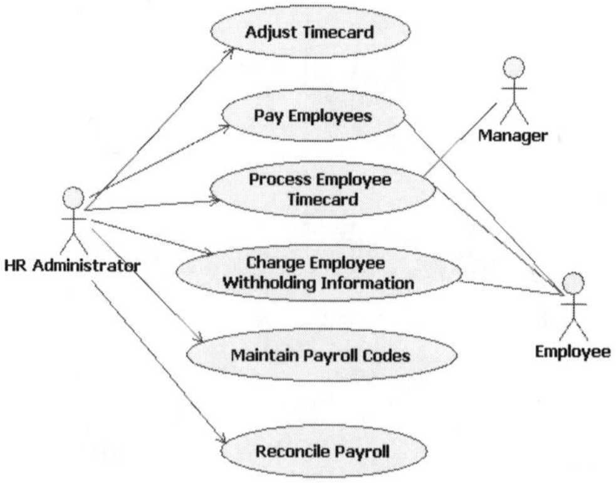

FIGURE 3.6

Human Resources business use cases

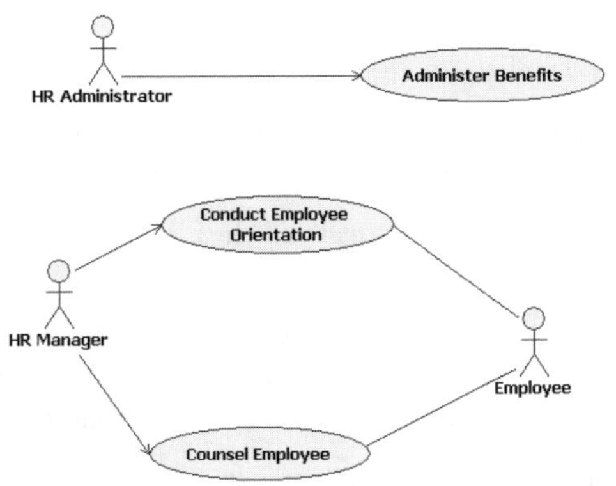

NOTE *If you are familiar with Rose or other UML modeling tools, you may be used to seeing business actors and use cases with a slash. XDE does not include this notation, and it makes no distinction between business use cases and system use cases.*

Because this project will automate the timekeeping portion of the business, the team then built an activity diagram for the current timekeeping process. Figure 3.7 is an activity diagram of the current process, which is largely manual.

FIGURE 3.7

Current timekeeping process

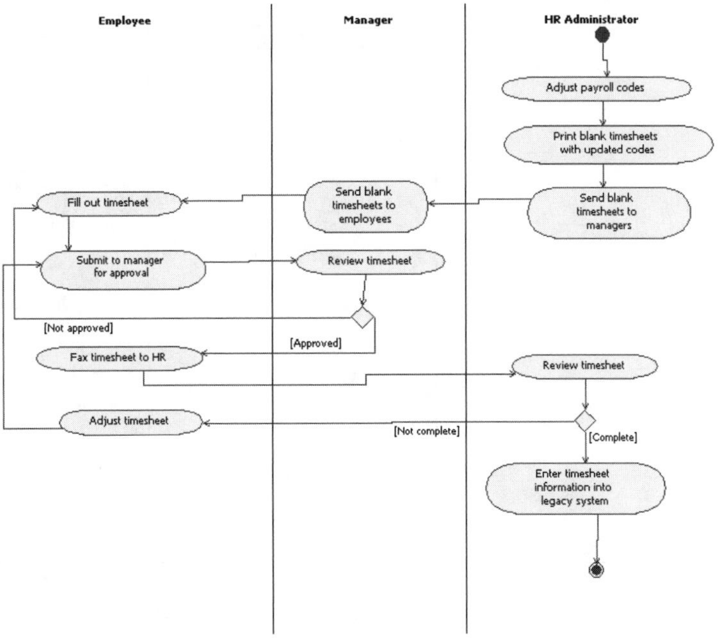

Some of the major problems with this process include:

- Any time anyone has trouble with a fax machine or doesn't have immediate access to one, the whole process slows down.
- The HR department spends hours and hours reprinting and sending blank timesheets anytime a payroll code changes, which occurs fairly frequently.
- The separate reviews by the manager and the HR administrator are redundant and time-consuming.
- The HR department has to manually enter each employee's timesheet into the timekeeping system, in addition to the employees manually entering their time on the timesheet. This increases the amount of time needed for the process and increases the potential for error.
- Validation errors have to be caught manually. The HR manager has been noticing an increase in the number of errors that were slipping through the cracks.

By analyzing this diagram, the team was able to come up with ways of improving and automating the current process. The new workflow is shown in Figure 3.8.

Through this analysis, the team hoped to automate and simplify timekeeping as much as possible. Some of the major improvements were the addition of automatic validation, and the ability for employees to enter their time directly into the system, removing the double entry. The HR department no longer had to print and distribute new timesheets with updated payroll codes, and the managers no longer had to distribute the new timesheets to their employees.

FIGURE 3.8
Proposed timekeeping process

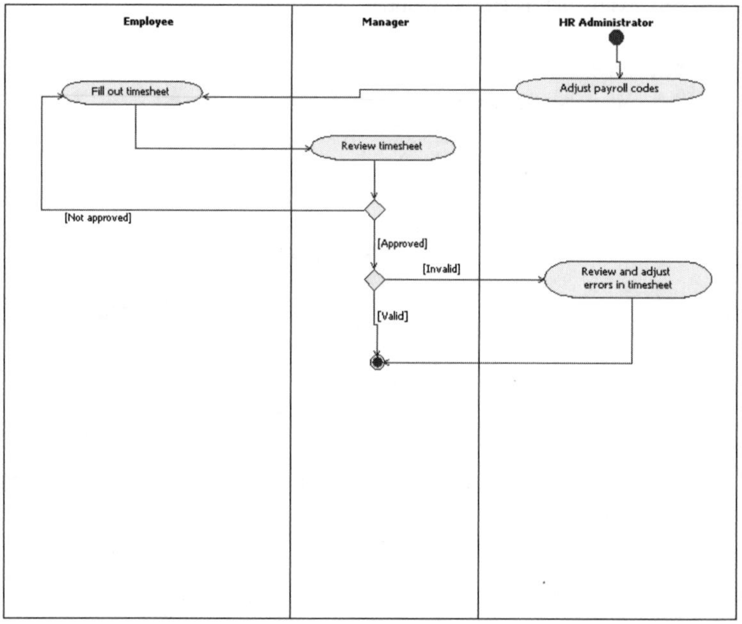

Proposed Architectural Alternatives

Later in the Inception phase, the team did some brainstorming related to the system architecture and came up with a few high-level alternatives. They did not want to make a final decision until later in the project, but by analyzing the alternatives, they were able to estimate costs and identify some initial architectural risks.

We've gone down both the Java and the .NET paths in this book. To complete the project using J2EE, see Chapter 5, "Modeling Java and J2EE Elements in XDE." To complete the project using .NET, see Chapter 6, "Modeling Visual Studio .NET Elements in XDE." Exercises in the remaining chapters can be done in either technology.

NOTE *Note that architectural decisions are better left to the Elaboration phase. We are showing the options here simply to provide background for the problem.*

Use Cases

Before getting into architectural decisions, the team first needed to analyze the problem itself, and gather some requirements. After several brainstorming sessions with user representatives, the first draft of the use case diagram was created and is shown in Figure 3.9.

FIGURE 3.9

Use cases for the timekeeping system

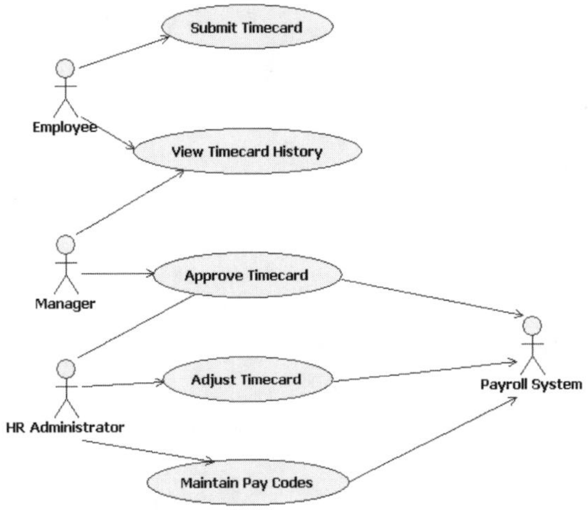

Summary

This chapter provided some background for the timekeeping exercise that is used in the remainder of this book. In the RUP process, which is being used in this example, the vision statement, business use case diagram, and initial use case diagram are created in the Inception phase. Architectural decisions are made in Elaboration.

We looked here at a small hotel chain that, like many other organizations, needed an automated-way to record and keep track of its employees' time. In the remainder of this book, we use XDE to model and build the application.

Part II

Visual Modeling with XDE

In this part:

- Chapter 4: Integrated Use Case Management
- Chapter 5: Modeling Java and J2EE Elements in XDE
- Chapter 6: Modeling Visual Studio .NET Elements in XDE
- Chapter 7: Modeling Databases with XDE
- Chapter 8: Publishing and Reporting Models

Chapter 4

Integrated Use Case Management

ALTHOUGH XDE IS MAINLY a design and development tool, it does play a critical role in requirements management. Specifically, it helps to tie the design and code of the project back to the requirements. This is a crucial step for any project team that wants to be sure all of the requirements were met and that every piece of the design is there because of a requirement. It also gives the developers the added benefit of a deeper understanding of the user's needs. This link between design and requirements is referred to as *Integrated Use Case Management (IUCM)*.

XDE is also valuable in developing and documenting pieces of the use case model, in particular the use case diagrams. XDE can be used to define use cases and actors, establish relationships between them, and group them into packages.

In this chapter, we look at use case modeling and requirements management, but from a developer's perspective. We're assuming that you are familiar with use cases, but we do provide a quick introduction to use cases and actors for those who are not.

We also talk about how to build an analysis model in XDE. An *analysis model* is an implementation-independent view of the system structure. It's started early in the project, before the team has decided what programming languages or other tools and technologies to use. It is made up of analysis classes, analysis-level sequence diagrams, and analysis-level class diagrams. We discuss each of these diagrams, their purpose, and how to create them in XDE.

At the end of the chapter is an exercise designed to give you some practice in implementing all of these concepts in XDE.

Featured in this chapter:

- Introduction to requirements management
- Building use case diagrams in XDE
- Packaging use cases and actors
- Integrated use case management with XDE and RequisitePro
- Building activity diagrams in XDE

- Creating an analysis model in XDE
- Packaging classes and other analysis model elements in XDE
- Building analysis-level sequence diagrams in XDE
- Building analysis-level class diagrams in XDE

Introduction to Requirements Management

Why should developers worry about requirements? After all, it's the analysts' job to gather requirements; developers just implement them, right?

Well, sort of. One of the problems we seem to encounter is a "throw it over the wall" mentality between the analysis group and the development group. The trouble is, what we're missing in this situation is any sort of a deep understanding of the users' needs by the developers, and any sort of understanding of the system structure by the analysts. So, we can end up with a system with requirements that can't be met by the design, or with a design that doesn't really meet the users' needs. Either way, we've got some unhappy customers.

To help get around this problem, the team can trace the use cases in XDE to the detailed system requirements in RequisitePro or some other requirements management repository.

NOTE *XDE interfaces directly with RequisitePro, Rational's requirements management tool. If you aren't using RequisitePro, you can still trace the requirements, but it will be more of a manual process. See the section "Integrated Use Case Management" later in this chapter.*

Linking XDE to a requirements management tool helps you trace requirements more completely. You can trace the design in the use case realizations to the use cases themselves, and trace the use cases to the detailed requirements. You will then find it easier to ensure that every requirement was met, and that every part of the design is there because of a requirement.

The essential pieces of a use case model are:

Use case diagrams Modeled in XDE, these provide a visual representation of the project's scope.

Use case documentation Maintained outside of XDE, these documents provide a detailed description of the flow of events through the use cases.

Supplementary Specification Maintained outside of XDE, this artifact is a repository for all of the detailed nonfunctional requirements of the system.

Software Requirements Specification (SRS) Maintained outside of XDE, the SRS is a repository of detailed functional and nonfunctional requirements for the use cases. Commonly, the SRS is a *virtual artifact* consisting of the use case diagrams, use case specifications, and the Supplementary Specification.

In this chapter, we focus on use case diagrams but also discuss how to link XDE to the use case documents and SRS. Let's start with use case diagrams.

Building a Use Case Diagram in XDE

A *use case diagram* is a way to display some of the actors and/or use cases in a system. The notation is, by design, very simple, so the use case diagrams are an effective way to communicate with the project team without getting into technical details or jargon.

A typical project has multiple use case diagrams: some for actors, some for use cases, and some showing both actors and use cases. Create as many diagrams as you need to fully express the functionality of the system. Some recommended diagrams include the following:

- A diagram for each package, showing all actors and/or use cases in that package, and their relationships.
- A diagram showing the inheritance hierarchy of actors.
- A diagram showing the inheritance hierarchy of use cases.
- A diagram showing only the packages, and their relationships to one another.
- A diagram showing a use case and all actors and use cases with relationships to that use case.
- (For smaller systems) a diagram showing all use cases and actors in the system, and their relationships.

Because XDE maintains everything in a repository, changing an item on one use case diagram automatically changes the item on all of them. This makes maintenance of the model much simpler if everyone is sharing the same XDE files. Note, however, that if multiple people are each working off of their own XDE model, you need to synchronize everyone's changes periodically.

Creating Use Case Diagrams

A use case diagram may contain actors, use cases, packages, notes, constraints, or one of several different types of relationships. Use case diagrams can also include a box that delineates the boundary of the system. Use cases are drawn within the box, while actors are drawn outside of it.

As we mentioned earlier, you can create as many different diagrams as you need. Start with one diagram for the system. As you identify more and more use cases, you may want to create packages and more diagrams. Figure 4.1 shows the use case diagram for the timekeeping system that will be referred to in this book's exercises. (This system was described in detail in Chapter 3, "Introduction to the Exercises: A Study for Real-World Application Development.")

To create a use case diagram in XDE, follow these steps:

1. In the Explorer window, right-click the element (model, package, use case, or actor) to which you'd like to add the diagram.
2. Select Add Diagram ➢ Use Case. A new entry appears in the tree, with the symbol shown here: 
3. Type the name of the new diagram.

XDE automatically opens the new diagram for you. To rename the diagram, right-click it in the Explorer window, and select Rename, or select the diagram in the Explorer window, click it so that the cursor appears in the window, and type the new name. While you can create two diagrams with the same name, we recommend that you use unique diagram names.

FIGURE 4.1
Timekeeping system use cases

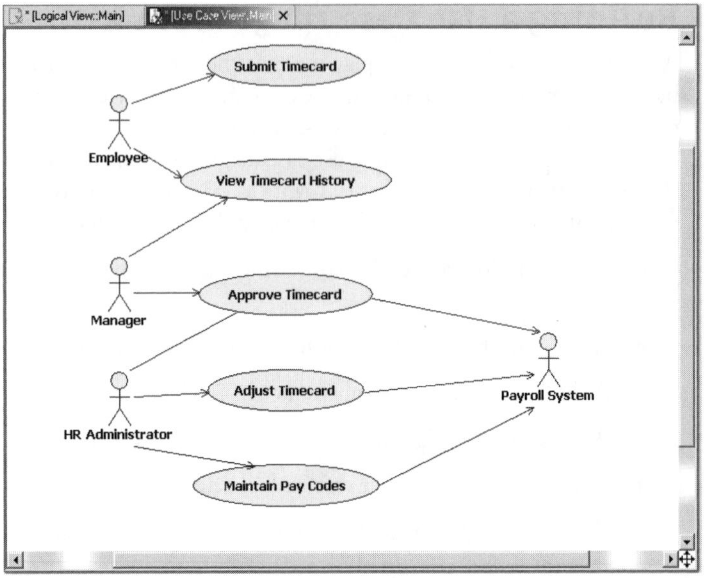

The UML Use Case Toolbox

The toolbox provides buttons that can be used to create the use cases, actors, relationships, and other elements discussed in the remainder of this chapter. Table 4.1 lists the toolbox options and their meanings, and which sections of this chapter to see for more detail.

TABLE 4.1: UML USE CASE TOOLBOX

ICON	MEANING	SEE SECTION
Pointer	Returns the mouse to the standard pointer	
Package	Creates a UML package, which can be used to group use cases and/or actors together	"Packaging Use Cases and Actors"
Use Case	Creates a use case, which describes part of the system's behavior	"Finding Use Cases"
Actor	Creates an actor, which is an entity outside the system scope	"Finding Actors"
Dependency	Creates a dependency, which signifies that one package needs to access or add the public contents of another	"Defining Relationships between Packages"
Access	Allows one package to access the public contents of another	"Defining Relationships between Packages"

Continued on next page

TABLE 4.1: UML USE CASE TOOLBOX *(continued)*

ICON	MEANING	SEE SECTION
Import	Allows one package to add the public contents of another	"Defining Relationships between Packages"
Include	Allows one use case to include the functionality provided by another	"Defining Use Case Relationships"
Extend	Allows one use case to optionally add to the functionality provided by another	"Defining Use Case Relationships"
Association	Defines relationship between an actor and a use case with bidirectional navigability	"Defining Association Relationships between Actors and Use Cases"
Directed Association	Defines relationship between an actor and a use case with navigability in one direction	"Defining Association Relationships between Actors and Use Cases"
Generalization	Defines an inheritance relationship for actors or use cases	"Defining Use Case Relationships" and "Defining Actor Relationships"
Note	Adds a simple note to the diagram	
Note Attachment	Attaches a note to a use case or other element	
Constraint	Refines the structure or behavior of an element	
Constraint Attachment	Attaches a constraint to an element	
Text	Adds text to the diagram	

LINKING USE CASE DIAGRAMS

As you create more and more use case diagrams, you may want to link some of them together. For example, you may have a package on one diagram that has a more detailed use case diagram behind it. With XDE, you can easily set up these links. Just follow these steps:

1. On the high-level diagram, add a note using the Note icon in the UML Use Case toolbox.
2. Use the Note Attachment icon in the toolbox to attach the note to a package, use case, or other element on the diagram. You don't have to attach the note to anything; if you'd rather use a free-floating note, you can do that.
3. In the Model Explorer, right-click the model, a package, a use case, or an actor, and select Add Diagram ➢ Use Case.
4. Build the detailed use case diagram, using the steps described in the rest of this "Building a Use Case Diagram in XDE" section.

5. On the high-level diagram, drag and drop the detailed use case diagram to the note. The name of the detailed diagram appears in the note. Now when you double-click the note, the detailed diagram opens.

TIP *This process works on other types of diagrams, too. Just create a note and drag and drop a diagram from the Explorer onto the note. Double-clicking the note then opens the linked diagram.*

FINDING USE CASES

The UML version 1.4 defines a *use case* as "the specification of a sequence of actions, including variants, that a system (or another entity) can perform, interacting with actors of the system." In essence, a use case is a textual description of a piece of functionality within the system. It represents a "conversation" between the system and an actor, and this conversation provides some observable result of value to the actor. To determine what the use case is, it helps to answer the question, "What can you do with the system?" For instance, the classic examples of use cases for an Automated Teller Machine (ATM) include Withdraw Cash, Deposit Check, and Transfer Funds. Each use case contains the details, from the user's point of view, for completing the appropriate transaction. A use case is drawn as an oval:

The list of features in the vision statement is a good place to start looking for use cases. The features give you a high-level understanding of what the system is supposed to do, and from this, you might be able to start identifying some slightly lower-level pieces of functionality that will become your use cases. Look at any actors you have identified so far, and answer the question, "What will this actor do with the system?" A great way to identify use cases is through a use case workshop with the stakeholders. It may take a little while, but by the end of the workshop, everyone should have a common understanding of the use cases. Be sure to write a short, one- or two-sentence description of each use case so that everyone stays on the same page as the project goes along. At this point, identify all of the candidate use cases you can. As the iterations progress, you may end up combining or even eliminating some of the use cases.

Use cases are containers for the functional requirements of the system. While XDE can be used to draw the use cases themselves, it is not used to manage all of the detailed requirements within each use case. See the "Integrated Use Case Management" section later in this chapter for details related to managing requirements.

XDE allows you to have two use cases with the same name, but we recommend that each use case be given a unique name. Use cases are typically named using the format <*verb*><*noun*>, such as "Deposit Check," and they should be named using business terminology, not technical terminology. Use cases are related to actors via association relationships (see the section "Defining Association Relationships between Actors and Use Cases" later in this chapter) and may be related to other use cases via include, extend, or generalization relationships (see the section "Defining Use Case Relationships" later in this chapter).

Use cases have a number of properties in XDE, including the ones listed in Table 4.2.

TABLE 4.2: USE CASE PROPERTIES IN XDE

CATEGORY	PROPERTY	DESCRIPTION
ClassicRose	Rank	The Rank property is used to prioritize the use case. You can use whatever prioritization scheme you'd like—numeric, alphabetic, or a high, medium, or low ranking.
UML	Name	Sets the name of the use case.
UML	IsAbstract	Controls whether or not the use case is abstract. An abstract use case, like an abstract class, is one that is never directly instantiated. Abstract use cases are typically parents in a generalization relationship, and they exist only to hold some common functionality.
RequisitePro	ReqProProjectPath	Displays the path and filename of the RequisitePro project associated with the use case.

To add use cases to a use case diagram in XDE, follow these steps:

1. Select the Use Case option from the UML Use Case area of the toolbox.
2. Click anywhere inside the use case diagram to place the new use case.
3. Type the name of the new use case.
4. Edit the properties of the new use case if necessary.
5. Repeat steps 1–4 for each use case you'd like to add to the model.

The new use case appears on the diagram and also in the Explorer window. A use case in the Explorer window has this symbol: 

FINDING ACTORS

The UML 1.4 defines an *actor* as "a coherent set of roles that users of use cases play when interacting with these use cases." In other words, an actor is a role that someone or something plays when interacting with the system. By definition, an actor is outside the system scope, but an actor must directly interact with the system.

Many of your actors will be users of the system. To begin identifying actors, consider the roles people play when using the system. For example, someone may play the role of customer, while someone else plays the role of salesperson. There may also be roles for a manager, an accounting clerk, a vendor, a warehouse staff member, and so on. The specific names of these actors obviously depend on your problem domain, but remember that actors should be named with roles, not positions. It can be too confusing to try to tie a position to specific use cases; a position typically includes so many roles that the model can get pretty complex. You can also run into the problem of changes to the model. Positions and their responsibilities tend to change a lot, while roles stay fairly stable. Take a look at the vision statement and business case to begin identifying actors. The business case documents the economic justification for the project, including the return on investment. The users in the vision statement are typically actors, although the vision statement may list positions and not roles. To add them as actors, just change their names to role names. You might find other actors from the business case, or from general discussions with the users and team members. List any potential actor you find. As the project goes along and you refine the model, you can always combine actors or delete actors that are no longer needed.

Also, consider the roles other systems play when interacting with your system. You may have an actor, for example, called Accounting System. Having that actor lets you know that your system must interface with the accounting system, but that the accounting system itself is outside the scope of this project.

A good trick is to go through the list of use cases and ask yourself, "Who will be using this use case?" The answer may be a person, a group of people, or another system. Define the role that's being played, and add an actor with that role name. This is, of course, an iterative process. As new use cases are added, you'll add new actors as well.

In our timekeeping example, there were three users identified in the vision statement: the HR manager, the HR administrator, and the hotel's employees. These are roles, not positions; the person playing the role of the HR manager is, after all, also playing the role of an employee. In looking through the vision statement and other documents, we notice that there's a legacy payroll system we're going to have to interface with. So we add another actor for the payroll system. This is a good start to our actor list, but chances are the list will change as the project goes along.

It's a good idea to write a short definition for each actor, so that no one is confused about the actor or their role in the system. Actors are drawn with stick figures:

Actors may have association relationships with use cases or generalization relationships with other actors. See "Defining Association Relationships between Actors and Use Cases" and "Defining Actor Relationships" later in this chapter for further details.

XDE includes a number of properties for actors, as shown in Table 4.3.

TABLE 4.3: ACTOR PROPERTIES IN XDE

CATEGORY	PROPERTY	DESCRIPTION
UML	Name	Sets the name of the actor.
UML	IsAbstract	An abstract actor is one that is never directly instantiated. It exists only to hold the commonality between other actors, and it is related to those actors via a generalization.
UML	Multiplicity	Sets the number of instances of the actor that may exist simultaneously.
UML	Stereotype	Sets the stereotype of the actor. This property is generally not used, but it is helpful if you have different types of actors.

To add actors to a use case diagram in XDE, follow these steps:

1. Select the Actor option from the UML Use Case area of the toolbox.
2. Click anywhere inside the diagram to add the new actor and type its name. The actor is also added to the Explorer window, with the following symbol:
3. Edit the properties of the new actor if necessary.
4. Repeat steps 1–3 for each actor you'd like to add to the model.

DEFINING ASSOCIATION RELATIONSHIPS BETWEEN ACTORS AND USE CASES

Use cases and actors are connected via *association* relationships. An association on a use case diagram indicates that the use case and actor communicate, and it is drawn as a single line between the actor and use case. In this example, an employee initiates the Submit Timecard process:

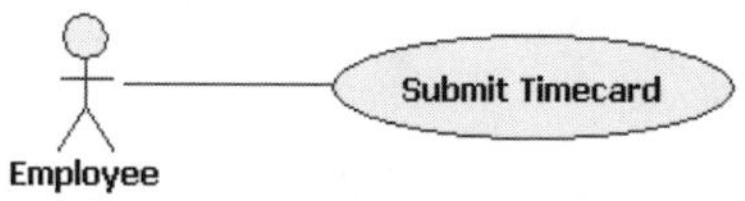

Associations let you know which actors participate in which use cases. A single actor may have associations with many use cases, and a single use case may have associations with many actors.

If you want, you can add multiplicity settings to the ends of the relationship. The multiplicity lets you know how many instances of an actor may be using the use case, and how many instances of the use case an actor may use. In this example, an employee can enter many timecards, but only one employee is associated with a particular timecard:

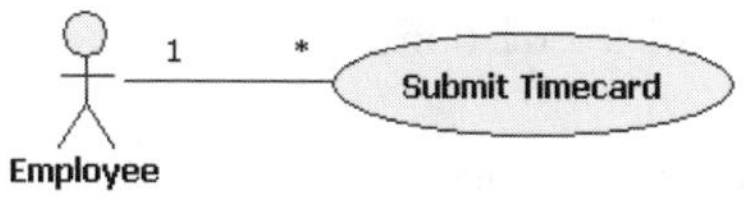

TIP *XDE automatically adds multiplicity and association names to the new associations. To hide them on the diagram, select the associations, right-click, and then select Hide Connector Labels.*

"TO ARROW IS HUMAN!"

"Do I add arrowheads to the association?" Good question! Let's talk...

The UML is not specific about whether to include arrowheads on the associations between use cases and actors, and as a result, there has been quite a bit of debate and confusion about this topic. Adding the arrowheads can clutter the diagram a little, but they can also clarify who initiates the communication. If you use a directed association, general conventions suggest that an arrow from the actor to the use case indicates that the actor initiates the use case, while an arrow from the use case to an actor indicates that the use case initiates the communication with the actor.

The arrowheads on an association between a use case and actor show only who initiates the communication. Do not confuse this with data flow.

On the other hand, leaving out the arrowheads can simplify the diagram and help prevent people from thinking that this is a data flow diagram. However, with this approach, you don't get the information about who initiates communication with whom.

There is nothing in the UML 1.4 specification that specifically prohibits using a directed association. Some organizations always use arrowheads, others never use them, and some use them only when necessary to clarify the relationships. The bottom line is that it is up to you.

XDE supports either option; you can use either the Association or Directed Association relationships from the UML Use Case toolbox. We suggest that the team decide early in the project whether to use directed or nondirected associations and to stick with the selected convention.

Associations on use case diagrams should only be used to show relationships between use cases and actors, never between two actors or two use cases. In the "Defining Use Case Relationships" and "Defining Actor Relationships" sections later in this chapter, we discuss other types of relationships that you can use between actors or between use cases.

WARNING *XDE allows you to draw associations between two use cases or between two actors. But this does not follow the UML 1.4 specification and is not recommended.*

To add associations between actors and use cases on a use case diagram in XDE, follow these steps:

1. Select the Association or Directed Association option from the UML Use Case area of the toolbox.
2. Drag and drop between the actor and the use case. For a directed association, drag and drop from the actor to the use case to create a relationship pointing toward the use case. Drag and drop from the use case to the actor to create an association pointing toward the actor.
3. (Optional) Set the values of the End1Multiplicity and End2Multiplicity properties to reflect the multiplicity of the relationship.

DEFINING THE SYSTEM BOUNDARY

In the UML, you can optionally draw a box around the use cases on a use case diagram to show where the system boundary lies. By definition, the boundary between the system and the outside world lies between the use cases and the actors, but using a box can help clearly delineate the scope. Figure 4.2 shows a boundary definition box.

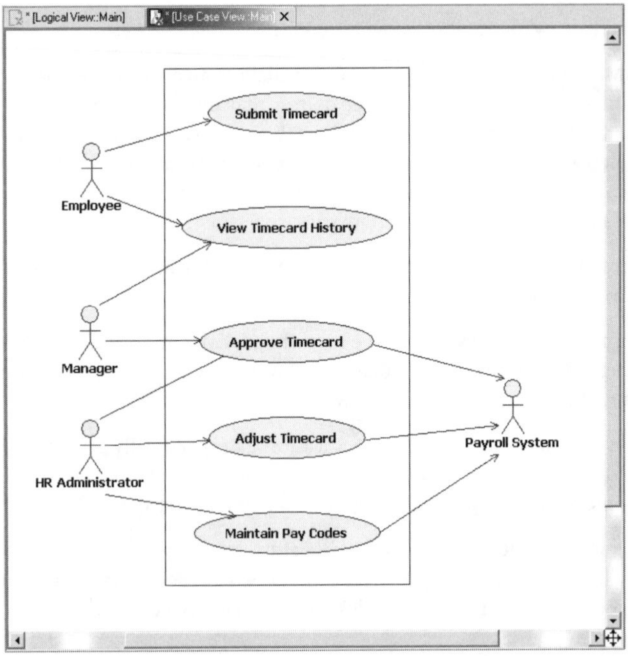

FIGURE 4.2
System boundary on a use case diagram

As you can see, the rectangle really just serves to explicitly state where the system boundary lies. This is optional notation.

To draw the system boundary on a use case diagram in XDE, follow these steps:

1. Right-click inside the use case diagram, and select Add Geometric Shapes ➢ Rectangle.
2. Right-click the new rectangle and select Order ➢ Send to Back.
3. Move and resize the rectangle so that the use cases are enclosed within it and the actors lie outside of it.

TIP *To change the fill color of the rectangle, use the Fill color picker button on the Appearance toolbar:*  .

PRIORITIZING USE CASES

If you are in an architect's role, you are most likely involved in the use case prioritization process. In a perfect world, we'd be able to implement all of the requirements within the time and budget constraints of the project. Unfortunately, the real world doesn't usually work that way, so we need some sort of prioritization. The prioritization of use cases is really a balance between three perspectives: the user's perspective, the project manager's perspective, and the architect's perspective.

The user's perspective lets everyone know how important the use case is for the end users. There's usually some critical functionality that the users absolutely must have, whatever the risk.

The project manager's perspective factors in things such as the cost and time needed to implement the use case. A discussion of estimation techniques is outside the scope of this book, but the project manager typically uses a method such as the Constructive Cost Model (COCOMO) method developed by Barry Boehm or function point analysis to estimate the time and cost for each use case (or a group of use cases in a larger system). The project manager is also very concerned with risk. The risk level of a use case affects its priority from the project manager's point-of-view.

The final perspective is that of the architect. The architect is concerned with how difficult the use case is to implement and how much architectural risk the use case imposes on the project. For example, a use case may seem simple on the surface, but to implement it you may have to build interfaces to multiple other systems.

It's usually up to the project manager to carefully balance these three perspectives and come up with a final prioritization that everyone should agree on before continuing with the project. The project manager needs to consider situations such as a use case that's very critical to the users, but one that also introduces a lot of risk. These types of use cases are usually given a higher priority so that the team can mitigate the risk as early as possible. There are also situations where a use case is of very low importance to the users, and introduces a lot of risk. Here, the team may reexamine the business value of the use case and may decide not to include the use case in the project at all. The same type of analysis is usually conducted for the requirements themselves, which may be given a priority of "must have," "should have," or "nice to have."

We're focusing here, though, on the prioritization of use cases, which can be tracked using XDE. You can record a use case's priority in XDE by using the Rank property for each use case. This won't affect the appearance of the diagram at all, but it helps you keep track of the use case priorities. Keep in mind that as the project goes along, use case priorities can (and do) change.

Defining Use Case Relationships

Many of the relationships in your use case model are those between use cases and actors, but there are times when you may need to define relationships between the use cases themselves. There are only three types of relationships allowed between use cases: an extend relationship, an include relationship, or a generalization relationship. These aren't always needed for a project, but they can help when there is some common functionality among use cases. Look through your use case model and try to identify areas of commonality between the use cases. If you find some very minor functionality in common, it probably isn't necessary to define use case relationships. However, if there is a significant chunk of functionality that's common among several use cases, setting up use case relationships can help you during analysis, design, and coding.

EXTEND RELATIONSHIP

An *extend relationship* indicates that one use case (the *base use case*) is conditionally augmented by another (the *extending use case*). An extend relationship is shown as a dependency with an <<extend>> stereotype, pointing toward the base use case. In the following example, the base use case Conduct Employee Review is extended by the use case Promote Employee. In other words, when a manager is completing an employee review, certain conditions trigger a promotion.

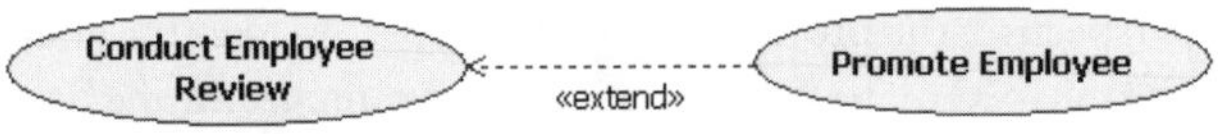

You use an extend relationship when there is some (typically large) piece of functionality that may or may not run when another use case is run. It's a good way of dividing a very complex use case into two parts: the required and the optional. It is also a good way of showing commonality between the use cases. If two or more base use cases have some functionality in common, you can split the common functionality into its own use case, the extending use case, rather than document the common functionality in each of the base use cases.

One extending use case can extend many base use cases, and each base use case may be extended by many extending use cases. The base use case has *extension points*, which are points where the logic of the extending use case is inserted. The extend relationship references those extension points, and also contains a condition. The condition defines when the extending use case should run. In UML notation, the extension points are listed in a compartment inside the use case, and the condition is written along the extend relationship arrow.

XDE does not support the direct modeling of extension points or conditions. However, you can document these in a note, and attach the note to the extend relationship:

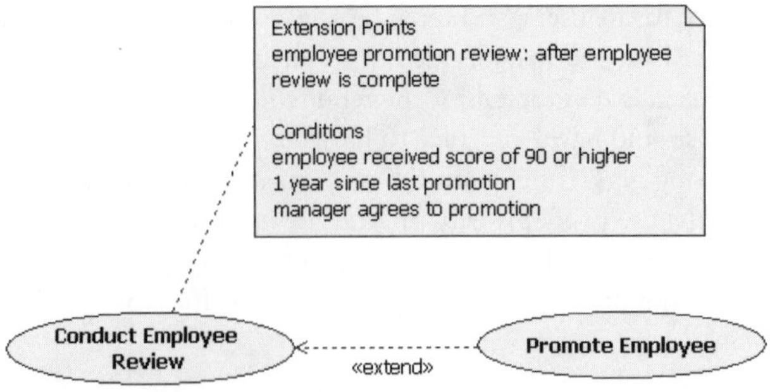

TIP *Use Ctrl+Enter to insert a line break in a note.*

You can also use attributes to model extension points. Create an attribute for each extension point, and give it the stereotype of <<extension point>>.

The extension points and condition are also included in the documentation for the base use case.

To add an extend relationship in XDE:

1. Select the Extend option from the UML Use Case toolbox.
2. Click first on the extending use case and then on the base use case.

Include Relationship

An *include relationship* indicates that the base use case includes the functionality provided by another (the *inclusion* use case). The inclusion use case is sometimes also referred to as an addition use case. The difference between an include and an extend relationship is the condition. While an extending use case runs if a particular condition is true, an inclusion use case always runs. In other words, an extend relationship implies "optional," while an include relationship implies "mandatory." An include relationship is shown as a dependency with an <<include>> stereotype, pointing toward the inclusion use case. In this example, while we're paying employees, we're also running the payroll reporting process:

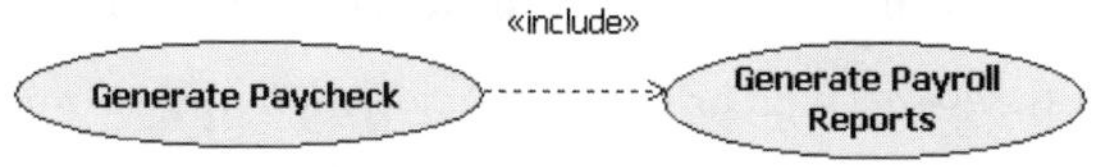

With an include relationship, the base use case runs, and at some point in the base use case, the inclusion use case runs. The flow then returns back to the base use case. Like extend relationships, include relationships are used when there is some amount of functionality that is common between two or more use cases. The common functionality is moved into its own use case, and include relationships are set up between the base use cases and this new use case.

To add an include relationship in XDE:

1. Select the Include option from the UML Use Case toolbox.
2. Click first on the base use case and then on the inclusion use case.

Generalization Relationship

A *generalization relationship* indicates that a child use case is a more specific form of the parent use case. A generalization relationship is shown as an arrow with a triangular arrowhead, pointing toward the parent use case:

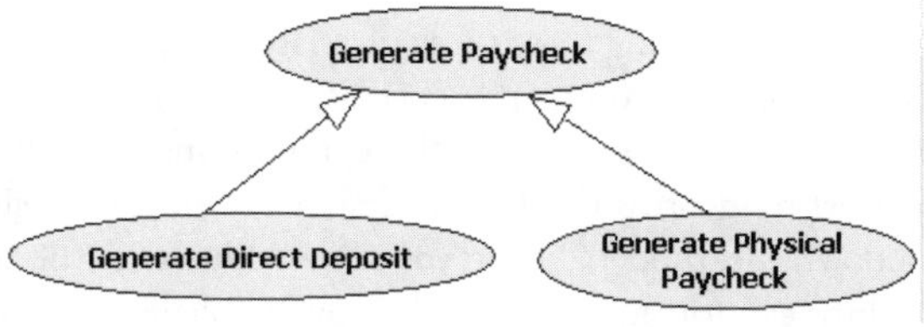

In this example, the Generate Paycheck use case holds all of the generic functionality that runs regardless of whether a direct deposit or a physical check is being created: calculating the pay, calculating taxes, incorporating sick leave and vacation pay, and recording the results. The two children use cases include all of this functionality, plus a little more detail related to generating a direct deposit transaction or printing a paycheck.

As with the other relationships, a generalization is used to show some commonality between two or more use cases. Each child use case inherits the behavior, attributes, extension points, and relationships of the parent. Each parent can have multiple children, and each child can have multiple parents. Typically, however, a child has only one parent. Note that this is a little different from generalizations for classes. In some languages, the concept of a child having more than one parent, referred to as *multiple inheritance*, is not supported. In other languages, multiple inheritance is allowed. The UML does allow for multiple inheritance with use cases, although it is fairly rarely used. The idea is that each parent would define some generic functionality, and the child would define a more specific version of the functionality in each of the parents.

To add a generalization relationship in XDE:

1. Select the Generalization option from the UML Use Case toolbox.
2. Click first on the child use case and then on the parent use case.
3. Review the child use cases, and look for common associations.
4. Select the Association or Directed Association option from the UML Use Case toolbox.
5. Add the common associations to the parent use case.
6. Delete the common associations from the children by right-clicking each association and selecting Delete from Model.

Abstract Use Cases

Sometimes the parent use case in a generalization relationship is never really intended to run. All it does is hold some generic functionality that is common to its children. These types of use cases, which are never directly instantiated, are referred to as *abstract use cases*. On a use case diagram, abstract use cases have their names italicized.

To create an abstract use case in XDE:

1. Select the use case in a diagram or in the Explorer window.
2. In the Properties window, set the value of the IsAbstract property to True. Note that the name of the use case is now italicized, according to the UML standards.

Should I Use Include, Extend, and Generalization Relationships?

There is an advantage to using these types of relationships on a use case diagram. They help you easily see what functionality is common between two or more use cases. They can help to simplify each individual use case, by removing extraneous, common functionality. When you get to design, they can also help you start to identify areas of the design that might be reused.

There is a downside, though. When you are working with the stakeholders to identify use cases, these relationships can sometimes get in the way, especially if the stakeholders are new to the idea of use cases. You can end up spending most of your time worrying about these relationships, rather than the more fundamental task of identifying use cases, actors, and the associations between them.

In short, use caution. We generally recommend against including these relationships in discussions with your end users. Once you've worked with the users to identify the use cases, actors, and associations, though, you can go back through without the users and add the other relationships if they will help the technical team. Our experience has shown that the users more easily understand these relationships after the use case diagram is drawn, rather than when a discussion of the relationships is incorporated into a discussion on eliciting the use cases.

Defining Actor Relationships

Having the actors and their use cases gives us a lot of information about the system, but it doesn't say anything about any commonality between the actors. It can be one thing to build a system where each actor pretty much does his or her own thing, and quite another to build a system where the actors share a lot of functionality. There is only one type of relationship, the generalization relationship, that can be used to connect two actors. It is used primarily when there is a lot of commonality between the actors. Be careful not to get carried away, though. A common trap is to create too many actors and too complex an inheritance structure for them. You end up with many actors that all really play the same role, and an inheritance structure that's difficult to understand. As a general guideline, add actor relationships (generalizations) only when two or more actors share a number of relationships with use cases. Also watch that you don't create an organizational structure as an actor hierarchy. Actor generalizations, as in classes, still need to follow the "is a..." test. For instance, is a manager a type of employee? Possibly so. Is an order taker a type of vice president? Not in most organizational structures with which we're familiar.

Generalization Relationship for Actors

A generalization relationship for actors is the same in principle as a generalization relationship for use cases. A parent actor holds some common features of its children.

Actor generalizations can help simplify a use case diagram. If there are several actors that communicate with some common use cases, you can create a parent actor to hold those common relationships. Figure 4.3 shows a portion of a use case diagram without actor generalizations.

Figure 4.4 is the same portion of a use case diagram, but this time an actor generalization was used to simplify the diagram.

A child actor can, in turn, have children. Be careful setting up an actor hierarchy with too many levels, however. It can sometimes add complexity to the model. Two to three levels of inheritance are usually sufficient.

To add a generalization relationship between actors in XDE, follow these steps:

1. Select the Generalization option from the UML Use Case toolbox.
2. Click the child actor.
3. Click the parent actor.
4. Repeat steps 1–3 for all children of this parent actor.
5. Review the association relationships of the children, and identify any common associations.

6. Select the Association or Directed Association option from the UML Use Case toolbox.
7. Click the parent actor, and then click a use case common to all children. Repeat this for any additional common use cases.
8. Right-click each common association on each child actor, and select Delete From Model.

FIGURE 4.3
Use case diagram without actor generalization

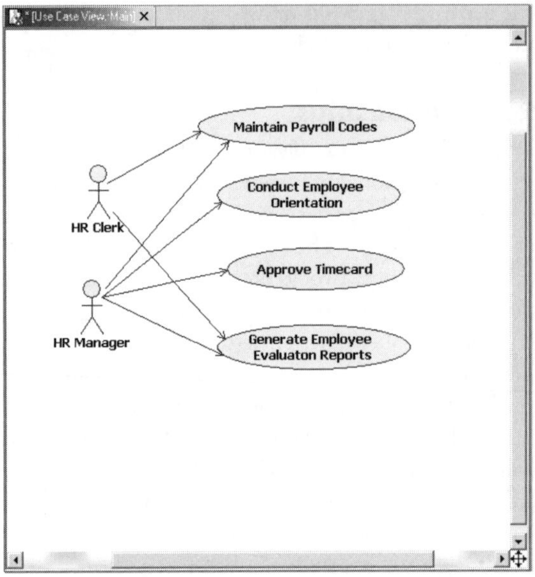

FIGURE 4.4
Use case diagram with actor generalization

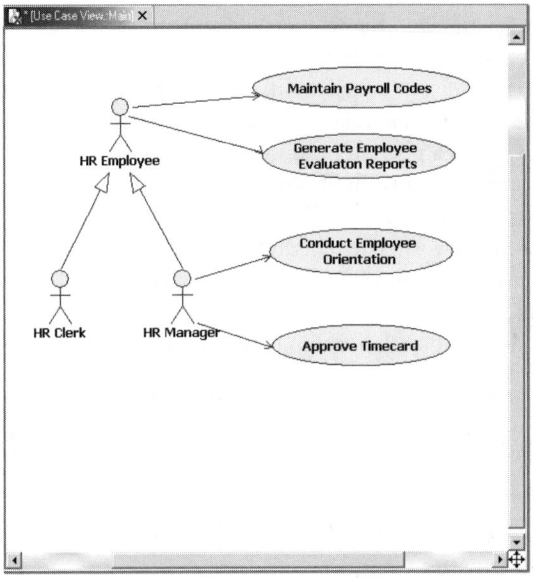

Abstract Actors

A parent actor that is never directly instantiated (that is, no person, system, or other entity ever plays the role of that actor) is referred to as an *abstract actor*. An abstract actor exists only to hold some commonality between its children. For example, let's look at the following diagram:

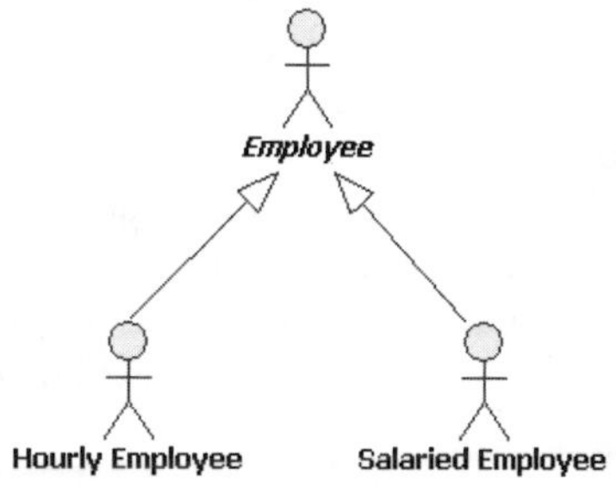

In this example, no person ever plays the role of an Employee. Everyone is either an Hourly or a Salaried Employee. Because the role Employee is never directly used, the Employee actor is abstract. Note the italicized name in this diagram; an abstract actor has its name italicized on a use case diagram. An actor without children should not be marked as an abstract actor.

To create an abstract actor in XDE:

1. Select the actor in a diagram or in the Explorer window.
2. In the Properties window, set the value of the IsAbstract property to True.

Packaging Use Cases and Actors

As you dive deeper into the problem, and discover more and more actors and use cases, the model can become cluttered. Packaging is a good way of organizing the use case model and of seeing the dependencies between the groups of use cases and actors.

A *package* is a generic UML mechanism used to group model elements together. It is shown using the following symbol:

In the use case model, a package can contain use cases, actors, and their relationships. A package does not have to contain both use cases and actors; the contents depend upon your packaging strategy. There are several different package stereotypes in the UML, including façade, framework, modelLibrary, profile, stub, and topLevel. XDE has added a few other stereotypes as well. In particular, the three we consider here are the Use Case Package, Use Case Storyboard, and Use Case System stereotypes.

Defining Packages in the Use Case Model

When we work on detailed design later, we may package items in accordance with the system architecture, but here we're dealing with things at a more conceptual level. Look for a group of use cases, actors, and/or relationships that logically go together from the user's point of view. For example, in building an accounting system, you may want to group all of the Accounts Receivable use cases and actors in one package and all of the Accounts Payable use cases and actors in another. Another strategy is to look for inheritance structures of either use cases or actors. Group the whole inheritance tree into a single package.

Packages can contain packages, so you can create several different layers of abstraction for your system. The highest-level packages describe the system at an extremely high, conceptual level, while the lower-level packages contain the actual use cases and actors. Each use case, actor, or other model element may only be contained in one package. Let's quickly discuss the three use case package stereotypes.

TIP *You can change the stereotype of a package by modifying its Stereotype property.*

USE CASE PACKAGE

A *use case package* is a package that contains use cases, actors, and their relationships. Such packages don't contain other packages, so they represent the system at a detailed level. Most of the examples and discussion in this section focus on use case packages. A use case package in XDE is represented on a diagram and in the Explorer with the following symbol:

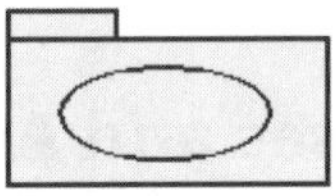

Use Case Package

USE CASE SYSTEM PACKAGE

A *use case system package* is a high-level package that contains one or more use case packages, or one or more other use case system packages. It provides a high-level perspective of the system, without getting into the details of any of the specific use cases or actors. You can create several layers of abstraction in your model through the use of use case system packages. Each of these packages contains other use case system packages, breaking down the system into a more and more granular view, until finally the lowest-level use case system packages hold use case packages. In XDE, a use case system package is drawn on a diagram or in the Explorer with the following symbol:

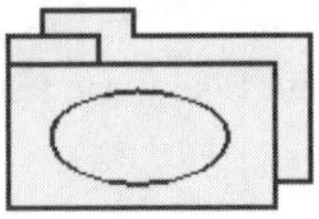

Use Case System

USE CASE STORYBOARD PACKAGE

A *storyboard* is a conceptual description of the user interface for a use case. A use case storyboard package holds the boundary classes and relationships needed for the user interface for that use case. It may also contain some sequence and class diagrams with those boundary classes and relationships. (See the section "Identifying Analysis-Level Classes" later in this chapter for a definition of boundary classes.) You can also attach other files, such as a sketch of the user interface in a drawing program, directly to the use case storyboard package by right-clicking the package in the Explorer and selecting Add UML ➢ URL. A use case storyboard package in XDE is represented by the following symbol on a diagram or in the Explorer:

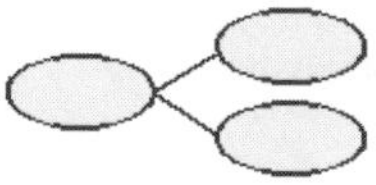

Use Case Storyboard

Generally speaking, you won't need a use case storyboard package for every use case. However, it can be very helpful in eliciting requirements if the user interface is expected to be very complex, or the requirements are expected to change. And, let's face it, many customers are simply more comfortable seeing something tangible related to the user interface, even if it is just a storyboard.

You can add as many use case packages, use case system packages, and use case storyboard packages as you need. Most applications, particularly larger applications, will have several use case packages, and possibly some use case system and use case storyboard packages as well.

To add a new package to a use case diagram in XDE:

1. Select the Package option from the UML Use Case toolbox.
2. Click anywhere inside the diagram to place the new package. Type the name of the package. Note that the package also appeared in the Explorer window, with the following symbol next to it: 
3. To add use cases and actors to the package, in the Explorer window, drag them from their current location and drop them into the new package.
4. To add other packages to the package, use the Explorer window to drag and drop the other packages into the new package.
5. (Optional) Change the value of the Stereotype property for the package to Use Case Package, Use Case System, or Use Case Storyboard. The symbol used on the diagram and in the Explorer also changes.

Defining Relationships between Packages

Keep in mind as you review these relationships that we are working with the use case model. We revisit these relationships later, while building the design model. While these relationships have essentially the same meaning in both the use case and design models, the perspective you view them through changes. Here we are looking at things from the users' perspective, later we look at things from an implementation perspective.

The different relationships between packages include the following:

- Access relationship

- Import relationship

- Friend permission relationship

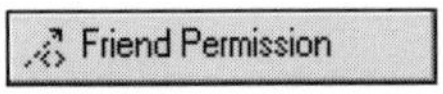

- Dependency relationship

- Generalization relationship

ACCESS RELATIONSHIP

An *access relationship* is a stereotyped dependency that allows one namespace to gain access to the public contents of another. When used to link packages, it indicates that one package has access to the public contents of the other. It is drawn using the following notation:

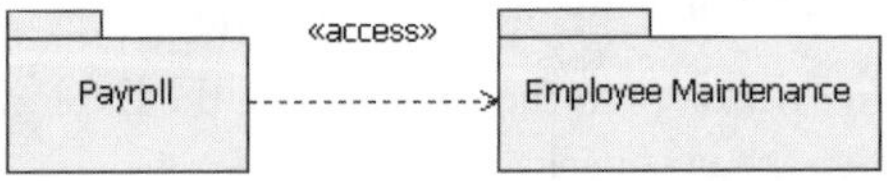

On a use case diagram, we are not yet dealing with the architecture of the system; everything is written from the users' perspective. So, at this point, don't think of an access relationship in terms of one package of classes accessing public classes in another. Think of it more as a logical relationship; the functionality in one group (package) of use cases needs to access the functionality in another group. For example, Figure 4.5 shows a system where the packages of use cases are fairly well independent of one another.

FIGURE 4.5

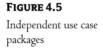

Independent use case packages

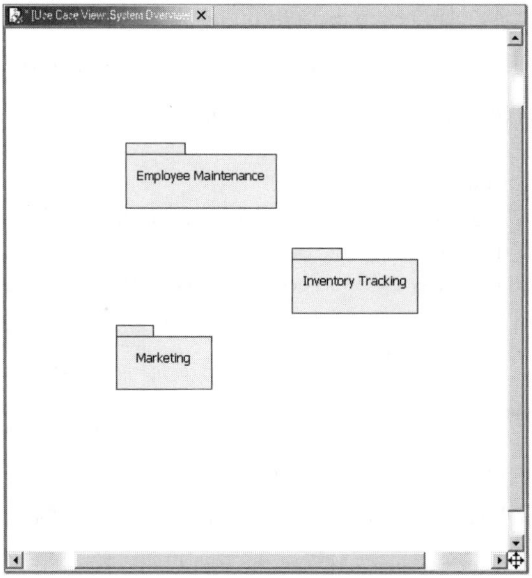

Figure 4.6 shows another system in which the use cases in one package access the functionality of the use cases in another. By the time we get to implementation, this will probably translate into classes from the use case realizations in Accounts Receivable accessing public classes in the use case realizations from General Ledger, but don't worry about that yet. At this point, all we know is that while we're running some of the functionality in Accounts Receivable, we may need to use some of the functionality in General Ledger.

FIGURE 4.6

Use case packages with access relationships

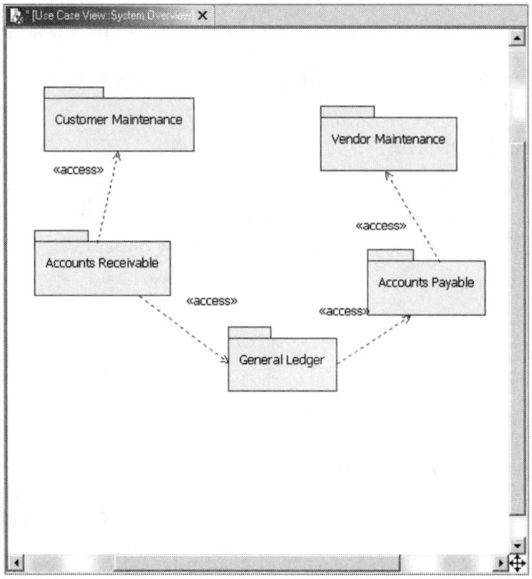

To add an access relationship in XDE:

1. Select the Access option from the UML Use Case toolbox.
2. Click the client package and then the supplier package.

IMPORT RELATIONSHIP

An *import relationship* is very similar to an access relationship. In this relationship, however, rather than simply accessing the public contents of another package, one package adds the public contents of another. It is also drawn as a stereotyped dependency, using the stereotype <<import>>:

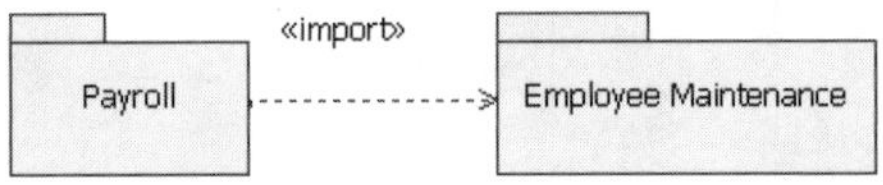

To add an import relationship in XDE:

1. Select the Import option from the UML Use Case toolbox.
2. Click the client package and then the supplier package.

FRIEND RELATIONSHIP

A *friend relationship* at the package level is essentially the same as a C++ friend relationship at the class level. We all tell our friends everything; similarly, this type of relationship allows one package to see the contents of another, even if those contents do not have public visibility.

XDE does not have an icon for a friend relationship in the UML Use Case toolbox, but there is one in the UML Class toolbox.

To add a friend relationship in XDE:

1. Select the Friend Permission option from the UML Class toolbox.
2. Click the client package and then the supplier package.

DEPENDENCY RELATIONSHIP

A *dependency relationship* between two packages of use cases lets you know that one package needs to access or import elements from another. In other words, you know you have an access, import, or friend relationship, but you're not sure which one. A dependency without a stereotype is a more generic relationship.

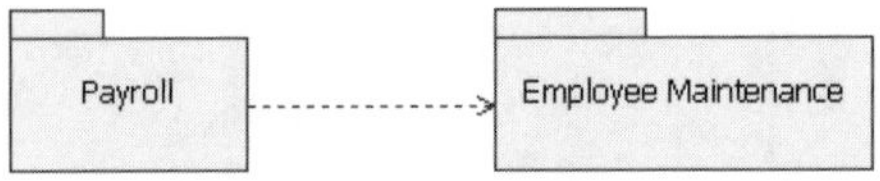

To add a dependency relationship in XDE:

1. Select the Dependency option from the UML Use Case toolbox.
2. Click the client package and then the supplier package.

GENERALIZATION RELATIONSHIP

Like actors and use cases, packages can be inherited. A child package inherits all of the public and protected elements of its parent. The inherited elements have the same visibility (public or protected) in the child package as they had in the parent package. You can use a generalization relationship to show that one package is inherited from another.

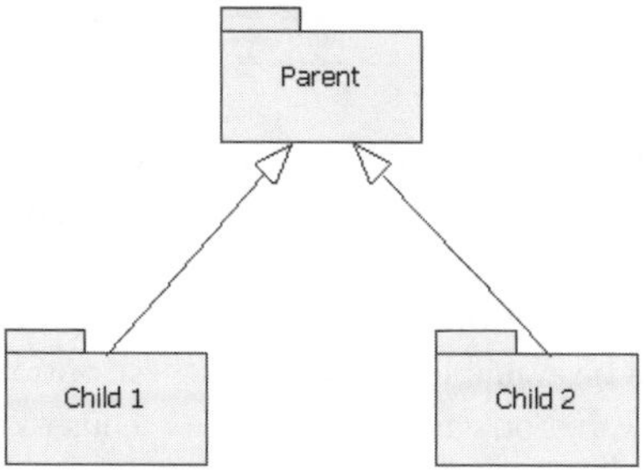

To add a package generalization relationship in XDE:

1. Select the Generalization option from the UML Use Case toolbox.
2. Click the client package and then the supplier package.

Integrated Use Case Management

Integrated Use Case Management (IUCM) is the process of connecting use case diagrams in XDE with detailed requirements information stored in RequisitePro. We're also going to apply IUCM here to requirements that are stored in a format other than RequisitePro, such as a word-processing document or a spreadsheet.

Why bother with IUCM? Well, as we mentioned before, often you have a problem where the requirements and the design don't quite match up. If you don't trace the use cases from XDE back to the requirements, there's the risk that the rest of the design won't trace back, either. IUCM has a couple of other advantages as well. By integrating with RequisitePro, you can make changes to the use case attributes, such as Priority or Risk, without leaving XDE. Any changes you make are automatically added to an audit trail. You can also create use case specification documents or open existing documents right through XDE, rather than having to switch back and forth between XDE and RequisitePro.

There's one final benefit of IUCM that may not be apparent until later in the project. Have you ever been a designer or developer on a project where the analysis team keeps saying, "Oops, I forgot to tell you about that requirement change"? Having earned more than our fair share of five-alarm headaches from that one, we can attest to the fact that having real-time access to the ever-changing requirements is extremely beneficial. With IUCM, a designer or developer working on a use case constantly has access not only to the use case text, but to the requirements and their attributes (status, priority, and so on) as well.

Before you can use any of the IUCM features on your model, you need to activate IUCM in XDE.

1. Select the model in the Explorer window.

2. Look for the AppliedProfiles property in the UML section of the Properties window.
3. Add **RequisitePro** to the AppliedProfiles property. If there are already entries in Applied-Profiles, separate them with commas.

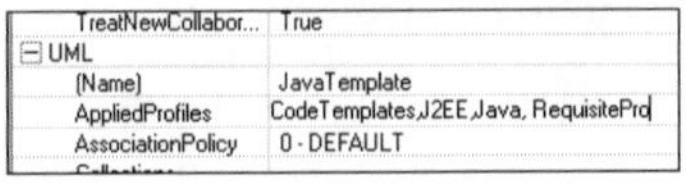

The IUCM features are now activated. You should have three new menus available. First, on the Tools menu, there should now be a submenu called Rational RequisitePro. Second, when you right-click a use case, you should see menu options for Use Case Document, Requirement Properties, and View RequisitePro Association. Finally, when you right-click a package, a Rational RequisitePro menu option should be available. You can use these options to set up and maintain links between RequisitePro and XDE. You can also use these menus to maintain the detailed attributes for each use case.

Linking to RequisitePro

The first step in the IUCM process is to decide which RequisitePro project to use to manage the requirements for your XDE model. You may have more than one RequisitePro project that you want to use, and XDE supports this. We'll return to that in just a minute.

To associate your XDE model with a RequisitePro project:

1. Select Tools ➢ Rational RequisitePro ➢ Associate Model To Project.

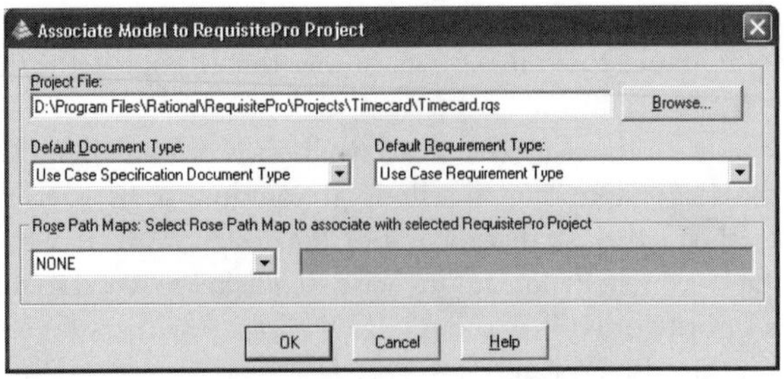

2. In the Project File field, enter the full path and name of the RequisitePro project to use.

The Default Document Type is the type of RequisitePro artifact (such as a use case specification, vision, SRS, and so on) that XDE uses for a use case document template. We recommend using the Use Case Specification type, unless you have created your own use case document template in RequisitePro. The Default Requirement Type lets XDE know what type of requirement (feature, use case, and so on) to use by default when you are creating requirements in a use case document. Here, we recommend that you use Use Case (functional requirement), unless you have created a different requirement type in RequisitePro.

As we mentioned before, you do have the option of associating some use cases to one RequisitePro project and other use cases to a different project. To do so, you must first package the use cases and save each package as a separate unit. You can then associate each package with a different RequisitePro project. Once you've packaged your use cases:

1. Right-click each package and select Make A Separate Unit.
2. Save the model, and then right-click each package and select Rational RequisitePro ➢ Associate Package to Project.
3. As you did when you associated a RequisitePro project to the model, select the RequisitePro project, the default document type, and the default requirement type. These settings apply to all use cases in the package.

Managing Use Cases in XDE

Now that you've set up the associations between XDE and RequisitePro, you're ready to manage the use cases. There are three things you can do by right-clicking a use case:

- Manage the requirement properties for the use case.
- Create or associate a use case document.
- View the RequisitePro association.

Managing Requirement Properties

A use case has several properties in a RequisitePro project. These include general properties, revision information, attributes of the use case, traceability relationships of the use case, and hierarchy information. To view or edit these properties, right-click a use case and select Requirement Properties ➢ Open. You'll see the requirement Properties window for the use case:

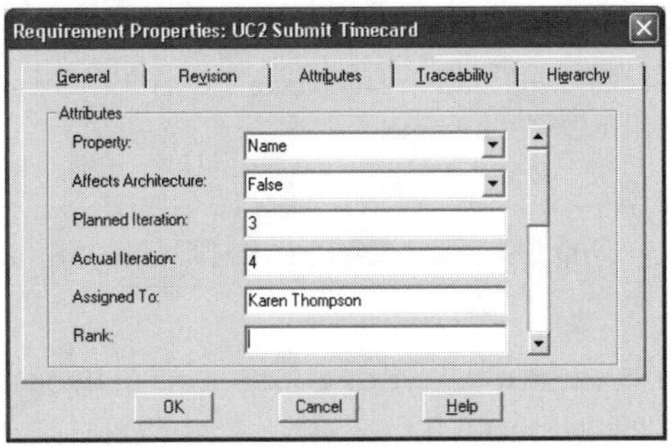

On the General tab, you can edit the type of requirement (although we recommend leaving it as a Use Case requirement), the name and text of the requirement, the package in which the requirement resides, and the location of the requirement (use case document, or database if the requirement resides only in the RequisitePro database). The Revision tab displays the version history of the requirement.

The Attributes tab (the one shown in the previous graphic) is the one you're most likely to use in XDE. It includes attributes of the use case, which typically include items such as the priority, status, cost, and difficulty of the use case, and who the use case is assigned to. In RequisitePro, you can define the attributes you'd like to track for a use case. When you bring up the Attributes tab in XDE, you'll see the different attribute types you created in RequisitePro.

Use the Traceability tab to view or edit the traceability between this use case and other requirements. Using RequisitePro, you can create detailed reports for the traceability between the requirements, or you can view a matrix of requirements and their traceability relationships. Finally, use the Hierarchy tab to view or modify hierarchical relationships between the use case and other requirements.

WORKING WITH USE CASE DOCUMENTS

The attributes of a use case are good to have, but to really be able to design and code the use case, we need some more detailed information. Typically, this detailed information is stored in the use case document, or use case specification. It includes the following:

- A brief description of the use case.
- The flow of events for the use case, which describe, step-by-step, how the logic flows through the use case. The flow of events is written from the user's point of view and is independent of programming language and other implementation details. There is one basic flow, which is the most common path through the use case, and several alternate flows, which describe the alternate paths through the use case.
- Preconditions, which are conditions that must be true before the use case begins.
- Post-conditions, which are conditions that must be true when the use case ends.
- Extension points of the use case.
- Any special requirements for the use case.

This is just a brief overview. A complete discussion of the documentation for a use case would require a book of its own (and, in fact, there are several). Here, we focus on how to link the use cases in XDE to the use case documents.

NOTE *This book only covers using XDE to model use cases. For more information about identifying and writing use cases, please see* Applying Use Cases: A Practical Guide, Second Edition *by Geri Schneider and Jason P. Winters (Addison-Wesley, 2001).*

If you've already created the use case documents in RequisitePro, all you need to do is associate these existing documents with the use cases in XDE. Once you've done that, you can view or edit the documents directly through XDE.

To associate an existing use case document to a use case in XDE, follow these steps:

1. Right-click the use case and select Use Case Document ➢ Associate.
2. Select the document to associate to the use case.

If you need to create new use case documents, you can also do that directly through XDE. Once they've been created, you can view or edit them using XDE. To create a new use case document in XDE, right-click the use case and select Use Case Document ➢ New. XDE launches Microsoft Word, and your new document loads. The template it uses depends upon which Default Document type you chose when you linked the model to a RequisitePro project.

Once you have attached a use case document to a use case, you can open the document by right-clicking the use case and selecting Use Case Document ➢ Open. When you do, Microsoft Word launches, and you can use all of the RequisitePro functionality to create, edit, or delete requirements.

If you need to dissociate a use case document from a use case in XDE, simply right-click the use case and select Use Case Document ➢ Dissociate.

WARNING *If you move a use case to another package that is associated to a different RequisitePro project, it loses its use case document association.*

What If I Don't Have RequisitePro?

If you aren't using RequisitePro, you can still apply the concepts of IUCM, but you have to perform the steps manually. The first step, linking the model to a RequisitePro project, can obviously be omitted, but you may want to link the model to a directory that contains the use case documents. If so, you have a couple of options. You could right-click the model in Model Explorer, and select Add UML ➢ URL. Then, attach a document or URL with an index of the use case documents for the project. Another option is to select the model in the Explorer window, and then use the Model Documentation window to enter the name of the directory that contains the use case documents.

TIP *To link to a bookmark within a Word document, type # followed by the bookmark name. For example,* `C:\Documents and Settings\user1\mydocument.doc#bookmark1`.

To manage the attributes of the use cases, such as their priority, status, or difficulty, there are a few things you can do. Again, you won't get all the functionality of RequisitePro, but you can capture some information about the use case attributes. The first approach to this problem is to create attributes for the use cases by right-clicking each use case in the Model Explorer and selecting Add UML ➢ Attribute. Add attributes such as Priority, Status, Assigned To, and so on. Select the attribute in the Model Explorer, and in the Properties window, set the value of the attribute through the Default-ValueExpression property. For example, here we've set the priority of a use case to High:

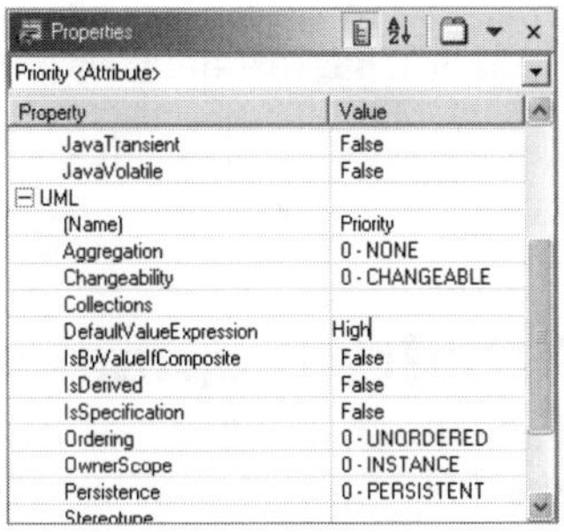

You can display these attributes on a use case diagram by selecting the use case, and then using the Show/Hide Compartment button to show the attribute compartment:

Now you can see the use case's attributes, as well as the attribute values, on the use case diagram. It does clutter up the diagram a little bit, so we suggest creating some use case diagrams with this detail and some without.

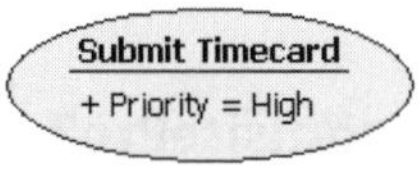

There are quite a few steps to go through here, but you can maintain the use case attributes with this method. Another option is to document the attributes in the Model Documentation window for the use case. Finally, you can create a document outside of XDE that contains the attributes for the use case and then attach it to the use case in XDE by choosing Add UML ➢ URL.

The most difficult part of this manual form of IUCM is linking the use cases to their detailed requirements. The simplest approach is to build a matrix with the requirements on one side and the use cases along the top. Then mark the appropriate use case/requirement intersections to show which requirements map to which use cases. You won't be able to maintain any of this in XDE, but you can attach this matrix to the model or to a package of use cases in XDE by right-clicking the model or package and selecting Add UML ➢ URL. This won't provide all the functionality that RequisitePro supplies, but it does give you some basic traceability. Another approach involves listing the requirements directly in the use case documents and linking the documents to the use cases by choosing Add UML ➢ URL. The downside here is that there is no easy way to determine which requirements apply to multiple use cases. If you change a requirement, you may need to change several use case documents.

The final piece of IUCM requires you to link the use case documents to the use cases themselves. To link a use case document to a use case:

1. Right-click the use case in XDE and choose Add UML ➢ URL.
2. Select the document or URL that holds the use case specification.
3. To open the use case specification, double-click the linked filename or URL in the Explorer window.

Building an Activity Diagram in XDE

Most of the documentation for a use case is contained within the use case specification, but sometimes it helps to draw the flow of logic in another format. Especially when the flow is complex, or there are a lot of decision points, an activity diagram can be easier to read and understand than the flow-of-events text. An *activity diagram* is a specialized form of a state machine that is used to model processes. It is typically used in three situations:

- In business modeling, activity diagrams can be used to model the workflow through a business process.
- In use case modeling, activity diagrams can be used to show the flow of events through a use case.
- You can use the activity diagram as you would a typical flowchart—to show the logical steps the code goes through to accomplish a task.

An activity diagram is contained within an activity graph. An activity graph can contain one or more activity diagrams. One pattern creates an activity graph for each use case that holds all of the activity diagrams for the use case. The states, activities, and transitions that are shown on the diagram are actually owned by the activity graph, not the diagram. This allows multiple diagrams to use the same states, activities, transitions, and other elements.

To create an activity diagram, right-click the model, a package, an activity graph, a use case, an actor, or a class and select Add Diagram ➢ Activity. XDE creates an activity graph, and adds the new diagram to it. It also creates a composite state called TOP, which holds all of the activities and other elements in the diagram.

The activity graph appears in the Explorer with the following symbol: . The activity diagram appears in the Explorer with the following symbol: .

The Activity Diagram Toolbox

The activity diagram toolbox is used to add activities, decision points, transitions, and other elements to an activity diagram. Table 4.4 lists the toolbox options and their meanings, and which sections of this chapter to see for more detail.

TABLE 4.4: ACTIVITY DIAGRAM TOOLBOX

Icon	Meaning	See Section
Pointer	Returns the mouse to the standard pointer	
Activity	Adds an activity, which is a step in a workflow	"Activity"
Transition	Adds a transition from one activity to the next	"Transition"
SelfTransition	Adds a transition from one activity to itself	"Transition"
Decision	Adds a decision point to the workflow	"Decision Point"
Initial State	Indicates where the workflow begins	"Initial State"
Final State	Indicates where the workflow ends	"Final State"
Swimlane	Divides the workflow into different areas for each of the different roles involved in the workflow	"Swimlane"
Synchronization	Adds a synchronization point, which splits the workflow into parallel flows, or brings parallel flows back together	"Synchronization"

Continued on next page

TABLE 4.4: ACTIVITY DIAGRAM TOOLBOX *(continued)*

ICON	MEANING	SEE SECTION
Subactivity State	Creates a subactivity state, which is an activity with its own subworkflow (activity diagram)	"Activity"
ObjectFlow State	Adds an object flow state, which shows how the workflow affects an object	"Object Flow State"
Proxy State	Adds a proxy state, which is a placeholder for another activity or state from a different diagram	"Proxy State"
Stub State	Adds a stub state, which shows the entry and exit points in the subworkflow of a subactivity state	"Stub State"
Note	Adds a simple note to the diagram	
Note Attachment	Attaches a note to a use case or other element	
Constraint	Refines the structure or behavior of an element	
Constraint Attachment	Attaches a constraint to an element	
Text	Adds text to the diagram	

Activity

An *activity* is a step in the process being modeled in the activity diagram. For the most part, each step in the flow of events becomes an activity on the diagram. An activity is different from a state in that a *state* is used to define different situations in the lifecycle of an object, while an activity is a step in a process. For example, states of an Employee object might be "hired," "on leave," "fired," or "quit." The activity diagrams would show the processes of hiring, going on leave, firing, or quitting. An activity is shown on the diagram as a rounded rectangle:

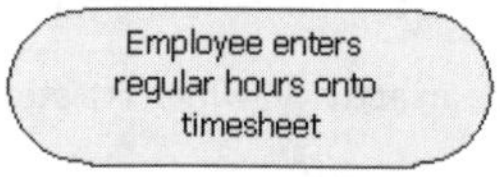

To add an activity, select Activity from the UML Activity toolbox, and click anywhere inside the diagram to place the activity. Type the name of the new activity. The activity is added to both the diagram and the Explorer. There are very few properties for an activity, but you may want to use the IsDynamic and DynamicMultiplicity properties. If IsDynamic is set to True, this implies that the activity can run multiple times concurrently. The DynamicMultiplicity property controls how many concurrent instances of the activity you can have.

Activities may contain *actions*. An action is a noninterruptible, atomic task that occurs during the activity. There are four types of actions:

- Entry

- Exit
- Do
- Upon event

An entry action occurs as the workflow enters the activity. An exit action occurs as the workflow is leaving the activity. A do action occurs while the workflow is in the activity, and an upon event action occurs when a specific event happens. All entry, exit, and do actions must be completed before the workflow leaves the activity. Using actions is a good way to break down an activity into its basic steps. The actions appear on an activity diagram in a compartment of the activity:

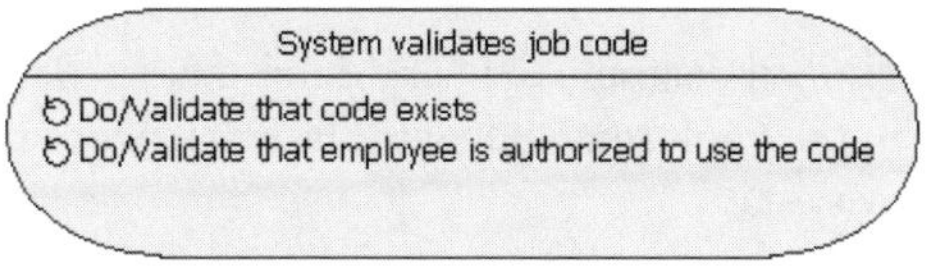

To create an action, follow these steps:

1. Right-click the activity and select Add UML, and then Do Action, Entry Action, or Exit Action. The new action appears inside the activity, preceded by Do/, Entry/, or Exit/. Type the name of the new action.
2. To create an upon event action, add a do action, but remove the Do/ from the action name. The syntax for an upon event action is as follows:

```
event-name(comma-separated parameter list)[guard condition]_
/action or expression
```

3. (Optional) If the action is recurring, edit the Recurrence property in the Properties window. The Recurrence property can be set to a numeric value (indicating the number of times the action should be performed) or to an expression.

If you need to delete an action, find it in the Explorer window underneath the activity in which it is located. Right-click the action and select Delete From Model.

SUBACTIVITY STATE

You can create activity diagrams at different levels of abstraction. If there is a high-level activity that you'd like to break down into its own activity diagram, you can do this by creating a subactivity state. A *subactivity state* is an activity that has its own activity diagram behind it. It looks like an activity but with a small icon representing an activity diagram:

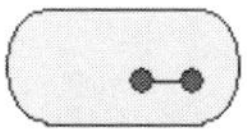

Note that the name of the subactivity state is not displayed on the diagram. Once the subactivity state is created, you can create the detailed diagram and then link the high-level and detailed diagrams together. The name of the detailed diagram will then appear in the subactivity state. Just follow these steps:

1. On the high-level diagram, select Subactivity State from the UML Activity toolbox, and place the new state on the diagram.
2. Create the detailed activity graph and activity diagram for the subactivity state. Right-click the model or a package in the Model Explorer and select Add Diagram ➢ Activity. Name the new activity diagram.
3. Build the new activity diagram, adding activities, transitions, and other elements as described in this chapter.
4. On the high-level diagram, drag and drop the detailed activity graph (the graph, not the diagram) from the Explorer window to the subactivity state. The activity graph name appears in the subactivity state.

Transition

A *transition* moves the workflow from one activity or decision point to the next. In its simplest form, it is drawn as an arrow between the activities or decision points:

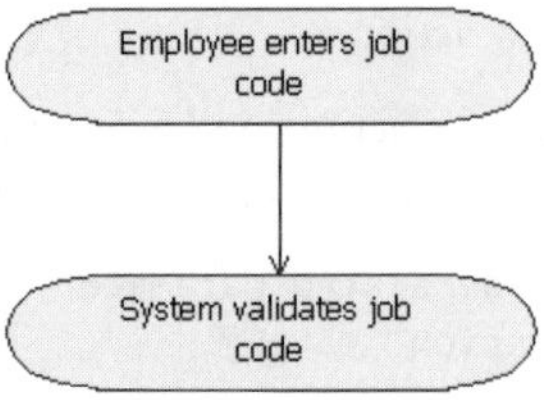

In this case, as soon as the first activity finishes, the second begins. You can add some additional details to the transitions if you need to. The first item you can add is a *guard condition,* which controls when the transition may or may not occur. The guard condition must be true for the transition to occur.

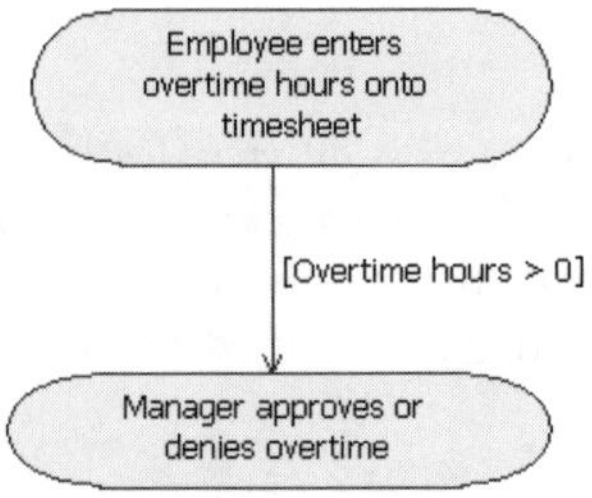

There can be multiple transitions for exiting an activity or a decision point. If so, the guard conditions on them must be mutually exclusive. The other element you can add to the transition is an *event,* where an event is an observable occurrence. If an event is added, the transition occurs only when the event occurs. There are four types of events you can add:

Call event A *call event* is an event that occurs when the object receives a request to run a specific operation.

Change event A *change event* is an event that occurs when some condition changes from False to True. This is different from a guard condition in that a guard is evaluated only when the workflow is leaving the activity. A change event, on the other hand, is constantly evaluated.

Signal event A *signal event* is an event that occurs when a signal is received.

Time event A *time event* is an event that occurs at some predefined date or time, or after a specific duration of time has passed.

To add a transition, complete the following steps:

1. Select the Transition icon in the UML Activity toolbox.
2. Click the source activity (or other shape), and then on the destination activity (or other shape).
3. (Optional) To add a guard condition, select the transition and enter the condition in the GuardCondition property in the Properties window.
4. (Optional) To add an event, right-click the transition, and select Add UML, and then the appropriate type of event. Type in the name of the new event.
5. If you added a change event, set the change condition using the Change property of the event. Note that you may need to select the event in the Explorer window to see the event properties.
6. If you added a time event, set the trigger time using the When property of the event. Note that you may need to select the event in the Explorer window to see the event properties.

To delete a guard condition, clear the contents of the GuardCondition property. To delete an event, locate it in the Explorer window. It will appear underneath the transition in the tree. Right-click the event and select Delete From Model.

TIP *To make a transition with straight lines, draw the transition and then select Format ➢ Line Style ➢ Rectilinear Line Style. Or draw the transition and then use the Line Style toolbar button. This works with relationships on other types of diagrams as well.*

A transition does not have to go between activities; you can have a transition from an activity to itself. These types of transitions, referred to as *self-transitions,* can also have guard conditions and events:

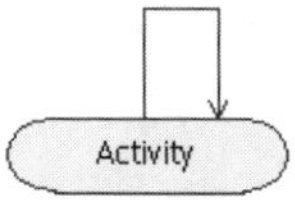

Decision Point

A *decision point* is a conditional expression that controls where the workflow goes. At a decision point, the workflow may split into several alternate paths, or merge back to a common path. If there is more than one outgoing transition from a decision point, there should be events or mutually exclusive guard conditions on them. A decision point is represented as a diamond:

To add a decision point, select the Decision icon in the UML Activity toolbox. Click anywhere inside the diagram to place the decision point. You can add transitions to or from the decision point by selecting the Transition icon in the toolbox, clicking the source decision point or activity, and then clicking the destination decision point or activity.

Initial State

Every activity diagram should have an *initial state*. This is a single solid dot that lets the reader know where the workflow begins, as shown in the left margin.

The initial state may also be referred to as the *start state*. A start state is required, and there may be only one per activity diagram. To add an initial state, select Initial State from the toolbox, and then click anywhere inside the diagram.

Final State

The *final state*, also sometimes called the *end state* or *stop state*, lets the reader know where the workflow ends. It appears on the diagram as a bulls-eye, as shown in the left margin.

Final states are optional and there may be more than one. To add a final state, select the Final State icon from the toolbox, and click anywhere inside the diagram to place it.

Synchronization

A *synchronization* is used to show some parallel processing in the workflow. There are two ways to use synchronizations: to fork the workflow into two or more parallel paths, and to join the workflow paths again. When the workflow forks, there is one transition entering the synchronization, and two or more exiting:

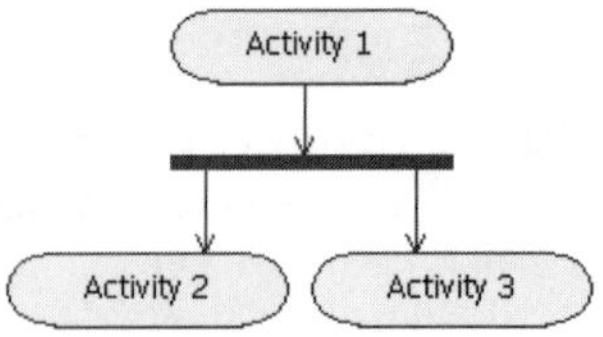

Each of the resulting workflow paths can occur in parallel. When the workflow joins again, two or more transitions enter a synchronization but there is only one exiting transition:

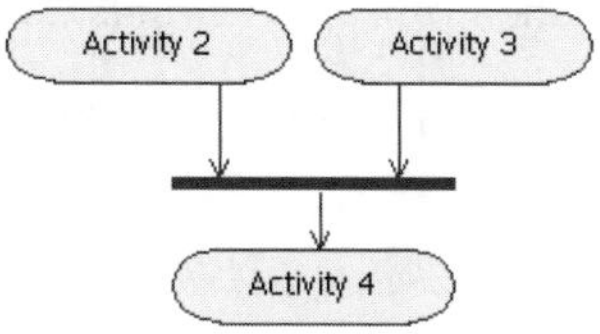

Swimlane

So far, we've looked at how an activity diagram can be used to model the steps, transitions, and decision points in a workflow. What we haven't yet discussed is the notation for describing who is responsible for doing what in the process. That's what swimlanes are used for. *Swimlanes* divide the diagram into pieces, where each piece is performed by a different role or organizational unit (see Figure 4.7 for an example). Note that this is just an initial, high-level activity diagram. The team goes through and builds a more detailed activity diagram from the flow of events as the details of the flow of events are uncovered.

FIGURE 4.7

Swimlanes in an activity diagram

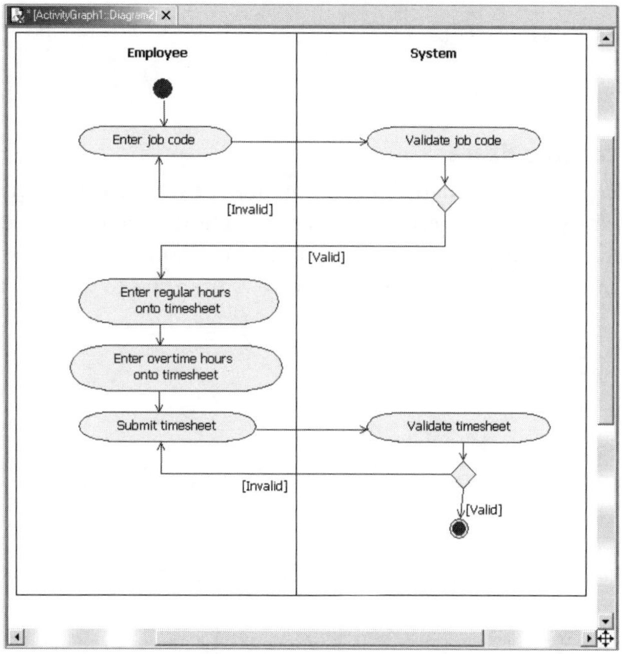

The use of swimlanes is optional. If they are used, each activity is placed in the appropriate swimlane to show who is responsible for performing that activity. The order of the swimlanes does not matter.

To add a swimlane in XDE:

1. Select the Swimlane icon in the toolbox, and click anywhere inside the diagram to place it. Type the name of the swimlane. A swimlane appears as a free-floating rectangle.
2. Drag and drop the appropriate activities into the swimlane. XDE automatically resizes the swimlane as needed.

TIP *To move an element out of a swimlane, hold down the Alt key while dragging and dropping the element.*

TIP *To see the transitions, you may need to move the swimlane to the back. Select Format ➢ Order ➢ Send to Back.*

3. To line up the swimlanes vertically, select each swimlane to align, right-click, and select Swimlane ➢ Merge Swimlanes. Or simply drag and drop one swimlane into another.
4. To reorder attached swimlanes, drag and drop the swimlane you'd like to move into its new location.
5. To detach the swimlanes again so that each is a free-floating rectangle, right-click the merged swimlanes and select Swimlane ➢ Detach Swimlanes.
6. To delete a swimlane, right-click it in the diagram, and select Delete From Model.

NOTE *Deleting a swimlane does not delete the activities and other elements within it. These are still available in the Explorer window.*

Object Flow State

An *object flow state* is used to show how an object's state changes during the workflow. A particular activity may take an object as input and output that same object, but in a different state. The changed object may then serve as input into additional states. These types of situations are modeled using an object flow state and dashed arrows from and to the activities:

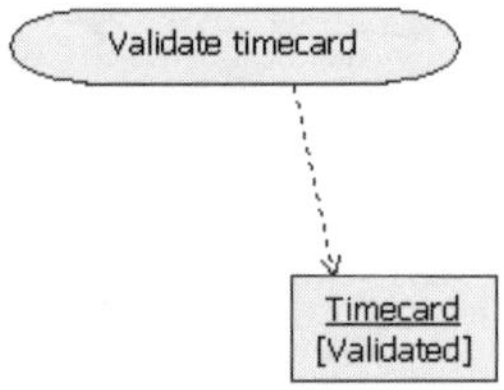

When using an object flow state, you must specify the class that the object is an instance of, and the state the object is in. To add an object flow state:

1. Select the ObjectFlow State icon from the toolbox, and click anywhere on the diagram to place it.

2. Drag and drop a class from the Model Explorer onto the ObjectFlow State.
3. Drag and drop a state from the Explorer onto the ObjectFlow State. States may have been created on a statechart diagram; if not, you need to create the state before performing this step.
4. Select the Transition relationship icon from the UML Class toolbox.
5. Create a transition between the activity and the object flow state. The transition should go from the activity to the object flow state if the activity changes the state of the object, and from the object flow state to the activity if the activity uses the object as an input.

NOTE *You cannot dissociate a class or state from an object flow state, but you can change the class or state. Simply drag and drop the new class or state from the Explorer onto the object flow state.*

Proxy State

A *proxy state* is a "placeholder" activity that is used to represent an activity or state from another state machine or activity graph. This is not a standard UML element but was added into XDE to help support reuse across state machines, activity graphs, and models. Rather than having to duplicate an activity or state in several areas, you can maintain the activity or state in one place and just reference it with proxy states wherever else it is used. A proxy state in XDE appears as an activity with a "T" at the bottom:

To add a proxy state:

1. Select Proxy State from the toolbox, and click anywhere inside the diagram to place it.
2. Drag the appropriate state or activity from the Explorer window to the proxy state on the diagram. The name of the state or activity appears in the proxy state.

NOTE *You cannot dissociate a proxy state from the associated state or activity, but you can replace the associated state or activity with another. Just drag and drop the new state or activity from the Explorer window to the proxy state on the diagram.*

Stub State

If you are working on an activity diagram with one or more subactivity states, you may want to show where the workflow starts on the diagram for the subactivity state. For example, you may want to enter a subactivity at activity A1 if a certain condition is true but enter the subactivity at activity A2 if a different condition is true. A *stub state* is used to identify the entry and exit points in the subactivity workflow. A stub state appears on the diagram with the subactivity and shows which activity will be the entry point:

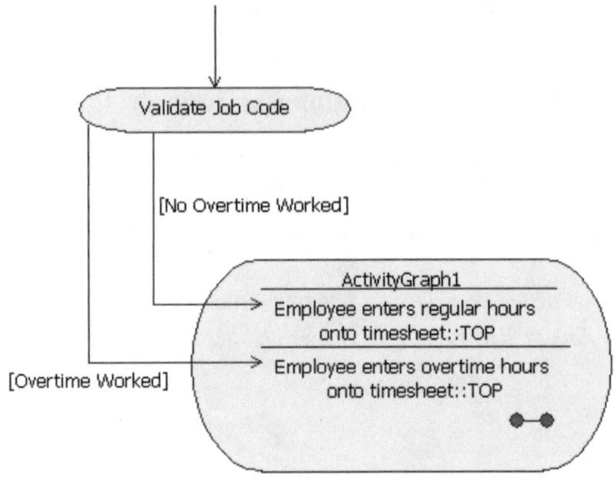

To add a stub state, follow these steps:

1. Select the Stub State icon from the toolbox and click inside the subactivity on the diagram.
2. Drag and drop the appropriate state or activity from the Explorer window onto the stub state in the diagram. The name of the state or activity appears in the stub state.
3. Drag and drop the stub state onto the subactivity state on the diagram.

TIP *An alternate method is to drag and drop the appropriate state or activity directly onto the subactivity state in the diagram. A stub state is created automatically.*

Summary: Activity Diagrams

This section provided an overview of the different elements you can add to an activity diagram. We look at statechart diagrams later, but these same elements also apply to statecharts. For the most part, activity diagrams contain activities, transitions, decision points, and swimlanes (and, of course, an initial and a final state). The other types of elements are useful in some situations, but they tend to be used more in statecharts than in activity diagrams.

Activity diagrams have several audiences:

- The customers review them to make sure that they accurately capture the workflow.
- The design team reviews them to make sure that the steps in the workflow can be implemented in the system, given the current design decisions and system architecture.
- The testing team uses them as a flow representing the way the system is supposed to work and tests to be sure that this is the way the system does work.

Sometimes you may find it helpful to create two sets of diagrams: one for the current workflow, and one for the future workflow. This process can help uncover problems with the current processes and elicit more requirements. The bottom line is that an activity diagram in the use case model should be an implementation-independent representation of the flow of events through a use case. Communication is the major issue here; be sure the diagrams are clear to their audiences, and avoid using too many different types of elements if your reader is unfamiliar with activity diagrams.

When we get to statechart diagrams, you'll see a lot of similarities. The essential difference is that an activity diagram shows workflow, while a statechart diagram shows the different states in which an object can exist in its lifetime. A statechart diagram is more technical, while an activity diagram is more from the user's point of view.

Use Case Analysis

Before we move on to really designing the use case, it helps to take a quick initial look at how the use case might work. The process of examining the functional requirements of a use case and building an initial, implementation-independent "design" is referred to as *use case analysis*. It bridges the gap between requirements (*What* do we want the system to do?) and design (*How* is the system going to do it?).

NOTE *Use case analysis is also sometimes referred to as robustness analysis.*

The primary output of this step is an *analysis model*, which is an abstraction of the design model. While the design model must take into account the programming language being used, architectural decisions made, and architectural constraints, the analysis model focuses on identifying the conceptual classes and other elements that are needed to implement the functionality in a use case.

Let's look at a quick example. In our timecard application, we have a use case called Submit Timecard. Now, we'll assume that it's still pretty early in the project, so we're not sure yet whether we're building this application in Java, C#, Visual Basic, or whatever. But we would at least like to start looking at how we're going to put this thing together. So we begin to identify some conceptual classes. We know, for example, that we're going to need something called Timecard to store the information and behavior of a timecard, and something called Employee to store the information and behavior associated with an employee. We'll also probably need things such as Payroll Code and Pay Period. We also know we'll need a couple of forms: one for the employee, on which they will enter their time, and another for their manager to use to approve the timecard. We have no idea yet what we're going to build all this in, but it's still very helpful to look at these initial pieces of the system, begin to assign responsibilities to each piece, and look at the relationships between them. This whole process is use case analysis.

There are three types of UML diagrams that are typically used in use case analysis: activity diagrams, which we've already discussed, sequence diagrams, and class diagrams. We'll go through an analysis of the timecard application using these diagrams.

Before we dive into the diagrams, though, there are a couple of other things we need to do. We can assume that at this point in the project we've got a pretty complete use case document and a list of requirements for that use case. If not, someone on the team needs to revisit the use case and get the details ironed out. Assuming we're using an iterative rather than a waterfall process, it's okay if we don't have 100 percent of the requirements for the use case, so long as we have all of the architecturally significant requirements. However, we should have enough to get a general sense of what the use case needs to do (say 40–50 percent or so). More is great if you know the requirements, but if not, we can still create an initial analysis model and refine it as we uncover more requirements.

We're also going to need to begin structuring the analysis model by creating packages. As we mentioned earlier, a package is just a UML construct that lets you group things together. How you organize the model elements into packages is completely up to you. Keep in mind, though, that our audience has changed. When we were packaging use cases, we were looking at it from the perspective of the end user and what would make sense from a business perspective. Now we're slowly transitioning into the design of the system, so we need to start focusing on its internal organization. Therefore, packaging here tends to take into account the relationships between the classes, the responsibilities of the classes, and the hierarchies of these classes more than the business perspective. Generally speaking, you create packages at a couple of levels of abstraction to define the high-level and the more detailed structure of your system. As always in analysis, keep in mind that this structure will be refined as you get into the design; this is just an initial organization of the system.

The highest-level package diagrams will, after design, represent the architectural layers in the system. During analysis, you can be fairly generic:

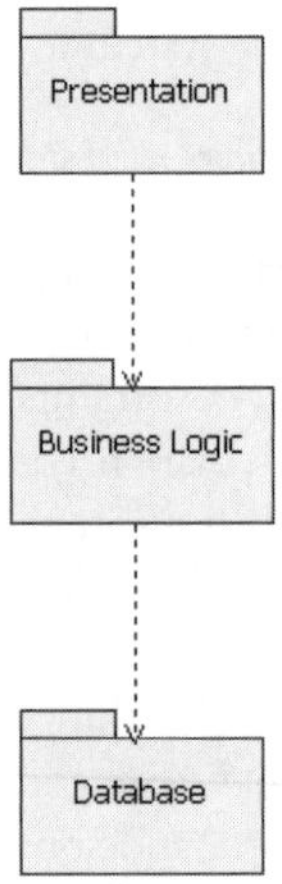

Then, in design, we'll refine these to take into account the specific architecture we'll be using. More detailed packages are typically created for each subsystem in the system. We'll get into the details of this in design.

One final note: let's be realistic for a minute. You're not always going to have the luxury of time to go through each use case and create an analysis model for it and then go through the use cases again to create the design. In some projects, especially shorter projects, the team doesn't really create an analysis model at all. Even if one is created, it's not usually kept up-to-date once the design model has been built, so it is, at best, a transitory artifact. That's okay, though. Part of the purpose of the analysis model is to get you to design—if it has served that purpose, then it was worth the time it took to build. If you decide to leave the analysis model completely out of your project, just be aware of the risk. The design model has a lot of architecture and implementation considerations (whether to use .NET or Java, ASP or HTML, and so on), while the analysis model helps the team be sure that all of the requirements are met, without having to worry about all those pesky implementation details. If the team jumps straight into design with no use case analysis, you'll have to put some extra effort into mapping back to the requirements to make sure they were all met.

Identifying Analysis-Level Classes

To begin, we need to start defining a "dictionary" of analysis classes we can use in our sequence and class diagrams. This is a little bit of art and a little bit of science, but there are a few places you can start. First, however, let's briefly discuss the three types of analysis classes:

Boundary classes These are your forms, windows, and interfaces to other systems. The classes that actors interface with are the boundary classes.

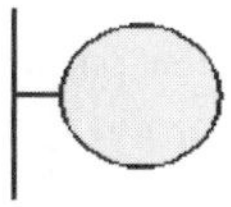

Boundary

Entity classes These are primarily responsible for holding information. Typically, the information they hold is made persistent, although this isn't a requirement.

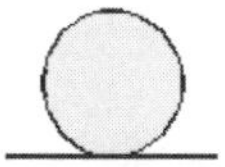

Entity

Control classes These are responsible for controlling the flow of logic through a use case. They don't actually carry out any business functionality; instead they coordinate the behavior of other classes.

Control

The symbols shown here are used during the analysis effort. Once we get into design, we'll replace these with the traditional UML box for each class.

The best way to start finding these classes is to go through the flow of events for the use case. Take a look at the nouns. Not all of them will become classes, of course, but many may be good candidates. In our example, the terms Timecard, Employee, Payroll Code, and Pay Period can all be found in the flow of events. Another good place to look is a database structure, if it exists. If you are re-engineering or enhancing an existing system, look at the tables in the existing database. Some of these may be good candidates for entity objects.

To find boundary classes, just look at the use case diagram. A boundary class must exist for each arrow between an actor and a use case. They do not need to be unique; a single boundary class can serve more than one arrow, but each relationship must have a boundary class. The reason is that actors can interact only with boundary classes. Therefore, in order for an actor to interact with the system, a boundary class must exist.

Control classes won't show up in the flow of events. They're more of a pattern you can use to manage the flow through a use case. In analysis, it is common to create one control class per use case, although a use case can have more than one control class. By the time we get to design, we may remove the control classes.

To add analysis classes to the Model Explorer, follow these steps:

1. (Optional) Create packages to hold the classes. Right-click an existing package and select Add UML ➢ Package. Name the new package.
2. (Optional) If you created new packages, edit the Stereotype property in the Properties window. Select the "..." button, and then select Analysis Package from the drop-down list of stereotypes. The symbol used in XDE changes to that of an Analysis package:

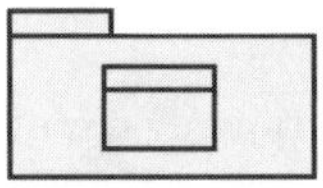

Analysis Package

3. Right-click a package in the Explorer window.
4. Select Add UML ➢ Class.
5. Type the name of the new class.
6. Use the Stereotype property in the UML section of the Properties window to set the class to Boundary, Entity, Control, or another stereotype.

TIP *As an alternate to this approach, in step 5, include the stereotype when you enter the class name. For example, instead of entering **Class1** and then modifying the stereotype property, you would type **<<boundary>>Class1** in step 5.*

TIP *If the classes appear as boxes rather than one of the symbols shown at the beginning of this section, select Format ➢ Stereotype And Visibility Style ➢ Shape Stereotype: Icon from the menu.*

After going through this process, we have an initial list of candidate classes in our XDE model. Let's look at these classes in the context of sequence and class diagrams.

NOTE *You can create sequence and class diagrams in either order. In our experience, teams usually have defined sequence diagrams first, followed by class diagrams, but the two activities occur somewhat in parallel.*

Building an Analysis-Level Sequence Diagram in XDE

In the UML, an *interaction diagram* shows the objects, actors, and messages required to implement the functionality in a flow of events. A *sequence diagram* is a type of interaction diagram that is arranged in time sequence.

There is another type of interaction diagram, the *collaboration diagram*, that also shows this information, but in a slightly different format. XDE does not currently support collaboration diagrams, so we focus on sequence diagrams here.

In analysis, the objects that appear on the diagram may not be objects in the eventual code. These are analysis-level objects from analysis-level classes, meant to give the team just a rough idea of the types of classes and messages they might need. Figure 4.8 is an example of an analysis-level sequence diagram.

FIGURE 4.8

Sequence diagram

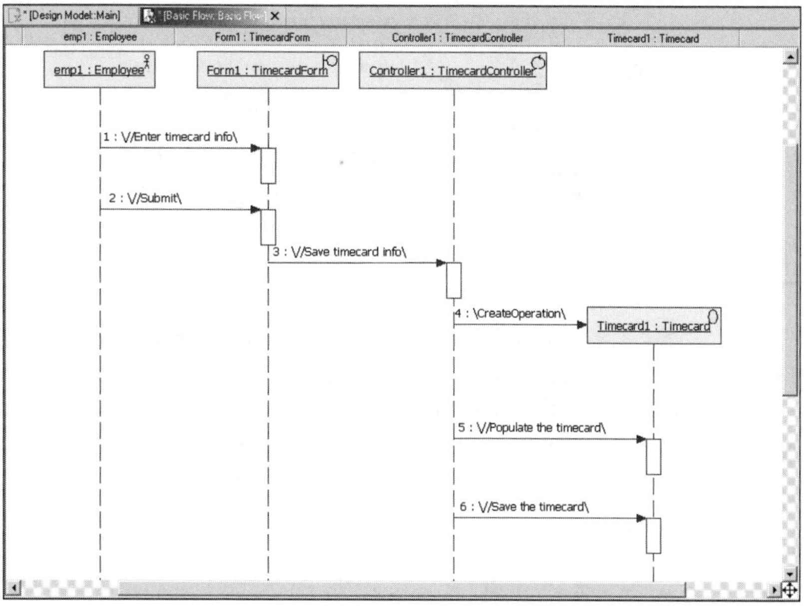

Typically, the team creates a couple of sequence diagrams: one for the basic flow of events and one for each significant alternate flow.

THE SEQUENCE DIAGRAM TOOLBOX

The sequence diagram toolbox includes options for creating objects, instances of actors, messages, and other elements on a sequence diagram. Table 4.5 lists the toolbox options and their meanings, and which sections of this chapter to see for more detail.

TABLE 4.5: SEQUENCE DIAGRAM TOOLBOX

ICON	MEANING	SEE SECTION
Pointer	Returns the mouse to the standard pointer	
Lifeline	Adds an object to the diagram	"Adding Objects and Actors"
Lifeline Actor	Adds an actor instance to the diagram	"Adding Objects and Actors"
→ Message	Adds a message between objects, between actors, or between an object and an actor	"Adding Messages"
← Return Message	Shows the return of a message	"Adding Messages"

Continued on next page

TABLE 4.5: SEQUENCE DIAGRAM TOOLBOX *(continued)*

ICON	MEANING	SEE SECTION
Create	Creates an object in memory	"Adding Messages"
Destroy	Removes an object from memory	"Adding Messages"
Note	Adds a simple note to the diagram	
Note Attachment	Attaches a note to a use case or other element	
Constraint	Refines the structure or behavior of an element	
Text	Adds text to the diagram	

CREATING COLLABORATION INSTANCES AND INTERACTION INSTANCES

In XDE, a sequence diagram is created in an *interaction instance,* which is contained within a *collaboration instance.* A collaboration instance is sometimes referred to as a *use-case realization* and a relationship can exist between the collaboration instance and the use case it realizes. We show this as a realizes relationship.

Here is an example of the structure of collaboration instances in XDE:

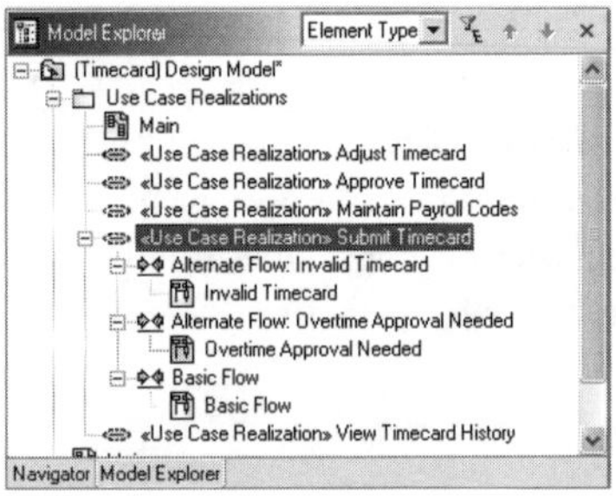

In this example, the collaboration instance is the use case realization Submit Timecard. The use case realizations for the other use cases are also collaboration instances. For the Submit Timecard use case, the interaction instances are Alternate Flow: Invalid Timecard, Alternate Flow: Overtime Approval Needed, and Basic Flow. The actual sequence diagrams are Invalid Timecard, Overtime Approval Needed, and Basic Flow.

A collaboration instance owns the objects that are used in a set of sequence diagrams. Note that we said *objects* and not classes. A single class may have instances in many collaboration instances, and a collaboration instance may use objects instantiated from classes anywhere in the model. There is typically one collaboration instance per use case that holds the objects for all of the sequence diagrams in the use case.

Placing an interaction instance within a collaboration instance allows you to model the stimuli exchanged between objects to perform a task. You can have multiple interaction instances within a collaboration instance. Each usually corresponds to a basic or alternate flow in the flow of events. Each of the interaction instances contains a single sequence diagram, as well as all of the messages on that sequence diagram. The objects on the diagram are owned by the collaboration instance.

If a collaboration instance does not yet exist (in other words, if you want to create the first sequence diagram for a use case), XDE can create the collaboration instance, interaction instance, and sequence diagram all at once. To do this, follow these steps:

1. Right-click a package and select Add Diagram ➢ Sequence: Instance.
2. Type the name of the new sequence diagram.
3. If a collaboration instance and interaction instance do not already exist, XDE automatically creates them for you. You can rename the collaboration instance (usually with the name of the use case) and interaction instance (usually with the name of the basic or alternate flow) if you'd like.

To create a new sequence diagram if the collaboration instance already exists (in other words, to create a new sequence diagram for a use case that already has some sequence diagrams), follow these steps:

1. Right-click the existing collaboration instance in the Explorer and select Add UML ➢ Interaction Instance.
2. Name the new interaction instance (usually with the name of the basic or alternate flow).
3. Right-click the new interaction instance and select Add Diagram ➢ Sequence: Instance.
4. Name the new sequence diagram.

We were assuming here that you opted to put your collaboration instances into a separate package, which isn't required. Here are a few notes on creating sequence diagrams:

- You do not have to create the collaboration instances under a package. You can right-click any model element and select Add Diagram ➢ Sequence: Instance. This creates the collaboration instance, interaction instance, and sequence diagram under the selected model element. A pattern that project teams frequently use, however, involves creating a package that holds all of the collaboration instances.
- You can create collaboration instances or interaction instances independently of creating a sequence diagram.
    1. Right-click an element in the Explorer and select Add UML ➢ Collaboration Instance.
    2. Then, right-click the new collaboration instance and select Add UML ➢ Interaction Instance.

    To add a sequence diagram to the interaction instance later, right-click the interaction instance and select Add Diagram ➢ Sequence: Instance.

ADDING OBJECTS AND ACTORS

Now that we've created the structure and added a new sequence diagram, the next step is to add objects, actors, and messages to the new diagram. The general process is to go through the flow of events one step at a time, and determine how we're going to implement that functionality. For example, if a line in the flow of events reads, "the system validates the timecard entries," we need to decide four things.

- First, what objects will be needed to validate a timecard?
- Second, what messages must be sent between the objects to validate a timecard?
- Third, what order should the messages be sent in?
- Finally, what actors, if any, must send or receive messages to validate a timecard?

Again, because this is analysis, try not to think J2EE, or .NET, or ASP, or whatever. We're just using conceptual classes here. Once we've answered the four questions for this step in the flow, we can add the actors, objects, and messages needed to implement the step. Then, we can continue through the scenario, going through step-by-step and adding objects and messages until we've finished this diagram.

The boxes on a sequence diagram represent the different objects that participate in this particular scenario. In XDE, you can include the boundary, entity, and control symbols to show what type of objects you're dealing with. The actor(s) in the scenario are also shown in boxes. By convention, you would show the actor on the far left, followed by boundary classes, then control classes, and finally entity classes. The reason for this is that in the analysis of a typical three-tier application, boundary classes send messages to control classes, which send messages to entity classes. This is just a convention, however. You can place the objects, including the actors, in any order you like.

NOTE *If the actor is another system, you may want to model it as a boundary class (representing the interface to the other system) as opposed to an actor on a sequence diagram. This isn't necessary in analysis, but is common in design.*

The dashed line descending from each object is its *lifeline*. The object is placed vertically at the point it is instantiated into memory. The lifeline ends when the object is removed from memory. In analysis, it isn't necessary to explicitly state when objects are created and destroyed, but we will do so in design.

To add actors and objects to the sequence diagram, follow these steps:

1. Add instances of existing actors or classes. To do so,
   A. Drag and drop the actor or class from the Explorer window to the sequence diagram.
   B. (Optional) Name an actor instance or an object by right-clicking it and selecting Rename.
2. If need be, add other objects (that are not instances of existing classes, or have not yet been mapped to existing classes). To do so,
   A. Select the Lifeline option from the toolbox.
   B. Click the diagram to place the new object.
   C. Type the new object name.

3. If need be, add new actor instances (that are not instances of existing actors, or have not yet been mapped to existing actors). To do this,

   A. Select the Lifeline Actor option from the toolbox.

   B. Click the diagram to place the new actor instance.

   C. Type the name of the new actor instance.

ADDING MESSAGES

The arrows between the lifelines are *messages*, or stimuli sent from one object to another. These may be method calls, or a signal being raised. In analysis, though, we don't need to worry about method names yet. All we need to do is state, in simple language, what the message is for:

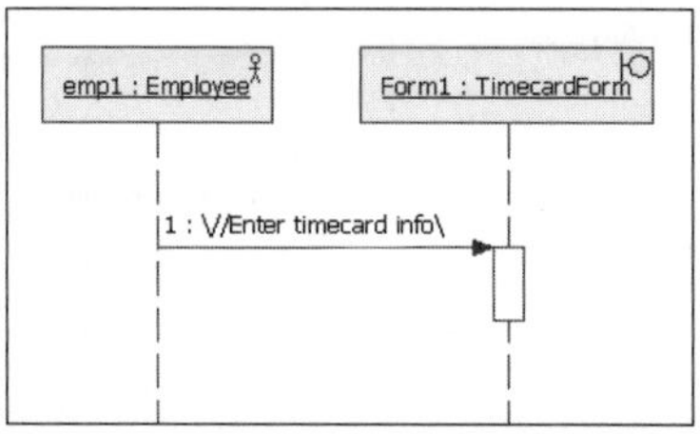

By convention, messages in an analysis diagram start with a double-slash (//). This signals the reader, saying, "We're in the analysis model—these aren't method names." The messages on the analysis diagrams will become *analysis operations* for the classes. An analysis operation really just defines a responsibility of a class (for example, "hold timecard information," "validate timecard," and so on).

It is assumed that each message on the diagram returns some value. You can look at the operation signature to see the return type of the operation. There are times, though, when it is helpful to explicitly show the return of a message. This is done by using a *return message*.

To add messages to a sequence diagram:

1. Add messages between objects, between actors, or between an object and an actor. To do so,

   A. Select the Message icon from the toolbox.

   B. Click the lifeline of the actor or object sending the message.

   C. Click the lifeline of the actor or object receiving the message.

   D. Click the message text to modify it. By convention, analysis messages start with a double-slash (//), but this isn't required.

   E. To reorder the messages, simply drag and drop a message higher or lower in the diagram. XDE automatically renumbers the messages.

2. To show that one object instantiates another, use a create message from the lifeline of one object to the object it is creating. To do this,

   A. Move the object being created vertically on the diagram until it corresponds to the point in time it will be created.

B. Select the Create option on the toolbox.

C. Click the lifeline of the object that is instantiating another.

D. Click the object (the box, not the lifeline) being created. XDE creates a new message called \CreateOperation\. You can optionally rename this message.

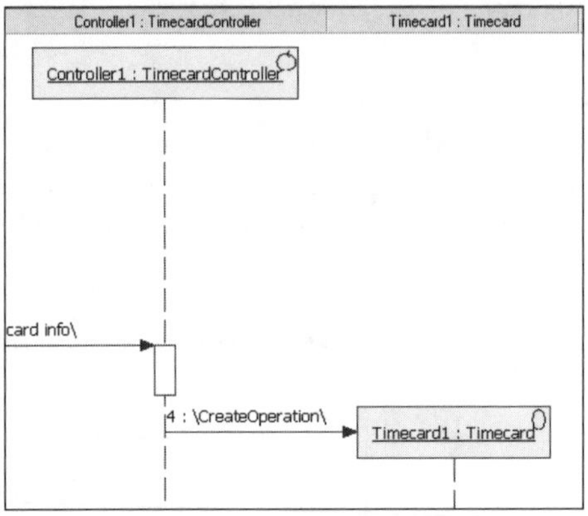

3. To show that one object destroys another, use a destroy message from the lifeline of one object to the lifeline of the object it is removing from memory. In order to do this,

   A. Select the Destroy option on the toolbox.

   B. Click the lifeline of the object that will destroy another.

   C. Click the lifeline of the object to be destroyed. XDE automatically shortens that object's lifeline and adds a destruction marker (a large "X").

4. Show return messages if needed. To do this,

   A. Select the Return Message option from the toolbox.

   B. Click the lifeline of the object sending the return.

   C. Click the lifeline of the object receiving the return message.

5. Map the analysis messages to analysis operations. To do this,

   A. Right-click a message on the diagram (the arrow, not the text).

   B. Select Create Operation From Message. (This option will not appear unless the object is mapped to a class.)

NOTE *You can't create an operation from a Create or Destroy message. A Create message will become a constructor for the class, and a Destroy message will become a destructor.*

You can add a number of other details to a sequence diagram, but these aren't relevant in analysis and will be covered when we get to design.

Building an Analysis-Level Class Diagram in XDE

A sequence diagram gives you a good view of how objects collaborate to carry out functionality, but a class diagram is better for viewing classes and their relationships across many scenarios and many use cases. A class diagram shows classes, packages of classes, or subsystems. It may also optionally include one or more of the following: attributes of the classes, operations of the classes, class interfaces, relationships between classes, relationships between packages, relationships between subsystems, subsystem interfaces, notes, and constraints. Whew!

Fortunately for us, there are a lot of design details that we don't have to worry about yet. Until we get to design, we won't know what programming language, database management system (DBMS), or other architectural constraints we're facing. At this point, we just need to document the logical structure of the system. We can create as many different class diagrams as we need: some to show the architectural layers, others to show a set of classes. A common pattern is to create a View of Participating Classes (VOPC) for each use case. This diagram contains all of the classes that a particular use case needs, along with the attributes, operations, and relationships of those classes. Some common class diagrams you might want to consider include:

- A diagram showing the high-level architectural layers
- Diagrams showing the packages of classes and their relationships
- Diagrams showing the inheritance hierarchy of the classes
- VOPC diagrams for the use cases
- Diagrams showing classes and relationships, but no attributes or operations
- Diagrams showing reusable classes
- Diagrams showing classes being reused from other sources, and dependencies between the new system's classes and the reused classes

Of course, we won't create all of these in analysis. As the project moves along, we'll build more and more diagrams and refine the ones we've already created. Figure 4.9 is an example of an analysis-level class diagram.

FIGURE 4.9

Analysis-level class diagram

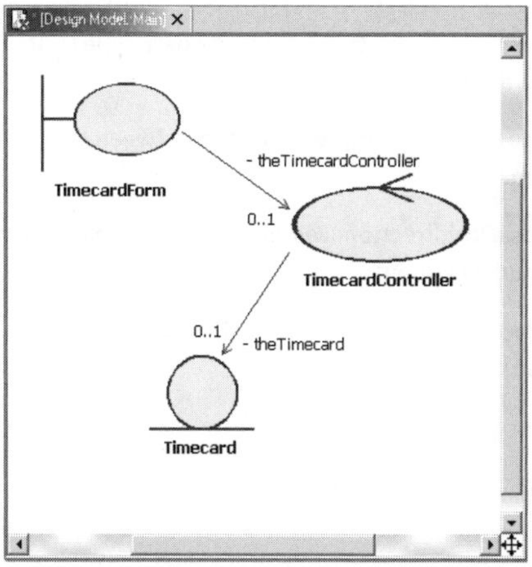

To create a class diagram in XDE:

1. Right-click the model or a package and select Add Diagram ➢ Class. You can also add a class diagram to a class, subsystem, operation, use case, or actor.
2. Name the new diagram.

TIP *The following sections describe how to create classes and packages using a class diagram. To add an existing class or package to a class diagram, simply drag and drop the existing class or package from the Explorer onto the diagram.*

THE CLASS DIAGRAM TOOLBOX

The class diagram toolbox is used to add classes, relationships, and other elements to a class diagram. We won't need all of these options in analysis, but they will all be used by the time we get to design. Table 4.6 lists the toolbox options and their meanings, and which chapters or sections of this chapter to see for more detail.

TABLE 4.6: CLASS DIAGRAM TOOLBOX

ICON	MEANING	SEE SECTION
Pointer	Returns the mouse to the standard pointer	
Package	Creates a package of classes	"Creating Packages and Architectural Layers"
Class	Creates a class	"Adding Analysis Classes"
Interface	Creates an interface for a class or subsystem	See Chapter 5, "Modeling Java and J2EE Elements on XDE," and Chapter 6, "Modeling Visual Studio .NET Elements in XDE."
Signal	Creates a signal, which is an asynchronous communication between objects	See Chapters 5 and 6.
Enumeration	Creates an enumeration, which is a data type containing a list of values	See Chapters 5 and 6.
Association	Creates an association relationship between two model elements	"Adding Class Relationships"
Directed Association	Creates a unidirectional association relationship between two model elements	"Adding Class Relationships"
Aggregation Association	Creates an aggregation relationship between two model elements	"Adding Class Relationships"

Continued on next page

TABLE 4.6: CLASS DIAGRAM TOOLBOX *(continued)*

ICON	**MEANING**	**SEE SECTION**
Composition Association	Creates a composition relationship between two model elements	"Adding Class Relationships"
Association Class	Creates an association class, used to hold information and/or behavior related to an association	"Adding Class Relationships"
Generalization	Creates an inheritance relationship between two model elements	"Adding Class Relationships"
Realization	Creates a realization relationship between two model elements	See Chapters 5 and 6.
Dependency	Creates a dependency relationship between two model elements	"Adding Package Relationships"; also see the sections of Chapters 5 and 6 having to do with class dependencies.
Bind	Creates a bind relationship between an element and a template	See Chapters 5 and 6.
Usage	Creates a usage relationship between two model elements, in which one element requires the presence of the other	See Chapters 5 and 6.
Friend Permission	Creates a friend relationship between model elements, giving one element access to the contents of the other	"Adding Package Relationships"; also see the sections of Chapters 5 and 6 having to do with class friend relationships.
Abstraction	Creates an abstraction relationship between two elements, showing that the elements contain the same information at different levels of abstraction	See Chapters 5 and 6.
Instantiate	Shows that one element instantiates another	See Chapters 5 and 6.
Subsystem	Creates a subsystem, which is a package with a defined interface	See Chapters 5 and 6.
Note	Adds a simple note to the diagram	
Note Attachment	Attaches a note to a use case or other element	
Constraint	Refines the structure or behavior of an element	
Constraint Attachment	Attaches a constraint to an element	
Text	Adds text to the diagram	

CREATING PACKAGES AND ARCHITECTURAL LAYERS

Let's begin at the high level. We may not know what implementation mechanisms we're using yet, but we can still develop a general picture of our architectural layers. These layers can be documented in a class diagram, using packages with a stereotype of <<layer>>.

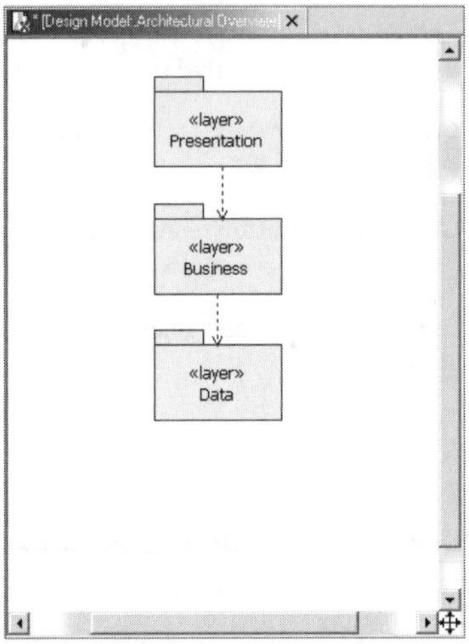

This example is a standard approach based on the Model-View-Controller (MVC) idea. MVC is an architectural pattern that separates data and data logic into a Model layer, presentation logic into a View layer, and application or business logic into a Controller layer. This fits in really well when you are working with the analysis model. The boundary, entity, and control classes map to the View, Model, and Controller layers, respectively.

Of course, it is more common today to use an *n*-tiered approach. Once you've analyzed your distribution requirements, security issues, reuse issues, implementation mechanisms, and other design decisions, you may decide to create four, five, or more architectural layers. A complete discussion of how to partition your application is beyond our scope, but here are some of the things you need to consider:

Distribution How will the application be physically distributed across nodes?

Security Are there areas of the architecture that have special security requirements? What are the security implications of each dependency between the layers?

Likelihood of change How likely are the elements in one layer to change? Try to build your architecture to minimize the impact on the other layers.

Scalability If the system were to experience an increase in workload in the future, would this layering approach support it?

Efficiency How will the layers communicate? Upon distribution, will there be a geographic separation between layers that might slow system performance? Are there security or other issues that might slow the communication between layers?

Reuse Are there specific things you'd like to reuse? If so, minimize the number of other elements that the reusable items depend on.

To create an architectural layer in XDE, you need to create a package and then assign it a stereotype of <<layer>>.

1. Right-click an existing package in the Explorer and select Add UML ➢ Package.
2. Name the new package.
3. Change the value in the Stereotype property to layer.

At a more detailed level, we can create packages to hold the classes in our analysis model. Although the packages themselves are likely to change during design, it is important to pick a packaging strategy now. As with layering, some of the things to consider include:

Reuse Which classes are likely to be reused? You might want to group them together.

Maintenance What would the dependencies between packages look like with different packaging strategies? Try to minimize the impact of a change to one package.

Flexibility and scalability Does the packaging strategy allow for enhancements and workload increases?

Deployment Where will the classes be physically deployed?

Security Are there special security requirements for certain groups of classes?

One option for organizing classes into packages is to group the classes by stereotype. Using this approach, you'd have separate packages for your boundary, entity, and control classes. This approach is good for finding items; it's really easy to find all of your forms, for example. It's not such a good approach, though, when dealing with reuse.

Another option is to group the classes by functionality. In our timecard example, we might have one package called TimeCard, which deals with entering and validating timecards. Another package called Payroll might deal with maintaining payroll codes and dealing with other payroll-specific functionality in the system. A Security package might deal with the security logic in the system. We would follow this type of pattern, breaking the system down into more manageable, functional pieces. If we take this approach, we will most likely create some subsystems in design, where a *subsystem* is a package that has a well-defined interface. But more on that later. Whatever approach you take, be sure the design team understands the packaging guidelines you've established.

To add a package in XDE, follow these steps:

1. Right-click the model or an existing package in the Explorer window and select New UML ➢ Package.
2. Type the name of the new package.
3. In the Explorer window, drag and drop classes into or out of that package. You can also nest packages by dragging and dropping another package into the new package.

ADDING PACKAGE RELATIONSHIPS

In the section "Packaging Actors and Use Cases" within our discussion of use cases, we talked about the different types of relationships between packages. Here, we briefly review them. Generally speaking, we use simple dependencies between layers. We may use dependencies or the other types of relationships between packages.

Access relationship Allows one package to access the public contents of another.

Import relationship Allows one package to add the public contents of another.

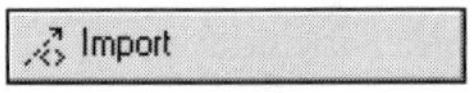

Friend relationship Allows one package to view the contents of another, regardless of the visibility settings of the contents.

Dependency relationship Specifies that one package needs to access or import the public contents of another.

Generalization relationship Allows the contents of one package to inherit from the contents of another.

To add a relationship between packages:

1. Select the appropriate relationship from the UML Class toolbox. If you are creating an access or import relationship, select the appropriate option from the UML Use Case toolbox.
2. Click the client package.
3. Click the supplier package.

ADDING ANALYSIS CLASSES

Our analysis classes are the boundary, entity, and control classes that we found while reviewing the flow of events and building the sequence diagrams. We've already added the analysis classes to our model (by right-clicking a package and selecting Add UML ➢ Class). What remains is to add some details to the classes, such as attributes, operations, and relationships.

To add an analysis class to a class diagram:

1. Drag and drop the class from the Explorer onto the diagram. Because XDE maintains all elements in a central repository, any relationships that class has with other classes on the diagram will also be shown.
2. If the analysis class does not exist in the Explorer,
   A. Select the Class option from the toolbox and click in the diagram to place the new class.
   B. Type the name of the class, and modify the Stereotype property to set the appropriate stereotype.

Analysis Attributes

An *attribute* is a piece of information associated with a class. Attributes will eventually become the class members, and we'll define details such as the visibility, data type, and default value of each. For now, though, it's sufficient to add the attributes and their names. To add an analysis attribute to a class:

1. Right-click the class in the Explorer or on a class diagram and select Add UML ➢ Attribute.
2. Type the name of the new attribute.
3. (Optional) Set the initial data type of the new attribute by modifying the TypeExpression property.

TIP *To hide the attributes on the diagram, or to show them again if they are hidden, select the class on the diagram and then select Format ➢ Compartment ➢ Attribute Compartment.*

Analysis Operations

As we discussed earlier, an analysis operation just identifies a responsibility that the class has. It eventually maps to one or more "official" class methods. In analysis, parameters and return types are optional. Don't spend too much time worrying about the signature of an operation; just identify any obvious, significant parameters that the operation has. If you want to assign a data type to a parameter, you can, but stick with language-independent types such as String or Integer. We'll refine the data types later. Also, don't worry about giving the operation an "official" name. Stick with the informal name you used in the sequence diagrams until you get to design.

To add an analysis operation to a class:

1. Right-click the class in the Explorer or on a class diagram and select Add UML ➢ Operation.
2. Type the name of the new operation.

TIP *An alternate way to add an analysis operation to a class is to right-click the messages on the sequence diagrams and select Create Operation from Message.*

3. (Optional) Right-click the new operation and select Add UML ➢ Parameter. Type the name of the new parameter.
4. (Optional) Set the data type of the new parameter by modifying its TypeExpression property.

Analysis Operation Display Options on Class Diagrams

You have a few options when you are displaying analysis operations on a class diagram.

To show the whole operation signature rather than just the operation name on the class diagram, select the class on the diagram and then choose Format ➢ Signature ➢ Operation Signature.

To hide the operations completely or to show them again if they are hidden, select the class on the diagram and then choose Format ➢ Compartment ➢ Operation Compartment.

To change the order of the parameters, you need to directly edit the operation's signature on the class diagram. Single-click the operation to highlight it and edit the text. Then, edit the signature as needed to reorder the parameters.

ADDING CLASS RELATIONSHIPS

In design, we'll add all sorts of details to these relationships: multiplicity, navigation, names, and so on. But in analysis, all we need to do is define the relationships we have.

A good place to look is the sequence diagrams. If an instance of class A and an instance of class B send messages to one another on a sequence diagram, they'll need a relationship on a class diagram. If all the messages are sent in one direction, we can use a directed association; otherwise, we'll just use an association.

If classes from different packages need an association, be sure that a relationship has been set up between the packages, in addition to the relationship between the classes.

Associations

An *association* is a semantic relationship between classes. It allows instances of one class to send messages to instances of another class. It is drawn as a line connecting the two classes:

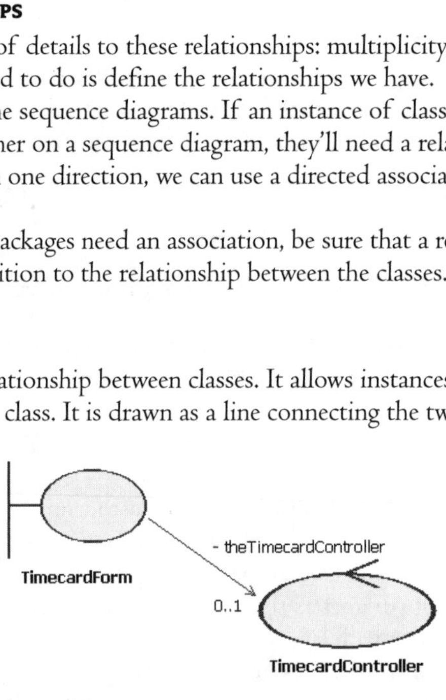

A directed association appears as an arrow connecting the two classes, pointing from the client to the supplier. Associations are fairly easy to find. Just examine the sequence diagram; any two objects that send messages to one another need an association between their classes on the class diagram.

To add an association or a directed association:

1. Select the Association or Directed Association option from the toolbox.
2. Click one class, and then the other. If you are adding a directed association, click the client class first and then the supplier. Don't worry about the multiplicity or association names that are automatically added; we'll get to those in design.

NOTE *The UML 1.4 specification allows for* n-ary associations, *which are associations that join more than two classes. This feature is not currently supported in XDE.*

Association Classes

An *association class* is an association that has information and behavior of its own. That is, it is an association that is also a class and is used when there is some information and behavior related to the relationship between two classes, rather than to one class by itself. For example, let's assume that in our problem domain, each company employs many people, and each person can work for more than one company. But if we have only a Person and a Company class, where can we store the Salary attribute? If we put it in Person, we need a separate attribute for each company they work for. If we put it in Company, we need a separate attribute for each person that works for the company. Because Salary is more of an attribute of the relationship between those two classes, we can put it in an association class. An association class is connected directly to the association between two other classes:

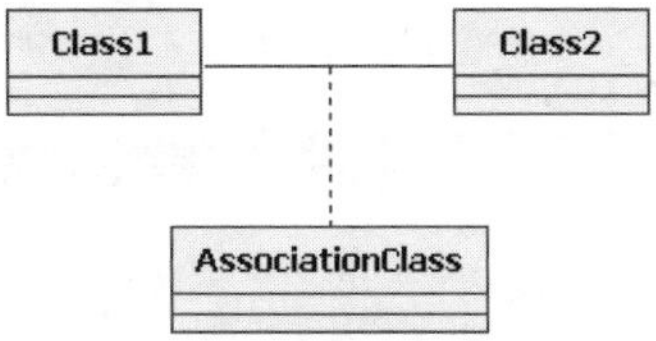

If you're familiar with database design, you'll have noticed that association classes tend to show up on some many-to-many relationships between classes. We won't necessarily find a lot of these in analysis, but we may find some in design.

To add an association class:

1. Create an association relationship between the two primary classes.
2. Use the Class option in the toolbox to create an association class on the diagram or drag and drop an existing class from the Explorer.
3. Select the Association Class option from the toolbox.
4. Click the association class and then the association to create the relationship.

Aggregations

An *aggregation* is a special form of association that connects two classes with a "whole/part" relationship. For example, a timecard is made up of time entries. A time entry consists of the job number, the number of hours worked, and the date. A collection of time entries is a timecard, so an aggregation relationship exists between them. An aggregation is shown as an association with a diamond next to the class representing the whole (the composite class):

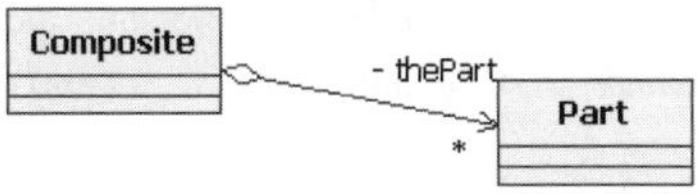

There are two types of aggregations. A *standard aggregation* is one in which instances of the part class and composite class are created and destroyed independently of one another. These relationships are shown with a hollow diamond, as shown earlier. A *composite aggregation*, also known as a *composition relationship*, is one in which an instance of the part class can be included in only one composite at a time, and the composite instance is responsible for creating and destroying instances of the parts. These relationships are shown with a filled diamond:

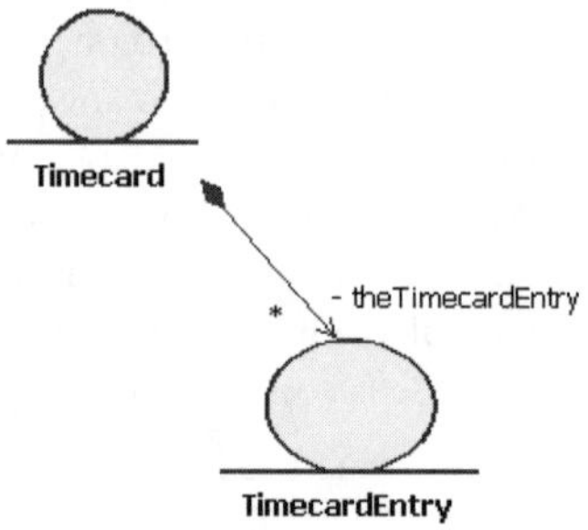

To create an aggregation or composition association:

1. Select the Aggregation Association or Composition Association relationship from the toolbox.
2. Click the composite class first, then click the part class.

TIP *To change an aggregation to a composition, or a composition to an aggregation, modify the Kind property in the UML section of the Properties window.*

Generalizations

A generalization between classes is similar in purpose to a generalization between use cases or a generalization between packages. One key difference is that a generalization between classes affects the source code. In a generalization, the child class inherits all of the attributes, operations, and relationships of the parent. For the purposes of analysis, that's all we need to worry about at this point. A generalization between classes is modeled as shown here:

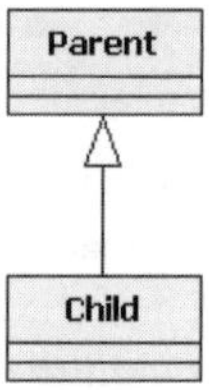

NOTE ***For Rose users:*** *In XDE, each child/parent generalization has its own arrow. In Rose, the tool can combine all the arrowheads into one to make the diagram a little less cluttered. This functionality isn't currently included in XDE.*

To add a generalization:

1. Select the Generalization option from the toolbox.
2. Click the child class first, then the parent class.

Review and Refine

The whole idea of switching easily between code and model perspectives is to give you the flexibility to make changes. As you build more and more of your analysis model, chances are that you'll want to change some things that you've already done. You may find that a few of the analysis classes should be combined, or that a single analysis class is getting too large and should be split apart. You may discover that your initial packaging strategy isn't working and you want to restructure your packages.

This is a constant process; always keep in the back of your mind the idea of refining your analysis model. The general concept is known as *refactoring*, and there are a number of books and articles out there that can provide guidance in this area.

NOTE *For more information on refactoring, see* Refactoring: Improving the Design of Existing Code *by Martin Fowler et al. (Addison-Wesley, 1999) and* `www.refactoring.com`*, a website maintained by Fowler.*

For the analysis model, some of the things to think about are as follows:

- Do any of the classes have too many responsibilities? Too few?
- Are there classes that depend on too many other classes?
- Are there classes that all of the other classes seem to depend on? Are there changes to this one class that could drastically affect the system?
- Are there packages with no classes, or with only one or two? Are there packages with too many classes?
- Is the inheritance structure appropriate? Do the attributes, operations, and relationships of the parent class really apply to each of the children?
- Are the classes, attributes, and operations named appropriately? Do they make sense to the reader of the model?

Go through these types of questions as you're building, reviewing, and refining the analysis model. We'll go through the same type of exercise in the design model, but from an implementation perspective.

Now What?

Where do we go from here? We've reached a fork in the road. Using traditional tools, the designers would take all of this information and build sequence diagrams and class diagrams in a design model. From the design model, the developers would then build the code.

With XDE, you've got another option. If you are more comfortable working with the design, you can start with the design model. If you are more comfortable working with the code, you can start with the code. The two approaches are briefly described here.

One option is to take the analysis model and use case documents, and create sequence and class diagrams with initial design classes. (Some people prefer to build sequence diagrams first, others prefer to build class diagrams first—either works.) You may then want to synchronize with the code to create and refine these classes a little bit. Then, you can go back to the design model to build some more of the detailed design. With this approach, you switch back and forth between the modeling perspective and the coding perspective, building a little bit of the design and then working with the code.

A second option is to start with the code. Review the analysis model and use case documents, and begin building classes to support the logic in them. Switch to the design model and update it with the structure of the code you've created. As with the first option, switch back and forth between the two perspectives, building a little bit of code and working with the design each time.

Exercise: Creating the Use Case and Analysis Models for the Timekeeping System

In the following exercise, we create the use case model for the timekeeping system that was laid out in Chapter 3. We begin by first creating an XDE project. We then add packages to organize the use cases and actors, and create some use case diagrams. Next, we detail the use case diagrams, adding actors, use cases, and their relationships. We also add a new use case and relationship to handle a change in the requirements. We link the requirements and the XDE model using the principles of integrated use case management, either with RequisitePro or without. Finally, we create a design model, and add an activity diagram, sequence diagram, and class diagram.

Creating the Project and Use Case Model

In the first part of this exercise, we create a use case model according to the guidelines for model hierarchy as published by Rational Software. We add packages to organize the use cases, and create use case diagrams that we detail later in this exercise.

1. Start Rational XDE.
2. If you are not currently in the modeling perspective, select Perspective ➢ Open ➢ Modeling.
3. Choose File ➢ New ➢ Project. This displays the New Project window:

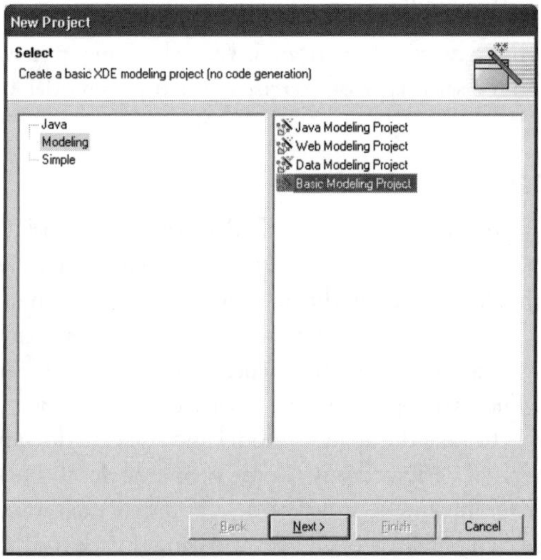

4. Select Basic from the list of project types, and choose Basic Modeling Project. Then click Next. This creates a modeling project without code generation capabilities. Since this will be the use case model, the code generation option is not required.

5. Name the project **Timekeeping System** and click Finish. The project is created and the Model Explorer opens with the default name XDE Model.

6. In the Model Explorer, right-click XDE Model and choose Rename. Rename XDE Model to **Use-Case Model**.

7. You also need to rename the filename for the model. Open the Navigator view by choosing Perspective ➢ Show View ➢ Navigator or by selecting the Navigator tab in the Model Explorer to display the Navigator.

8. Right-click the model file in the Timekeeping System project. The model file will likely be `XDE Model.mdx`. Select Rename from the context menu.

9. Rename the model file to **Use-Case Model.mdx**. Open the Model Explorer.

10. Since this is a use case model, you should change the Main diagram for the model to a use case diagram instead of the default freeform diagram. Select the Main diagram in the Model Explorer. In the Properties window, choose UML ➢ Type. Change the value of the Type property from 0 - FREE_FORM to 2 - USE_CASE:

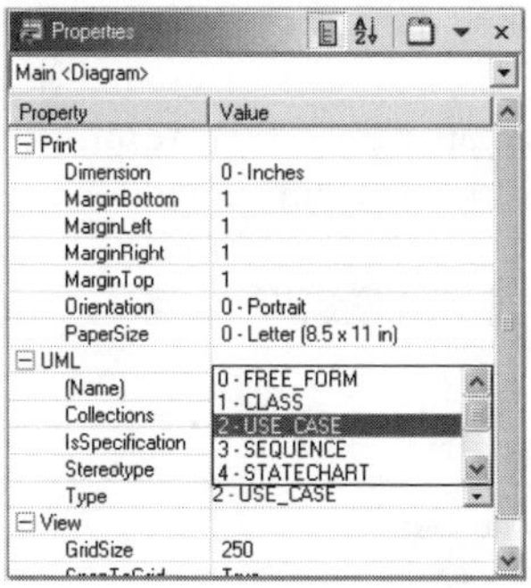

11. In order to follow the guidelines, you will need to create packages for actors and use cases. To do so, right-click Use-Case Model in the Model Explorer, then select Add UML ➢ Package from the context menu. Name the package **Actors**. Repeat this process to add the Use Cases package to the model. Expand both packages by clicking the plus (+) symbol next to each one. A Main diagram is automatically created for each package. Change this Main diagram in each package from a freeform diagram to a use case diagram using the process outlined in step 10.

12. These two packages are use case packages and should be stereotyped. To stereotype them, select the Actors package and choose UML ➢ Stereotype in the Properties window. Set the Stereotype property to Use Case Package. Repeat this process for the Use Cases package. Note the different icon in the Model Explorer for the use case packages.

13. Next you need to create two use case diagrams to represent the Global View and Use-Case View of the architecture. To create a use case diagram, right-click Use-Case Model in the Model Explorer, then select Add Diagram ➢ Use Case. Name the diagram **Global View Of Actors And Use Cases.** Repeat this process to add the Use-Case View use case diagram to the model.

14. Click the disk toolbar icon to save the model.

At this point, the structure of the Use-Case Model is now in place. Next you add actors and use cases and place them in the appropriate packages.

Creating the Use Case Diagram for a Global View of the System

The Global View Of Actors And Use Cases diagram covers all actors and use cases in the model and their interactions. In this portion of the exercise, you populate this diagram, create the actors and use cases, create the associations, and move the actors and use cases into their respective packages.

1. Double-click the Global View Of Actors And Use Cases diagram to open it in the diagram window.

2. Click the Actor toolbox button and click in the diagram to add an actor. Name the actor **Employee.**

3. Another method you can use to create actors (or other elements) uses the Model Explorer. Right-click the Actors package in the Model Explorer. Select Add UML ➢ Actor from the context menu. Name the actor **Manager.** Click and drag the actor onto the Global View Of Actors And Use Cases use case diagram. Use either this method or the process in step 2 to create two more actors named **HR Administrator** and **Payroll System.** When you have created all the actors, the diagram should look similar to this:

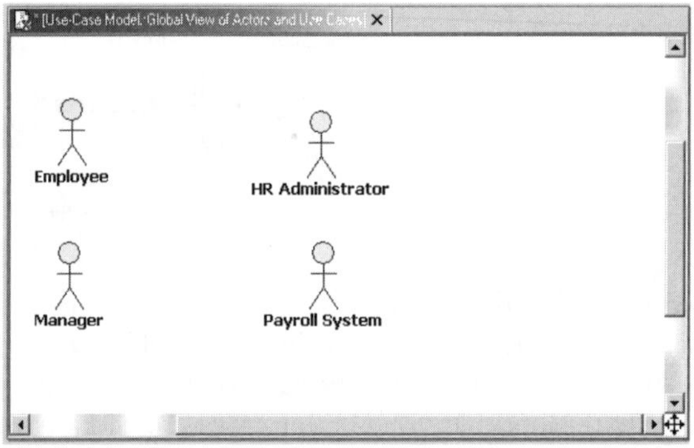

4. Click the Use Case toolbox button and click in the diagram to add a use case. Name the use case **Submit Timecard.**

5. Add the following additional use cases to the diagram:

   - **View Timecard History**

- **Approve Timecard**
- **Adjust Timecard**
- **Maintain Pay Codes**

6. Drag and arrange the actors and use cases to roughly the positions shown in the following illustration. You may want to change the Zoom factor in the toolbar depending on your screen size.

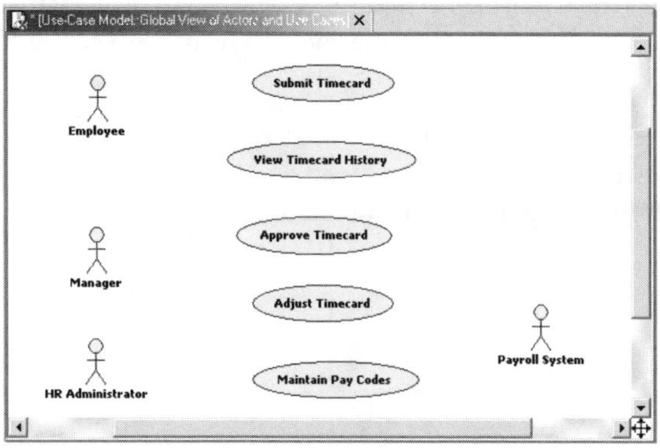

7. Click the Directed Association toolbox button and click the Employee actor to add an association from the Employee actor to the Submit Timecard use case. Drag the association to the Submit Timecard use case.
8. Add the following additional directed associations to the diagram:
   - From the Employee actor to the View Timecard History use case
   - From the Manager actor to the View Timecard History use case
   - From the Manager actor to the Approve Timecard use case
   - From the HR Administrator actor to the Adjust Timecard use case
   - From the HR Administrator actor to the Maintain Pay Codes use case
   - From the Approve Timecard use case to the Payroll System actor
   - From the Adjust Timecard use case to the Payroll System actor
   - From the Maintain Pay Codes use case to the Payroll System actor
9. Click the Association toolbox button and click the HR Administrator actor to add an association from the HR Administrator actor to the Approve Timecard use case. Drag the association to the HR Administrator actor. This association indicates that the HR Administrator actor participates in the Approve Timecard use case but does not initiate the use case.

10. Select Diagram ➢ Hide Connector Labels to hide the multiplicity and role name labels from the diagram.

11. XDE provides some capability to tidy up the diagrams. Drag a box around the Employee, Manager, and HR Administrator actors to select all three. Alternately, you can click one of the actors, and then Ctrl-click the other two. Select Format ➢ Align ➢ Centers to center all three actors. Do the same for the use cases to center them.

12. Create equal spacing between the elements. To do so, Ctrl-click the Employee, Manager, and HR Administrator actors and choose Format ➢ Vertical Spacing ➢ Make Equal. Do the same for the use cases.

13. Just for cosmetic appeal, move the Payroll System actor up a little. Click the Adjust Timecard use case and Ctrl-click the Payroll System actor. Select Format ➢ Align ➢ Middles. The completed diagram should appear as follows:

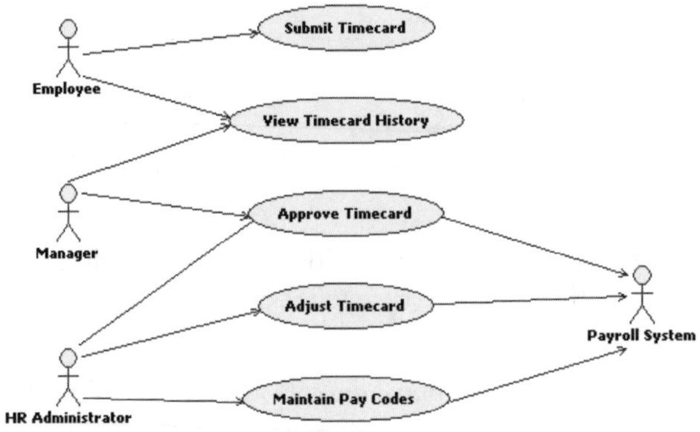

14. Now you should place the use cases and actors into their respective packages. To do so, select the Submit Timecard use case in the Model Explorer and drag it to the Use Cases package. Repeat this process to drag all of the actors and use cases into the appropriate packages.

Handle a New Requirement

After the initial use case diagram was presented to the stakeholders, they remembered some additional functionality—the timekeeping system also needs to maintain status reports. Employees can write status reports at any time, but if an employee submits a timecard without a status report for that period, they must write a status report at that time. You can show this requirement change on the diagram by adding a new use case and an extend relationship to the Submit Timecard use case. To make this change, follow these steps:

1. Add the Write Status Report use case to the Use Cases package using the Model Explorer.

2. Open the Global View Of Actors And Use Cases diagram.

3. Drag the Write Status Report use case to the diagram.

4. Create a directed association from the Employee actor to the Write Status Report use case.
5. Select the directed association and hide the connector labels.
6. Select the Extend toolbox button and create an extend relationship from the Write Status Report use case to the Submit Timecard use case. The revised diagram should appear as follows:

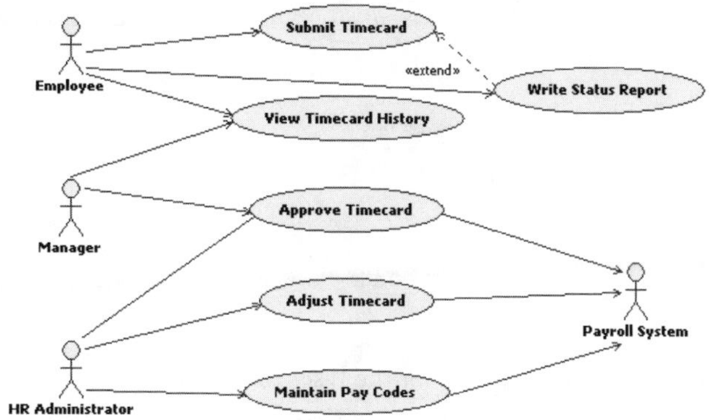

7. Save the model.

Create the Main Diagrams for Each Package

Each package contains a Main diagram on which you should show all elements within the package. For example, you should create a Main diagram in the Actors package that shows all of the actors in that package. In addition, you should show all use cases on the Main diagram in the Use Cases package, and all the Actors and Use Cases packages on the Main diagram of the Use-Case Model. To do all this, follow these steps:

1. Open the Main diagram in the Actors package.
2. Select all actors using either Shift-click or Ctrl-click.
3. Drag the actors to the diagram.
4. Choose Diagram ➢ Arrange to arrange the actors on the diagram. Fine-tune the arrangement any way you like. The diagram should look similar to this:

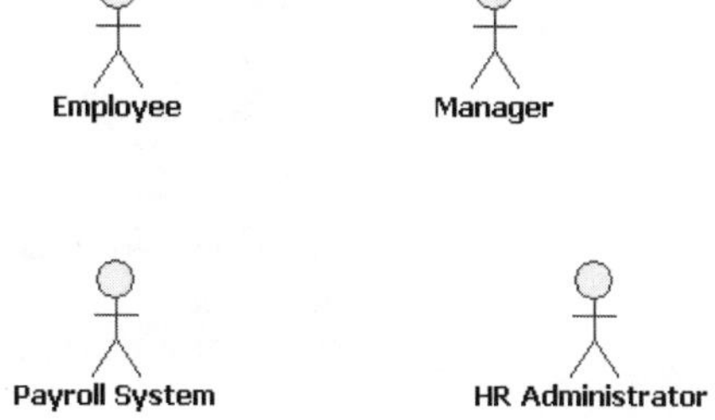

5. Follow the same process to create the Main diagram for the Use Cases package. This diagram appears as follows:

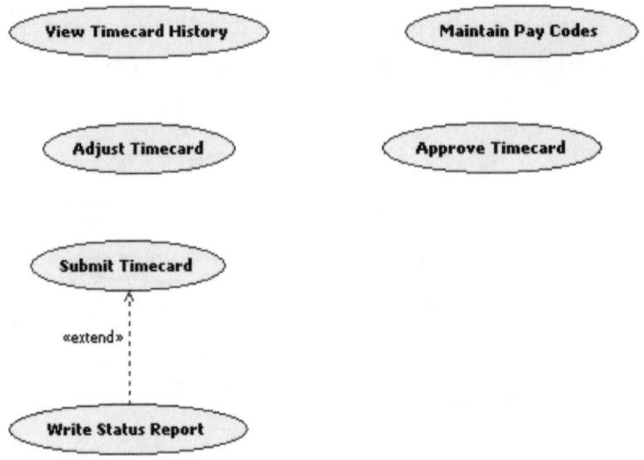

6. Open the Main diagram for the Use-Case Model.
7. Drag the Actors and Use Cases packages onto the diagram. Arrange the diagram to appear as follows:

Now you have defined the use case model and you have added use cases and actors and the relationships between them. You have also separated the model into packages for clarity and organization. The completed model should appear in the Model Explorer as shown in the following illustration. Further, this model follows the standard developed by Rational for use case models and you can use the same structure for your own use case models.

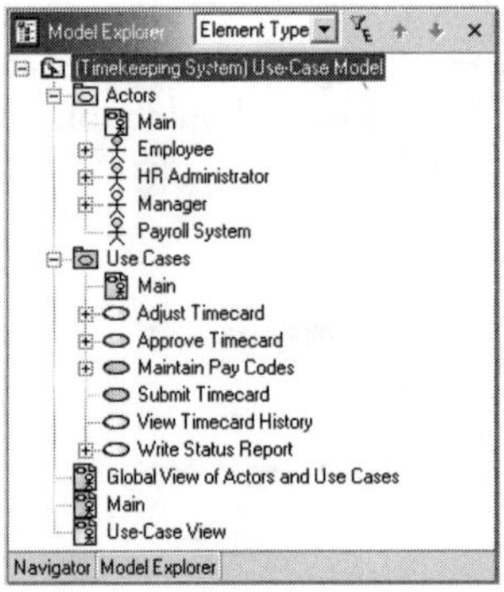

Integrated Use Case Management

XDE gives you two different methods to link use cases to their documents. If you are using Rational RequisitePro, this is the IUCM process. If you are not using RequisitePro, you can still link documents to use cases.

Before you continue with this exercise, copy the exercise files from the Sybex website (`www.sybex.com`). Search for the book by its ISBN number, 4205, or by its title, and download the files from the Download button.

Linking a Document to a Use Case without RequisitePro

If you aren't using RequisitePro, you can link documents to use cases by adding a URL to the use cases in XDE. Follow these steps to link the View Timecard History flow-of-events document to the View Timecard History use case.

1. Right-click the View Timecard History use case in the Model Explorer.
2. Choose Add UML ➢ URL from the context menu.
3. Assuming that you have already downloaded the exercise files to your `C:\Mastering XDE` directory, enter **`C:\Mastering XDE\Chapter 4\Flow of Events - View Timecard History.doc`** as the URL.

Although documents can be attached without a requirements management tool, such a tool gives you more options. With RequisitePro, you can also store attributes about the use case, establish requirements traceability, and launch RequisitePro directly from XDE.

NOTE *You must have Rational RequisitePro installed in order to complete the following two parts of the exercise. If you do not have RequisitePro, visit* `www.rational.com/tryit` *for an evaluation copy.*

Setting Up the RequisitePro/XDE Integration

The first step in IUCM with RequisitePro is to configure the XDE model's properties and associate the XDE model with a RequisitePro project. Follow these steps to configure the XDE model's properties:

1. Select the Use-Case Model in the Model Explorer.
2. In the Properties window, select the AppliedProfiles property and enter **RequisitePro** in this property. This adds model properties and menu items as shown here:

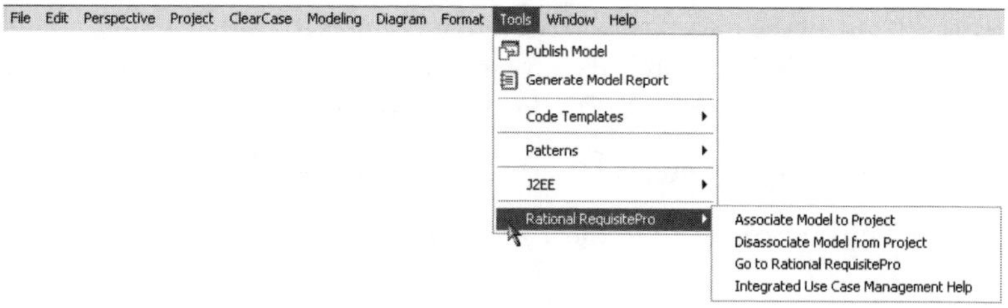

If your menu does not contain the RequisitePro items, the add-in for RequisitePro may be inactive. Follow these steps to reactivate it:

A. Choose Window ➢ Preferences from the menu.

B. Expand the Rational XDE preferences and select Add-Ins; then click the Add-In Manager button.

C. Ensure that the RequisitePro and COMServerAddIn add-ins are selected. Click the check boxes if they are not.

D. Click OK twice.

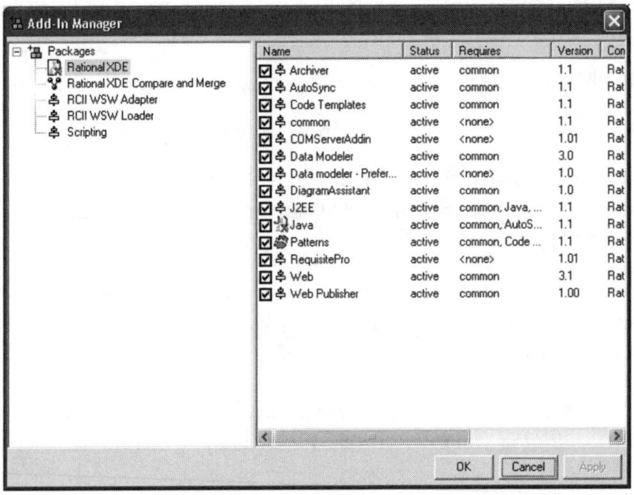

3. Select Tools ➢ RequisitePro ➢ Associate Model To Project.

4. Enter the Project File as **`C:\Mastering XDE\Chapter 4\Timekeeping System\Timekeeping System.RQS`**.

5. Select Use Case Specification Document Type as the default document type and Use Case Requirement Type as the default requirement type. Click OK.

Link XDE Use Case to RequisitePro Use Case Document

After setting up the integration between XDE and RequisitePro, you can link use cases to the use case documents in RequisitePro. You can also create documents and access and update the requirement properties through XDE. To do all of this, follow these steps:

1. Right-click the Submit Timecard use case in the Model Explorer.

2. Choose Use Case Document ➢ Associate from the context menu.

3. Ensure that the display document type is UCS: Use Case Specification Document Type as shown here:

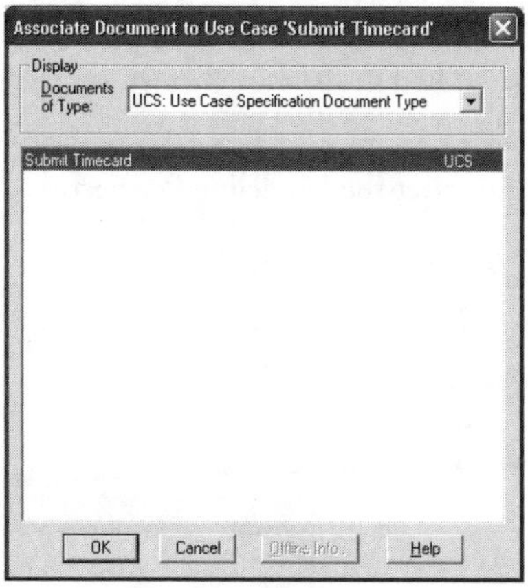

4. Click the Submit Timecard document, and then click OK.
5. Right-click the Submit Timecard use case in the Model Explorer.
6. Select Requirement Properties ➢ Open from the context menu. This will display the Requirement properties:

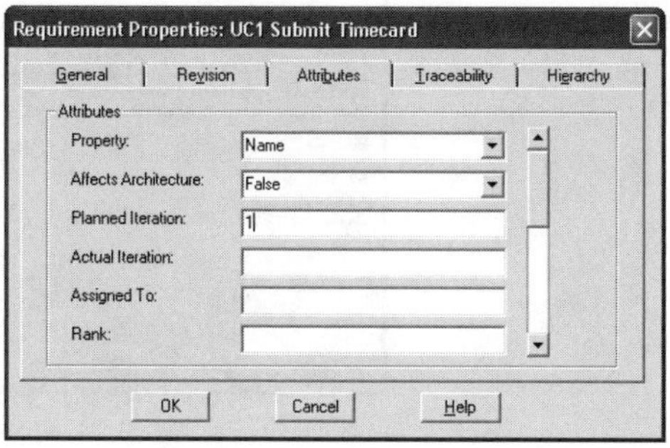

7. Set the Planned Iteration attribute to Iteration 1.
8. Set the Priority to High.
9. Set the Status to Approved.
10. Click OK. The requirement properties will be updated.

Creating the Design Model

After the Use-Case Model has been defined, you turn next to the Analysis Model. The recommended structure for the Analysis Model is to store the model elements in a Design Model under the Analysis Elements. You will create the Design Model with this structure. Use case realizations and analysis classes are stored in the model; later, the design elements of the project will be stored here. Follow these steps to create the Design Model:

1. Open XDE and select the Modeling Perspective.
2. Open the Navigator view and right-click the Timekeeping System project.
3. Choose New ➢ Model from the context menu.
4. Choose Java Content Model and set the filename to Design Model, as shown in the following illustration, and then click Finish.

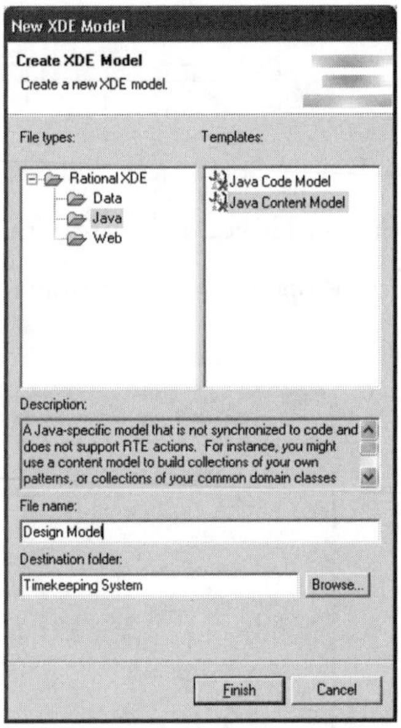

5. Create an Analysis Elements package in the Design Model.
6. Set the stereotype of the Analysis Elements package to Analysis Package.
7. Add the Analysis Elements package to the Main diagram of the Design Model.

Creating an Activity Diagram

An activity diagram can be used to graphically show the flow of events through a use case. Just follow these steps:

1. In the Use-Case Model, right-click the Submit Timecard use case.

2. Select Add Diagram ➢ Activity from the context menu.
3. Name the activity diagram Submit Timecard. Name the ActivityGraph Submit Timecard as well.
4. Select the Initial State toolbar button and add an initial state to the activity diagram.
5. Select the Activity toolbar button and add an activity to the activity diagram. Name the activity "**Select option to submit a timecard**".
6. Add another activity named "**Request period for the timecard**".
7. Add additional activities named as follows:
   - **"Enter period for the timecard"**
   - **"Display timecard and available status"**
   - **"Enter hours and pay codes"**
   - **"Submit timecard for approval"**
8. Add a final state to the diagram.
9. Add a transition between the initial state and the Select option to submit a timecard activity by selecting the Transition toolbar button and dragging a transition between the elements.
10. Add additional transitions:

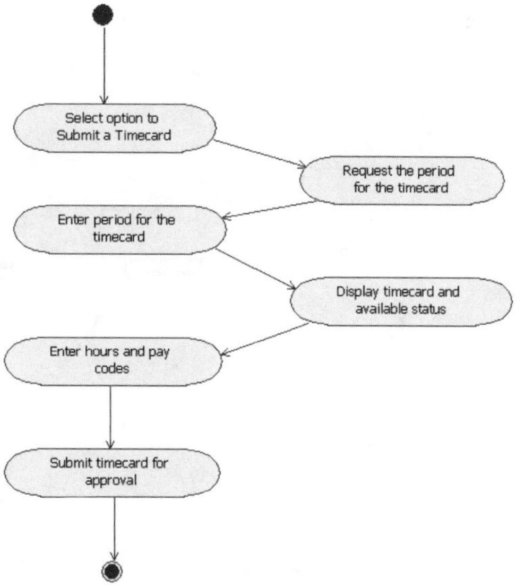

ADDING ALTERNATE FLOWS TO AN ACTIVITY DIAGRAM

Next, you add the alternate flows to the diagram, along with guard conditions on the transitions so that you can indicate which flow to use. You can also do this using decision points, but you use the guard conditions here.

1. Add the following activities to the diagram:
   - **"Display 'Invalid Period' error message"**
   - **"Display list of valid periods"**
   - **"Select valid period from the list"**
2. Add transitions between the following activities:
   - "Enter period for the timecard" and "Display 'Invalid Period' error message"
   - "Display 'Invalid Period' error message" and "Display list of valid periods"
   - "Display list of valid periods" and "Select valid period from the list"
   - "Select valid period from the list" and "Display timecard and available status"
3. Select the transition between "Enter period for the timecard" and "Display 'Invalid Period' error message."
4. In the Properties window, enter **invalid period** as the guard condition.
5. Enter **valid period** as the guard condition for the transition between "Enter period for the timecard" and "Display timecard and available status." The activity diagram should appear as shown here:

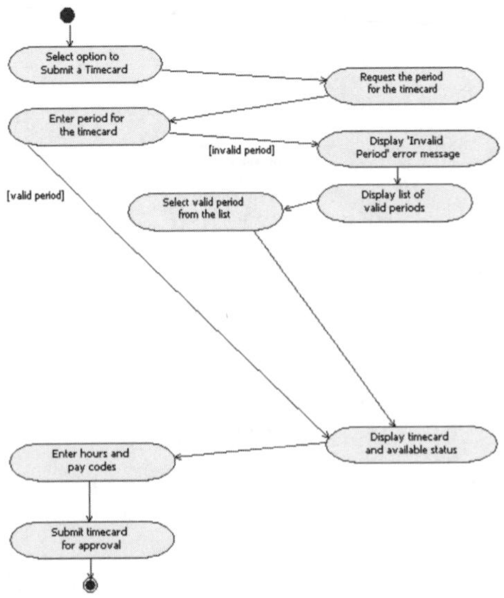

6. Add activities named as follows:
   - **"Display 'Hours too high' error message"**
   - **"Display 'Invalid Pay Code' error message"**
   - **"Display 'Too Few Hours' error message"**
7. Add a Proxy State from the toolbox to the diagram.
8. Create an activity diagram for the Write Status Report use case in the Model Explorer.
9. Add an initial state, final state, and Write Status Report activity to the Write Status Report activity diagram. Add transitions so that the diagram appears like this:

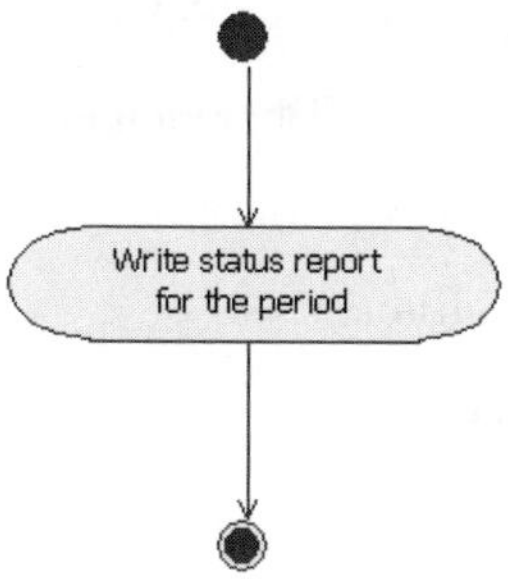

10. Open the Submit Timecard activity diagram.
11. Drag the Write Status Report activity from the Model Explorer to the proxy state in the diagram.
12. Add transitions and guard conditions as shown in the following illustrations:

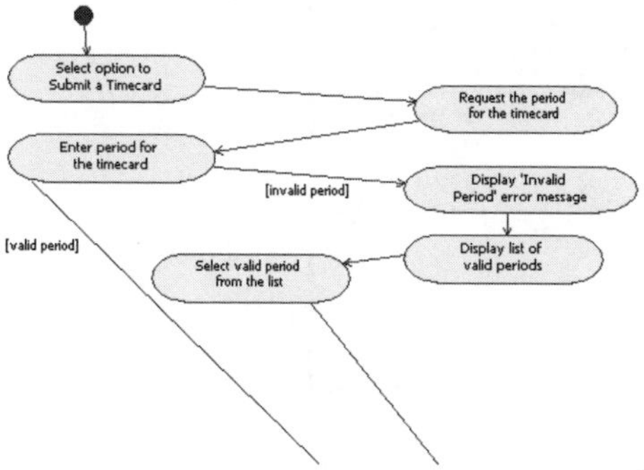

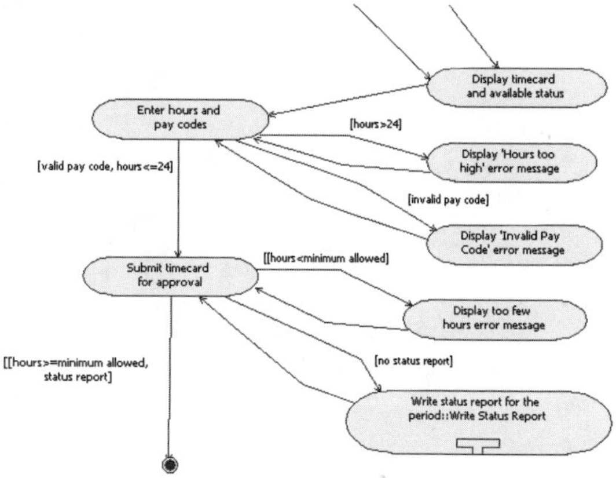

Creating a Sequence Diagram

During analysis, you can use a sequence diagram to identify some initial objects that you need for a flow of events, and you can assign responsibilities to them. Sequence diagrams are contained within interaction instances, which are contained within collaboration instances.

1. In the Design Model, right-click the Analysis Elements package.
2. Select Add UML ➢ Package from the context menu.
3. Name the package **Use-Case Realizations**.
4. Right-click the Use-Case Realizations package and choose Add UML ➢ Collaboration Instance.
5. Name the collaboration instance **Submit Timecard**.
6. Set the stereotype of the collaboration instance to Use-Case Realization.
7. Add collaboration instances for each of the following:
   - View Timecard History
   - Approve Timecard
   - Adjust Timecard
   - Maintain Pay Codes
   - Write Status Report
8. At this point, the Explorer should look like the following illustration. Right-click the Submit Timecard use case, and select Add UML ➢ Interaction Instance from the context menu.

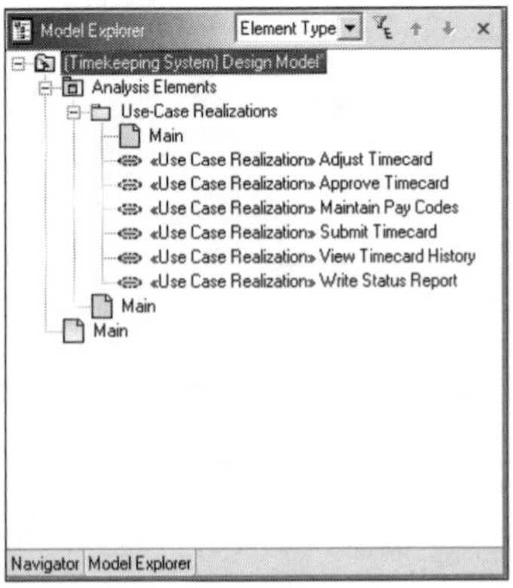

9. Rename the interaction instance **Basic Flow**.

10. Right-click the Basic Flow interaction instance and choose Add Diagram ➢ Sequence: Instance from the context menu.
11. Name the sequence diagram **Basic Flow.**
12. Add the following additional interaction instances to the Submit Timecard use case. When complete, the Explorer window should look like the following illustration.
    - **Alternate Flow: Invalid Period**
    - **Alternate Flow: Hours Too High**
    - **Alternate Flow: Invalid Pay Code**
    - **Alternate Flow: Submission of Too Few Hours**
    - **Alternate Flow: Submission Without Status Report**

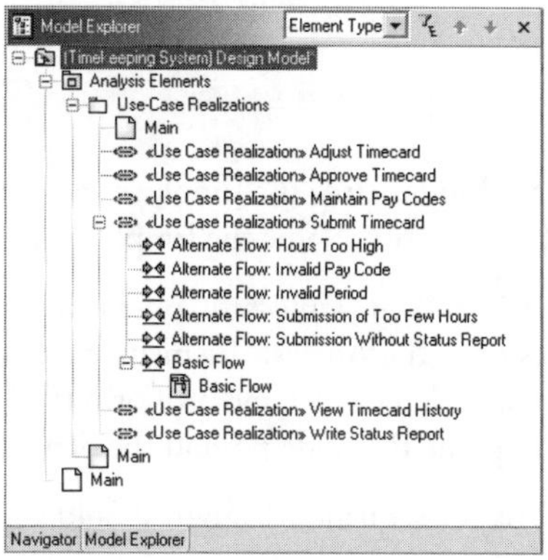

ADDING OBJECTS AND ACTORS

Now that you've created a sequence diagram, the next step is to add the classes and actors you need so that you can add objects and actor instances to the diagram.

1. Right-click the Analysis Elements package and select Add UML ➢ Class from the context menu.
2. Name the class **<<boundary>> TimecardForm.** This will name the class and set its stereotype.
3. Add the following other classes:
    - <<control>> TimecardController
    - <<entity>> Timecard
    - <<entity>> PayPeriod
    - <<entity>> StatusReport

4. When complete, the Explorer should look like this:

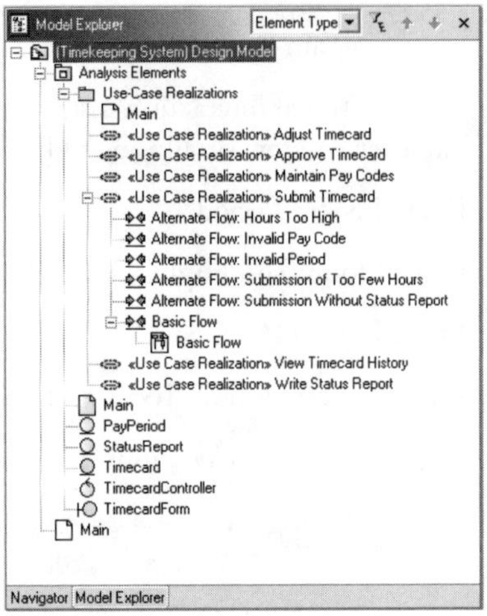

5. In the Use-Case Model, drag the Employee actor to the Basic Flow sequence diagram to create a lifeline for the actor. Name the Employee **E**.

6. Drag the TimecardForm, TimecardController, Timecard, PayPeriod, PayCode, and StatusReport objects from the Analysis Elements package in the Design Model to the Basic Flow sequence diagram. Name the TimecardForm **tf**, the TimecardController **tc**, the Timecard **tce**, the PayPeriod **pp**, the PayCode **pc**, and the StatusReport **sr**.

   When complete, the sequence diagram should appear as shown here:

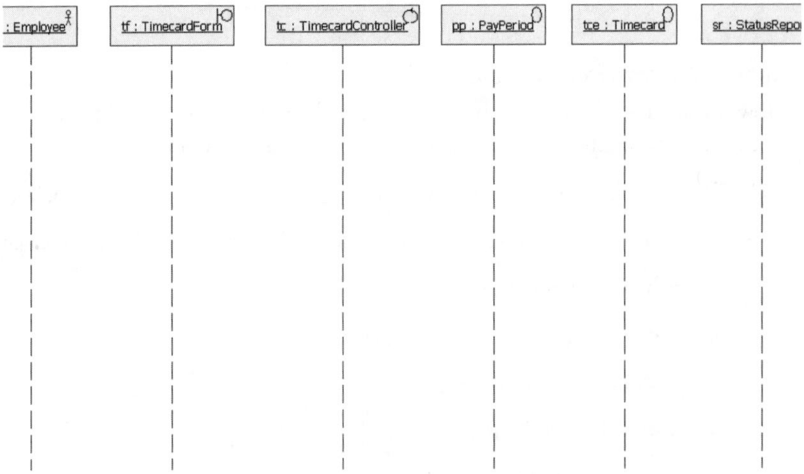

7. Select the Message toolbar button and add a message between the Employee and the TimecardForm.

8. Name the message **// Enter a timecard.** The double-slash indicates that the message is a comment, not an operation. (To edit the message on the diagram, you may need to single-click twice on the text.)

9. Add messages between the objects as shown here:

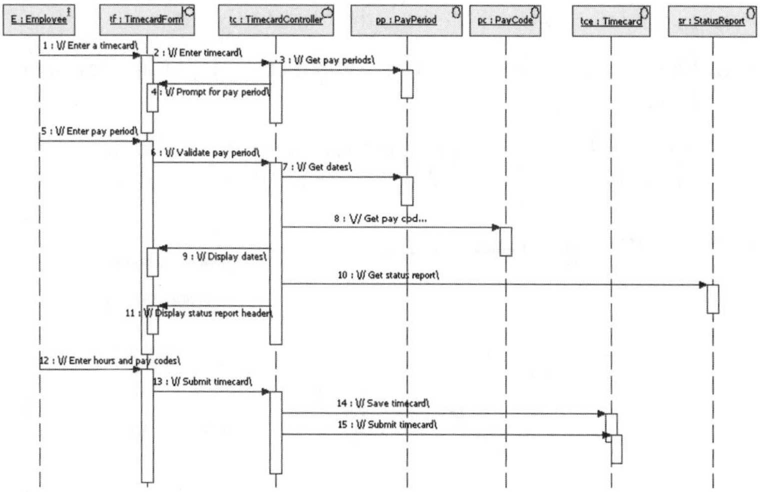

10. Create analysis operations from the messages by right-clicking each message arrow and selecting Create Operation From Message. The messages will then end with parentheses and analysis operations will be created on the analysis classes. The sequence diagram should appear as shown here:

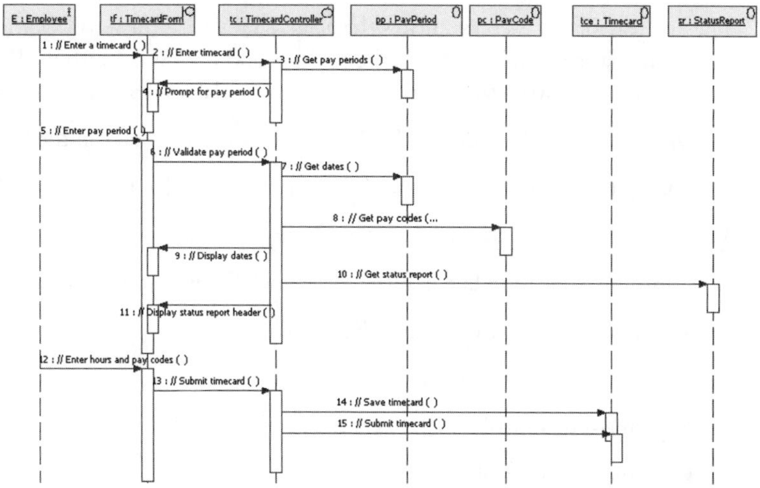

11. Save the model.

Next, you should complete the Main diagram of the Use-Case Realizations package. Here you show the use-case realizations (collaboration instances) and those use cases they realize.

1. Open the Main diagram of the Use-Case Realizations package in the Design Model.
2. Drag each collaboration instance to the Main diagram.
3. Expand the Use-Case Model in the Model Explorer.
4. Drag each use case to the Main diagram of the Use-Case Realizations package in the Design Model.
5. Select the Realization toolbar button and create a realization from each collaboration instance to the use case it realizes. When complete, the diagram should look like this:

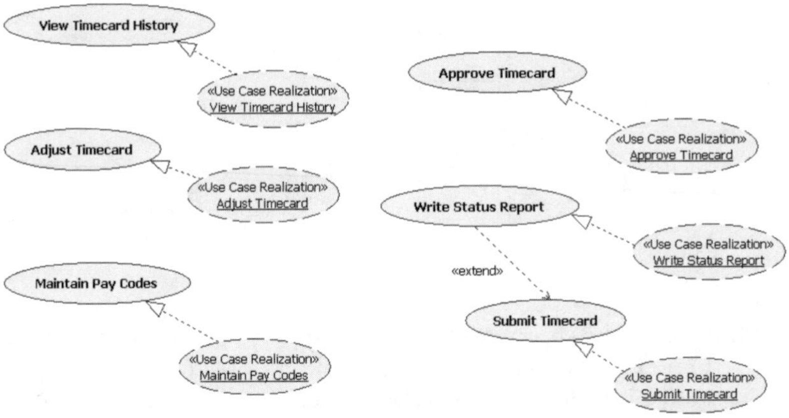

The last part of the exercise creates the class diagram for the Analysis Elements package. Here you show all of the analysis classes in the package and their relationships. If a message appears on a sequence diagram between two analysis classes, those classes must have an association between them.

1. Open the Main diagram for the Analysis Elements package in the Design Model.
2. Change the Main diagram from freeform to a class diagram.
3. Drag each analysis class to the Main diagram.
4. Create an association between the following classes that have corresponding messages:
   - TimecardForm and TimecardController
   - TimecardController and Timecard
   - TimecardController and PayPeriod
   - TimecardController and PayCode
   - TimecardController and StatusReport

5. The diagram should look like this:

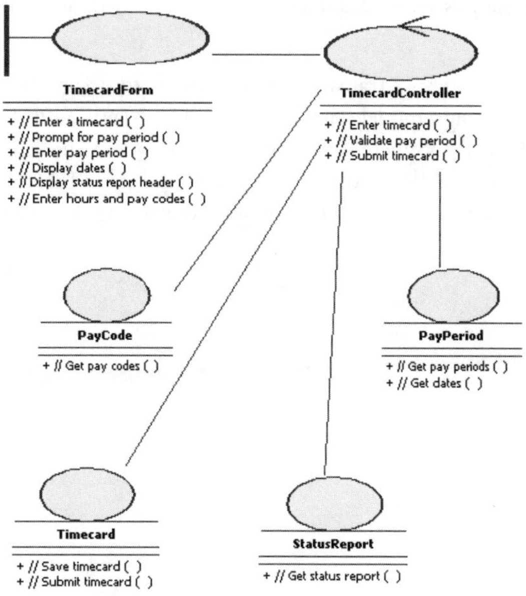

6. Save the model.

Summary

This chapter was devoted to gathering requirements and building the analysis model using XDE. In addition to being a powerful analysis and design tool, XDE can be used in the requirements process. Specifically, it can be used to

- Diagram use cases, actors, and their relationships, along with packages of use cases and actors.
- Store information about a use case, such as its priority and a brief description.
- Attach a document with the use case specification.
- Integrate with RequisitePro to manage the attributes of the use cases, link to use case documentation and other analysis artifacts, and manage requirements and their attributes.

During the analysis process, you can use XDE for many functions. XDE's features can help you build a robust analysis model, which gives the team a better understanding of the implementation-independent structure of the system. XDE can be used in the analysis model to

- Create activity diagrams to model the flow of events in a use case.
- Create and manage analysis classes.

- Build analysis-level sequence diagrams to model the collaborations in a scenario.
- Build analysis-level class diagrams, complete with attributes, operations, relationships, and packages.

In the next chapter, we transition from analysis to design. Specifically, we discuss how to create and maintain a design model and code in XDE for Java. XDE for Java supports two platforms: Eclipse and IBM WebSphere. We look at modeling Java and J2EE constructs in these two platforms, discuss how to model these constructs in the UML, and look at how the code is created and maintained. We also discuss code generation and reverse engineering in XDE for Java.

Chapter 5

Modeling Java and J2EE Elements in XDE

In this chapter, we talk about how XDE can be used to model and generate a Java application. Chapter 4, "Integrated Use Case Management," dealt with analysis, which is language-independent. For this chapter, we know we're using Java, so we need to refine our model to incorporate Java concepts and constructs. We can generate some code or reverse engineer some existing code to further expand our model.

NOTE *This chapter and the next ("Modeling Visual Studio .NET Elements in XDE") are the only platform-specific chapters in this book. Everything else applies to both programming environments.*

Featured in this chapter:

- Creating projects for a Java application
- Setting Java preferences
- Modeling Java elements in the UML
- Modeling Java elements in XDE
- Building a design model
- Designing J2EE elements
- Working with Java code

Creating Projects for a Java Application

We begin this chapter by creating a Java project in XDE. A *project* is the container used to hold all of the models for your Java application. There are five different types of projects you can use in XDE, but the available types vary slightly depending upon whether you are working with WebSphere Studio Application Developer or Eclipse. The available project types are as follows (we have noted where a project type is only available for WebSphere or Eclipse):

Basic modeling projects These are used primarily as analysis models. You cannot generate code or reverse engineer from a basic modeling project. However, you can create all of the UML diagrams. A basic modeling project, by default, contains only an XDE analysis model.

Java modeling projects These are used to model and generate code for a Java application. Using these projects, you can reverse engineer and generate code, as well as create the different types of UML diagrams. By default, a Java modeling project contains a Java code model.

Web modeling projects These are used to model and generate code for a web application. As with Java modeling projects, you can reverse engineer, generate code, and create UML diagrams in a web modeling project. A web modeling project contains a Java code model; a virtual directory model, which is used to hold Java Server Pages (JSP) pages and other web elements; and a tag library model, which is used to model custom tag libraries.

Data modeling projects These are used to model and generate the database for your application. You can generate the data definition language (DDL) or update the database structure by directly connecting to the database management system (DBMS). A data modeling project contains a data model and a Java code model.

Enterprise application modeling projects These projects are used to represent an Enterprise Archive (EAR) file that will be deployed. The project contains up to three subordinate projects: a Java modeling project, a web modeling project, and an Enterprise JavaBeans (EJB) modeling project. Each of these projects, in turn, contains the models that you use in XDE. An Enterprise application modeling project is only available using WebSphere Studio Application Developer.

EJB modeling projects These are used to model projects that include Enterprise JavaBeans. Such projects include Java code models. This type of project is only available using WebSphere Studio Application Developer.

The type(s) of projects you use depends upon the Java platform you are using and the nature of the application you are building. A typical business application needs a Java modeling project for the code, a data modeling project for the database, and a web modeling project for any web components. In WebSphere, you may use an EJB modeling project rather than a standard Java modeling project, and you will most likely use an Enterprise application modeling project to hold the other projects. Just keep in mind that you can always add new projects as the need arises, or you can remove projects that you find you aren't using.

To create a new project, follow these steps:

1. Choose File ➢ New ➢ Project. XDE displays the New Project dialog box:

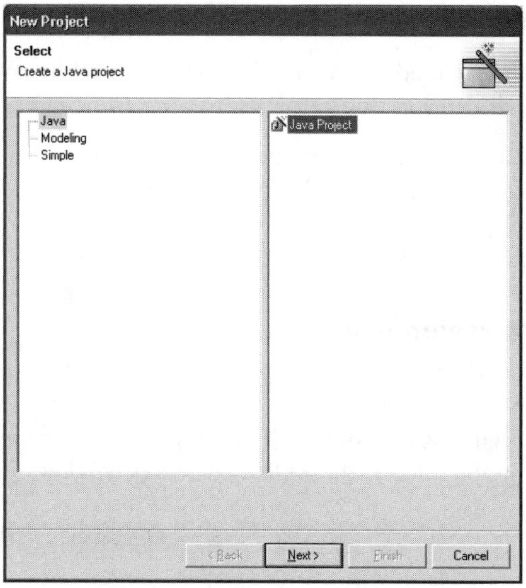

2. Select Modeling from the left-hand list box, and then select the appropriate project type from the right-hand list box. Click Next.
3. Enter the name of the new project and the root directory for your application, and click Finish.

Using Models

Now that you have your project(s) set up, the next step is to add models. The models are contained within the projects, and they directly hold the classes, EJBs, UML diagrams, and other pieces of your application. There are six different types of models available:

Blank model The blank model, as its name implies, is an empty model. You can use packages to structure this model however you like.

Getting started model You can use this model to become more familiar with XDE. It includes packages for the analysis, design, deployment, architecture, and implementation pieces of your model, and it includes comments describing each piece.

Java code model A code model is used to round-trip engineer a Java application. An XDE project can contain at most one Java code model.

Java content model A content model can be used to create UML diagrams, but it cannot be used to generate code or reverse engineer.

JSP tag library model A tag library model is used to create custom tags for JSP-based web applications.

Virtual directory model A virtual directory model holds JSP pages, HTML pages, servlets, and other web elements. It can be used to generate or reverse engineer a web application.

You can create as many different models as you need for your application. Blank models tend to be used more for the analysis portion of the modeling effort, such as when you are developing use cases. Java content models can be used to design diagrams and use case realizations, and code models can be used to model and generate implementation classes.

Setting Java Preferences

The final step in setting up your Java project involves setting the different preferences that XDE makes available. You can, of course, change any of these at any time, but we find it easier to set all of this up at the beginning of a project. You can view or set the preferences using the Window ➢ Preferences menu option. Here is the XDE Preferences window:

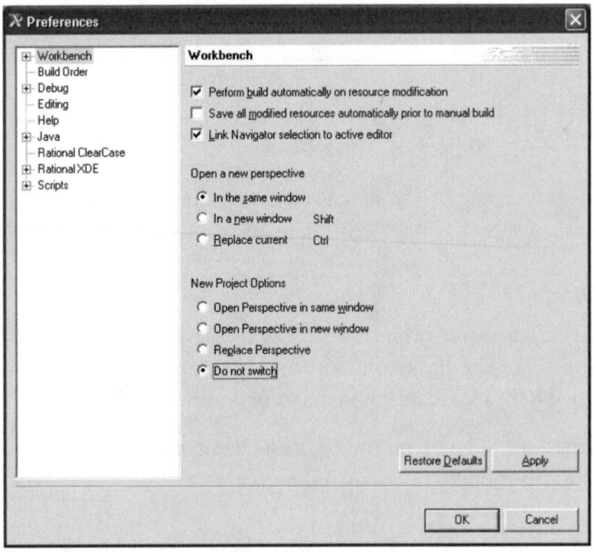

There are a great number of options and settings here; we discuss selected settings that you might want to consider.

The first category of settings includes the code generation options. These can be found in two areas: under Java ➢ Code Formatter and under Rational XDE ➢ Java. We begin with the Java ➢ Code Formatter options. Here is the Code Formatter options window:

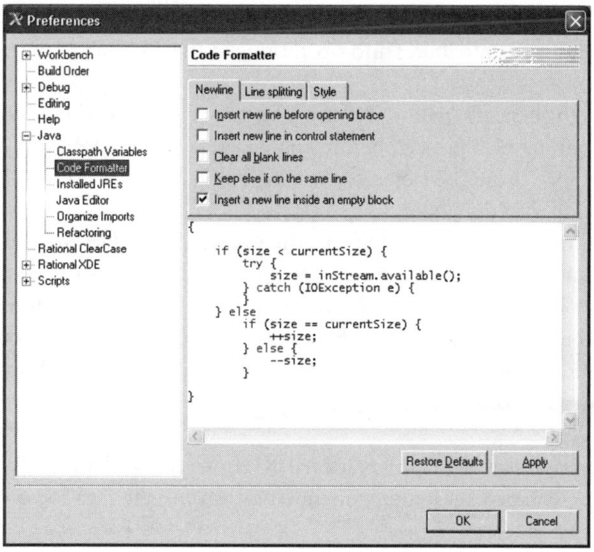

Using this window, you can control where new lines are used. For example, you can set the Insert New Line Before Opening Brace property to ensure that an opening brace always appears at the beginning of a new line. You can also control the maximum line length and indentation settings. At the bottom of the window, XDE provides you with a code preview based on the current settings.

The Code Generation Options and Code Styles areas under Rational XDE ➢ Java provide you with some additional code generation options:

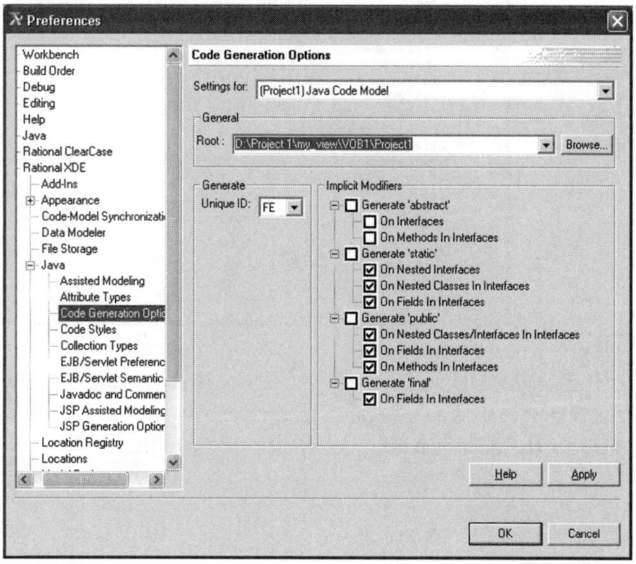

For example, you can control when abstract, static, public, and final modifiers are used, you can set the ordering of attributes and operations in the code, and you can further specify indentation settings.

Although these are mainly stylistic issues, we recommend that you go through all of these settings at the beginning of a project, before you generate any code. If you don't, you run the risk of having each developer create their own formatting rules, and as a result, the code can become inconsistent from developer to developer.

Another option to check early in the project is the Java attribute types under Rational XDE ➢ Java ➢ Attribute Types. This is the list of the Java types recognized by XDE. If you have your own Java class libraries, you may want to consider adding the classes here. When you reverse engineer, any element with a data type from this list is modeled as an attribute; a variable with a data type not on this list is modeled as a relationship. Also look at the collection types listed under Rational XDE ➢ Java ➢ Collection Types. These are the Java collections recognized by XDE.

Javadoc styles are set using Rational XDE ➢ Java ➢ Javadoc And Comment Styles. Using this screen, you can set default documentation for the Javadoc tags or add your own Javadoc tags:

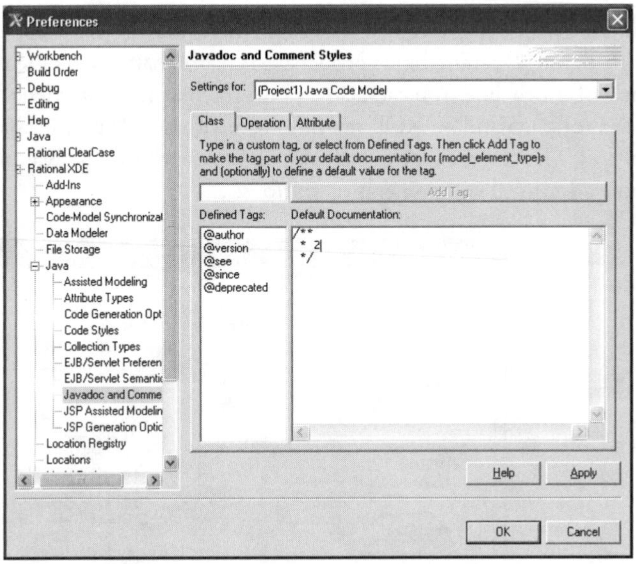

Under Rational XDE ➢ Java ➢ EJB/Servlet Preferences, set the version of J2EE you will be using. This is a critical setting because it directly affects the code that is generated. Using this screen, you can also set the default naming conventions for EJBs:

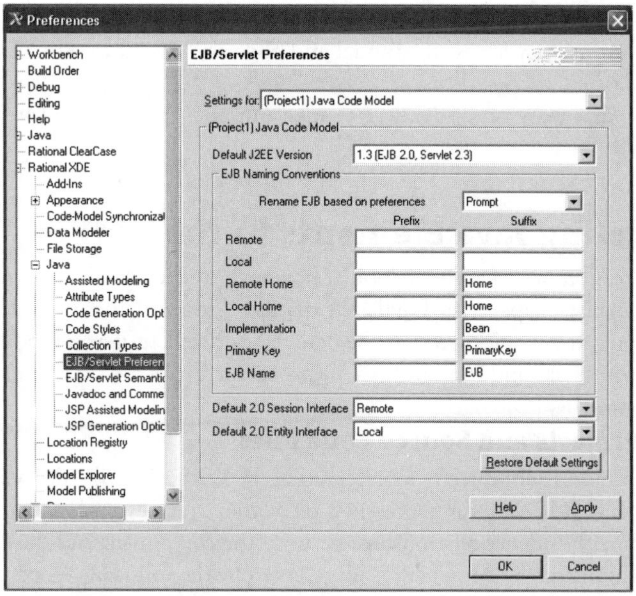

Finally, the settings available under Rational XDE ➢ Java ➢ EJB/Servlet Semantic Rules let you view and edit the rules that will be used to validate EJBs in your model. For example, you can enable or disable a rule requiring every bean to have a remote or local interface. The rules on this screen can be enabled or disabled, but they cannot be changed.

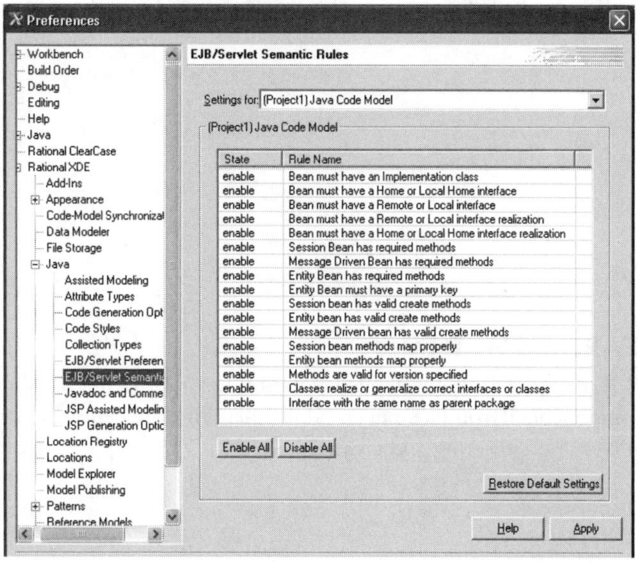

As we mentioned earlier, it's a good idea to set all of these options up front. This helps ensure consistency across the model and code and that the code XDE generates is the code you want.

Now that we've set up XDE, let's take a moment to see how Java elements are mapped to the UML.

Modeling Java Elements in the UML

In this section, we take a brief look at how each of the significant constructs in the Java programming language maps to the UML. We discussed some of these topics from an analysis standpoint in Chapter 4. We quickly review the definitions here, but if you need further clarification of these UML constructs and relationships, please revisit Chapter 4.

Java Projects and Source Code Files

A Java project is not directly represented in the UML, but the files with a `.java` extension are modeled in the UML. You can represent a file with a `.java` extension as a component in the UML. There are ElementResidence relationships between the component and the class(es) defined in the file for that component. A component is represented by the following icon:

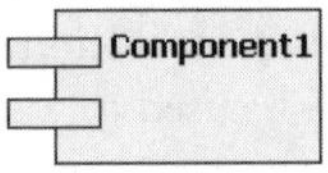

An *ElementResidence relationship* is a stereotyped dependency that lets you know which classes are included in a particular component. Here is an example:

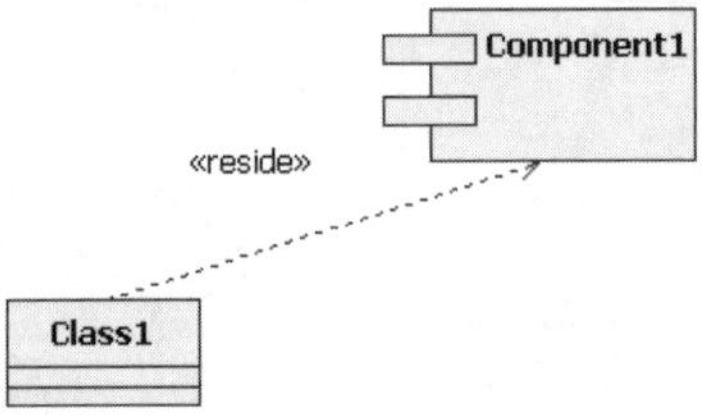

JAR, EAR, and WAR Files

The UML does not have any explicit notation for JAR, EAR, or WAR files. You can model them using components if you like, but in XDE, these files are generally not modeled. However, XDE uses them in reverse engineering and creates them during the deployment process.

Classes

In the UML, a Java class is represented as a rectangle with three compartments. The top compartment (the name compartment in the UML) displays the class name and, optionally, its stereotype. The name is italicized if the class is abstract. The middle compartment displays the fields, or attributes, of the class. The lower compartment displays the methods, or operations, of the class. This is standard UML notation for any class, not just Java classes. Here is an example of some Java code, as well as the UML representation of that code:

```
Public class Timecard
{
}
```

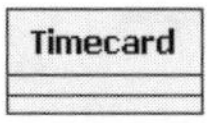

This is the default notation, but the UML does allow you to suppress the attributes and/or operations on a class diagram to keep the diagram from getting too cluttered. See the "Building a Design-Level Class Diagram" section later in this chapter for instructions.

As we just saw, the UML representation of a class gives us some detailed information about the class. We can see the fields and methods in the class, the visibility of the fields and methods, and the stereotype of the class itself. We discuss each of these in the following sections.

Class Stereotypes

There are a number of stereotypes for classes, such as interface, utility, thread, and, of course, the boundary, entity, and control stereotypes we used in analysis. These help us figure out what types of classes we're dealing with in our model. Boundary classes, for example, are used in analysis to distinguish the forms, windows, and system interfaces from the other classes in the model. An interface stereotype is used to mark the Java interfaces in the model. We don't have to assign a stereotype to every class in design; those without a stereotype become standard Java classes. If a class is given a stereotype, it appears in the Name compartment of the class:

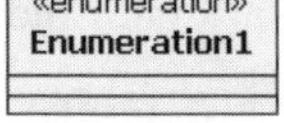

Fields

In the UML, a Java field is modeled in one of two ways: as an attribute of the class that contains it or as a relationship between two classes (semantically, an attribute and a composition association are the same, so we can use either). Attributes are displayed in the middle compartment of a class on a class diagram. Here is some Java code, represented first as an attribute and then as a relationship. An attribute is listed on a class diagram in the format *`AttributeName:DataType = DefaultValue`*, where the default value is optional.

```
Public class Timecard
{
   public int Totalhours;
}
```

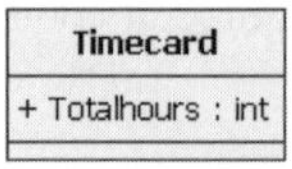

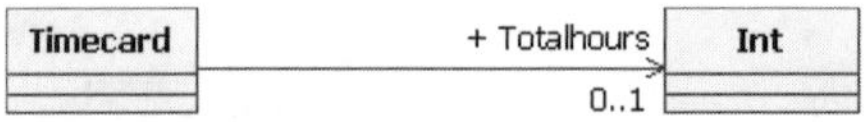

So which should we use? Although all attributes are technically relationships to objects of other classes, simple data types such as `float` or `int` tend to be modeled as attributes. More complex field data types, such as `Employee`, tend to be modeled as relationships between classes.

Visibility

In the UML, the scope, or visibility, of a field is documented using one of four symbols. A field in Java may be set to Public, Private, Protected, or Package visibility. The visibility notation appears just to the left of the field name on a class diagram. The UML visibility notation includes the following:

+	Public
–	Private
#	Protected
~	Package

METHODS

Java methods map to operations in the UML. The operations for a class are listed in the lower compartment of the class on a class diagram, and have the following format:

`MethodName([Parm1Kind]Parm1:DataType, [Parm2Kind]Parm2:DataType):ReturnType`

Let's take a quick look at the pieces of an operation signature in the UML:

- *`MethodName`* is the name of the method or operation. Be sure to use the Java naming conventions from your organization; the name you enter here will be the name used in the code.
- *`Parm1Kind`* identifies the first parameter as an input parameter, output parameter, or input and output parameter. *`Parm1Kind`* should be replaced with the term `in`, `out`, or `inout`.
- *`Parm1`* is the name of the first parameter. Again, be sure to follow Java naming conventions.

- *DataType* is the type (`int`, `float`, and so on) of the parameter.
- *ReturnType* is the data type of the return of the operation.

Parameters should be separated by commas. If there are no parameters, just use empty parentheses. On a class diagram, you can display just the operation name or the full signature. A few examples of methods in UML format are listed here:

- `Add([in] X:int, [in] Y:float):float`
- `PrintEmployeeTimecard([in] CurrentEmp:Employee):int`
- `Deposit([inout] MyAccount:Account, [in] Amount:float):void`

Here is an example of the code for a method and the corresponding UML:

```
Public class Timecard
{
   public float CalculateTimeForJob(int JobCode)
   {
   }
}
```

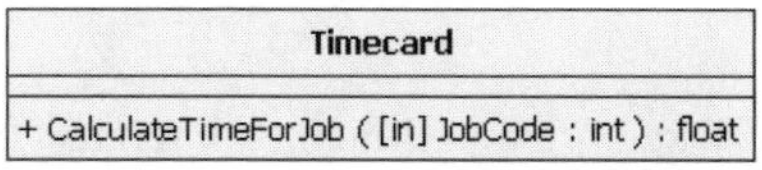

Like attributes, visibility for methods is indicated using a + for Public, – for Private, # for Protected, or ~ for Package. Method names in design should follow your organization's Java naming conventions and standards.

Interfaces

A Java interface is modeled in the UML as a class with a stereotype of interface. There are two ways to represent an interface: using the standard UML class (box) representation or using a circle icon:

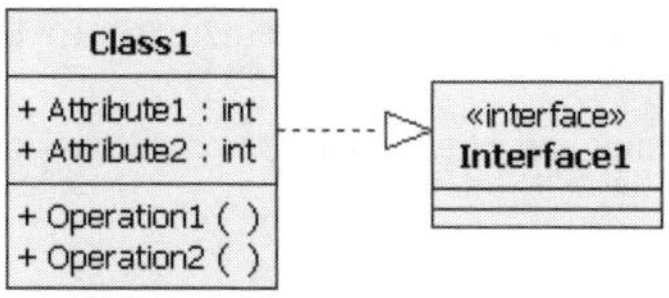

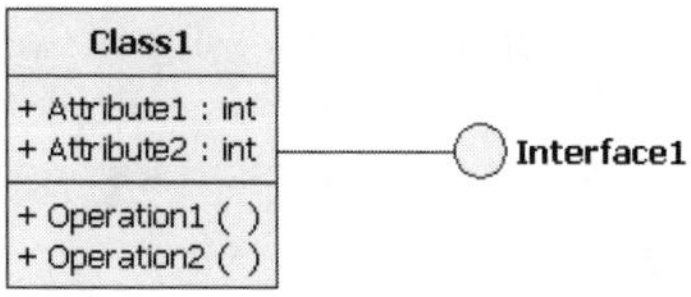

Implements Relationships

In Java, we use the `implements` keyword when an interface is realized by a class. In the UML, we use a *realization relationship* to show the relationship between a class and an interface. Here is an example of Java code and the corresponding UML:

```
Public class Timecard implements TimecardInterface
{
}
```

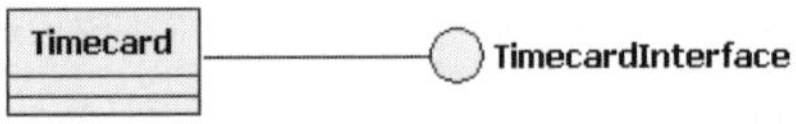

Packages and Subsystems

A *package* is a UML construct that allows you to group model elements together. In a Java project, a package maps to a directory on your filesystem. A package in the UML is represented as a folder:

A *subsystem* is a package with a well-defined interface. It is a logical construct that lets you group some classes together and define an interface for the whole group. Although a subsystem doesn't have a corresponding construct in Java, it can still be a good pattern to follow.

Relationships

In analysis, we got as far as defining the classes and the relationships between them. We identified each relationship as an association, an aggregation, or a generalization; we decided if each association was unidirectional or bidirectional; and we decided whether each aggregation was a composite aggregation. Now, we add some more detail to the relationships and also discuss a couple of new types of relationships. While analysis was language-independent, we're using Java now, so the relationships discussed in the next several sections map specifically to Java.

NOTE *The following sections apply to both WebSphere and Eclipse, so we don't make a distinction between platforms here.*

ASSOCIATION RELATIONSHIPS

An *association relationship* is a structural relationship between two classes. When expressed in code, the relationship is supported by fields. Here is an example of an association relationship expressed in some Java code and followed by its UML representation:

```
Public class Employee
{
   private Timecard myTimecard;
}
```

```
Public class Timecard
{
   private Employee TimecardOwner;
}
```

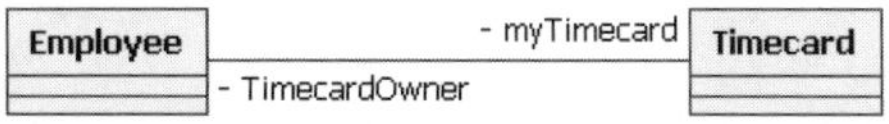

As you can see, attributes exist to support both sides of the relationship. For Employee to access its instance of Timecard, it need only use its own myTimecard field. For Timecard to access its Employee, it can use its own TimecardOwner field. The preceding example is bidirectional; each class is a client of the other, and a supplier for the other. Most associations, however, are unidirectional:

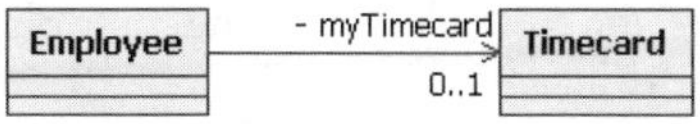

In this case, there is only an attribute created at one end of the relationship. Using the preceding example, if the association goes from Employee to Timecard, the myTimecard field still exists in Employee, but the TimecardOwner field does not exist in Timecard.

You can also create a *reflexive association,* which is an association between a class and itself. This simply suggests that one instance of the class has an association with another instance of the class. The following is the UML representation for a reflexive association:

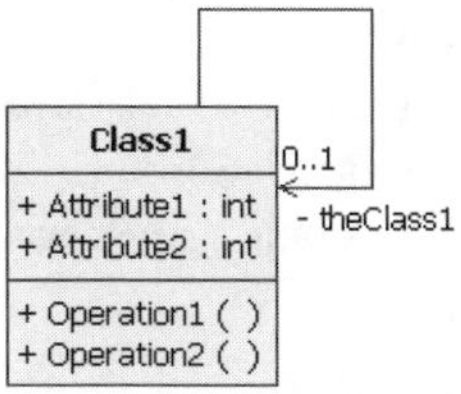

Aggregation Relationships

An *aggregation* is an association relationship that logically fits the "whole/part" pattern. For example, a tire is part of a car, an Employee is part of an EmployeeList, a book is part of a library, and so on. Anytime you have a "part of" relationship, you can use an aggregation.

There are two types of aggregations: standard aggregations and compositions.

Standard Aggregation Relationships

A *standard aggregation* connects two objects whose lifetimes are independent. That is, the "whole" object and "part" object are created and destroyed independently of one another. A *composition* connects two objects whose lifetimes are linked (the whole creates the part, and the part cannot exist without the whole). A standard aggregation is drawn as an association with a diamond next to the whole class. A composition is drawn as an aggregation with a filled diamond. The following is the notation for a standard aggregation in the UML:

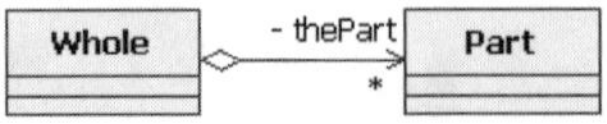

In a standard aggregation, each part object can be a part of more than one whole object.

Composition Relationships

A *composition* is an aggregation in which the lifetimes of the part object and the whole object are linked. When the whole is created, an instance of the part is also created; when the whole is destroyed, the part is also destroyed. A composition requires that a part instance be included in at most one composite at a time; therefore, the multiplicity on the composite end of the relationship must be exactly one:

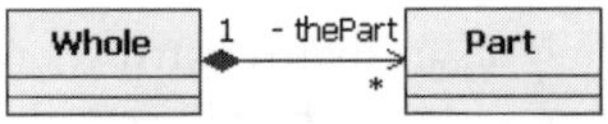

Note that, as we discussed earlier, there is no semantic difference between an attribute and a composition relationship. The entity Name, for example, could be modeled as an attribute of an Employee class, or as a relationship between the Employee class and a String class.

DEPENDENCY RELATIONSHIPS

A *dependency relationship* is a weaker type of relationship than an association. With an association, an attribute is created to support the relationship. A dependency, on the other hand, does not create an attribute. Therefore, the client object must access the supplier object through other means. The possibilities include

- The supplier object is global, and is therefore accessible to the client.
- The supplier object is passed to the client as a parameter to an operation.
- The supplier object is declared locally within an operation of the client.

In the UML, a dependency is shown as a dashed arrow, pointing from the client to the supplier:

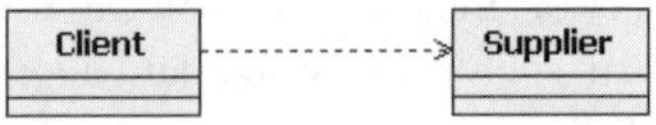

A dependency relationship between packages indicates that at least one element in the client package is dependent upon at least one element in the supplier package.

EXTENDS RELATIONSHIP

In the UML, the Java `extends` keyword is modeled as a generalization relationship. The generalization points from the child class to the parent class. The child inherits all of the attributes, operations, and relationships of the parent. The following is the UML representation for a generalization:

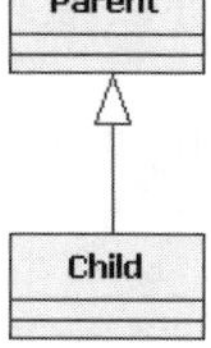

IMPORT RELATIONSHIP

The `import` keyword in Java translates to an access relationship in the UML. During code generation, an access relationship generates an import statement. In reverse engineering, an import or import-on-demand statement generates an access relationship. An access relationship is shown as a dependency with a stereotype of <<Access>>:

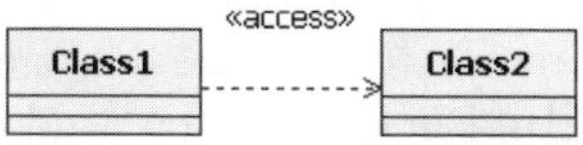

Modeling Java Elements in XDE

Now that we've discussed how Java elements map to the UML, it's time to look at how to add and manage these elements in an XDE model. In this section, we cover adding, editing, and deleting elements, as well as setting element properties in XDE.

Java Projects and Source Code Files

In XDE, a Java project maps directly to a Java code model. Each of the files with a `.java` extension in the Java project is represented as a component in the XDE model. As you generate code from your UML model, XDE automatically creates the components.

An ElementResidence relationship is a stereotyped dependency that lets you know which classes are included in a particular component:

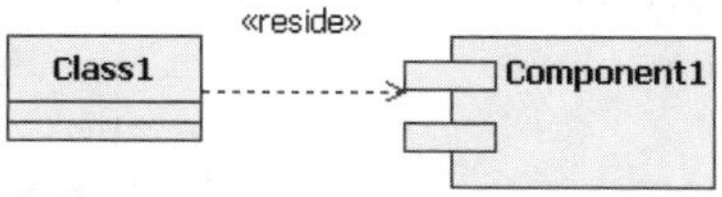

When you generate code and XDE creates components in the model, it also automatically adds residence relationships. To view a relationship, add a class and its component to a class diagram. XDE displays the residence relationship between them.

NOTE *As mentioned earlier, JAR, EAR, and WAR files are not modeled in XDE, so there is no need to manually enter the information into XDE. However, XDE looks at these files when reverse engineering, and it creates them for you when you deploy your application (if the files do not already exist).*

Classes

In XDE, you can add, view, or delete classes using either class diagrams or the Explorer window. Each class appears as a compartmentalized rectangle, as described earlier in this chapter in the "Modeling Java Elements in the UML" section. Each class contains compartments for the class name, attributes, and operations.

XDE also includes a fourth compartment, the *Signal Compartment,* that you can use. Select the class on a class diagram, and then choose Format ➢ Compartment ➢ Signal Compartment to show or hide the signal compartment. The signal compartment displays signal receptions for the class. A *signal* is defined as a one-way, asynchronous communication between objects, and is most frequently modeled when working with real-time systems.

To add a signal reception to a class:

1. First, add the signal to the model. Right-click a class diagram or a package in the Explorer window, and select Add UML ➢ Signal.
2. Name the signal, and add any needed attributes and operations.
3. To add a signal reception to a class called Class1, for example, drag the new signal from the Explorer window to Class1 on a class diagram. The signal appears on the class diagram, and also underneath Class1 in the Explorer window:

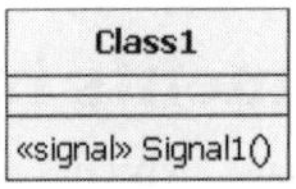

Although the UML allows you to add other new compartments to a class, this feature is not supported in XDE (or in any other UML modeling tool that we are aware of). If you need an extra compartment, you can attach a note to the class with the extra information, or you can attach a file to the class in the Explorer window.

There are a number of Java class properties you can set for a class in XDE. These directly affect the code generated and are listed in Table 5.1.

TABLE 5.1: JAVA CLASS PROPERTIES IN XDE

CATEGORY	PROPERTY	DESCRIPTION
Java	JavaAbstract	If True, marks the class as an abstract class, and adds the `abstract` keyword to the code. The name of an abstract class is italicized on class diagrams. Note that changing this property also changes the UML ➢ IsAbstract property, and vice versa.
Java	JavaFilename	Displays the path and filename of the source code file associated with the class.
Java	JavaFinal	If True, adds the `final` keyword to the code. The setting of the JavaFinal property doesn't affect how the class appears on class diagrams. Note that changing this property also changes the UML ➢ IsLeaf property, and vice versa.

Continued on next page

TABLE 5.1: JAVA CLASS PROPERTIES IN XDE *(continued)*

CATEGORY	**PROPERTY**	**DESCRIPTION**
Java	JavaScope	Sets the scope (visibility) of the class to Public, Private, Protected, or Package. Note that changing this property also changes the UML ➢ Visibility property, and vice versa.
Java	JavaStatic	If True, marks the class as a static class, and adds the `static` keyword to the code. This property should only be set to True for member classes. The setting of the JavaStatic property doesn't affect how the class appears on class diagrams.
Java	JavaStrictFP	If True, adds the `strictfp` keyword to the code. The setting of the JavaStrictFP property doesn't affect how the class appears on class diagrams.
Java	Synchronization	Controls round-trip engineering for the class. Possible values are: 0: Not included in forward or reverse-engineering 1: Included only in code generation 2: Included only in reverse-engineering 3: Included in forward and reverse-engineering
UML	IsAbstract	See JavaAbstract.
UML	IsActive	Creates an active class, which is used to model a thread. See the "Building a Component Diagram" section later in this chapter.
UML	IsLeaf	See JavaFinal.
UML	IsRoot	Notes that the class may not have parents in a generalization.
UML	IsSpecification	If True, the class is part of the model's specification. If False, the class is part of the model's implementation.
UML	Multiplicity	Sets the number of instances of the class that may occur simultaneously.
UML	Persistence	If set to Persistent, the class is made persistent (that is, in a database) outside of the system.
UML	Stereotype	Sets the stereotype of the class.
UML	Visibility	See JavaScope.

To add a new class in XDE:

1. Right-click a package in the Explorer or right-click a class diagram and choose Add Java ➢ Class.
2. Type the name of the new class, and edit the properties as needed.

TIP *On a class diagram, add a new Java class by using the Class option in the Java toolbox.*

CLASS STEREOTYPES

Stereotypes are a means of classifying the different types of elements you have in your model. For example, some of the class stereotypes available in XDE include JavaInterface, ImplementationClass, Utility, EJBEntityHomeInterface, EJBEntityLocalHomeInterface, EJBImplementation, EJBLocalInterface, EJBRemoteInterface, EJBSessionHomeInterface, EJBSessionLocalHomeInterface, GenericServlet, HttpServlet, ServletFilter, ServletListener, Process, Thread, Metaclass, and Powertype. By looking at a class's stereotype, you can easily see what type of class you're dealing with. By default, the class stereotype is displayed in the name compartment on a class diagram, and is enclosed in guillemets (<< >>):

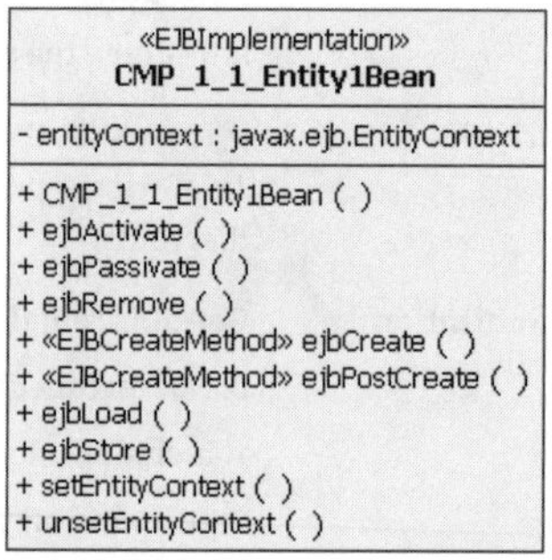

To assign a stereotype to a class, modify its UML ➢ Stereotype property. You can select from one of XDE's predefined stereotypes, or enter your own. Stereotypes can be displayed on a class diagram using either text or an icon. See "Building a Design-Level Class Diagram" later in this chapter for instructions related to displaying icons and adding your own customized icons.

NOTE *If you right-click a class diagram or a package in the Explorer window, select Add Java, and then add a Java interface, bean, or servlet, XDE automatically sets the stereotype for you. Similarly, if you right-click and select Add UML, and then Enumeration, Interface, Signal, or Subsystem, the stereotype is set automatically.*

MEMBER CLASSES

A member class in XDE is modeled much the same as any other class. It appears underneath its containing class in the Explorer, and has the same properties as a standard Java class. It is created a little differently, however. Rather than right-clicking a package or right-clicking on a class diagram and selecting Add Java ➢ Class, right-click an existing Java class and select Add Java ➢ Class. The new class does not appear on the class diagram by default but is added to the Explorer.

JAVADOC

You can enter Javadoc documentation directly into the XDE tool. Then, using a Javadoc tool, you can generate HTML documentation for your system. XDE does not include the Javadoc tool, but it does provide you with a way to enter Javadoc information. Specifically, XDE includes the following Javadoc fields:

- For a class: @author, @version, @see, @since, @deprecated
- For an operation: @param, @return, @exception, @see, @since, @deprecated
- For an attribute: @see, @since, @deprecated

To add Javadoc comments to a class, operation, or attribute, follow these steps:

1. Right-click the class, operation, or attribute and select More Java Actions ➢ Javadoc. XDE displays the Javadoc window. Here is the window displayed for a class:

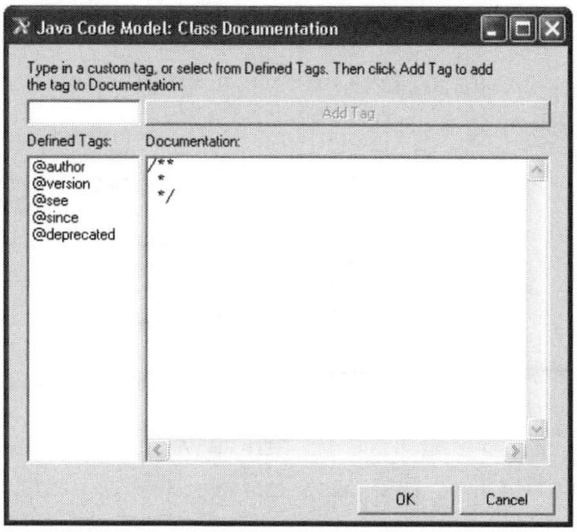

2. In the list of defined tags, select the tag to edit.
3. (Optional) Add your own tag by using the Add Tag button.
4. Edit the comment in the Documentation area of the window.

If you'd like, you can also add a new tag for all classes, attributes, or operations. You can do this using the Window ➢ Preferences menu option. In the Preferences window, select Rational XDE, Java, and then Javadoc and Comment Styles:

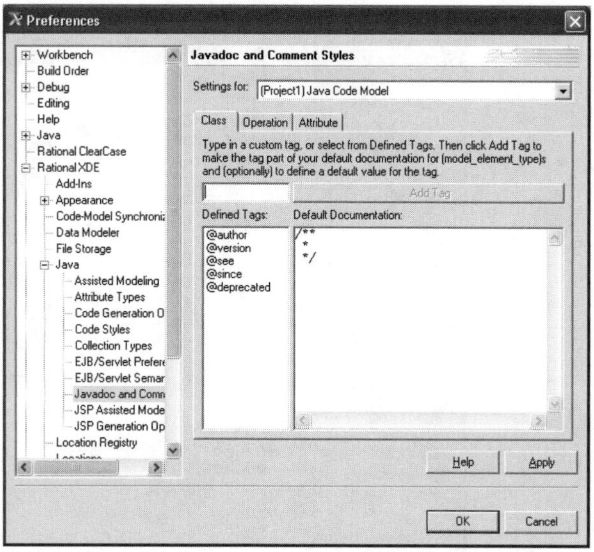

Any new tags you add here are available for all classes, attributes, or operations in the model.

USING THE NEW JAVA CLASS WIZARD

We've already described how to add a class and set its properties through a class diagram or the Model Explorer. Now, we take a quick look at a third option: a class wizard provided with XDE for Java.

To use the wizard to add a class to package:

1. First, open the Packages view. This is a Java view that shows you the structure of your Java packages, files with a `.java` extension, and models. From the Perspective menu, select Show View ➢ Other.
2. In the Java section, select Packages. The packages perspective is opened:

3. To add a class to a package with the wizard, right-click a package in the Packages view and select New ➢ Class. The Java Class window appears, as shown in Figure 5.1.
4. Enter the following information:

   Folder The name of the project that will contain the class. By default, this is the current project.

   Package The name of the package that will contain the class. You can either enter a package here or enter a value in the Enclosing Type field.

   Enclosing Type The name of the type that will contain the class. You can either enter a type here or enter a value in the Package field.

   Name The name of the new class.

FIGURE 5.1

New Java Class wizard

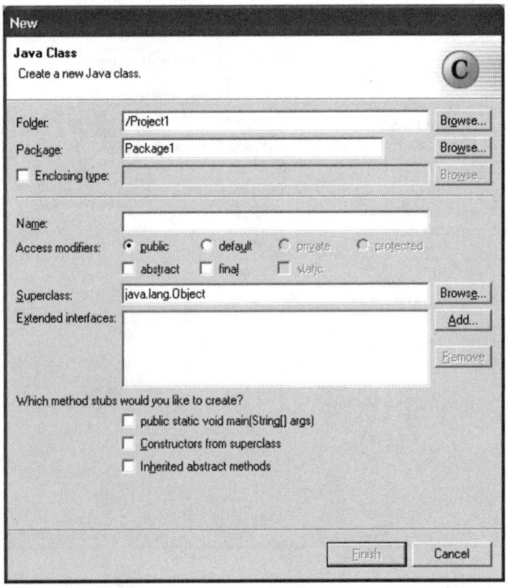

Access Modifiers Miscellaneous modifiers for the class. Select a visibility option (Public, Default, Private, or Protected). Note that Private and Protected can only be selected if you entered an enclosing type. Select the Abstract, Final, or Static check boxes if any of these apply to the new class.

Superclass The parent class for the new class. By default, this is `java.lang.Object`.

Extended Interfaces The names of any interfaces that the class will realize. Click the Add button to select existing interfaces.

Method Stubs The names of any method stubs you want XDE to automatically create for you. XDE can create a main method, with the signature `public static void main(String[]:args)`. It can also create constructors and abstract methods from the parent class.

5. Press Finish after you've entered all the necessary information. The new class appears in the Packages view. You can then add attributes, operations, and relationships to the new class.

FIELDS

As we discussed earlier, a Java field may be modeled as an attribute, or as a relationship between classes. When you're creating the model, you can select either option. When reverse engineering, XDE looks at the Attribute Types list. If the data type of the field is on the list, XDE models it as an attribute. Otherwise, XDE models it as a relationship.

To modify the Attribute Types list in XDE:

1. Choose Window ➢ Preferences.
2. Look in the section Rational XDE ➢ Java ➢ Attribute Types.
3. Select the model to edit, and then add, remove, or edit the attribute types.

Don't panic if you used the attribute notation and want to switch to using a relationship, or if you used a relationship and would now like to use an attribute. XDE lets you switch back and forth between the two.

To change an attribute into a relationship:

1. Right-click the attribute in the Explorer.
2. Select More Java Actions ➢ Convert To Association.

NOTE *This option is only available if the attribute doesn't have a data type on the Attribute Types list.*

To change a relationship to an attribute:

1. Right-click the relationship in the Explorer or on a diagram.
2. Select More Java Actions ➢ Convert To Attribute. The relationship disappears and is replaced by an attribute.

Like classes, attributes have a number of properties in XDE that directly affect how code is generated. For example, you can create static fields, add the `volatile` keyword, or set the default value for the field by setting specific Java field properties. Table 5.2 lists some of the attribute properties and their meanings. Note that to view or edit the properties for an attribute, you need to select the attribute in the Explorer window, not on a diagram.

TABLE 5.2: JAVA FIELD PROPERTIES IN XDE

CATEGORY	PROPERTY	DESCRIPTION
Java	JavaCollection	Sets the name of the collection type to use if the attribute is implementing a relationship with a multiplicity greater than one.
Java	JavaDimensions	If the attribute is an array, sets the number of dimensions in the array.
Java	JavaFinal	Adds the `final` keyword to the code. Note that changing this property also changes the UML ➢ Changeable property, and vice versa.
Java	JavaScope	Sets the scope (visibility) of the attribute to Public, Private, Protected, or Package. Note that changing this property also changes the UML ➢ Visibility property, and vice versa.
Java	JavaStatic	Adds the `static` keyword to the code. The attribute is underlined on a class diagram.
Java	JavaTransient	Adds the `transient` keyword to the code.
Java	JavaVolatile	Adds the `volatile` keyword to the code.
UML	Changeability	See JavaFinal.
UML	DefaultValueExpression	Sets the default value of the attribute.
UML	IsDerived	Notes that the value of the attribute is derived from the values of one or more other attributes.
UML	Ordering	If the attribute is a list or other collection, indicates whether the elements within it are ordered or unordered. Options are: 0: Unordered 1: Ordered 2: Sorted
UML	OwnerScope	See JavaStatic.
UML	Persistence	If set to Persistent, the attribute is made persistent (that is, in a database) outside of the system.
UML	TargetScope	Sets whether the target of the attribute is an instance of the classifier or the classifier itself.
UML	TypeExpression	Sets the data type of the attribute.
UML	Visibility	See JavaScope.

To add an attribute in XDE:

1. Right-click the class in the Explorer or on a diagram.
2. Choose Add Java ➢ Field. XDE creates a new attribute with a default data type of `int`. Name the attribute. To set the data type, follow the name with a colon and then the data type. For example, type in **Address:string**.
3. Set the attribute properties as needed.

NOTE *You can also add an attribute by right-clicking a class and selecting Add UML ➢ Attribute. However, the new attribute will not have a default data type (you can always set the data type manually).*

Reordering Fields

By default, fields are listed on the diagram, and generated in the code, in the order you enter them. While it isn't typically necessary, you can change the order if you like:

1. Right-click the class on a diagram or in the Explorer, and choose Collection Editor to see the following window:

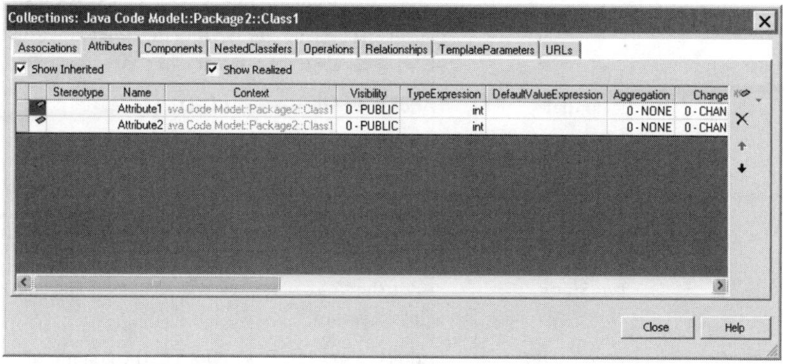

2. Select the Attributes tab, then use the up and down buttons on the right-hand side of the window to move attributes up or down in the list. When you close the window, XDE reorders the attributes.

WARNING *If you've already generated the code, reordering the attributes in the model may not reorder them in the code, even after a synchronization.*

Visibility

The UML notation for field scope is as follows: a + for Public, a – for Private, a # for Protected, and a ~ for Package. In XDE, the Explorer window uses different notation to show the visibility. To the left of the attribute name in the Explorer, you will see one of the following four symbols:

 Public

 Private

 Protected

 Package

If you'd like, you can also use these symbols on a class diagram, rather than the +, –, #, and ~ symbols used in the UML. Select the class(es) to change, and then choose Format ➢ Stereotype And Visibility Style ➢ Visibility Style: Icon.

METHODS

Methods, or operations, appear in the third compartment of a class on a class diagram. When reverse engineering, XDE creates operations for all of the methods in the code. During code generation, XDE creates the method signatures and any Javadoc comments you've added for the method.

The properties for a method are listed in Table 5.3.

TABLE 5.3: JAVA METHOD PROPERTIES IN XDE

CATEGORY	PROPERTY	DESCRIPTION
Java	JavaAbstract	If True, marks the operation as an abstract operation, and adds the `abstract` keyword to the code. The name of an abstract operation is italicized on class diagrams. Note that changing this property also changes the UML ➢ IsAbstract property, and vice versa.
	JavaFinal	Adds the `final` keyword to the code.
	JavaNative	
	JavaScope	Sets the scope (visibility) of the operation to Public, Private, Protected, or Package. Note that changing this property also changes the UML ➢ Visibility property, and vice versa.
	JavaStatic	Adds the `static` keyword to the code. The operation is underlined on a class diagram.
	JavaStrictFP	Adds the `strictfp` keyword to the generated operation.
	JavaSynchronized	Adds the `synchronized` keyword to the generated operation.
	JavaThrows	Lists the exceptions that the operation throws.
UML	Concurrency	Specifies what should happen if there are simultaneous calls to the same instance of a classifier that is not active. Options are:
		0: Sequential
		1: Guarded
		2: Concurrent
	IsAbstract	See JavaAbstract.
	IsQuery	If True, suggests that the operation return a value but does not change the state of the system.
	OwnerScope	See JavaStatic.
	Visibility	See JavaScope.

Reordering Methods

Like fields, methods are listed on the diagram, and generated in the code, in the order you enter them. XDE lets you change the order of the method declarations, however:

1. Right-click the class on a diagram or in the Explorer, and choose Collection Editor to see the following window:

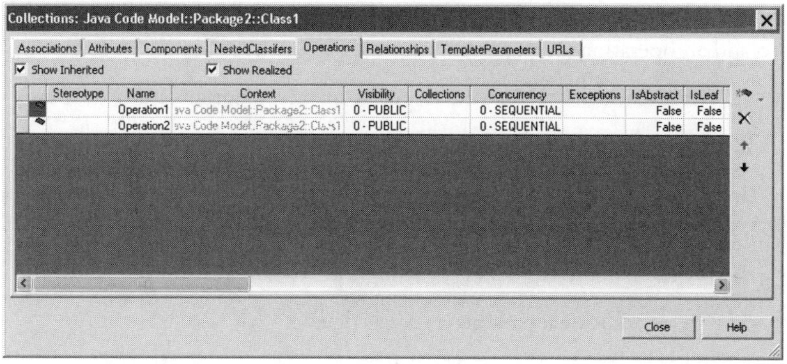

2. Select the Operations tab, then use the up and down buttons on the right-hand side of the window to move operations up or down in the list. When you close the window, XDE reorders the operations.

WARNING *If you've already generated the code, reordering the operations in the model may not reorder them in the code, even after a synchronization.*

Parameters and Return Values

In XDE, methods, their parameters, and their return values are all modeled as separate elements. The parameters and return bodies appear underneath the operation in the Explorer. Parameters have the following icon next to them: ◆ . Return bodies use this icon: ↵ .

Table 5.4 lists the properties for a parameter.

TABLE 5.4: JAVA METHOD PARAMETER PROPERTIES IN XDE

CATEGORY	PROPERTY	DESCRIPTION
Java	JavaDimensions	Specifies the number of array dimensions declared by the parameter.
	JavaFinal	Adds the `final` keyword to the parameter.
UML	DefaultValueExpression	Sets the default value of the parameter.
	Kind	Sets the type of parameter. Options are: 0: In 1: Out 2: InOut 3: Return (for a return value)
	TypeExpression	Sets the data type of the parameter.

Adding Methods

To add an operation (with parameters and a return type) in XDE, follow these steps:

1. Right-click the class in the Explorer or on a diagram and choose Add Java ➢ Method.
2. Enter the name of the new operation.
3. Add a parameter by right-clicking the operation in the Explorer and selecting Add Java ➢ Parameter.
4. Set the parameter's data type using the TypeExpression property.
5. Create additional parameters as needed.
6. Add a return body by right-clicking the operation in the Explorer and choosing Add Java ➢ Return Body.
7. Set the operation's return type by modifying the return body's TypeExpression property.

TIP *A quicker way to create an operation is to type the whole signature at once. Right-click the class and select Add Java ➢ Method. Then, rather than just typing the method name, type the full signature, using the format* `Name([Parm1Kind] Parm1:datatype, [Parm2Kind]Parm2:datatype):returntype`.

CONSTRUCTORS AND FINALIZERS

XDE includes options for adding a constructor and a finalizer to a class. Right-click the class, and choose Add Java ➢ Constructor or Add Java ➢ Finalizer. For the constructor, XDE creates code similar to the following:

```
Public Class1()
{
}
```

The destructor includes a little more code. XDE generates code similar to the following for a destructor:

```
protected void finalize() throws Throwable
    {

        try {
        }
        catch (Exception e) {
        }
        finally {
           super.finalize();
        }
    }
```

Interfaces

In XDE, Java interfaces are modeled as classes with a stereotype of <<JavaInterface>>. On a class diagram, you can view the interface using the standard class notation (a box), or using the UML icon for an interface. The following graphics show these two options, with the box notation on top and the UML interface icon on the bottom:

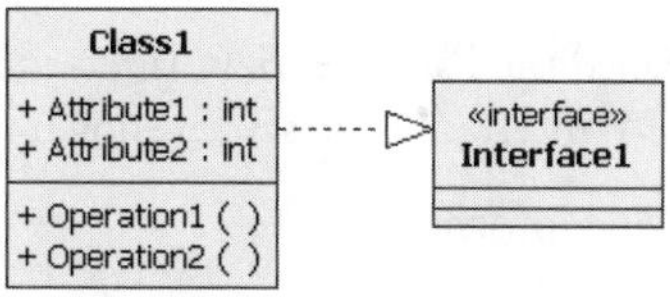

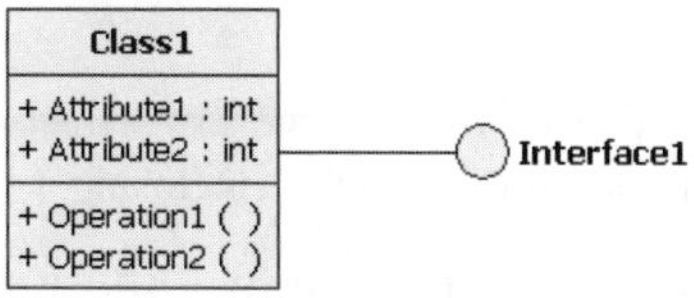

Because they are stereotyped classes, interfaces have the same property set as classes. However, there are a few properties that must be set for interfaces. XDE sets them for you by default.

- The JavaAbstract property must be set to True. Note that you can also set the UML IsAbstract property.
- The UML Stereotype property must be set to JavaInterface.
- The JavaStatic property should not be set to True unless the interface is directly contained by a Java class or interface.
- The JavaScope property should not be set to Protected or Private unless the interface is directly contained by a Java class.

WARNING *If you create an interface using the Interface button in the Class toolbox, this creates a UML interface, not a Java interface, and the Java properties are not available. Use the Java Interface option in the Java toolbox instead.*

To add an interface:

1. Right-click a package or class in the Explorer, or right-click inside a class diagram, and choose Add Java ➢ Interface.
2. Type the name of the new interface, and edit the properties if necessary.
3. Add implements relationships (see the following section) between the interface and the classes that realize it.

TIP *On a class diagram, you can also add a Java interface by selecting the Java Interface option in the Java toolbox.*

USING THE NEW JAVA INTERFACE WIZARD

XDE for Java includes a wizard that you can use to create an interface. To use the wizard:

1. First, open the Packages view if you haven't already done so by choosing Perspective ➢ Show View ➢ Other.
2. Select the Packages view in the Java section.
3. Once you've opened the Packages view, right-click the package that will contain the interface and select New ➢ Interface. The screen shown in Figure 5.2 appears.
4. Enter the following information:

   Folder The name of the project that will contain the interface. By default, this is the current project.

   Package The name of the package that will contain the interface. You can either enter a package here or enter a value in the Enclosing Type field.

   Enclosing Type The name of the type that will contain the interface. You can either enter a type here or enter a value in the Package field.

   Name The name of the new interface.

   Access Modifiers Miscellaneous modifiers for the interface. Select a visibility option (Public, Default, Private, or Protected). Note that Private and Protected can be selected only if you enter an enclosing type. Choose the Static check box if the interface is static.

   Extended Interfaces The names of any interfaces that the interface extends. Click the Add button to select existing interfaces.

5. Press Finish when you're done. The new interface is added to the Packages view.

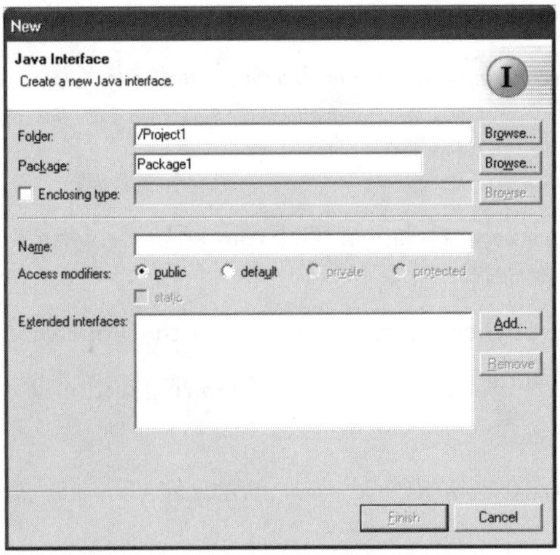

FIGURE 5.2

New Java Interface wizard

IMPLEMENTS RELATIONSHIPS

An implements relationship is used to show that a class, component, or subsystem implements the functionality specified in an interface. It appears on a class diagram as a dashed arrow from the interface to the class, component, or subsystem. To add an implements (realization) relationship to a class diagram,

1. Select the Realization option from the UML Class toolbox or the Java toolbox.
2. Click the class, and then choose the interface it realizes.

Packages

As we mentioned earlier, a Java package maps directly to a UML package in XDE. When reverse engineering, XDE reads the package structure and create the necessary packages in the model. When generating code, XDE uses the package structure in the model to automatically create the directory structure for you.

To create a package:

1. Right-click the model name or an existing package in the Explorer and select Add Java ➢ Package. Or, use the Package option from the toolbox to add a package to a class diagram.
2. If you need to, drag and drop classes and other elements in the Explorer into or out of the package.

TIP *To move an element into a package, you can also right-click an element in the Explorer window and choose Cut, and then right-click the package and select Paste.*

If you added the package using the toolbox and a class diagram, XDE automatically created a class diagram called Main inside the new package. If you added the package directly to the Explorer, you need to manually add a Main diagram (right-click the package and choose Add Diagram ➢ Class). You don't have to name this diagram "Main," but you should have one diagram that provides an overview of the package. If the package contains only classes, the Main diagram typically shows all classes (although not necessarily all attributes, operations, and relationships) in the package. If the package contains other packages, the Main diagram typically shows the subpackages and their dependencies.

PACKAGE RELATIONSHIPS

There are three types of relationships, known as *permission relationships*, that can be set up between packages:

- Access
- Friend
- Import

Friend relationships, however, are typically used between classes, not between packages, and are not used in Java. Therefore, we only discuss access and import relationships here.

An *access relationship* indicates that the classifiers in one package can access the public elements in another package. It is drawn as a dependency from the client to the supplier, with a stereotype of <<Access>>. An *import relationship* indicates that the public contents of one package are added to the namespace of another. It is drawn as a dependency from the client to the supplier, with a stereotype of <<Import>>.

To add an access or import relationship in XDE:

1. Select the Access option from the Java toolbox, or the Access Or Import option from the UML Use Case toolbox.
2. Click the client package, and then choose the supplier package.

Association Relationships

An *association relationship* is a semantic relationship connecting two classifiers, allowing instances of the classifiers to communicate. An association is drawn as an arrow between the two classifiers, and may be unidirectional or bidirectional. The association may be labeled with details, such as the multiplicity of the association, the role names at the association ends, and the scope of the roles at the association ends. When code is generated, attributes are created to support the association. In a bidirectional association, an attribute is created at both ends of the association, using the role names. In a unidirectional association, only one attribute is created. Table 5.5 lists the properties of an association.

TABLE 5.5: ASSOCIATION PROPERTIES IN XDE

CATEGORY	PROPERTY	DESCRIPTION
End1, End2	End1Changeability, End2Changeability	See JavaFinal.
End1, End2	End1InitialValueExpression, End2InitialValueExpression	Sets the initial value of the attribute created to support the relationship. Generally not used unless the supplier class is an elementary data type.
End1, End2	End1IsNavigable, End2IsNavigable	Controls whether the association is unidirectional or bidirectional.
End1, End2	End1Multiplicity, End2Multiplicity	Sets the number of instances of one class associated with each instance of the other class.
End1, End2	End1Name, End2Name	Sets the name(s) of the attribute(s) that will be generated to support the relationship. Required in order to generate code for the relationship.
End1, End2	End1OwnerScope, End2OwnerScope	Controls whether the generated attribute is static. Options are: 0: Instance (attribute is not static) 1: Classifier (attribute is static)

Continued on next page

TABLE 5.5: ASSOCIATION PROPERTIES IN XDE

CATEGORY	PROPERTY	DESCRIPTION
End1, End2	End1SupplierName, End2SupplierName	Read-only property. Displays the name of the supplier class.
End1, End2	End1Visibility, End2Visibility	See JavaScope.
End1-Java, End2-Java	JavaCollection	Sets the name of the collection type to use if the generated attribute is implementing an association with a multiplicity greater than one.
End1-Java, End2-Java	JavaDimensions	If the generated attribute is an array, sets the number of dimensions of the array.
End1-Java, End2-Java	JavaFinal	Adds the `final` keyword to the generated attribute. Note that changing this property also changes the End1 ➢ End1Changeability property, and vice versa.
End1-Java, End2-Java	JavaScope	Sets the scope of the generated attribute. Options are: 0: Public 1: Protected 2: Private 3: Package
End1-Java, End2-Java	JavaStatic	Adds the `static` keyword to the generated attribute. The role name is also underlined on the class diagram.
End1-Java, End2-Java	JavaTransient	Adds the `transient` keyword to the generated attribute.
End1-Java, End2-Java	JavaVolatile	Adds the `volatile` keyword to the generated attribute.

NOTE *If the JavaStatic property is set to True, the End1OwnerScope property must be set to 1—Classifier. If the JavaStatic property is set to False, the End1OwnerScope property must be set to 0—Instance. If you change one property, XDE automatically changes the other.*

To add an association in XDE:

1. Select the Association or Directed Association option from the UML Class toolbox, or select the Directed Association option from the Java toolbox.
2. Choose one class, then the other.

3. If you did not use a directed association, check the End1Name and End2Name properties in the End1 and the End2 sections of the Properties window. For the association to be generated in the code, there must be a name at both ends. If you used a directed association, XDE automatically creates the name for you.
4. Set the multiplicity and other association properties as needed.

ASSOCIATION CLASSES

An *association class* is used to hold attributes, operations, or relationships that pertain to an association, rather than to an individual class. They are generated like any other Java class, and are indistinguishable in code from other classes. During the reverse-engineering process, an association class is brought into the XDE model as a Java class, but not as an association class. An association class is connected via a dashed line to an association, and has the same properties as a standard Java class.

To add an association class in XDE:

1. Create an association between two classes.
2. Create an association class as you would any other Java class.
3. Use the Association Class option from the UML Class toolbox to connect the association class to the association.

Aggregation Relationships

An *aggregation* is used to model a "whole/part" relationship between classes. This is really just a specialized form of association, and therefore has exactly the same properties we described for an association. In fact, you can even change an aggregation to an association (or change an association to an aggregation) by modifying the UML ➢ Kind property. Your choices for this property are Simple (creates an association), Aggregation, or Composition.

To create an aggregation relationship:

1. Select the Aggregation Association icon from the toolbox.
2. Choose the "whole" class and then the "part" class.
3. By default, the aggregation is unidirectional, but you can create a bidirectional aggregation as well. Modify the End1IsNavigable or End2IsNavigable properties as necessary.
4. Modify the other aggregation properties as needed.

Composition Relationships

A *composition relationship* is an aggregation in which the lifetimes of the "whole" object and the "part" object are dependent. To add a composition relationship in XDE:

1. Select the Composition Association icon from the toolbox.
2. Choose the "whole" class and then the "part" class.

3. By default, the composition is unidirectional, but you can create a bidirectional composition as well. Modify the End1IsNavigable or End2IsNavigable properties as necessary.
4. Modify the other composition properties as needed.

TIP *To change a composition to an aggregation, or an aggregation to a composition, modify the UML ➢ Kind property.*

Dependency Relationships

A *dependency relationship* is a weaker form of association. With an association, attributes are created in the code to support the relationship. With a dependency, no attributes are created. This means that the client object must access the supplier object through some other method—the supplier is global, the supplier is passed in to an operation of the client as a parameter, or the supplier is declared locally within an operation of the client. In any event, the dependency is drawn as a dashed arrow from the client to the supplier. It can have multiplicity settings, but not role names.

To create a dependency relationship:

1. Select the Dependency option from the toolbox.
2. Choose the client class first, then the supplier.

Extends Relationship

An extends (UML generalization) relationship is used to show an inheritance relationship between model elements. You can mark an element as the root of an inheritance tree, or as a leaf using the IsRoot and IsLeaf class properties.

To create a generalization relationship:

1. Select the Generalization option from the UML Class toolbox or the Java toolbox.
2. Choose the child class first, then the parent.

Import Relationship

A Java import statement is modeled as an access relationship between classes. An access relationship is a stereotyped dependency, and does not add attributes to the generated code.

To add an access relationship between classes in XDE:

1. Select the Access option from the Java toolbox (not the UML Class toolbox).
2. Choose the client class first, then the supplier class.

Building a Design Model

In object-oriented analysis and design, the team typically needs two different perspectives of the system: the *analysis model*, which is an implementation-independent view, and the *design model*, which is an implementation-dependent view. The analysis model focuses on *what* the system will do, while the design model focuses on *how* the system will do it.

Maintaining these two perspectives is especially helpful when you aren't yet sure what programming language you will use. The team can still capture the significant concepts in an analysis model and then add the implementation-specific design details to the design model once a programming language has been selected.

The design model is made up of a number of diagrams. A typical design model contains one or more of the following:

- Sequence diagram
- Class diagram
- Statechart diagram
- Component diagram
- Deployment diagram
- Freeform diagram

In this section, we discuss each of these types of diagrams, how they are used, and how to create them in XDE. First, however, let's look at the transition from analysis to design.

Moving from Analysis to Design

In a particular project, you may or may not have gone through the effort of creating an analysis model. If you've got one, begin the design by reviewing it. Map the analysis-level classes to design-level classes—this won't necessarily be a one-to-one mapping. For example, in analysis we may have created a generic boundary class called "timecard form." Now, we decide that we need an HTML form to collect the employee's name and ID and a server page to validate the information. Review each of the classes in the analysis model, and determine what design classes you need.

Boundary classes are the forms and windows in the system, as well as the interfaces to other systems or hardware. Each of the analysis-level boundary classes maps to one or more Java classes. The same is true of the entity classes we identified in analysis. Control classes may or may not be carried over one-to-one into design. They are frequently used as business logic placeholders in analysis, and during design, the responsibilities of the control classes are mapped to business logic Java classes such as servlets. In design, we give all of these classes Java-specific names, and these are the names that are ultimately used in the code.

The transition from analysis classes to design classes is iterative. As time goes on, you may end up combining two or more analysis classes to form one design class, or you may merge design classes that are similar. This process is called *refactoring*, and it is used to refine and optimize your design as the project goes along.

Building a Design-Level Sequence Diagram

In Chapter 4, we discuss how to create sequence diagrams at an analysis level. A *sequence diagram* is a type of interaction diagram in the UML, and it shows you, conceptually, what objects you need to implement a particular scenario in a use case. Now that we're in design, we can refine those analysis diagrams and create new design-level diagrams to see the specific objects that we need in order to implement a scenario. Where analysis was language-independent, we can assume in design that we're using Java. We also know the IDE, DBMS, and other specific technologies that we'll be using, so we can build the diagrams in the context of these technologies.

NOTE *There is another type of interaction diagram in the UML called a* collaboration diagram. *Collaboration diagrams are not supported by XDE at this time.*

To build a design-level sequence diagram, first select a use case scenario or a particular flow through a use case. Review the requirements, the flow of events, and any analysis-level diagrams created for the scenario. Now, consider the scenario in the context of Eclipse, WebSphere, or whatever IDE you are using. Go through each step in the flow of events and decide, specifically, what objects you need to implement the logic in that step. Add the classes to the model, and then create objects on the sequence diagram. Next, look through the messages on the analysis-level sequence diagram. In design, each message corresponds to an operation on the class receiving the message. Consider each analysis-level message, and create the operation(s) you need to implement each. On the design-level sequence diagram, show the operations and their order of execution by adding messages.

You will most likely need a number of sequence diagrams for each use case. Typically, you'd create one for the primary, or basic, flow and one for each significant alternate flow.

Patterns are an essential part of this process. If you have created a pattern for error handling, use the pattern consistently as you build your diagram. The more patterns you establish, the more you minimize the risk of different designers taking different approaches to similar problems.

In XDE, sequence diagrams are created within an interaction instance, which is itself contained within a collaboration instance. A collaboration instance, also known as a use case realization, is an implementation-specific view of the design for the use case.

Here is an example of the structure of collaboration instances in XDE:

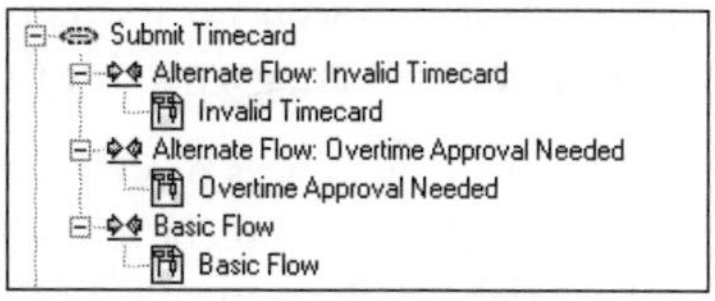

In this example, the collaboration instance is the use case realization Submit Timecard. The use case realizations for the other use cases are also collaboration instances. For the Submit Timecard use case, the interaction instances are Alternate Flow: Invalid Timecard, Alternate Flow: Overtime Approval Needed, and Basic Flow. The actual sequence diagrams are Invalid Timecard, Overtime Approval Needed, and Basic Flow.

All of the objects from the sequence diagrams for a use case are owned by the use case realization (the collaboration instance). The classes themselves are not owned by any specific collaboration instance because a single class is frequently used by multiple use cases. A single class may have instances in many collaboration instances, and a collaboration instance may use objects instantiated from classes anywhere in the model.

An interaction instance within a collaboration instance models the design for a single flow of events (the basic flow or an alternate flow). A single collaboration instance typically has a number of interaction instances, one for each flow in the use case. Each of the collaboration instances contains a single sequence diagram, which helps you visualize the design for that flow of events.

To create a sequence diagram in XDE when a collaboration instance does not yet exist (that is, to create the first sequence diagram for a use case), follow these steps:

1. To create a new collaboration instance, interaction instance, and sequence diagram, right-click a package and select Add Diagram ➢ Sequence: Instance.
2. Type the name of the new sequence diagram.
3. If a collaboration instance and interaction instance do not already exist, XDE automatically creates them for you. You can rename the collaboration instance (usually with the name of the use case) and interaction instance (usually with the name of the basic or alternate flow) if you like.

To create a new sequence diagram if the collaboration instance already exists (that is, to create a new sequence diagram for a use case that already has some sequence diagrams), follow these steps:

1. Right-click the existing collaboration instance in the Explorer and choose Add UML ➢ Interaction Instance.
2. Name the new interaction instance (usually with the name of the basic or alternate flow).
3. Right-click the new interaction instance and select Add Diagram ➢ Sequence: Instance.
4. Name the new sequence diagram.

We are assuming here that you opted to put your collaboration instances into a separate package, which isn't required. A few notes on creating sequence diagrams:

- You do not have to create the collaboration instances under a package. You can right-click any model element and select Add Diagram ➢ Sequence: Instance. This creates the collaboration instance, interaction instance, and sequence diagram under the selected model element. A frequently used pattern, however, involves creating a package that holds all of the collaboration instances.
- You can create collaboration instances or interaction instances independently of creating a sequence diagram. Right-click an element in the Explorer and choose Add UML ➢ Collaboration Instance. Then, right-click the new collaboration instance and select Add UML ➢ Interaction Instance. To add a sequence diagram to the interaction instance later, right-click the interaction instance and choose Add Diagram ➢ Sequence: Instance.

To delete a sequence diagram in XDE:

1. Locate the sequence diagram in the Explorer window.
2. Right-click the diagram and select Delete From Model.

Design-level sequence diagrams can frequently be long and complex. If this is the case, it helps to break the diagram down into smaller ones. Create several different diagrams, and then link them using these steps:

1. To link sequence diagram B to sequence diagram A, first open sequence diagram A.
2. Add a note to sequence diagram A.
3. Drag and drop sequence diagram B from the Explorer window onto the note. The text "Double-click to bring up the linked diagram sequence diagram B" appears in the note.

4. Double-click the note to open the linked diagram.
5. To remove the link, simply delete the note.

THE SEQUENCE DIAGRAM TOOLBOX

The sequence diagram toolbox includes options for creating objects, instances of actors, messages, and other elements on a sequence diagram. Table 5.6 lists the toolbox options and their meanings.

TABLE 5.6: SEQUENCE DIAGRAM TOOLBOX

ICON	MEANING
Pointer	Returns the mouse to the standard pointer
Lifeline	Adds an object to the diagram
Lifeline Actor	Adds an actor instance to the diagram
Message	Adds a message between objects, actors, or between an object and an actor
Return Message	Shows the return of a message
Create	Creates an object in memory
Destroy	Removes an object from memory
Note	Adds a simple note to the diagram
Note Attachment	Attaches a note to a use case or other element
Constraint	Refines the structure or behavior of an element
Text	Adds text to the diagram

ADDING OBJECTS AND ACTORS

If you are building a design-level diagram from your analysis model, you can start with the analysis-level sequence diagram to identify actors and classes. However, don't assume there is a one-to-one mapping between analysis classes and design classes. Go through each step on the analysis diagram and determine what design-level classes you need to implement the step. We'll translate the analysis messages into design messages, which correspond to methods on the Java classes.

If you are building a design-level diagram without an analysis model, start with the flow of events. Read through each step in the flow of events, and answer the following four questions:

- What objects will be needed to implement the step?
- What messages must be sent between the objects to implement the step?
- What order must the messages be in?
- What actors must send or receive messages to implement the step?

As you answer these questions, add objects, messages, and actors to the diagram. Then, move to the next step in the flow.

Objects are shown as boxes on the diagram. They are usually arranged at the top of the diagram, but they may be moved down to the point in the flow at which they are instantiated. There is a dashed line below each object, representing its lifeline. You can add an "X" to an object's lifeline to indicate where in the flow the object is destroyed from memory.

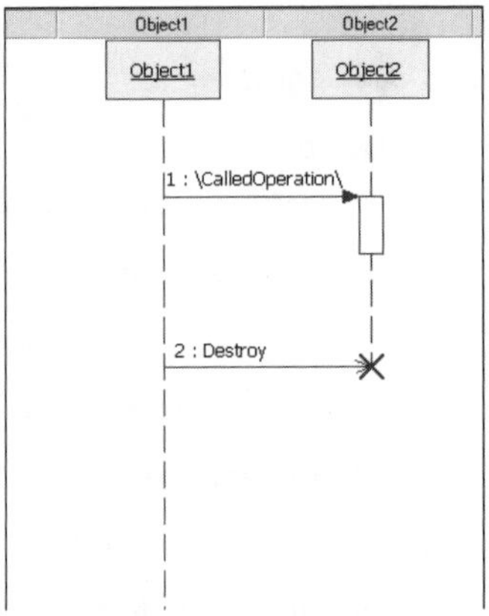

To add an object to a sequence diagram:

1. Add instances of existing classes.
   - **A.** Drag and drop the class from the Explorer window to the sequence diagram.
   - **B.** (Optional) Name an object by right-clicking it and selecting Rename. This is generally not done in design.
2. If you need to, add other objects (that are not instances of existing classes or have not yet been mapped to existing classes). Generally speaking, this shouldn't be done in design; all objects should map to classes in the design model.
   - **A.** Select the Lifeline option from the toolbox.
   - **B.** Click on the diagram to place the new object.
   - **C.** Type the new object name.

Actors are also shown as boxes on the diagram. A small actor symbol on the right-hand side of the box lets you know that the object is an instance of an actor. Like objects, actor instances can be named.

To add an instance of an actor to a sequence diagram:

1. Add instances of existing actors.
   - **A.** Drag and drop the actor from the Explorer window to the sequence diagram.
   - **B.** (Optional) Name an actor instance by right-clicking it and selecting Rename. This is generally not done in design.

2. If you need to, add other actor instances. By the time the design model is complete, all actor instances should map to actors in the model.
   - A. Select the Lifeline Actor option from the toolbox.
   - B. Click on the diagram to place the new actor instance.
   - C. Type the new actor instance name.

When an actor is another system, rather than a person, you need one or more classes to interface with that actor. On the sequence diagram, you should always show these interface classes. You can then show the interface classes communicating with the other classes in the system, as shown in Figure 5.3.

FIGURE 5.3

Actors on a sequence diagram

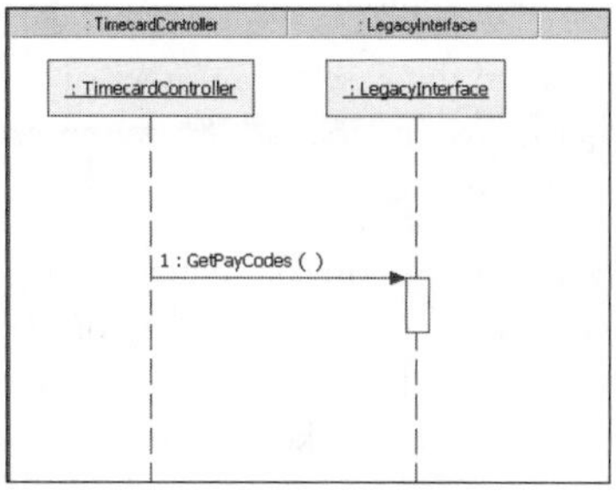

ADDING MESSAGES

Messages on a design-level sequence diagram correspond to the methods, or operations, on the Java classes. A message from a client object to a supplier object means that the client is calling a method of the supplier. Messages can also be reflexive; a message from an object to itself means that the object is calling one of its own methods.

If you are working from an analysis model, translate each analysis-level message to an operation. In analysis, we wrote text messages such as "Validate ID and password." Now, we identify the specific operations that we need, such as `Validate(ID:string, Pwd: string):int`. Obviously, we also need to identify the parameters and return types of the operations, if we haven't already done so.

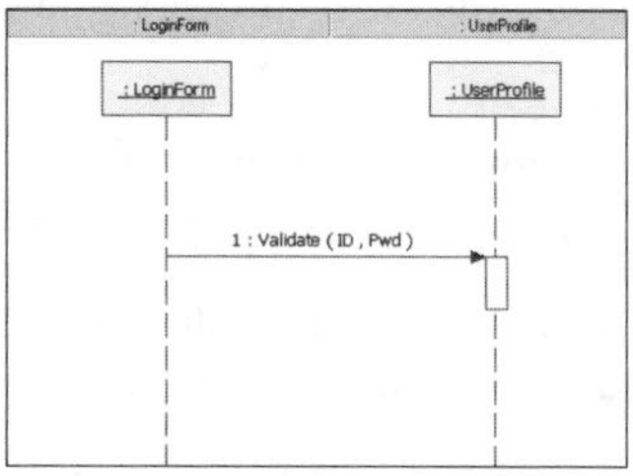

When you perform this translation, you usually create a number of new operations and you frequently create new classes as well. In the validation example just mentioned, we may have put the validation responsibility on a form in analysis. Now that we're in design, we may want to create a separate class to handle this responsibility.

So, we're making a great deal of the design decisions here, determining what classes we need and what the responsibilities of each class should be. Responsibilities are a primary focus of these diagrams. Always keep in mind as you're building these diagrams that you're allocating the responsibilities of the system to the various classes. Be sure you aren't violating any architectural guidelines here, such as putting database responsibilities on an HTML page, or putting display logic on an entity bean. There are two extremes to design: creating a few classes that have a lot of responsibilities, or creating lots of classes with fewer responsibilities. There are advantages and disadvantages to each approach, and most designers fall somewhere in the middle. Here are a few things to consider:

- Creating a few large classes can make each individual class difficult to understand, maintain, or reuse. However, there won't be as many relationships to set up or maintain, so the overall system structure can be easier to understand.
- Creating a lot of small classes can increase the number of relationships between the classes, making the overall model harder to understand. However, each individual class will be easier to understand, maintain, and reuse.
- Consider the direction of the messages on the sequence diagram. If two objects both send messages to each other, there will be a bidirectional association between their classes on the class diagram. Neither class can then be reused without the other, and a change to one can affect the other. Whenever possible, try to keep all messages between a given pair of objects going in the same direction.

It is assumed that each message on the diagram returns some value. You can look at the operation signature to see the return type of the operation. There are times, though, when it helps to explicitly show the return of a message. This is done by using a *return message*.

To add messages to a sequence diagram:

1. Add messages between objects, between actors, or between an object and an actor.
   - **A.** Select the Message icon from the toolbox.
   - **B.** Click the lifeline of the actor or object sending the message.
   - **C.** Click the lifeline of the actor or object receiving the message. To create a reflexive message, again click the lifeline of the object sending the message.
   - **D.** Click the message text to display a drop-down list box of the methods of the supplier class. Select the appropriate method from the drop-down list box. Alternatively, locate the method in the Explorer window, and drag and drop the method onto the message.
   - **E.** To reorder the messages, simply drag and drop a message higher or lower in the diagram. XDE automatically renumbers the messages.
2. To show that one object instantiates another, use a create message from the lifeline of one object to the object it is creating:
   - **A.** Move the object being created vertically on the diagram until it corresponds to the point in time when it will be created.
   - **B.** Select the Create option on the toolbox.

C. Click the lifeline of the object that is instantiating another.

D. Click the object (the box, not the lifeline) being created. As a result, XDE creates a new message called \CreateOperation\. Optionally rename this message.

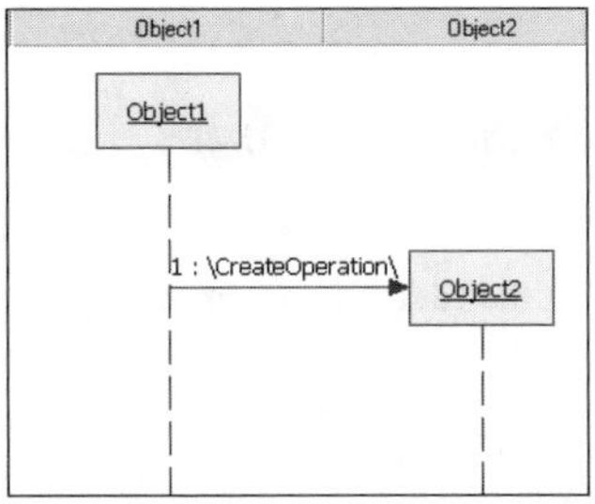

3. To show that one object destroys another, use a destroy message from the lifeline of one object to the lifeline of the object it is removing from memory.

   A. Select the Destroy option on the toolbox.

   B. Click the lifeline of the object that will destroy another.

   C. Click the lifeline of the object to be destroyed. XDE automatically shortens that object's lifeline and add a destruction marker (a large "X").

NOTE *A destroy message can also be reflexive, indicating that an object destroys itself.*

4. Show return messages if needed.

   A. Select the Return Message option from the toolbox.

   B. Click the lifeline of the object sending the return.

   C. Click the lifeline of the object receiving the return message.

5. To delete a message, right-click the arrow (not the text of the message), and select Delete From Model.

To change the display options for a message's parameters:

1. Select the message on the sequence diagram.
2. Modify the MessageSignature property.
   - Choosing Name Only displays the parameter names, but not their data types.
   - Selecting Type Only displays the parameters' data types, but not their names.
   - Choosing Name and Type displays both the names and types.
   - Selecting None hides the parameters on the diagram.

The UML does include some notation not yet supported by XDE. Specifically, the UML allows you to hide or display sequence numbers on a sequence diagram. XDE always displays the numbers and does not include an option for hiding them. The UML also supports variations on the message arrows for different types of messages. Table 5.7 lists these variations, which are not supported by XDE at this time.

TABLE 5.7: MESSAGE VARIATIONS IN THE UML

VARIATION	DESCRIPTION
Filled solid arrowhead rather than a standard arrowhead	Used to show a nested flow of control. All of the messages in the nested flow must be completed before the outer level sequence can resume.
Message arrow slanted downward	If a message will take a significant amount of time to arrive, the message arrow can be slanted downward to signify this.
Branching of messages	Branching can be used to show conditions on a sequence diagram. Each branch is labeled with a condition.

Although these options are not directly supported by XDE, you can always use a note or text on the diagram to show these variations.

FORMATTING A SEQUENCE DIAGRAM

There are a few menu options you can use to format your sequence diagram. These won't affect the meaning of the diagram at all and are simply used to make the diagrams more readable.

To align objects vertically:

1. Select the objects to align.
2. Choose Format ➢ Align ➢ Tops.

To adjust the horizontal spacing between objects:

1. Select the objects.
2. Choose Format ➢ Horizontal Spacing ➢ Make Equal to evenly space the objects. Select Increase or Decrease to fine-tune the spacing between objects, or select Remove to place the objects next to each other.

Building a Design-Level Class Diagram

The elements on a design-level class diagram are similar to those we used for the analysis-level class diagrams, but here everything is language-dependent. We'll remove the boundary, entity, and control stereotypes we used in analysis, and use Java-specific stereotypes instead.

While a sequence diagram provides a view of the objects within a specific use case scenario, a class diagram is used to view a set of classes, not necessarily from the same use case scenario. Because many classes will be used in many different use cases, a class diagram is a good way to consolidate and view all of the behavior and information in the class, as well as the relationships between the classes. As we mentioned in analysis, you typically create many class diagrams. Some show classes, others show packages of classes.

To create a class diagram in XDE:

1. Right-click a package, class (any type of class, including a JavaBean, interface, servlet, and so on), operation, component, use case, or actor, and choose Add Diagram ➢ Class.
2. Name the new diagram. XDE does not require that class diagrams have unique names, but we recommend that they do.

To delete a class diagram in XDE:

1. Right-click the diagram in the Explorer window.
2. Select Delete From Model.

To change another type of diagram into a class diagram:

1. Open the other diagram.
2. Edit the diagram's UML ➢ Type property, setting it to 1–Class.

The Class Diagram Toolbox

The class diagram toolbox is used to add classes, relationships, and other elements to a class diagram. Table 5.8 lists the toolbox options and their meanings.

Table 5.8: Class Diagram Toolbox

Icon	Meaning
Pointer	Returns the mouse to the standard pointer
Package	Creates a package of classes
Class	Creates a class
Interface	Creates an interface for a class or subsystem
Signal	Creates a signal, which is an asynchronous communication between objects
Enumeration	Creates an enumeration, which is a data type containing a list of values
Association	Creates an association relationship between two model elements
Directed Association	Creates a unidirectional association relationship between two model elements
Aggregation Association	Creates an aggregation relationship between two model elements
Composition Association	Creates a composition relationship between two model elements
Association Class	Creates an association class, used to hold information and/or behavior related to an association

Continued on next page

TABLE 5.8: CLASS DIAGRAM TOOLBOX *(continued)*

ICON	MEANING
Generalization	Creates an inheritance relationship between two model elements
Realization	Creates a realization relationship between two model elements
Dependency	Creates a dependency relationship between two model elements
Bind	Creates a bind relationship between an element and a template
Usage	Creates a usage relationship between two model elements, in which one element requires the presence of the other
Friend Permission	Creates a friend relationship between model elements, giving one element access to the contents of the other
Abstraction	Creates an abstraction relationship between two elements, showing that the elements contain the same information at different levels of abstraction
Instantiate	Shows that one element instantiates another
Subsystem	Creates a subsystem, which is a package with a defined interface
Note	Adds a simple note to the diagram
Note Attachment	Attaches a note to a use case or other element
Constraint	Refines the structure or behavior of an element
Constraint Attachment	Attaches a constraint to an element
Text	Adds text to the diagram

WORKING WITH ELEMENTS ON A CLASS DIAGRAM

You can add classes, including interfaces and other stereotyped classes, using the Explorer window or directly on a class diagram. Once you've added a class or other element, you can use it on as many different class diagrams as you need. XDE maintains only one copy of the class in a central repository. Any changes you make to the class are automatically reflected on all class diagrams that contain the class. Relationships are added using a class diagram and are also maintained in the central repository.

To add a class or relationship, select the appropriate item from the Java toolbox or the UML Class toolbox, and then click inside the diagram. See the appropriate section elsewhere in this chapter for instructions related to adding specific types of classes or relationships.

To delete an element from one diagram:

1. Right-click the element on the diagram.
2. Select Delete From Diagram.

To delete an element from the model:

1. Right-click the element on a class diagram or in the Explorer window.
2. Select Delete From Model.

TIP *If you accidentally delete an element from the model, you can undo the deletion using Edit ➢ Undo.*

FORMATTING A CLASS DIAGRAM

There are various options you can set to change the look of your class diagrams. None of these options has any syntactic meaning, and none affects any of the generated code. They are simply used to make the diagrams more readable.

The following instructions cover how to format specific classes or other elements on a class diagram. To change these settings for all classes or other elements, choose Window ➢ Preferences. Use the settings under Rational XDE ➢ Appearance to affect all elements.

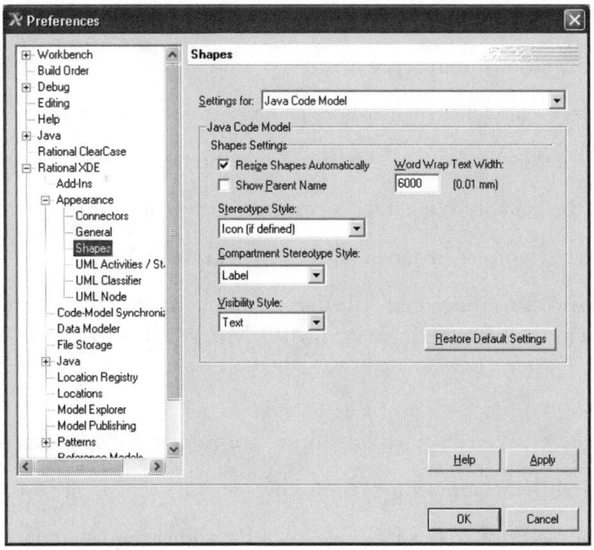

Attributes and Operations

Follow these steps to show or hide attributes or operations on a class diagram:

1. Select the class(es) to show or hide attributes or operations.
2. Choose Format ➢ Compartment, and then Attribute Compartment or Operation Compartment to show or hide the attributes and/or operations for the selected class(es). Hiding attributes or operations from one diagram does not delete them from the model.

To view the full operation signatures on a class diagram:

1. Select the class(es) to modify.
2. Choose Format ➢ Signature ➢ Operation Signature to show the full operation signature, or deselect this option to show only the operation names.

Stereotypes

Follow these steps to view stereotypes as icons:

1. Select the class(es) to modify.
2. Choose Format ➢ Stereotype and Visibility Style. Select from the following options:

   Shape Stereotype: None Lets you hide the stereotype completely.

   Shape Stereotype: Label Lets you view the stereotype as a label in the Name compartment of the class.

   Shape Stereotype: Icon Lets you view the stereotype using the UML icons.

To add your own stereotype icons:

1. Select a model element whose stereotype you want to modify.
2. Click the ellipsis ("…") button in the Stereotype property for that element.
3. In the Stereotype list, type a new stereotype name or select from the list of existing stereotypes.
4. In the Explorer Image field, click the ellipsis button.
5. Navigate to the graphic file that contains the icon for the stereotype. XDE supports the following graphic file formats: BMP, EMF, WMF, GIF, JPG, PNG, TIF.

Relationships

To alternate between diagonal lines for relationships and squared (rectilinear) lines:

1. Select the relationship(s) to modify.
2. Choose Format ➢ Line Style, then Rectilinear or Oblique.

Layout Options

To lay out items on a class diagram:

1. Select the classes or other elements to align.
2. Choose Format ➢ Align, and then the alignment method (tops, centers, and so on).

To resize items on a class diagram:

1. Select the classes or other elements to resize.
2. Choose Format ➢ Make Same Size to change the width, height, or both of the selected items.

To change the spacing on a class diagram:

1. Select the elements to modify.
2. Choose Format ➢ Horizontal Spacing (or Vertical Spacing) to change the spacing between elements.

To have XDE automatically lay out the diagram:

1. Open the diagram.
2. (Optional) Select the elements to arrange. If none are selected, XDE arranges all elements on the diagram.
3. Choose Diagram ➢ Arrange.

To add a (non-UML) geometric shape to the diagram:

1. Open the diagram.
2. Choose Modeling ➢ Add Geometric Shapes to add a shape.

VALIDATING A CLASS DIAGRAM

Before you generate code, it's a good idea to verify that the relationships and other elements you've added to a diagram are valid. Although XDE uses the repository rather than the diagrams to generate code (technically, you don't need a class diagram at all!), any changes you make on a class diagram update the information in the repository.

Choose Diagram ➢ Validate Diagram or right-click the diagram in the Explorer and select Validate. This checks the diagram to see if it conforms to the UML and Java language syntax rules. Any errors or warnings are listed in the Tasks window. You should correct all errors before code is generated.

Building a Statechart Diagram

A statechart diagram shows the lifecycle of a single object, from the time it is created until it is destroyed. These diagrams are a good way to model the dynamic behavior of a class. In a typical project, you do not create a statechart diagram for every class. In fact, many projects do not use them at all, but if you have a class that has some significant dynamic behavior, it helps to create a statechart diagram for it.

A class with significant dynamic behavior is one that can exist in many states. To decide whether a class has significant dynamic behavior, begin by looking at its attributes. Consider how an instance of the class might behave differently with different values in an attribute. If you have an attribute called Status, this can be a good indicator of various states. How does the object behave differently as different values are placed in this attribute?

You can also examine the relationships of a class. Look for any relationships with a zero in the multiplicity. Zeroes indicate that the relationship is optional. Does an instance of the class behave differently when the relationship does or does not exist? If it does, you may have multiple states. For example, let's look at a relationship between a person and a company. If there is a relationship, the person is in an employed state. If there is no relationship, the person may have been fired or may have retired.

In XDE, no source code is generated from a statechart diagram. These diagrams serve to document the dynamic behavior of a class so that developers and analysts will have a clear understanding of this behavior. The developers are ultimately responsible for implementing the logic outlined in this diagram. As with the other UML diagrams, statechart diagrams give the team a chance to discuss and document the logic before it is coded.

To create a statechart diagram, right-click a package, class, or operation and choose Add Diagram ➢ Statechart. The diagram will appear in the browser with the following symbol:

THE STATECHART DIAGRAM TOOLBOX

The statechart diagram toolbox is used to add states, transitions, and other elements to a statechart diagram. Table 5.9 lists the toolbox options and their meanings.

TABLE 5.9: STATECHART DIAGRAM TOOLBOX

ICON	MEANING
Pointer	Returns the mouse to the standard pointer
State	Creates a state
Transition	Creates a transition between two states or other elements
SelfTransition	Creates a transition from a state to itself
Initial State	Marks the starting point of the diagram
Final State	Marks the ending state for the object, which is the state the object is in before it is destroyed
Junction Point	Brings branches of the flow on the diagram back together
Shallow History	Notation to keep track of the most recent state within a substate so that the flow can return to that state when the substate is re-entered
Deep History	Notation to keep track of the most recent state within a substate no matter how far nested the recent state is
Choice Point	Marks a decision point on the diagram
Synchronization	Used to show concurrent states
Submachine State	Used to reference another state machine, defined elsewhere
Stub State	Used to show entry or exit points in a submachine state
Synch State	Shows synchronization points between layers in a concurrent state
Concurrent State	Shows two or more branches of the flow executing concurrently
Note	Adds a simple note to the diagram
Note Attachment	Attaches a note to a use case or other element
Constraint	Refines the structure or behavior of an element
Text	Adds text to the diagram

ADDING STATES

A *state* is one of the possible conditions in which an object may exist. As we discussed earlier, you can examine two areas to determine the state of an object: the values of the attributes and the relationships to other objects. Consider the different values that can be placed in the attributes and the state of the object if a relationship does or does not exist.

As with other XDE elements, you can add documentation to a state. However, because code is not generated from these diagrams, comments are not inserted into generated code for state documentation.

In UML, a state is shown as a rounded rectangle:

To add a state, use the State option in the UML Statechart toolbox.

ADDING STATE DETAILS

While an object is in a particular state, there may be some activity that it performs. A report may be generated, some calculation may occur, or an event may be sent to another object. There are five types of information you can include for a state: a do action, an entry action, an exit action, an event, or state history. We discuss each of these here.

Do Action

A *do action* is some behavior that an object carries out while it is in a particular state. For example, when an account is in the closed state, the account holder's signature card is pulled. When a flight is in a cancelled state, the airline tries to find alternate flights for its customers. A do action is an interruptible behavior. It may run to completion while the object is in that state, or it may be interrupted by the object moving to another state.

A do action is shown inside the state itself, preceded by the word *do*.

To add a do action, right-click the state and choose Add UML ➢ Do Action.

Entry Action

An *entry action* is a behavior that occurs while the object is transitioning into the state. As soon as a flight becomes scheduled, the system posts the schedule to the Internet. This happens while the flight is transitioned to the Scheduled state. Unlike a do action, an entry action is considered to be non-interruptible. Although the posting of a schedule record for use on the Internet is technically interruptible, it happens very fast, and the user does not have the ability to easily cancel the transaction while it is occurring. Therefore, it can be modeled as an entry action.

An entry action is shown inside the state, preceded by the word *entry*.

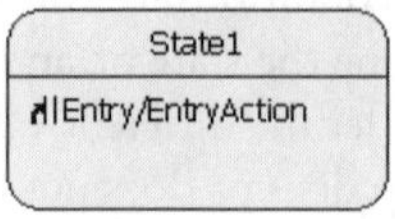

To add an entry action, right-click the state and choose Add UML ➢ Entry Action.

Exit Action

An *exit action* is similar to an entry action. However, an exit action occurs as part of the transition out of a state. For example, when the plane lands and transitions out of the In Flight state, the system records the landing time. Like an entry action, an exit action is considered to be noninterruptible.

An exit action is shown inside the state, preceded by the word *exit*.

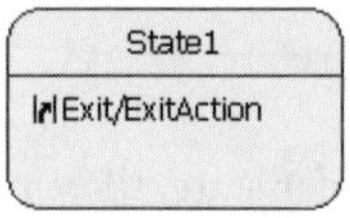

To add an exit action, right-click the state and choose Add UML ➢ Exit Action.

The behavior in an activity, entry action, or exit action can include sending an event to some other object. For example, if the flight is delayed for more than four hours, the flight object may need to send an event to a flight scheduler object, which will automatically reschedule the flight for another day. In this case, the activity, entry action, or exit action is preceded by a ^. The diagram would then read as follows:

Do: ^Target.Event(Arguments)

where Target is the object receiving the event, Event is the message being sent, and Arguments are parameters of the message being sent.

ADDING TRANSITIONS

A *transition* is a movement from one state to another. The set of transitions on a diagram shows how the object moves from one state to another. On the diagram, each transition is drawn as an arrow from the originating state to the succeeding state.

Transitions can also be reflexive. Something may happen that causes an object to transition back to the state it is currently in. A reflexive transition causes the exit action and the entry action to be executed. Reflexive transitions are shown as an arrow starting and ending on the same state.

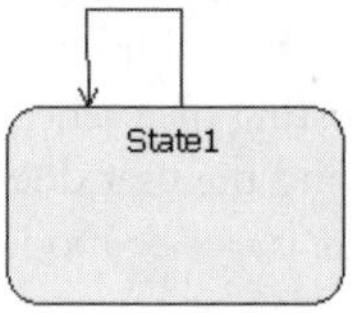

To add a transition:

1. Select Transition from the UML Statechart toolbox.
2. Click the state where the transition begins.
3. Click the state where the transition ends.

To add a reflexive transition:

1. Select SelfTransition from the toolbox.
2. Click the state where the reflexive transition occurs.

Adding Transition Details

There are various specifications you can include for each transition. These include events, guard conditions, actions, and send events. We look at each of these in this section.

Event

An *event* is something that occurs that causes a transition from one state to another. In the airline example, the Land event transitions the flight from an In Flight status to a Landed status. If the flight was delayed, it becomes closed if the Plane Arrived event happens. An event is shown on the diagram along the transition arrow.

XDE supports four types of events:

Call events Used when you trigger a transition by calling an operation. Call events use the following icon:

Time events Used when you trigger a transition by the passage of a specified amount of time, or at a specified date and time. Time events use the following icon:

Signal events Used when you trigger a transition by the receipt of a signal. Signal events use the following icon:

Change events Used when you trigger a transition by a condition changing from False to True. Change events use the following icon:

On a statechart diagram, events (regardless of type) are drawn along the transition arrow:

Most transitions will have events—the events are what cause the transition to occur in the first place. However, you can also have an automatic transition, which has no event. With an automatic transition, an object automatically moves from one state to another as soon as all the entry actions, do actions, and exit actions have occurred.

To add an event, right-click the transition line on the statechart diagram, and choose Add UML, followed by Call Event, Change Event, Signal Event, or Time Event.

Guard Condition

A *guard condition* controls when a transition can or cannot occur. In the airline example, adding a passenger moves the flight from the Open to the Full state, but *only if* the last seat was sold. The guard condition in this example is "Last seat was sold."

A guard condition is drawn along the transition line, after the event name, and is enclosed in square brackets.

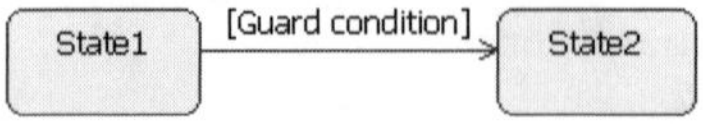

Guard conditions are optional. However, if there is more than one automatic transition out of a state, there must be mutually exclusive guard conditions on each automatic transition. This helps the reader of the diagram understand which path is automatically taken.

To add a guard condition, modify the GuardCondition property of the transition.

Action

An *action* is a noninterruptible behavior that occurs as part of a transition. Entry and exit actions are shown inside states because they define what happens every time an object enters or leaves a state. Other actions, however, are drawn along the transition line because they won't apply every time an object enters or leaves a state.

An action is shown along the transition line, after the event name, and preceded by a slash:

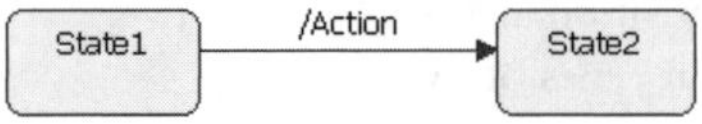

To add an action, modify the Action property of the transition. Do not enter the slash; XDE adds that for you when it adds the action to the diagram.

ADDING SPECIAL STATES

There are two special states that can be added to the diagram: the initial state and the final state.

Initial State

The *initial state* is the state the object is in when it is first created. An account object, for example, may start in a pending state until all of the paperwork is completed. The initial state is drawn on a statechart diagram as a filled circle. A transition is then drawn from the circle to the initial state:

An initial state is mandatory: the reader of the diagram needs to know what state a new object is in. There can be only one initial state on the diagram, although nested states may contain additional initial states. We'll get to nested states in a moment. To add an initial state, use the Initial State option in the UML Statechart toolbox.

Final State

The *final state* is the state an object is in when it is destroyed. A final state is shown on the diagram as a bull's-eye. Final states are optional, and you can add as many final states as you need.

To add a final state, use the Final State option on the UML Statechart toolbox.

Adding Choice Points, Junction Points, and Synchronizations

Choice points, junction points, and synchronizations are used to show how the flow of logic branches and merges as you go through the diagram. A *choice point* (also referred to as a *dynamic choice point* in the UML) shows the branching of paths on a statechart diagram. The transitions exiting a choice point must have mutually exclusive guard conditions. The choice point itself is shown as a circle:

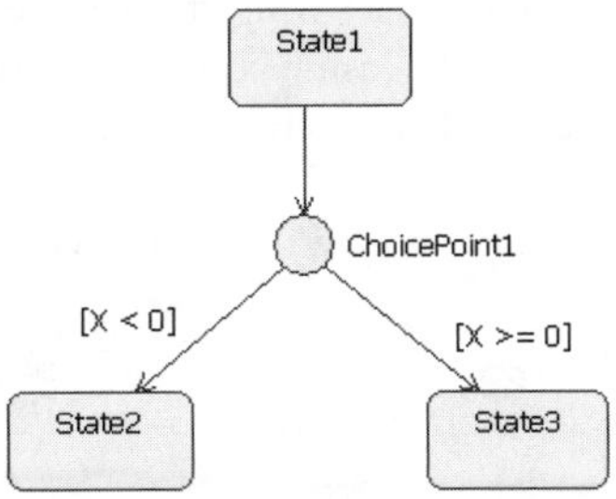

A *junction point* shows how different branches merge back together. Two or more states may have transitions into the junction point, and one or more transitions may leave. A junction point is shown as a filled circle:

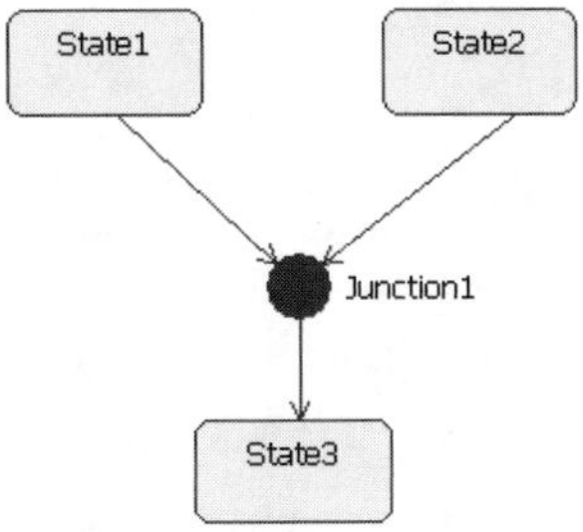

A *synchronization* is similar to a choice or junction point in that it branches the flow or joins it back together. The difference is that a choice point divides the flow into mutually exclusive paths, while a synchronization divides the flow into paths that execute simultaneously. When the simultaneous paths have finished, the flow can join again using another synchronization:

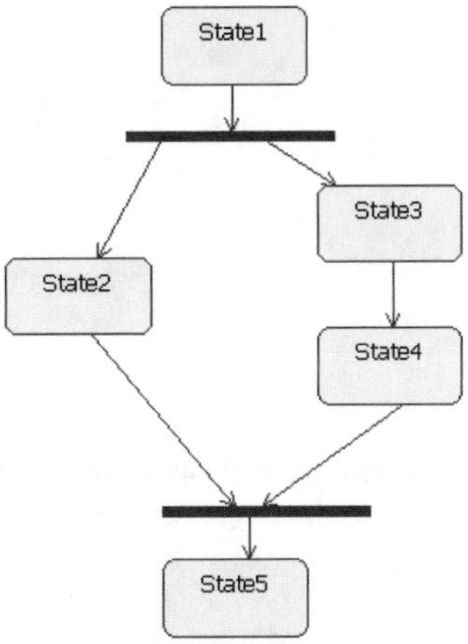

Choice points, junction points, and synchronizations can all be added using the UML Statechart toolbox.

ADDING SYNCH STATES AND CONCURRENT STATES

Sometimes, there are two or more states that happen concurrently. For example, in building a house, the electrician may be installing the wiring at the same time the plumber is installing the plumbing. This type of situation is modeled using concurrent states. Concurrent states are shown inside a rounded rectangle, with dashed lines separating their paths:

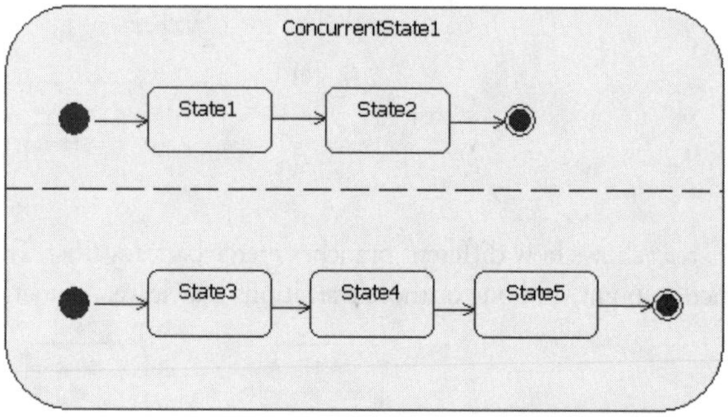

A synch state is used to show synchronizations between the different regions in a concurrent state. A synch state has incoming transitions from a source region, and outgoing transitions to a target region. For example, if a specific state in one region cannot be entered until a state in another region is complete, a synch state can be used.

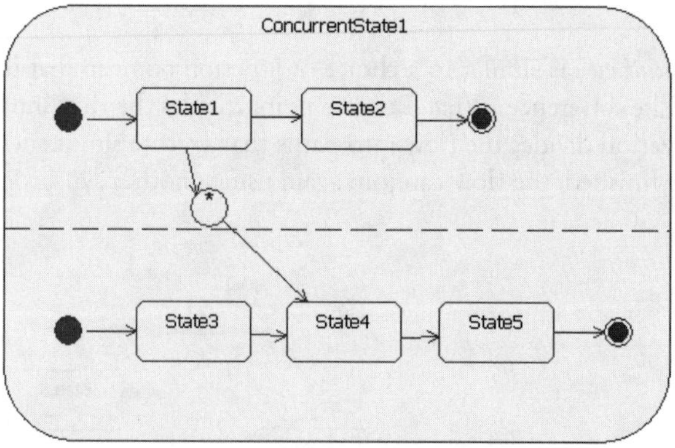

USING NESTED STATES

To reduce clutter on your diagram, you can nest one or more states inside another. The nested states are referred to as *substates*, while the larger state is referred to as a *superstate*.

If two or more states have an identical transition, they can be grouped together into a superstate. Then, rather than maintaining two identical transitions (one for each state) the transition can be moved to the superstate.

At times, you may need the system to remember which state it was last in. If you have three states in a superstate, and the object leaves the superstate, you may want the system to remember where you left off. In our example, if we want to temporarily suspend reservations while the system is undergoing routine maintenance, we may transition to a SuspendReservations state while the maintenance is occurring. Once the maintenance is done, we want to return to whatever state the flight was in before the maintenance started.

There are two things you can do to resolve this issue. The first is to add a start state inside the superstate. The start state indicates where the default starting point is in the superstate. The first time the object enters that superstate, this is where the object will be.

The second is to use state history to remember where the object was. If the history option is set, an object can leave a superstate, then return and pick up right where it left off. The History option is shown with a small "H" in a circle at the corner of the diagram:

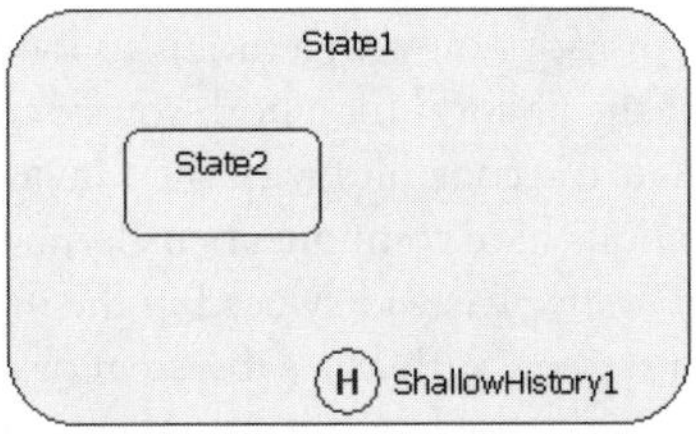

There are two types of history icons. A shallow history, as just shown, keeps track of the substate the object was last in, and resumes at that substate the next time control returns to the superstate. A deep history, shown as an "H*", suggests that we need to keep track of the last state, even if it was a substate inside a substate inside another substate. With a deep history, the object resumes at the last state, regardless of how deep that state is. The following is the symbol for a deep history:

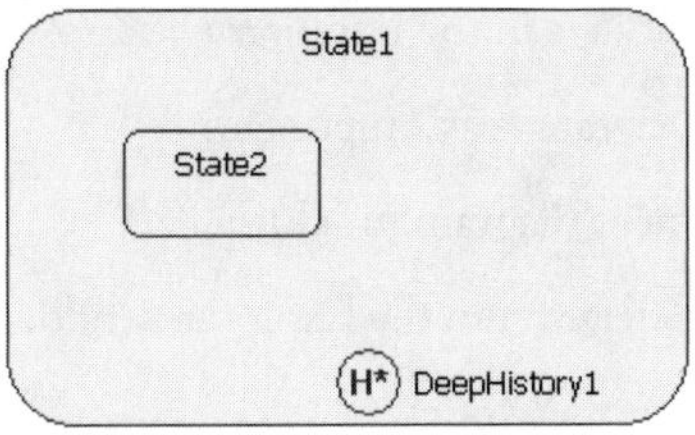

To add either a deep or a shallow history, select Shallow History or Deep History from the UML Statechart toolbox, and then click the superstate to which it applies.

USING SUBMACHINE STATES

A final piece of notation you can add to a statechart diagram is a *submachine state*. This notation simply suggests that the current state machine is invoking another state machine, defined elsewhere.

Stub states are used to show where you enter or exit the submachine state. For example, if we enter a submachine state at SubMachState2, the submachine state notation is as follows:

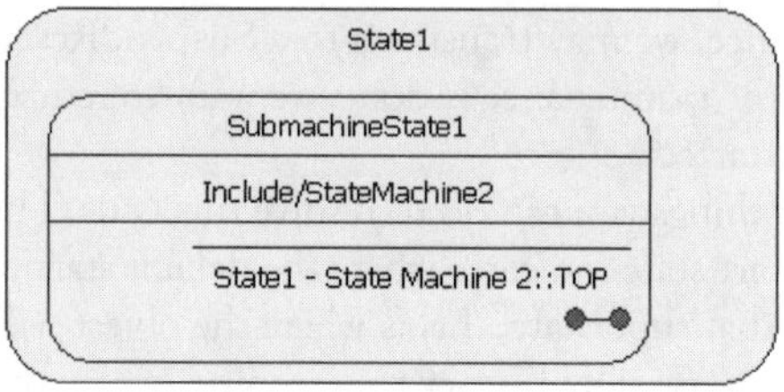

Building a Component Diagram

Component diagrams provide you with a means to look at the implementation model of the project. Components represent the physical files, both source code and executable, in your application. In Java, components include the code files with the `.java` extension, JAR files, EAR files, WAR files, and EJBs. Web applications have components including HTML files, JSP files, and ASP files.

Note that the term *component* is widely used in the industry to mean any relatively independent, encapsulated part of a system (such as a subsystem or a group of classes working together to accomplish some goal). Although these logical components are still a big part of design, this section deals strictly with physical components—in other words, files.

Component diagrams show you the dependencies between the components that make up the system. In XDE, component diagrams may contain packages, components, component instances, and interfaces. Dependency, realization, association, and residency relationships may be made between elements on a component diagram.

To create a component diagram in XDE:

1. Right-click a package in the Explorer window.
2. Choose Add Diagram ➢ Component.

To delete a component diagram in XDE:

1. Right-click the diagram in the Explorer window.
2. Choose Delete From Model.

THE COMPONENT DIAGRAM TOOLBOX

The component diagram toolbox is used to add components, relationships, and other elements to a component diagram. Table 5.10 lists the toolbox options and their meanings.

TABLE 5.10: COMPONENT DIAGRAM TOOLBOX

ICON	MEANING
Pointer	Returns the mouse to the standard pointer
Package	Creates a package of components
Component	Creates a component
Component Instance	Creates a component instance
Interface	Creates an interface
Dependency	Creates a dependency relationship between two model elements
Realization	Creates a realization relationship between two model elements
Association	Creates an association relationship between two model elements
Reside	Creates a residency relationship between two model elements
Note	Adds a simple note to the diagram
Note Attachment	Attaches a note to a use case or other element
Constraint	Refines the structure or behavior of an element
Constraint Attachment	Attaches a constraint to an element
Text	Adds text to the diagram

WORKING WITH ELEMENTS ON A COMPONENT DIAGRAM

We can use component diagrams to show the components in our system, the relationships between them, and the interfaces they implement. All of these options are available in the UML Component toolbox. In this section, we discuss the available options. In XDE, a component diagram appears in the Explorer window with the following symbol: 

We begin with components themselves. A component is a physical, replaceable part of a system. It corresponds to a physical file, such as a code file with a `.java` extension, JAR file, or HTML page. It may hold only a single class, or it may contain a number of classes and other model elements that work together. In the UML, you draw a component using the following notation:

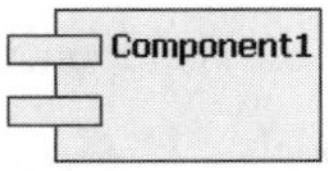

For the most part, you won't need to manually add a component. When you add a class or EJB and generate code, XDE automatically creates a component for the class or EJB. When you reverse engineer, XDE automatically creates components for you.

If you do need to add a component manually, you can use the Component option in the UML Component toolbox.

There are three primary types of relationships to use on a component diagram.

- A dependency indicates that an element in one component must access an element in another component:

- A resides relationship indicates that a class or other model element resides in a component:

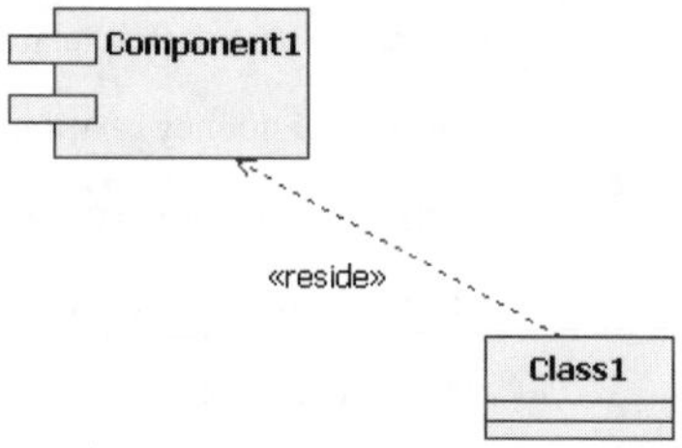

- A realizes relationship connects a component to an interface that it realizes. An interface is drawn as a stereotyped class, just as it was on a class diagram, or as a lollipop icon.

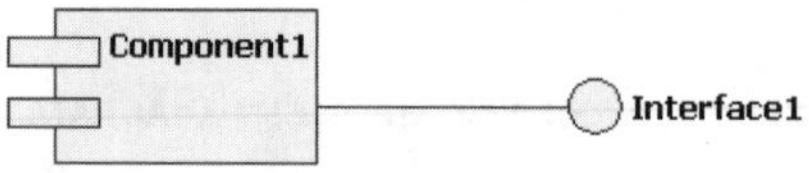

To add a component or a relationship, select the appropriate item from the UML Component toolbox, and then click inside the diagram.

To delete an element from one diagram:

1. Right-click the element on the diagram.
2. Select Delete From Diagram.

To delete an element from the model:

1. Right-click the element on a component diagram or in the Explorer window.
2. Select Delete From Model.

TIP *Deleting an element from a diagram does not delete it from the model. This also applies to relationships. Be careful that you do not delete elements from the diagram when you intended to delete them from the model.*

Building a Deployment Diagram

A deployment diagram is used to model how the application will be deployed on a network. We've defined our components, and the deployment diagram will be used to map the run-time components to the hardware on which they run. Until now, we haven't focused on things such as network bandwidth or backup servers; a deployment diagram is a good place to incorporate issues like these.

THE DEPLOYMENT DIAGRAM TOOLBOX

The deployment diagram toolbox is used to add elements to a deployment diagram. Table 5.11 lists the toolbox options and their meanings.

TABLE 5.11: DEPLOYMENT DIAGRAM TOOLBOX

ICON	MEANING
Pointer	Returns the mouse to the standard pointer
Node	Adds a processing node type to the diagram
Node Instance	Adds an instance of a node type to the diagram
Deploy	Shows the relationship between a component and the hardware on which it executes
Association	Used to show a physical connection between nodes
Note	Adds a simple note to the diagram
Note Attachment	Attaches a note to a use case or other element
Constraint	Refines the structure or behavior of an element
Constraint Attachment	Attaches a constraint to an element
Text	Adds text to the diagram
Cloud	Adds an Internet "cloud" to the diagram
Communication Link	Adds a link between nodes (not necessarily a physical link)
Desktop	Adds a desktop computer to the diagram
Ethernet	Adds an Ethernet to the diagram
Fax	Adds a fax machine to the diagram
FDDI	Adds a fiber distributed data interface network backbone to the diagram
Hub	Adds a network hub to the diagram
Laptop	Adds a laptop computer to the diagram
Mainframe	Adds a mainframe computer to the diagram
Mini Computer	Adds a mini to the diagram

Continued on next page

TABLE 5.11: DEPLOYMENT DIAGRAM TOOLBOX *(continued)*

ICON	MEANING
Modem	Adds a modem to the diagram
Plotter	Adds a plotter to the diagram
Printer	Adds a printer to the diagram
Radio Tower	Adds a radio tower to the diagram
Router	Adds a network router to the diagram
Satellite	Adds a satellite to the diagram
Satellite Dish	Adds a satellite dish to the diagram
Scanner	Adds a scanner to the diagram
Tower	Adds a tower computer to the diagram

WORKING WITH ELEMENTS ON A DEPLOYMENT DIAGRAM

In the UML, a deployment diagram is very simple. It consists of only a few pieces of notation. The first is a *node*, which is a type of processing resource. For example, an application may have nodes called "server" and "workstation." A *node instance* is simply an instance of a particular type of node. For example, each workstation on a LAN is an instance of the "workstation" node. Both nodes and node instances are drawn as cubes, but the name of a node instance is underlined. A node instance is named using the instance name, followed by a colon, followed by the node name:

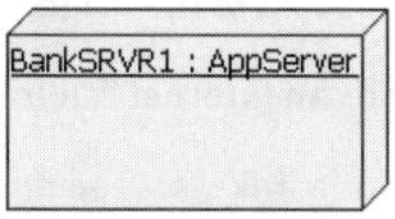

NOTE *From this point on, we use the term* node *to refer to both* nodes *and* node instances.

Communication associations are used to connect the nodes on the diagram. Each association represents a physical connection between nodes. If you like, you can create stereotypes such as <<LAN>> or <<Internet>> to show what type of connection exists. A communication association is drawn as an association relationship:

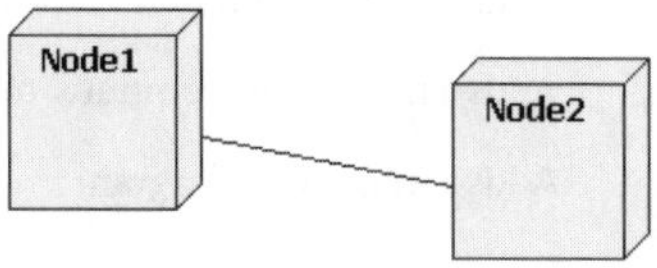

Inside each node instance, you can show the run-time component(s) that execute on that node, along with their interfaces and dependencies. Graphically, the components are displayed inside the node:

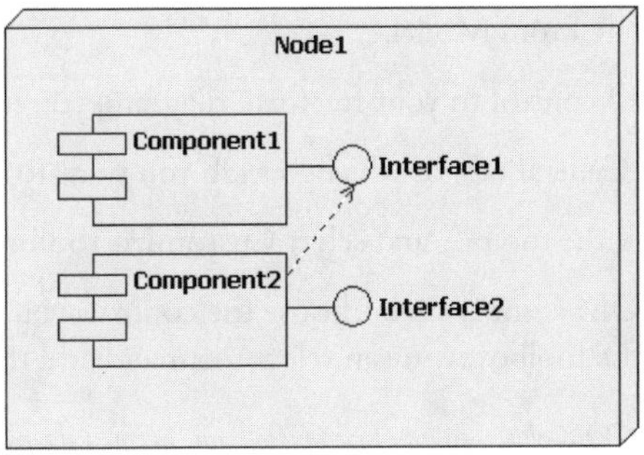

However, there is alternate notation. Rather than display a component inside a node, you can draw a dependency between the component and the node and give the dependency the stereotype <<Deploy>>. Here is an example of a deployment diagram:

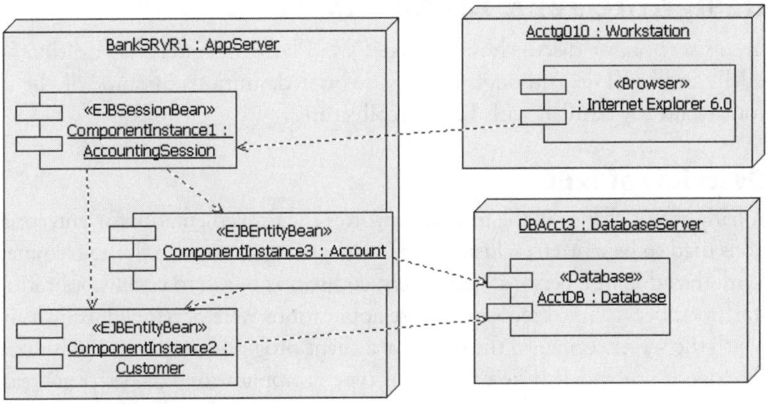

XDE goes beyond the standard UML notation to provide some extra icons that you can use on your deployment diagram. These icons, listed earlier in Table 5.11, can help you and the project team more clearly understand the hardware needed for deployment.

Building a Freeform Diagram

Although the UML provides a number of different views of a system, there are times when you may need additional views. XDE includes the ability to create a freeform diagram. A freeform diagram can contain any of the elements displayed on any of the other types of diagrams, geometric shapes, or COM controls.

To create a freeform diagram in XDE:

1. Right-click a package in the Explorer window.
2. Choose Add Diagram ➢ Freeform.

To delete a freeform diagram in XDE:

1. Right-click the diagram in the Explorer window.
2. Select Delete From Model.

To add a COM control to your freeform diagram, you must first customize the toolbox:

1. Select the General tab, or whichever tab you want to hold the COM controls.
2. Right-click the toolbox and select Customize Toolbox.
3. On the COM Controls tab, choose the controls you want to use. Once the controls have been added to the toolbox, you can select them and add them to the diagram.

TIP *You can add COM objects to any type of diagram, not just the freeform diagrams.*

You can add other elements to your freeform diagram using the different tabs in the toolbox. To add geometric shapes, right-click anywhere inside the diagram and select Add Geometric Shapes.

Designing J2EE Elements

In this section, we discuss how to model Java Platform Enterprise Edition (J2EE) elements in the UML and in XDE. Although we provide brief definitions of some of the concepts, we assume that you are already familiar with J2EE architecture.

Overview of J2EE

A fairly recent change in the industry involves the implementation of enterprise applications. Applications used to be written exclusively on mainframe systems with dumb terminals to access the programs. With the advent of personal computers, companies began to create applications for a single or a few staff members to use. Frequently, these applications were developed using a client/server model in which the server contained the data and a client program contained the functionality to connect and use the data. It was widely believed that this type of application was better and easier to change than the mainframe systems, at least according to the personal computer programmers.

As these applications matured and changes were needed, they became more difficult to change. The code encompassing the business rules was sometimes in the client program and sometimes in the server program. One method to avoid this was an architectural model called *three-tier* or *n-tier*. In this model, the business rules are separated from the data and the presentation layer. Most of the changes were now easier to incorporate into any layer because of the clear separation.

When Java came of age as a language for developing full-scale production applications, project teams needed an easier method of deployment and consistency. Also, more and more applications were developed using the Hypertext Transfer Protocol (HTTP) and the Internet. This was a substantial improvement from just using an *n*-tier architecture because it made deployment easier and it standardized many aspects of the applications. The consistent approach made the applications much more resilient to change. This was the foundation of J2EE.

The J2EE framework is designed to capitalize on the *n*-tier architecture as well as to use a consistent, standardized set of objects to build applications. The J2EE constructs include

- Servlets

- Java Server Pages (JSPs)
- Enterprise JavaBeans (EJBs)

These constructs build standardized applications that can be used on the Internet or on a private intranet. They can be used to access databases and execute business functionality easily once project teams understand the patterns for usage.

NOTE *Unique modeling elements for the modeling of EJBs have not explicitly been defined in the UML version 1.4. XDE follows an emerging specification, the JSR-26, UML Profile for EJB.*

Servlets

Servlets are the J2EE constructs that can generate dynamic content for web pages. Prior to the servlet, the standard method used to generate dynamic web pages or show data on a web page involved writing Common Gateway Interface (CGI) scripts. Using servlets is quite a bit easier than writing CGI scripts for this type of functionality.

In XDE, servlets are modeled as classes with stereotypes of <<HTTPServlet>> or <<GenericServlet>>, depending on the type of servlet you are creating:

A typical example of a servlet used in a sequence diagram is shown here:

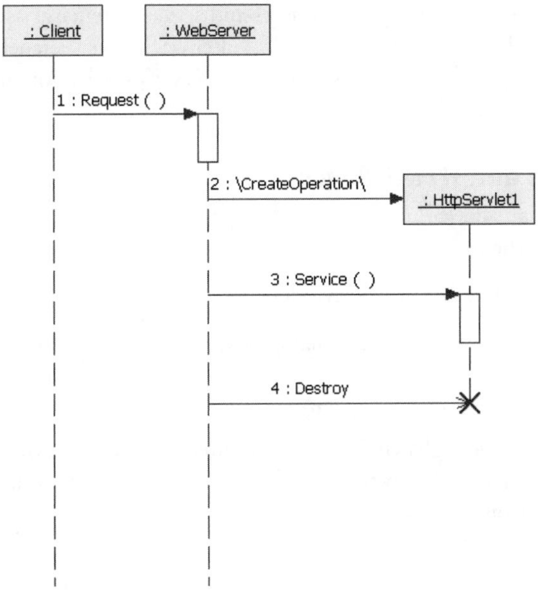

HTTP servlets, by default, include a `doGet()` and a `doPost()` method to handle the HTTP get and post requests. You can add other standard HTTP servlet methods by right-clicking the class, selecting Add Java, and then choosing the type of method you want to add. The methods available for HTTP servlets include

- `init()`
- `destroy()`
- `service()`
- `getServletInfo()`
- `doDelete()`
- `doOptions()`
- `doPut()`
- `doTrace()`

You can, of course, add your own methods to the HTTP servlet as well. To add an HTTP servlet, right-click a package and choose Add Java ➢ HTTP Servlet. Or, you can use the HTTP Servlet option on the Java toolbox.

The other type of supported servlet is a generic servlet. By default, a generic servlet includes a `service()` operation. By right-clicking the class, selecting Add Java, and then choosing the method name, you can also add `init()`, `destroy()`, and `getServletInfo()` methods to the generic servlet.

To create a generic servlet, right-click the package and choose Add Java ➢ Generic Servlet. Or, you can use the Generic Servlet option on the Java toolbox. To enter the URL for either an HTTP servlet or a generic servlet, edit the servlet's ServletURLPattern property.

You can also add servlet filter classes and servlet listener classes to your XDE model. Right-click a package and choose Add Java ➢ Servlet Filter or Servlet Listener.

Although servlets execute inside the web server's servlet container, the container is not explicitly modeled in XDE.

JSP Pages and HTML Pages

Before you can add JSP pages or HTML pages to your model, you will need to create a virtual directory to hold the files:

1. Choose File ➢ New ➢ Model.
2. In the New XDE model dialog box, select Web, and then Virtual Directory Model.

JSP Pages: Server and Client Pages

To add a JSP page, right-click the virtual directory model in the Explorer window, and choose Add Java ➢ Server Page. Or, open a class diagram from the virtual directory model, and use the Server Page option from the Web toolbox.

If we look conceptually at a JSP page, it is really made up of two logical elements. There is some behavior that is executed on the server side. This is typically the *business logic*, and the JSP page may need to communicate with business objects or other JSP pages to carry out this functionality. The JSP page may also have some *presentation logic*, which is the conceptual client-side piece of the JSP. Because there is this logical division, we model a JSP in XDE as two classes, one with a <<ServerPage>> stereotype, and one with a <<ClientPage>> stereotype. In the model, the client page is contained within the server page.

When you create a server page in XDE, a client page is created automatically inside the server page, and a Build relationship is automatically added between them:

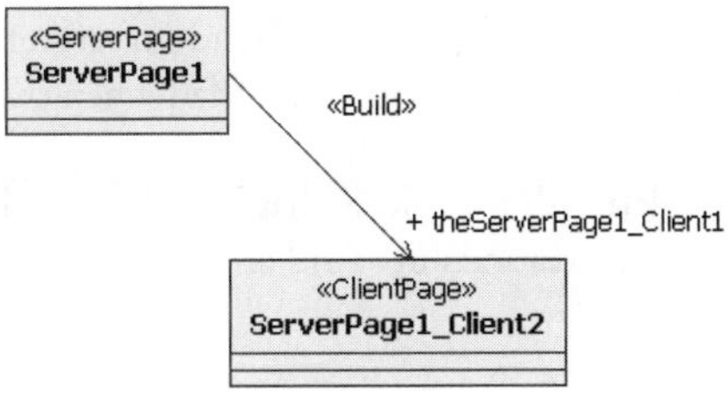

HTML Pages

We'll discuss other types of server and client page relationships in just a moment. First, however, let's quickly look at how a simple HTML page is modeled in the UML and in XDE. An HTML page is modeled as a class with a stereotype of <<HTMLForm>>. To add an HTML page to the model:

1. Select the HTML Form option from the Web toolbox, and click inside a class diagram. XDE displays the Add Form dialog box:

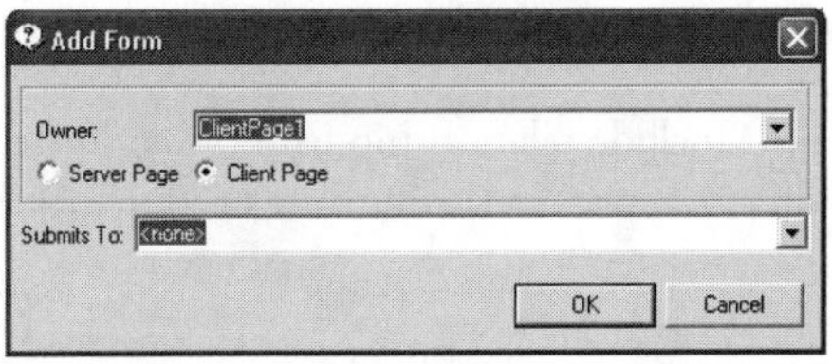

2. Select the form's owner. The owner may be either a server page or a client page.
3. (Optional) Select the server page to which this new form will submit its information. Click OK to finish.

Attributes on an HTMLForm class represent the HTML input fields that are on the form, and have a stereotype of <<HTMLInput>>, <<HTMLSelect>>, or <<HTMLTextArea>>. To add a field, right-click the form and select Add Java, followed by HTML Input, HTML Select, or HTML TextArea.

When a form is added, XDE automatically creates an aggregation relationship between the form and its owner. In addition, XDE creates a relationship with a stereotype of <<HTMLSubmit>> between the form and the server page to which the form submits:

JSP AND HTML PAGE RELATIONSHIPS

There are a few types of relationships we can add to server pages, client pages, and HTML forms. Some, as we've discussed, are automatically added when these elements are created in the XDE model. Others we have to add manually.

You use a Build relationship to show that a server page builds a client page. Use a stereotyped dependency to draw this relationship. Add an association using the UML Class toolbox, and assign it a stereotype <<Build>>.

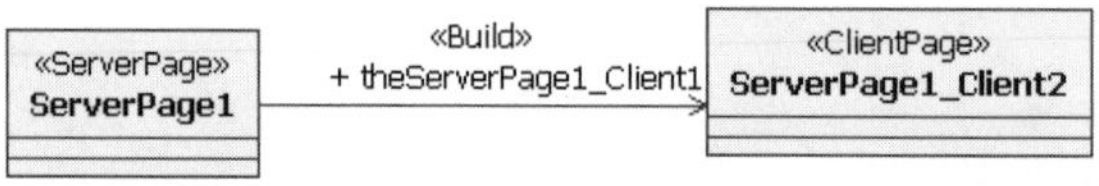

You can use an HTML Link relationship to show a hypertext link (the `A HREF` tag) between two client pages or between a server page and a client page. You can add it to the diagram using the HTMLLink Relation option on the Web toolbox.

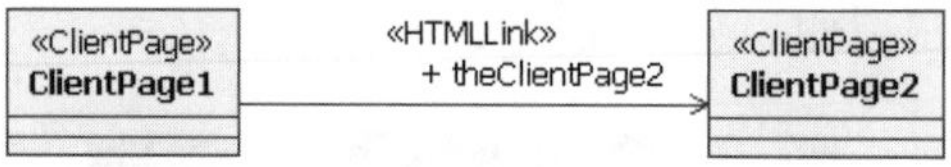

You can use a JSP Include relationship to show an inclusion of a client page by a server page (the `jsp:include` command in code). Add it using the JSPInclude Relation option on the Web toolbox.

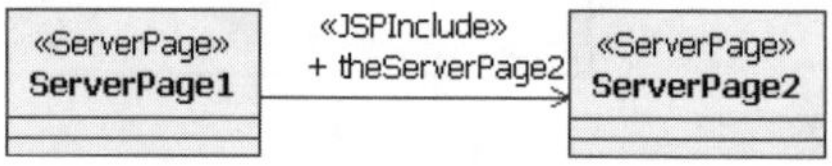

You can use a JSP Forward relationship to show that one server page forwards control to another. Add it using the JSPForward Relation option on the Web toolbox.

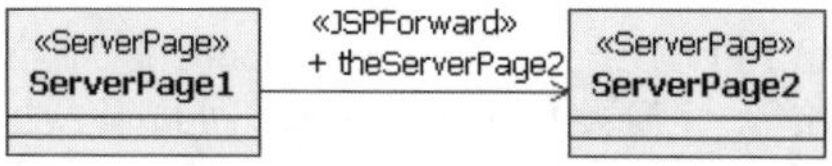

JavaBeans

In XDE, a JavaBean (not an Enterprise JavaBean) is modeled as an attribute of a class. To create a bean:

1. Right-click a class and choose Add Java ➢ Bean Property. XDE displays the Create Bean Property dialog box:

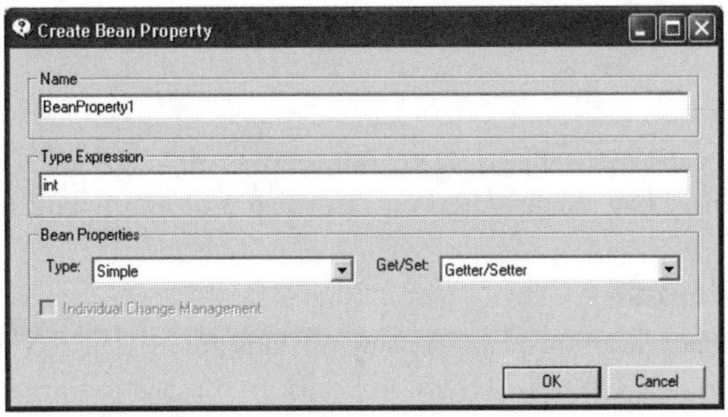

2. Enter the bean's name and data type. If you leave the type blank, the default type is `int`.
3. Enter the bean type (simple, constrained, or bound).
4. In the Get/Set field, indicate which methods (get and/or set) should automatically be added to the model for the bean.

The following is an example of the code generated for bean Bean1 in class Class1. The bean's data type was set to `int`.

```
package Package1;
/**
 *
 * @modelguid {98E1B66B-37E4-4E68-8604-58123A93BDD5}
 */
public class Class1
{
    /**
     *
     * @modelguid {F58C2965-56C2-4FC0-B107-85A5D6CC565A}
     */
    private int bean1;

    /** @modelguid {1A4406CB-1ACE-4686-97A2-1B9D6AF9FF1C} */
    public int getBean1()
    {
        /*Begin Template Expansion{9A0448E9-A403-4CE3-8CC6-E5BBB53CCC0E}*/

        return bean1;
        /*End Template Expansion{9A0448E9-A403-4CE3-8CC6-E5BBB53CCC0E}*/
    }
```

```
    /** @modelguid {06CCA90B-6208-48D5-B38B-4AB3457B94D5} */
    public void setBean1(int aBean1)
    {
        /*Begin Template Expansion{29CE507E-049A-4E76-AB8E-F2371317EEAA}*/
        bean1 = aBean1;
        /*End Template Expansion{29CE507E-049A-4E76-AB8E-F2371317EEAA}*/
    }

}
```

Because beans are modeled as attributes rather than classes, they are not typically used in interaction diagrams. They are displayed on class diagrams as attributes of their class.

Session Beans

Unlike standard JavaBeans, Enterprise JavaBeans are modeled as separate components. XDE supports both EJB versions 1.0 and 2.0 session beans. In this section, we look at how both stateful and stateless session beans are modeled and used in the UML. To begin, though, let's look at the classes created to support the session bean.

When you create a new session bean, whether stateful or stateless, XDE creates a component with a stereotype of <<EJBSessionBean>>. The component is a container for the classes that make up the session bean. The classes in the session bean are the home interface, the remote interface, and the implementation class. The following is an example of the structure for a stateful session bean (we discuss the relationships later in this chapter in the section "Bean Relationships"):

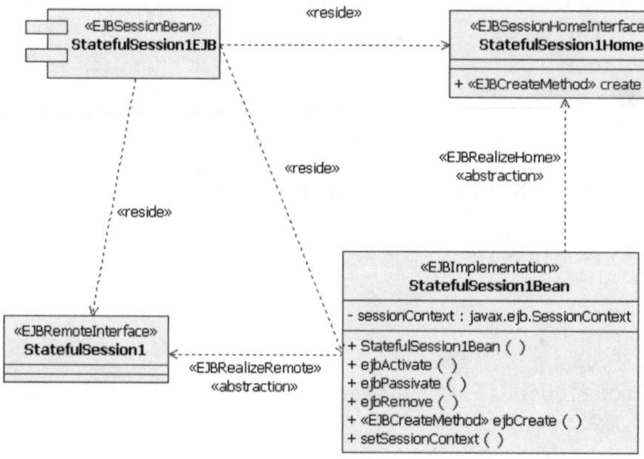

In addition to holding the classes, the component is used to store information related to the deployment descriptor. The component itself does not map to a code construct, but the deployment descriptor information in the component properties will be used during deployment.

The home interface is modeled as a class with a stereotype of <<EJBSessionHomeInterface>>. XDE automatically adds a `create()` method to the home interface. Note that although XDE allows you to define additional `create()` methods for a stateless session, this is generally not recommended.

You can, however, define more `create()` methods, with differing parameters, for a stateful session. Right-click the home interface, and choose Add Java ➢ Create Method.

The remote interface is modeled as a class with a stereotype of <<EJBRemoteInterface>>. Because the remote interface typically includes signatures for business-specific methods, XDE does not automatically add any operations to this class. You can add your own methods by right-clicking the remote interface and choosing Add Java ➢ Business Method. Note that as you add methods to the remote interface, XDE also automatically adds those methods to the implementation class.

Finally, the implementation piece of the EJB is created as its own class as well. This is a class with a stereotype of <<EJBImplementation>>. A `create()` method is automatically added to the class to implement the `create()` operation from the home interface. As you add methods to the remote interface, they are automatically added to the implementation class as well. XDE automatically adds the following:

- `ejbActivate()`, which is implemented only in stateful beans but is present in stateless beans as well
- `ejbPassivate()`, which is implemented only in stateful beans but is present in stateless beans as well
- `ejbRemove()`
- `setSessionContext()`

You can create a session bean from scratch, or you can transform an existing class into a session bean. If you create a bean from scratch, XDE creates default names for the component and classes. Otherwise, XDE uses the original class name as a basis for the component and class names. For example, if we transform a class called Class1 into a session bean, the component is named Class1EJB, the home interface is Class1Home, the remote interface is Class1, and the implementation class is Class1Bean.

To create a session bean from scratch:

1. Open a class diagram.
2. Use the Stateful Session Bean or Stateless Session Bean option from the Java toolbox.

To transform an existing class into a session bean:

1. Right-click the class to transform.
2. Select Transform, followed by Stateless Session Bean or Stateful Session Bean.

Entity Beans

Like a session bean, an entity bean is modeled as a component containing a series of classes. XDE has support for container-managed persistence (CMP) 1.1 and 2.0 and bean-managed persistence (BMP) entity beans. To add any of these to your model, right-click a package or a class diagram, and select Add Java, followed by BMP Entity Bean, CMP 1.1 Entity Bean, or CMP 2.0 Entity Bean. You can also transform an existing class into an entity bean by right-clicking and selecting Transform, followed by BMP Entity Bean, CMP 1.1 Entity Bean, or CMP 2.0 Entity Bean.

The specific classes that are created depend upon the type of entity bean you are creating. Let's begin with BMP entity beans. The following is an example of the elements created to support a BMP:

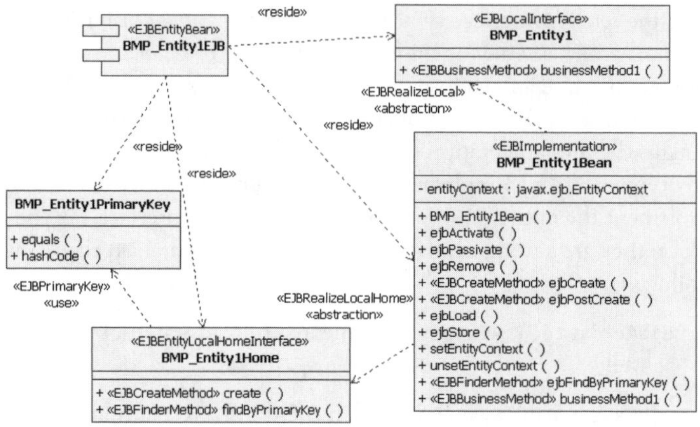

The home interface is modeled as a class with a stereotype of <<EJBEntityLocalHomeInterface>>. There are two methods added by default: the `create()` method and the `findbyPrimaryKey()` method, which is used to find an instance of the BMP entity bean. The remote interface is modeled as a class with a stereotype of <<EJBLocalInterface>>, and it does not include any default methods.

XDE adds a number of methods to the implementation class. As is the case with session beans, when you add a method to the remote interface, it is added to the implementation class as well. The following methods are created in the implementation class:

- `ejbActivate()`
- `ejbPassivate()`
- `ejbRemove()`
- `ejbCreate()`
- `ejbPostCreate()`
- `ejbLoad()`
- `ejbStore()`
- `setEntityContext()` (Note that default code is added to this method during code generation.)
- `unsetEntityContext()`
- `ejbFindByPrimaryKey()`

The final class created for a BMP entity bean is a primary key class. This is a class that contains two methods, `equals()` and `hashcode()`, and at least one attribute for the entity's primary key. If the entity has only one primary key field, it can be modeled on the implementation class rather than needing a separate primary key class. If, however, the entity has a primary key made up of two or more fields, a primary key class is required.

To add a primary key to the implementation class, right-click it and choose Add Java ➢ Primary Key Field.

The preceding discussion was related to BMP entity beans. Let's turn now to CMP entity beans. As we mentioned earlier, XDE supports CMP 1.1 and CMP 2.0 beans. Most of the following discussion applies to both of these types; we make a note where the modeling is different for CMP 1.1 or 2.0.

An entity bean is mapped to a component and three classes: a home interface, a remote interface, and an implementation class. The following is an example of the entities created for a CMP 2.0 entity bean:

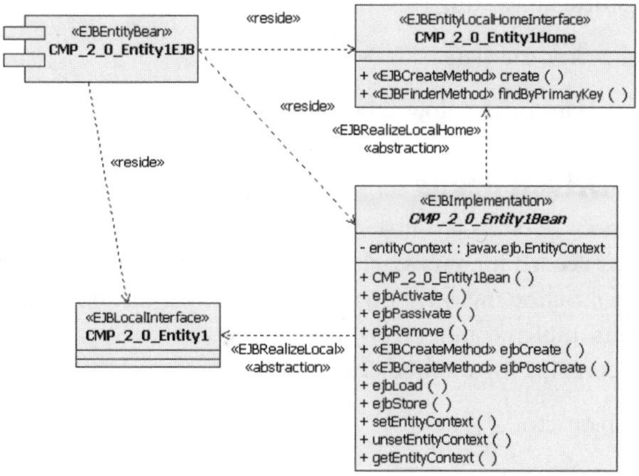

The home interface is a class with a stereotype of <<EJBEntityHomeInterface>> for a CMP 1.1 bean, or <<EJBEntityLocalHomeInterface>> for a CMP 2.0 bean. The home interface contains two methods: `create()` and `findByPrimaryKey()`.

The remote interface is a class with a stereotype of <<EJBRemoteInterface>> for a CMP 1.1 bean, or <<EJBLocalInterface>> for a CMP 2.0 bean. The remote interface does not contain any default methods.

The implementation class has a stereotype of <<EJBImplementation>>, and contains a number of default methods. As with other beans, when you add a method to the remote interface, it is automatically added to the implementation class as well. XDE adds the following methods to an entity bean's implementation class:

- `ejbActivate()`
- `ejbPassivate()`
- `ejbRemove()`
- `ejbCreate()`
- `ejbPostCreate()`
- `ejbLoad()`
- `ejbStore()`
- `setEntityContext()` (Note that default code is added to this method during code generation.)

- `unsetEntityContext()`
- `getEntityContext()` (Note that this method is only for CMP 2.0 beans.)

To create an entity bean:

1. Right-click a package in the Explorer, or right-click inside a diagram.
2. Select Add Java, followed by BMP Entity Bean, CMP 1.1 Entity Bean, or CMP 2.0 Entity Bean.

To transform an existing class into an entity bean:

1. Right-click the class.
2. Select Transform, followed by BMP Entity Bean, CMP 1.1 Entity Bean, or CMP 2.0 Entity Bean.

Message-Driven Beans

Modeling message beans is a little bit simpler than modeling entity or session beans. There are only two elements needed for a message bean: a component and an implementation class. To create a message bean, right-click anywhere on a class diagram and choose Add Java ➢ Message-Driven Bean.

The bean's implementation class is modeled as a class with the stereotype <<EJBImplementation>>. It contains five methods by default:

- A constructor
- `onMessage()`
- `ejbCreate()`
- `ejbRemove()`
- `setMessageDrivenContext()`

You can add new methods by right-clicking the implementation class and choosing Add Java ➢ Method.

On a sequence diagram, you can show the message bean as an object receiving messages from an EJB container or JMS destination:

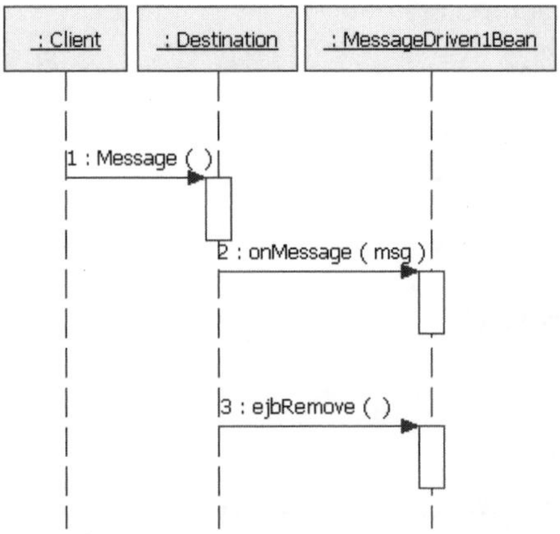

Bean Relationships

In this section, we look at four different types of relationships you can set up between EJBs in XDE: the reside relationship, the realize relationship, the reference relationship, and the persistence relationship.

Reside Relationship

One of the more frequently used relationships, a *reside relationship,* is drawn between a class and a component and is used to show that the class is contained within the component. In the diagrams we saw earlier, each of a bean's classes had a reside relationship with that bean's component. A reside relationship is a stereotyped dependency:

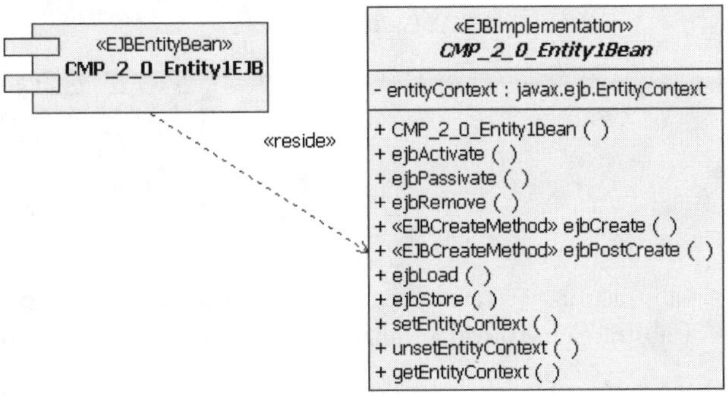

Realize Relationship

A *realize relationship* is used to model the relationship between a class and the interface(s) it implements. When XDE adds realization relationships, the specific stereotypes will vary a little, depending upon the type of bean. The relationship between the implementation class and the home interface is stereotyped as follows:

- In a BMP bean: <<EJBRealizeLocalHome>>
- In a CMP 1.1 bean: <<EJBRealizeHome>>
- In a CMP 2.0 bean: <<EJBRealizeLocalHome>>

The relationship between the implementation class and the remote interface is stereotyped as follows:

- In a BMP bean: <<EJBRealizeLocal>>
- In a CMP 1.1 bean: <<EJBRealizeRemote>>
- In a CMP 2.0 bean: <<EJBRealizeLocal>>

A realize relationship is drawn as a stereotyped dependency:

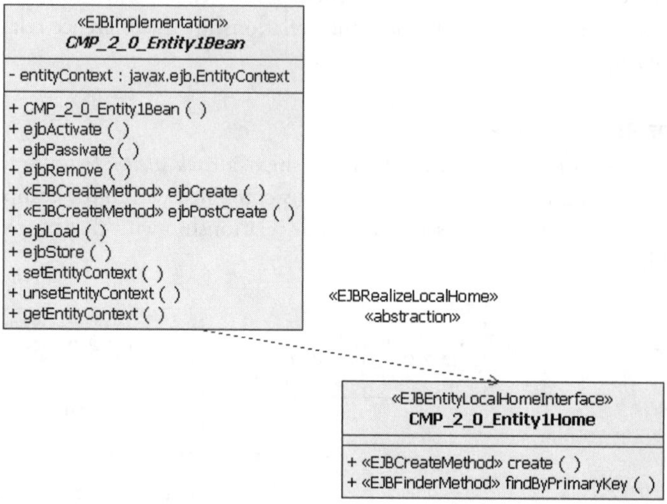

The <<abstraction>> stereotype indicates that the two classes present the same concepts at different levels of abstraction. To add a realize relationship, use the Realization option in the Java toolbox.

REFERENCE RELATIONSHIP

A *reference relationship* between EJBs is similar to an association relationship between classes. It allows one EJB to use the services provided by another. When you set up a reference relationship, XDE automatically creates the appropriate information in the deployment descriptors to support the relationships. A reference relationship is drawn as a stereotyped association:

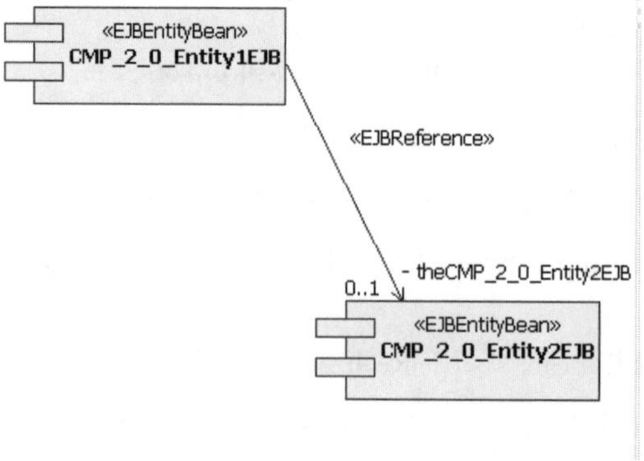

The stereotype on the relationship will be <<EJBReference>> if the client EJB has remote interfaces, or <<EJBLocalReference>> if the client EJB has local interfaces. To add a reference relationship, use the EJB Reference option in the Java toolbox.

PERSISTENCE RELATIONSHIP

The final type of EJB relationship is a *persistence relationship*. These are used only between CMP 2.0 entity beans and are used to show permanent, persistent links between entity beans. For example, we may want to establish a link between a Company entity and an Employee entity. Like associations, persistence relationships may be unidirectional or bidirectional and will have multiplicity settings.

To add a bidirectional persistence relationship, use one of the following options in the Java toolbox:

- 1:1 CMP Relationship
- 1:M CMP Relationship
- M:M CMP Relationship

To add a unidirectional relationship, use one of the following:

- 1:1 Directed CMP Relationship
- 1:M Directed CMP Relationship
- M:M Directed CMP Relationship

These relationships are drawn as stereotyped associations, with multiplicity shown on the ends.

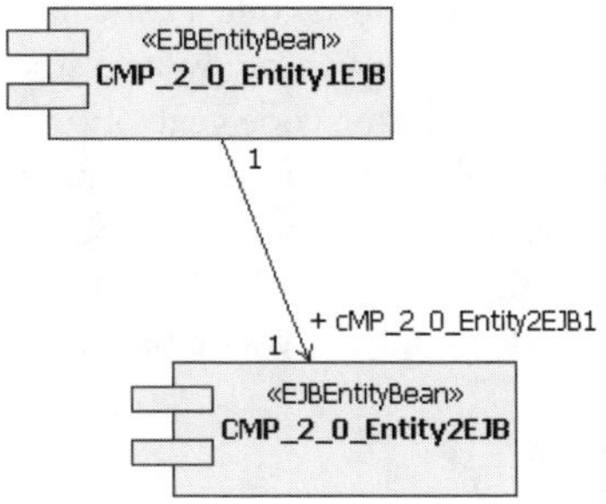

XDE adds accessor methods to the EJBs to support the relationship. If the relationship is bidirectional, accessors are added to both ends. If the relationship is unidirectional, the accessors are added only to the client EJB. Accessors will have signatures similar to the following:

- One-to-one relationship

```
Public abstract Entity1 getEntity1EJB2();
Public abstract void setEntity1EJB2(Entity1 Parameter);
```

- Many-to-many relationship

```
Public abstract java.util.Collection getEntity1EJB2();
Public abstract void setEntity1EJB2(java.util.Collection Parameter);
```

Working with Java Code

Until now, we've focused on the modeling side of application development. Now, we take a look at the code itself and discuss how the code and model are kept in sync. We also cover code templates, which are useful when you are inserting standard code into the application; they also help ensure consistency among the different parts of the application.

Code Templates

There are several UML tools out there that create some minimal code during the code generation process. Typically, the tool generates code for constructors, destructors, and get and set operations. That's very helpful, but it still does leave a lot of coding up to the developers. Of course, there's no way for any tool to read your mind and code the business operations for you, but if you do have some code templates already developed, incorporating them into the tool can save a lot of time. The code in the template is automatically added to the methods during the code generation process.

A code template is simply some predefined code that you'd like inserted into one or more operation bodies during code generation. For example, maybe you have some pre-existing code that you always use in exception handling for message beans. By associating this pre-existing code with an `onMessage()` method, for example, XDE can insert the code during code generation. The process of associating a template to a model element is referred to as *binding*.

NOTE *Code templates are different from patterns. Patterns are developed for reuse among models; code templates are developed for reuse in code.*

XDE takes this idea of predefined code a little bit further. You can enter static text that is inserted as code into a method, or you can write a small program in JavaScript as the code template. The JavaScript program runs during code generation and its results are inserted into the method code. We'll look at an example of this in just a minute.

Either of these approaches (static code or JavaScript) saves the developers a lot of time and trouble, and increases the consistency of your code. As you complete more and more projects, look for opportunities to create these code templates to save time in the future.

CODE TEMPLATE SYNTAX

The simplest syntax for a template is to simply enter the code that you want included in the method. The code you enter is exactly what appears in the generated operation. This is a useful option for both static code and static comments, such as copyright information.

Another option is to add some JavaScript to the template body. The JavaScript scriptlet is enclosed in <% and %> tags. During code generation, XDE runs the scriptlet to create the code for the operation. For example, if we enter the following scriptlet into the template body:

```
return <%=thisElement.getName()%>;
```

the following is the code for the generated operation:

```
public void Operation1()
{
    /*Begin Template Expansion{DA882CA9-5A4B-4828-9038-E4B108B4712E}*/
    return Operation1;
    /*End Template Expansion{DA882CA9-5A4B-4828-9038-E4B108B4712E}*/
}
```

A great feature of using scriptlets is their ability to reference items within the XDE model itself. For example, if you wanted to generate an operation that would print the name of the class, you could use the syntax `thiselement.getname()`. The variable `thiselement` always refers to the element containing the operation.

You can use static code, scriptlets, or both in a template body. Code templates can also contain parameters, which can be strings or of type ModelElement. Ways to add and edit parameters are discussed in the upcoming "Creating and Binding Templates" section.

Internal and External Templates

There are two types of templates you can create: internal and external. An *internal template* is bound to only one operation and is stored within the XDE model itself. To edit this kind of template, you must work through XDE.

An *external template* is stored in an XML file outside of XDE. It can be bound to one or more operations in XDE but does not have to be bound to an operation at all.

Creating and Binding Templates

Because an internal template is bound to one and only one operation, the template creation process and the binding process are the same. When you remove the binding between an internal template and the operation, the template is completely removed.

To add an internal template, follow these steps:

1. In the Explorer window, right-click the operation and choose Code Templates ➢ Bind. XDE displays the Bind Code Template dialog box.
2. Select New to add a new template, or choose Browse to select an existing one.
3. If you are adding a new template, complete steps 4–13. If you are using an existing template, skip to step 14.
4. Select the New button. XDE displays a window for the first part of the template definition process:

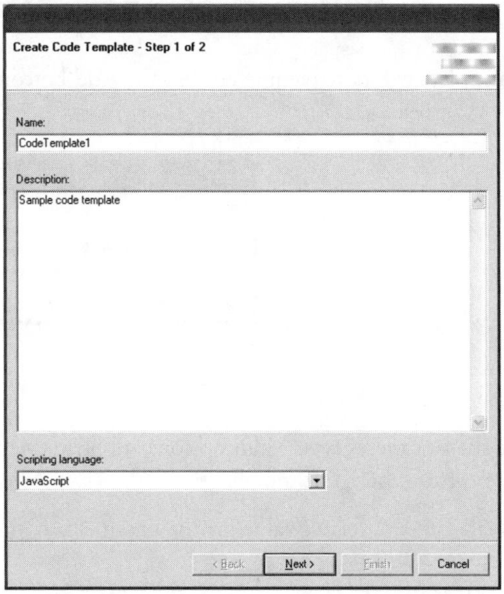

5. Enter the name of the template, and a description. The description is optional, but recommended.
6. In the Scripting Language list box, select the appropriate language. At this time, JavaScript is the only supported scripting language.
7. Click Next to continue. XDE displays a window for the second part of the template definition process:

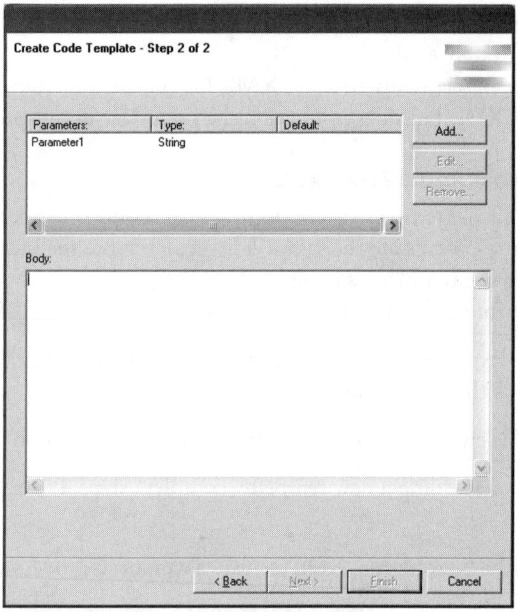

8. If the template will have parameters, use the Add button. This action causes the Add Parameter window to appear:

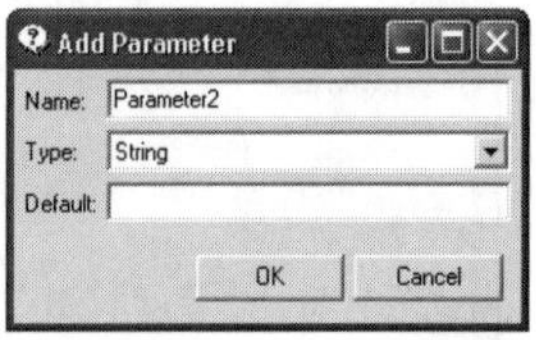

9. Enter the parameter name.
10. Choose the parameter type. Valid options are String or ModelItem. Use ModelItem to pass in an element from the XDE model.
11. (Optional) Enter a default value for the parameter if the parameter type is String.

12. Click OK. Repeat steps 8–11 for any additional parameters.
13. Enter the body of the template and click Finish.
14. On the Bind Code Template dialog box, set the actual values to pass into the template as parameters. Select a parameter, and click the Edit button. Type a value in the Use Custom Value field or select Use Default Value. Repeat for any additional parameters.
15. When you have finished, click the Bind button.

The process for adding an external template is very similar to that used to add an internal template. The differences are that you save the template to an XML file, and you create and bind the template in two separate processes rather than one. To add an external template and bind it to an operation, follow these steps:

1. Add the template:
   - A. Choose Tools ➢ Code Template ➢ Create. XDE displays a window for the first part of the template definition process:

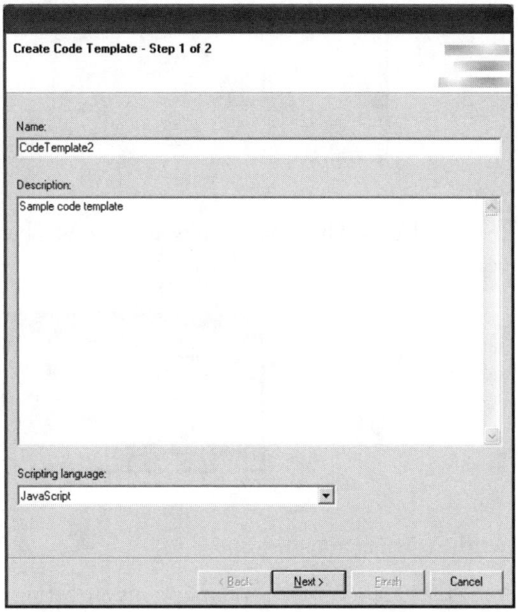

   - B. Enter the name of the template, and a description. The description is optional, but recommended.
   - C. In the Scripting Language list box, select the appropriate language. At this time, JavaScript is the only supported scripting language.

D. Click Next to continue. XDE displays a window for the second part of the template definition process:

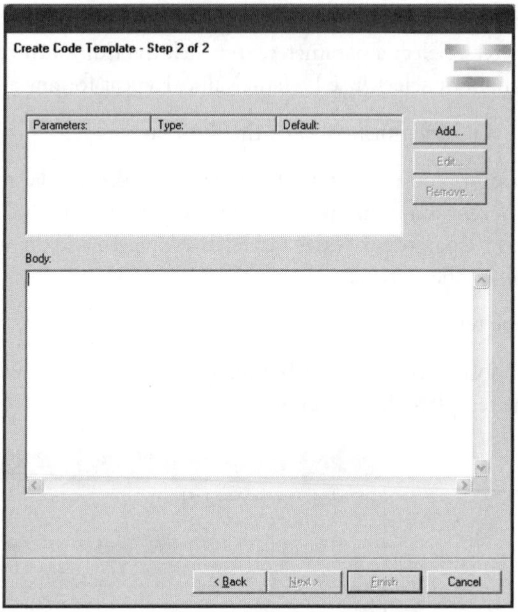

E. If the template will have parameters, use the Add button. The Add Parameter window appears:

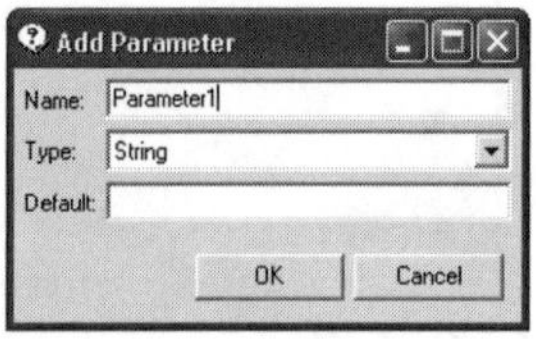

F. Enter the parameter name.

G. Choose the parameter type. Valid options are String or ModelItem. Use ModelItem to pass in an element from the XDE model.

H. (Optional) Enter a default value for the parameter if the parameter type is String.

I. Click OK. Repeat steps E–H for any additional parameters.

J. Enter the body of the template and click Finish.

K. Enter the name of the XML file for the template.

2. Bind the template to an element by following these steps:

   A. In the Explorer window, right-click the element and choose Code Templates ➢ Bind. XDE displays the Bind Code Template dialog box.

   B. Select the Browse button.

   C. Navigate to the new template and select the file.

   D. Edit the value of each parameter by selecting the parameter on the lower portion of the screen and clicking the Edit button. Select the Use Default Value option to use the default value of the parameter, if one was defined. Use the Use Custom Value option to add your own value.

   E. When you have finished, click the Bind button.

Editing a Code Template

If a code template needs to be changed, the process you follow depends upon whether the template is internal or external.

To edit an internal template, right-click the operation in the Explorer window and choose Code Templates ➢ Edit Binding. XDE displays the Edit Code Template Binding window, as shown here. Make any needed changes to the template, and click Save.

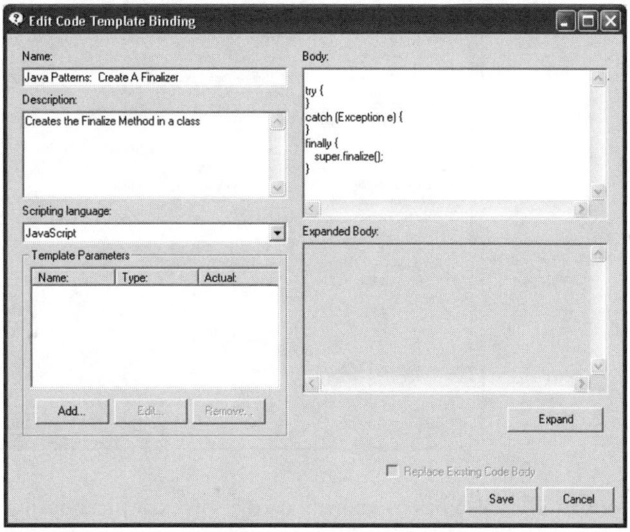

To edit an external template:

1. Choose Tools ➢ Code Templates ➢ Edit File.

2. Navigate to the appropriate XML file. XDE displays the Edit Code Template File dialog box.

3. Make any needed changes to the template, and select Save or Save As.

If you changed any of the template parameters, you need to rebind the template to any operations that were bound to it. As soon as you save the template, XDE notifies you of any operations that should be rebound by producing a list of these operations. To rebind these operations:

1. Select an operation to rebind, and click Rebind. XDE displays the Bind Code Template window for the selected operation.
2. Add actual values to any changed operations.
3. Repeat steps 1 and 2 for any additional operations that need to be rebound.

Synchronizing the Model and Code

Because of the tight integration between the XDE models and the code, synchronizing the two is a very straightforward process. You can opt to manually start the synchronization, or you can have XDE automatically synchronize whenever anything changes.

To automatically synchronize the code and the model when changes are made, open the Preferences window by choosing Window ➢ Preferences. In the tree browser, select Rational XDE, and then Code-Model Synchronization. Click the AutoSync check box to automatically synchronize.

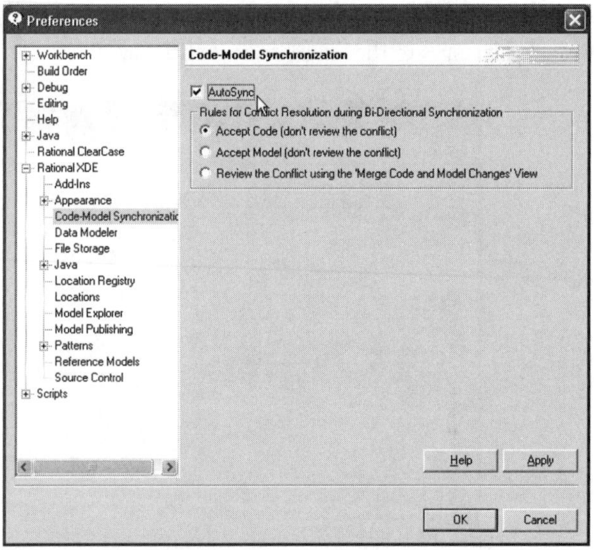

Of course, XDE also has to know how to resolve conflicts during synchronization (this is true whether you are using automatic or manual synchronization). If both the code and model have been updated but are different, which should be changed? In the Code-Model Synchronization Preferences dialog box, indicate how XDE should handle conflicts:

- Accept the code and update the model
- Accept the model and update the code
- Present you with a list of changes so that you can decide, change by change, which one should be updated

CODE GENERATION

Back in the "Setting Java Preferences" section at the beginning of this chapter, we talked about setting up preferences, including code generation options. Later, we talked about the different properties you can set for classes and other model elements, and how to add Javadoc to your model. Once you've set all of these preferences and entered any Javadoc comments, you're ready to generate code.

Almost. There is one other important step—validating the model to be sure the code you end up with is the code you really want. XDE includes a model validation utility that checks your code to make sure it is compliant with the UML with Java syntax. To see a list of the rules used to perform the validation, refer to the "Java Validation Rules" topic in the XDE help. To validate a single element or a selected group of elements, first select the element(s) in the Explorer or on a diagram. Then, right-click and select Validate. To validate everything on a diagram, open the diagram and then choose Diagram ➢ Validate Diagram.

A final step you can take is to assign classes to source code files. By default, XDE generates files with `.java` and `.class` extensions using the class name. It also creates a component in the model representing that file. For example, a Class1 class will generate `Class1.java`, `Class1.class`, and a component called `Class1.java`. Again, XDE uses the class name by default, but if you'd rather use a different file, you can. To use a different file:

1. Right-click a class and choose More Java Actions ➢ Assign to Source File. This brings up the Assign Class To File dialog box:

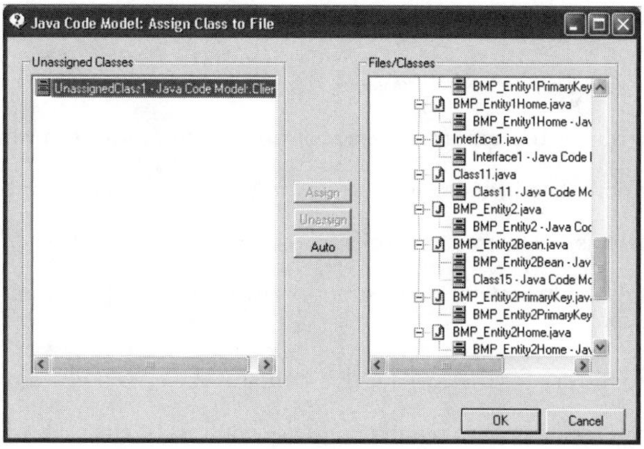

2. In the Unassigned Classes list, select the class(es) to assign to a file.
3. Select the file you want to use from the Files/Classes list, and click the Assign button. The unassigned class(es) are then moved to the Files/Classes list, underneath the file you selected.

Once the model has been validated and classes optionally assigned to source code files, you can generate code. If you have automatic synchronization turned on, the code will have already been updated when you changed the model. If you are manually generating code, right-click the element(s) you'd like to generate, and select Generate Code.

To summarize, here are the steps to follow to generate code:

1. Set the Java code generation preferences.

2. Set the properties of the elements to generate.
3. (Optional) Add Javadoc documentation.
4. Validate the model.
5. (Optional) Assign classes to source files.
6. Right-click the selected element(s) and select Generate Code.
7. Right-click an element and select Browse Code to view the generated code.

What Gets Generated?

In this section, we discuss the code elements that are generated for the different types of model elements.

Classes For each class, XDE creates:

- A Java class of the appropriate type (interface, class, and so on)
- Attributes, an attribute scope, an attribute data type, and a default value if one was specified
- Operation signatures, including parameters and return types
- Any Javadoc that was entered into the model
- A file with a `.java` extension
- A file with a `.class` extension
- Attributes to support any associations or aggregations in which the class participated
- Import statements to support any import relationships for the class
- Extends statements to support any generalization relationships for the class
- Implements statements to support any implements relationships between the class and an interface
- A directory for the package that contains the class if the directory does not already exist

If you've used any code templates, the operations of the class will have the template's code inserted into them. By default, the `finalize()` method of the class will also contain code.

Server Pages and Client Pages A class in the model with a stereotype of <<Server Page>> generates a JSP file. Any methods added to the class are added to the JSP file. If the server page includes a nested client page, the tags from the client page are also added to the JSP file.

If a client page exists that is not nested within a server page, XDE generates an HTML or HTM file.

REVERSE ENGINEERING

Although code generation updates the code from the model, reverse engineering updates the model from the code. A typical pattern begins with a legacy system, reverse engineers it into XDE to examine its architecture, and then generates code as changes are made.

The process you follow depends on whether you are updating the model from code that was previously generated from XDE, or if you are adding new classes. Before you can reverse engineer a web application, you must create a virtual directory model to hold the web elements.

To reverse engineer code that was generated from XDE, right-click a model element (class, package, component, or model) and select Reverse Engineer. You can also add new classes to your model through the reverse-engineering process. To reverse engineer new JAVA, CLASS, or web files into your model:

1. Right-click the model, and choose More Java Actions ➢ Add/Remove Modeled Files. XDE displays the Add/Remove Modeled Files dialog box:

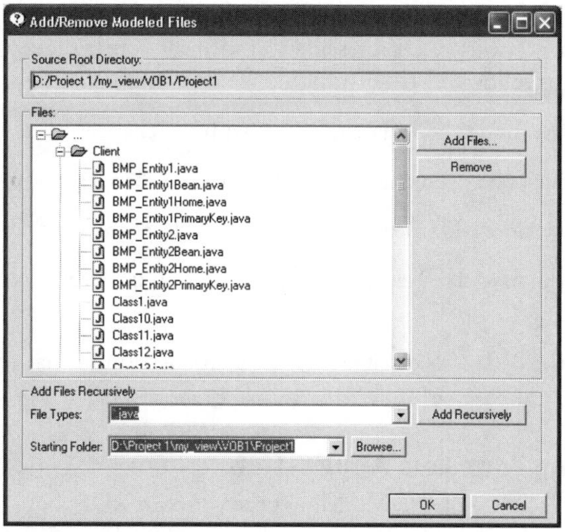

2 Click the Add Files button, and select the files to add.

3. Add or remove files, then click the OK button to start the reverse-engineering process.

Reverse engineering a new EJB JAR file follows a very similar process (to reverse engineer an EJB created from XDE, simply right-click and select Reverse Engineer). During the reverse-engineering process, any classes and interfaces contained within the JAR are added to the model. Information from the deployment descriptor is also added to the model, inside a component. If you generate code later, XDE can then use the information in the component to update the deployment descriptor. If the EJB is not contained within a JAR, you will need to import its deployment descriptor separately.

To reverse engineer a new JAR:

1. Right-click a package and choose More Java Actions ➢ Add/Remove Modeled Files.

2. Click the Add Files button, and select the files to add.

3. Add or remove files, then click the OK button to start the reverse-engineering process.

To import a deployment descriptor:

1. Right-click a package and choose More Java Actions ➢ Import EJB Deployment Descriptor. XDE displays a file selection dialog box.
2. Select the file to reverse engineer, and click Open to begin the reverse-engineering process.

SYNCHRONIZING

Although code generation updates the code and reverse engineering updates the model, the synchronization process may update both. During synchronization, XDE looks for changes in the model or in the code, updating each with changes made to the other. If the same element has been updated in both the model and the code, but different changes were made in the model and the code, you need to resolve the conflict. XDE presents you with the conflict and asks what you want to do. Your options are as follows:

Accept the model Update the code with the changes made to the model.

Accept the code Update the model with the changes made to the code.

Take no action Don't update either the code or the model.

Browse the model Navigate to the element in question so that you can manually review it and make changes.

Browse the code Navigate to the code in question so that you can manually review it and make changes.

Debugging Your Java Application

We've been focusing on the Modeling perspective in XDE, but we switch now to the Debug perspective to view the code and debug the application. The debug functionality in XDE works much the same as debugging in most IDEs. You can walk through the code, set breakpoints, and check the values of variables.

To begin, switch to the Debug perspective by choosing Perspective ➢ Open ➢ Other and then the Debug option. The perspective is added to the perspective toolbar, if it isn't already there, and it has the following symbol: 

The Debug perspective is shown in Figure 5.4. It is broken down into several windows.

The Navigator window Used to locate and select the code files to view.

The Processes window Used to view the processes within the application.

The Breakpoints window Used to view the breakpoints in the code.

The Debug window Used to view the contents of the thread being examined.

The Code window Used to view the application code.

The Outline window Used to view the methods and variables within the current class.

The Variables window Used to view the variables within the current stack frame and their current values.

The Inspector window Used to view the results of inspecting (executing) a specific line of code.

The Tasks window Used to view and edit the debugging tasks that must be completed.

FIGURE 5.4

Debug perspective

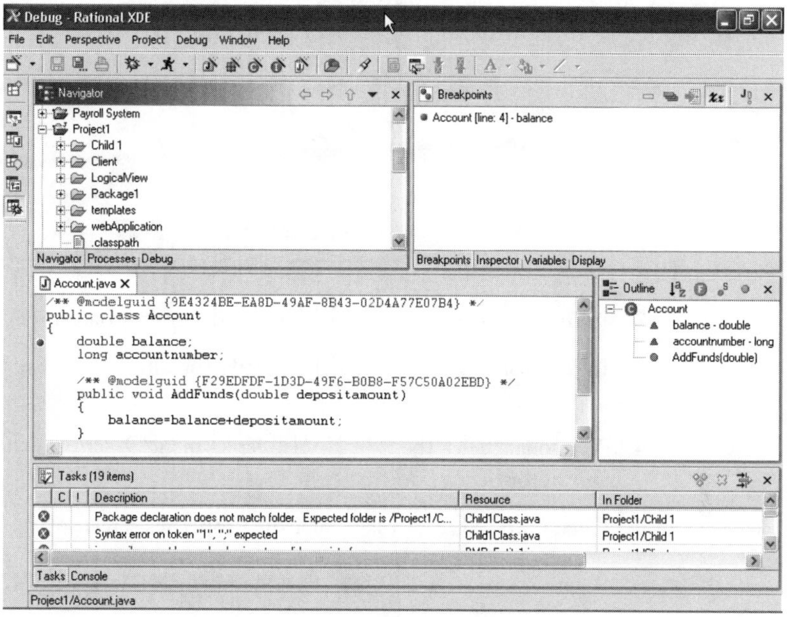

Note that the windows can be combined into a tab folder, as with the Navigator, Process, and Debug windows shown earlier in Figure 5.4. To add a breakpoint, double-click a line of code. Use the Step Into, Step Over, and Step Return options in the Debug menu to walk through the code and debug it. To see the results of running a single line of code as you are debugging, right-click the line and select Inspect. The results are shown in the Inspector window.

Deploying Your Java Application

XDE can automatically generate EAR, JAR, and WAR files to help you deploy your application. To create EAR files, follow these steps:

1. Right-click an element and choose More Java Actions ➢ Deploy. XDE displays the XDE - J2EE Application Deployer dialog box.

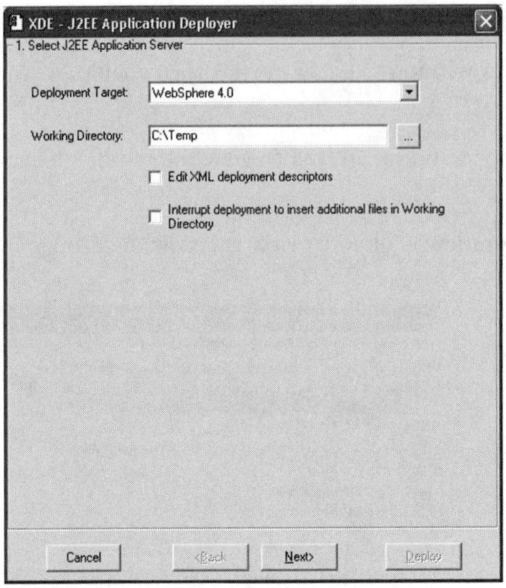

2. In the Deployment Target field, select the appropriate application server or web server.
3. In the Working Directory field, specify the directory to use for temporary files during the deployment process.
4. (Optional) Click the Edit XML Deployment Descriptor check box to edit the deployment descriptor before you create the files.
5. Click Next. XDE displays the Edit Properties screen:

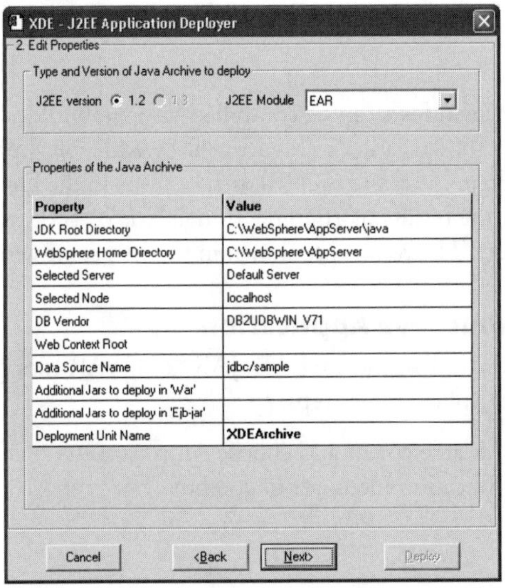

6. Choose the version of J2EE to use. The options are 1.2 or 1.3.
7. In the J2EE Module list, select EAR, EJB-JAR, or WAR.
8. Edit the properties of the file, and click Next.
9. If you selected EAR or WAR files in step 7, XDE prompts you for the contents of the web tier. Select the package(s) and class(es) to include in the WAR file, and click Next to continue.

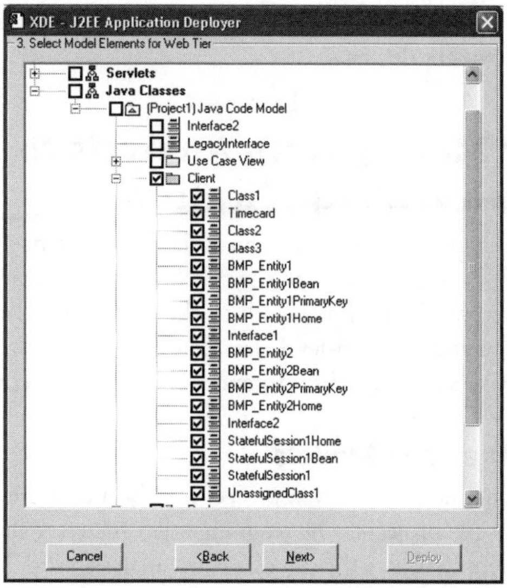

10. If you selected EAR or EJB-JAR files in step 7, XDE prompts you for the contents of the EJB tier. Select the package(s) and class(es) to include in the JAR file, and click Next to continue.

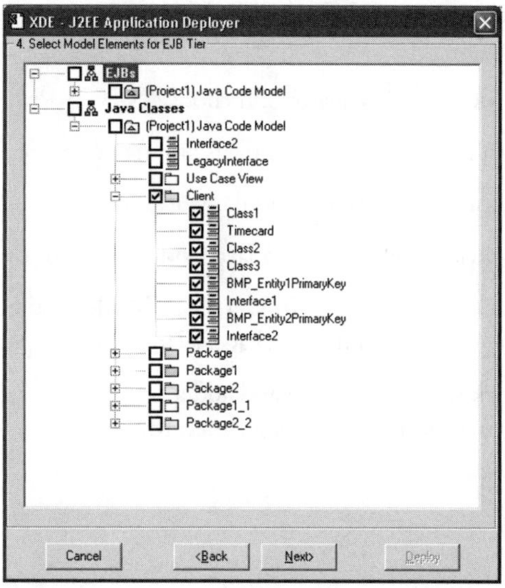

11. XDE displays a summary of the deployment actions. Click Back to make any changes or Deploy to finish the process.
12. If you selected the Edit XML Deployment Descriptor check box, XDE prompts you for the deployment descriptor to edit, and allows you to make changes and save the deployment descriptor.
13. When the process is complete, the results are displayed in the Output window.

When this process is finished, XDE creates the appropriate JAR, EAR, and WAR files for you, as well as the deployment descriptors.

Exercise: Moving from Analysis to Design in a J2EE Application

In the previous chapter, we created an analysis-level sequence diagram and an analysis class diagram for the Submit Timecard use case in the timekeeping application. In this exercise, we continue working on this design model, adding details to the analysis-level sequence diagram to create a design-level sequence diagram and a design-level class diagram. Before starting all of this, we will verify the Java properties to make sure that XDE generates the code properly.

Setting Up the Code Models

In XDE, only one model in a given project may be a code model. Because of this restriction, you must create multiple projects. The recommended structure has you create a project for the non–code generation elements, such as the use cases and analysis model. Then, you create a project for each code model that will be needed. For a J2EE project with EJBs, you need an EJB project and a web project. To begin, follow these steps to add the projects, models, and packages for this exercise:

1. Start Rational XDE.
2. If you are not currently in the Modeling perspective, choose Perspective ➢ Open ➢ Modeling.
3. Right-click in the Navigator and choose New ➢ Project.
4. Select Java Project from the options and name the new project **TimekeepingEJB**.
5. Create another Java project and name it **TimekeepingWeb**.
6. Double-click TimekeepingEJB Java Code Model to open it in the Model Explorer.
7. Right-click TimekeepingEJB Java Code Model in the Model Explorer and choose Add Java ➢ Package to create a new package. Name the new package **com**.
8. Right-click the new package and add a new Java package named **timekeeping**. Then add another package; name this one **timecard**.

9. Add new packages to the timekeeping package named **PayCode**, **PayPeriod**, **StatusReport**, and **TimecardControl**.

10. Open the Design Model in the Timekeeping System project.

11. Right-click the Design Model in the Model Explorer and choose Add UML ➢ Package. Create a layer package named Business by typing **<<layer>> Business**.

12. Create two more layer packages named **Presentation** and **Integration**.

13. Right-click the Business layer and choose Add UML ➢ Subsystem. Create a subsystem named **Timecard**.

14. Create a package within the subsystem named **Interface Operation Realizations**.

15. Copy the Submit Timecard use case realization from the Analysis Elements package and paste it into the Interface Operation Realizations package.

16. Right-click the TimekeepingWeb project in the Navigator and choose Add New ➢ Model. Select Virtual Directory Model and name it **Timekeeping Virtual Directory Model**.

17. Open the Timekeeping Virtual Directory Model in the Model Explorer and choose Add UML ➢ Package to create a new package. Name the new package **Timekeeping**.

18. Right-click the TimekeepingWeb Java Code Model in the Model Explorer and choose Add Java ➢ Package to create a new package. Name the new package **com**.

19. Right-click the new package and add a new Java package named **timekeeping**. Then add another package; name this one **presentation**.

20. The structure of the models should be as shown here:

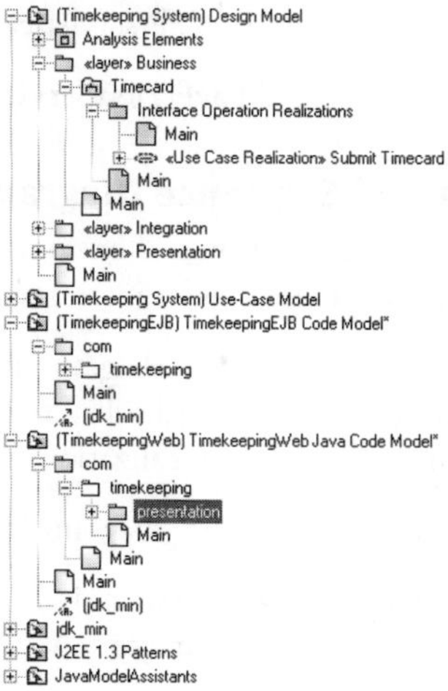

Create the EJBs

Now that the structure for the projects is set up, you need to create the EJBs. In the Analysis Elements package, you created entity classes for the entities in the system. Now you need to create EJBs for these entities. You also need to create a session bean for the operation.

1. Right-click the Timecard entity class in the Analysis Elements package. Choose Transform ➢ CMP 2.0 Entity Bean.
2. Select `TimekeepingEJB Code Model/com/timekeeping/Timecard` as the EJB location.
3. Repeat the creation of entity beans for the other entity classes.
4. Right-click the TimecardController control class in the Analysis Elements package. Choose Transform ➢ Stateful Session Bean.
5. Select `TimekeepingEJB Code Model/com/timekeeping/TimecardControl` as the EJB location.

Create the Presentation Layer

Now that you have created the EJBs, you need to create the presentation layer. You do this by creating server pages in the Virtual Directory Model. Then, you need to create the servlets for the application.

1. Open the Main diagram in the Timekeeping package of the Virtual Directory Model.
2. Select the Web toolbox and add a Server Page to the Main diagram. Name the server page **Main.JSP**.
3. Add two more Server Pages to the Main diagram and name them **PayPeriods.jsp** and **Timecard.jsp**.
4. Open the Main diagram in the presentation package of the TimekeepingWeb Java Code Model.
5. From the Java toolbox, add an HTTP servlet called **MainServlet** to the Main diagram.
6. Add additional servlets named **PayPeriodServlet** and **TimecardServlet** to the Main diagram.

Create the Design-Level Sequence Diagram

You have already created the presentation and business layers. The next step is to create a design-level sequence diagram to show how these objects interact.

1. Navigate to the Basic Flow sequence diagram in the Timekeeping Design Model. Open the Business layer, and then the Timecard subsystem, the Interface Operation Realizations package, the Submit Timecard use-case realization, and the Basic Flow interaction instance.
2. Create a new lifeline in the sequence diagram called **Main**.
3. Map the Main lifeline to the `Main.jsp_client1` client page located within the `Main.jsp` server page in the Timekeeping Virtual Directory Model.
4. Drag the MainServlet class to the sequence diagram to add a new object mapped to the MainServlet to the sequence diagram.

5. Drag the PayPeriodServlet, TimecardServlet, Timecard.jsp_client1, and PayPeriod.jsp_client1 classes to the sequence diagram.
6. Map the TimecardController object to the TimecardController EJBRemoteInterface from the Timekeeping EJB Code Model.
7. Map the PayPeriod object to the PayPeriod EJBLocalInterface from the Timekeeping EJB Code Model.
8. Map the PayCode object to the PayCode EJBLocalInterface from the Timekeeping EJB Code Model.
9. Map the Timecard object to the Timecard EJBLocalInterface from the Timekeeping EJB Code Model.
10. Map the StatusReport object to the StatusReport EJBLocalInterface from the Timekeeping EJB Code Model.
11. Drag the PayPeriodHome, PayCodeHome, TimecardHome, and StatusReportHome interfaces from the Timekeeping EJB Code Model to the sequence diagram to create objects mapped to these interfaces. The lifelines in the sequence diagram should be as shown here:

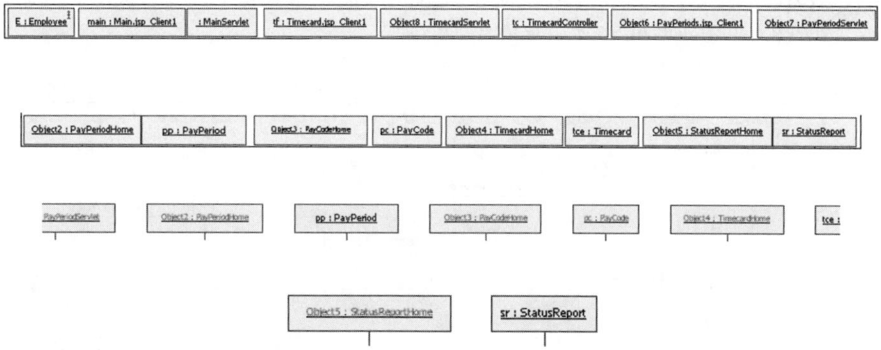

Add Messages to the Design-Level Sequence Diagram

Now that you have set up the lifelines, you need to create the messages to go between the objects.

1. Drag the end of the analysis message \//Enter a Timecard\ from the Timecard.jsp_Client1 object to the Main.jsp_Client1 object. The message should now originate with the actor and end on Main.jsp_Client1.
2. Just under message 1, add a message from Main.jsp_Client1 to MainServlet. Click the message text to display a drop-down list box. Select the `DoGet()` method from the drop-down list box.

3. Right-click message 3, an analysis message called //Enter Timecard( ), and select Delete From Model. This analysis message is no longer needed.
4. Delete the analysis message called //Get Pay Periods from the TimecardController to the PayPeriod object.
5. Create a new message under message 2, from the MainServlet object to the TimecardController object. Click the text of the message to change it. Type **GetPayPeriods**.
6. Right-click the new message and select Create Operation From Message.
7. Add new messages and delete analysis messages until the diagram appears as in the following graphic. Be sure to create new operations from messages for any new messages added (except the <<forward>> messages or any remaining analysis messages, as shown in the graphic). Note that the `doPost()` and `FindByPrimaryKey()` methods already exist, and can be selected from a message's drop-down list box when needed.

   Also, to add parameters to a new method, find the method in the Explorer, right-click, and choose Add Java ➢ Parameter. Do not type in the parenthesis and parameters on the sequence diagram as you are naming the message.

NOTE *These two sections of the sequence diagram are meant to be read side-by-side, with the Employee actor at the top far left and the StatusReport object at the top far right.*

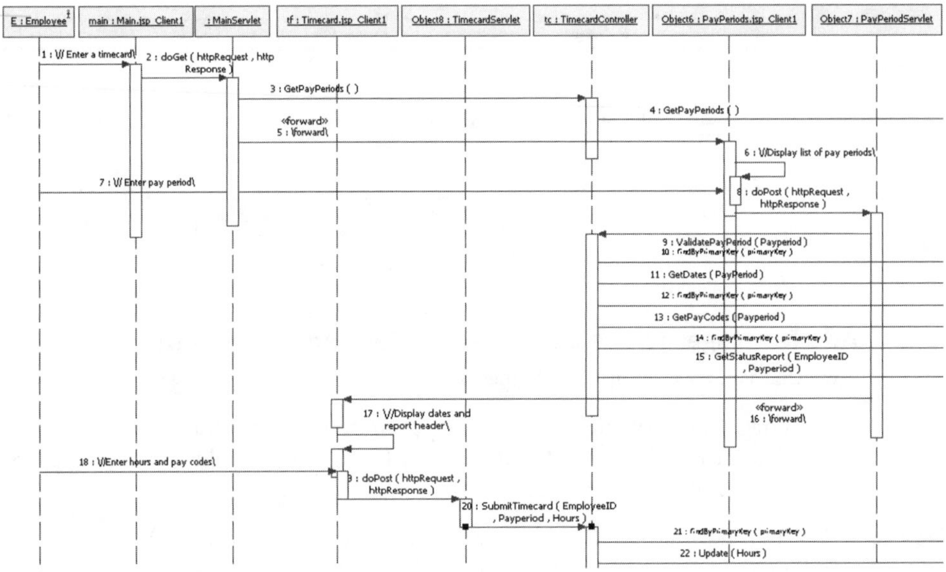

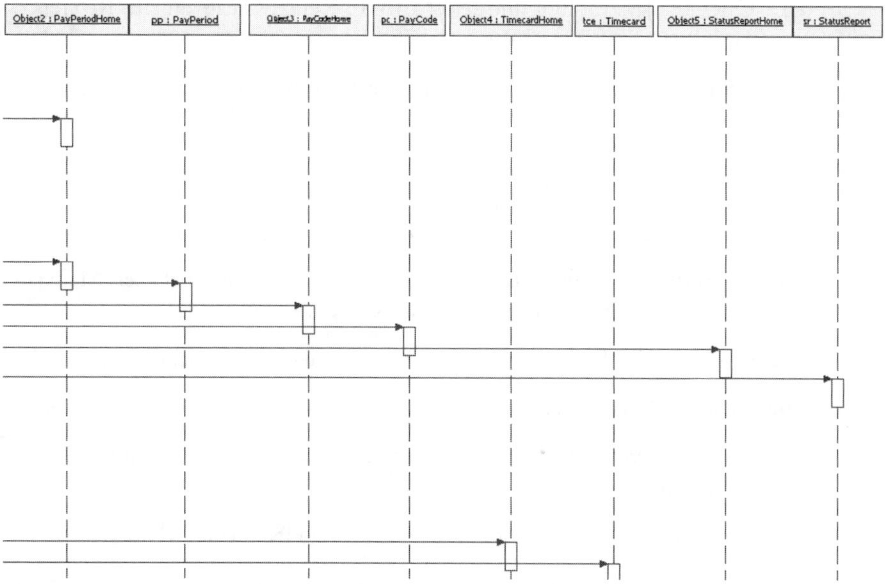

Create a Design-Level Class Diagram

The next step in the exercise is to create a class diagram to display all of the classes you've just created.

1. In the Timekeeping Design Model, right-click the package Interface Operation Realizations, and choose Add Diagram ➢ Class. Name the new diagram **Submit Timecard**.

2. Drag and drop the PayCodeEJB, PayPeriodEJB, StatusReportEJB, TimecardEJB, and TimecardControllerEJB components from the timekeeping package in the TimekeepingEJB Code Model to the diagram.

3. Drag and drop the MainServlet, PayPeriodServlet, and TimecardServlet classes from the TimekeepingWeb Java Code Model to the diagram.

4. Drag and drop the Main.jsp and Main.jsp_client1 pages from the Timekeeping Virtual Directory Model to the diagram.

5. Drag and drop the PayPeriods.jsp and PayPeriods.jsp_client1 pages from the Timekeeping Virtual Directory Model to the diagram.

6. Drag and drop the Timecard.jsp and Timecard.jsp_client1 pages from the Timekeeping Virtual Directory Model to the diagram.

Add Relationships to the Class Diagram

In the final step, you add the remaining relationships to the class diagram. These relationships include the EJB references, forwards, submits, and dependencies.

1. Open the Java toolbox and select EJB Reference. Create an EJB Reference between the TimecardControllerEJB and PayCodeEJB components.
2. Create EJB references between TimecardControllerEJB and the following:
   - PayPeriodEJB
   - StatusReportEJB
   - TimecardEJB
3. Open the Java toolbox and create a directed association between Main.jsp_client1 and MainServlet. Stereotype this relationship as **<<submit>>**.
4. Create an EJB Reference between MainServlet and TimecardControllerEJB.
5. Create a directed association between MainServlet and PayPeriod.jsp stereotyped as **forward.**
6. Create a directed association between PayPeriod.jsp_client1 and PayPeriodServlet stereotyped as **submit**.
7. Create a directed association between PayPeriodServlet and Timecard.jsp stereotyped as **forward.**
8. Create an EJB Reference from PayPeriodServlet to TimecardControllerEJB.
9. Create a directed association from Timecard.jsp_client1 to TimecardServlet stereotyped as **submit.**
10. Create an EJB Reference from TimecardServlet to TimecardControllerEJB. The class diagram should appear as follows:

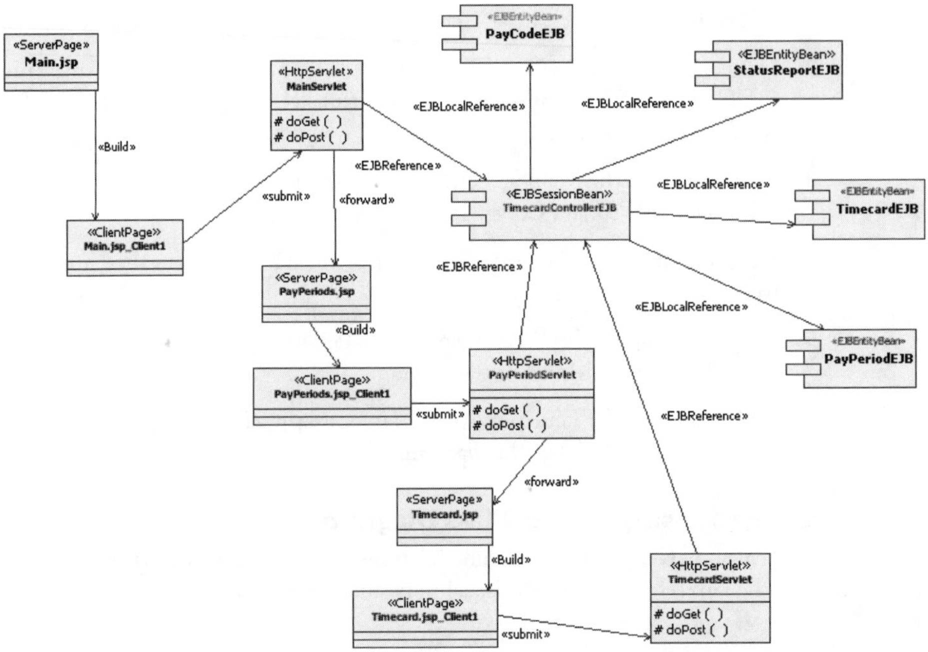

Summary

In this chapter, we examined the different pieces of a design model for Java. We walked through the process, from defining the Java model and setting preferences, to creating the UML diagrams, to generating code and deploying an application. The sequence of topics, however, is not rigid. In XDE, you may start with the code, and then work on the diagrams. You will most likely switch from the diagrams to the code and back again many times before the end of the project.

In the next chapter, we discuss these same topics, but from the perspective of a .NET application rather than from a Java application.

Chapter 6

Modeling Visual Studio .NET Elements in XDE

THIS CHAPTER EXPLORES HOW to model ASP .NET, C#, and Visual Basic .NET applications using XDE. Just as XDE for Java runs directly from the WebSphere IDE, XDE for .NET is used directly in the Visual Studio .NET IDE. In this chapter, we discuss how to model, reverse engineer, and generate code for a .NET application.

Featured in this chapter:

- Creating projects for a .NET application
- Setting .NET preferences
- Modeling .NET elements in the UML
- Modeling .NET elements in XDE
- Building a design model
- Working with .NET code

A Word about Terminology

Before we get into the details of modeling Visual Studio applications, let's go through a little terminology. Because UML, XDE, and Visual Studio often use the same terms to mean different things, you may find such terminology confusing.

For instance, a *field* in C# or Visual Basic is equivalent to what the UML calls an *attribute*. Visual Studio provides another definition of attribute—a means of defining some declarative information about C# code. In other words, an attribute in Visual Studio functions as a way to define and use metadata in a .NET application. In this chapter, when we use the word *attribute*, we're referring to an attribute as defined by the UML. When we are referring to an attribute as defined by Visual Studio, we'll use the term *Visual Studio attribute*.

Properties in Visual Studio are equivalent to an attribute and its *get* and *set* operations (accessor methods) in the UML. XDE has an alternate meaning for the term properties. In XDE, a property refers to one of a set of code-generation properties that control how code is generated from the model. We make it clear from the context of the term which definition we are referring to. In general, the tables in this chapter list the XDE properties, while the text discusses Visual Studio properties.

Methods, functions, and *sub procedures* in Visual Studio are all equivalent to an *operation* in the UML. We use the term *operation* to generically refer to any of these three items.

Creating Projects for a .NET Application

XDE runs directly from within Visual Studio .NET, so you can continue to work in the Visual Studio IDE with which you are already familiar. XDE simply adds some new menu options and views that allow you to create the UML, reverse engineer, and generate code from within Visual Studio.

You can use an XDE project to manage the design and code for an application, including the source files and UML diagrams. In this regard, using XDE is no different from using Visual Studio. You create an XDE project by first creating a Visual Studio solution and then creating a Visual Studio C#, C++, or Visual Basic project. In Visual Studio, simply choose File ➢ New ➢ Project.

Once you've created a project, right-click it in the Solution Explorer. You should see options called Synchronize, Reverse Engineer, and Browse Model, which XDE has added.

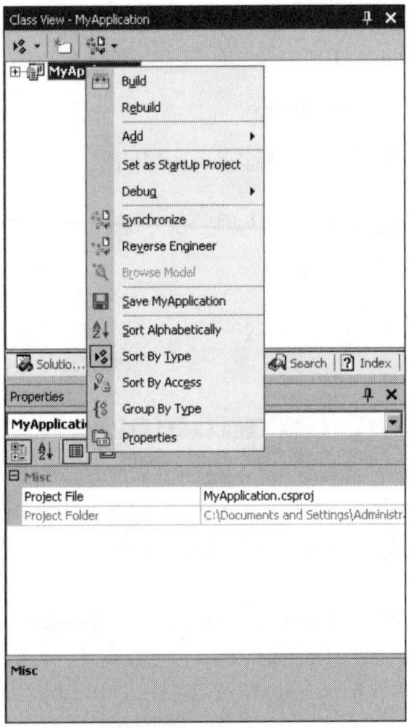

Using Models

Now that you have created your project, the next step is to create the model(s) that you will use to maintain the application design. In XDE, models are contained within the Visual Studio projects, and it is the model that contains the actual UML diagrams and other elements. Here are three types of models you may want to use on your project:

Blank model This model can hold UML elements, but you cannot use it to generate code or reverse engineer.

Code model You can use a code model to forward engineer code from the model, reverse engineer code into the model, and keep the model and the code synchronized. Each project can have only one code model.

Reference model You can use a reference model to include external resources, either models or code, in your project. You cannot modify reference models but you can use them in multiple projects.

You can see the models and their contents in the Model Explorer:

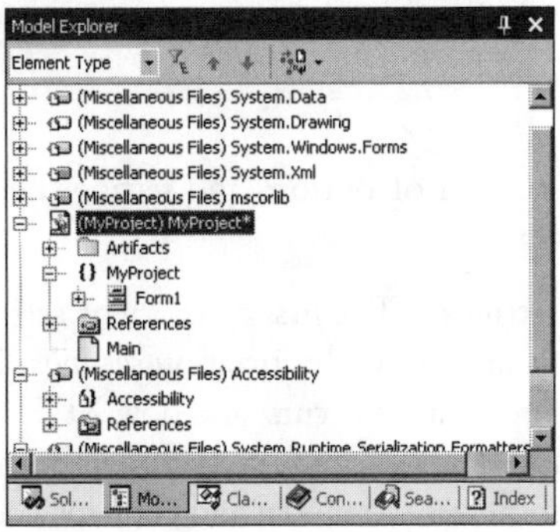

As you can see, the individual files and directories of your application all appear under the model in the Model Explorer, as do the classes and relationships in the model.

In addition, all of the standard .NET system namespaces and classes are listed in the Model Explorer, ready to be referenced and used in your model. You cannot change them, of course, but you can include them in a project to save yourself from having to model them manually so that you can use them in your application.

You can create as many different models as you need for your application, but each project may contain only one code model. The simplest way to create a code model is to right-click the project in the Solution Explorer window, and select Synchronize. When you do this, XDE automatically creates a model for you.

To manually create a model:

1. Choose File ➢ Add New Item.
2. Select the Rational XDE folder and the type of model you want to create. If you don't have an existing solution, choose File ➢ New ➢ File, and then the type of XDE model you want to create. Either way, XDE creates a new model for you, with the extension `.mdx`.

Setting .NET Preferences

The final step in setting up your project is setting the different preferences that XDE makes available. You can, of course, change any of these at any time, but we've found it easier to set all of this up at the beginning of a project. You can view or set the preferences by choosing Tools ➢ Options and selecting the Rational XDE folder from the left-hand side of the dialog box:

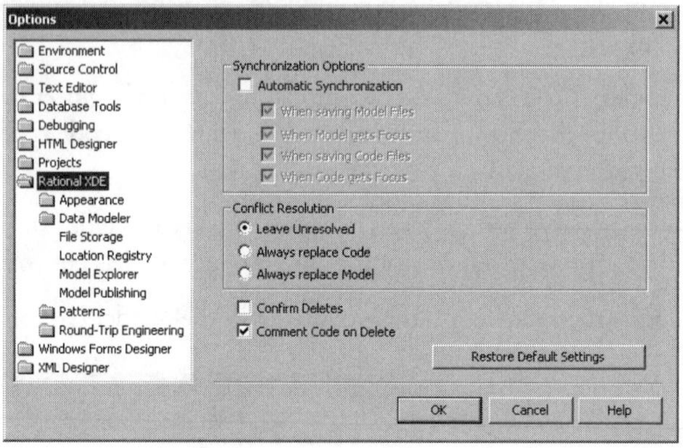

There are a great number of options and settings here; let's discuss selected settings that you might want to consider.

Synchronization settings The first category of settings, which can be found in the Round-Trip Engineering section, are the synchronization settings. The Synchronization Settings area is used to control when synchronization occurs, and how XDE should resolve conflicts between the model and code during synchronization. The Automatic Synchronization check box controls whether XDE automatically synchronizes the model and code for you, or whether you'd rather manually synchronize them. You can use the Conflict Resolution area to let XDE know how you want to handle conflicts. If an item has been changed in both the code and the model but has been changed differently in each, this option tells XDE whether to accept changes in the code or in the model. If you select Leave Unresolved, XDE won't change either the code or the model during synchronization.

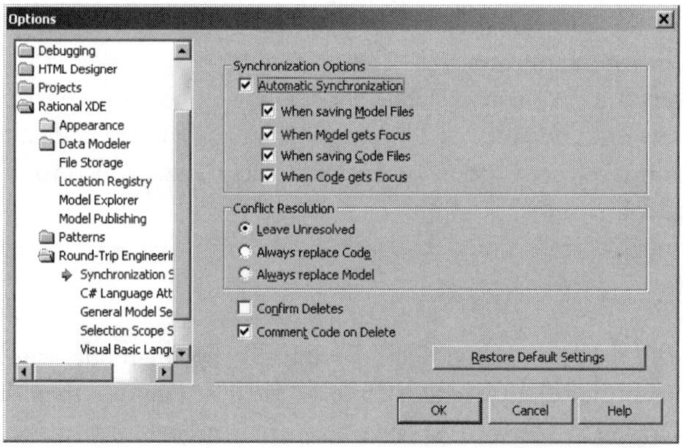

C# and Visual Basic language attributes options The C# Language Attributes and Visual Basic Language Attributes options specify the data types that are recognized from each of these languages. These options are also found in the Round-Trip Engineering section. During reverse engineering, fields and properties with a data type listed here are reverse engineered as an attribute; fields and properties with other data types are reverse engineered as a relationship.

Appearance settings Let's move out of the Round-Trip Engineering section now and look at the appearance settings. The Appearance folder is used to control how the different UML diagrams look by default. For example, you can set whether attributes and operations are shown by default on a class diagram and whether stereotypes should be displayed as an icon or as a label. Of course, you can change these appearance settings for any number of elements in the model.

Model Explorer settings Another of the areas directly under the Rational XDE folder is the Model Explorer area. The Model Explorer area controls how elements are displayed in the Model Explorer window. You can, for example, change how the elements are sorted and filter elements out of the window.

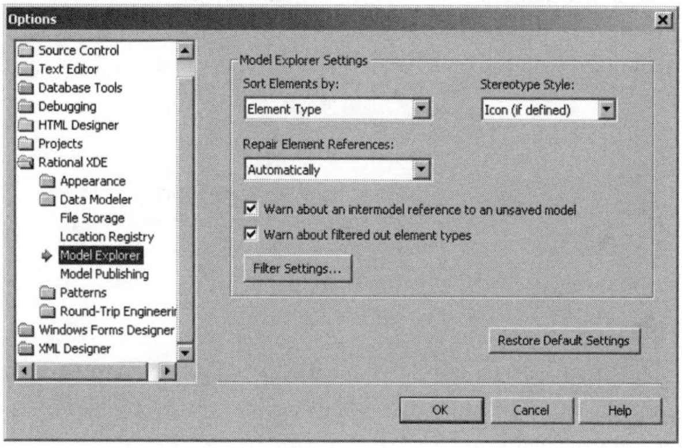

TIP *As we mentioned earlier, it's a good idea to set all of these options up front. This helps ensure consistency across the model and code and that the code XDE generates is the code you want.*

Now that we've set up XDE, let's take a moment to see how .NET elements are mapped to the UML.

Modeling .NET Elements in the UML

In this section, we take a brief look at how each of the significant constructs in the C# and Visual Basic .NET programming languages map to the UML. We discussed some of these topics from an analysis standpoint in Chapter 4, "Integrated Use Case Management." We quickly review the definitions here, but if you need further information about the UML constructs and relationships, please refer back to Chapter 4.

Solutions and Projects

A Visual Studio solution does not have any direct UML representation. If you need to create a diagram that includes a solution, you can create a component with a stereotype of <<solution>>, but you won't generally need this.

The projects within a solution are also generally not modeled in the UML. As we'll see later, each project is added to XDE, and a code model is created for each. The projects themselves, though, are not typically modeled. If you need to model a project, you can create a component with a stereotype of <<project>>.

Namespaces

A namespace is modeled as a package, which is a generic UML construct that allows you to group items together. It is similar in purpose to a directory on a filesystem. In the UML, each namespace can be represented as a package with a stereotype of <<namespace>>, as shown here:

Directories

The physical directories in your Visual Studio solution map to stereotyped packages in the UML. Each package that represents a directory is given the stereotype <<directory>>, and contains the classes that are physically located in that directory.

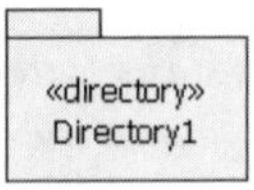

Source Code Files

Your project's source code files, such as the files with the `.cs` extension files in C#, can be modeled in the UML as components with a stereotype of <<file>>. Each file is its own component, and dependencies between the components show the compilation dependencies between the source code files. In the UML, a component is modeled using the following symbol:

The components will show you the physical source files that you have. However, they don't show you which classes are actually implemented in those components; you may need to add ElementResidence relationships to see this information. An ElementResidence relationship is a stereotyped dependency that lets you know which classes are included in a particular component. Here is an example:

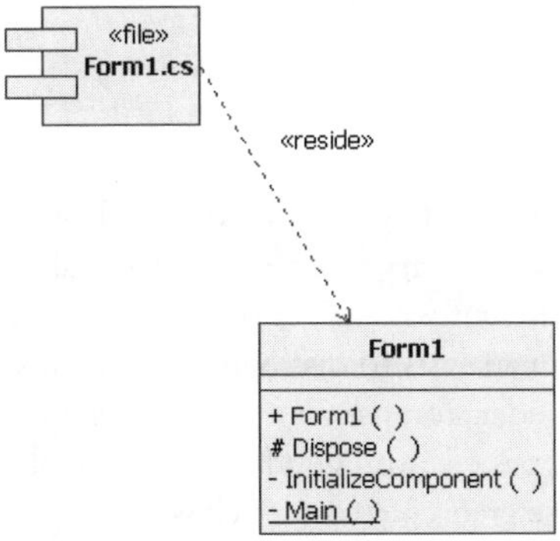

Classes

In the UML, a class is represented as a rectangle with three compartments. The top compartment (the name compartment in the UML) displays the class name and, optionally, its stereotype. The name is italicized if the class is abstract. The middle compartment displays the fields, or attributes, of the class. The lower compartment displays the methods, or operations, of the class. Here is an example of some C# code, as well as the UML representation of that code:

```
Public class Timecard {
      public double TotalHours;
      public double GetTotalHours() {
         return TotalHours;
      }
}
```

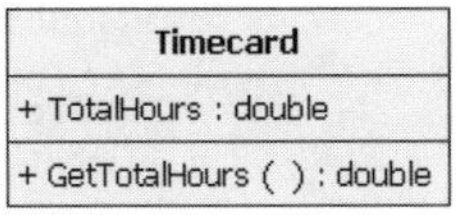

The Visual Basic code for this class would be as follows:

```
Public Class TimeCard
   Public TotalHours as Double
   Public Function GetTotalHours() as Double
      Return TotalHours
   End Function
End Class
```

As you can see, there's nothing in the UML representation that specifically marks the class as Visual Basic or C#. However, the data types used can suggest a language, and the model that contains the class has a stereotype that tells you what language is being used.

TIP *This is the default notation, but the UML does allow you to suppress the attributes and/or operations on a class diagram to keep the diagram from getting too cluttered. See the "Building a Design-Level Class Diagram" section later in this chapter for instructions.*

CLASS STEREOTYPES

There are a number of stereotypes for classes, such as <<interface>>, <<utility>>, <<thread>>, and of course, the <<boundary>>, <<entity>>, and <<control>> stereotypes we used in analysis. These help us figure out what types of classes we're dealing with in our model. You use boundary classes, for example, in analysis to distinguish the forms, windows, and system interfaces from the other classes in the model. You use an interface stereotype to mark the interfaces in the model. Although the stereotypes give you good information about the type of class you're working with, we don't have to assign a stereotype to every class in design. If a class is given a stereotype, it appears in the name compartment of the class:

FIELDS AND PROPERTIES

In the UML, a field is modeled in one of two ways: as an attribute of the class that contains it, or as a relationship between two classes (semantically, an attribute and a composition association are the same, so we can use either). A property is modeled only as an attribute, along with the get and set operations for the property. Attributes are displayed in the middle compartment of a class on a class diagram. Here is some code, which is represented first as an attribute and then as a relationship in the UML in the graphics that follow:

C#

```
Public Class Timecard
{
   publicintTotalHours
}
```

Visual Basic

```
Public class Timecard
   Public TotalHours as Integer
End Class
```

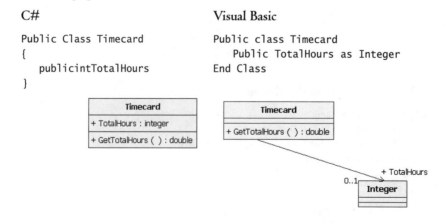

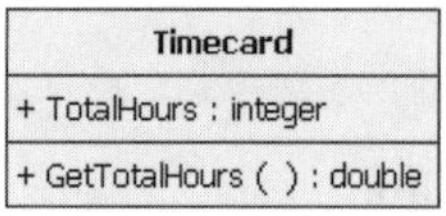

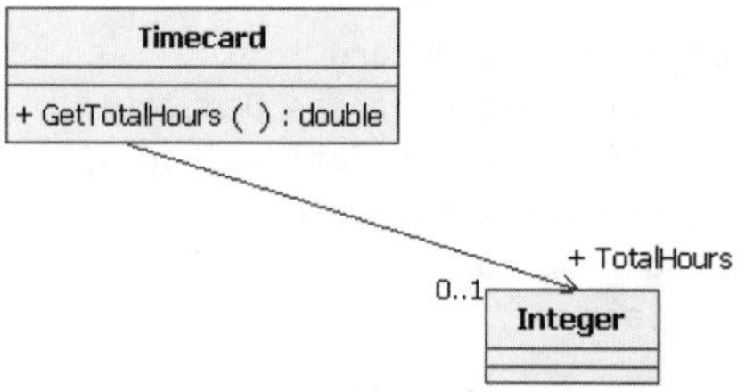

An attribute is listed on a class diagram in the following format:

```
AttributeName:DataType = DefaultValue
```

where the default value is optional.

So should we model a field as an attribute or a relationship? Although all attributes are technically relationships to objects of other classes, simple data types such as `float` or `int` tend to be modeled as attributes. More complex field data types, such as `Employee`, tend to be modeled as relationships between classes.

Visibility

In the UML, the scope, or visibility, of an attribute is documented using one of four symbols. The UML visibility notation includes the following:

+	Public
–	Private
#	Protected
~	Package (Internal in C# or Friend in Visual Basic)

An attribute in C# or Visual Basic may be set to Public, Private, or Protected visibility. In addition, C# supports Internal visibility, and Visual Basic supports Friend visibility. The visibility notation appears just to the left of the attribute name on a class diagram.

Methods, Delegates, and Events

In the UML, methods and functions are represented as operations of a class or interface. The operations for a class are listed in the lower compartment of the class on a class diagram, and have the following format:

```
MethodName([Parm1Kind]Parm1:DataType, [Parm2Kind]Parm2:DataType):ReturnType
```

Let's take a quick look at the pieces of an operation signature in the UML:

`MethodName` The name of the method or operation. Be sure to use the naming conventions from your organization. The name you enter here is the name used in the code.

`Parm1Kind` Identifies the first parameter as an input parameter, output parameter, or input and output parameter. *`Parm1Kind`* should be replaced with `in`, `out`, or `inout`.

`Parm1` The name of the first parameter. Again, be sure to follow your organization's naming conventions.

`DataType` The data type (`int`, `float`, and so on) of the parameter.

`ReturnType` The data type of the return of the operation.

Parameters should be separated by commas. If there are no parameters, just use empty parentheses. On a class diagram, you can display just the operation name or the full signature. A few examples of methods in UML format are listed here:

- `Add([in] X:int, [in] Y:float):float`
- `PrintEmployeeTimecard([in] CurrentEmp:Employee):int`
- `Deposit([inout] MyAccount:Account, [in] Amount:float):void`

Here is an example of the code for a method, and the corresponding UML:

C#

```
Public int Method1 (int parm1) {
   Return 0
}
```

Visual Basic

```
Public function Method1(parm1 as Integer)
   Return 0
End Function
```

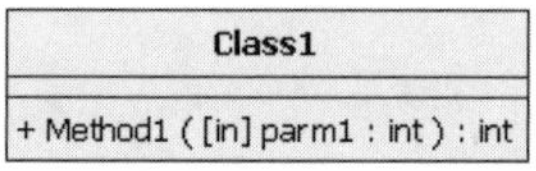

As with attributes, visibility is indicated using a + for Public, – for Private, # for Protected, or ~ for Package. Method names in design should follow your organization's naming conventions and standards.

Delegates are modeled as separate classes in the UML, and are given the stereotype <<delegate>>. The delegate class has one operation by default, called `Invoke`. The `Invoke` operation is given the same operation signature as the delegate. An event is modeled as an association between a class and a delegate.

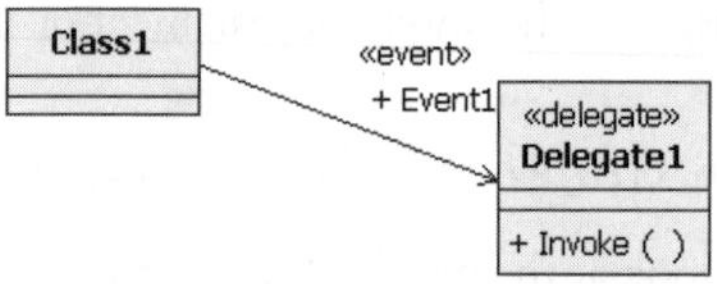

Interfaces

An interface is modeled in the UML as a class with a stereotype of <<interface>>. Here is the code for this:

C#

```
Interface Interface1 {
   Void Method1();
}
```

Visual Basic

```
Interface Interface1
   Sub Method1()
   End Sub
End Interface
```

There are two ways to represent an interface: using the standard UML class (box) representation, or using a circle icon:

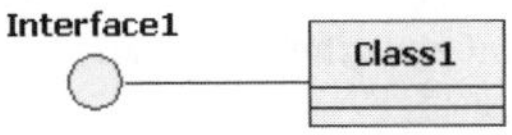

Implements Relationships and Interface Realization

In Visual Basic, we use the `implements` keyword when an interface is realized by a class. In C#, we use the syntax `class : interface`. In the UML, we use a realization relationship to show the relationship between a class and an interface. Here is an example of some code and the corresponding UML:

C#

```
Interface Interface1 {
   Void Method1();
}

Public Class Class1 : Interface1 {
   Public void Method1() {
   }
}
```

Visual Basic

```
Interface Interface1
   Sub Method1(
   End Sub
End Interface

Public Class Class1
   Implements Interface1
   Public Sub Method1() implements
➥Interface1.Method1
   End Sub
End Class
```

Relationships

In analysis, we got as far as defining the classes and the relationships between them. We identified each relationship as an association, aggregation, or generalization; decided if each association was unidirectional or bidirectional; and decided if each aggregation was a composite aggregation. Now, we add some more detail to the relationships, and we also discuss a couple of new types of relationships. Although analysis was language-independent, we now know what language we're using, so the relationships discussed in the next several sections will map specifically to .NET.

ASSOCIATION RELATIONSHIPS

An *association relationship* is a structural relationship between two classes. In the code, the relationship is supported by fields. Listings 6.1 and 6.2 are examples of some code, followed by the UML representation.

LISTING 6.1: C# CODE EXAMPLE—ASSOCIATION

```
public class Employee
{
        private TimeCard theTimeCard;

   public void RecordTime(DateTime Date, long NumHours)
   {
      theTimeCard.AddTCEntry(Date, NumHours);
   }
}

public class Timecard
{
   private Employee theEmployee;

   public void AddTCEntry(DateTime Workdate, long Hours)
   {
   int ErrorCode;
TimeCardEntry newTimeCardEntry;

      newTimeCardEntry = new TimeCardEntry(Workdate,Hours);
      ErrorCode = newTimeCardEntry.Validate();
   }
}
```

LISTING 6.2: VISUAL BASIC CODE EXAMPLE—ASSOCIATION

```
Public Class Employee
   Private theTimeCard as TimeCard

   Public Sub RecordTime(ByVal WorkDate As DateTime, ByVal Hours As Long)
        theTimeCard.AddTCEntry(WorkDate, Hours)
    End Sub
End Class

Public Class TimeCard
   Private theEmployee as Employee

   Public Sub AddTCEntry(ByVal Workdate As DateTime, ByVal Hours As Long)
        Dim myTCEntry As TimeCardEntry
        Dim ErrorCode As Integer
```

```
        myTCEntry = New TimeCardEntry(WorkDate, Hours)
        ErrorCode = myTCEntry.Validate()
    End Sub
End Class
```

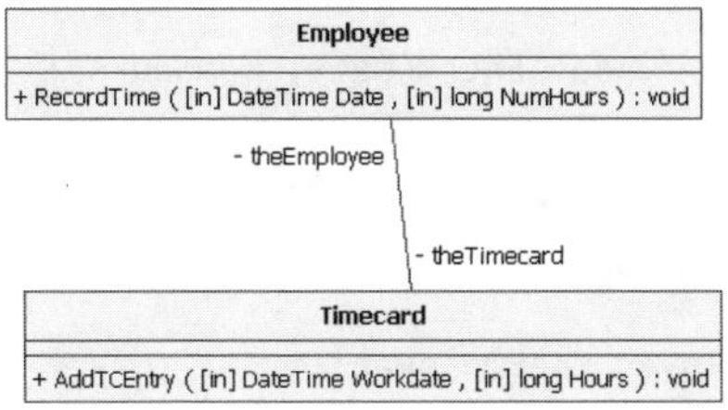

As you can see, attributes exist to support both sides of the relationship. For Employee to access its instance of Timecard, it need only use its own theTimecard field. For Timecard to access its Employee, it can use the theTimecard field. The example above is bidirectional; each class is a client of the other, and a supplier for the other. Most associations, however, are unidirectional. In this case, there is a field created at only one end of the relationship. Using the examples in Listings 6.1 and 6.2, if the association goes from Employee to Timecard, the theTimecard field will still exist in Employee, but the theTimecard field will not exist in Timecard.

You can also create a *reflexive association,* which is an association between a class and itself. This simply suggests that one instance of the class has an association with another instance of the class. The following is the UML representation for a reflexive association:

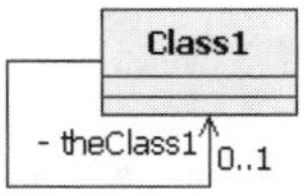

Aggregation Relationships

An aggregation is an association relationship that logically fits the "whole/part" pattern. For example, a tire is part of a car, an Employee is part of an EmployeeList, a book is part of a library, and so on. Anytime you have a "part of" relationship, you can use an aggregation. The code generated for an aggregation is exactly the same as that generated for an association.

There are two types of aggregations: standard aggregations and compositions.

Standard Aggregation Relationships

A *standard aggregation* connects two objects whose lifetimes are independent. That is, the "whole" object and the "part" object are created and destroyed independently of one another. A standard aggregation is drawn as an association with a diamond next to the "whole" class. Listings 6.3 and 6.4 show the code, and they are followed by the UML notation for an aggregation.

LISTING 6.3: C# CODE EXAMPLE—AGGREGATION

```
public class Employee
{
         private TimeCard theTimeCard;

   public void RecordTime(DateTime Date, long NumHours)
   {
      theTimeCard.AddTCEntry(Date, NumHours);
   }
}

public class Timecard
{
   private Employee theEmployee;

   public void AddTCEntry(DateTime Workdate, long Hours)
   {
      int ErrorCode;
TimeCardEntry newTimeCardEntry;

      newTimeCardEntry = new TimeCardEntry(Workdate,Hours);
      ErrorCode = newTimeCardEntry.Validate();
   }
}
```

LISTING 6.4: VISUAL BASIC CODE EXAMPLE—AGGREGATION

```
Public Class Employee
   Private theTimeCard as TimeCard

   Public Sub RecordTime(ByVal WorkDate As DateTime, ByVal Hours As Long)
        theTimeCard.AddTCEntry(WorkDate, Hours)
    End Sub
End Class

Public Class TimeCard
   Private theEmployee as Employee

   Public Sub AddTCEntry(ByVal Workdate As DateTime, ByVal Hours As Long)
        Dim myTCEntry As TimeCardEntry
        Dim ErrorCode As Integer

        myTCEntry = New TimeCardEntry(WorkDate, Hours)
        ErrorCode = myTCEntry.Validate()
    End Sub
End Class
```

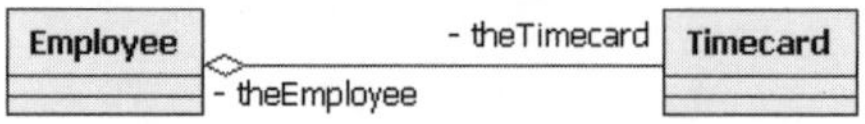

NOTE *In a standard aggregation, each "part" object can be a part of more than one "whole" object.*

Composition Relationships

A *composition* is an aggregation in which the lifetimes of the part object and the whole object are linked. When an instance of the whole is created, an instance of the part is also created; when the instance of the whole is destroyed, the part is also destroyed. The composition is drawn as an aggregation with a filled diamond. A composition requires that a part instance be included in at most one composite at a time, so therefore the multiplicity on the composite end of the relationship must be exactly one. As with an aggregation, the code generated is exactly the same as for an association (see Listings 6.5 and 6.6 and the following illustration).

LISTING 6.5: C# CODE EXAMPLE—COMPOSITION

```
public class Employee
{
         private TimeCard theTimeCard;

   public void RecordTime(DateTime Date, long NumHours)
   {
      theTimeCard.AddTCEntry(Date, NumHours);
   }
}

public class Timecard
{
   private Employee theEmployee;

   public void AddTCEntry(DateTime Workdate, long Hours)
   {
      int ErrorCode;
TimeCardEntry newTimeCardEntry;

      newTimeCardEntry = new TimeCardEntry(Workdate,Hours);
      ErrorCode = newTimeCardEntry.Validate();
   }
}
```

LISTING 6.6: VISUAL BASIC CODE EXAMPLE—COMPOSITION

```
Public Class Employee
   Private theTimeCard as TimeCard

   Public Sub RecordTime(ByVal WorkDate As DateTime, ByVal Hours As Long)
        theTimeCard.AddTCEntry(WorkDate, Hours)
```

Continued on next page

LISTING 6.6: VISUAL BASIC CODE EXAMPLE—COMPOSITION *(continued)*

```
    End Sub
End Class

Public Class TimeCard
   Private theEmployee as Employee

   Public Sub AddTCEntry(ByVal Workdate As DateTime, ByVal Hours As Long)
        Dim myTCEntry As TimeCardEntry
        Dim ErrorCode As Integer

        myTCEntry = New TimeCardEntry(WorkDate, Hours)
        ErrorCode = myTCEntry.Validate()
    End Sub
End Class
```

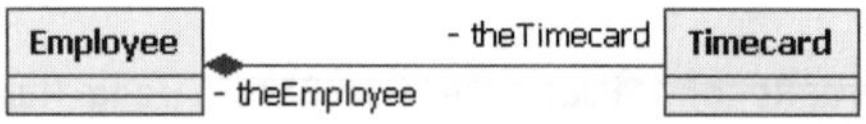

NOTE *As we discussed earlier, there is no difference in the code between an attribute and a composition relationship. The entity Name, for example, could be modeled as an attribute of an Employee class, or as a relationship between the Employee class and a String class.*

DEPENDENCY RELATIONSHIPS

A dependency relationship is a weaker form of association. With an association, an attribute is created to support the relationship. A dependency, on the other hand, does not create an attribute. Therefore, the client object must access the supplier object through another means. The possibilities include the following:

- The supplier object is global and is therefore accessible to the client.
- The supplier object is passed to the client as a parameter to an operation.
- The supplier object is declared locally within an operation of the client.

In the UML, a dependency is shown as a dashed arrow, pointing from the client to the supplier (see the following illustration). Listings 6.7 and 6.8 show the code for a dependency. Note that there are no supporting attributes.

LISTING 6.7: C# CODE EXAMPLE—DEPENDENCY

```
public class Employee
{

   public void RecordTime(DateTime Date, long NumHours)
```

Continued on next page

LISTING 6.7: C# CODE EXAMPLE—DEPENDENCY *(continued)*

```
    {
       TimeCard theTimeCard = new Timecard();
       theTimeCard.AddTCEntry(Date, NumHours);
    }
}

public class Timecard
{
    public void AddTCEntry(DateTime Workdate, long Hours)
    {
       int ErrorCode;
TimeCardEntry newTimeCardEntry;

       newTimeCardEntry = new TimeCardEntry(Workdate,Hours);
       ErrorCode = newTimeCardEntry.Validate();
    }
}
```

LISTING 6.8: VISUAL BASIC CODE EXAMPLE—DEPENDENCY

```
Public Class Employee
   Public Sub RecordTime(ByVal WorkDate As DateTime, ByVal Hours As Long)
        Dim theTimeCard As TimeCard
        theTimeCard = New TimeCard()
        theTimeCard.AddTCEntry(WorkDate, Hours)
    End Sub
End Class

Public Class TimeCard
    Public Sub AddTCEntry(ByVal Workdate As DateTime, ByVal Hours As Long)
        Dim myTCEntry As TimeCardEntry
        Dim ErrorCode As Integer

        myTCEntry = New TimeCardEntry(WorkDate, Hours)
        ErrorCode = myTCEntry.Validate()
    End Sub
End Class
```

A dependency relationship between packages indicates that at least one element in the client package is dependent upon at least one element in the supplier package.

INHERITANCE

In the UML, an inheritance structure is modeled as a generalization relationship. The generalization points from the child class to the parent class. The child inherits all of the attributes, operations, and relationships of the parent. The following graphic is the UML representation for a generalization:

C#

```
Public class Class1 : Class2 {
}
```

Visual Basic

```
Public class Class1
   Inherits Class2
End Class
```

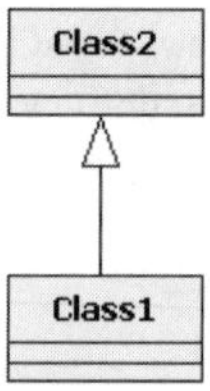

ASP .NET Applications

To model an ASP .NET application in the UML, the scripts and HTML from a file with an `.aspx` extension are represented as separate classes, one with a stereotype of <<ClientPage>> and one with a stereotype of <<ServerPage>>. The <<ClientPage>> stereotype is used to represent any client-side scripts, HTML markup, dynamic HTML, and text. It corresponds to the `body` section of the page. The <<ServerPage>> stereotype is used to represent server-side processing. In the UML, a directed build association from the server page to the client page is used to indicate which server page builds which client page. A client page may or may not have a build relationship (a client page without the relationship is a standard HTML file), but a server page always does. By logically separating the client-side logic from the server-side logic, you can make the application easier to maintain, and you can assign the appropriate resources to develop the logical portions of each page. Developers of the client-side portions typically need skills in graphics, text formatting, and other user interface items, while server-side developers need skills in business logic programming, database interaction, and so on.

The code-behind file (XDE currently supports Visual Basic and C#) contains the business logic for the ASPX page. Depending upon the programming language, the code-behind file has an extension of `.aspx.cs` or `.aspx.vb`. Whatever the language, the code-behind file is represented as an unstereotyped class. The server page builds the client page, and has a generalization relationship to the code-behind class, indicating the one it inherits from the class. Any HTML forms on the client page are related to the client page via an aggregation.

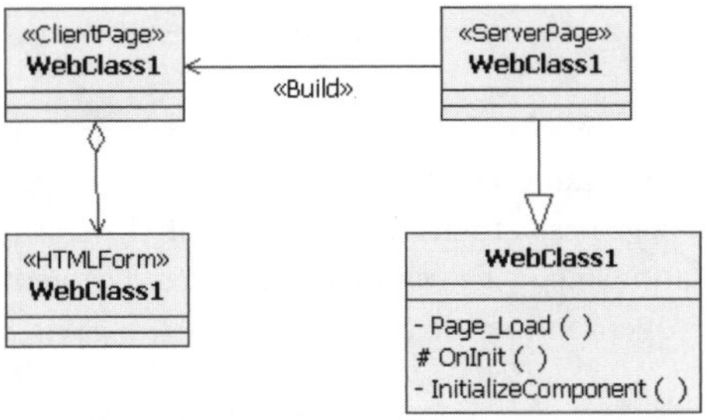

There are several other relationships that you may need. These are discussed in the following sections.

Link Relationship

An HTML Link relationship is used to show a hypertext link between two client pages or between a server page and a client page. The corresponding code will be something like `<a href="mypage.htm">`. The relationship can be added to the diagram using the Link Relation option on the Web toolbox.

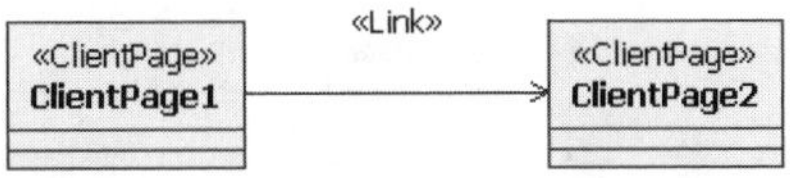

A very similar relationship is the NETLink relationship used to model the relationship between a web form and a server page or HTML page. The NETLink relationship is drawn as a directed association, from the web form to the server page or HTML page, and it has the stereotype <<NetLink>>. It corresponds to the `asp:Hyperlink` tag in the code.

Redirect, NETTransfer, and NETExecute Relationships

The redirect relationship is a directed association used to show the passing of control from a server page to another server page or to a client page. It is added using the Redirect Relation option on the Web toolbox.

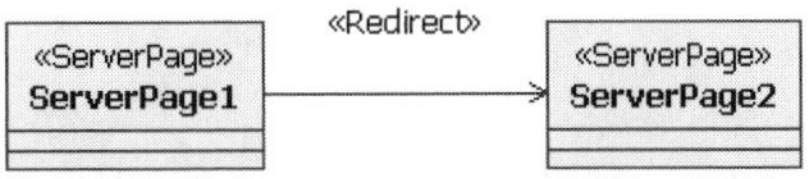

This relationship corresponds to the `Response.Redirect` command in the code. For example, `<% Response.Redirect("mypage.aspx") %>` redirects control to `mypage.aspx`.

A given server page automatically has access to certain objects, including the request and response objects, the server object, and the session and application objects. With a redirect relationship, the page that is given control does not have access to the same objects (the new page has its own corresponding objects, rather than having access to the specific session, application, and so on, objects of the original page).

The NETTransfer relationship is very similar, but in this relationship the page receiving control does have access to the same set of objects as the original page. This is a useful relationship when, for example, the new page needs to access a variable of the session object, such as the session ID. The NETTransfer relationship is also shown as a directed, stereotyped association. It corresponds to the `server.transfer` operation in the code.

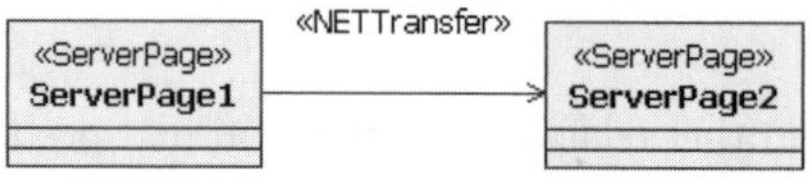

Finally, the NETExecute relationship can be used to show that control passes from one server page to another server page or an HTML page, but that control returns to the original server page once the new page has finished its processing. As with the NETTransfer relationship, the new page has access to the same set of objects (request, response, and so on) as the original page. A NETExecute relationship is drawn as a stereotyped association, as shown here:

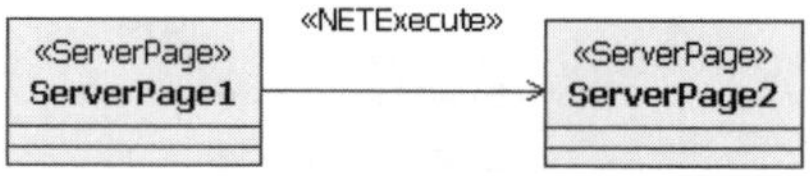

SUBMIT RELATIONSHIP

A submit relationship is used to show a form submitting its values to a server page:

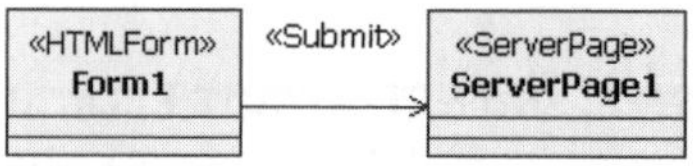

In the code, this corresponds to a line similar to the following:

```
<form action="myform.aspx" id="myform" method="post"></form>
```

Web Services

In the UML, a web service can be modeled as a component with its interface. In XDE, we can add methods to the interface, but these are not typically shown on a class diagram. The interface is connected to the web services component that realizes it.

XML web services in Visual Studio are defined in ASMX files, with the business logic in code-behind files. Although the business logic may also be present in the ASMX file, XDE currently only supports business logic in code-behind files. You use two classes to represent the web service: a class with an interface of <<NETWebService>> to represent the ASMX file itself, and an unstereotyped class to represent the code-behind file, like so:

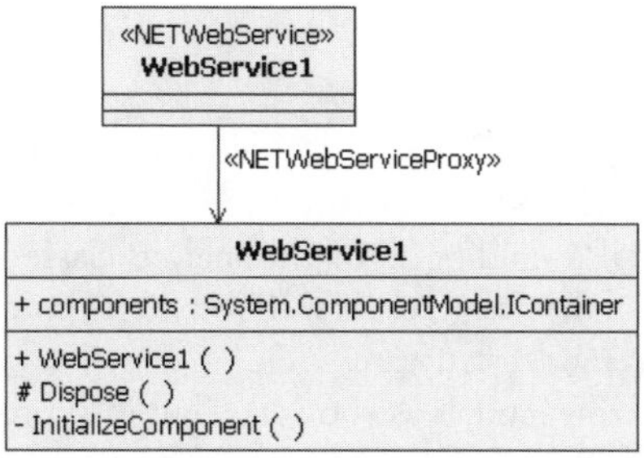

The Web Services Description Language (WSDL) used to locate the web service is also modeled as a class, with a stereotype of <<WebServiceReference>>.

As you can see, the relationship between the service and its code-behind class is modeled as an association with a stereotype of <<NETWebServiceProxy>>. The request and the service's XML SOAP response are not modeled on a class diagram, but they are frequently shown on a sequence diagram. The sequence diagram typically indicates when the service is called, by what class, and what the system does with the response—the focus is less on how the WSDL and web service communicate.

Modeling .NET Elements in XDE

Now that we've discussed how .NET elements map to the UML, it's time to look at how to add and manage these elements in an XDE model. In this section, we cover adding, editing, and deleting elements, as well as setting element properties in XDE.

Visual Studio Solutions and Projects

The Visual Studio solution itself is not modeled using XDE, but the projects within the solution are. When you use Visual Studio with XDE, you create solutions just as you would if you weren't using XDE.

The projects within a solution are modeled in XDE. Using the Solution Explorer, you can view the projects within a solution. The projects, in turn, contain the XDE models. Each project may include many models, but only one can be a code model.

A good thing about this structure is that it allows you to use multiple languages within an application. Each project can have a different language, and its code model holds the UML representation of the code for that language.

XDE Models

You can create multiple XDE models to hold information about the analysis and design of your application. One XDE model, for example, may correspond to the analysis model in the Rational Unified Process (RUP), holding all of the analysis classes. Another may correspond to the design model, holding all of the design classes. If you are a Rational customer, contact Rational for their recommended XDE model structure.

You can add as many models as you'd like, but each project can contain only one code model. Visual Studio and XDE create a code model for you; simply right-click the solution in the Solution Explorer and select Synchronize. XDE creates a new code model (if one does not already exist) and synchronizes it with the code.

To add a model manually:

1. Right-click the project in the Solution Explorer window and choose Add ➢ Add New Item.
2. In the Add New Item dialog box, select the Rational XDE folder and then the type of model (blank model, data model, or getting started model).
3. Select Open. XDE adds the model to the Solution Explorer and Model Explorer windows.

Using the Model Explorer, you can drag and drop elements between models, add new model elements, and delete model elements. Each project can contain multiple models. On a class diagram, a model is represented as a stereotyped package.

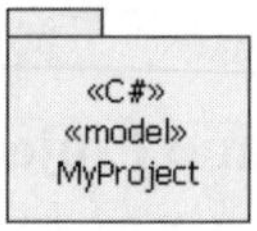

Namespaces

In the UML, a namespace is represented as a stereotyped package. In XDE, you can add a namespace using the Namespace option on either the C# or the Visual Basic toolbox. Once you've added a namespace, you can drag and drop existing classes, interfaces, structs, enums, or other namespaces into the new namespace in the Model Explorer.

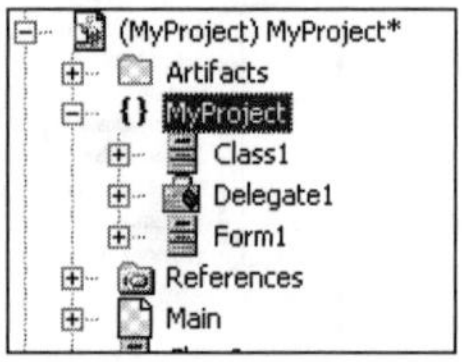

Within a namespace, no two model elements of the same type should have the same name. For example, you can't have two classes called Employee within the same namespace, but you can have a class called Employee and an actor called Employee.

WARNING *XDE lets you create two model elements with the same name within the same namespace. You see a warning, however, when you validate the model.*

When you right-click a namespace and generate code or synchronize, XDE generates or updates code for all of the classes and other elements in the namespace. For example, if a C# class called Class1 is in a namespace called Namespace1, XDE generates the following:

```
Namespace Namespace1
{
   public class Class1
   {
   }
}
```

When you are reverse engineering, XDE creates a stereotyped package for each namespace in the code and places the classes and other elements in the appropriate namespace. It often helps to add a class diagram (right-click the namespace and choose Add Diagram ➢ Class) for the namespace. The class diagram contains all of the classes and other elements in the namespace.

Source Code Files

The source code files are represented in the XDE model as components and are given the stereotype of <<file>>:

When you synchronize your code from the Solution Explorer, XDE automatically creates or updates the components in the model. You can see the components in the Artifacts package within each XDE model. If you'd like to create components manually, you can do so by right-clicking a package in the Model Explorer and choosing Add UML ➢ Component.

The source code components can be displayed on a component diagram (right-click a package and choose Add Diagram ➢ Component). Dependencies between the components show the compilation dependencies between the source code files.

You can use a reside relationship to show which class(es) are contained within a component, as shown here:

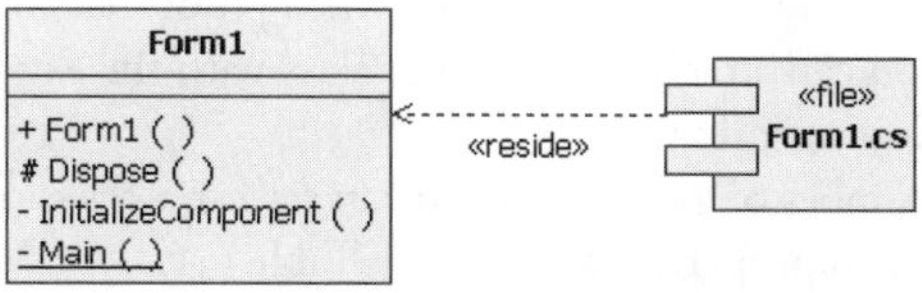

These relationships are automatically added for you when you generate code for a class, but you can also add them manually using the Reside option on the C# or Visual Basic toolbox.

You can also see which interface(s) a component realizes by including the interfaces on the component diagram. A realizes relationship between a component and an interface suggests that the component realizes the methods in the interface.

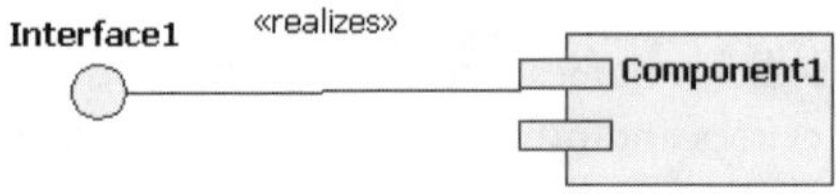

Classes

In XDE, you can add, view, or delete classes using either class diagrams or the Model Explorer window. Each class appears as a compartmentalized rectangle, as described in the "Modeling .NET Elements in the UML" section earlier in this chapter. Each class contains compartments for the class name, attributes, and operations.

XDE also includes a fourth compartment, the *Signal Compartment,* that you can use. Select the class on a class diagram, and then choose Format ➢ Compartment ➢ Signal Compartment to show or hide the signal compartment. The signal compartment displays signal receptions for the class. A *signal* is a one-way, asynchronous communication between objects and is most frequently modeled when you are working with real-time systems.

To add a signal reception to a class:

1. First, add the signal itself to the model. Right-click a class diagram in the diagram window or a package in the Explorer window, and choose Add UML ➢ Signal.
2. Name the signal, and add any needed attributes and operations.
3. Add the signal reception to a class by dragging it from the Explorer window to the class on a class diagram.

For example, to add a signal reception to a class called Class1, drag the new signal from the Explorer window to Class1 on a class diagram. The signal appears on the class diagram, and also underneath Class1 in the Explorer window, as shown here:

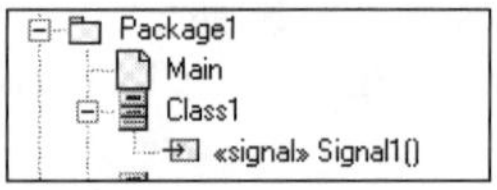

Although the UML allows you to add other new compartments to a class, this feature is not supported in XDE (or in any other UML modeling tool that we are aware of). If you need an extra compartment, you can attach a note to the class with the extra information, or attach a file to the class in the Explorer window.

There are a number of properties you can set for a class in XDE. These directly affect the code generated. The main properties are listed in Table 6.1.

TABLE 6.1: CLASS PROPERTIES IN XDE

CATEGORY	PROPERTY	DESCRIPTION
Round-Trip Engineering	ImplementationFile	Sets the filename for the source code file containing the class. Note that this is the same as the XDE code property called Source File.
Round-Trip Engineering	SynchronizationPolicy	Determines how code is synchronized with the model for this class. If the same item has been changed in both the model and code, "Accept code changes" updates the model with the code, and "Accept model changes" updates the code with the model. The Synchronize option prompts you to determine whether you should accept the model or code. The Disabled option prevents the code and model from being synchronized for this class.
UML	IsAbstract	If True, marks the class as an abstract class, and adds the `abstract` keyword (C#) or `mustinherit` keyword (Visual Basic) to the code. The name of an abstract class is italicized on class diagrams. Note that changing this property also changes the XDE code property called Abstract, and vice versa.
UML	IsActive	Marks the class as an active class. An active class is used to model a thread.
UML	IsLeaf	If True, the class is at the lowest level of an inheritance tree and can't have children in a generalization relationship. This property does not affect the generated code.
UML	IsRoot	If True, the class is at the root of a inheritance tree and can't have a parent in a generalization relationship. This property does not affect the generated code.
UML	IsSpecification	If True, the class is part of the model's specification. If False, the class is part of the model's implementation. This property does not affect the generated code.
UML	Multiplicity	Sets the number of instances of the class expected to be in memory. This property does not affect the generated code.
UML	Persistence	Marks the class as persistent, which allows XDE to generate a database table definition for it.
UML	Stereotype	Sets the stereotype of the class.
UML	Visibility	Sets the scope (visibility) of the class to Public, Private, Protected, or Package. Note that changing this property also changes the XDE code property called Access.
XDE Code Properties	Name	Name of the class.

Continued on next page

TABLE 6.1: CLASS PROPERTIES IN XDE *(continued)*

CATEGORY	PROPERTY	DESCRIPTION
XDE Code Properties	Namespace	Displays the namespace that contains the class.
XDE Code Properties	Access	See UML ➢ Visibility.
XDE Code Properties	Source File	See Round Trip Engineering ➢ Implementation File.
XDE Code Properties	Abstract (C# only)	See UML ➢ IsAbstract.
XDE Code Properties	New (C# only)	Adds the `New` modifier to the class.
XDE Code Properties	Sealed (C# only)	Adds the `Sealed` modifier to the class.
XDE Code Properties	Unsafe (C# only)	Adds the `Unsafe` modifier to the class.
XDE Code Properties	MustInherit (Visual Basic only)	See UML ➢ IsAbstract.
XDE Code Properties	Shadows (Visual Basic only)	Adds the `Shadows` modifier to the generated code. This property can only be set to True for a class if it is contained within another class.
XDE Code Properties	NonInheritable	Adds the `NotInheritable` modifier to the generated code.

To add a new class in XDE:

1. Right-click a package in the Explorer, or right-click a class diagram and choose Add C# ➢ Class or Add Visual Basic ➢ Class.
2. Type the name of the new class, and edit the properties as needed.

TIP *On a class diagram, add a new C# or Visual Basic class by using the Class option in the C# or Visual Basic toolbox.*

CLASS STEREOTYPES

Stereotypes are a means of classifying the different types of elements you have in your model. For example, some of the class stereotypes available in XDE include <<NETWebService>>, <<NETWebUserControl>>, <<ClientPage>>, <<ServerPage>>, <<delegate>>, and <<WebServiceReference>>. By looking at a class's stereotype, you can easily see what type of class you're dealing with. By default, the class stereotype is displayed in the name compartment on a class diagram, and is enclosed in guillemets (<< >>), as shown here:

To assign a stereotype to a class, modify its UML ➢ Stereotype property. You can select from one of XDE's predefined stereotypes, or you can enter your own. Stereotypes can be displayed on a class diagram using either text or an icon. See "Building a Design-Level Class Diagram" later in this chapter for instructions related to displaying icons and adding your own customized icons.

FIELDS AND PROPERTIES

A field may be modeled as an attribute in the UML or as a relationship between classes. When you're adding a field to your model, you can select either option. The code that results is the same in either case. A property may only be added as an attribute.

To add a property:

1. Right-click the class and choose Add C-Sharp ➢ Property or Add Visual Basic ➢ Property. The Add Property screen appears (this screen looks very similar to a Visual Basic property, but it also has a Parameters section):

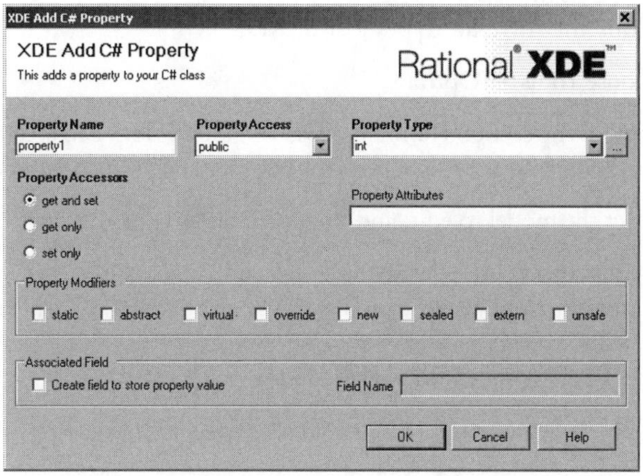

2. Use the Add Property screen to define the name, data type, access, modifiers, and other information for the property. Depending upon what you select in the Property Accessors area, XDE creates the appropriate methods for you. If you select the "Create field to store property value" check box, XDE creates an additional attribute for you. The property you just added will also be modeled as an attribute with a stereotype of <<property>>.

To add a field as an attribute:

1. Right-click the class and choose Add UML ➢ Attribute.
2. Name the attribute and set its data type using the following format:

   ```
   Name:Datatype = Initial Value
   ```

   where the initial value is optional. Remember that the name you use here is the name in the generated code.

To add a field as a relationship, create an association between two classes. During code generation, XDE automatically adds the field for you (on both ends of a bidirectional association, or at the client end of a unidirectional association).

You can also convert a field to a property. Right-click the field in the Model Explorer window, and select Convert To Property. XDE creates the property as well as the get and set methods. The property appears on a class diagram as an attribute with a stereotype of <<property>>, as shown here:

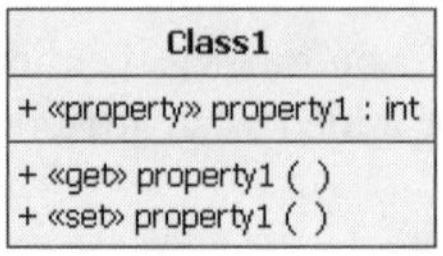

When reverse engineering, XDE looks at the Attribute Types List available in Tools ➢ Options ➢ Round-Trip Engineering. If the data type of the field is on the list, XDE models it as an attribute. Otherwise, XDE models it as a relationship.

To modify the Attribute Types List in XDE:

1. Choose Tools ➢ Options.
2. Look in the section Rational XDE ➢ Round-Trip Engineering ➢ C# Language Attributes or Rational XDE ➢ Round-Trip Engineering ➢ Visual Basic Language Attributes.
3. Select the model to edit, and then add, remove, or edit attribute types.

Don't panic if you used the attribute notation and want to switch to using a relationship or if you used a relationship and would now like to use an attribute. XDE lets you switch back and forth between the two.

To change an attribute into a relationship:

1. Right-click the attribute in the Model Explorer.
2. Select Convert To Association.

To change a relationship to an attribute:

1. Right-click the relationship in the Explorer or on a diagram.
2. Select Convert To Attribute. The relationship disappears and is replaced by an attribute.

Like classes, attributes have a number of code generation properties in XDE that directly affect how code is generated. These code generation properties vary slightly for fields and Visual Studio properties. Table 6.2 lists some of the attribute properties and their meanings. Note that to view or edit the properties for an attribute, you need to select the attribute in the Explorer window, not on a diagram.

TABLE 6.2: ATTRIBUTE PROPERTIES IN XDE

CATEGORY	**PROPERTY**	**DESCRIPTION**
Round-Trip Engineering	LanguageAttributes	Used to add C# or Visual Basic attributes to the field or property.
Round-Trip Engineering	SynchronizationPolicy	Determines how code is synchronized with the model for this attribute. If the same item has been changed in both the model and code, "Accept code changes" updates the model with the code, and "Accept model changes" updates the code with the model. The Synchronize option prompts you to determine whether you should accept the model or code. The Disabled option prevents the code and model from being synchronized for this attribute.
UML	Name	Sets the name of the attribute.
UML	Aggregation	Indicates how the lifetime of the attribute instance and its containing object are related. Aggregation suggests that the object and attribute instance are not necessarily instantiated at the same time. Composition suggests that the object and attribute are instantiated and destroyed at the same time.
UML	Changeability	Controls whether the value of the attribute can be changed after the object containing it is instantiated. The options are Changeable, which allows the value to be changed; Add_Only, which allows a value to be added if no default value was provided; and Frozen, which does not allow the attribute to be modified.
UML	Collections	Allows you to attach URLs to the attribute.
UML	DefaultValueExpression	An expression that sets the default value of the attribute when its containing object is instantiated.
UML	IsByValueIfComposite	If the value of the Aggregation property is set to Composite, this property determines whether the composition is implemented by value or by reference.
UML	IsDerived	Notes whether the value of the attribute is calculated from the value of one or more other attributes.
UML	IsSpecification	If True, the attribute is part of the model's specification. If False, the attribute is part of the model's implementation.

Continued on next page

TABLE 6.2: ATTRIBUTE PROPERTIES IN XDE *(continued)*

CATEGORY	PROPERTY	DESCRIPTION
UML	Ordering	If the attribute is a list or other collection, indicates whether the elements within it are ordered or unordered. Options are: 0: Unordered 1: Ordered 2: Sorted
UML	OwnerScope	Notes whether the attribute is static. If set to Classifier, the attribute is static.
UML	Persistence	If set to Persistent, the attribute is made persistent (that is, in a database) outside of the system.
UML	Stereotype	Sets the stereotype of the attribute. Fields have no stereotype; properties have a stereotype of <<property>>.
UML	TargetScope	Sets whether the instance of the attribute is an instance of a class or the class itself.
UML	TypeExpression	The data type of the attribute.
UML	Visibility	Sets the accessibility (Public, Private, Protected, or Package) of the attribute. See the "Visibility" section later in this chapter.
XDE Code Properties	Name	Sets the name of the attribute.
XDE Code Properties	Type	Sets the data type of the attribute.
XDE Code Properties	Access	See UML ➢ Visibility.
XDE Code Properties	Initial Value	Sets the initial value of the attribute.
XDE Code Properties	Readonly	Determines whether the value of the attribute can be changed.
XDE Code Properties	New (C#)	Adds the `new` keyword to the code.
XDE Code Properties	Static (C#)	Adds the `static` keyword to the code.
XDE Code Properties	Volatile (C#)	Adds the `volatile` keyword to the code.
XDE Code Properties	Unsafe (C#)	Adds the `unsafe` keyword to the code.
XDE Code Properties	Shadows (Visual Basic)	Adds the `shadows` keyword to the code.
XDE Code Properties	Shared (Visual Basic)	Adds the `shared` keyword to the code.
XDE Code Properties	Attributes	Defines any additional declarative information for the field or property.

Reordering Fields

By default, fields are listed on the diagram, and generated in the code, in the order that you entered them. While it isn't typically necessary, you can change the order if you want to. To change the order of the fields:

1. Right-click the class on a diagram or in the Explorer, and select Collection Editor. The following window appears:

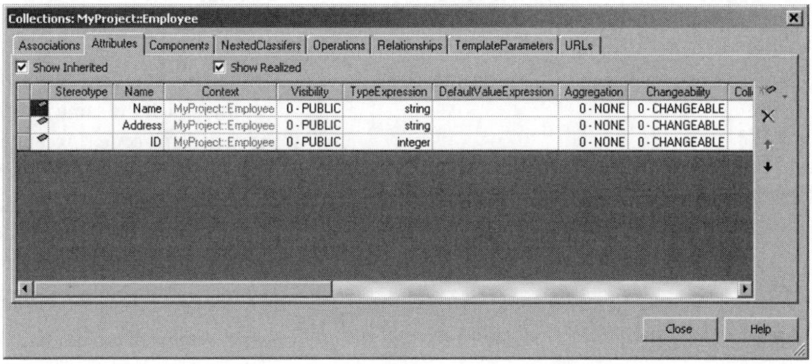

2. Select the Attributes tab, then use the up and down buttons on the right-hand side of the window to move attributes up or down in the list. You can also add or delete attributes using this window. When you close the window, XDE reorders the attributes.

WARNING *If you've already generated the code, reordering the attributes in the model may not reorder them in the code, even after a synchronization.*

Visibility

The UML notation for field scope is as follows: + for Public, – for Private, # for Protected, and ~ for Package. In XDE, the Explorer window uses different notation to show the visibility. To the left of the attribute name in the Explorer, you will see one of the following four symbols:

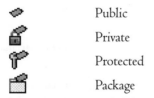

 Public

 Private

 Protected

 Package

If you'd like, you can also use these symbols on a class diagram, rather than the +, –, #, and ~ symbols used in the UML. Select the class(es) to change, and then choose Format ➢ Stereotype and Visibility Style ➢ Visibility Style: Icon.

METHODS, DELEGATES, AND EVENTS

Methods, or operations, appear in the third compartment of a class on a class diagram. When reverse engineering, XDE creates operations for all of the methods in the code. During code generation, XDE creates the method signatures for you. The properties for a method are listed in Table 6.3.

TABLE 6.3: METHOD PROPERTIES IN XDE

CATEGORY	PROPERTY	DESCRIPTION
Round-Trip Engineering	LanguageAttributes	Used to add C# or Visual Basic attributes to the method.
Round-Trip Engineering	SynchronizationPolicy	Determines how code is synchronized with the model for this method. If the same item has been changed in both the model and code, "Accept code changes" updates the model with the code, and "Accept model changes" updates the code with the model. The Synchronize option prompts you to determine whether you should accept the model or code. The Disabled option prevents the code and model from being synchronized for this method.
UML	Name	Sets the name of the method.
UML	Collections	Used to attach URLs to the method.
UML	Concurrency	Specifies what occurs when there are simultaneous calls to the same instance of a classifier that is not active. The options are Sequential, which indicates that calls should be made sequentially and the integrity of the system is not guaranteed if simultaneous calls are made; Guarded, which indicates that calls may occur simultaneously but are executed sequentially; and Concurrent, which indicates that calls may be made and executed concurrently.
UML	IsAbstract	Adds the `abstract` keyword to the method.
UML	IsLeaf	If True, the operation may not be overridden when it is inherited.
UML	IsQuery	Marks the method as an operation that does not affect the state of the system.
UML	IsRoot	If True, the class may not inherit a declaration of the same operation.
UML	IsSpecification	If True, the method is part of the model's specification. If False, the method is part of the model's implementation.
UML	OwnerScope	Notes whether the method is static. If set to Classifier, the method is static.
UML	Stereotype	Sets the stereotype of the method. Examples are <<add>>, <<destroy>>, <<get>>, <<set>>, and <<remove>>. Setting this property does not affect the generated code.

Continued on next page

TABLE 6.3: METHOD PROPERTIES IN XDE *(continued)*

CATEGORY	**PROPERTY**	**DESCRIPTION**
UML	Visibility	Sets the scope (Public, Private, Protected, or Package) of the method.
XDE Code Properties	Name	See UML ➢ Name.
XDE Code Properties	Return Type	Sets the return type of the operation.
XDE Code Properties	Access	See UML ➢ Visibility.
XDE Code Properties	Sealed (C#)	Adds the `sealed` keyword to the generated code.
XDE Code Properties	Virtual (C#)	Adds the `virtual` keyword to the generated code.
XDE Code Properties	Override (C#)	Adds the `override` keyword to the generated code.
XDE Code Properties	New (C#)	Adds the `new` keyword to the generated code.
XDE Code Properties	Static (C#)	See UML ➢ OwnerScope.
XDE Code Properties	Extern (C#)	Adds the `extern` keyword to the generated code.
XDE Code Properties	Unsafe (C#)	Adds the `unsafe` keyword to the generated code.
XDE Code Properties	MustOverride (Visual Basic)	See UML ➢ IsAbstract. Setting MustOverride to True sets IsAbstract to True and adds the `mustoverride` keyword to the generated code. If MustOverride is True, NotOverridable, Overridable, Overrides, and Shared are disabled and set to False.
XDE Code Properties	NotOverridable (Visual Basic)	Adds the `notoverrideable` keyword to the generated code. If NotOverridable is set to True, Overrides should also be set to True. If NotOverridable is set to True, MustOverride and Overridable are set to False and disabled.
XDE Code Properties	Overridable (Visual Basic)	Adds the `overrideable` keyword to the generated code. If Overridable is set to True, MustOverride, NotOverridable, Overrides, and Shared are set to False and disabled.
XDE Code Properties	Overrides (Visual Basic)	Adds the `overrides` keyword to the generated code. If Overrides is set to True, NotOverridable should also be set to True. If Overrides is set to True, MustOverride, Overridable, Shadows, and Shared are set to False and disabled.
XDE Code Properties	Shadows (Visual Basic)	Adds the `shadows` keyword to the generated code. If Shadows is set to True, Overrides is set to False and disabled.
XDE Code Properties	Shared (Visual Basic)	Adds the `shared` keyword to the generated code. If Shared is set to True, MustOverride, Overridable, and Overrides are set to False and disabled.
XDE Code Properties	Attributes	Defines any additional declarative information for the method.

Reordering Methods

Like fields, methods are listed on the diagram, and generated in the code, in the order you entered them. XDE lets you change the order of the method declarations, however. Right-click the class on a diagram or in the Explorer, and select Collection Editor. You'll see the following window:

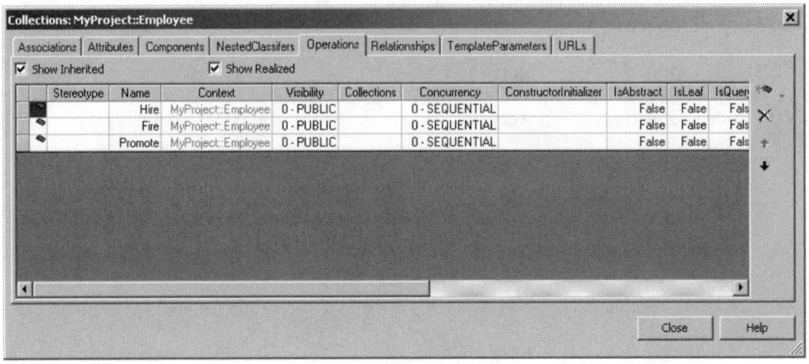

Select the Operations tab, then use the up and down buttons on the right-hand side of the window to move operations up or down in the list. When you close the window, XDE reorders the operations.

WARNING *If you've already generated the code, reordering the operations in the model may not reorder them in the code, even after a synchronization.*

Parameters and Return Values

In XDE, methods, their parameters, and their return values are all modeled as separate elements. The parameters and return bodies appear underneath the operation in the Explorer. Parameters have the following icon next to them: . Return bodies use this icon: .

Table 6.4 lists the properties for a parameter.

TABLE 6.4: METHOD PARAMETER PROPERTIES IN XDE

CATEGORY	PROPERTY	DESCRIPTION
UML	Name	Sets the name of the parameter.
UML	Collections	Used to attach URLs to the parameter.
UML	DefaultValueExpression	Sets the default value of the parameter.
UML	IsSpecification	If True, the parameter is part of the model's specification. If False, the parameter is part of the model's implementation.

UML	Kind	Sets the type of parameter. Options are:
		`in`
		`out`
		`inout`
		return (for a return value)

Continued on next page

TABLE 6.4: METHOD PARAMETER PROPERTIES IN XDE *(continued)*

CATEGORY	PROPERTY	DESCRIPTION
UML	Stereotype	Sets the stereotype of the parameter.
UML	TypeExpression	Sets the data type of the parameter.
XDE Code Properties	Name	Sets the name of the parameter.
XDE Code Properties	Type	See UML ➢ TypeExpression.
XDE Code Properties	Kind	Controls whether the parameter is passed by value or by reference.
XDE Code Properties	Attributes	Defines any additional declarative information for the parameter.
XDE Code Properties	Optional (Visual Basic)	Sets the parameter as optional or required. Adds the `optional` keyword to the generated parameter if this property is set to True.
XDE Code Properties	Initial Value (Visual Basic)	Sets the initial value of the parameter. Available only if Optional is set to True. Adds code to the method signature to set the default value of the parameter.

Adding Methods

To add an operation (with parameters and a return type) in XDE:

1. Right-click the class in the Explorer or on a diagram and choose Add UML ➢ Operation.
2. Enter the name of the new operation.
3. Add a parameter by right-clicking the operation in the Explorer and choosing Add UML ➢ Parameter.
4. Set the parameter's data type using the TypeExpression property.
5. Create additional parameters as needed.
6. Set the operation's return type by modifying the Return Type property in the XDE Code Properties window.

TIP *A quicker way to create an operation is to type the whole signature at once. Right-click the class and choose Add UML ➢ Operation. Then, rather than just type the method name, type the full signature, using the format* **`Name([Parm1Kind]Parm1:datatype, [Parm2Kind]Parm2:datatype):returntype`**.

Delegates and Events

A Visual Studio delegate is modeled as a separate class, with a stereotype of <<delegate>> and an operation called `Invoke`. The parameters of the delegate are modeled as parameters of the `Invoke` operation. For example, the following delegate:

```
Public Delegate Sub MyDelegate(ByVal Parm1 as Integer)
```

is modeled in XDE as a class with a stereotype of <<delegate>>. It has a single operation, called `Invoke`, which has one Integer parameter called Parm1:

To add a delegate:

1. Right-click a class and choose Add C-Sharp ➢ Delegate or Add Visual Basic ➢ Delegate. XDE displays the Delegate definition dialog box that is shown here:

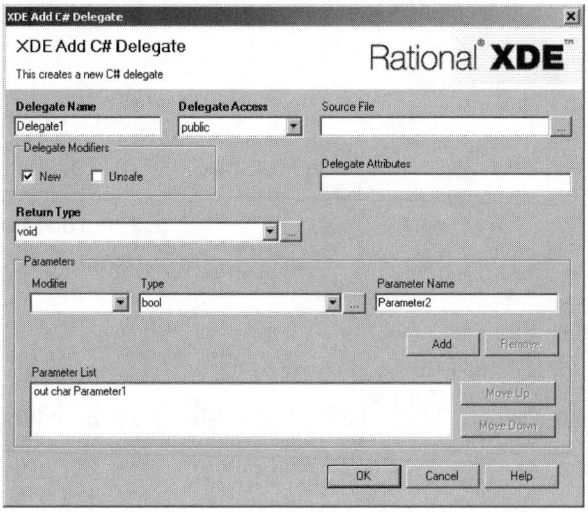

2. Enter the delegate name, access, and return type. Optionally, enter the other information on the dialog box and click OK.

An event is modeled as a relationship between the delegate and the client class. Specifically, it is modeled as a unidirectional association, from the client to the delegate, with a stereotype of <<event>>.

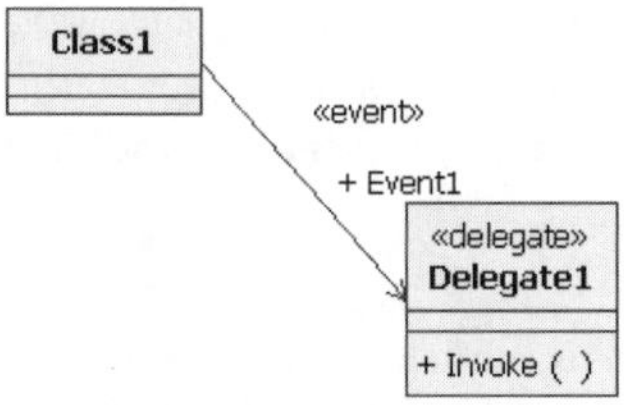

To add an event:

1. Right-click a class and choose Add C-Sharp ➢ Event or Add Visual Basic ➢ Event. XDE displays the following Event definition dialog box:

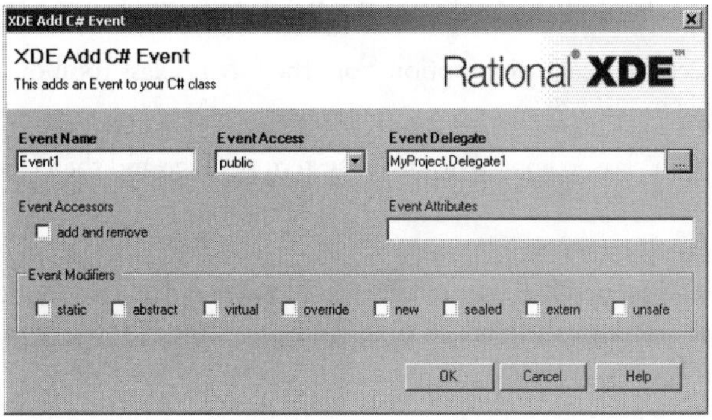

2. Enter the event name, delegate, and other information, and click OK. XDE adds the event as an association between the class and the delegate.

Interfaces

In XDE, interfaces are modeled as classes with a stereotype of <<Interface>>. On a class diagram, you can view the interface using the standard class notation (a box), or using the UML icon for an interface:

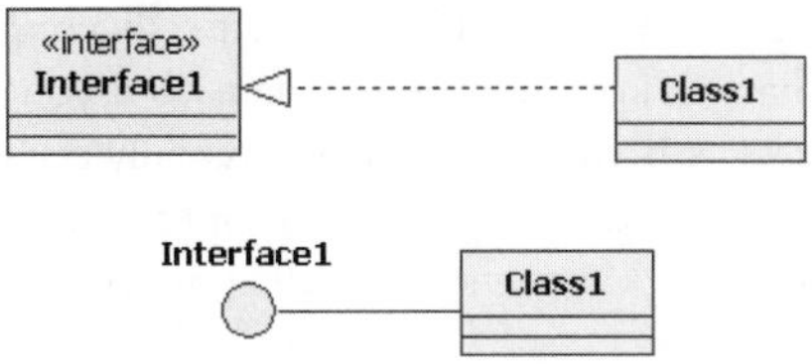

To add an interface:

1. Right-click a package or class in the Explorer, or right-click inside a class diagram, and choose Add C-Sharp ➢ Interface or Add Visual Basic ➢ Interface.
2. Type the name of the new interface, and edit the properties if necessary.
3. Add implements relationships (see next section) between the interface and the classes that realize it.

TIP *On a class diagram, you can also add an interface by selecting the Interface option in the C# or Visual Basic toolbox.*

Implements Relationships and Interface Realization

An interface realization (implements statement in Visual Basic) is used to show that a class, component, or subsystem implements the functionality specified in an interface. It appears on a class diagram as a dashed arrow from the class, component, or subsystem to the interface.

To add an implements (realization) relationship to a class diagram:

1. Select the Realization option from the UML Class toolbox, the C# toolbox, or the Visual Basic toolbox.
2. Click a class, component, or subsystem package and then click the interface it realizes.

Packages

A *package* is a generic UML construct that allows you to group model elements together. You can create as many packages as you need to organize the model, and you can nest packages within one another to further organize.

To create a package:

1. Right-click the model name or an existing package in the Explorer and choose Add UML ➢ Package. Or, use the Package option from the UML Class toolbox to add a package to a class diagram.
2. If you need to, drag and drop classes and other elements in the Explorer into or out of the package.

TIP *To move an element into a package, you can also right-click an element in the Explorer window and select Cut, and then right-click the package and select Paste.*

When you create the package, XDE automatically creates a freeform diagram called *Main* inside it for you. You don't have to keep the name "Main," but you should have one diagram that provides an overview of the package. If the package contains only classes, the Main diagram typically shows all classes (although not necessarily all attributes, operations, and relationships) in the package. If the package contains other packages, the Main diagram typically shows the subpackages and their dependencies.

PACKAGE RELATIONSHIPS

There are three types of relationships, known as permission relationships, that can be set up between packages:

Access relationship This relationship indicates that the classifiers in one package can access the public elements in another package. It is drawn as a dependency from the client to the supplier, with a stereotype of <<access>>.

Friend relationship This relationship indicates that the classifiers in one package can access the supplier package, regardless of the visibility of the contents of the supplier package. It is also drawn as a dependency from the client to the supplier, with a stereotype of <<friend>>.

Import relationship This relationship indicates that the public contents of one package are added to the namespace of another. It is drawn as a dependency from the client to the supplier, with a stereotype of <<import>>.

To add an access, friend, or import relationship in XDE:

1. Select the Access or Import option from the UML Use Case toolbox or the Friend Permission option from the UML Class toolbox.
2. Click the client package and then the supplier package.

Association Relationships

An association relationship is a semantic relationship connecting two classifiers, allowing instances of the classifiers to communicate. An association is drawn as an arrow between the two classifiers, and may be unidirectional or bidirectional. The association may be labeled with details, such as the multiplicity of the association, the role names at the association ends, and the scope of the roles at the association ends. When code is generated in Visual Studio, fields are created to support the association. In a bidirectional association, a field is created at both ends of the association, using the role names. In a unidirectional association, only one field is created. Table 6.5 lists the properties of an association.

TABLE 6.5: ASSOCIATION PROPERTIES IN XDE

CATEGORY	PROPERTY	DESCRIPTION
End1, End2	End1Changeability, End2Changeability	Controls whether the generated field may be changed. If set to changeable, a standard field is created. If set to add_only, the `static` keyword is added to the field and the XDE code property called Static is set to True (C# only). If set to frozen, the `const` keyword is added to the field.
End1, End2	End1InitialValueExpression, End2InitialValueExpression	Sets the initial value of the attribute created to support the relationship. Generally not used unless the supplier class is an elementary data type. Adds the default value to the generated field.
End1, End2	End1IsNavigable, End2IsNavigable	Controls whether the association is unidirectional or bidirectional. If unidirectional, a field is added to the client class. If bidirectional, a field is added to both classes.
End1, End2	End1Multiplicity, End2Multiplicity	Sets the number of instances of one class associated with each instance of the other class.
End1, End2	End1Name, End2Name	Sets the name(s) of the field(s) that are generated to support the relationship. Required in order to generate code for the relationship.

Continued on next page

TABLE 6.5: ASSOCIATION PROPERTIES IN XDE *(continued)*

CATEGORY	PROPERTY	DESCRIPTION
End1, End2	End1OwnerScope, End2OwnerScope	Controls whether the generated attribute is static. Options include: Instance (attribute is not static) Classifier (attribute is static)
End1, End2	Stereotype	The stereotype of the role played by the classifier at End1 or End2.
End1, End2	End1SupplierName, End2SupplierName	Read-only property. Displays the name of the classifier.
End1, End2	End1TypeExpression, End2TypeExpression	Data type of the generated field.
End1, End2	End1Visibility, End2Visibility	Sets the scope of the generated attribute. Options are Public, Protected, Private, and Package.
End1 Round-Trip Engineering, End2 Round-Trip Engineering	LanguageAttributes	Adds attributes to the fields generated to support the association.
End1 Round-Trip Engineering, End2 Round-Trip Engineering	LanguageModifiers	Adds modifiers to the fields generated to support the association.
End1 Round-Trip Engineering, End2 Round-Trip Engineering	SynchronizationPolicy	Determines how code is synchronized with the model for this end of the relationship. If the same item has been changed in both the model and code, "Accept code changes" updates the model with the code, and "Accept model changes" updates the code with the model. The Synchronize option prompts you to determine whether you should accept the model or code. The Disabled option prevents the code and model from being synchronized for this end of the association.
Round-Trip Engineering	SynchronizationPolicy	Determines how code is synchronized with the model for this association. If the same item has been changed in both the model and code, "Accept code changes" updates the model with the code, and "Accept model changes" updates the code with the model. The Synchronize option prompts you to determine whether you should accept the model or code. The Disabled option prevents the code and model from being synchronized for this association.
UML	Name	Sets the name of the association.

Continued on next page

TABLE 6.5: ASSOCIATION PROPERTIES IN XDE *(continued)*

CATEGORY	PROPERTY	DESCRIPTION
UML	Collections	Used to attach qualifiers and URLs to the association. A qualifier is used to partition the set of instances associated with an instance across an association.
UML	IsDerived	Indicates that the association is a concrete instance of a more conceptual association. This property does not affect the generated code.
UML	IsSpecification	If True, the method is part of the model's specification. If False, the method is part of the model's implementation.
UML	Kind	Sets the kind of association. The options are Simple, which creates an association; Aggregation, which creates an aggregation relationship (see the "Aggregation Relationships" section later in this chapter); or Composition, which creates a composition relationship (see the upcoming "Composition Relationships" section).
UML	Persistence	Indicates that the association is made persistent (that is, in a database).
UML	Stereotype	Sets the stereotype of the association.
XDE Code Properties	Name	Sets the name of the field generated to support the association.
XDE Code Properties	Supplier	Sets the supplier class in the unidirectional association.
XDE Code Properties	Type	Sets the data type of the field generated to support the association.
XDE Code Properties	Access	Sets the visibility of the field generated to support the association. Options are Public, Private, Protected, Friend (Visual Basic), Protected Friend (Visual Basic), Internal (C#), and Protected Internal (C#).
XDE Code Properties	Initial Value	Sets the initial value of the field generated to support the association.
XDE Code Properties	Readonly	Adds the `readonly` keyword to the generated field.
XDE Code Properties	New (C#)	Adds the `new` keyword to the generated field.
XDE Code Properties	Static (C#)	Adds the `static` keyword to the generated field.

Continued on next page

TABLE 6.5: ASSOCIATION PROPERTIES IN XDE *(continued)*

CATEGORY	PROPERTY	DESCRIPTION
XDE Code Properties	Volatile (C#)	Adds the `volatile` keyword to the generated field.
XDE Code Properties	Unsafe (C#)	Adds the `unsafe` keyword to the generated field.
XDE Code Properties	Shadows (Visual Basic)	Adds the `shadows` keyword to the generated field.
XDE Code Properties	Shared (Visual Basic)	Adds the `shared` keyword to the generated field.
XDE Code Properties	Attributes	Adds Visual Studio attributes to the generated field.

NOTE *The XDE code properties are available only for unidirectional associations.*

To add an association in XDE:

1. Select the Association or Directed Association option from the UML Class toolbox, or select the Directed Association option from the C# or Visual Basic toolbox.
2. Click one class, then the other. For a unidirectional relationship, click the client class first, then click the supplier.
3. Check the End1Name and End2Name properties in the End1 and the End2 sections of the Properties window. These names will be used to create the field(s) needed to support the relationship.
4. Set the multiplicity and other association properties as needed.

ASSOCIATION CLASSES

An association class is used to hold attributes, operations, or relationships that pertain to an association, rather than to an individual class. They are generated like any other class and are indistinguishable in code from other classes. During the reverse-engineering process, an association class is brought into the XDE model as a class but not as an association class. An association class is connected via a dashed line to an association, and it has the same properties as a standard class.

To add an association class in XDE:

1. Create an association between two classes.
2. Create an association class as you would any other class.
3. Use the Association Class option from the UML Class toolbox to connect the association class to the association.

Aggregation Relationships

An aggregation is used to model a "whole/part" relationship between classes. This is really just a specialized form of association, and therefore it has exactly the same properties we described for an association. In fact, you can even change an aggregation to an association (or change an association to an aggregation) by modifying the UML ➢ Kind property. Your choices for this property are Simple (creates an association), Aggregation, or Composition.

To create an aggregation relationship, follow these steps:

1. Select the Aggregation Association icon from the UML Class toolbox.
2. Click the "whole" class, and then the "part" class.
3. By default, the aggregation will be unidirectional, but you can create a bidirectional aggregation as well. Modify the End1IsNavigable or End2IsNavigable properties as necessary.
4. Modify the other properties as needed.

Composition Relationships

A composition relationship is an aggregation in which the lifetimes of the "whole" object and the "part" object are dependent. Follow these steps to add a composition relationship in XDE:

1. Select the Composition Association icon from the toolbox.
2. Click the "whole" class and then the "part" class.
3. By default, the composition is unidirectional, but you can create a bidirectional composition as well. To do so, modify the End1IsNavigable or End2IsNavigable properties as necessary.
4. Modify the other properties as needed.

TIP *To change a composition to an aggregation, or an aggregation to a composition, modify the UML ➢ Kind property.*

Dependency Relationships

A dependency relationship is a weaker form of association. With an association, attributes are created in the code to support the relationship. With a dependency, no attributes are created. This means the client object must access the supplier object through some other method: the supplier is global, the supplier is passed in to an operation of the client as a parameter, or the supplier is declared locally within an operation of the client. In any event, the dependency is drawn as a dashed arrow from the client to the supplier. It does not have multiplicity or role names.

To create a dependency relationship:

1. Select the Dependency option from the UML Class toolbox.
2. Click the client class first, and then the supplier.

Generalization Relationship

A UML generalization relationship is used to show an inheritance relationship between model elements. You can mark an element as the root of an inheritance tree, or as a leaf using the IsRoot and IsLeaf class properties.

To create a generalization relationship:

1. Select the Generalization option from the UML Class toolbox, the C# toolbox, or the Visual Basic toolbox.
2. Click the child class first, then the parent.

ASP .NET Applications

XDE provides an easy way to add the elements in a file with an `.aspx` extension to your application. A Web toolbox includes options for server pages with code-behind files, user controls with code-behind files, web services, server pages, client pages, HTML forms, and the relationships between these elements.

Let's begin with server pages with code-behind files. If you select this option and click anywhere on a class diagram, XDE first prompts you for a name to use for the generated classes. Enter a name, and XDE creates a server page, a client page, an HTML form, and a code-behind file, as shown here:

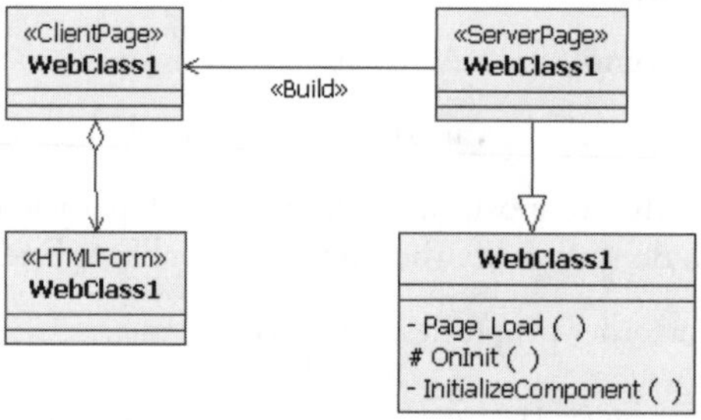

Notice that XDE also created the relationship stereotyped <<build>>, the aggregation, and the generalization you need to complete the model. If you synchronize at this point, XDE creates the files for these classes. You can add fields and methods from the class diagram or simply open the file with the `.aspx` extension using the Solution Explorer, and edit the files there.

Creating a user control with a code-behind file is a very similar process:

1. Select the User Control With Code-Behind option from the Web toolbox, and click anywhere inside a class diagram.
2. XDE prompts you for the name to use in the generated classes. Enter the name to use. XDE will create a class representing the user control, and will give it a stereotype of <<NETWebUser-Control>>. XDE also generates the code-behind file as a nonstereotyped class, as shown here:

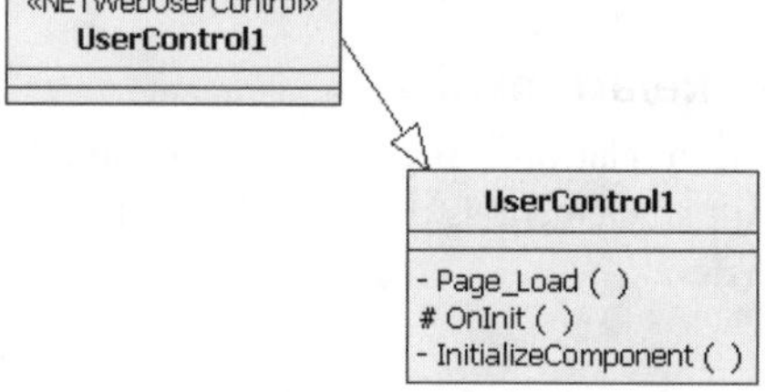

You can create the code-behind file in either Visual Basic or C#. Look at the stereotype of the model containing the code-behind file; the language of the model's stereotype is the language used to create the code-behind file. If you are working in a C# model and want to create a Visual Basic code-behind file, create a new model and place the server page with code-behind or user control with code-behind in this new model. You can use the Server Page, Client Page, and HTMLForm toolbox options from the Web toolbox to add additional elements to the ASP portion of your model. You can also add the following relationships:

Submit relationship Shows a form submitting its values to a server page.

Build relationship Indicates a server page building a client page.

Link relationship Shows a hypertext link between two client pages or between a server page and a client page.

NETLink relationship Models the relationship between a web form and a server page or HTML page.

NETRegister relationship Shows a server page containing a web user control.

NETTransfer Relationship Similar to a redirect relationship, but in this relationship, the page receiving control does have access to the same set of inherent objects (session, request, response, server, and application) as the original page.

NETExecute relationship Shows that control passes from one server page to another server page or an HTML page but that control returns to the original server page once the new page has finished its processing.

Redirect relationship A directed association that shows control passing from a server page to another server page or to a client page.

Each of the ASP .NET class stereotypes (ServerPage, ClientPage, HTMLForm, NETWebUser-Control) have the same properties and XDE code generation properties as those that were discussed in the "Classes" section earlier in this chapter. When you synchronize the code and the model, XDE creates the appropriate code files.

Web Services

Web services are modeled in XDE using the Web Service With Code-Behind option from the Web toolbox. XDE prompts you for the name of the web service, and then creates two classes: one with a stereotype of <<NETWebService>>, and an unstereotyped class representing the code-behind file. The classes are linked using an association with a stereotype of <<NetWebServiceProxy>>, as shown here:

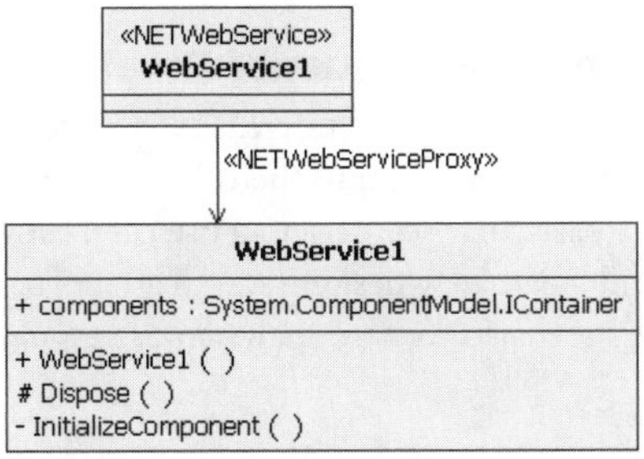

When you synchronize the code and model, XDE creates a file with an `.asmx` extension and the code-behind file containing the new web service for you.

To consume the service, use the Solution Explorer. Right-click the project and select Add Web Reference. Enter the path to the new file with an `.asmx` extension to use the service.

Building a Design Model

The analysis model is an implementation-independent view of the system you'll be building. It includes many of the salient entities and concepts of the system, but it doesn't get into the details of how these concepts are implemented in a programming language.

Once you've decided to use .NET, your team needs to translate the analysis model into the design model. The analysis model isn't always necessary; if you know from day one that you will be using .NET, you may decide to create just the design model. The design model is the implementation-specific view of the system. It defines specifically what classes and other elements you will need to implement the system, and it describes exactly how the system will work.

In this section, we examine the different diagrams that constitute the design model. Not every project needs all of these diagrams, but most need at least the sequence and class diagrams.

Moving from Analysis to Design

In a particular project, you may or may not have gone through the effort of creating an analysis model. If you've got one, begin the design by reviewing the analysis model. Map the analysis-level classes to design-level classes. This won't necessarily be a one-to-one mapping. For example, in analysis we may have created a generic boundary class called Timecard Form. Now, we decide that we need an HTML form to collect the employee's name and ID, and a server page to validate the information. Review each of the classes in the analysis model, and determine what design classes you need.

Boundary classes are the forms and windows in the system, as well as the interfaces to other systems or hardware. Each of the analysis-level boundary classes maps to one or more design classes. The same is true of the entity classes we identified in analysis. Control classes may or may not be carried over one-to-one into design. They are frequently used as business logic placeholders in analysis, and during design, the responsibilities of the control classes are mapped to business logic classes. In design, we give all of these classes language-specific names, and these are the names that are ultimately used in the code.

The transition from analysis classes to design classes is iterative. As time goes on, you may end up combining two or more analysis classes to form one design class, or you may merge design classes that are similar. This process is called *refactoring*, and is used to refine and optimize your design as the project goes along.

Building a Design-Level Sequence Diagram

Back in Chapter 4, we discussed how to create sequence diagrams at an analysis level. A *sequence diagram* is a type of interaction diagram in the UML, and it shows you, conceptually, what objects you need to implement a particular scenario in a use case. Now that we're in design, we can refine those analysis diagrams and create new design-level diagrams to see the specific objects that we need in order to implement a scenario. Where analysis was language-independent, we can assume in design that we're using C# or Visual Basic. We also know which DBMS and which other specific technologies we'll be using, so we can build the diagrams in the context of these technologies.

NOTE *There is another type of interaction diagram in the UML, called a collaboration diagram. Collaboration diagrams are not supported by XDE at this time.*

To build a design-level sequence diagram, follow these steps:

1. Select a use case scenario or a particular flow through a use case. Review the requirements and the flow of events for that scenario, and review any analysis-level diagrams created for the scenario.
2. Consider the scenario in the context of ASP .NET, C# .NET, and/or Visual Basic .NET. Go through each step in the flow of events and decide, specifically, what objects you need to implement the logic in that step.
3. Add the classes to the model, and then create objects on the sequence diagram.
4. Look through the messages on the analysis-level sequence diagram. In design, each message corresponds to an operation on the class receiving the message. Consider each analysis-level message, and create the operation(s) needed to implement each.
5. On the design-level sequence diagram, show the operations and their order of execution by adding messages.

You will most likely need a number of sequence diagrams for each use case. Typically, you'd create one for the primary, or basic, flow and one for each significant alternate flow.

Patterns are an essential part of this process. If you have created a pattern for error handling, use the pattern consistently as you build your diagram. The more patterns you establish, the more you minimize the risk of different designers taking different approaches to similar problems.

In XDE, sequence diagrams are created within an interaction instance, which is itself contained within a collaboration instance. A collaboration instance, also known as a use case realization, is an implementation-specific view of the design for the use case.

Here is an example of the structure of collaboration instances in XDE:

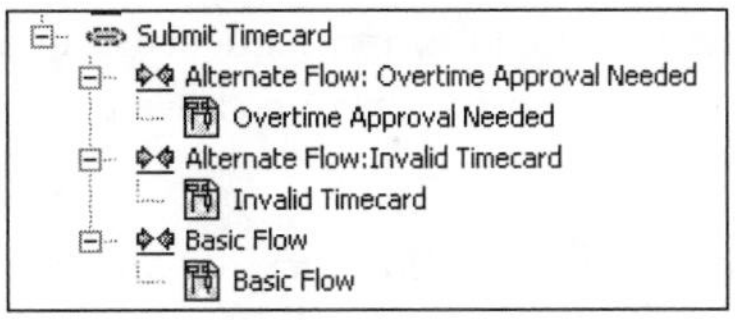

In this example, the collaboration instance is the use case realization Submit Timecard. The use case realizations for the other use cases are also collaboration instances. For the Submit Timecard use case, the interaction instances are Alternate Flow: Invalid Timecard, Alternate Flow: Overtime Approval Needed, and Basic Flow. The actual sequence diagrams are Invalid Timecard, Overtime Approval Needed, and Basic Flow.

All of the objects from the sequence diagrams for a use case are owned by the use case realization (the collaboration instance). The classes themselves are not owned by any specific collaboration instance because a single class is frequently used by multiple use cases. A single class may have instances in many collaboration instances, and a collaboration instance may use objects instantiated from classes anywhere in the model.

An interaction instance within a collaboration instance is used to model the design for a single flow of events (the basic flow or an alternate flow). A single collaboration instance typically has a number of interaction instances, one for each flow in the use case. Each of the collaboration instances contains a single sequence diagram, which helps you visualize the design for that flow of events.

To create a sequence diagram in XDE when a collaboration instance does not yet exist (that is, to create the first sequence diagram for a use case), follow these steps:

1. To create a new collaboration instance, interaction instance, and sequence diagram, right-click a package and choose Add Diagram ➢ Sequence: Instance.
2. Type the name of the new sequence diagram.

If a collaboration instance and interaction instance do not already exist, XDE automatically creates them for you. You can rename the collaboration instance (usually with the name of the use case) and interaction instance (usually with the name of the basic or alternate flow) if you like.

To create a new sequence diagram if the collaboration instance already exists (that is, to create a new sequence diagram for a use case that already has some sequence diagrams), follow these steps:

1. Right-click the existing collaboration instance in the Explorer and choose Add UML ➢ Interaction Instance.
2. Name the new interaction instance (usually with the name of the basic or alternate flow).
3. Right-click the new interaction instance and choose Add Diagram ➢ Sequence: Instance.
4. Name the new sequence diagram.

We were assuming here that you opted to put your collaboration instances into a separate package, which isn't required. Here are a few notes on creating sequence diagrams:

- You do not have to create the collaboration instances under a package. You can right-click any model element and select Add Diagram ➢ Sequence: Instance. This creates the collaboration instance, interaction instance, and sequence diagram under the selected model element. A frequently used pattern, however, is to create a package that holds all of the collaboration instances.
- You can create collaboration instances or interaction instances independently of creating a sequence diagram. Right-click an element in the Explorer and choose Add UML ➢ Collaboration Instance. Then, right-click the new collaboration instance and choose Add UML ➢ Interaction Instance. To add a sequence diagram to the interaction instance later, right-click the interaction instance and choose Add Diagram ➢ Sequence: Instance.

To delete a sequence diagram in XDE:

1. Locate the sequence diagram in the Explorer window.
2. Right-click the diagram and select Delete From Model.

Design-level sequence diagrams can frequently be long and complex. If this is the case, it can be helpful to break the diagram down into smaller ones. Create several different diagrams, and then link them using the following steps:

1. To link sequence diagram B to sequence diagram A, first open sequence diagram A.
2. Add a note to sequence diagram A.
3. Drag and drop sequence diagram B from the Explorer window onto the note. The text "Double-click to bring up the linked diagram sequence diagram B" will appear in the note.
4. Double-click the note to open the linked diagram.
5. To remove the link, simply delete the note.

The Sequence Diagram Toolbox

The sequence diagram toolbox includes options for creating objects, instances of actors, messages, and other elements on a sequence diagram. Table 6.6 lists the toolbox options and their meanings.

Table 6.6: Sequence Diagram Toolbox

Icon	Meaning
Pointer	Returns the mouse to the standard pointer
Lifeline	Adds an object to the diagram
Lifeline Actor	Adds an actor instance to the diagram
Message	Adds a message between objects, actors, or between an object and an actor
Return Message	Shows the return of a message
Create	Creates an object in memory
Destroy	Removes an object from memory
Note	Adds a simple note to the diagram
Note Attachment	Attaches a note to a use case or other element
Constraint	Refines the structure or behavior of an element
Text	Adds text to the diagram

Adding Objects and Actors

If you are building a design-level diagram from your analysis model, you can start with the analysis-level sequence diagram to identify actors and classes. However, don't assume that there is a one-to-one mapping between analysis classes and design classes. Go through each step on the analysis diagram, and determine what design-level classes will be needed to implement the step. We'll translate the analysis messages into design messages, which correspond to methods on the design classes.

If you are building a design-level diagram without an analysis model, start with the flow of events. Read through each step in the flow of events, and answer the following four questions:

- What objects will be needed to implement the step?
- What messages must be sent between the objects to implement the step?
- What order must the messages be in?
- What actors must send or receive messages to implement the step?

As you answer these questions, add objects, messages, and actors to the diagram. Then, move to the next step in the flow.

Objects are shown as boxes on the diagram. They are usually arranged at the top of the diagram, but they may be moved down to the point in the flow at which they are instantiated. There is a dashed line below each object, representing its lifeline. An "X" can be added to an object's lifeline, indicating where in the flow the object is destroyed from memory.

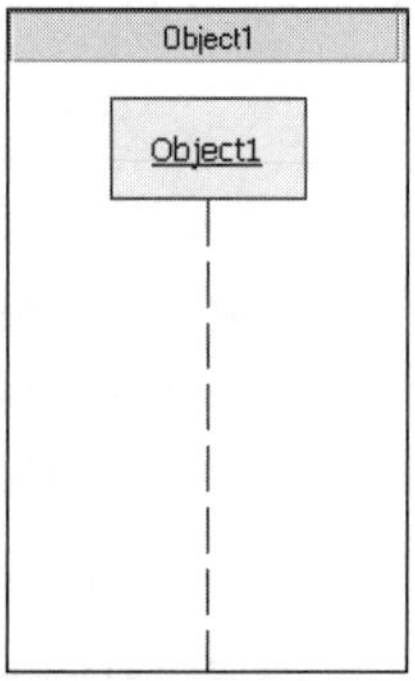

To add an object to a sequence diagram:

1. Add instances of existing classes by following these steps:
   - **A.** Drag and drop the class from the Explorer window to the sequence diagram.
   - **B.** (Optional) Name an object by right-clicking it and selecting Rename. This is generally not done in design.
2. If you need to, add other objects (that are not instances of existing classes, or have not yet been mapped to existing classes) using the following steps. Generally speaking, this shouldn't be done in design; all objects should map to classes in the design model.
   - **A.** Select the Lifeline option from the toolbox.
   - **B.** Click the diagram to place the new object.
   - **C.** Type the new object name.

Actors are also shown as boxes on the diagram. A small actor symbol on the right-hand side of the box lets you know that the object is an instance of an actor. Like objects, actor instances can be named.

To add an instance of an actor to a sequence diagram:

1. Add instances of existing actors:
   - **A.** Drag and drop the actor from the Explorer window to the sequence diagram.
   - **B.** (Optional) Name an actor instance by right-clicking it and selecting Rename. This is generally not done in design.
2. If you need to, add other actor instances. As with objects, this shouldn't generally be done in design. All actor instances should map to actors in the model.
   - **A.** Select the Lifeline Actor option from the toolbox.
   - **B.** Click the diagram to place the new actor instance.
   - **C.** Type the new actor instance name.

When an actor is another system, rather than a person, you need one or more classes to interface with that actor. On the sequence diagram, you should always show these interface classes. You can then show the interface classes communicating with the other classes in the system, as shown in Figure 6.1.

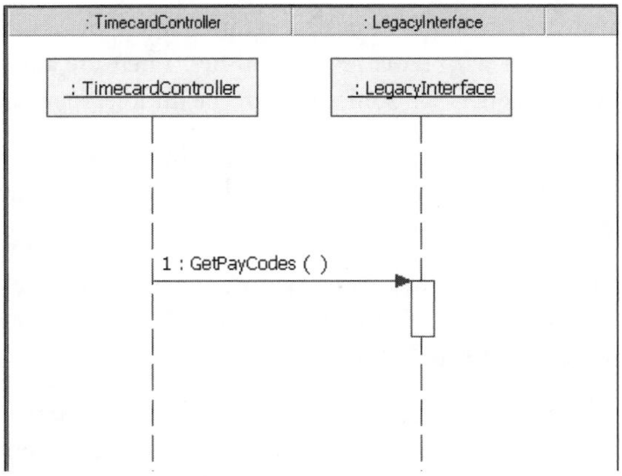

FIGURE 6.1

Actors on a sequence diagram

ADDING MESSAGES

Messages on a design-level sequence diagram correspond to the methods, or operations, on the design classes. A message from a client object to a supplier object means that the client is calling a method of the supplier. Messages can also be reflexive; a message from an object to itself means that the object is calling one of its own methods.

If you are working from an analysis model, translate each analysis-level message to an operation. In analysis, we wrote text messages, such as "Validate ID and password." Now, we identify the specific operations that we need, such as `Validate(ID:string, Pwd: string):int`. Obviously, we also need to identify the parameters and return types of the operations, if we haven't already done so. The message is drawn between the objects, as shown here:

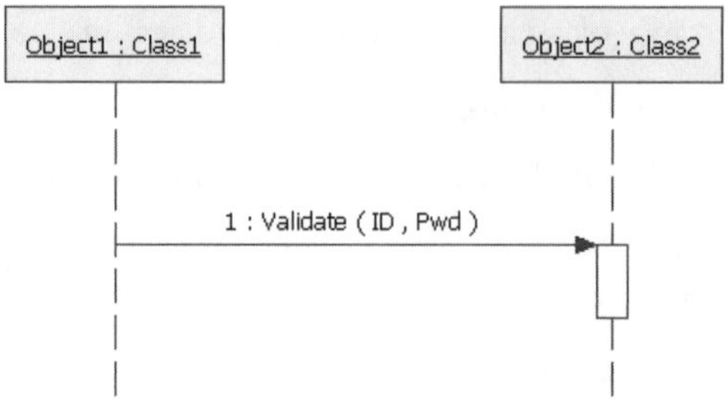

This translation effort usually results in a number of new operations being created, and frequently, it also results in new classes being created. In the validation example just described, we may have put the validation responsibility on a form in analysis. Now that we're in design, we may want to create a separate class to handle this responsibility.

So, we're making a great deal of the design decisions here, determining what classes we need and what the responsibilities of each class should be. Responsibilities are a primary focus of these diagrams. Always keep in mind as you're building these diagrams that you're allocating the responsibilities of the system to the various classes. Be sure that you aren't violating any architectural guidelines here, such as putting database responsibilities on an HTML page, or putting display logic on a business class. There are two extremes to design: creating a few classes that have a lot of responsibilities, or creating lots of classes with fewer responsibilities. There are advantages and disadvantages to each approach, and most designers fall somewhere in the middle. Here are a few things to consider:

- Creating a few large classes can make each individual class difficult to understand, maintain, or reuse. However, there won't be as many relationships to set up or maintain, so the overall system structure can be easier to understand.
- Creating a lot of small classes can increase the number of relationships between the classes, making the overall model harder to understand. However, each individual class is easier to understand, maintain, and reuse.
- Consider the direction of the messages on the sequence diagram. If two objects both send messages to each other, a bidirectional association between their classes on the class diagram results. Neither class can then be reused without the other, and a change to one can affect the other. Whenever possible, try to keep all messages between a given pair of objects going in the same direction.

The UML assumes that each message on the diagram returns some value. You can look at the operation signature to see the return type of the operation. There are times, though, when it helps to explicitly show the return of a message. You do this using a *return message*.

To add messages to a sequence diagram, follow these steps:

1. Add messages between objects, between actors, or between an object and an actor by following these steps:

   A. Select the Message icon from the toolbox.

B. Click the lifeline of the actor or object sending the message.

C. Click the lifeline of the actor or object receiving the message. To create a reflexive message, click again on the lifeline of the object sending the message.

D. Click the message text to display a drop-down list box of the methods of the supplier class. Select the appropriate method from the drop-down list box. Alternatively, locate the method in the Explorer window, and drag and drop the method onto the message.

E. To reorder the messages, simply drag and drop a message higher or lower in the diagram. XDE automatically renumbers the messages.

2. To show that one object instantiates another, use a create message from the lifeline of one object to the object it is creating:

   A. Move the object being created vertically on the diagram, until it corresponds to the point in time in which it will be created.

   B. Select the Create option on the toolbox.

   C. Click the lifeline of the object that is instantiating another.

   D. Click the object (the box, not the lifeline) being created. XDE creates a new message called \CreateOperation\. Optionally rename this message.

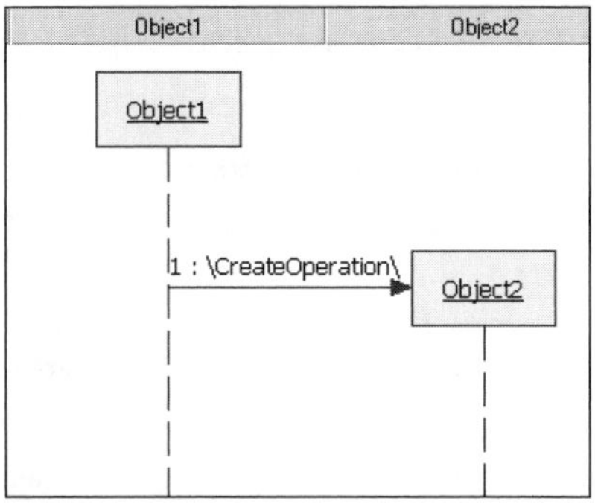

3. To show that one object destroys another, use a destroy message from the lifeline of one object to the lifeline of the object it is removing from memory (you can set this up using the following steps). An object can also destroy itself. In this case, the message both originates and ends on the same object.

   A. Select the Destroy option on the toolbox.

   B. Click the lifeline of the object that will destroy another.

   C. Click the lifeline of the object to be destroyed. XDE automatically shortens that object's lifeline and adds a destruction marker (a large "X").

4. Show return messages if you need to by following these steps:
    A. Select the Return Message option from the toolbox.
    B. Click the lifeline of the object sending the return.
    C. Click the lifeline of the object receiving the return message.
5. To delete a message, right-click it and select Delete From Model.

To change the display options for a message's parameters:

1. Select the message on the sequence diagram.
2. Modify the MessageSignature property. Selecting Name Only displays the parameter names but not their data types. Selecting Type Only displays the parameters' data types but not their names. Selecting Name and Type displays both the names and types, and selecting None hides the parameters on the diagram.

The UML does include some notation that is not yet supported by XDE. Specifically, the UML allows you to hide or display sequence numbers on a sequence diagram. XDE always displays the numbers and does not include an option for hiding them. The UML also supports variations on the message arrows for different types of messages. Table 6.7 lists these variations, which are not supported by XDE at this time.

TABLE 6.7: MESSAGE VARIATIONS IN THE UML

VARIATION	DESCRIPTION
Filled solid arrowhead rather than a standard arrowhead	Used to show a nested flow of control. All of the messages in the nested flow must be completed before the outer level sequence can resume.
Message arrow slanted downward	If a message will take a significant amount of time to arrive, the message arrow can be slanted downward to signify this.
Branching of messages	Branching can be used to show conditions on a sequence diagram. Each branch is labeled with a condition.

Although these options are not directly supported by XDE, you can always use a note or text on the diagram to show these variations.

FORMATTING A SEQUENCE DIAGRAM

There are a few menu options you can use to format your sequence diagram. These won't affect the meaning of the diagram at all, and are simply used to make the diagrams more readable.

To align objects vertically:

1. Select the objects to align.
2. Choose Format ➢ Align ➢ Tops.

To adjust the horizontal spacing between objects:

1. Select the objects.
2. Choose Format ➢ Horizontal Spacing ➢ Make Equal to evenly space the objects. Select Increase or Decrease to fine-tune the spacing between objects, or select Remove to place the objects next to each other.

Building a Design-Level Class Diagram

The elements on a design-level class diagram are similar to those we used for the analysis-level class diagrams, but here everything is language-dependent. Here, we remove the <<boundary>>, <<entity>>, and <<control>> stereotypes we used in analysis and use language-specific stereotypes instead.

Although a sequence diagram provides a view of the objects within a specific use case scenario, you use a class diagram to view a set of classes, not necessarily from the same use case scenario. Because you will use many classes in many different use cases, you will find that using a class diagram is a good way to consolidate and view all of the behavior and information in the class, as well as the relationships between the classes. As we mentioned in analysis, you typically create many class diagrams. Some show classes, others show packages of classes.

To create a class diagram in XDE:

1. Right-click a package, class, operation, component, use case, or actor, and choose Add Diagram ➢ Class.
2. Name the new diagram. XDE does not require that class diagrams have unique names, but we recommend that they do.

To delete a class diagram in XDE:

1. Right-click the diagram in the Explorer window.
2. Select Delete From Model.

To change another type of diagram into a class diagram:

1. Open the other diagram.
2. Edit the diagram's UML ➢ Type property, setting it to 1- Class.

The Class Diagram Toolbox

You can use the class diagram toolbox to add classes, relationships, and other elements to a class diagram. Table 6.8 lists the toolbox options and their meanings.

TABLE 6.8: CLASS DIAGRAM TOOLBOX

ICON	MEANING
Pointer	Returns the mouse to the standard pointer
Package	Creates a package of classes
Class	Creates a class
Interface	Creates an interface for a class or subsystem
Signal	Creates a signal, which is an asynchronous communication between objects
Enumeration	Creates an enumeration, which is a data type containing a list of values
Association	Creates an association relationship between two model elements
Directed Association	Creates a unidirectional association relationship between two model elements
Aggregation Association	Creates an aggregation relationship between two model elements
Composition Association	Creates a composition relationship between two model elements
Association Class	Creates an association class, which is used to hold information and/or behavior related to an association
Generalization	Creates an inheritance relationship between two model elements
Realization	Creates a realization relationship between two model elements
Dependency	Creates a dependency relationship between two model elements
Bind	Creates a bind relationship between an element and a template
Usage	Creates a usage relationship between two model elements in which one element requires the presence of the other
Friend Permission	Creates a friend relationship between model elements, giving one element access to the contents of the other
Abstraction	Creates an abstraction relationship between two elements, showing that the elements contain the same information at different levels of abstraction
Instantiate	Shows that one element instantiates another
Subsystem	Creates a subsystem, which is a package with a defined interface
Note	Adds a simple note to the diagram
Note Attachment	Attaches a note to a use case or other element
Constraint	Refines the structure or behavior of an element
Constraint Attachment	Attaches a constraint to an element
Text	Adds text to the diagram

WORKING WITH ELEMENTS ON A CLASS DIAGRAM

You can add classes, including interfaces and other stereotyped classes, using the Explorer window or directly on a class diagram. Once you've added a class or other element, you can use it on as many different class diagrams as you need. XDE maintains only one copy of the class in a central repository. Any changes you make to the class are automatically reflected on all class diagrams that contain the class. Relationships are added using a class diagram and are also maintained in the central repository.

To add a class or a relationship, select the appropriate item from the UML Class toolbox, and then click inside the diagram. See the appropriate section elsewhere in this chapter for instructions related to adding specific types of classes or relationships.

To delete an element from one diagram:

1. Right-click the element on the diagram.
2. Select Delete From Diagram.

To delete an element from the model:

1. Right-click the element on a class diagram or in the Explorer window.
2. Select Delete From Model.

TIP *If you accidentally delete an element from the model, you can undo the deletion by choosing Edit ➢ Undo.*

FORMATTING A CLASS DIAGRAM

There are various options you can set to change the look of your class diagrams. None of these options has any syntactic meaning, and none affects any of the generated code. They are simply used to make the diagrams more readable.

The following instructions cover how to format specific classes or other elements on a class diagram. To change these settings for all classes or other elements, choose Tools ➢ Options. Use the settings under Rational XDE ➢ Appearance to affect all elements.

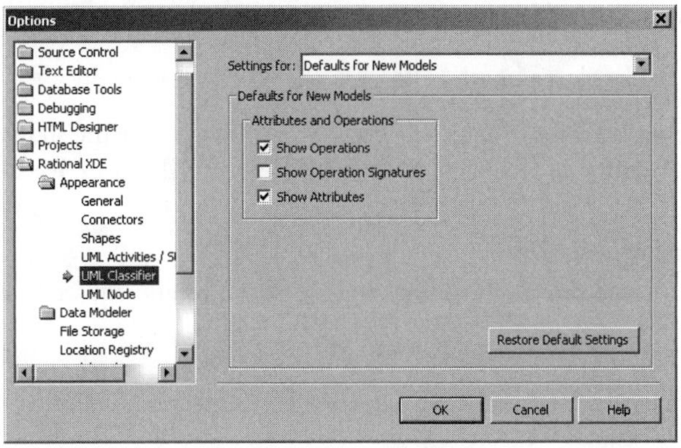

Formatting Attributes and Operations

To show or hide attributes or operations on a class diagram:

1. Select the class(es) to show or hide attributes or operations.
2. Choose Format ➢ Compartment and then Attribute Compartment or Operation Compartment to show or hide the attributes and/or operations for the selected class(es). Hiding attributes or operations from one diagram does not delete them from the model.

To view the full operation signatures on a class diagram:

1. Select the class(es) to modify.
2. Choose Format ➢ Signature ➢ Operation Signature to show the full operation signature, or deselect this option to show only the operation names.

Formatting Stereotypes

To view stereotypes as icons:

1. Select the class(es) to modify.
2. Choose Format ➢ Stereotype and Visibility Style. Select from the following options:

   Shape Stereotype: None Hides the stereotype completely.

   Shape Stereotype: Label Lets you view the stereotype as a label in the Name compartment of the class.

   Shape Stereotype: Icon Lets you view the stereotype using the UML icons.

To add your own stereotype icons:

1. Select a model element whose stereotype you want to modify.
2. Click the ellipsis (…) button in the Stereotype property for that element.
3. In the Stereotype list, type a new stereotype name or select from the list of existing stereotypes.
4. In the Explorer Image field, click the ellipsis button.
5. Navigate to the graphic file containing the icon for the stereotype. XDE supports the following graphic file formats: BMP, EMF, WMF, GIF, JPG, PNG, and TIF.

Formatting Relationships

To alternate between diagonal lines for relationships and squared (rectilinear) lines:

1. Select the relationship(s) to modify.
2. Choose Format ➢ Line Style, then Rectilinear or Oblique.

Layout Options

To layout items on a class diagram:

1. Select the classes or other elements to align.
2. Choose Format ➢ Align, and then the alignment method (tops, centers, and so on).

To resize items on a class diagram:

1. Select the classes or other elements to resize.
2. Choose Format ➢ Make Same Size to change the width, height, or both of the selected items.

To change the spacing on a class diagram:

1. Select the elements to modify.
2. Choose Format ➢ Horizontal Spacing (or Vertical Spacing) to change the spacing between elements.

To have XDE automatically lay out the diagram:

1. Open the diagram.
2. (Optional) Select the elements to arrange. If none are selected, XDE arranges all elements on the diagram.
3. Choose Diagram ➢ Arrange.

To add a geometric shape to the diagram:

1. Open the diagram.
2. Choose Modeling ➢ Add Geometric Shapes to add a shape.

Building a Statechart Diagram

A statechart diagram shows the lifecycle of a single object, from the time it is created until it is destroyed. These diagrams provide a good way to model the dynamic behavior of a class. In a typical project, you do not create a statechart diagram for every class; in fact, many projects do not use them at all. But if you have a class that has some significant dynamic behavior, it helps to create a statechart diagram for it. A class with significant dynamic behavior is one that can exist in many states. To decide whether a class has significant dynamic behavior, begin by looking at its attributes. Consider how an instance of the class might behave differently with different values in an attribute. For instance, an attribute called Status can be a good indicator of various states. How does the object behave differently as different values are placed in this attribute?

You can also examine the relationships of a class. Look for any relationships with a zero in the multiplicity. Zeroes indicate that the relationship is optional. Does an instance of the class behave differently when the relationship does or does not exist? If it does, you may have multiple states. For example, let's look at a relationship between a person and a company. If there is a relationship, the person is in an employed state. If there is no relationship, the person may have been fired or have retired.

In XDE, no source code is generated from a statechart diagram. These diagrams serve to document the dynamic behavior of a class so that developers and analysts have a clear understanding of this behavior. The developers are ultimately responsible for implementing the logic outlined in this diagram. As with the other UML diagrams, statechart diagrams give the team a chance to discuss and document the logic before it is coded.

To create a statechart diagram, right-click a package, class, or operation and choose Add Diagram ➢ Statechart. The diagram will appear in the browser with the following symbol: .

THE STATECHART DIAGRAM TOOLBOX

You can use the statechart diagram toolbox to add states, transitions, and other elements to a statechart diagram. Table 6.9 lists the toolbox options and their meanings.

TABLE 6.9: STATECHART DIAGRAM TOOLBOX

ICON	MEANING
Pointer	Returns the mouse to the standard pointer
State	Creates a state
Transition	Creates a transition between two states or other elements
SelfTransition	Creates a transition from a state to itself
Initial State	Marks the starting point of the diagram
Final State	Marks the ending state for the object, which is the state the object is in before it is destroyed
Junction Point	Brings branches of the flow on the diagram back together
Shallow History	Notation that keeps track of the most recent state within a substate so that the flow can return to that state when the substate is re-entered
Deep History	Notation that keeps track of the most recent state within a substate, no matter how far nested the recent state is
Choice Point	Marks a decision point on the diagram
Synchronization	Used to show concurrent states
Submachine State	Used to reference another state machine, defined elsewhere
Stub State	Used to show entry or exit points in a submachine state
Synch State	Shows synchronization points between layers in a concurrent state
Concurrent State	Shows two or more branches of the flow executing concurrently
Note	Adds a simple note to the diagram
Note Attachment	Attaches a note to a use case or other element
Constraint	Refines the structure or behavior of an element
Text	Adds text to the diagram

Adding States

A *state* is one of the possible conditions in which an object may exist. As we discussed earlier, you can examine two areas to determine the state of an object: the values of the attributes and the relationships to other objects. Consider the different values that can be placed in the attributes and the state of the object if a relationship does or does not exist.

As with other XDE elements, you can add documentation to a state. However, because code is not generated from these diagrams, comments are not inserted into generated code for state documentation.

In UML, a state is shown as a rounded rectangle, like so:

To add a state, use the State option in the UML Statechart toolbox.

Adding State Details

While an object is in a particular state, there may be some activity that it performs. A report may be generated, some calculation may occur, or an event may be sent to another object. There are five types of information you can include for a state: a do action, an entry action, an exit action, an event, or state history. We'll discuss each of these here.

Do Action

A *do action* is some behavior that an object carries out while it is in a particular state. For example, when an account is in the closed state, the account holder's signature card is pulled. When a flight is in a cancelled state, the airline tries to find alternate flights for its customers. A do action is an interruptible behavior. It may run to completion while the object is in that state, or it may be interrupted when the object moves to another state.

A do action is shown inside the state itself, preceded by the word *do*.

To add a do action, right-click the state and choose Add UML ➢ Do Action.

Entry Action

An *entry action* is a behavior that occurs while the object is transitioning into the state. As soon as a flight becomes scheduled, the system posts the schedule to the Internet. This happens while the flight is transitioned to the Scheduled state. Unlike a do action, an entry action is considered to be noninterruptible. Although posting a schedule record for use on the Internet is technically interruptible, it happens very fast, and the user is not able to easily cancel the transaction while it is occurring. Therefore, it can be modeled as an entry action.

An entry action is shown inside the state, preceded by the word *entry*.

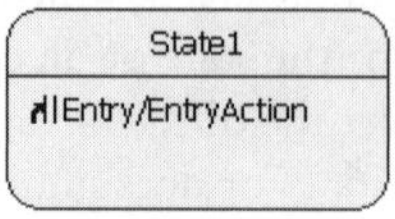

To add an entry action, right-click the state and choose Add UML ➢ Entry Action.

Exit Action

An *exit action* is similar to an entry action; however, an exit action occurs as part of the transition out of a state. For example, when the plane lands and transitions out of the In Flight state, the system records the landing time. Like an entry action, an exit action is considered to be noninterruptible.

An exit action is shown inside the state, preceded by the word *exit*.

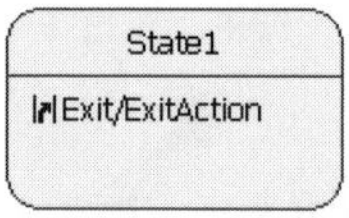

To add an exit action, right-click the state and choose Add UML ➢ Exit Action.

The behavior in an activity, entry action, or exit action can include sending an event to some other object. For example, if the flight is delayed for more than four hours, the flight object may need to send an event to a flight scheduler object, which will automatically reschedule the flight for another day. In this case, the activity, entry action, or exit action is preceded by a ^. The diagram would then read

Do: ^Target.Event(Arguments)

where Target is the object receiving the event, Event is the message being sent, and Arguments are the parameters of the message being sent.

ADDING TRANSITIONS

A *transition* is a movement from one state to another. The set of transitions on a diagram show how the object moves from one state to another. On the diagram, each transition is drawn as an arrow from the originating state to the succeeding state.

Transitions can also be reflexive. Something may happen that causes an object to transition back to the state it is currently in. Reflexive transitions are shown as an arrow starting and ending on the same state.

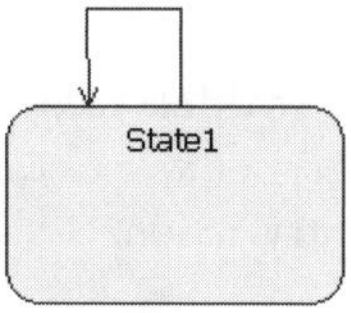

To add a transition:

1. Select Transition from the UML Statechart toolbox.
2. Click the state where the transition begins.
3. Click the state where the transition ends.

To add a reflexive transition:

1. Select SelfTransition from the toolbox.
2. Click the state where the reflexive transition occurs.

ADDING TRANSITION DETAILS

There are various specifications you can include for each transition. These include events, guard conditions, actions, and send events. We look at each of these in this section.

Event

An *event* is something that occurs that causes a transition from one state to another. In the airline example, the Land event transitions the flight from an In Flight status to a Landed status. If the flight was delayed, it becomes closed if the Plane Arrived event happens. An event is shown on the diagram along the transition arrow. XDE supports four types of events:

Call Events Used when you trigger a transition by calling an operation. Call events use the following icon: .

Time Events Used when you trigger a transition by the passage of a specified amount of time, or at a specified date and time. Time events use the following icon: .

Signal Events Used when you trigger a transition by the receipt of a signal. Signal events use the following icon: .

Change Events Used when you trigger a transition by a condition changing from False to True. Change events use the following icon: .

On a statechart diagram, events (regardless of type) are drawn along the transition arrow, as shown here:

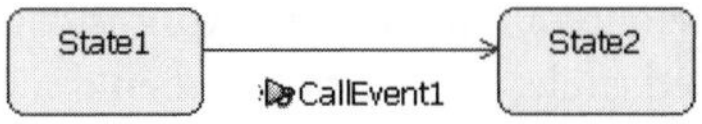

Most transitions have events—the events are what cause the transition to occur in the first place. However, you can also have an *automatic transition*, which has no event. With an automatic transition, an object automatically moves from one state to another as soon as all the entry actions, do actions, and exit actions have occurred.

To add an event, right-click the transition line on the statechart diagram, and select Add UML, followed by Call Event, Change Event, Signal Event, or Time Event.

Guard Condition

A *guard condition* controls when a transition can or cannot occur. In the airline example, adding a passenger moves the flight from the Open to the Full state, but *only if* the last seat was sold. The guard condition in this example is "Last seat was sold."

A guard condition is drawn along the transition line, after the event name, and is enclosed in square brackets.

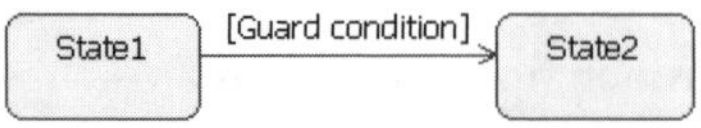

Guard conditions are optional. However, if there is more than one automatic transition out of a state, there must be mutually exclusive guard conditions on each automatic transition. This helps the reader of the diagram understand which path is taken automatically.

To add a guard condition, modify the GuardCondition property of the transition.

Action

An *action* is a noninterruptible behavior that occurs as part of a transition. Entry and exit actions are shown inside states because they define what happens every time an object enters or leaves a state. Other actions, however, are drawn along the transition line because they won't apply every time an object enters or leaves a state.

An action is shown along the transition line, after the event name, and preceded by a slash.

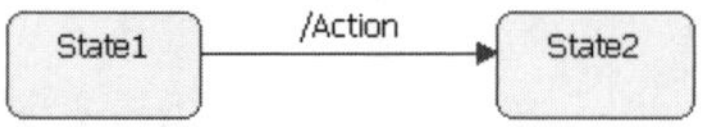

To add an action, modify the Action property of the transition. Do not enter the slash; XDE adds that for you when it adds the action to the diagram.

ADDING SPECIAL STATES

There are two special states that can be added to the diagram: the initial state and the final state.

Initial State

The *initial state* is the state the object is in when it is first created. An account object, for example, may start in a pending state until all of the paperwork is completed. The initial state is drawn on a statechart diagram as a filled circle. A transition is then drawn from the circle to the initial state:

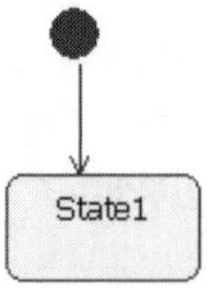

An initial state is mandatory: the reader of the diagram needs to know what state a new object is in. There can be only one initial state on the diagram, although nested states may contain additional initial states. We'll get to nested states in a moment. To add an initial state, use the Initial State option in the UML Statechart toolbox.

Final State

The *final state* is the state an object is in when it is destroyed. A final state is shown on the diagram as a bull's-eye. Final states are optional, and you can add as many final states as you need.

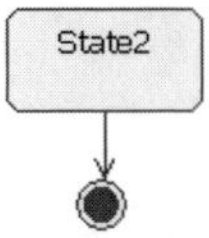

To add a final state, use the Final State option on the UML Statechart toolbox.

ADDING CHOICE POINTS, JUNCTION POINTS, AND SYNCHRONIZATIONS

Choice points, junction points, and synchronizations are used to show how the flow of logic branches and merges as you go through the diagram. A *choice point* (also referred to as a *dynamic choice point* in the UML) is used to show the branching of paths on a statechart diagram. The transitions exiting a choice point must have mutually exclusive guard conditions. The choice point itself is shown as a circle.

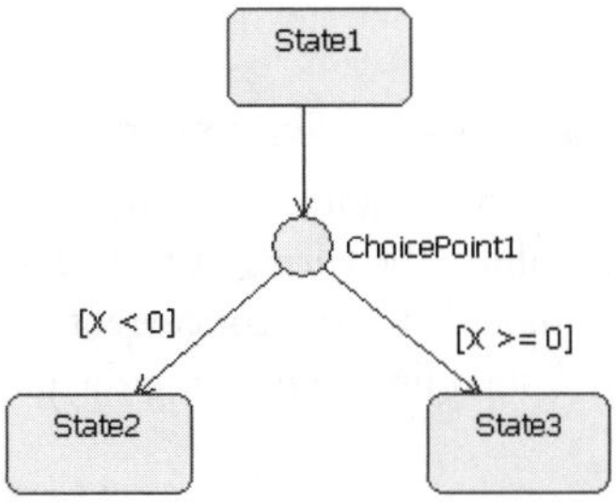

A *junction point* is used to show how different branches merge back together. Two or more states may have transitions into the junction point, and one or more transitions may leave. A junction point is shown as a filled circle:

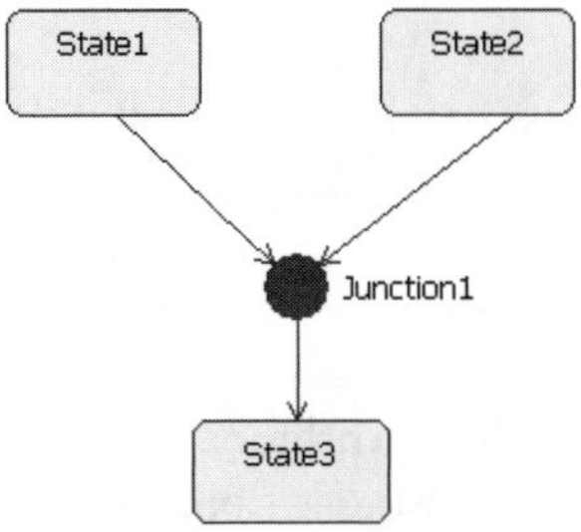

A *synchronization* is similar to a choice or junction point in that it is used to branch the flow or join it back together. The difference is that a choice point divides the flow into mutually exclusive paths, while a synchronization divides the flow into paths that execute simultaneously. When the simultaneous paths have finished, the flow can join again using another synchronization:

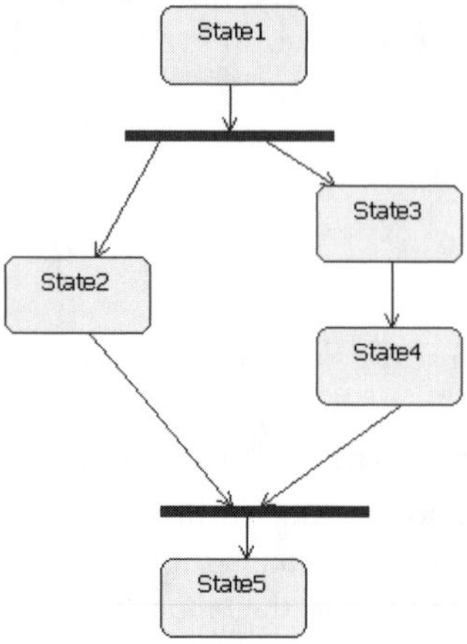

Choice points, junction points, and synchronizations can all be added using the UML Statechart toolbox.

Adding Synch States and Concurrent States

Sometimes, there are two or more states that happen concurrently. For example, in building a house, the electrician may be installing the wiring at the same time the plumber is installing the plumbing. This type of situation is modeled using concurrent states. Concurrent states are shown inside a rounded rectangle, with dashed lines separating the paths of the concurrent states:

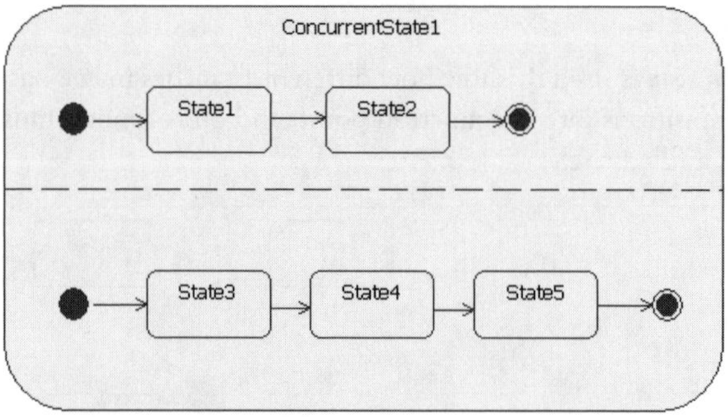

A synch state is used to show synchronizations between the different regions in a concurrent state. A synch state has incoming transitions from a source region, and outgoing transitions to a target region. For example, if a specific state in one region cannot be entered until a state in another region is complete, a synch state can be used:

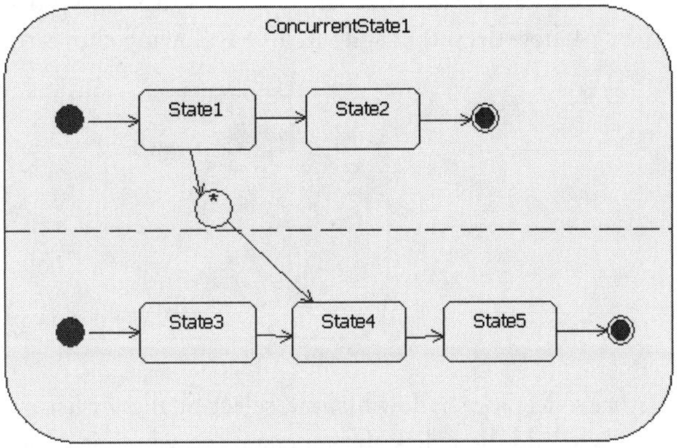

Using Nested States

To reduce clutter on your diagram, you can nest one or more states inside another. The nested states are referred to as *substates,* while the larger state is referred to as a *superstate.* If two or more states have an identical transition, they can be grouped together into a superstate. Then, rather than maintaining two identical transitions (one for each state), the transition can be moved to the superstate.

At times, you may need the system to remember which state it was last in. If you have three states in a superstate, and then you leave the superstate, you may want the system to remember where you left off. In our example, if we want to temporarily suspend reservations while the system is undergoing routine maintenance, we may transition to a SuspendReservations state while the maintenance is occurring. Once the maintenance is done, we want to return to whatever state the flight was in before the maintenance started.

There are two things you can do to resolve this issue. The first is to add a start state inside the superstate. The start state indicates where the default starting point is in the superstate. The first time the object enters that superstate, this is where the object will be.

The second is to use state history to remember where the object was. If the history option is set, an object can leave a superstate, then return and pick up right where it left off. The History option is shown with a small H in a circle:

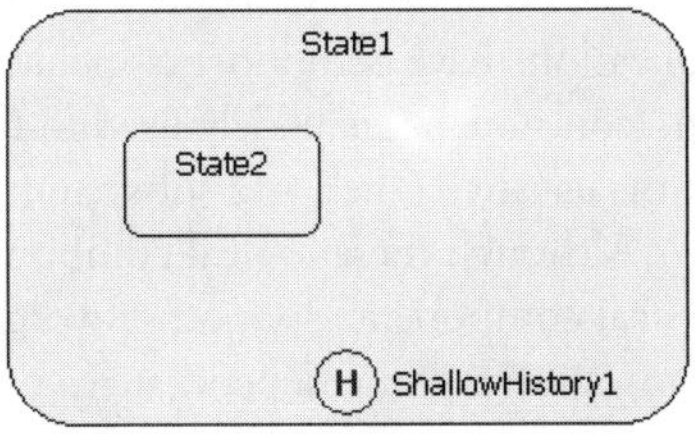

There are two types of history icons. A shallow history, as just shown, keeps track of the substate the object was last in, and resumes at that substate the next time control returns to the superstate. A deep history, shown as an H*, suggests that we need to keep track of the last state, even if it was a substate inside a substate inside another substate. With a deep history, the object resumes at the last state, regardless of how deep that state is. The following shows the symbol for a deep history:

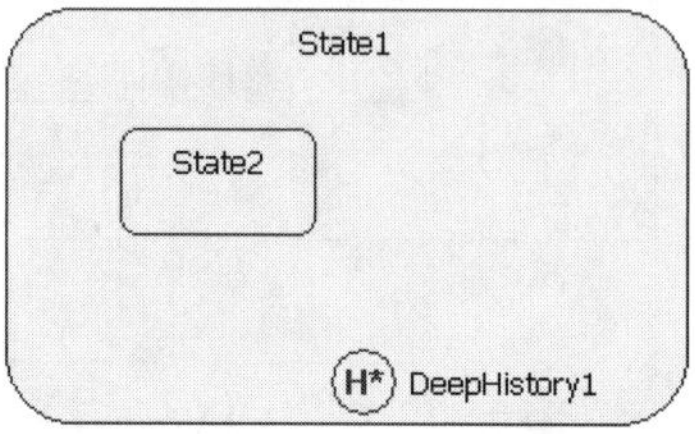

To add either a deep or shallow history, select Shallow History or Deep History from the UML Statechart toolbox, and then click the superstate to which it applies.

USING SUBMACHINE STATES

A *submachine state* is a final piece of notation you can add to a statechart diagram. This notation simply suggests that the current state machine is invoking another state machine, which is defined elsewhere.

Stub states are used to show where you enter or exit the submachine state. For example, if we enter a submachine state at SubMachState2, the submachine state notation would be as follows:

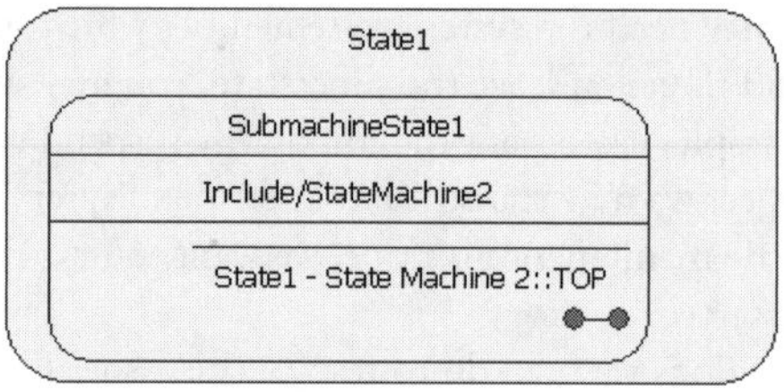

Building a Component Diagram

Component diagrams provide you with a means to look at the implementation model of the project. Components represent the physical files, both source code and executable, in your application. In .NET applications, components include files such as those with an extension of `.aspx`, `.cs`, `.vb`, or `.exe`. Web applications have components including HTML files, JSP files, and ASP files.

Note that the term "component" is widely used in the industry to mean any relatively independent, encapsulated part of a system (such as a subsystem or a group of classes working together to accomplish some goal). Although these logical components are still a big part of design, this section deals strictly with physical components—in other words, files.

Component diagrams show you the dependencies between the components that make up the system. In XDE, component diagrams may contain packages, components, component instances, and interfaces. Dependency, realization, association, and residency relationships may be made between elements on a component diagram.

To create a component diagram in XDE:

1. Right-click a package in the Explorer window.
2. Choose Add Diagram ➢ Component.

To delete a component diagram in XDE:

1. Right-click the diagram in the Explorer window.
2. Choose Delete From Model.

The Component Diagram Toolbox

The component diagram toolbox is used to add components, relationships, and other elements to a component diagram. Table 6.10 lists the toolbox options and their meanings.

Table 6.10: Component Diagram Toolbox

Icon	Meaning
Pointer	Returns the mouse to the standard pointer
Package	Creates a package of components
Component	Creates a component
Component Instance	Creates a component instance
Interface	Creates an interface
Dependency	Creates a dependency relationship between two model elements
Realization	Creates a realization relationship between two model elements
Association	Creates an association relationship between two model elements
Reside	Creates a residency relationship between two model elements
Note	Adds a simple note to the diagram
Note Attachment	Attaches a note to a use case or other element
Constraint	Refines the structure or behavior of an element
Constraint Attachment	Attaches a constraint to an element
Text	Adds text to the diagram

Working with Elements on a Component Diagram

We can use component diagrams to show the components in our system, the relationships between them, and the interfaces they implement. All of these options are available in the UML Component toolbox. In this section, we discuss the available options. In XDE, a component diagram appears in the Explorer window with the following symbol: 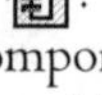.

Let's begin with components themselves. A component is a physical, replaceable part of a system. It corresponds to a physical file, such as a CS file or HTML page. It may hold only a single class, or it may contain a number of classes and other model elements that work together. In the UML, a component is drawn using the following notation:

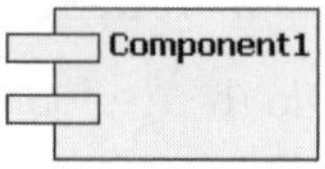

For the most part, you won't need to manually add a component. When you reverse engineer a .NET application or generate code from your model, XDE automatically creates the appropriate components for you.

If you do need to add a component manually, you can use the Component option in the UML Component toolbox.

There are three primary types of relationships to use on a component diagram: a dependency, a resides relationship, and a realizes relationship. A dependency indicates that an element in one component must access an element in another component, and it is represented as follows:

A resides relationship indicates that a class or other model element resides in a component:

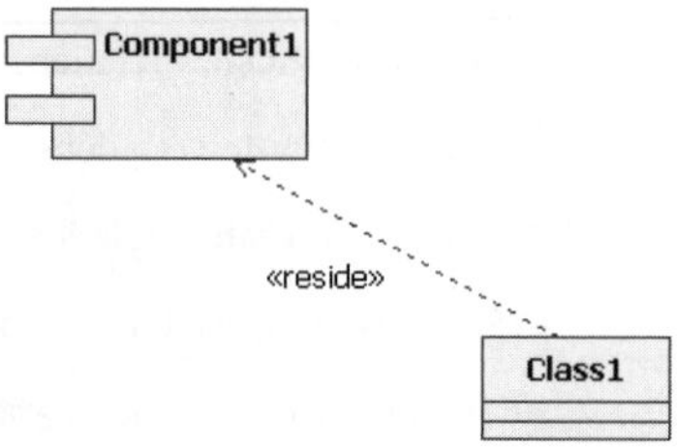

A realizes relationship connects a component to an interface that it realizes. An interface is drawn as a stereotyped class, just as it was on a class diagram.

To add a component or relationship, select the appropriate item from the UML Component toolbox, and then click inside the diagram.

To delete an element from one diagram:

1. Right-click the element on the diagram.
2. Choose Delete From Diagram.

To delete an element from the model:

1. Right-click the element on a component diagram or in the Explorer window.
2. Choose Delete From Model.

TIP *Deleting an element from a diagram does not delete it from the model. This also applies to relationships. Be careful that you do not delete elements from the diagram when you intended to delete them from the model.*

Building a Deployment Diagram

A deployment diagram is used to model how the application will be deployed on a network. We've defined our components, and the deployment diagram will be used to map the run-time components to the hardware on which they will run. Until now, we haven't focused on things such as network bandwidth or backup servers; a deployment diagram is a good place to incorporate issues like this.

The Deployment Diagram Toolbox

The deployment diagram toolbox is used to add elements to a deployment diagram. Table 6.11 lists the toolbox options and their meanings.

TABLE 6.11: DEPLOYMENT DIAGRAM TOOLBOX

Icon	Meaning
Pointer	Returns the mouse to the standard pointer
Node	Adds a processing node type to the diagram
Node Instance	Adds an instance of a node type to the diagram
Deploy	Shows the relationship between a component and the hardware it executes on
Association	Shows a physical connection between nodes
Note	Adds a simple note to the diagram
Note Attachment	Attaches a note to a use case or other element
Constraint	Refines the structure or behavior of an element
Constraint Attachment	Attaches a constraint to an element
Text	Adds text to the diagram
Cloud	Adds an Internet "cloud" to the diagram
Communication Link	Adds a link between nodes (not necessarily a physical link)

Continued on next page

TABLE 6.11: DEPLOYMENT DIAGRAM TOOLBOX *(continued)*

ICON	MEANING
Desktop	Adds a desktop computer to the diagram
Ethernet	Adds an Ethernet to the diagram
Fax	Adds a fax machine to the diagram
FDDI	Adds a fiber distributed data interface (FDDI) network backbone to the diagram
Hub	Adds a network hub to the diagram
Laptop	Adds a laptop computer to the diagram
Mainframe	Adds a mainframe computer to the diagram
Mini Computer	Adds a mini to the diagram
Modem	Adds a modem to the diagram
Plotter	Adds a plotter to the diagram
Printer	Adds a printer to the diagram
Radio Tower	Adds a radio tower to the diagram
Router	Adds a network router to the diagram
Satellite	Adds a satellite to the diagram
Satellite Dish	Adds a satellite dish to the diagram
Scanner	Adds a scanner to the diagram
Tower	Adds a tower computer to the diagram

WORKING WITH ELEMENTS ON A DEPLOYMENT DIAGRAM

In the UML, a deployment diagram is very simple. It consists of only a few pieces of notation. The first is a *node*, which is a type of processing resource. For example, an application may have nodes called "server" and "workstation." A *node instance* is simply an instance of a particular type of node. For example, each workstation on a LAN is an instance of the "workstation" node. Both nodes and node instances are drawn as cubes, but the name of a node instance is underlined. A node instance is named using the instance name, followed by a colon, followed by the node name.

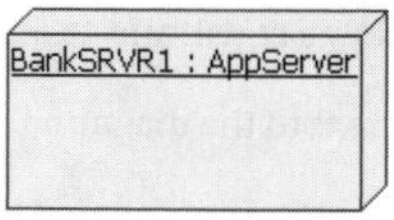

NOTE *From this point on, we use the term "node" to refer to both nodes and node instances.*

Communication associations are used to connect the nodes on the diagram. Each association represents a physical connection between nodes. If you'd like, you can create stereotypes such as <<LAN>> or <<Internet>> to show what type of connection exists. A communication relationship is drawn as an association, as shown here:

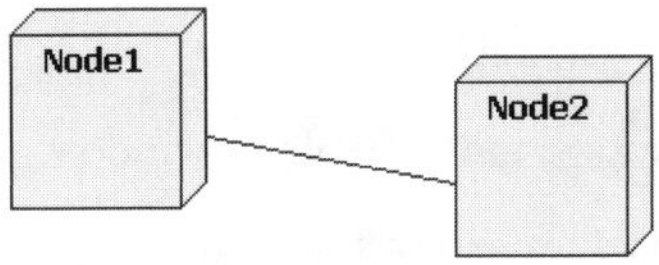

Inside each node instance, you can show the run-time component(s) that execute on that node, along with their interfaces and dependencies. Graphically, the components are displayed inside the node, like so:

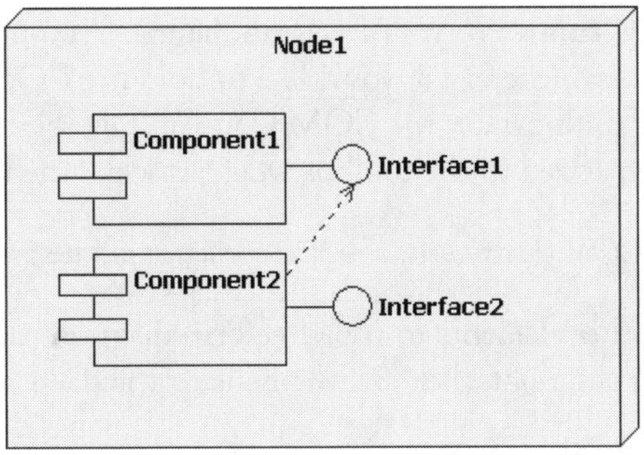

However, there is alternate notation. Rather than display a component inside a node, you can draw a dependency between the component and the node, and give the dependency the stereotype <<deploy>>. The following is an example of a deployment diagram:

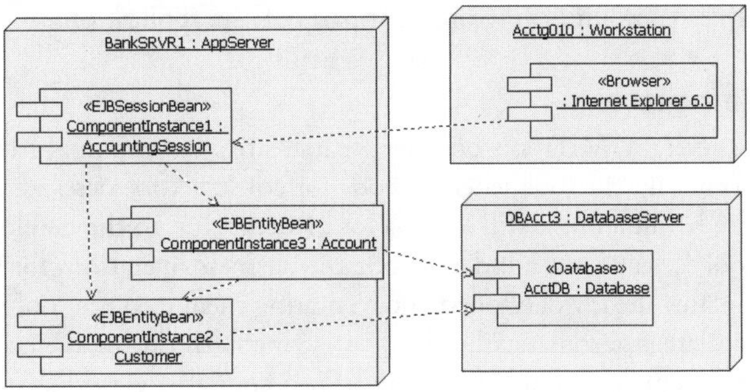

XDE goes beyond the standard UML notation to provide some extra icons that you can use on your deployment diagram. These icons, listed previously in Table 6.11, can help you and the team obtain a clearer understanding of the hardware needed for deployment.

Building a Freeform Diagram

Although the UML provides a number of different views of a system, there are times when you may need additional views. XDE includes the ability to create a freeform diagram. A freeform diagram can contain any of the elements displayed on any of the other types of diagrams, geometric shapes, or COM controls.

To create a freeform diagram in XDE:

1. Right-click a package in the Explorer window.
2. Choose Add Diagram ➢ Freeform.

To delete a freeform diagram in XDE:

1. Right-click the diagram in the Explorer window.
2. Select Delete From Model.

To add a COM control to your freeform diagram, you must first customize the toolbox. Select the General tab, or whichever tab you'd like to hold the COM controls. Right-click the toolbox and select Customize Toolbox. On the COM Controls tab, select the controls you want to use. Once the controls have been added to the toolbox, you can select them and add them to the diagram.

TIP *You can add COM objects to any type of diagram, not just the freeform diagrams.*

You can add other elements to your freeform diagram using the different tabs in the toolbox. To add geometric shapes, right-click anywhere inside the diagram and select Add Geometric Shapes.

Working with .NET Code

Until now, we've focused on the modeling side of application development. Now, let's take a look at the code itself and discuss how the code and model are kept in sync. In this section, we also cover code templates, which are a useful way of inserting standard code into the application and helping to ensure consistency among the different parts of the application.

Code Templates

There are several UML tools out there that create some minimal code during the code generation process. Typically, the tool generates code for constructors, destructors, and get and set operations. That's very helpful, but it still leaves a lot of coding up to the developers. Of course, there's no way for any tool to read your mind and code the business operations for you, but if you do have some code templates already developed, incorporating them into the tool can save a lot of time. The code in the template is automatically added to the methods during the code generation process.

A code template is simply some predefined code that you'd like inserted into one or more operation bodies during code generation. For example, maybe you have some pre-existing code that you always use in exception handling. By associating this pre-existing code with an exception handling method, XDE will insert the code during code generation. The process of associating a template to a model element is referred to as *binding*.

NOTE *Code templates are different from patterns; patterns are developed for reuse among models, while code templates are developed for reuse in code.*

XDE takes this idea a little bit further. You can enter static text that will be inserted as code into a method, or you can write a small program in JavaScript as the code template. The JavaScript program runs during code generation, and its results are inserted into the method code. We'll look at an example in just a minute.

Either of these approaches (static code or JavaScript) save the developers a lot of time and trouble and increase the consistency of your code. As you complete more and more projects, look for opportunities to create these code templates to save time in the future.

Code Template Syntax

Producing the simplest syntax for a template involves simply entering the code that you want included in the method. The code you enter is exactly what appears in the generated operation. This practice is useful for both static code or static comments, such as copyright information.

Another option is to add some JavaScript to the template body. The JavaScript scriptlet is enclosed in `<%` and `%>` tags. During code generation, XDE runs the scriptlet to create the code for the operation. For example, if we enter the following scriptlet into the template body:

```
//Copyright 2002 YourCompany
//Return statement generated from a code template

Return "<%=thisElement.getName()%>";
```

the following is the code for the generated operation:

```
Public string Operation1()
{
//Copyright 2002 YourCompany
//Return statement generated from a code template

Return "Operation1";
}
```

A great feature of using scriptlets is that they let you reference items within the XDE model. For example, if you wanted to generate an operation that would print the name of the class, you could use the syntax `thiselement.getname()`. The variable *`thiselement`* always refers to the element containing the operation.

You can use static code, scriptlets, or both in a template body. Code templates can also contain parameters, which can be strings or be of type ModelElement. Adding and editing parameters are discussed shortly in the "Creating and Binding Templates" section.

Internal and External Templates

There are two types of templates you can create: internal and external. An *internal template* is bound to only one operation and is stored within the XDE model. To edit this kind of template, you must work through XDE.

An *external template* is stored in an XML file outside of XDE. It can be bound to one or more operations in XDE but does not have to be bound to an operation at all.

CREATING AND BINDING TEMPLATES

Because an internal template is bound to one and only one operation, the template creation process and the binding process are the same. When you remove the binding between an internal template and the operation, the template is completely removed.

To add an internal template:

1. In the Model Explorer window, right-click the operation, and choose Code Templates ➢ Bind. XDE displays the Bind Code Template dialog box.
2. Select New to add a new template, or Browse to select an existing one.
3. If you are adding a new template, complete steps 4–13.
4. Select the New button. XDE displays a window for the first part of the template definition process:

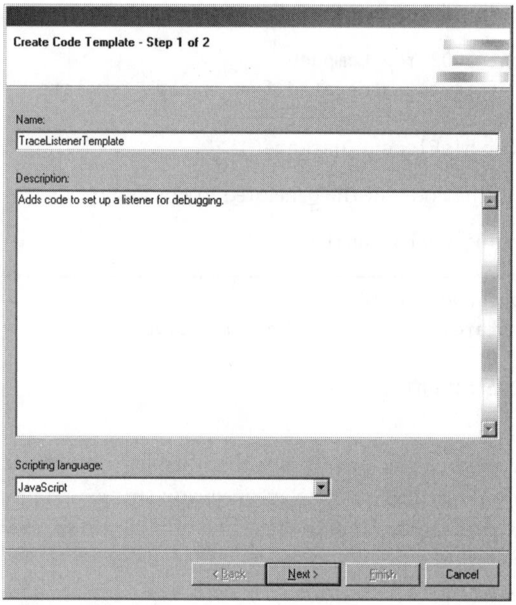

5. Enter the name of the template and a description. The description is optional, but recommended.
6. In the Scripting Language list box, select the appropriate language. At this time, JavaScript is the only supported scripting language.

7. Click Next to continue. XDE displays a window for the second part of the template definition process:

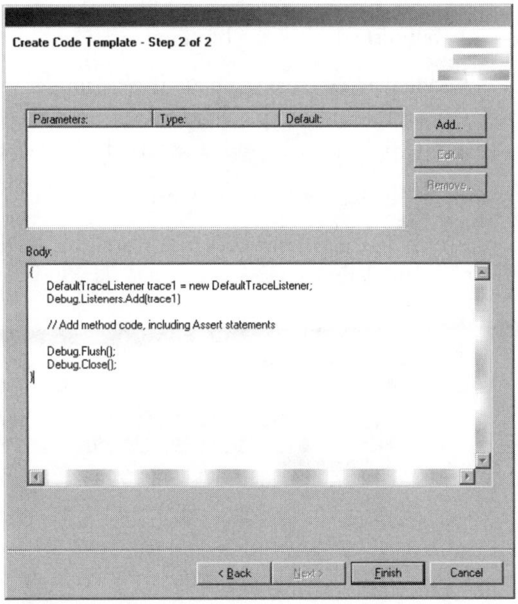

8. If the template will have parameters, use the Add button. The parameter window appears:

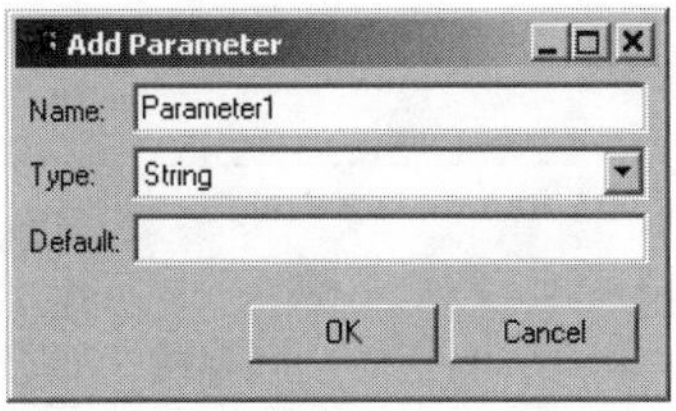

9. Enter the parameter name.
10. Enter the parameter type. Valid options are String or ModelItem. Use ModelItem to pass in an element from the XDE model.
11. (Optional) Enter a default value for the parameter if the parameter type is String.
12. Click OK. Repeat steps 8–11 for any additional parameters.
13. Enter the body of the template and click Finish.

14. On the Bind Code Template dialog box, set the actual values to pass into the template as parameters. Select a parameter, and click the Edit button. Type a value in the Use Custom Value field, or select Use Default Value. Repeat for any additional parameters.

15. When you have finished, click the Bind button.

The process for adding an external template is very similar to that used to add an internal template. The differences are that the template is saved to an XML file, and you create and bind the template in two separate processes. To add an external template and bind it to an operation:

1. Add the template by following these steps:

   A. Choose Tools ➢ Code Templates ➢ Create File. XDE displays a window for the first part of the template definition process:

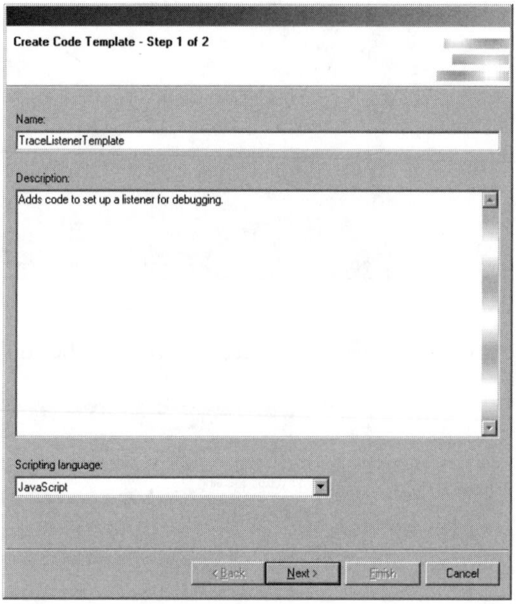

   B. Enter the name of the template and a description. The description is optional, but recommended.

   C. In the Scripting Language list box, select the appropriate language. At this time, JavaScript is the only supported scripting language.

   D. Click Next to continue. XDE displays a window for the second part of the template definition process:

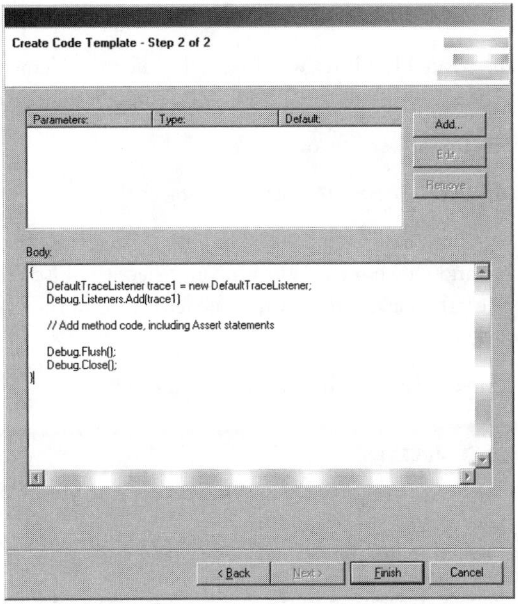

E. If the template will have parameters, use the Add button, which brings up the parameter window:

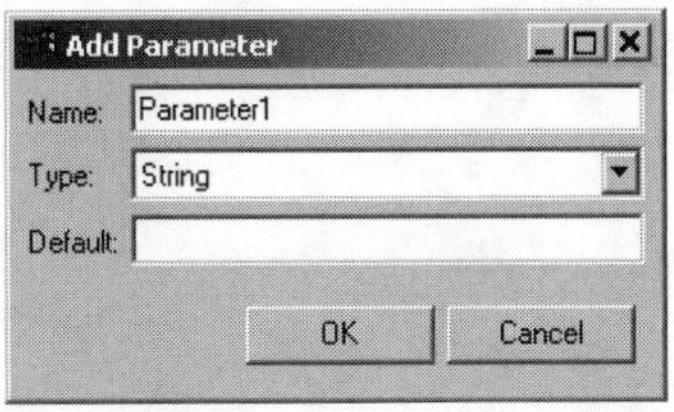

F. Enter the parameter name.

G. Enter the parameter type. Valid options are String or ModelItem. Use ModelItem to pass in an element from the XDE model.

H. (Optional) Enter a default value for the parameter if the parameter type is String.

I. Click OK. Repeat steps E–H for any additional parameters.

J. Enter the body of the template and click Finish.

K. Enter the name of the XML file for the template.

2. Bind the template to an element, by following these steps:
   - A. In the Model Explorer window, right-click the element and choose Code Templates ➢ Bind. XDE displays the Bind Code Template dialog box.
   - B. Select the Browse button.
   - C. Navigate to the new template and select the file.
   - D. Edit the value of each parameter by selecting the parameter on the lower portion of the screen and clicking the Edit button. Select the Use Default Value option to use the default value of the parameter if one was defined. Use the Use Custom Value option to add your own value.
   - E. When you have finished, click the Bind button.

EDITING A CODE TEMPLATE

If a code template needs to be changed, the process you follow depends upon whether the template is internal or external.

To edit an internal template:

1. Right-click the operation in the Explorer window and choose Code Templates ➢ Edit Binding. XDE displays the Edit Code Template Binding window.

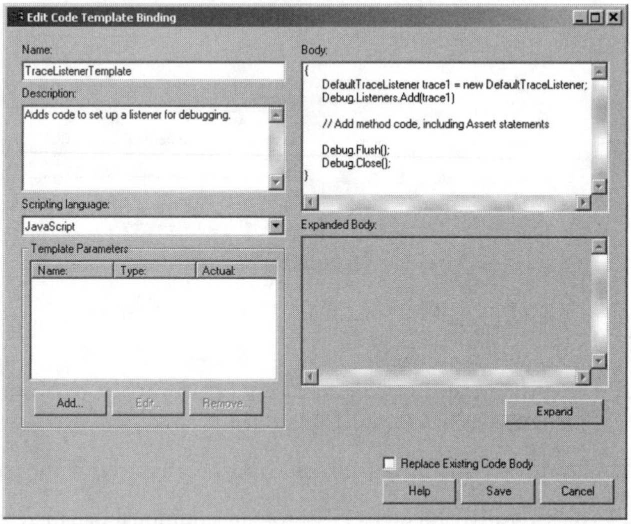

2. Make any needed changes to the template, and click Save.

To edit an external template:

1. Choose Tools ➢ Code Templates ➢ Edit File.
2. Navigate to the appropriate XML file. XDE displays the Edit Code Template File dialog box.
3. Make any needed changes to the template, and select Save or Save As.

If you changed any of the template parameters, you need to rebind the template to any operations that were bound to it. As soon as you save the template, XDE notifies you of any operations that should be rebound and provides you with a list of the operations that need to be rebound. To rebind the template to these operations:

1. Select an operation to rebind, and click Rebind. XDE displays the Bind Code Template window for the selected operation.
2. Add actual values to any changed operations.
3. Repeat steps 1–2 for any additional operations that need to be rebound.

Synchronizing the Model and Code

Because of the tight integration between the XDE models and the code, synchronizing the two is a very straightforward process. You can opt to manually start the synchronization or have XDE automatically synchronize whenever anything changes.

To automatically synchronize the code and model when changes are made:

1. Open the Options window by choosing Tools ➢ Options.
2. In the tree browser, choose Rational XDE ➢ Round-Trip Engineering ➢ Synchronization Settings.
3. Check the Automatic Synchronization box to automatically synchronize.

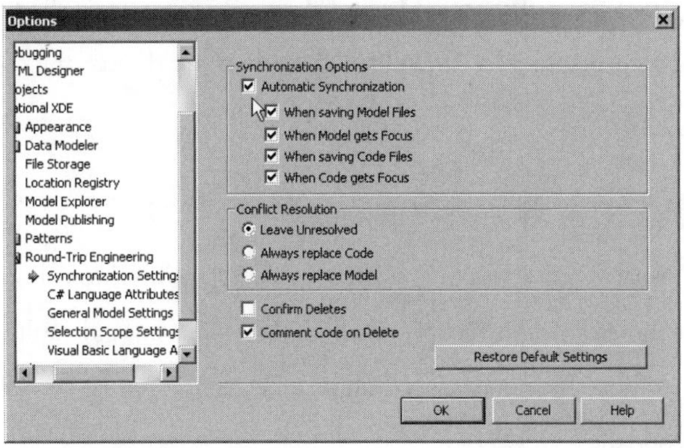

Of course, XDE also has to know how to resolve conflicts during synchronization (this is true whether you are using automatic or manual synchronization). If the code and model have both been updated but are different, which should be changed? In the Conflict Resolution area, indicate how

XDE should handle conflicts: accept the code and update the model, accept the model and update the code, or leave the conflict unresolved.

CODE GENERATION

Earlier in this chapter, in the "Setting .NET Preferences" section, we talked about setting up preferences, including code generation options. Later, in the "Modeling .NET Elements in XDE" section, we talked about the different properties you can set for classes and other model elements. Once you've set all of these preferences, you're ready to generate code.

Almost. One other important step involves validating the model to be sure that the code you end up with is the code you really want. XDE includes a model validation utility that checks for compliance to the UML and to Visual Studio constraints. To validate a single element, or a selected group of elements:

1. Select the element(s) in the Model Explorer or on a diagram.
2. Right-click and select Validate.
3. To validate everything on a diagram, open the diagram and then choose Diagram ➢ Validate Diagram.

Once the model has been validated, you can generate code. If you have automatic synchronization turned on, the code was updated when you changed the model. If you are manually generating code, right-click the element(s) you'd like to generate, and select Generate Code.

To summarize, here are the steps to follow for code generation:

1. Set the code generation preferences.
2. Set the properties of the elements to generate.
3. Validate the model.
4. Right-click the selected element(s) and select Generate Code.
5. Right-click an element and select Browse Code to view the generated code.

What gets generated? In the following sections, we discuss the code elements that are generated for the different types of model elements.

Classes

For each class, XDE creates the following:

- A Visual Studio class of the appropriate type (interface, class, and so on)
- Attributes, attribute scope, attribute data type, and a default value if one was specified
- Operation signatures, including parameters and return types
- A code file
- Attributes to support any associations or aggregations in which the class participated
- Inherits statements (Visual Basic) or <class>:<base class> statements (C#) to support any generalization relationships for the class

- Implements statements (Visual Basic) or <class>:<interface> statements (C#) to support any implements relationships between the class and an interface

If you've used any code templates, the operations of the class have the template's code inserted into them.

Server Pages and Client Pages

A server page with a code-behind file generates files with an extension of `.aspx`, `.cs`, or `.vb`. Any methods added to the code-behind class are added to the CS or VB file. If the server page includes a nested client page, the tags from the client page are also added to the ASPX file.

If a client page exists that is not nested within a server page, XDE generates an HTML or HTM file.

Reverse Engineering

While code generation updates the code from the model, reverse engineering updates the model from the code. Typically you begin with a legacy system, reverse engineer it into XDE to examine its architecture, and then generate code as changes are made.

The process you follow depends on whether you are updating the model from code that was previously generated from XDE or are adding new classes. Before you can reverse engineer a web application, you must create a virtual directory model to hold the web elements.

To reverse engineer code that was generated from XDE, right-click a file in the Solution Explorer and select Reverse Engineer.

Synchronizing

Although code generation updates the code and reverse engineering updates the model, the synchronization process may update both. During synchronization, XDE looks for changes in the model or in the code, updating each with changes made to the other. If the same element has been updated in both the model and the code, but different changes were made in the model and the code, you will need to resolve the conflict. There are four ways to resolve each conflict:

Generate the code Update the code with the changes made to the model.

Reverse engineer Update the model with the changes made to the code.

Browse the model Navigate to the element in question so that you can manually review it and make changes.

Browse the code Navigate to the code in question so that you can manually review it and make changes.

When you synchronize, XDE places any conflicts found into the Task List window. Right-click each conflict and select one of the four options just listed.

Debugging Your Application

XDE does not alter the debugging and deployment features provided by Visual Studio. Use Visual Studio's Debug menu to step through and debug your code. See the Visual Studio reference materials for further information.

Exercise: Moving from Analysis to Design in a .NET Application

In Chapter 4, we created an analysis-level sequence diagram and an analysis class diagram for the Submit Timecard use case in the timekeeping application. In this exercise, we continue working on this design model, adding details to the analysis-level sequence diagram to create a design-level sequence diagram. We also create a design-level class diagram. Before starting all of this, we verify the code-generation properties to make sure that XDE generates the code properly.

Setting Up the Code Models

In XDE, only one model in a given project may be a code model. Due to this restriction, you must create multiple projects. The recommended structure is to create a project for the non-code generation elements, such as the use cases and analysis model. Then create a project for each code model that you need. To do so, follow these steps:

1. Start Visual Studio .NET.
2. Choose File ➢ New ➢ Blank Solution to create a new Visual Studio solution.
3. In the New Project dialog box, select Visual Basic Projects, then Windows Application. Name the new project **Timekeeping** and click OK.
4. In the Solution Explorer, right-click the new solution and select Synchronize. This creates a code model.

Creating Classes

Next, you create the classes that you'll use to build the sequence diagram and class diagram in the remainder of this exercise. Classes can be added on a class diagram or using the Model Explorer; in this exercise, you use the Model Explorer.

1. In the Model Explorer, expand the Timekeeping namespace.
2. Right-click the Timekeeping namespace, and choose Add Visual Basic ➢ Class.
3. Name the new class **frmMain**.
4. Create two additional classes, named **frmTimecard** and **DBAccess**.

Creating an Initial Design Class Diagram

Before you build the sequence diagram, you need to show that your DBAccess class imports the System.Data namespace. The easiest way to do this is on a class diagram, so you should build an initial class diagram.

1. Right-click the Timekeeping namespace, and choose Add Diagram ➢ Class. Name the new diagram **Timekeeping Overview**.
2. Drag the DBAccess class from the Model Explorer onto the diagram.

3. Expand the (Miscellaneous Files) System.Data node on the treeview in the Model Explorer. Expand the System node. You should see nodes called Data and Xml. Expand the Data node and locate the SqlClient namespace.
4. Drag the SqlClient namespace from the Model Explorer onto the diagram. It should appear as a stereotyped package.
5. In the UML Use Case toolbox, find the Import option and use it to add an import relationship from DBAccess to the SqlClient namespace. Your initial class diagram should now look like this:

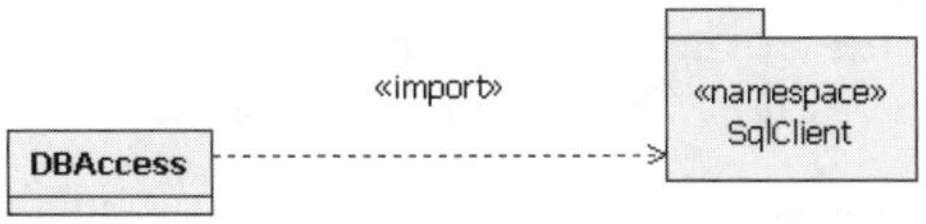

Creating the Design-Level Sequence Diagram

The classes you need have now been created. The next step is to create a design-level sequence diagram to show how these classes will interact.

1. Right-click the Timekeeping namespace and choose Add Diagram ➢ Sequence: Instance. Name the new diagram **Submit Timecard**.
2. Right-click the solution in the Solution Explorer and choose Add ➢ Add Existing Item. Navigate to the MDX file you created in the exercise for Chapter 4. This model contains the actors and use cases for this project.
3. If you did not complete the Chapter 4 exercise, right-click the Timekeeping namespace and choose Add UML ➢ Actor. Name the actor **Employee**. Otherwise, skip to step 4.
4. Drag the Employee actor to the sequence diagram. Once the object has been created, double-click it to remove the object name.
5. Drag the frmMain class to the sequence diagram, and remove the object name.
6. Drag the frmTimecard and DBAccess classes to the diagram, and remove the object names.
7. Locate the SqlConnection class in the SqlClient namespace in the Model Explorer treeview. Drag the SqlConnection class to the diagram, and remove the object name.
8. Locate the SqlDataAdapter class in the SqlClient namespace in the Model Explorer treeview. Drag the SqlDataAdapter class to the diagram, and name the object **PayPeriodAdapter**.
9. Locate the SqlCommandBuilder class in the SqlClient namespace in the Model Explorer treeview. Drag the SqlCommandBuilder class to the diagram, and name the object **PayPeriodBuilder**.
10. Repeat steps 8 and 9 to add three additional instances of SqlDataAdapter and SqlCommandBuilder. Name these objects **PayCodeAdapter**, **PayCodeBuilder**, **StatusReportAdapter**, **StatusReportBuilder**, **TimecardAdapter**, and **TimecardBuilder**.

11. Use the Message option in the UML Sequence toolbox to add a message from the Employee actor to the frmMain object. Click the lifeline leading down from the Employee actor first, and then click the lifeline of the frmMain object.

12. Click the message text CalledOperation to edit it. Name this message **Submit timecard**.

13. Add a message from the frmMain object to the frmTimecard object. Name this message **New**. Right-click the new message arrow, and select Create Operation From Message.

14. Add the messages shown in the following illustrations to complete the diagram. There are several things to note.

    - First, after creating message numbers 2, 3, 4, 5, 6, 13, 17, and 23, right-click the message and select Create Operation From Message.
    - When you create a message that ends on the SqlConncection instance, or any instance of SqlDataAdapter or SqlCommandBuilder, you do not need to manually create an operation. Create the message arrow, then use the drop-down list box to select the appropriate message.
    - Finally, when you create an operation with a parameter, such as in message 13, first run Create Operation From Message without the parameter. Then, right-click the new operation in the Model Explorer to add the parameter.

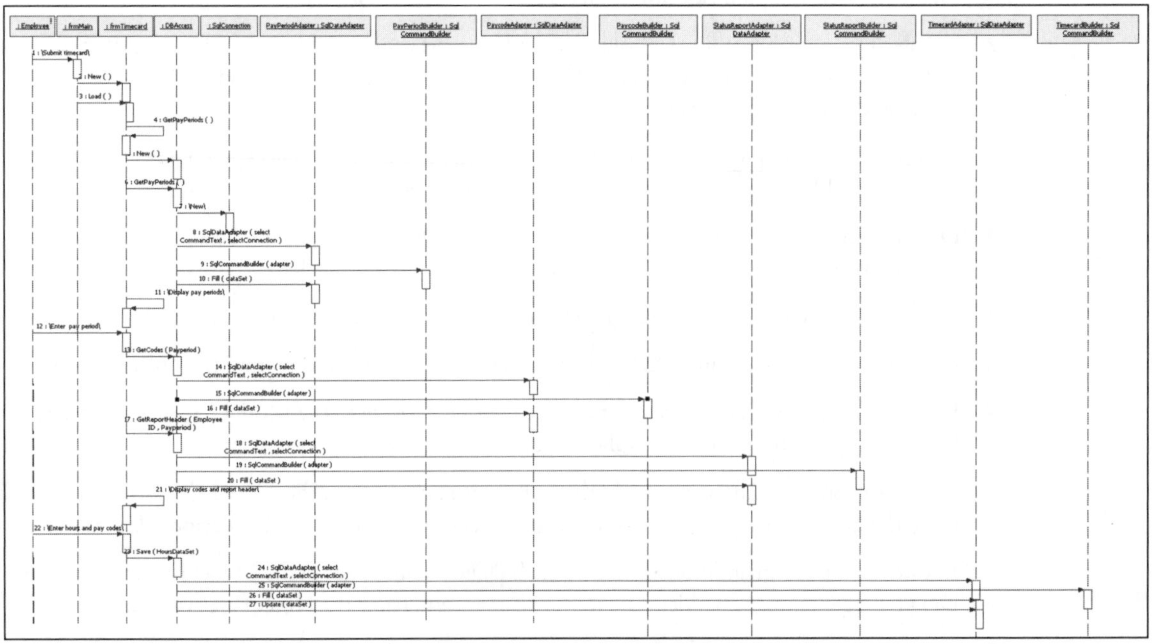

Creating the Class Diagram

The final step is to complete your class diagram, adding the relationships you established through the sequence diagram.

1. Open the Timekeeping class diagram.
2. Drag the frmMain and frmTimecard classes from the Model Explorer onto the diagram.
3. Drag the SqlConnection, SqlDataAdapter, and SqlCommandBuilder classes from the Model Explorer onto the diagram.
4. Create a directed association from the frmTimecard class to the DBAdapter class.
5. Create a directed association from the DBAdapter class to the SqlConnection class.
6. Create dependencies from the DBAdapter class to the SqlDataAdapter and SqlCommand-Builder classes.
7. Create a dependency from the frmMain class to the frmTimecard class. The diagram should now look like this:

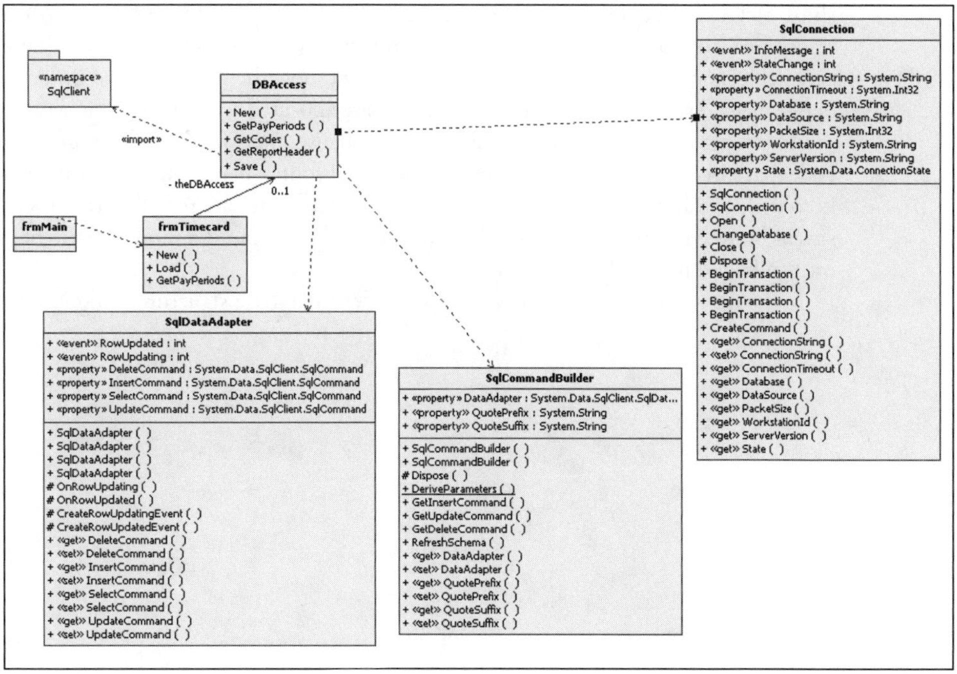

Summary

In this chapter, we examined the different pieces of a design model for C# or Visual Basic .NET applications. We walked through the process, from defining the code model and setting preferences, to creating the UML diagrams, to generating code and deploying it. The sequence of topics, however, is not rigid. In XDE, you may start with the code, and then work on the diagrams. You will most likely switch from the diagrams to the code and back again many times before the end of the project.

The classes, interfaces, components, and other constructs in your Visual Studio .NET project can be modeled directly in XDE. These constructs in the Visual Studio languages translate to UML classes, attributes, operations, interfaces, components, and other modeling elements. By modeling your application before coding it, you can be sure it is well-architected and that you have access to a more abstract representation of your system. This view of the system helps you not only create the system, but maintain it as well.

The design model is made up of one or more diagrams: sequence diagrams, class diagrams, statechart diagrams, component diagrams, and deployment diagrams. Sequence diagrams show you the objects needed for a scenario, and the messages sent between them. Class diagrams show a subset of the classes, packages, and interfaces in the system, along with their attributes, operations, and relationships. Statechart diagrams show you the various states in which an object can exist, and how the object transitions from one state to another. Component diagrams show you the physical files (source code, executable, and so on) that make up the system, and how these files depend on one another. Finally, deployment diagrams show you how processes are allocated to nodes on the network.

As you are modeling your application, you can also generate code for it and reverse engineer any code that's been written. XDE provides a powerful round-trip engineering capability that helps you keep the code and the model synchronized. Code templates are useful in that they keep the code consistent between developers. All of these features help you build a more consistent, reliable application on a solid architectural foundation.

In the next chapter, we examine how to model a database structure using XDE.

Chapter 7

Modeling Databases with XDE

So far, we've focused on modeling the application itself—creating the use case diagrams, interaction diagrams, class diagrams, and other artifacts needed to really understand how the system works. An essential element to nearly every system, however, is some form of persistent storage, typically a database.

Using XDE, you can model not only the application, but also the database or databases that support the application.

Featured in this chapter:

- Comparing object models and data models
- Creating a data model
- Modeling views
- Generating an object model from a data model
- Generating a data model from an object model
- Creating the database from a data model
- Reverse engineering a database into a data model

Object Models and Data Models

An object model is used for all of the pieces of the application that we have discussed so far—the classes, attributes, operations, relationships, components, and other constructs—*except* for the data. The primary emphasis of an object model is on memory—answering questions such as what objects are created in memory, how these objects communicate, and what each object is responsible for doing. The focus of the data model is, as the name implies, the database rather than the application.

While object modeling is concerned with memory efficiency, data modeling is more concerned with database efficiency. Table 7.1 lists some of the differences in perspective between the data model and the object model.

TABLE 7.1: DATA MODELING VS. OBJECT MODELING

OBJECT MODEL	DATA MODEL
How can I design the classes to be memory efficient?	How can I design the database to be storage efficient?
What objects need relationships in the object model?	What tables need relationships in the data model?
How can I structure the data on the user interface to make the most sense to the end user?	How can I structure the data to speed access times?
How can I package the data with behavior to create classes?	How can I normalize the data?
What data will be used throughout the application, and what data will be used in only one area?	What data will be retrieved frequently?
How can I use generalizations or other design strategies to reuse code?	How can I incorporate the concept of inheritance into my data model if my database management system (DBMS) doesn't directly support inheritance?

There is a definite disparity between the data model and the object model. The primary reason for this is the nature of the models themselves; objects are, by definition, focused on behavior *and* data, while the data model is focused on data alone. The object model, in most languages, supports inheritance, while the data model does not. Data types in programming languages and DBMS packages are different. Join tables do not need to be included in the object model as a general rule (although association classes are sometimes needed). Two classes need to have a relationship if one needs to access the attributes or the operations of the other; two tables need to have a relationship if there is a logical connection between the data in the two tables. Two entity classes may have a relationship in the object model, but their tables may not be related in the data model. To account for these natural differences, XDE supports the creation of both an object model and a separate data model.

So, which comes first: the data model or the object model? In many cases, the two models are developed concurrently. In the Inception phase, the team can develop both a (very) rough data model and a (very) rough object model, or a domain model. As Elaboration and Construction progress, the team can fill in the details of both models. Many of the entity classes from the class diagrams become database tables. There is not, however, a one-to-one correspondence. Because of the differences in perspective between the two models, a single entity class may become two or more database tables. Conversely, a single database table may be supported by two or more classes in the application.

Many projects, especially maintenance projects, begin with some sort of existing data model. Using XDE, you can reverse engineer the existing data model to use as a starting point. If you have an object model but no data model, you can automatically generate a data model from the classes in your object model.

Creating a Data Model

In XDE, the database design is contained in a separate model. The data model includes databases, tables, stored procedures, triggers, primary keys, relationships, and domains. Each database is modeled as a component with a <<database>> stereotype. XDE supports modeling databases for DB2, SQL Server, Sybase, Oracle, or ANSI SQL. Using ANSI SQL allows you to generate data definition language (DDL) scripts for the databases, but it does not actually create tables and other database items. You can reverse engineer from all of the database types except ANSI SQL.

It's important to note that XDE lets you create one or more data models. Although a single data model may be enough for a relatively small application, you may want to create more than one, especially in a very complex application or in a situation where multiple DBMS packages are being used.

Inside each data model, you can use one or more DBMS packages. As you create new tables or stored procedures, you can attach them via a realization relationship to the appropriate database component. The DBMS of the table or stored procedure is then set to the same DBMS as the database component.

Here are the primary steps you need to follow to create a data model:

1. Add a new model to your project by choosing New ➢ Model from the menu in the Navigator window.
2. Select the Data Model template to add a data model to your project.

After you create the data model, you can add elements (databases, domains, stored procedures, tables, and views) by selecting Add Data Modeler from the menu.

It isn't necessary to follow all of the steps in this order, but by creating the database and schema first, you set the DBMS that you will use. When you create tables, fields, and other data-modeling elements, the appropriate data types become available. In the remainder of this chapter, we discuss each of these steps. Before we do, however, let's look at what logic might be incorporated into the data model.

Logic in a Data Model

Database management systems are becoming more sophisticated every year. It's becoming easier to add logic to the database—so easy that you may become confused about what logic should go in the database and what logic should go in the application.

There is no simple way to determine what logic should go where, and a complete analysis of database design principles is outside the scope of this book, but here are four points to consider:

- General object-oriented practices suggest keeping at least some of the business logic in an application layer rather than in the database.

- In general, only logic related to the data itself should be housed in the database. This includes items such as required fields, valid values for fields, and field lengths.
- Many business rules can be enforced directly in the database through the use of constraints. Although the database is an appropriate location for this type of logic, the application must gather information from the end user, pass it through the business layer, and then across a network connection, which may be slow, before the data is validated. Keeping this logic in the business layer can sometimes help reduce unnecessary network traffic.

  However, if a number of areas within the application, or even a number of different applications, need to use the same constraint, placing the logic in the database can help ensure that the rule is applied consistently.
- Some of the system logic can be carried out directly in the database through the use of stored procedures. There are advantages to this approach; if you have functionality that is very data-intensive, it will typically run more efficiently as a stored procedure. If the functionality is strictly data manipulation, programming it as a stored procedure might be significantly faster than loading all the records into memory, having the application do the processing, and then storing the results back to the database.

  However, there are some disadvantages to this strategy as well. Using stored procedures to implement any business logic inherently divides the business logic across at least two layers: the business layer and the database layer. When business logic changes, you may need to update both of these layers. You also run the risk of duplicate logic across the layers or, even worse, contradictory business logic across the two layers.

  Too many stored procedures can also cause difficulties in migrating from one DBMS to another. Many database management packages have slightly different syntax, and migrating from one to another may necessitate rewriting of the stored procedures.

Again, there isn't necessarily an easy way to distinguish between the logic that should reside in the database and the logic that should reside in the application. Once you have decided to place logic in the database, you can model that logic by modeling stored procedures, constraints, and triggers in XDE. First, however, you must create a database.

Adding a Database

A database is modeled in XDE as a stereotyped component. It is given a unique name, and assigned to a specific DBMS. In the current version at the time of this writing, XDE supports the following DBMS products:

ANSI SQL 92	Microsoft SQL Server 7.*x*
IBM DB2 5.*x*	Microsoft SQL Server 2000.*x*
IBM DB2 6.*x*	Oracle 7.*x*
IBM DB2 7.*x*	Oracle 8.*x*

IBM DB2 OS390 5.*x* Oracle 9.*x*

IBM DB2 OS390 6.*x* Sybase Adaptive Server 12.*x*

Microsoft SQL Server 6.*x*

You can set the DBMS for a database using the Database Specification window. As we mentioned earlier, each XDE project can contain multiple data models, and each data model can contain multiple databases using one or more DBMS packages.

To add a database:

1. Right-click the data model in the Model Explorer.
2. Choose Add Data Modeler ➢ Database.
3. Name the database.
4. Right-click the new database in the browser and select Open Specification.
5. In the Target field, select the appropriate DBMS.

Adding Tablespaces

When using DB2, Oracle, or SQL Server, you can add tablespaces to your database. A *tablespace* is a logical unit of storage for your tables. Within each tablespace are one or more containers, where a *container* is a physical storage device such as a hard drive. Each container is divided into smaller units called *extents*. Tables in the tablespace are evenly distributed across the containers within the tablespace.

NOTE *In Microsoft SQL Server, tablespaces are called filegroups, and containers are called files. In Oracle, containers are known as data files.*

Each tablespace has an initial size, in kilobytes (KB). Once that space has been used, the DBMS can automatically increase the size of the tablespace in preset increments. The size of the increments (in KB) can be set in XDE. Even when increments are set, the container cannot grow beyond its maximum size, which can also be set in XDE. Once tablespaces are established, you can assign tables to them.

Adding Tablespaces to Databases

The following are procedures for adding tablespaces to SQL Server, DB2, and Oracle databases.

Adding a Tablespace in SQL Server

The process of adding a tablespace in SQL Server is fairly straightforward. You only need to define the tablespace name, add comments, and optionally mark the tablespace as the default tablespace. To add a tablespace in SQL Server, follow these steps:

1. Right-click the database in the browser.
2. Choose Add Data Modeler ➢ Tablespace.
3. Name the tablespace.

4. Right-click the new tablespace in the browser and select Open Specification. The namespace specification window that appears will depend on your DBMS:

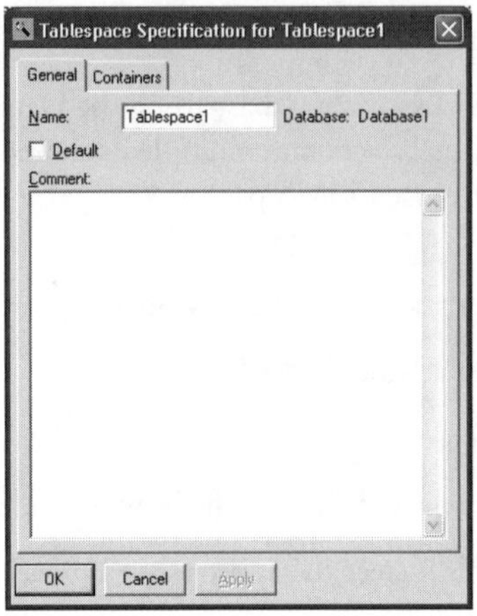

5. Check the Default field if you want this to be the default tablespace. Any tables that are not assigned to another tablespace are assigned to the default tablespace.

Adding a Tablespace in Oracle

When you create an Oracle tablespace, you need to define the tablespace name, optionally add comments, and set the tablespace type to Permanent or Temporary. To add a tablespace in Oracle, follow these steps:

1. Right-click the database in the browser.
2. Choose Add Data Modeler ➢ Tablespace.
3. Name the tablespace.
4. Right-click the new tablespace in the browser and select Open Specification. The namespace specification window appears:

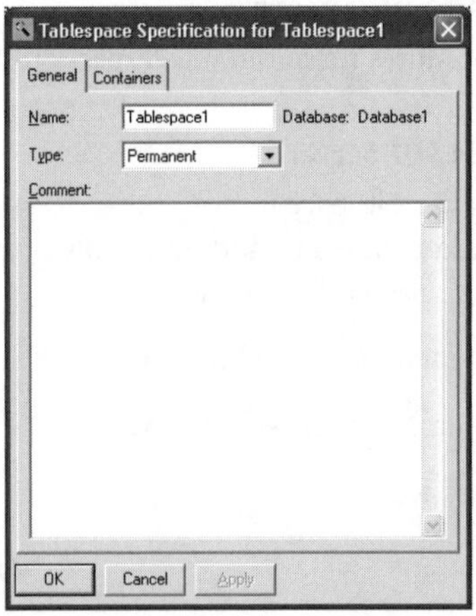

5. Set the tablespace type to Permanent or Temporary. A temporary tablespace allocates space for only the duration of the current database session. A permanent tablespace remains in existence even after the end of the database session.

Adding a Tablespace in DB2

Creating a DB2 tablespace is a little more involved than adding a SQL Server or Oracle tablespace. To add a tablespace in DB2, follow these steps:

1. Right-click the database in the browser.
2. Choose Add Data Modeler ➢ Tablespace.
3. Name the tablespace.
4. Right-click the new tablespace in the browser and select Open Specification. The namespace specification window appears:

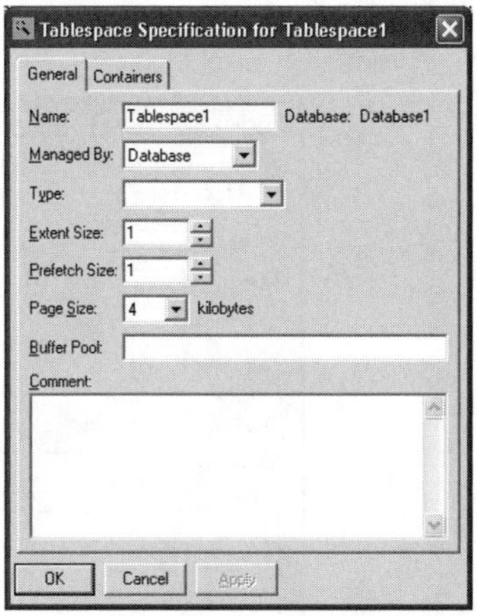

5. Set whether the tablespace is managed by the DBMS or by the operating system. If it is managed by the operating system, you cannot add new containers after creating the tablespace, but you can expand the existing tablespaces. If it is managed by the DBMS, then you cannot expand existing tablespaces, but you can add new containers.
6. Set the tablespace type to Regular or Temporary. A temporary tablespace allocates space only for the duration of the current database session. A regular tablespace remains in existence even after the end of the database session.
7. Set the extent size of the containers assigned to the tablespace.
8. Set the prefetch size for your designated extent size. The extent size is the tablespace increment amount in number of pages. A prefetch can speed up a query by fetching more pages than are currently being read by the query. The Prefetch Size field shows the number of pages to be prefetched.

9. Set the page size (in KB) for each extent in your container. The page size is the amount of space (in KB) per page.
10. Enter a buffer pool name in the Buffer Pool field. The *buffer pool* is a memory buffer that can be used to hold the prefetched pages.
11. (Optional) Enter comments about the tablespace.

Adding a Tablespace in DB2 OS/390

To add a tablespace in DB2 OS/390, follow these steps:

1. Right-click the database in the browser.
2. Choose Add Data Modeler ➢ Tablespace.
3. Name the tablespace.
4. Right-click the new tablespace in the browser and select Open Specification. The namespace specification window appears:

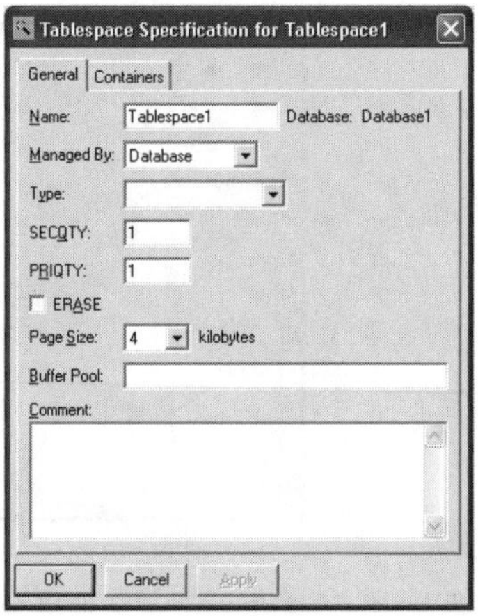

5. Set whether the tablespace is managed by the DBMS or by the operating system. If it is managed by the operating system, you cannot add new containers after creating the tablespace, but you can expand the existing tablespaces. If it is managed by the DBMS, you cannot expand the existing tablespaces, but you can add new containers.
6. Set the tablespace type to Regular, LARGE, or LOB as needed by your DBMS.
7. Set SECQTY and PRIQTY for the tablespace.
8. Set the ERASE flag if necessary by selecting the ERASE check box.
9. Set the page size (in KB) for each extent in your container.

10. Enter a buffer pool name in the Buffer Pool field.
11. (Optional) Enter comments about the tablespace.

SETTING UP CONTAINERS

The following are procedures for setting up containers within tablespaces for SQL Server, DB2, and Oracle databases.

Setting Up Containers within a Tablespace in SQL Server

To set up containers within a tablespace in SQL Server, follow these steps:

1. Right-click the tablespace in the browser and select Open Specification.
2. Select the Containers tab on the specification window.
3. Right-click anywhere in the white space and select New.
4. Enter the tablespace filename, initial size, maximum size, and file growth (increment amount).

Setting Up Containers within a Tablespace in Oracle

To set up containers within a tablespace in Oracle, follow these steps:

1. Right-click the tablespace in the browser and select Open Specification.
2. Select the Containers tab on the specification window.
3. Right-click anywhere in the white space and select New.
4. Enter the tablespace filename, initial size, maximum size, and extent size (increment amount).

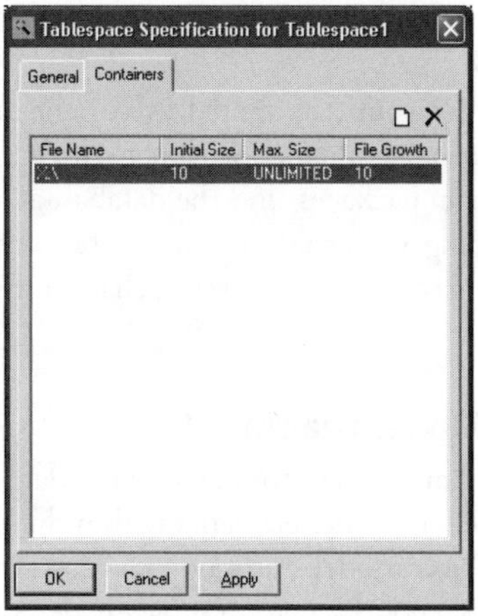

Setting Up Containers within a Tablespace in DB2 and DB2 OS/390

To set up containers within a tablespace in DB2 and DB2 OS/390, follow these steps:

1. Right-click the tablespace in the browser and select Open Specification.
2. Select the Containers tab on the specification window.
3. Right-click anywhere in the white space and select New.
4. Enter the filename.

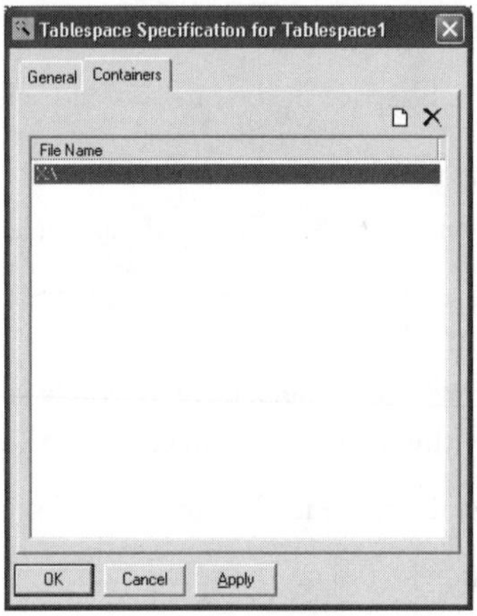

See the upcoming "Adding Tables" section in this chapter for information about assigning a table to a tablespace.

Adding a Schema

A *schema* is a container for your data model. All of the tables, fields, triggers, constraints, and other data-modeling elements are contained within a schema. The two exceptions are domains, which are contained within domain packages, and the database itself. Although XDE does not explicitly provide an option for adding a schema, you can create a schema by adding a package and giving it a stereotype of <<schema>>. Note, however, that XDE will not generate the schema during forward engineering.

Creating a Data Model Diagram

You can create a freeform diagram to illustrate the data model elements. This diagram is also used to add, edit, or view tables and other elements within the data model; it serves a similar purpose as the class diagram in the object model. Although you can add data-modeling elements directly into the browser, the diagram is a good way to graphically depict the elements and their relationships. You can create as many diagrams as you need for each database.

As with other features of XDE, the Data Modeler has a toolbox that you can use to add tables, relationships, and other data-modeling elements. Table 7.2 lists the buttons available on this toolbox.

TABLE 7.2: ICONS IN THE DATA MODEL DIAGRAM TOOLBAR

ICON	PURPOSE
Pointer	Returns the cursor to an arrow to select an item
Table	Adds a new table to the diagram
Identifying Relationship	Draws an identifying relationship between two tables
Non-Identifying Relationship	Draws a non-identifying relationship between two tables
Stored Procedure Container	Creates a container to organize stored procedures in the model
View	Adds a new view to the diagram
Domain	Adds a domain to the diagram
Many To Many Relationship	Adds a many-to-many relationship between two tables
Database	Adds a new database component
Dependency	Draws a dependency between two tables or views
Realization	Draws a realization between a table and database

Creating Domains

A domain can be used to enforce business rules such as required fields, valid values for the fields, and default values for the fields. A *domain* is a pattern that, once established, can be applied to one or more fields in the database. For example, assume you are working with a system that stores many types of phone numbers. You can set up a domain called Phone that would include all of the business rules that apply to all types of phone numbers. In the details of the domain, you can set the data type to `long`, set the default value to 0 and indicate that a value is required. Once the domain is set up, you can apply it to various fields in the database: Home_Phone, Work_Phone, Fax_Number, and so on. Each of these fields now has a data type of `long`, a default value of 0, and is required.

Using domains is entirely optional, but two of the benefits of using domains are consistency and maintenance. Applying domains helps you ensure that the business rules are consistent across many fields—in this case, across all fields related to phone numbers. Domains also centralize the business rules, which can make them easier to change. If, for example, the business rules change and phone numbers are no longer required, you could change the domain and re-create the tables, rather than going into each table individually and making the change. Domains are modeled as classes with stereotypes of <<Domain>>.

To create a domain:

1. Right-click a package or the model in the browser.
2. Choose Add Data Modeler ➢ Domain.
3. In the Properties window, edit the targetdatabase property to set the DBMS.

3. Right-click the new domain and select Open Specification.
4. On the General tab, enter the name of the domain.

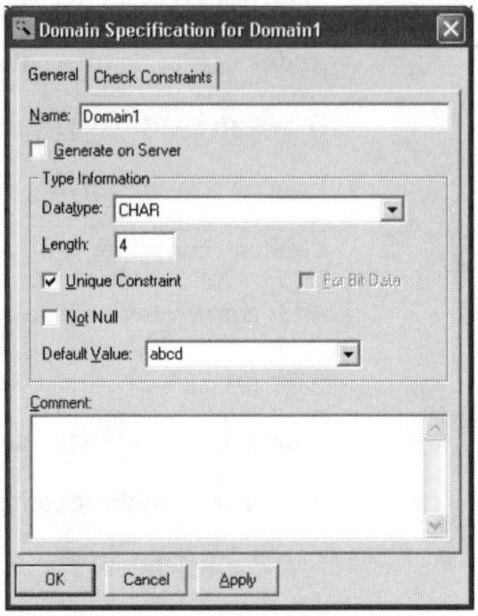

5. Check the Generate On Server check box to generate a server-based or distinct data type.
6. Select the domain's data type. The choices available in this list box depend upon the DBMS of the domain package.
7. Enter the field length for the domain. Not all data types require a field length.
8. Enter the precision and scale for the domain. *Precision* is the number of digits allowed in a numeric field. *Scale* is the number of digits to the right of the decimal point in the number. Not all data types require a precision or scale.
9. Check the Unique Constraint check box if fields that use the domain must have a unique value. A constraint is generated in the database if this box is checked. Note that not all data types allow a unique constraint.
10. Check the Not Null check box if fields that use this domain must contain a value.
11. Check the For Bit Data check box if the domain should support ForBitData (DB2 only).
12. Enter a default value or select a value from the list box if fields that use this domain should have a default.

On the Check Constraints tab of the specification window, you can set constraints for the domain. A *constraint* is an expression that must be true before data can be altered in the database. For example, you may want to enforce a business rule that requires all transactions in an accounting system to have a transaction number greater than 1000. You can create a domain called Transaction, and add a constraint that checks the value of the field and returns False if the value is less than 1000.

Constraints can also be added to individual tables; we discuss this in the next section, "Adding Tables." A domain constraint appears in the domain as an operation and the stereotype is <<Check Constraint>>.

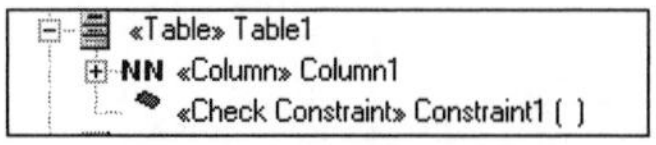

On the Check Constraints tab, select New to add a new constraint. XDE automatically creates a constraint name for you and populates the Name field. In the Expression field, enter the SQL statement for the constraint. To edit an existing constraint, select the constraint from the drop-down list in the Name field. You can optionally add a comment to the check constraint.

Adding Tables

Once you have established a database, you can create tables in it by adding realization relationships between the table and the database. Each table in a database is modeled as a persistent class with a stereotype of <<Table>>:

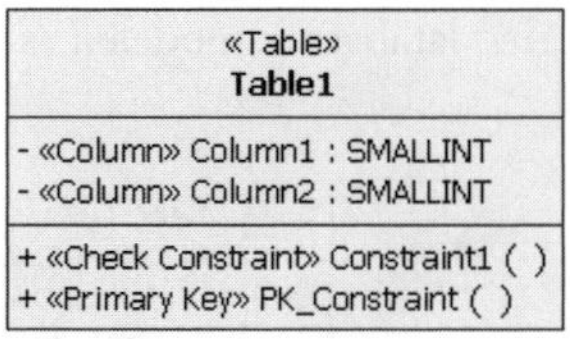

The DBMS for the table is set by modifying its targetdatabase property in the Properties window. When you add a realization relationship between a database component and a table, the DBMS of the table is automatically set to the DBMS of the database component.

To add a table:

1. Open a data model diagram.
2. Select the Table option from the Data Modeler toolbox.
3. Click anywhere inside the diagram to create the table.
4. Type the name of the new table.
5. Draw a realization relationship from the database component to the table in order to set the DBMS for the table.

OR

1. Right-click a package or model in the Model Explorer.
2. Choose Add Data Modeler ➢ Table.
3. Type the name of the new table.

4. Draw a realization relationship from the database component to the table in order to set the DBMS for the table.

To map a table to a database, we add a realization relationship from the database to the table. The realization relationship is drawn as follows:

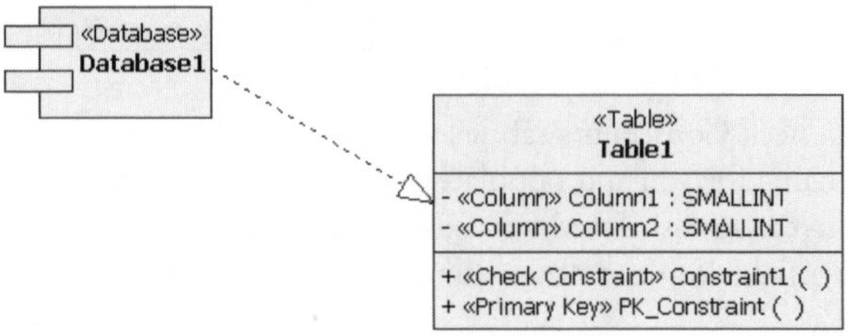

The next step in the process is to add details to the tables: fields, keys, indexes, constraints, and triggers.

ADDING COLUMNS

Each field, or column, in the database is modeled as an attribute in the Model Explorer under the table that contains it.

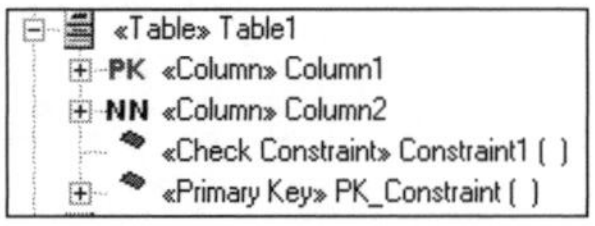

There are two types of columns: data columns and computed columns. A *computed column* uses a SQL statement to calculate its value from one or more other columns. For example, a company might have a retirement fund set up, and each employee is able to place a maximum of 4 percent of their annual salary into this fund. The table Employee would include the two columns: AnnualSalary and MaxRetirementContribution. The value in MaxRetirementContribution would be equal to 4 percent of the value in AnnualSalary. MaxRetirementContribution, therefore, is a computed column. A *data column* is any column that does not contain a calculated value.

Microsoft SQL Server also supports the concept of an *identity column*, which is a column with a system-generated value. For example, an identity column with a data type of `Integer` would assign the values 1, 2, 3, 4, and so on to the rows in the table.

To add a column for any DBMS:

1. Right-click the table and choose Add Data Modeler ➢ Column.
2. In the Model Explorer, right-click the new column and select Open Specification.
3. Enter the name of the new column, and an optional comment.
4. Select the Type tab.

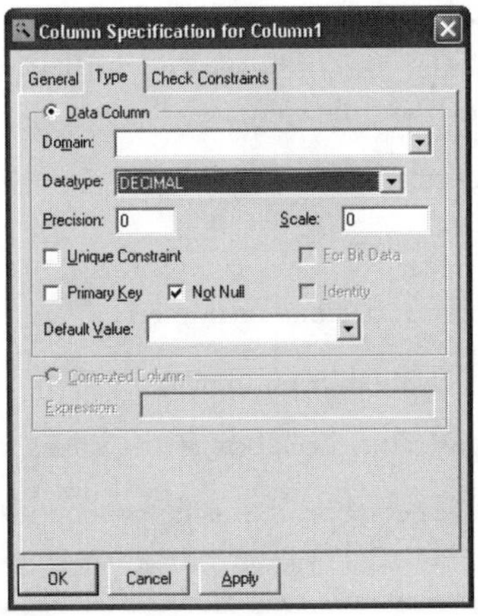

5. Select the Data Column or Computed Column radio button (SQL Server only).
6. If the column is a data column, complete the following fields:
   - Domain, if you have created a domain and wish to apply it to this column. If you use a domain, you do not need to enter any of the following fields other than Unique Constraint or Primary Key. The domain definition causes the other fields to be automatically filled in for you.
   - Data Type for the column. The choices available in this drop-down list box depend on the DBMS for this table.
   - Length, which is the number of characters allowed in the column. This value cannot be set for all data types. You will see this field if the data type is set to one of the following:

     For DB2: blob, character, clob, DBclob, graphic, varchar, or vargraphic

     For Oracle: char, nchar, nvarcahar2, raw, or varchar2

     For SQL Server: binary, car, nchar, nvarchar, varbinary, or varchar

     For Sybase: binary, char, nchar, nvarchar, varbinary, or varchar
   - Precision, which is the number of digits allowed in a numeric column. This value cannot be set for all data types. You will see this field if the data type is set to one of the following:

     For DB2: decimal

     For Oracle: float or number

     For SQL Server: decimal, float, or numeric

     For Sybase: decimal, float, or numeric

- Scale, which is the number of digits to the right of the decimal point in a numeric column. This value cannot be set for all data types. You will see this field if the data type is set to one of the following:

  For DB2: decimal

  For Oracle: number

  For SQL Server: decimal or numeric

  For Sybase: decimal or numeric
- Unique Constraint check box, if the values in the column must be unique.
- Primary Key check box, if this is the identifying column for the table. You can create a composite primary key by selecting this option for more than one column. When a column is a primary key, it has a red "PK" to the left of it in the browser.
- Not Null check box, if the column will not allow null values. If you set the Primary Key option, the Not Null option must also be set.
- Identity check box (SQL Server only), if this is an identity column. SQL Server automatically generates values for an identity column. Note that the data type must be a numeric type to allow this option.
- For Bit Data check box (DB2 only), if the column supports ForBitData.

7. If the column is a computed column (SQL Server only), enter the SQL statement that will be used to calculate the column value.
8. Select the Check Constraints tab and add constraints if necessary. See the upcoming section, "Adding Constraints," in this chapter.

SETTING A PRIMARY KEY

If a column is marked as a primary key, it is the identifying column for the table. In other words, it contains the unique values that distinguish the rows from each other. For example, the primary key in an Employee table might be the Social Security number.

To set the primary key for a table:

1. Right-click the column in the Model Explorer and select Open Specification.
2. Select the Type tab in the Column Specification window.
3. Select the Primary Key option.

NOTE *If you set a column as the primary key, the Not Null field is automatically checked and cannot be deselected. Primary keys cannot contain null values.*

ADDING CONSTRAINTS

A *constraint* is a conditional statement that must be true in order for a table to be updated. You can add a constraint either to a domain, as described earlier, or to a table. By using constraints, you can enforce business rules. An example of using constraints might involve checking to make sure that the value in a Birth_date field is prior to the current date. You can also check that the value in a State field is a valid state abbreviation or that the value in a Gender field is M or F.

Key Constraints

There are three types of key constraints: primary key constraints, unique constraints, and indexes. A *primary key constraint* ensures that the value entered into a primary key field is not null and is unique. XDE automatically creates a primary key constraint for you when you create a primary key for a table.

A *unique constraint* ensures that the value entered into a column is unique. XDE automatically creates a unique constraint for you when you select the Unique Constraint check box for a field in the Column Specification window.

An *index* provides quick access to records by searching only through a list of key columns when searching for rows in the table.

To add a key constraint:

1. Open the table or Column Specification window.
2. Select the Key Constraints tab.

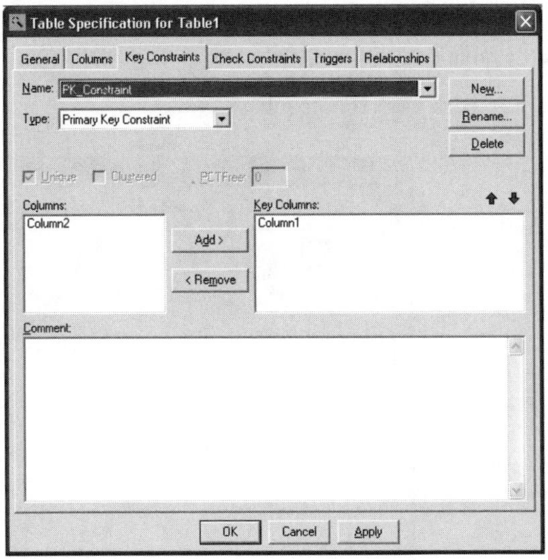

3. Click New.
4. Select the type: Primary Key Constraint, Unique Constraint, or Index.

5. In the Columns list box, select the column(s) to which the constraint applies. Use the Add button to move the selected columns to the Key Columns list box.
6. Select the Deferrable check box (Oracle and SQL 92 only) if you want to make the constraint deferred.
   - A nondeferred constraint runs at the end of a statement.
   - A deferred, initially immediate constraint runs at the beginning of a transaction.
   - A deferred, initially deferred constraint runs at the end of a transaction.
7. Select the Unique check box (index constraint) if the index is unique.
8. Select the Clustered check box if you want to make an index clustered.
9. In the Fill Factor/PCT Threshold/PCTFree field, optionally enter the free percentage (1–100) of the index. Each DBMS has a different name for this field.

Check Constraints

A *check constraint* is any constraint other than a primary key, unique, or index constraint. In other words, it is any constraint other than a key constraint. Check constraints are added on the specification window of either a column or table. The constraints themselves are linked to the table, but you can enter them in either location.

To add a check constraint:

1. Open the table or column specification window.
2. Select the Check Constraints tab.

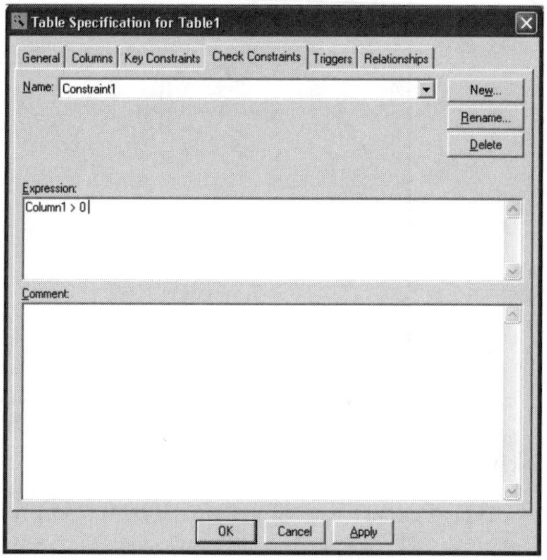

3. Click New.

4. In the Expression field, enter the SQL statement for the constraint.

5. If you are using Oracle or SQL 92, you can select the Deferrable option. Nondeferrable constraints are evaluated at the end of the SQL statement. For example, a nondeferrable constraint might be evaluated at the end of an insert statement.

   Deferrable constraints can be Initially Immediate, in which case they are evaluated at the beginning of the statement; or they can be Initially Deferred, in which case they are evaluated at the end of the transaction. The constraint also has a deferrable and an initially deferred property, which can be used to mark a constraint as deferrable, and optionally initially immediate.

Once a check constraint has been added, it appears in the Model Explorer underneath the table and has a stereotype of <<Check Constraint>>.

ADDING TRIGGERS

A *trigger* is a SQL procedure that runs upon a specific event. For example, you can set up a trigger to run every time a record is inserted into a specific table. Triggers can be set up to run when a row is inserted, changed, or deleted.

The specifications for a trigger vary depending on the DBMS you are using. A trigger is modeled in the Model Explorer under the table to which it applies and has the stereotype <<Trigger>>.

To add a trigger:

1. Open the Table Specification window.

2. Select the Triggers tab.

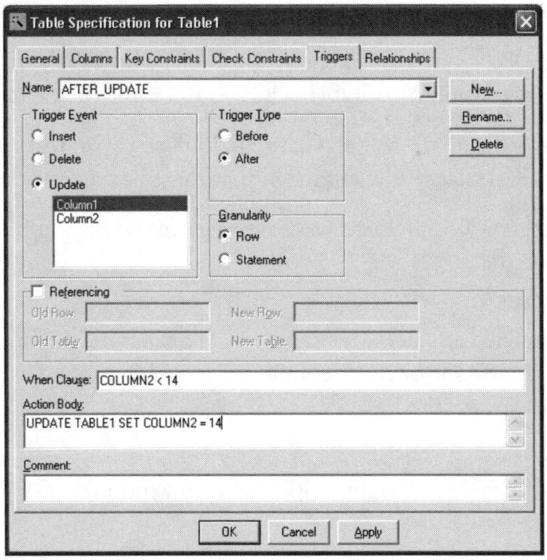

3. Click New.
4. Set the Trigger Event by choosing one of the following:
   - Select Insert if the trigger should run when a row is inserted.
   - Select Delete if the trigger should run when a row is removed.
   - Select Update if the trigger should run when a row is changed. If you select Update, enter the column that should be updated in order for the trigger to run.
5. Set the Trigger Type by choosing one of the following:
   - Select Before to run the trigger before the trigger event.
   - Select After to run the trigger after the trigger event.
   - Select Instead Of to run a view trigger instead of a table trigger. The Instead Of option does not appear on the graphic shown earlier because it is available only when you create a trigger for a SQL Server 2000 or Oracle view.
6. Set the Granularity (Oracle and DB2 only) to one of the following:
   - Select Row if the trigger should run after each row is inserted, updated, or deleted.
   - Select Statement if the trigger should run after the statement has executed.
7. Check the Referencing check box if you want to set up references in the trigger. Then, fill in the following information:
   - Enter the name of the Old Row, which is the name of the row before the trigger executes.
   - Enter the New Row, which is the name of the row after the trigger executes.
   - In DB2, you can also enter Old Table, which is the name of the table before the trigger executes, and New Table, which is the name of the table after the trigger executes.
8. Enter a value in the When Clause field if you wish to further refine when the trigger executes. The When Clause is a condition that must be true for the trigger to execute.
9. Enter the SQL statement for the trigger in the Action Body field.

Adding Indexes

An *index* is modeled as a key constraint in a table. An index is a structure that allows for quick searches of a table. One or more columns are used for an index; when a search is performed, only those columns are searched.

To add an index:

1. Open the table or Column Specification window.

2. Select the Key Constraints tab.

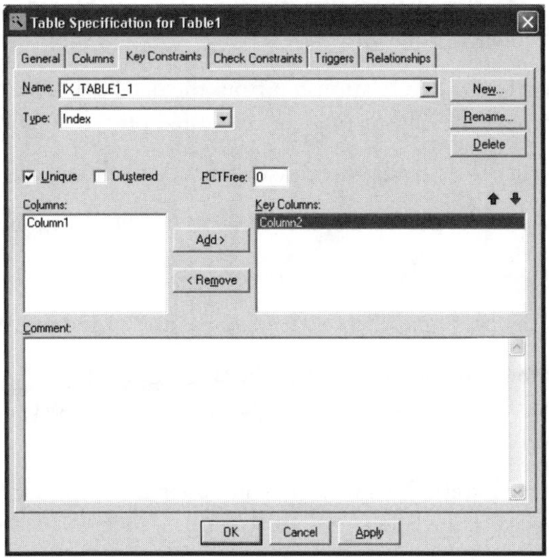

3. Click New.
4. Set the Type to Index.
5. In the Columns list box, select the column(s) that will be used in the index. Use the Add button to move the selected columns to the Key Columns list box.
6. Select the Unique check box (Index constraint) if the index is unique.
7. In the Fill Factor field (or PCT Threshold field for Oracle), optionally enter the free percentage (1–100) of the index.

Adding Stored Procedures

Like a trigger, a *stored procedure* is a piece of functionality in the database. It is essentially a small program that can be invoked directly by the application or by a trigger. It can accept input parameters and return one or more values, called output parameters.

Some DBMS packages support two types of stored procedures: regular stored procedures and functions. A function returns a value, while a stored procedure does not. A stored procedure can, however, return an output parameter.

In XDE, a stored procedure is modeled as an operation with the stereotype <<Stored Procedure>>. It is created within a special class with a stereotype of <<Stored Procedure Container>>. A stored procedure is not specific to a table, and is therefore created underneath the stored procedure container rather than underneath a table.

To add a stored procedure, follow these steps:

1. First, add a stored procedure container. Use the Stored Procedure Container option in the Data Modeler toolbox.
2. Create a realization relationship from the database component to the stored procedure container to set the DBMS type for the stored procedure container.
3. Right-click the stored procedure container and choose Add Data Modeler ➢ Stored Procedure.
4. Right-click the new stored procedure in the Model Explorer, and select Open Specification.
5. On the General tab, enter the following:
   - In the Name field, enter the name of the stored procedure.
   - In the Language field, enter the language for the stored procedure. In most cases, the language is SQL. Some DBMS packages also support other languages, such as C, Java, or COBOL.
   - In the External Name field, enter the path or library for the procedure. This field is not needed if the language is set to SQL.
   - In the Type field, enter the type (Procedure or Function) of stored procedure. A function returns a value while a stored procedure does not. Not all DBMS packages support functions.
   - In the Return Type field, enter the data type of the value returned from a function. This field is not needed unless the stored procedure is a function.
   - In the Length field, enter the number of characters in the return value. This field is not needed for all data types. You will see this field only if you use one of the following data types:

     For DB2: blob, character, clob, DBclob, graphic, varchar, or vargraphic

     For Oracle: char, nchar, nvarcahar2, raw, or varchar2

     For SQL Server: binary, car, nchar, nvarchar, varbinary, or varchar

     For Sybase: binary, char, nchar, nvarchar, varbinary, or varchar
   - In the Precision field, enter the number of digits to the right of the decimal point in the return value. This field is not needed for all data types. You will see this field only if you use one of the following data types:

     For DB2: decimal

     For Oracle: float or number

     For SQL Server: decimal, float, or numeric

     For Sybase: decimal, float, or numeric

- In the Scale field, enter the number of digits in the return value. This field is not needed for all data types. You will see this field only if you use one of the following data types:

  For DB2: decimal

  For Oracle: number

  For SQL Server: decimal or numeric

  For Sybase: decimal or numeric

- The Null Input Action (DB2) field controls what should happen if the function receives a null parameter. Return Null returns a null value from the function. Call Procedure causes the function to run even with a null parameter. This field appears only if you are defining a DB2 function.

- The Parameter Style (DB2) field sets the way parameters should be sent to and received from a stored procedure. This field appears only if you are defining a DB2 stored procedure.

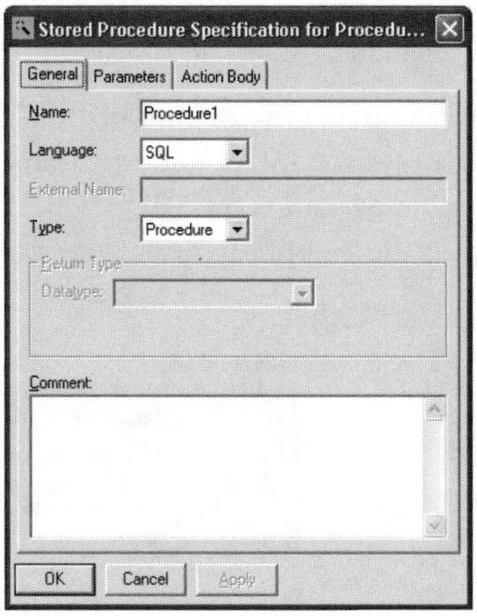

6. On the Parameters tab, enter any needed parameters. Right-click the white space and select Insert to add a new parameter. Enter the following:

   - Choose the parameter data type from the Data Type drop-down list.

   - In the Length field, enter the number of characters in the parameter. This field is not needed for all data types. You will see this field only if you use one of the following data types:

     For DB2: blob, character, clob, DBclob, graphic, varchar, or vargraphic

     For Oracle: char, nchar, nvarcahar2, raw, or varchar2

     For SQL Server: binary, car, nchar, nvarchar, varbinary, or varchar

     For Sybase: binary, char, nchar, nvarchar, varbinary, or varchar

- In the Precision field, enter the number of digits to the right of the decimal point in the parameter. This field is not needed for all data types. You will see this field only if you use one of the following data types:

  For DB2: decimal

  For Oracle: float or number

  For SQL Server: decimal, float, or numeric

  For Sybase: decimal, float, or numeric
- In the Scale field, enter the number of digits in the return value. This field is not needed for all data types. You will see this field only if you use one of the following data types:

  For DB2: decimal

  For Oracle: number

  For SQL Server: decimal or numeric

  For Sybase: decimal or numeric
- Direction: Choose In, Out, or In Out from the drop-down list. In is used for an input parameter. Out is used for an output parameter, which is similar to a return value. In Out is used for an input parameter that may be changed by the stored procedure and is then output to the calling application or trigger.
- Default Value, if needed.

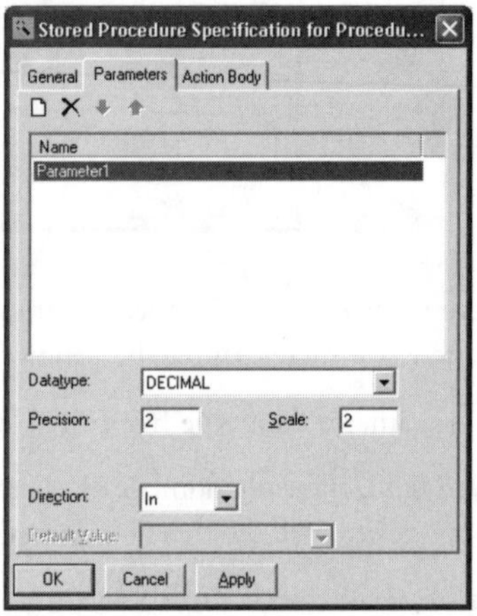

7. On the Action Body tab, enter the SQL for the stored procedure.

Adding Relationships

A relationship in the data model is similar to a relationship in the object model. Where a relationship in the object model joins two classes, a relationship in the data model joins two tables. There are two primary types of relationships supported by XDE: identifying relationships and non-identifying relationships.

In either case, a foreign key is added to the child table to support the relationship. With an identifying relationship, the foreign key becomes part of the primary key of the child table. In this situation, a record cannot exist in the child table without being linked to a record in the parent table. An identifying relationship is modeled as a composite aggregation, as shown here:

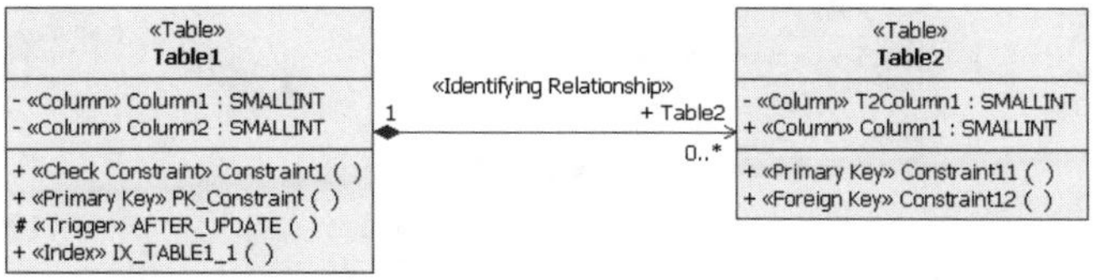

A non-identifying relationship still creates a foreign key in the child table, but the foreign key field does not become part of the primary key of the child table. In a non-identifying relationship, the relationship cardinality (multiplicity) controls whether a record in the child table can exist without a link to a record in the parent table. If the cardinality is 1, a parent record must exist. If the cardinality is 0..1, the parent record does not need to exist. A non-identifying relationship is modeled as an association, as shown here:

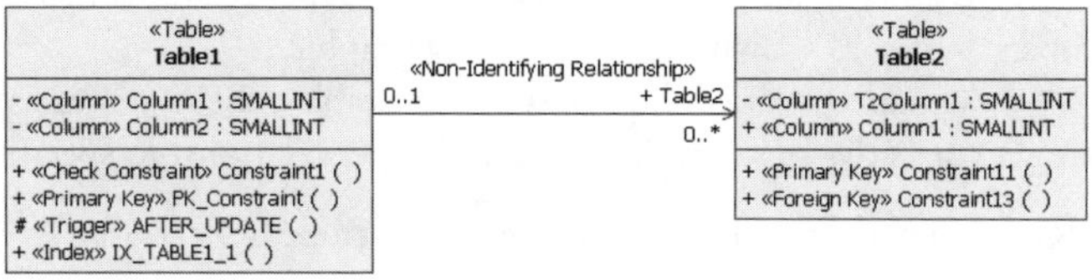

To add an identifying relationship:

1. Select the Identifying Relationship option from the Data Modeler toolbox.
2. Click first on the parent table and then on the child table. XDE automatically adds a primary key constraint and a foreign key constraint to the child table. If a primary key already existed in the child table, XDE adds the foreign key column to the primary key.

To add a non-identifying relationship:

1. Select the Non-Identifying Relationship toolbar button.
2. Click first on the parent table and then on the child table. XDE automatically adds a foreign key constraint to the child table.

Multiplicity defines the number of rows in one table related to a single row in another table. Multiplicity in the data model has much the same meaning as multiplicity in the object model. You set multiplicity options on both ends of the relationship. The multiplicity at the end of the relationship nearest the parent can be set to 1 if the relationship is mandatory, or set to 0..1 if the relationship is optional. The multiplicity nearest the child table controls how many records in the child table can be created for each record in the parent table.

A many-to-many relationship is modeled through the use of a join table, like so:

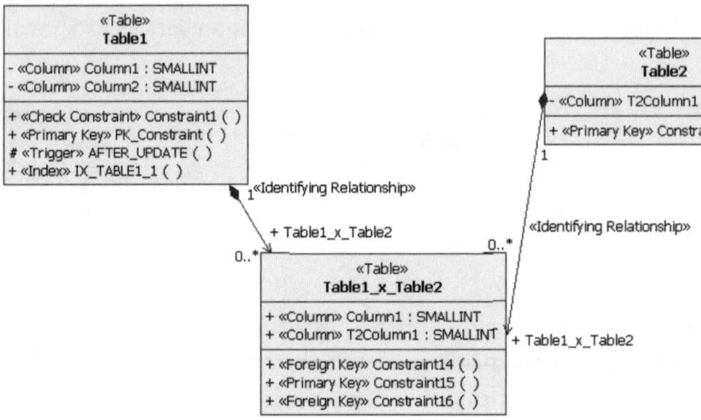

In XDE, adding a many-to-many relationship automatically adds a join table for you. Add the two tables to a diagram, and use the Many To Many Relationship option from the Data Modeler toolbox. XDE adds a join table, and creates identifying relationships between the join table and the two primary tables, as shown in the preceding graphic.

Once you've added relationships between the tables, the next step is to make sure the specifications are set correctly. To set multiplicity and other relationship specifications, follow these steps:

1. Right-click the relationship and select Open Specification.
2. Select the General tab.

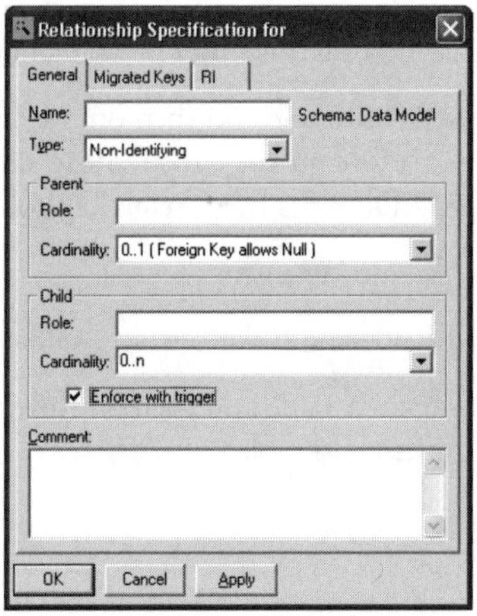

3. Enter the name of the relationship, if desired.
4. Select the type of relationship (Identifying or Non-Identifying).
5. Assign role names to the parent and child tables (optional).
6. Set the cardinality for both sides of the relationship.
7. Check the Enforce With Trigger check box to automatically generate a trigger that enforces the cardinality rules you just established.
8. Select the Migrated Keys tab. The names of the fields in the child and parent table that participate in the relationship are listed. You can change the field names here if needed.

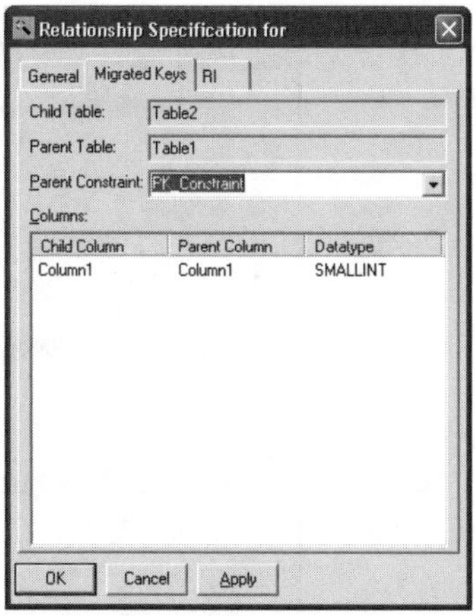

Adding Referential Integrity Rules

Referential integrity establishes a set of rules that help keep the data consistent. For John Doe, for example, you may have an employee record in the employee table and two address records (one for his home address and one for his work address) in the address table. If the John Doe record in the employee table is deleted, the address records will be "orphaned" (that is, they will no longer have an employee to refer to).

Referential integrity helps avoid these situations by specifying what should happen when the parent record is updated or deleted. You have several options. You can have the child record(s) automatically updated or deleted, you can prevent the parent from being updated or deleted at all, or you can run a trigger when you are updating or deleting the parent record. Once you choose your option, you enter this information on the relationship specification in XDE.

There are two primary types of referential integrity: trigger or declarative. Trigger-enforced referential integrity runs a trigger when the parent is updated or deleted. Declarative referential integrity includes the constraint as part of the foreign key clause. The following options are available when setting referential integrity:

Cascade Determines that when the parent is updated or deleted, all child records are updated or deleted.

Restrict Prevents the parent from being updated or deleted.

Set Null Sets the foreign keys in the child record to Null if the parent record is updated or deleted.

No Action Does not enforce referential integrity at all.

Set Default Sets the foreign keys in the child record to a default value if the parent record is updated or deleted.

To set referential integrity for a relationship, follow these steps:

1. Right-click the relationship and select Open Specification.
2. Select the RI (referential integrity) tab.

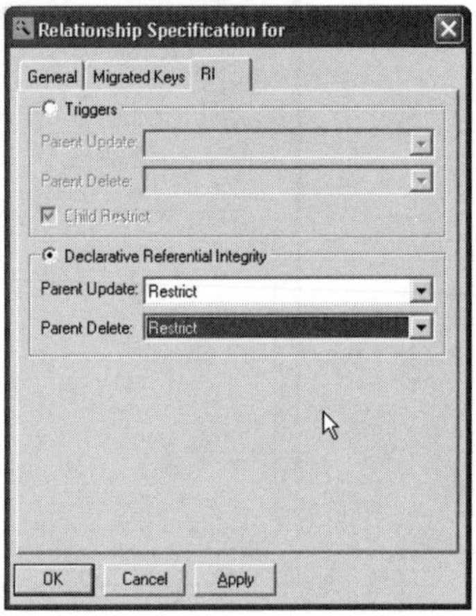

3. Select either the Triggers or the Declarative Referential Integrity radio button to control whether a trigger-enforced or declarative referential integrity rule will be used.
4. If you selected a trigger-enforced rule, enter the following:
   - Use the Parent Update drop-down list to set the option (Cascade, Restrict, Set Null, No Action, or Set Default) to use when the parent is updated. Note that not all options are supported by each DBMS.
   - Use the Parent Delete drop-down list to set the option (Cascade, Restrict, Set Null, No Action, or Set Default) to use when the parent is deleted. Note that not all options are supported by each DBMS.
   - Check the Child Restrict check box to prevent orphan child records from being created.
5. If you selected Declarative Referential Integrity, enter the following:
   - Use the Parent Update drop-down list to set the option (Cascade, Restrict, Set Null, No Action, or Set Default) to use when the parent is updated. Note that not all options are supported by each DBMS.

- Use the Parent Delete drop-down list to set the option (Cascade, Restrict, Set Null, No Action, or Set Default) to use when the parent is deleted. Note that not all options are supported by each DBMS.

Working with Views

A *view* is a way of looking at the data a little differently from the way it is structured in the database. You can create a "virtual" table using a view that contains data from one or more tables in the database. Views help secure the database; you can give a group of users read-only access to a view in order to prevent accidental modifications of the underlying data.

In XDE, a view is modeled as a class with a stereotype of <<Database View>>, as shown here:

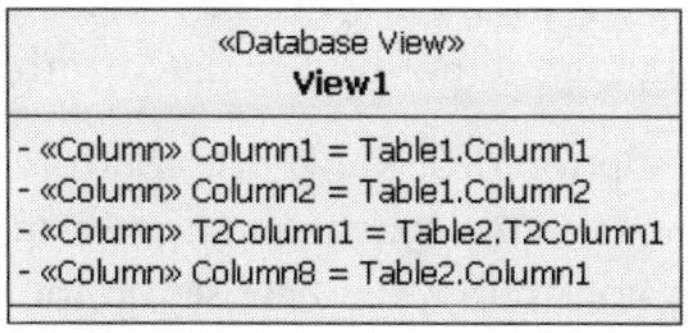

On the data model diagram, a dependency is drawn between the view and the table or tables that are the source of its data, as shown in Figure 7.1.

FIGURE 7.1
Modeling a view

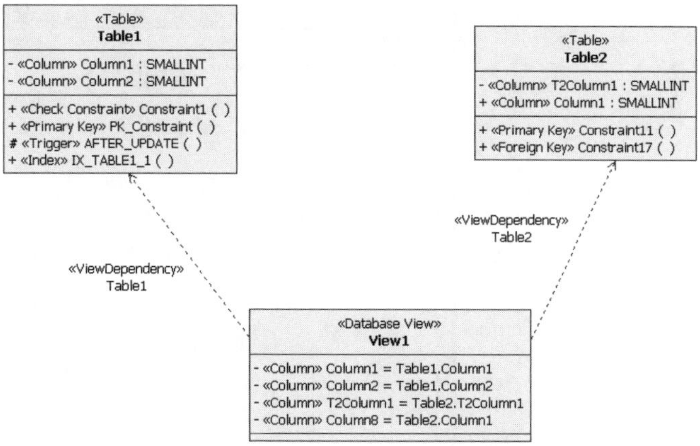

Follow these steps to create a view:

1. Use the View option from the Data Modeler toolbox to add a view.
2. Create dependency relationships from the view to the table(s) used by the view.
3. Right-click the view and select Open Specification.

4. On the General tab, explore the following fields:
   - The Name field is used to name or rename the view. Each view within a schema must have a unique name.
   - Schema displays the name of the schema that contains the view. This field cannot be changed.
   - The Updateable check box controls whether a user can modify data using the view. This field can be set only when you are using Oracle, DB2, or SQL 92.
   - When checked, the Distinct check box determines that only unique rows will be included in the view.
   - When checked, the Materialized (Oracle) check box means that the view will be populated when it is forward engineered from XDE. If this option is not set, the view will still be created, but it will not be populated with data.
   - The Check Option drop-down list controls what constraints are applied to the view. The None option prevents constraints from being enforced on the view; the Local option enforces any constraints you have set up for the view or for any views dependent on this view; and the Cascade option enforces any constraints you have set up for the view, constraints for dependent views, and constraints for the tables that contain the source data.

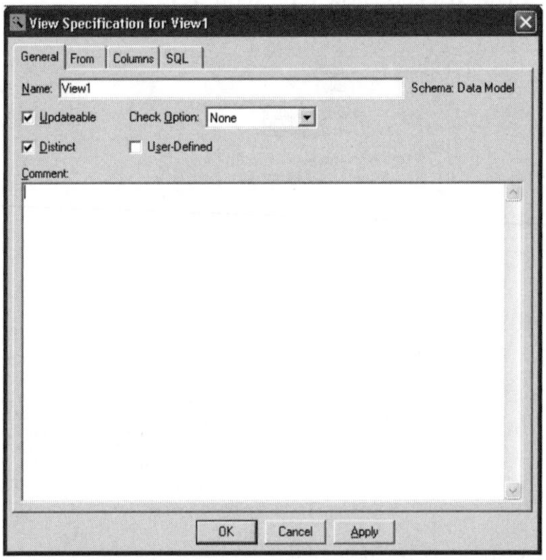

5. On the From tab, explore the following:
   - Select the table(s) and/or view(s) from the Available Members list box that you would like to use in the view. Click Add to move the selected tables or views to the View Members list box.
   - The Correlation Name field sets the alias you can use for the table or view in the current view's SQL statement.

- In the Where Clause field, enter a SQL `where` clause, `order by`, or `group by` statement to include in the view. Be sure to include the phrase `WHERE`, `ORDER BY`, or `GROUP BY`.

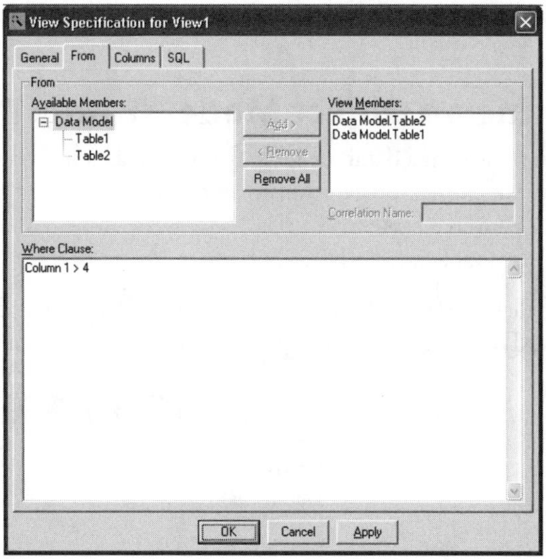

6. On the Columns tab, explore the following:
   - The View Columns field lists the columns that will be included in the view. To add a new column, select the Import Columns button. As a result, a list of all available columns appears. To remove a column, select it and click the Delete button on the toolbar.
   - Alias shows the alias name of the column.

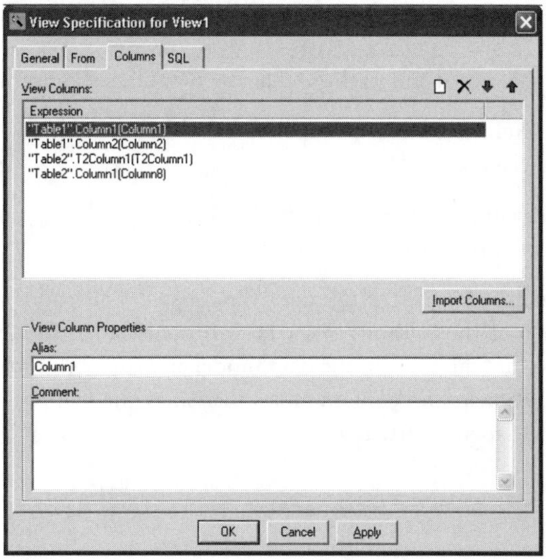

7. On the SQL tab, you can see the SQL statement that was built as you selected tables and columns on the other tabs. You can also enter a SQL statement directly into this window, or change the SQL statement XDE has generated for you. As you change the SQL statement, XDE updates the table and column selections on the other tabs.

Generating an Object Model from a Data Model

XDE lets you transform a database table from your data model into a class in your object model. In the Java version of XDE, you can transform a table into a class or an EJB. In the .NET version of XDE, you can convert a table into a class.

To transform a table into a class:

1. Right-click it in the Model Explorer or on a diagram, and choose Transform ➢ Transform To Class. XDE displays a transformation dialog box, similar to the following:

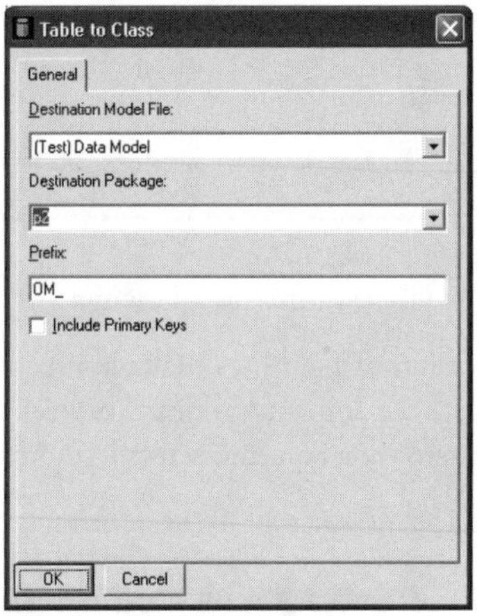

2. Enter the model and package that the new class should be added into.
3. In the Prefix field, you can optionally add a prefix that will be added to the table name to create the class name.
4. If the Include Primary Keys check box is checked, the primary key column(s) will be added as attributes in the generated class.

When you have finished, XDE adds the class, and also adds a dependency from the table to the new class. Each of the columns in the table becomes an attribute in the generated class. The data types, however, are different in the data model and the object model, so XDE needs to translate them. The XDE help files contain tables that show the mapping of the different data modeling types to the different language attribute types.

In the Java version of XDE, you can also transform a table to an EJB.

1. Right-click the table and choose Transform ➢ Transform To EJB. XDE displays the EJB transformation dialog box, as shown here:

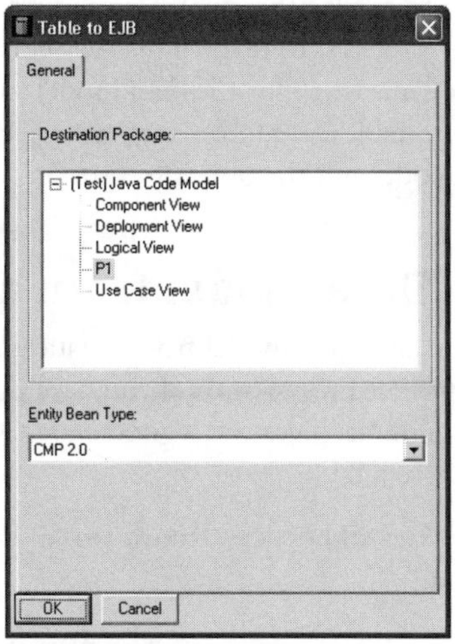

2. Enter the model and package for the new class.
3. From the Entity Bean Type drop-down list, select the type of EJB to create (CMP 1.1 or CMP 2.0).

When you have finished, XDE creates a home interface, a remote interface, and an implementation class for the new EJB. It also creates a component representing the EJB and a dependency between the component and the table, with a stereotype of <<EJBTableMapping>>, as shown in Figure 7.2.

FIGURE 7.2
EJB transformation

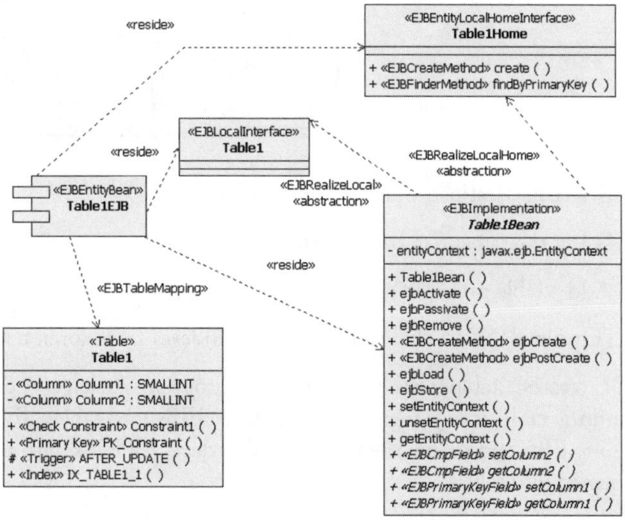

In a CMP 1.1 entity bean, XDE creates attributes in the EJB for all of the columns that were in the table. In CMP 2.0, XDE creates get and set operations in the EJB for each of the columns in the table. If the primary key in the table consisted of two or more columns, XDE also creates a primary key class for you.

These features help to resolve the "which came first, the data model or the object model?" question that plagues many projects. In reality, it is very common for the object model to feed into the data model and, at the same time, for the data model to feed into the object model. With the ability to transform classes into tables and tables into classes, it is easier to take advantage of the information in both the data model and the object model.

Generating a Data Model from an Object Model

Just as you can generate an object model from a data model, you can generate a data model from an object model. As the project progresses and you have discovered more entity classes, you will find that generating the data model gives you a good start to your database design.

To transform a class to a table:

1. Right-click the class and choose Transform ➢ Transform To Table. XDE displays the Class to Table dialog box:

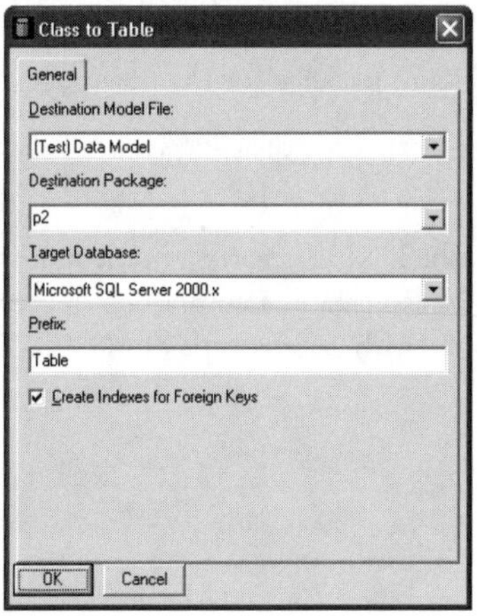

2. Select the destination model and package.
3. Select the target database for the table.
4. Add a table prefix, if desired.
5. (Optional) Select the option to create indexes from foreign keys.

XDE creates a table for the class in the appropriate package. A dependency is created between the class and the table, too. You can also transform EJBs into tables. To do so, select an EJB or package containing EJBs and follow the previous procedure. All EJBs within the package structure will be transformed into tables.

Generating a Database from a Data Model

At any point during the project, you can generate the database or DDL script from the data model. XDE gives you the choice of simply generating the DDL or running the DDL to create the database.

XDE includes a wizard that walks you through the steps of creating the database. Before running the wizard, however, be sure your data model is set up properly. Specifically, check to be sure:

- All stored procedures you want to generate have been included in a stored procedure container. A stored procedure outside a container will not be generated.
- The tables you want to generate have been associated via a realization relationship to a namespace in the database you are generating.
- There is a realization relationship between the namespace and the database you are generating.

Once you've checked to be sure that the appropriate relationships have been set up, follow these steps to generate the DDL:

1. Right-click a database, tablespace, or table in the Model Explorer and choose Data Modeler ➢ Forward Engineer.
2. After the welcome screen, put check marks in the boxes for the elements you wish to generate, and click Next to continue.

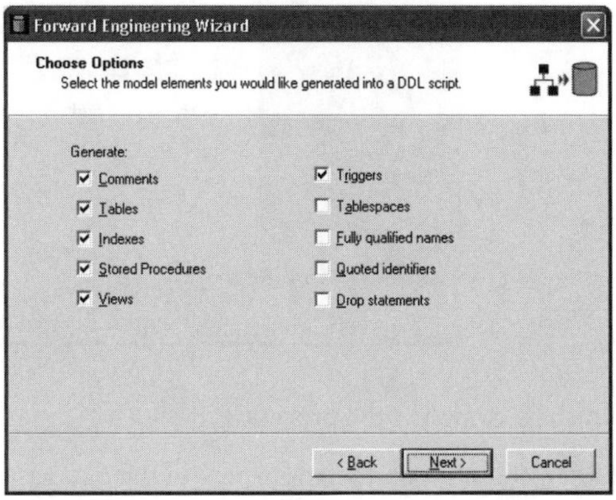

3. Next, enter the name of the DDL file to create.
4. If you want to create the DDL, but not run it, click Next.
5. If you want to run the new DDL against a database, select the Execute check box. Enter the connection information for your DBMS and click the Test Connection button to be sure that the connection is working properly.

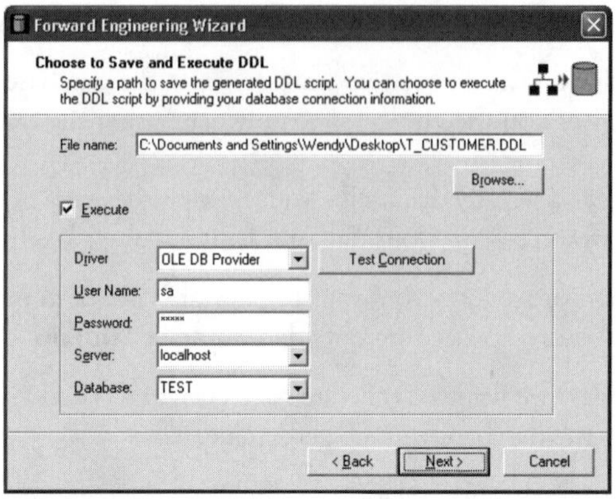

6. Click the Next button. XDE generates the DDL and optionally runs it against the database. If XDE encounters any errors, it adds them to the task list. Once the process finishes, XDE displays the completion screen.

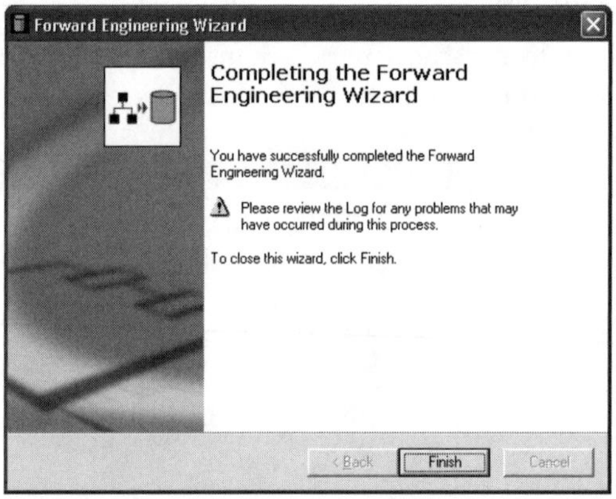

7. Click Finish to complete the process.

All of the tables, columns, and relationships in the database are generated in the DDL or database. The following example shows a table in the data model.

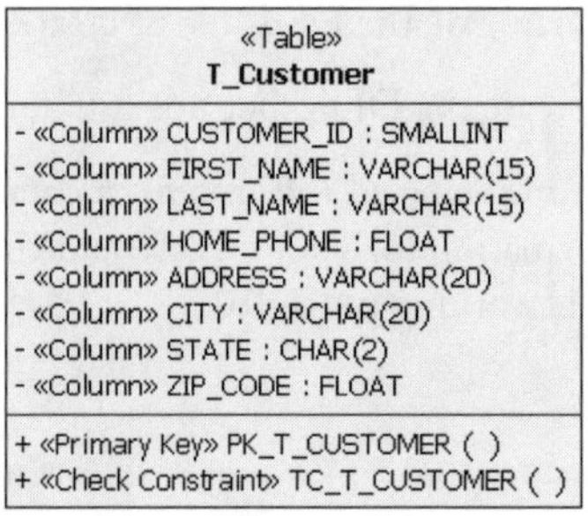

The following is the corresponding ANSI 92 DDL:

```
CREATE TABLE T_Customer (
   CUSTOMER_ID SMALLINT NOT NULL,
   FIRST_NAME VARCHAR ( 15 ) NOT NULL,
   LAST_NAME VARCHAR ( 15 ) NOT NULL,
   HOME_PHONE FLOAT NOT NULL,
   ADDRESS VARCHAR ( 20 ) NOT NULL,
   CITY VARCHAR ( 20 ) NOT NULL,
   STATE CHAR ( 2 ) NOT NULL,
   ZIP_CODE FLOAT NOT NULL,
   CONSTRAINT PK_T_CUSTOMER PRIMARY KEY (CUSTOMER_ID),
   CONSTRAINT TC_T_CUSTOMER CHECK (CUSTOMER_ID > 1000)
   );
```

Updating an Existing Database

Once a database has been created, you may make changes to either the data model or the database itself. Frequently, the two get out of synchronization, which can cause difficulties when you are trying to further modify the database design or maintain the application later. You can always forward engineer your data model again, but if you do, XDE will overwrite the DDL and database that were originally generated, which may not be what you want to do.

XDE includes a compare-and-synchronize feature to address this problem. The feature includes a graphical, side-by-side representation of the database and data model. Using this feature, you can select the changes to be made to the data model or database to synchronize the two again.

To begin the synchronization:

1. Right-click a database in the Model Explorer and choose Data Modeler ➢ Compare and Sync. Once you do, you are given the option of synchronizing with either a DDL script or a database.

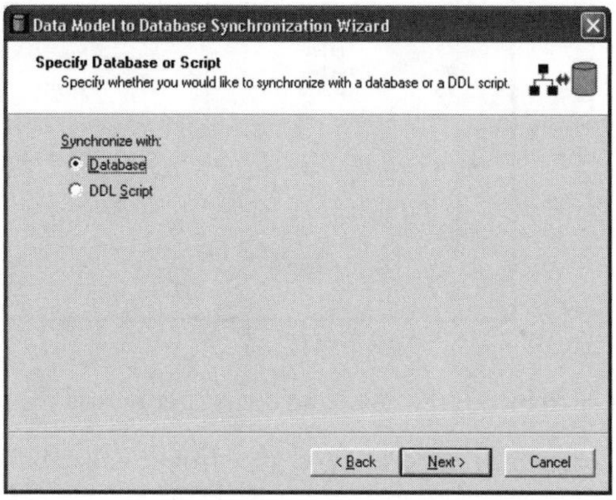

2. If you select DDL script, you are prompted for the name of the script. If you select Database, you are prompted for the database connection information.

3. Next, select the options you would like to synchronize. XDE always synchronizes tables and constraints, but you can also synchronize indexes, triggers, and other elements.

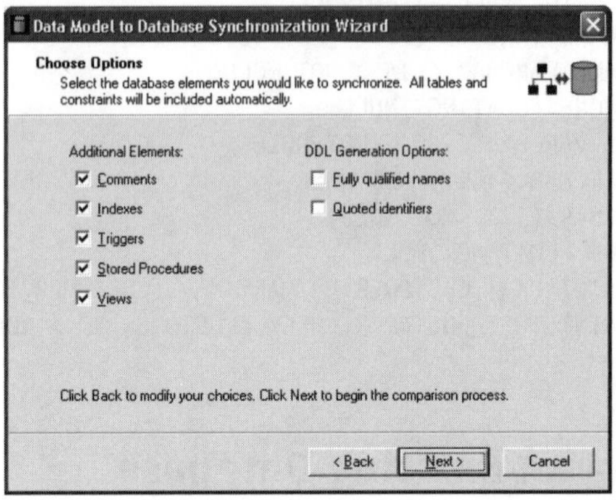

XDE then displays the differences between the model and the database, as shown in Figure 7.3.

FIGURE 7.3

The model and database compare-and-synchronize feature

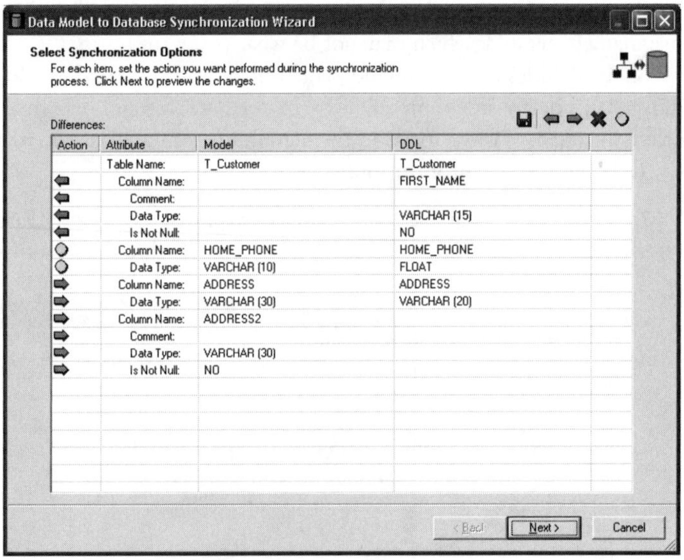

4. Select a difference in the table, and then select one of the following four options from the toolbar:
   - Import, which imports the change from the database into the data model
   - Export, which exports the change from the data model to the database
   - Delete, which removes the change from both the data model and the database
   - Ignore, which ignores the change

5. Once you finish the changes, select Next. At this point, XDE allows you to preview the changes you want to make.
6. When you are satisfied with the list of changes, click Next to commit the changes.

Reverse Engineering a Database

You can reverse engineer a database into a data model in XDE. When you reverse engineer the database, XDE creates the database component and the tables and other elements from the database. Once you have reverse engineered the database, you can generate an object model or perform a synchronization using the methods described earlier in this chapter.

To begin the process, right-click a package or the model in the Model Explorer and choose Data Modeler ➢ Reverse Engineer. After the welcome screen, you are asked whether to reverse engineer from a DDL script or a database. If you select DDL, you are prompted for the target DBMS and the name of the file. If you select database, you are prompted for the database connection information.

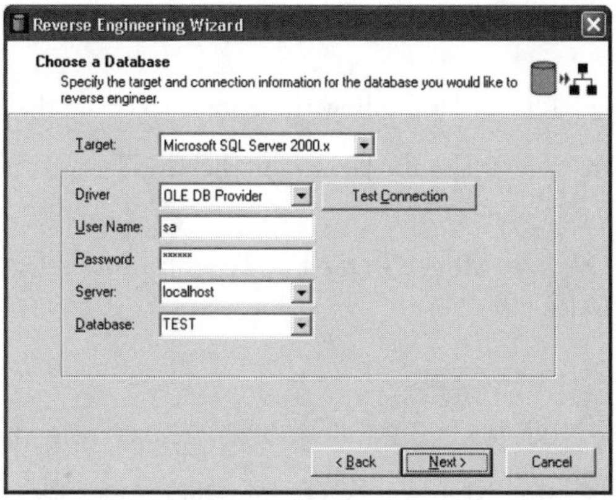

Next, select the item(s) to reverse engineer. Tables and constraints are always imported, but you can select other elements to reverse engineer.

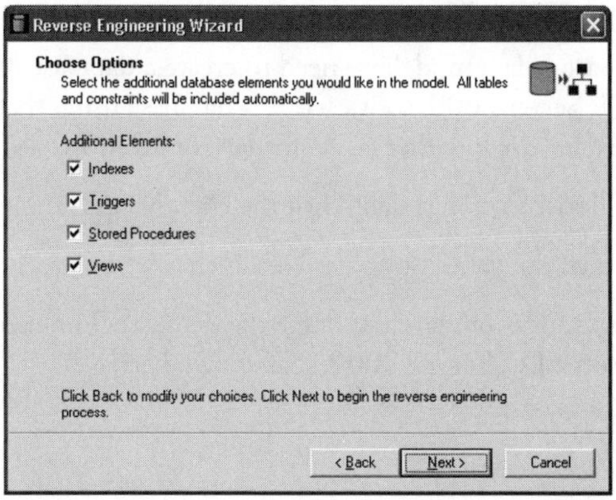

When you have finished, click Next. XDE creates the database component, along with the tables, constraints, and other model elements from your database. If XDE encounters any problems during the reverse-engineering process, these are noted in the task list.

Exercise: Creating a Database for the Timekeeping System

In previous chapters we created the design for the timekeeping system. In this exercise, we create a data model for the system. We add tables to store timecards and the detailed entries on the timecards, add a relationship between these tables, and create a view. Finally, we generate the SQL needed to implement the database.

Creating a Data Model

The first step in the process is to create a data model to hold the database design for the timekeeping system. In XDE, you can create more than one data model for a project, but in this exercise we create only one.

USING JAVA

If you are using XDE for Java, follow these steps to create the data model:

1. If you are using XDE for Java, right-click the Timekeeping System project in the Navigator window.
2. Choose New ➢ Model. In the File Types list box, select Data. In the Templates list box, select Data Model.

USING .NET

If you are using XDE for .NET, follow these steps to create the data model:

1. If you are using XDE for .NET, right-click the project in the Solution Explorer.
2. Choose Add ➢ Add New Item. In the Categories list box, select Rational XDE. In the Templates list box, select DataModel.

Adding a Database

Now that we have a data model, we need to create a database. Our fictional hotel chain uses Microsoft SQL Server 2000, so we set up a database using that DBMS.

To add the database in either XDE for Java or XDE for .NET, follow these steps:

1. In the Model Explorer, right-click the Data Model and choose Add Data Modeler ➢ Database.
2. Right-click the database and select Open Specification.
3. In the specification window, name the database **TimekeepingDB**, and set the target to **Microsoft SQL Server 2000.x**, as shown here:

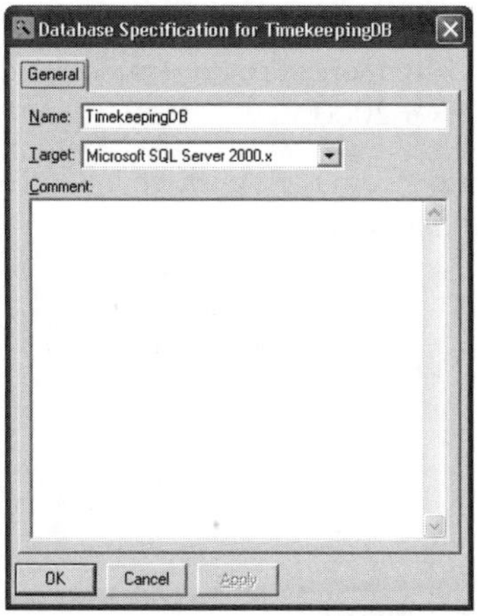

Creating a Data Model Diagram

We use the data model diagram to visualize the database, tables, columns, relationships, and views in the data model. To create a data model diagram for the timekeeping system, follow these steps:

1. In the Model Explorer, right-click the Data Model and choose Add Diagram ➢ Free Form.
2. Name the new diagram **Data Model Diagram**.
3. Select the Data Modeler portion of the toolbox to use the data modeling options.

Creating the Timecard and TimecardEntry Database Tables

Next, we create the Timecard and TimecardEntry tables for our example. The Timecard table holds general information about the timecard, such as the start date and end date, and the employee filling out the timecard. The TimecardEntry table holds the detailed items in each timecard. For example, if an employee spends two hours working at the front desk and another two hours working at the reservations desk, the employee would have two timecard entries.

Once we've created the tables, we use a realization relationship to show that the tables are contained in the database we just created. When we link the tables to the database via a realization relationship, XDE automatically sets the DBMS of the tables to SQL Server 2000.*x*.

To add the tables to our model, follow these steps:

1. Drag the TimekeepingDB component onto the data model diagram.
2. Select the Table option from the Data Modeler toolbox, and click inside the data model diagram to add the table. Name the new table **Timecard**.
3. Create another new table. Name this table **TimecardEntry**.

4. Use the Realization option in the Data Modeler toolbox to create a realization from the TimekeepingDB component to the Timecard table. This sets the DBMS of the Timecard table to SQL Server 2000.x.

5. Create a realization from the TimekeepingDB component to the TimecardEntry table. Your diagram should now look like this:

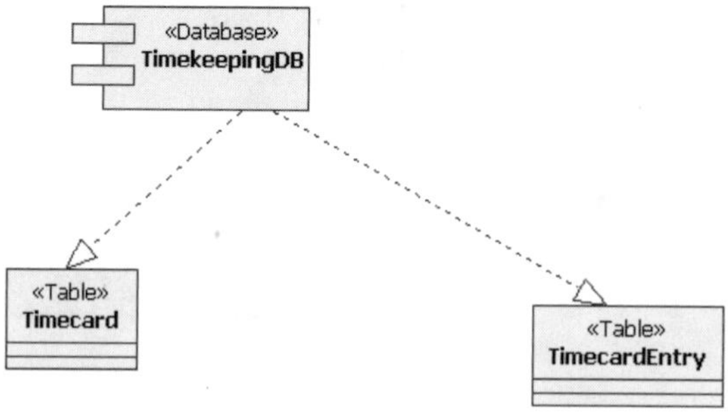

Adding Columns to the Timecard Table

We now have the tables we need, but we still need to add columns to them. In this part of the exercise, we add four columns to the Timecard table and four columns to the TimecardEntry table.

To add the columns, follow these steps:

1. Right-click the Timecard table and choose Add Data Modeler ➢ Column.

2. In the Model Explorer, right-click the new column and select Open Specification.

3. Name the new column **StartDate**.

4. Select the Type tab. Set the data type of the column to DATETIME, and be sure the Not Null check box is selected, as shown here:

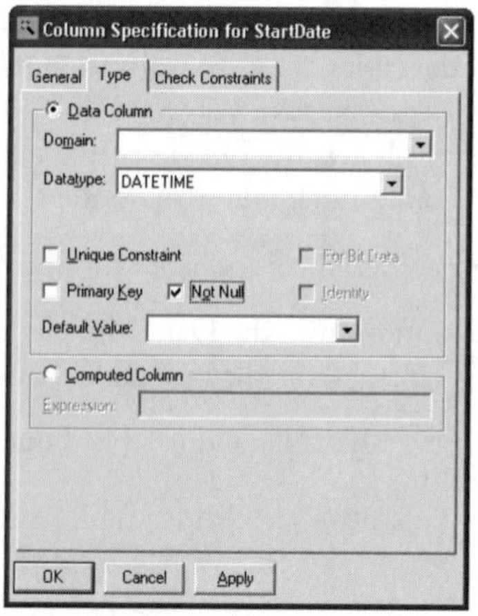

5. Repeat these steps to add a column called **EndDate**, which is a DATETIME, and a column called **TotalHours**, which is a REAL. The TotalHours column should have the Not Null check box selected, but the EndDate should not.

6. Add the following columns to the TimecardEntry table: **EntryDate (DATETIME)**, **JobCode (INT)**, **Hours (REAL)**.

7. Add a primary key column to the Timecard table. Add a new column called **TimecardID** with data type SMALLINT.

8. On the Type tab of the column specification window, check the Primary Key option and the Identity option. Note that XDE automatically creates a primary key constraint, and that the primary key has a red "PK" next to it in the Model Explorer.

9. Add a primary key called **EntryID** to the TimecardEntry table. Your diagram should now look like this:

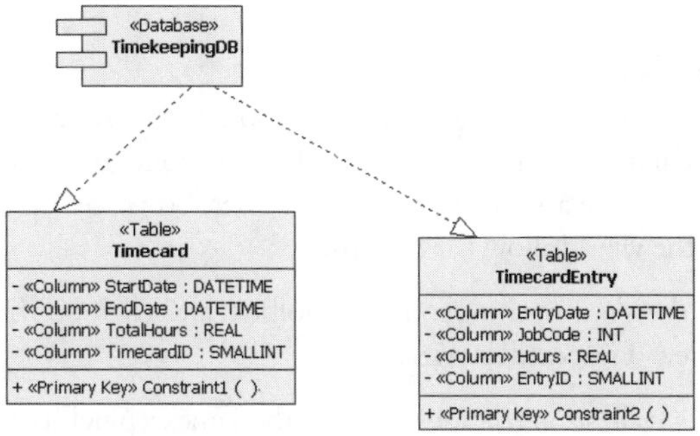

Adding a Relationship

Next we need to show that each timecard may have multiple timecard entries. We do this by setting up a non-identifying relationship between the two tables. In a non-identifying relationship, XDE adds the foreign keys for you, but the primary key of the parent table does not become part of the primary key of the child table. In our example, the TimecardID field is added to the TimecardEntry table, but doesn't become part of TimecardEntry's primary key. If we used an identifying relationship instead, TimecardID would become part of TimecardEntry's primary key.

To add the relationship, do the following:

1. Select the Non-Identifying Relationship option from the toolbox.

2. Click first on the Timecard table and then on the TimecardEntry table to create a non-identifying relationship between them. Note that XDE automatically adds the foreign key and foreign key constraint to the TimecardEntry table.

3. Select the new relationship on the diagram. Change the End2Multiplicity property to 1 in order to require that each timecard entry is associated with one and only one timecard.

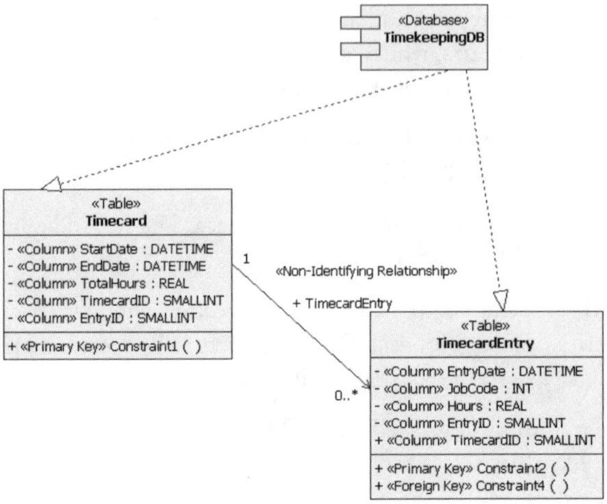

Creating a View

In complex database structures, a view is a good way to see a simplified version of data. In our example, the database structure is simple, but someone using the system may want an easy way to see the timecards and the associated timecard entries. So we set up a view using these two tables.

To create the view, follow these steps:

1. Select the View option from the toolbox, and click on the diagram to add the view. Name the new view **TimecardEntries.**
2. Create a realization relationship from the TimekeepingDB component to the TimecardEntries view.
3. Right-click the TimecardEntries view and select Open Specification.
4. On the From tab, add the Timecard and TimecardEntry tables.

TIP *You can also define what tables participate in a view by adding a dependency relationship from the view to the tables participating in the view.*

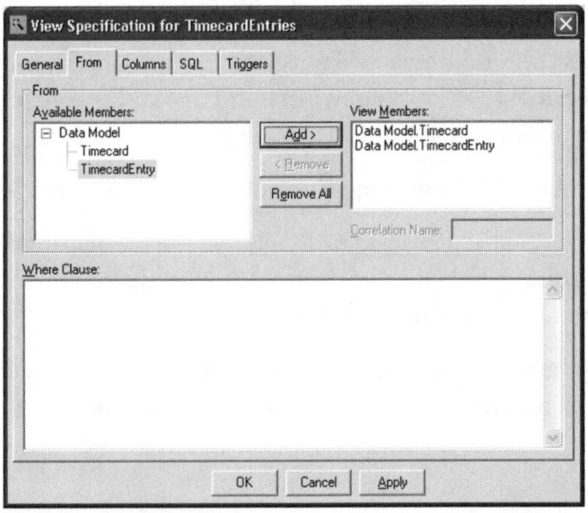

5. On the Columns tab, note that all columns have been selected by default. Highlight the TimecardEntry.EntryID column and click the Delete button to remove it.
6. Select the SQL tab. Note that the SQL for this view has automatically been created.
7. Click OK to finish.
8. Right-click the view on the diagram and select Add Related Shapes. On the Add Related Shapes dialog box, be sure Dependency is checked, and click OK. You can now see the dependencies between the view and the tables it uses:

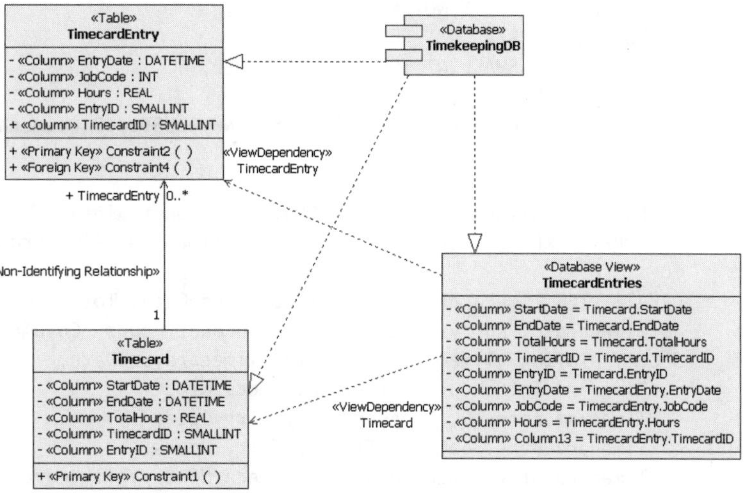

Generating DDL

Finally we need to generate DDL for the model. To generate the DDL, follow these steps:

1. In the Model Explorer, right-click the TimekeepingDB component. Perform one of the following procedures:
   - ◆ If you are using XDE for Java, choose Data Modeler ➢ Forward Engineer.
   - ◆ In XDE for .NET, choose Data Modeler Action ➢ Forward Engineer.
2. Click Next on the introductory screen.
3. Select the elements to generate. Select Comments, Tables, Indexes, Stored Procedures, Views, and Triggers. These should be selected for you by default. Click Next.
4. Enter a filename for the generated DDL. Note that you can also connect to a database on this screen and execute the script directly. Click Next to continue.
5. Click Finish to complete the wizard. Open the generated DDL file. It should look like this:

```
CREATE TABLE TimecardEntry (
   EntryDate DATETIME NOT NULL,
   JobCode INT NOT NULL,
```

```
   Hours REAL NOT NULL,
   EntryID SMALLINT IDENTITY NOT NULL,
   TimecardID SMALLINT NOT NULL,
   CONSTRAINT Constraint2 PRIMARY KEY NONCLUSTERED (EntryID)
   )
GO


CREATE TABLE Timecard (
   StartDate DATETIME NOT NULL,
   EndDate DATETIME NOT NULL,
   TotalHours REAL NOT NULL,
   TimecardID SMALLINT IDENTITY NOT NULL,
   EntryID SMALLINT,
   CONSTRAINT Constraint1 PRIMARY KEY NONCLUSTERED (TimecardID)
   )
GO
ALTER TABLE TimecardEntry ADD CONSTRAINT Constraint4
   FOREIGN KEY (TimecardID) REFERENCES Timecard (TimecardID)
GO
CREATE VIEW TimecardEntries(StartDate, EndDate, TotalHours,
   TimecardID, EntryID, EntryDate, JobCode, Hours, Column13) AS
SELECT DISTINCT Timecard.StartDate, Timecard.EndDate,
   Timecard.TotalHours, Timecard.TimecardID,
   Timecard.EntryID, TimecardEntry.EntryDate,
   TimecardEntry.JobCode, TimecardEntry.Hours,
   TimecardEntry.TimecardID FROM TimecardEntry, Timecard
GO
```

Summary

In this chapter, we examined the data-modeling capabilities of XDE. Combining the object model and data model into a single tool helps the team gain a more complete understanding of the system structure and organization. The forward- and reverse-engineering capabilities help you ensure that your object model, data model, and database stay synchronized.

In this chapter, we specifically discussed the following:

- The differences between an object model and a data model
- How to create a data model
- How to add data-modeling elements
- How to generate an object model from a data model
- How to generate a data model from an object model
- How to generate and reverse engineer a database
- How to keep your object model, data model, and database synchronized

In the next chapter, we look at the publishing and reporting features of XDE.

Chapter 8

Publishing and Reporting Models

WE'VE DISCUSSED HOW TO model your application in XDE and how to work with code and model the database through XDE. But there may be some people on your team who don't have access to XDE; they may still need information from XDE—this is where reporting and web publishing come in.

In this chapter, we look at the reports that can be generated from XDE. We also cover how you can publish an XDE model to HTML so that the rest of the team members can view it, whether or not they have XDE.

Featured in this chapter:

- Generating reports
- Publishing an XDE model

Generating Reports

There are four types of reports packaged with XDE:

- Detailed class report
- Detailed use case report
- Summary classifier and diagram report
- Summary classifier report

To generate any of these, choose Tools ➢ Generate Model Report. Select the type of report to generate, enter a filename, and click OK:

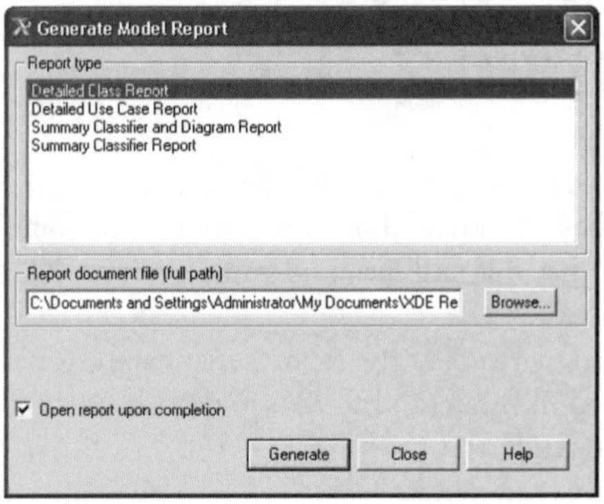

You can use the *detailed class report* when you need information about the classes, class diagrams, attributes, and operations. This type of report helps you build a library of reusable components; the report becomes a "dictionary" of available classes and interfaces. It also helps when you are working with someone who does not have direct access to the XDE model but needs some information about the classes. This report contains the following:

- The class diagrams
- Classes and interfaces, along with their package names, stereotypes, visibility, multiplicity, and persistence
- Enumerations and signals, along with their package names, stereotypes, visibility, multiplicity, and persistence
- Attributes, along with their data types and default values
- Operations, along with their visibility, parameters, parameter types and visibility, and return types
- Packages, along with their containing packages and stereotypes

A portion of a sample detailed class report is shown in Figure 8.1.

FIGURE 8.1
Detailed class report

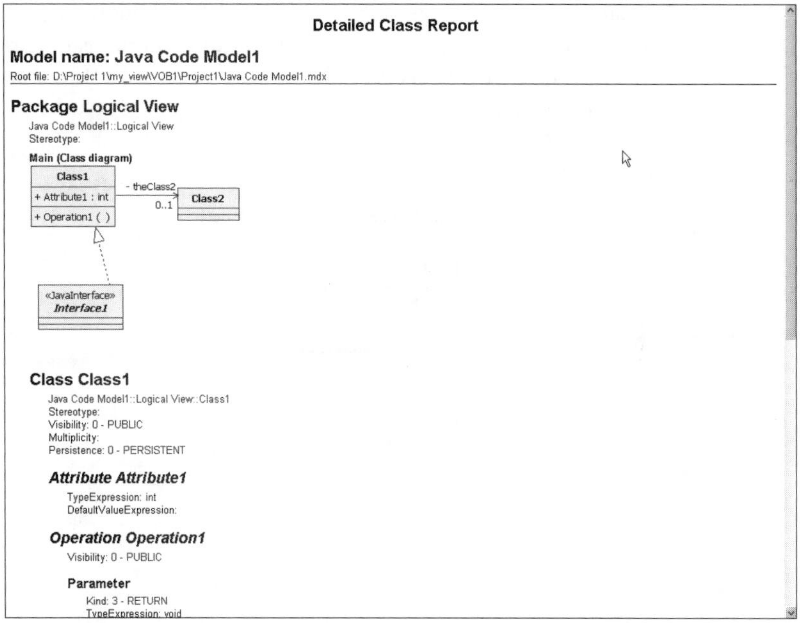

You can use the *detailed use case report* when you need information about the use case diagrams, use cases, and actors in the model. In particular, it helps you communicate with your customers, who typically do not have direct access to XDE. The detailed use case report contains the following:

- Use case diagrams
- Actors, along with their packages, stereotypes, visibility, and multiplicity
- Use cases, along with their packages, stereotypes, visibility, and multiplicity

A portion of a sample detailed use case report is shown in Figure 8.2.

You can use the *summary classifier and diagram report* to summarize information about all of the classifiers in the model. It contains the following:

- Actors, use cases, classes, interfaces, signals, subsystems, components, and nodes, along with their packages
- All of the diagrams in the model

A portion of a sample summary classifier and diagram report is shown in Figure 8.3.

The *summary classifier report* is the same as the summary classifier and diagram report, but it does not contain any of the diagrams. Like the summary classifier and diagram report, it helps give members of the team an overview of the pieces of the model, without having to give everyone access to XDE.

Using these four types of reports, you can communicate with other members of your team, whether or not they have access to XDE. At this time, XDE does not give you the option of creating your own customized reports.

FIGURE 8.2
Detailed use case report

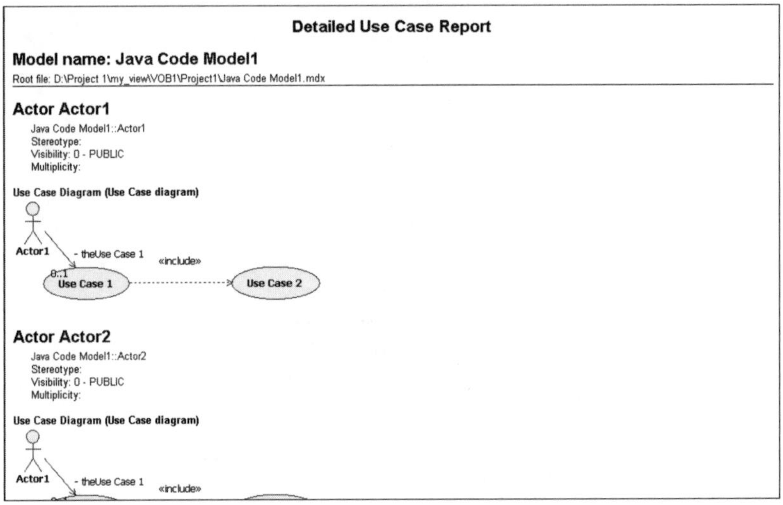
Detailed Use Case Report

Model name: Java Code Model1
Root file: D:\Project 1\my_view\VOB1\Project1\Java Code Model1.mdx

Actor Actor1
Java Code Model1::Actor1
Stereotype:
Visibility: 0 - PUBLIC
Multiplicity:

Use Case Diagram (Use Case diagram)

Actor Actor2
Java Code Model1::Actor2
Stereotype:
Visibility: 0 - PUBLIC
Multiplicity:

Use Case Diagram (Use Case diagram)

FIGURE 8.3
Summary classifier and diagram report

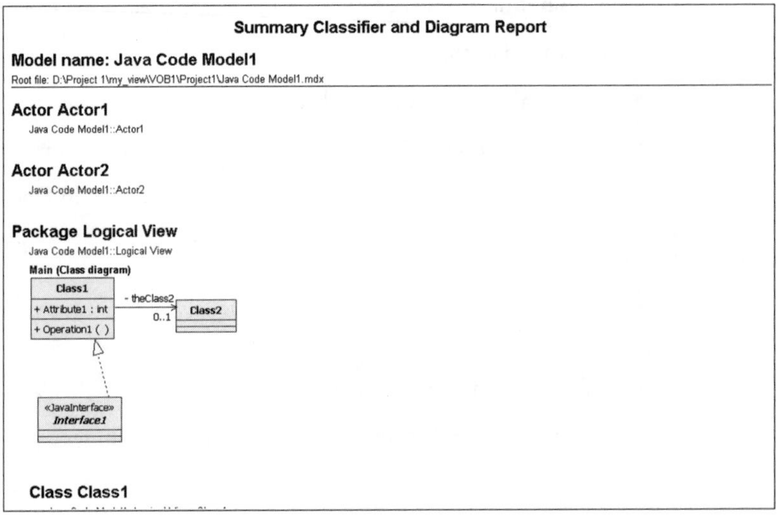
Summary Classifier and Diagram Report

Model name: Java Code Model1
Root file: D:\Project 1\my_view\VOB1\Project1\Java Code Model1.mdx

Actor Actor1
Java Code Model1::Actor1

Actor Actor2
Java Code Model1::Actor2

Package Logical View
Java Code Model1::Logical View

Main (Class diagram)

Class Class1

Publishing Your XDE Model

You can easily publish a model at various levels of detail to an intranet, Internet, or filesystem site using XDE. This way, many people who may need to view the model can do so without having to be XDE users and without printing a ream of model documentation. A model published to the Web is shown in Figure 8.4.

FIGURE 8.4

Published model

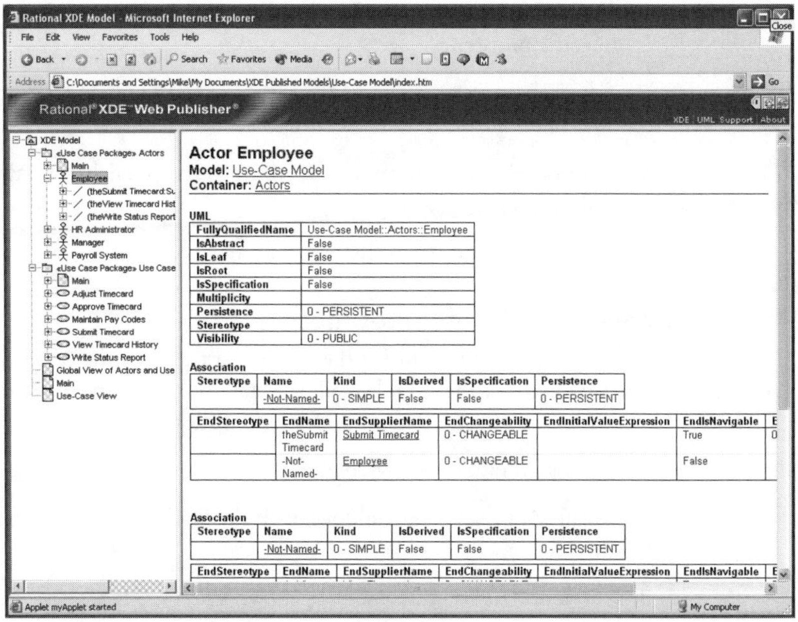

To publish a model, follow these steps:

1. Choose Tools ➢ Publish Model to display the Publish Model window (see Figure 8.5).

FIGURE 8.5

Model publisher

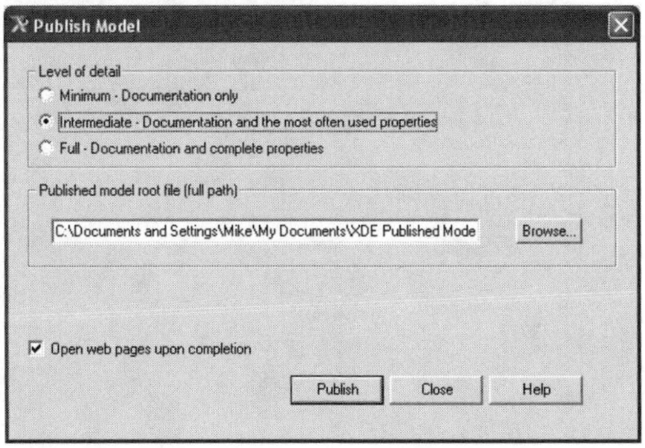

2. Select the desired level of detail.

   Minimum - Documentation only Includes high-level information and none of the properties of the model elements are displayed.

   Intermediate - Documentation and the most often used properties Display attributes, operations, relationships, associations, and stereotypes.

   Full - Documentation and complete properties Publish all properties, including language-specific properties.

3. Select the path to the HTML root file of the published model. This should be the `index.htm` file that non-XDE users can use to access the model.

4. Choose whether you want XDE to open the published model in your default browser once publication is complete.

5. Click Publish to begin the publication.

Model Publishing Preferences

XDE lets you set the default for the options available in the Model Publisher. From the Preferences window, you can set the default level of detail, the location of the root HTML file, and the name of the root file. To set these default preferences, follow these steps:

1. Choose Window ➢ Preferences.

2. From the Preferences window, open the Rational XDE preferences, and select Model Publishing preferences.

3. Set your default preferences, as shown in Figure 8.6.

FIGURE 8.6
Model publishing preferences

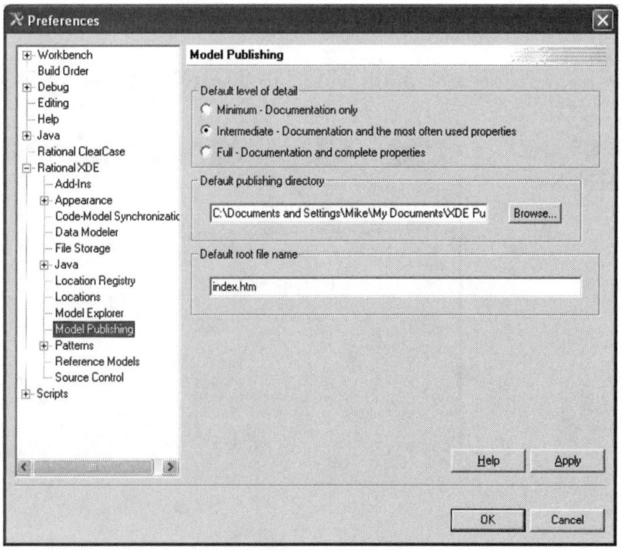

Exercise: Publishing and Reporting Models

In previous chapters, we created a model for the timekeeping system. In order to share this model with others, we now need to report on it. In this exercise, we create reports based on the model and publish it.

Reporting on a Model

In the first part of this exercise, we create the standard reports for a model available in XDE. There are four reports you can print and we will look at all four in this exercise.

1. Open the Design Model in the Timekeeping project.
2. Choose Tools ➢ Generate Model Report.
3. Select Summary Classifier Report as the report type.
4. Make sure the Open Report Upon Completion check box is checked, then click Generate. A section of this report is shown in Figure 8.7.
5. After you have read the summary classifier report, select the Summary Classifier and Diagram as the report type.
6. Change the filename for the report to `SummaryClassifierDiagrams.htm`. Make sure you maintain the full path to the file.

FIGURE 8.7

Excerpt of the summary classifier report

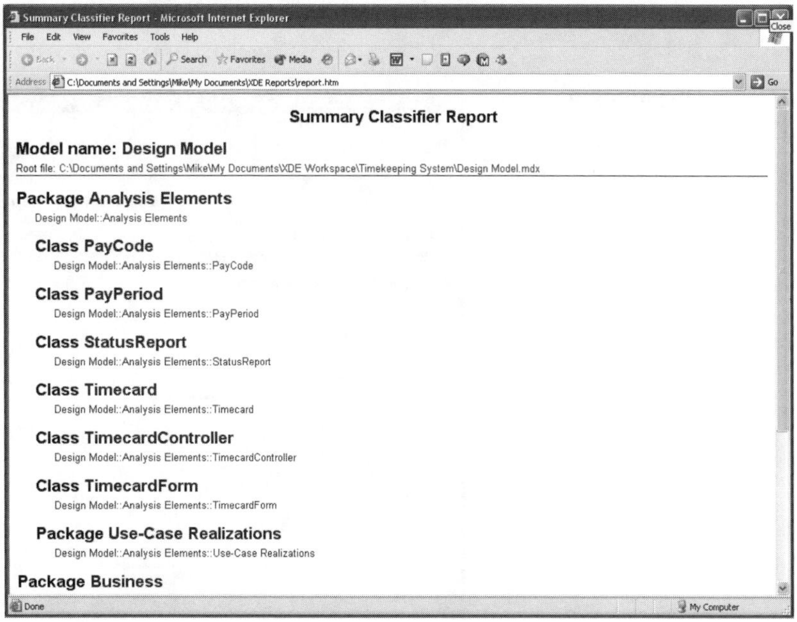

7. Click Generate and read the report. The summary classifier and diagram report contains the same information as the summary classifier report, but it also includes the diagrams in the model, as shown in Figure 8.8.

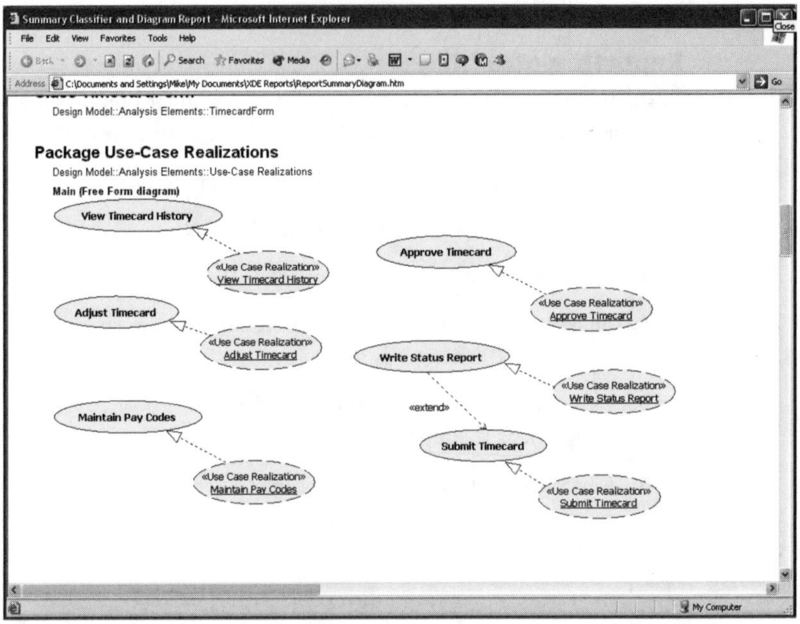

FIGURE 8.8

Excerpt of the summary classifier and diagram report

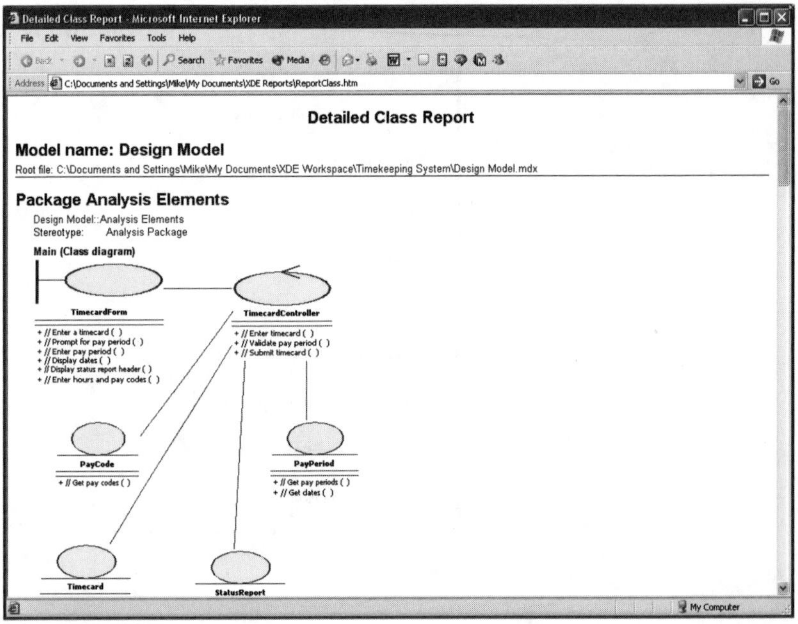

FIGURE 8.9

Excerpt of the detailed class report

8. Now let's look at the detail reports. Select Detailed Class Report as the report type.

9. Change the filename for the report to `DetailedClass.htm` and click Generate. The report will appear as shown in Figure 8.9.

10. Repeat steps 1–4 to print the detailed use case report, but open the Timekeeping Use Case model first, because the Design Model contains no use cases. The use case report should look like Figure 8.10.

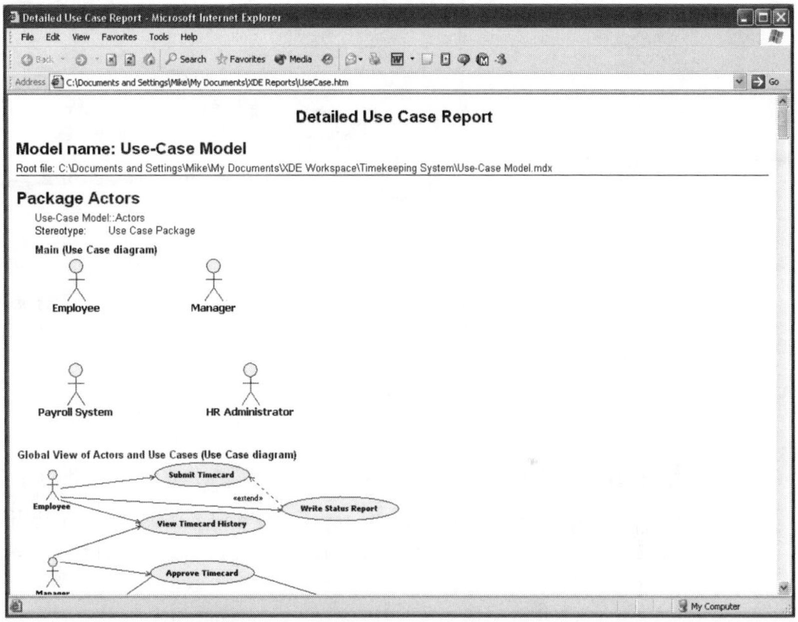

FIGURE 8.10

Excerpt of the detailed use case report

Publishing a Model

In this part of the exercise, we will publish the timekeeping model to web pages.

1. Re-open the Design Model.

2. Choose Tools ➢ Publish Model.

3. Select the intermediate level of detail.

4. Make sure the check box for Open Web Pages After Completion is checked, then Click Publish.

5. Navigate the published model. The published Submit Timecard interface operation realization diagram is shown in Figure 8.11.

FIGURE 8.11
Published model

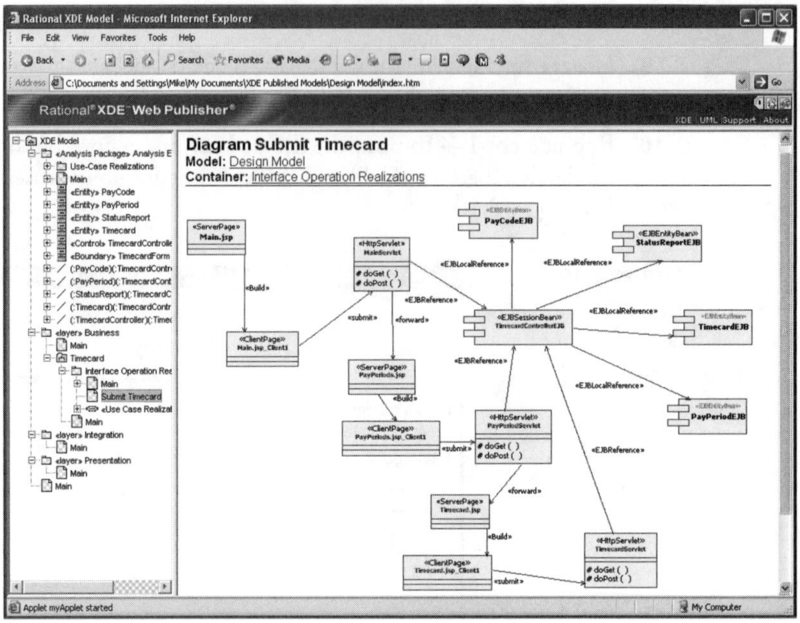

Summary

In this chapter, we looked at the reporting and publishing capabilities of XDE. Using these features, you can communicate information about the model to the entire team, even those members without XDE.

There are four types of reports you can generate:

- Detailed class report
- Detailed use case report
- Summary classifier and diagram report
- Summary classifier report

In addition, you can publish your entire model in HTML format to make it available on your company's intranet.

In the next chapter, we introduce patterns and discuss how you can use patterns to speed development time and standardize your applications.

Part III

Patterns

In this part:

Chapter 9

Using Patterns

PATTERNS ARE A POWERFUL feature of XDE that can reduce the amount of time and effort you need to put into designing and coding your application. Patterns define *best practices* and enable you to easily reuse superior designs and code. In this chapter, we define the term *pattern* and discuss how you can use patterns in XDE.

Featured in this chapter:

- What is a pattern?
- Why use patterns?
- The Pattern Explorer
- Applying patterns
- Binding and expanding patterns
- Pattern favorites

What Is a Pattern?

XDE defines a pattern as "a common solution to a common problem in a given context." In software, we can apply this concept to building an analysis model, building a design model, or building code.

A pattern can contain use cases, classes, interfaces, attributes, operations, relationships, or just about any other UML construct you'd like to reuse. Because patterns are so flexible, you can create patterns to use in analysis, design, or code. If you are building patterns for code, you can incorporate code templates.

A *design pattern* is a *collaboration,* where a collaboration is simply a group of objects that work together to accomplish some goal. Simple patterns may have only an object or two, while more complex patterns include multiple objects and their relationships.

In XDE, we use *parameterized collaborations* to create design patterns. Like a collaboration, a parameterized collaboration is a group of objects that work together to accomplish some goal. A parameterized collaboration, however, takes the specific objects as parameters. For example, one of the patterns we discuss in the next chapter is the Factory Method. In this pattern, one class (the creator) is responsible for creating the objects of another class (the product). Because this is a parameterized collaboration, it takes two arguments: the creator and the product. To use the pattern, you provide values for the parameters. For example, in a banking application you may want the creator to be called LoanCreator and the product to be called Loan.

The pattern collaborations in XDE also contain some components that aren't typically part of general design pattern definition outside of a tool. These are XDE-specific items that the tool uses to implement a pattern. These components are as follows:

Pattern applications These represent the bound instances of the pattern.

Advanced properties These set the defaults and dialog boxes that you use in the pattern wizard.

Root context This lists all non-parameterized elements.

Diagrams These are made up of class diagrams and the like that include pattern elements.

Parameters These are the classes or other UML elements that make up the pattern.

Why Use Patterns?

There are a number of reasons to use patterns in your organization. First and foremost, they can greatly decrease the amount of time you need to design and code a system. Rather than starting from scratch on each new project, the team can simply look for existing patterns and incorporate these into the design and code.

A second benefit is consistency. It can be extraordinarily frustrating to try to maintain someone else's code, especially when that code was written by a number of developers all using their own styles. Patterns can help ensure that everyone approaches the same problems the same way. The team can work together to find the most efficient solution to a common problem, and then they can document that solution in the form of a pattern.

One note of caution, though: a pattern may make it very easy to consistently reuse a great design, but it makes it just as easy to reuse a lousy one. It's very important for someone to keep an eye on all of the different patterns your organization is using and ensure that they are of sufficient quality. Who performs this responsibility varies from organization to organization. Essentially what you're doing here is establishing a reuse library. Some organizations have an object librarian, who is responsible for assessing patterns for quality and then making them available for use. Other organizations have an entire team involved in this effort. The number of people involved depends upon the size of your organization. Some very small organizations don't have an object librarian at all; it is up to the developers to share ideas and patterns without a formal reuse library.

Before adding a pattern to a reuse library, consider the following aspects of its quality:

- Is the pattern consistent with standards followed by the organization?

- Is the pattern consistent with enterprise-wide architectural decisions that have been made?
- Is this something that can really be reused, or it is too specific to a system?
- Has the pattern been sufficiently documented?

Of course, the degree of formality in the pattern review depends on the formality of your organization and the size of the pattern. The process of adding a large pattern for synchronizing data across multiple systems is a little more formal than adding a small pattern to display your company's logo on screens.

As a final note, remember that someone has to maintain the patterns that have been built. As technologies improve and new languages are released, you may want to alter some of your organization's existing patterns. Be sure that someone has been assigned this responsibility, and that any changed patterns are put through the same type of review as any new patterns.

The Pattern Explorer

The Pattern Explorer is an XDE window that allows you to display and organize your patterns. XDE comes with one pattern library, containing patterns commonly known as the *Gang-of-Four (GOF) patterns.* Although these were developed by four individuals—Erich Gamma, Richard Helm, Ralph Johnson, and John Vlissides—no one seems to know how the GOF title originated or why it stuck. GOF patterns are design patterns that are frequently used in real-world applications, and are documented in the book *Design Patterns: Elements of Reusable Object Oriented Software* (Addison-Wesley, 1995), written by the four individuals just mentioned. We discuss these patterns in detail in Chapter 10. In addition to the GOF patterns, you can create your own pattern libraries. The Pattern Explorer is shown here:

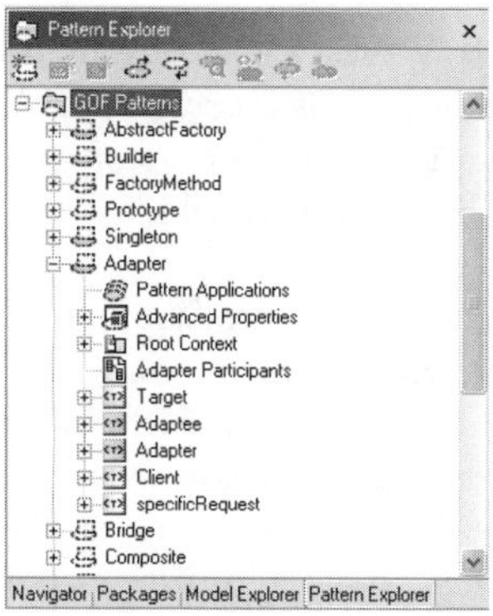

As you can see, this window displays the patterns themselves, as well as the parameters, diagrams, and other items that make up the pattern.

To open the Pattern Explorer, use the menu. In XDE for .NET, select View ➢ Other Windows ➢ Pattern Explorer. In XDE for Java, choose Perspective ➢ Show View ➢ Pattern Explorer.

Like model elements, patterns have properties associated with them. You can see and edit these properties through the Pattern Properties window, shown here:

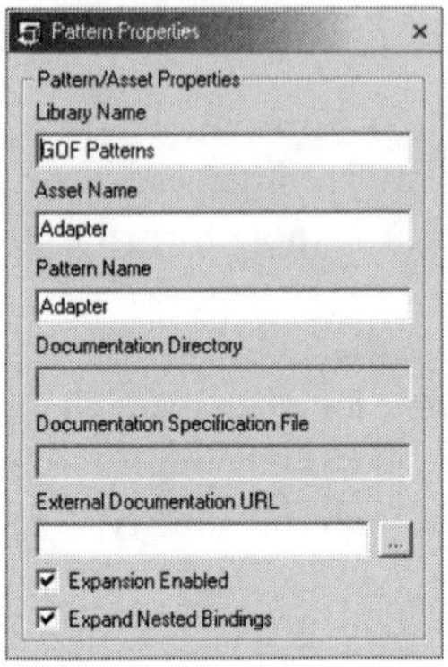

Each component of a pattern (parameter, diagram, and so on) has different properties. In the following sections, we look at each of these components in more detail. To view the Pattern Properties window in XDE for .NET, select View ➢ Other Windows ➢ Pattern Properties. In XDE for Java, choose Perspective ➢ Show View ➢ Pattern Properties.

Patterns

In the Pattern Explorer, a pattern is the container that holds all of the parameters, diagrams, and other elements in the pattern. The pattern is modeled as a parameterized collaboration, and has the following symbol next to it: .

According to the UML version 1.4, a collaboration "describes how an operation or a classifier, like a use case, is realized by a set of classifiers and associations used in a specific way." In other words, a collaboration describes how a group of objects, classes, or other UML elements interact to accomplish some goal. This is the essential idea of a pattern: describing how model elements interact to accomplish a goal.

A parameterized collaboration is a collaboration that receives parameters in order to be used. In XDE, the parameters it receives are the specific classes and other model elements to be used in the pattern. Let's take a look at a simple example to illustrate.

One of the GOF patterns included with XDE is the Singleton. A *Singleton* is a class that will be instantiated at most once. In our example, say we have a class called User. This class, similar to a session object, holds the ID and other information about the current user. We want only one instance of this class to be in memory at any time, so we apply the Singleton pattern.

If you look at the Singleton pattern in the Pattern Explorer, you'll notice that it takes two parameters, one called Singleton and one called Client:

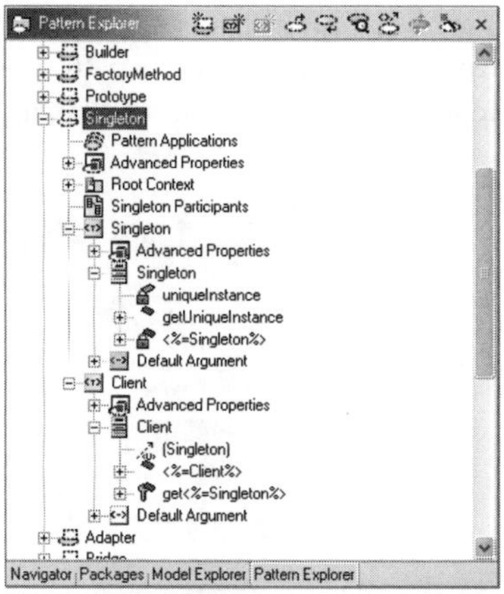

The Singleton parameter has some items associated with it, such as a `UniqueInstance` attribute and a `GetUniqueInstance` operation. In our example, we want to specify that our User class is the Singleton. When we apply the pattern, XDE asks us to provide a value for the Singleton parameter. We select the User class, and XDE uses this as a parameter. When we've finished, the User class has the `UniqueInstance` attribute and the `GetUniqueInstance` operation, as well as all of the other attributes, operations, and relationships defined for the Singleton parameter.

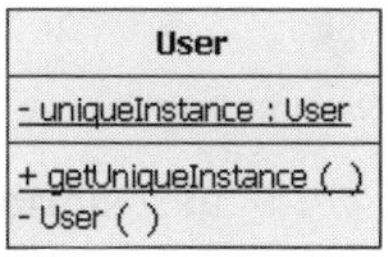

Pattern Parameters

As we just discussed, a *parameter* is a class or other UML element that is taken in by a pattern in order to implement it. A parameter is frequently a class, but it can be any number of UML elements. Figure 9.1 shows just a few parameter types.

FIGURE 9.1

Parameter types

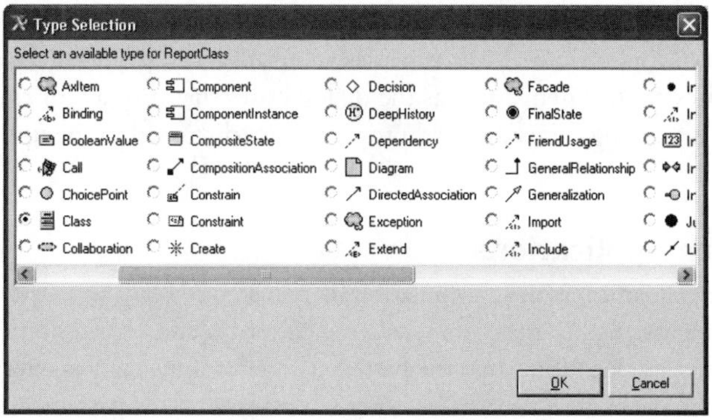

Pattern parameters are listed in the Pattern Explorer, underneath the pattern in which they are used. The following symbol is used to denote a pattern parameter: .

In the following Adapter pattern example, the parameters are Target, Adaptee, Adapter, Client, and specificRequest:

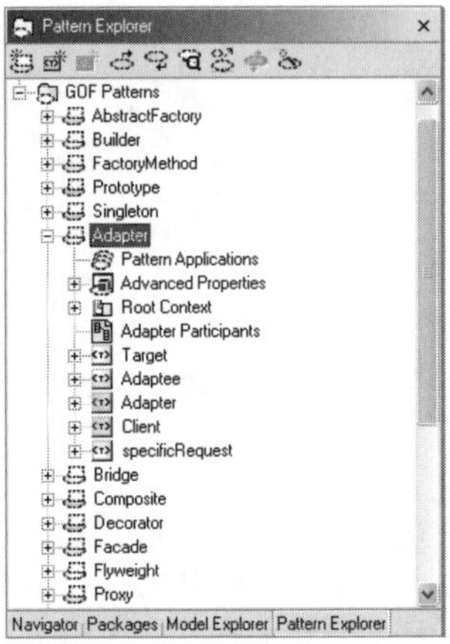

There are a number of properties you can set for a parameter. These fall into two categories: the basic properties and advanced properties. The basic properties are listed in Table 9.1.

TABLE 9.1: BASIC PARAMETER PROPERTIES

PROPERTY	DESCRIPTION
Name	The name of the parameter
Multiplicity	The number of values the parameter can take in
Type Name	Default parameter value
Type	Data type of the parameter
Parameter Documentation URL	URL to use when XDE generates documentation for the parameter

In addition to these, XDE provides some advanced properties for the parameters. These advanced properties control items such as the dialog boxes that display for the parameter when the pattern wizard is running. The advanced properties are discussed in the upcoming "Advanced Properties" section.

Pattern Applications

Applying a pattern is the combination of two steps: *binding* and *expanding* the pattern. When the arguments are assigned to the parameters, the pattern is considered bound. A copy of the pattern is placed in the binding location when the pattern is bound. This copy is referred to as the *pattern application*. If additional parameters need to be bound or aspects of the pattern need to be modified, they can be changed in the pattern application without affecting the pattern itself. Once all required parameters are bound, then the final step of using a pattern, pattern expansion, can occur. Once you bind a pattern, the pattern application appears in the binding location in the Model Explorer and in the Pattern Applications node of the Pattern Explorer.

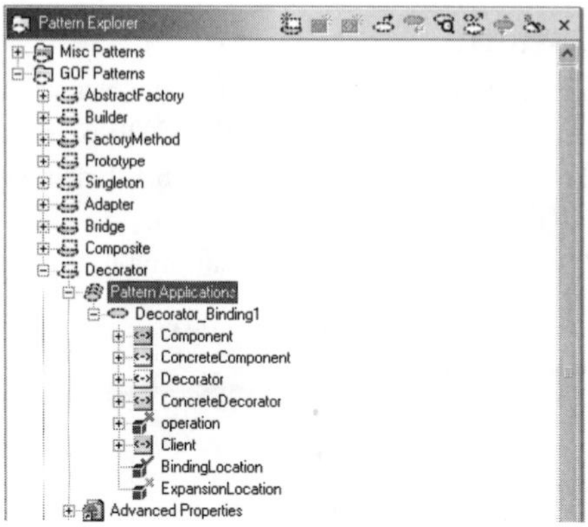

Advanced Properties

Advanced properties apply to either a pattern or a pattern parameter. They control items such as the dialog boxes to use in the Pattern Wizard, the default expansion location for a pattern, and the constraints to apply to a pattern or parameter. The advanced properties are listed in Table 9.2.

TABLE 9.2: ADVANCED PARAMETER PROPERTIES

PROPERTY	DESCRIPTION
Default Expansion Location	The default location in the model where the pattern is expanded
Default Bind Location	The default location in the model where the pattern is bound (that is, where the pattern application is placed)
Stereotype Application	Specifies what behavior occurs when the pattern is applied by stereotype (see Chapter 12, "Creating Your Own Patterns")
Custom Dialogs	Specifies information that is displayed in the dialog boxes for the Pattern Wizard (see Chapter 12)
Application Wizard Properties	Specifies behavior when the Pattern Wizard is used
Application Wizard Icons	Specifies the icons used to represent various concepts in the Pattern Wizard
Callouts	Specifies scripted behavior to be executed at various points during the pattern application process
Constraints	Specifies conditional scripted behavior to be executed at various points during the pattern application process
Value Sources	For a parameter (not a pattern), specifies where the value comes from: the user, the system, a collection, or a combination of these

Root Context

The root context of a pattern contains the non-parametric items of a pattern. It also contains any bound collaborations from other patterns that are used in the current pattern. In the GOF patterns, the root context contains sequence diagrams and pattern documentation.

Diagrams in Patterns

Some patterns contain diagrams in addition to the classes, relationships, and other elements that make up the pattern. For example, each of the GOF patterns contains a Participants class diagram, which displays all of the classes in the pattern and their relationships. Figure 9.2 is an example of the Participants class diagram for the Iterator pattern.

In Chapter 12, we discuss how to add diagrams to a pattern.

FIGURE 9.2

Participants diagram for the Iterator pattern

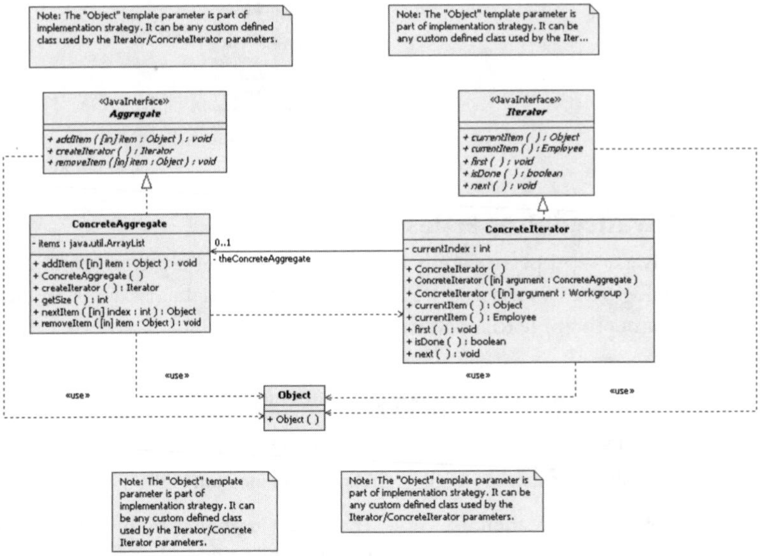

Applying Patterns

Applying a pattern transfers the pattern characteristics to selected elements in your model. In our earlier example, applying the Singleton pattern to the User class transferred all of the Singleton attributes, operations, and other characteristics to the User class. There are two ways you can use a pattern in XDE:

- Using the Apply Pattern wizard
- Using stereotypes associated with a pattern

Using the Apply Pattern Wizard

The Pattern Wizard lets you easily use a pattern in your XDE model. It walks you through all of the steps you need to apply the pattern and prompts you for all the needed information.

You can start the Pattern Wizard a number of ways:

- In the Pattern Explorer, right-click a pattern and select Apply This Pattern.
- In the Pattern Explorer, select a pattern and then click the Apply This Pattern toolbar button: .
- In the Model Explorer, right-click a pattern (a package with a stereotype of <<Asset>>), and select Apply This Pattern.
- In the Model Explorer, right-click an element and select Apply Favorite Pattern or Apply Recent Pattern, and then the pattern you want to apply.
- Choose Tools ➢ Patterns ➢ Apply Favorite Pattern, and then the pattern you'd like to apply.

Follow the steps in the wizard to apply the selected pattern to your model. The wizard prompts you for the parameters needed to apply the pattern. Let's look at an example. We'll apply the Iterator pattern to a model.

In our example, we've got a class called Employee, which holds the name, address, and other information about an employee. We also have a class called Workgroup, which is simply a collection of employees, and an interface for the Workgroup class. These classes are shown here:

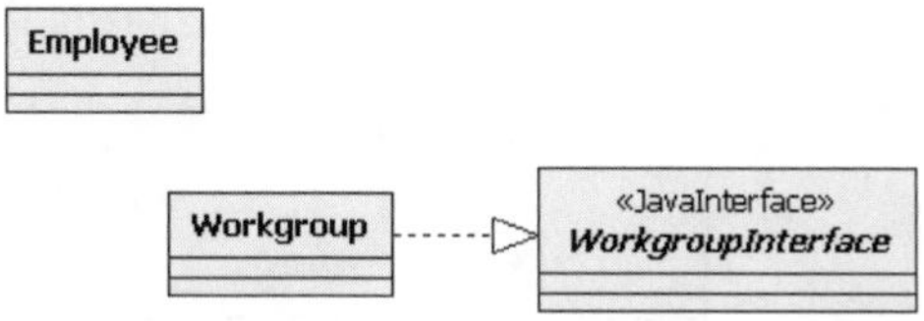

Now, suppose we're feeling generous and we'd like to give all of the employees in a workgroup a raise. We can use the Iterator pattern to create a class that iterates through all of the employees in the workgroup and gives a raise to each.

To start the wizard, right-click the Iterator pattern in the Pattern Explorer, and select Apply This Pattern. The first thing we see is the pattern welcome screen:

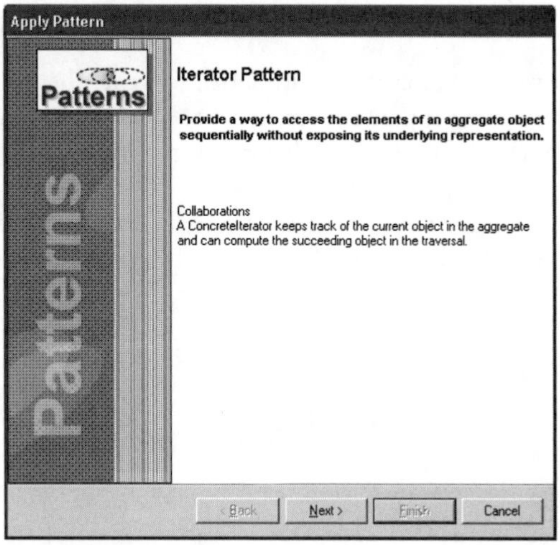

All patterns begin here. Next, we see one screen for each of the parameters in the pattern. In the Iterator pattern, there are five parameters: the `iterator` (iterator interface), the `concrete iterator`, the `aggregate` (in our example, the Workgroup interface), the `concrete aggregate` (in our example, the Workgroup), and the `object` (in our example, the Employee). Here is the first of the screens we see, prompting us for the name of the Iterator class to create:

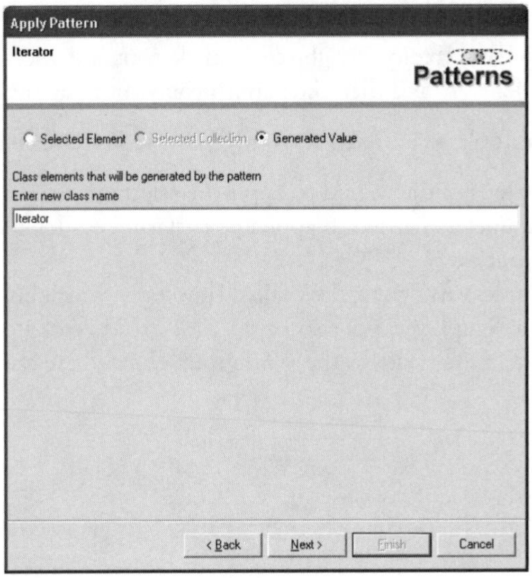

The radio buttons at the top of this screen control where the value for the parameter comes from. The choices are as follows:

Generated Value The wizard automatically creates a value.

Selected Element We have to manually supply a value.

Selected Collection We have to manually supply a collection.

We don't have an iterator yet in our model, so we let the wizard create one for us. We keep the radio buttons at the top of the screen set to Generated Value so that the wizard creates the class. We accept the default value of Iterator as the name of the class to create, and press Next to continue.

Now, we need a name for the concrete iterator class that will be generated by the wizard. We could enter a string on the left-hand side of the screen, but we just accept the default value of ConcreteIterator:

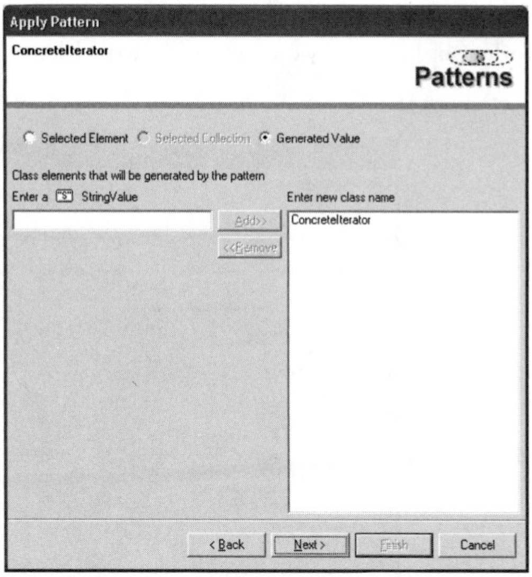

Next, we are prompted for the aggregate interface. We could accept the default value of Aggregate, which would cause the wizard to create a class called Aggregate. But we've already got an interface (WorkgroupInterface) for our aggregate class. So, we set the radio button to Selected Element, and then select the WorkgroupInterface class:

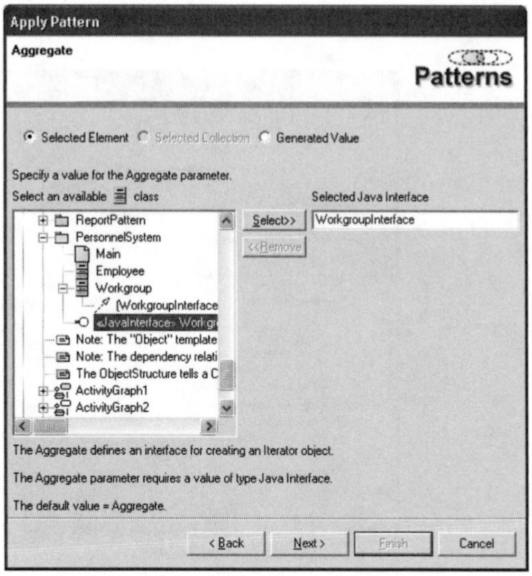

The wizard then asks for the concrete aggregate class. In our example, this is the Workgroup class. As with the WorkgroupInterface, we select the Selected Element radio button, and then the Workgroup class:

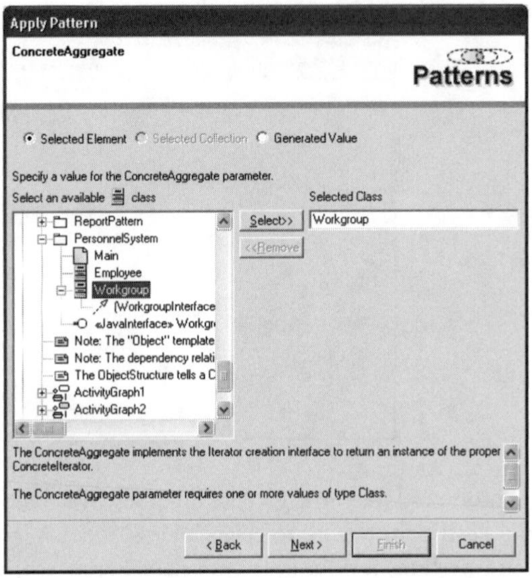

Finally, we are prompted for the object class. In our example, this is the Employee class. Once again, we use the Selected Element radio button, and select the Employee class:

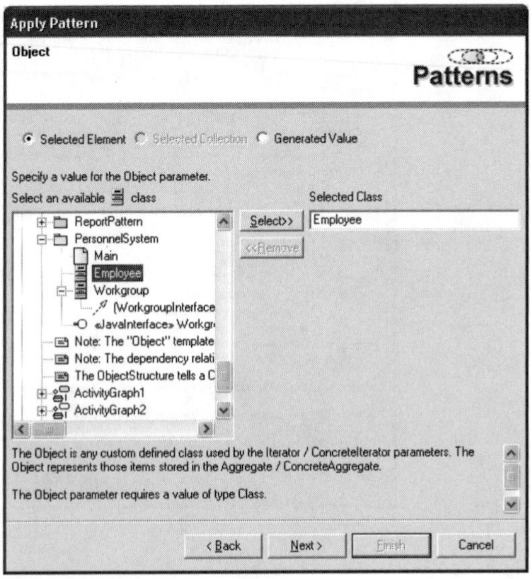

Now that we've supplied all of the parameters, XDE needs to know where to put the new classes it's going to generate. We select the model we want to use (if you like, you can also select a package within the model):

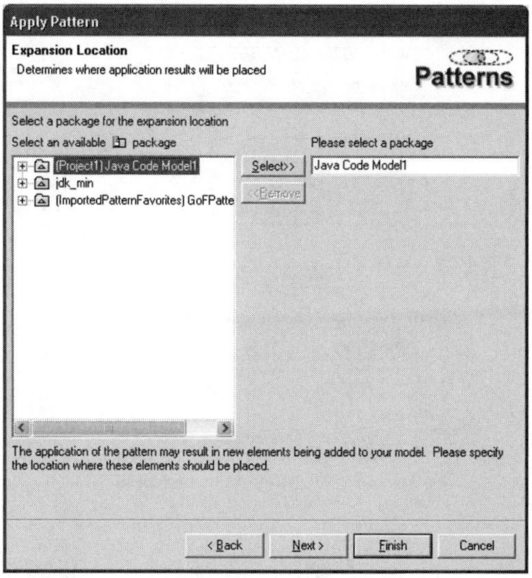

The last setting we need is the binding location. When XDE applies a pattern, it records the fact that the pattern was applied as a binding. The binding is just a copy of the pattern that is added to the model you specify on this dialog:

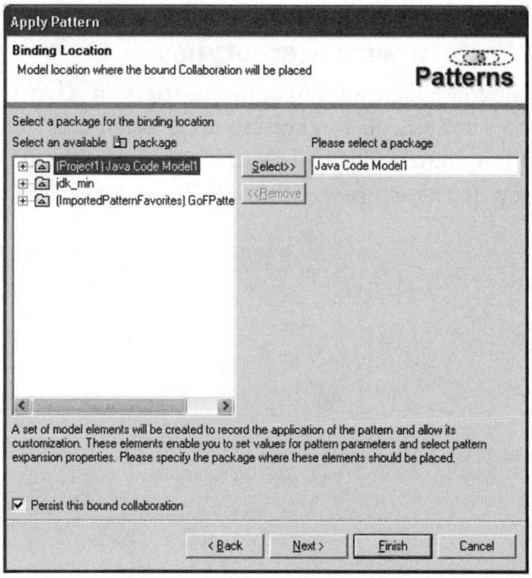

You can now change the bound pattern and re-apply it to your model, without affecting the original pattern.

When we select Next, XDE summarizes the changes it's about to make. Press Finish to apply the pattern. Figure 9.3 shows the results of running the wizard.

FIGURE 9.3

Iterator wizard results

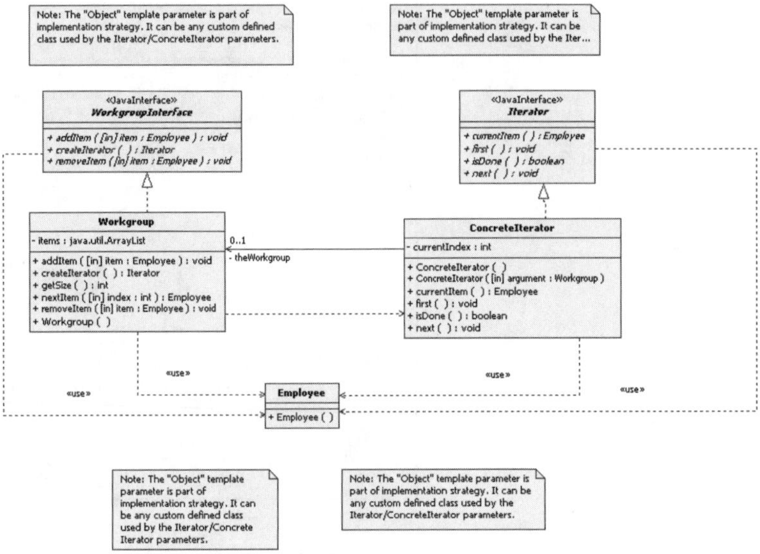

Wizards for the other patterns look very much the same. The basic steps are to supply the parameters, select the expansion location, select the binding location, and run the wizard.

Applying a Pattern with Stereotypes

One of the most convenient ways to apply a pattern in XDE is with stereotypes. If a stereotype has been assigned to a pattern, all you need to do is assign that stereotype to a model element; when you do, the pattern is automatically applied to that model element.

Let's look at a quick example to illustrate. Here, we created a simple pattern called ReportPattern:

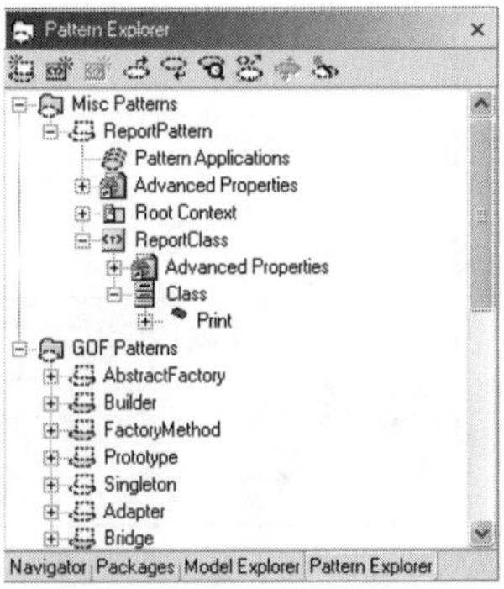

This pattern takes one class as a parameter. Because we want to be able to print all of our reports, all our pattern does is add a `Print()` method to reports. Next, we associate the stereotype <<Report>> with our new pattern by choosing Tools ➢ Patterns ➢ Update Pattern Stereotypes (see Chapter 12 for detailed instructions related to this).

Now, when we have a new report class, all we need to do is change its stereotype to <<Report>>. When we do, the ReportPattern is automatically applied, and XDE adds the `Print()` method to our new report class, as shown here:

Binding and Expanding a Pattern

When you are using a pattern, you can simply apply it to your model, using one of the procedures we just described. When building a pattern, however, you have the option of splitting the pattern application into two steps: binding and then expanding. This gives you the flexibility to test the pattern by binding and/or expanding as needed, until you are happy with the pattern's results.

Binding a pattern involves associating the parameters of the pattern to the arguments in the model. *Expanding a pattern* involves executing the scriptlets to create model elements that support the pattern. The binding process can be done separately from the expansion. As a general rule, you do not need to worry about the binding and expansion steps when applying a pattern. When applying a pattern through either the wizard or a stereotype, you bind and expand the pattern at the same time. The separation of these steps is important while you are building and testing your own patterns (this will be covered in Chapter 12).

Using Pattern Favorites

If you use certain patterns frequently, you can add these patterns to your Pattern Favorites. This functionality is similar to the Favorites functionality in the Microsoft Windows environment. It is a shortcut method to access the patterns you use most often. To use a favorite pattern, follow these steps:

1. Select the model element you want to apply the pattern against, then right-click and select Apply Favorite Pattern from the context menu.
2. Select the favorite pattern you want to apply and the Pattern Wizard starts for that pattern.

To add a pattern to your Pattern Favorites, follow these steps:

1. Select the pattern you want to add in the Model Explorer or the Pattern Explorer.

2. Right-click and select Add To Pattern Favorites from the context menu. Afterward, the pattern appears in the Pattern Favorites list, as shown here:

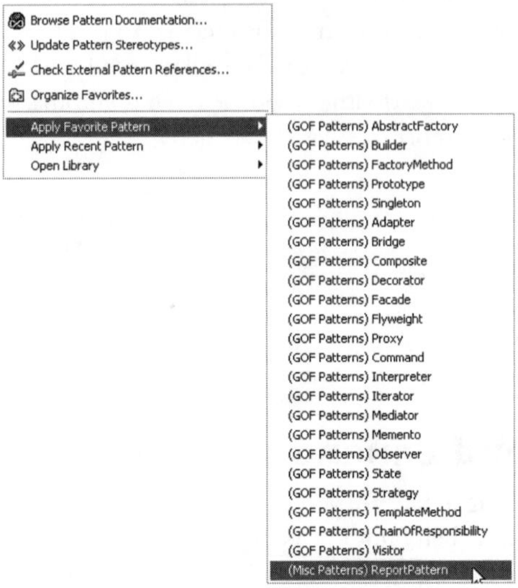

Pattern Favorites can be organized in any manner you need. You can move patterns up and down the list of Pattern Favorites. To do this, follow these steps:

1. Choose Tools ➢ Patterns ➢ Organize Favorites from the menu.
2. Move the patterns around on the list as desired by clicking the up or down button, or remove patterns from the list by clicking the Remove button. Note that removing a pattern with the Remove button does not delete the pattern, it simply removes it from the Pattern Favorites list.

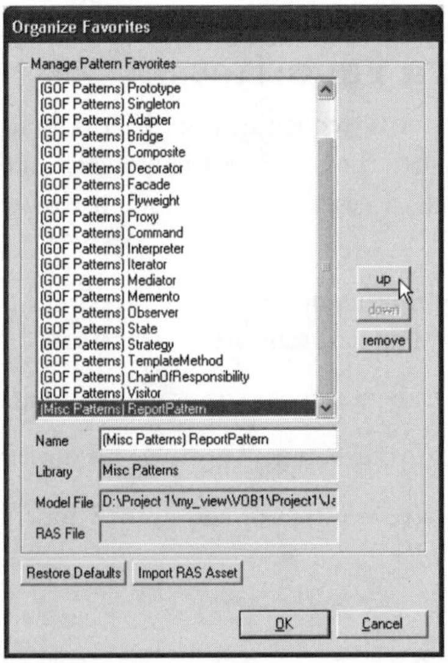

Exercise: Applying a Pattern

In this exercise, we revisit the Timecard Design Model we have been creating throughout this book. To put your newfound pattern knowledge to use, you will apply one of the Gang-of-Four patterns to your model. The Timecard Controller class is the class that controls the flow of events through the Submit Timecard use case. You might want to restrict the system to allow only one instance of this controller class through the use of the Singleton pattern.

Follow these steps to apply the Singleton pattern to the timekeeping system:

1. Open the Design Model in the Timekeeping project.
2. Open the Analysis Elements package.
3. Open the Main diagram in the Analysis Elements package. It should appear as in Figure 9.4.

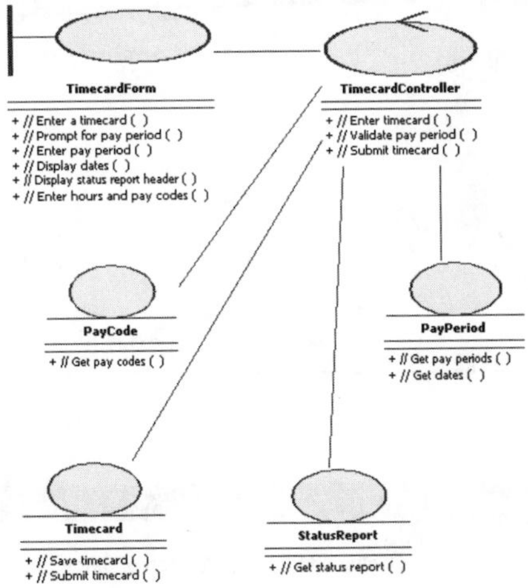

FIGURE 9.4 Analysis Elements class diagram

4. Right-click the TimecardController class and choose Apply Favorite Pattern ➢ (GOF Java Patterns) Singleton. The Pattern Wizard starts.
5. Figure 9.5 illustrates the welcome screen to the Pattern Wizard for the Singleton pattern. Click Next to begin associating model elements to the parameters of the pattern.
6. The selected class will already be filled in as the TimecardController class. Click Next to continue to the next screen of the wizard.
7. Set the client class by typing **TimecardControllerClient** and click Next.
8. The Analysis Elements package is automatically filled in as the expansion location. Click Next to continue.

9. The Analysis Elements package is automatically filled in as the binding location. Click Next to continue.
10. The confirmation screen of the Pattern Wizard is displayed. Verify that the settings appear as in Figure 9.6 and click Finish to complete applying the pattern.

FIGURE 9.5
Welcome screen

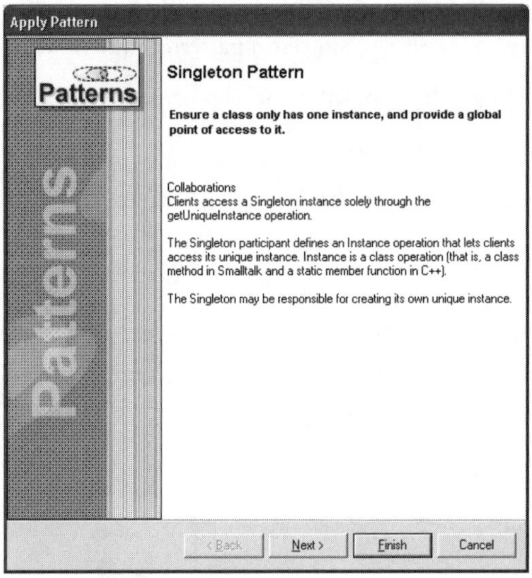

FIGURE 9.6
Pattern Wizard confirmation

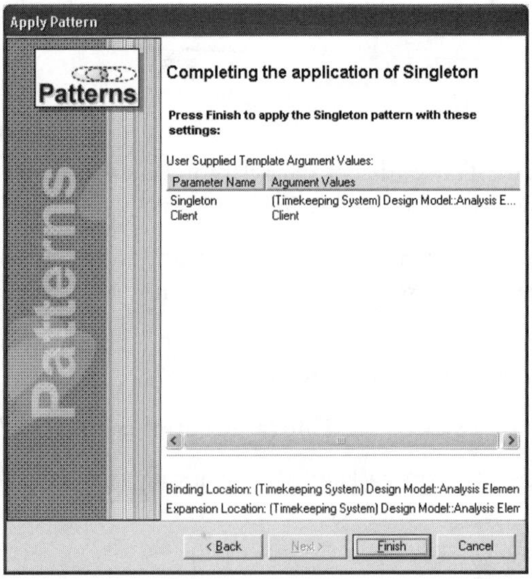

11. When the expansion is complete, a message is displayed indicating so. After this, notice the changes in the TimecardController class. They should be as shown here:

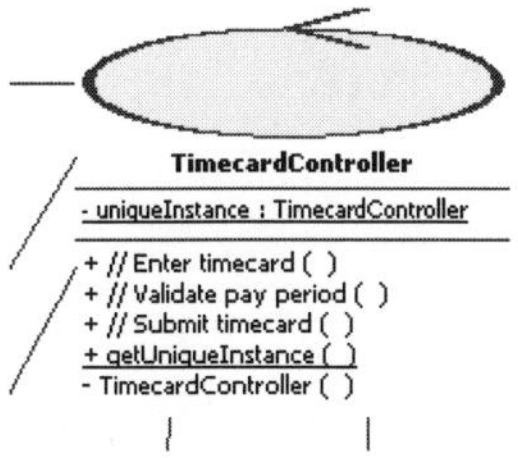

12. Open the Singleton Participants class diagram. This diagram should appear as in Figure 9.7.

FIGURE 9.7

Singleton Participants class diagram

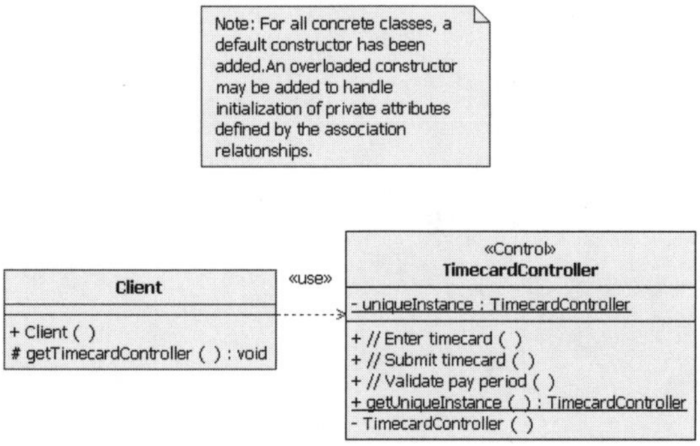

13. Save the Design Model.

Summary

In this chapter, we explored how to apply an existing pattern to your model. There are two fundamental ways to do this: by running the pattern wizard, or by applying a stereotype that has been associated with a pattern. You can start the Pattern Wizard in a number of ways: from the Pattern Explorer, the Model Explorer, the menus, or by right-clicking a model element.

When you run the Pattern Wizard, you supply values to all of the parameters that the pattern takes in. When the wizard has finished, the pattern is applied to your model.

In Chapter 12 we describe pattern properties in further detail and discuss how to add new patterns. First, however, we take a look at some very common patterns, the Gang-of-Four patterns, in Chapter 10.

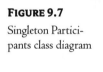

Chapter 10

Gang-of-Four Patterns

ALTHOUGH YOU CAN DEVELOP and use patterns yourself, a good place to start is with a library of patterns that comes with XDE. These patterns, developed by Erich Gamma, Richard Helm, Ralph Johnson, and John Vlissides and described in their book *Design Patterns: Elements of Reusable Object-Oriented Software* (Addison-Wesley, 1995), are commonly known as the *Gang-of-Four (GOF) patterns*. No one really seems to know where that moniker came from or why it stuck, but they are arguably the most well-known and commonly used patterns in object-oriented software. Part of the reason for this may be their wide applicability—they are specific enough to solve specific design problems, but generic enough to apply to any problem domain or object-oriented programming language. They have been used in hundreds, if not thousands, of software applications, and have been proven over time. This reason alone is a good reason to use them: you do not have to be concerned that you are using an unreliable or untested pattern.

As you learned in Chapter 9, "Using Patterns," a pattern is a sound, reusable solution to a common problem. Patterns can be applied to the analysis, design, coding, or architectural components of a project. Most of us use patterns, whether we realize it or not. By nature, most people approach a problem by applying the solution to a similar problem they've encountered before. Patterns can help:

- *Increase consistency across the application.* When everyone uses the same solutions to the same problems, the application design and code are more consistent.
- *Reduce testing time.* These patterns are proven, thus reducing the likelihood that they will cause problems during testing.
- *Reduce maintenance effort.* The consistency in the design and code helps the maintenance staff come up to speed more quickly.

There are twenty-three GOF patterns included with XDE. They are stored in a reusable asset specification that can be loaded into the tool for use in your applications. When you install XDE, the GOF patterns are automatically loaded and are available in the Pattern Explorer or by choosing Tools ➢ Patterns ➢ Apply Favorite Pattern.

If, for some reason, these patterns aren't available to you, you can reload them into XDE by choosing File ➢ Import. Import the file `GoF.ras`, which should be located in your `\XDE\Addins\Patterns\hshell\content` directory.

NOTE *Please note that there are a number of code samples in this chapter. The code samples we've listed here are in Java, but the code generated for C# .NET is very similar. On the Sybex web page for this book, you will find XDE models and code samples for the GOF patterns in both languages.*

Featured in this chapter:

- Creational patterns
- Structural patterns
- Behavioral patterns

Creational Patterns

The first group of GOF patterns is made up of *creational patterns*—patterns that are used to create classes and objects. These patterns separate the object creation logic from the other functionality in the system. Some of the creational patterns use inheritance to create classes while others use delegation or other methods to create objects.

By separating the creation logic into its own classes, you can allow the rest of the system to focus on the business logic and other functionality it needs to provide. You don't have to clutter all of your classes with this creation logic. On the other hand, you don't have to clutter your creational classes with business logic. Using these patterns, you can vary the business logic or the creation logic without affecting the other.

There are five creational patterns; the definitions of these patterns are as follows:

Factory method Provides a generic interface used to create objects, but allows the subclasses to decide which class should actually be instantiated. Decouples the use of an object from its creation.

Abstract factory Provides a generic interface used to create a family of related objects, without having to specify the concrete classes that should be instantiated. Like the factory method, this pattern decouples the use of an object from its creation.

Builder Encapsulates the logic of creating complex objects or groups of objects into a builder object. This protects clients from needing to know how the complex object is created, and allows the builder to create different versions of the complex object.

Prototype Provides a mechanism to create new objects by copying an existing object.

Singleton Allows you to enforce the rule that a particular class may be instantiated only once. The pattern also provides an access point to the singleton object.

In the following sections, we will take a closer look at each of these patterns and how they are applied in XDE.

Factory Method

The factory method pattern is a mechanism that creates application-specific objects, but one that doesn't require the creator to know which specific object will be created. Generally, the factory method pattern allows a created class to be instantiated in a subclass. For example, in a banking system, we may have the following different types of loans available for customers: fixed-rate mortgages, adjustable-rate mortgages, and personal loans. The loan officer can create these loans using the loan system's code.

If we use the factory method, all we need to do is create a new class. Without the factory method, we need to create some more complex code. If we did not use the factory method pattern, the code could potentially be a `case` statement or an `if/then/else` block that ran through the different types of loans and created (instantiated) the appropriate one. This seems like a workable solution, but it has a fundamental pitfall: change. For instance, consider what would happen if the bank decided to offer a new type of loan, a line-of-credit loan, which must now be supported by the system. In this case, we need to create the class and go back into the code block that creates loans, adding new `case` choices or another `if/then/else` block to accommodate the new type. If we implemented the factory pattern instead, we would only need to create the new class. The code block for creating loans would not change.

Pattern Strategy

The factory method pattern defines an interface for creating classes, but it lets the subclasses decide which class needs to be instantiated. To implement the pattern requires two key concepts: products and creators. A *product* is a class that is created using the factory pattern. A *creator* is a class that creates the product objects.

Figure 10.1 is a class diagram that shows the factory method participants.

The concrete product realizes the product interface. The concrete creator (inherited from the generic creator) uses the `factoryMethod` operation to create and return a concrete product. Typically, all of the different types of products that can be created using this pattern are subclasses of a common parent.

FIGURE 10.1

Factory method pattern class diagram

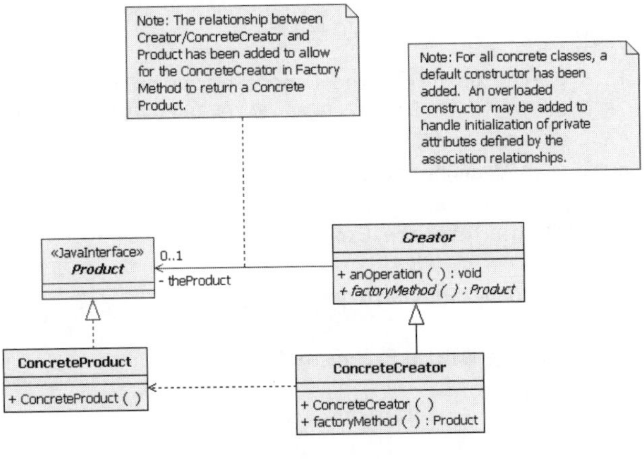

PROS AND CONS

Using the factory method is a good way to create multiple classes with a similar interface. The pattern separates the instantiation of a subclass from the particular subclass. This simplifies the process of adding new subclasses in the future.

The main disadvantage of this type of pattern is that you must subclass the creator for each new subclass to be created. This creates a hierarchy of creator classes that can be a challenge to maintain.

PARTICIPANT DETAILS

There are four parameters in XDE for this pattern:

- `Product`
- `Concrete product`
- `Creator`
- `Concrete creator`

The `product` parameter is the interface for the concrete product. Because all concrete products implement the same interface, the creator's `factoryMethod` operation can return a generic product rather than having to specify during coding which type of product will be returned.

The creator parameter is the abstract class that contains an abstract factory method, which is implemented in the concrete creators. The creator contains a reference to the product that will be created.

XDE generates code for the creator, as follows:

```
public abstract class Creator
{
    /** @modelguid {4E93064A-7F91-4B40-8022-F3B86B13A869} */
    private Product theProduct;

    /** @modelguid {85F8FB5F-1871-432D-B197-B32FD6991394} */
    public abstract Product factoryMethod();

    /**
    This operation calls the ConcreteCreator to create a ConcreteProduct.
     * @modelguid {B2D11687-9EAE-4A70-B898-F5470BAE118F}
    */
    public void anOperation()
    {
        /*Begin Template Expansion*/

        theProduct = factoryMethod();

        /*End Template Expansion*/
    }

}
```

The `anOperation` method in this code is a generic method that is used to generate a concrete product.

The `concrete creator` parameter is the class that creates the concrete product. It inherits from the creator and overrides the factory method to create the concrete product.

XDE generates code for the concrete creator as follows:

```
public class ConcreteCreator extends Creator
{
    /** @modelguid {29257837-D402-4E88-B404-1F69DA2F0A3A} */
    public ConcreteCreator()
    {
    }

    /**
    This operation returns an instance of the Product.
     * @modelguid {13C91DD5-52F1-4035-B27D-4C6A39D7B1F8}
    */
    public Product factoryMethod()
    {
        /*Begin Template Expansion*/

        // TO DO: The operation overrides the factory method to return
        an instance of a ConcreteProduct.
        // You can customize the operation based on your application needs.

        return new ConcreteProduct();

        /*End Template Expansion*/
    }

}
```

Abstract Factory

The abstract factory pattern is similar to the factory method in that it creates objects. However, the abstract factory is used to create families of similar objects. This pattern is used frequently in user interface design because you can create user interface objects that are not tightly coupled to the creators. If we follow the loan example we discussed earlier, we may want to create a user interface for the different types of loans. We could use an abstract factory to create the different pieces of the user interface, and to separate the creation of the user interface objects from their use.

PATTERN STRATEGY

The abstract factory pattern creates families of related objects without needing to specify the concrete objects that need to be created. There are five concepts in this pattern: the abstract factory, the concrete factory, the abstract product, the concrete product, and the client. The *abstract factory* is the interface for the factories. The *concrete factory* is the class that creates the concrete products. The *abstract product* is the interface for the objects to be created, and the *concrete products* are the specific objects to be created. The *client* is the class that needs to create the objects, and it uses only the abstract factory and the abstract product to create these objects.

Figure 10.2 is a class diagram that shows the abstract factory participants.

FIGURE 10.2

Abstract factory pattern class diagram

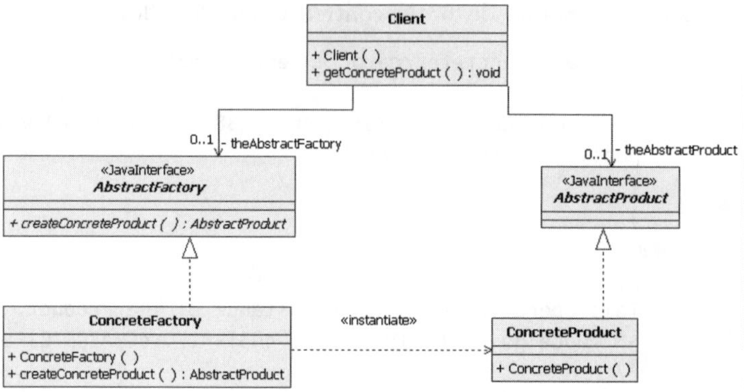

As you can see in this figure, the concrete product realizes the abstract product interface. The concrete factory realizes the abstract factory interface. When a client needs to have a product created, it calls the concrete factory's `createConcreteProduct` method. The concrete factory creates the concrete product and returns it to the client.

PROS AND CONS

By using the abstract factory method, you can abstract the use of families of products from the creation of those objects. Using this method lessens the impact of adding additional products of the same kind. Rather than creating a new product from scratch and re-programming all of the product creation logic, you can simply add a new product that implements the `AbstractProduct` interface.

PARTICIPANT DETAILS

There are five parameters in XDE for this pattern:

- `Abstract factory`
- `Concrete factory`
- `Abstract product`
- `Concrete product`
- `Client`

The `abstract factory` is the interface for the factory. It defines an abstract operation called `createConcreteProduct`, which is implemented by each of the concrete factories that implement the abstract factory interface. The `concrete factory` is the class that creates the actual concrete product. It implements the interface defined by the abstract factory, and implements the `createConcreteProduct` operation. This operation will create and return a concrete product.

The abstract product is the interface for the product. The concrete product is the object to be created. The client is the class that ultimately needs the concrete product. It has a private attribute called theAbstractProduct, which contains a reference to the concrete product once the concrete product is built.

The concrete factory contains an operation that can be used to create an instance of the concrete product. XDE generates code for the concrete factory such as the following:

```
public class ConcreteFactory implements AbstractFactory
{
    /** @modelguid {EDB58B90-F02F-4681-8DDC-BBF715FAC813} */
    public ConcreteFactory()
    {
    }

    /**
    This operation implements the createConcreteProduct operation from the
    superclass (AbstractFactory).
     * @modelguid {37EA5C56-B578-4898-8B0E-BDBEEE7F6447}
    */
    public AbstractProduct createConcreteProduct()
    {
        /*Begin Template Expansion*/

        // TO DO: Define a product object to be created by the
        corresponding concreteFactory.  This can be customized by your need.

        return new ConcreteProduct();

        /*End Template Expansion*/
    }

}
```

The client is the class that needs to create the objects. The client contains operations that call the concrete factory. The following is the code that XDE generates for the client:

```
public class Client
{
    /** @modelguid {1E878D3F-BFA1-4B19-9336-3A2030C0BEBB} */
    private AbstractFactory theAbstractFactory;

    /** @modelguid {47A7F240-A543-459E-B969-2A2C707F111D} */
    private AbstractProduct theAbstractProduct;

    /** @modelguid {4215063B-079A-41DE-94B4-D2E8EEF68069} */
    public Client()
    {
    }
```

```
        /**
        This is just an example how to use AbstractFactory pattern. The operation
        creates a ConcreteProduct by calling the corresponding ConcreteFactory
        class.
         * @modelguid {965D087C-F615-451D-82A5-6B5B96B3DDD3}
        */
        public void getConcreteProduct()
        {
            /*Begin Template Expansion*/

            // TO DO: You can  customize the code in order to define the call to the
            Concrete Factory.
            // The call should use only the interfaces declared by AbstractFactory
            and AbstractProduct classes.

            theAbstractProduct=theAbstractFactory.createConcreteProduct();

            /*End Template Expansion*/
        }

}
```

The abstract factory is an interface containing the operation signature for creating the concrete factory. XDE generates it as follows:

```
public interface AbstractFactory
{
    /** @modelguid {3E212D89-A5E1-4E18-92C9-363CF9E04762} */

    public AbstractProduct createConcreteProduct();

}
```

Builder

The builder pattern is used to separate the construction of an object from its representation so that the same construction process can create different representations. In other words, it allows a client to simply call a director class when a complex object needs to be constructed. The client does not need to know what is involved in creating the complex object.

PATTERN STRATEGY

The main participants in this pattern are the *builder*, the *director*, the *client*, and the *product*. The client begins the process by asking the director to build an object, and it is ultimately the client who needs the product that is being built. The director knows about the builders that exist, and tells the appropriate builder(s) to build the appropriate product piece(s). Each builder is responsible for constructing one or more pieces of the complex object. Once everything has been created, the client asks the concrete builder for the final product. Figure 10.3 shows the classes in the builder pattern.

FIGURE 10.3

Builder pattern class diagram

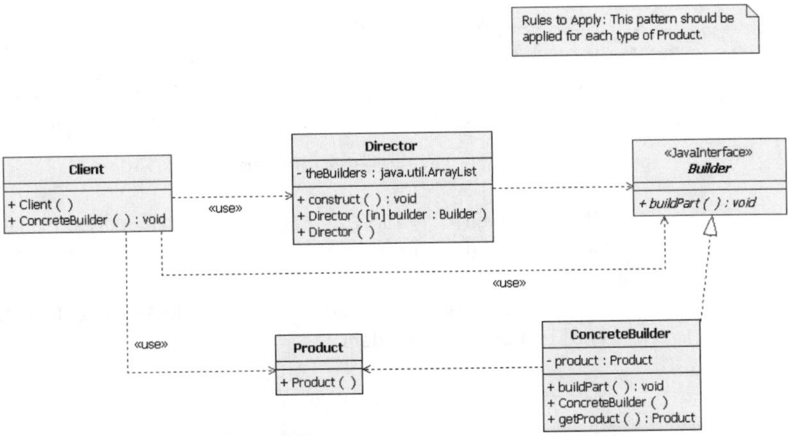

As you can see in the diagram, the builder concept is actually split into a concrete builder class and a builder interface. This allows the client and director to reference the builder without having to know specifically which type of builder is being used.

PROS AND CONS

The builder pattern helps separate the business logic in the client from the intricate details of creating complex objects. This gives you two benefits: first, the design of the client is simpler because it doesn't contain both the business and creation logic; secondly, it gives you the flexibility to change either the business or creation logic without impacting the other.

It also makes it easier to vary the complex object's composition. The individual concrete builders can create the components, and then the director can assemble them in a variety of ways.

The main thing you need to watch out for when using this pattern is the complexity of the director; you need to keep it from getting too complex. If the director needs to create a number of permutations of the complex object, the director may be a little more difficult to maintain. This typically isn't a problem but is worth keeping in mind.

PARTICIPANT DETAILS

In XDE, the builder pattern takes five parameters:

- `Builder`
- `Concrete builder`
- `Director`
- `Product`
- `Client`

The `builder` is an interface, implemented by the concrete builder, that is used to build a part of the complex object. Each concrete builder will implement this interface.

The `concrete builder` is the class that actually builds a part of the complex object. It implements the `buildPart` method that is declared in the `builder` interface. It may also assemble part of the product; the `getProduct` method is intended to assemble and return a part (or even all) of the `product` object. XDE provides some code for the concrete builder, as shown here:

```
public class ConcreteBuilder implements Builder
{
    /** @modelguid {F4902022-C809-45DB-BB76-9951877127B7} */
    private Product product;

    /** @modelguid {0E32AB20-8749-4DBE-8B8A-82C4D8F0A02C} */
    public ConcreteBuilder()
    {
        /*Begin Template Expansion*/

        // TO DO: Customize  the initialization of product class
        attribute as your custom application requests.

        product = new Product();


        /*End Template Expansion*/
    }

    /**
    This operation constructs and assembles the parts of the product.
     * @modelguid {C753DDEF-50B6-4823-80CD-9D12CFC5A7C3}
    */
    public void buildPart()
    {
        /*Begin Template Expansion*/

        // TO DO: Add your custom code to build/refine the product attribute(s).

        /*End Template Expansion*/
    }

    /**
    This operation retrieves the product.
     * @modelguid {F2FBF667-57B4-4772-8BC3-25E325B099A1}
    */
    public Product getProduct()
    {
        /*Begin Template Expansion*/

        // TO DO: Add your code here. This is your custom way to
        construct and return the product.
```

```
        return product;

        /*End Template Expansion*/
    }

}
```

The director is responsible for keeping track of the concrete builders, and for telling the builders to construct the product. It has a construct method, which calls the buildPart methods of the builders needed to construct the final object. The XDE-generated code for the construct method looks like this:

```
    public void construct()
    {
        /*Begin Template Expansion*/

        // TO DO: The operation constructs (an) object(s) using the
        Builder interface. You can customize the operation based
        on your application need.

        for (int i=1; i <= theBuilders.size(); i++) {
           ((Builder) this.theBuilders.get(i)).buildPart();
        }

        /*End Template Expansion*/
    }
```

Either the director creates an array of builders, or it is passed a builder as part of the constructor. If a builder is passed, the director creates an array for the builders and adds the builder that was passed into the constructor.

The product is the complex object that is constructed using this pattern. The client is the class that needs the complex object to be built. The client has a ConcreteBuilder method, which executes the pattern in two steps. First, it tells the director to tell the concrete builders to build the product. This is done through the construct method of the director. Once this is done, the client calls the getProduct method of the concrete builder to retrieve the completed product, as shown here:

```
public void ConcreteBuilder()
    {
        /*Begin Template Expansion*/

        // TO DO: This is an example how to use the pattern.
        You can customize the code based on your application needs.

        ConcreteBuilder theConcreteBuilder= new ConcreteBuilder();
        Director theDirector = new Director(theConcreteBuilder);
        theDirector.construct();
        Product theProduct = theConcreteBuilder.getProduct();

        /*End Template Expansion*/
    }
```

Prototype

The prototype pattern is used to make a copy of an object, rather than simply instantiating new ones. This is most helpful when the initialization of an object is time-consuming. For example, suppose we are working on an application to track stocks and averages in the market. We've got an object called Trend, which looks up the current value of the Dow Jones Industrial Average and performs several complex statistical calculations. Suppose that these calculations take several minutes to run. Now, suppose that our business rules state that we only need to be concerned with the changes in the DJIA every hour. When we need a new Trend object within an hour, we don't want to take the time to get the latest value of the DJIA and redo all of those statistical calculations. Since it hasn't yet been an hour, it would be easier to simply copy the existing Trend object, and use it. The prototype pattern helps us out here.

PATTERN STRATEGY

Figure 10.4 shows the classes that participate in the prototype pattern. The *client* is the class that needs a cloned object. The *concrete prototype* class is used for both the object that will be cloned, and for the cloned objects themselves. The concrete prototype implements the prototype interface.

The client contains a private attribute called `thePrototype`, which is used to store the object that will be cloned. When the client needs a clone, it calls the concrete prototype's `toClone` method.

FIGURE 10.4

Prototype pattern class diagram

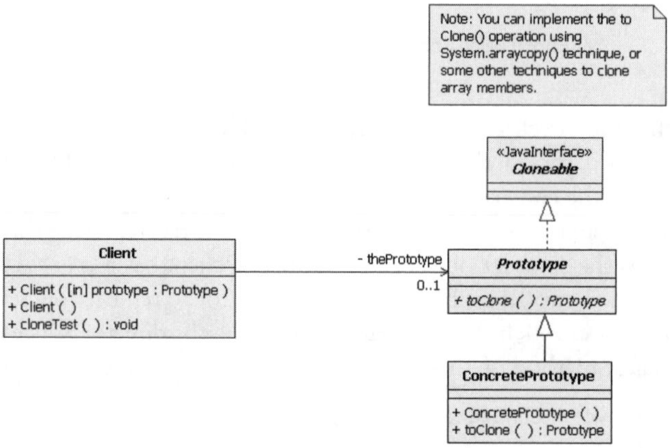

PROS AND CONS

The prototype pattern can help improve performance by allowing you to copy existing objects rather than take the time to initialize new ones. If two or more objects may be similar, the prototype pattern can be a little simpler to use than the builder.

There aren't typically any drawbacks to using this pattern. Just be sure that the cloning is more efficient than creating and initializing a new object.

PARTICIPANT DETAILS

This pattern has three participants:

- Prototype
- Concrete prototype
- Client

The `prototype` is the interface for the object that will be cloned. It contains one abstract method, called `toClone`, that the concrete prototype implements.

The `concrete prototype` is the class that is cloned. It implements the `toClone` method from the prototype interface. When a client needs a clone, it calls the `toClone` method.

The `client` is the class that needs the cloned object. It may create a new concrete prototype to clone or use an existing concrete prototype. Once it has a reference to a concrete prototype, it calls the `toClone` method, which returns a copy of the concrete prototype:

```
public void cloneTest() throws java.lang.CloneNotSupportedException
    {
        /*Begin Template Expansion*/

        // TO DO: This is just an example how to use Prototype pattern.
        You can customize the operation based on your application needs.

        thePrototype.toClone();

        /*End Template Expansion*/
    }
```

Singleton

Use the singleton pattern when you have a class that should only be instantiated once, and needs a global reference to that one instance. For example, you may want to create a single object to handle database transactions, and pass all database requests through that object. Another example is a print handler; typically, with a print handler, you need only one object to handle requests to the printer.

PATTERN STRATEGY

This is a fairly straightforward pattern. A *client* is any object in the application that needs to use the singleton object. A *singleton* is a class that can be instantiated at most once. Figure 10.5 shows the classes involved in the singleton pattern.

FIGURE 10.5

Singleton pattern class diagram

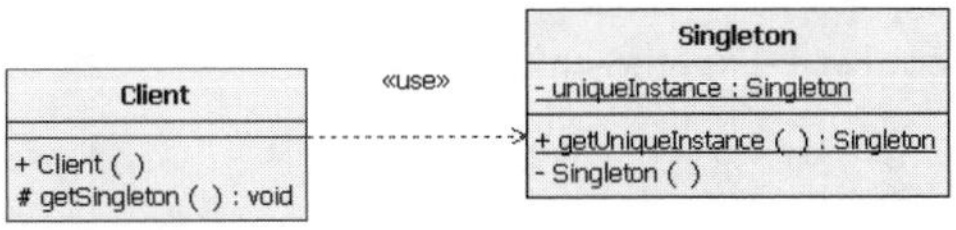

When the client needs to obtain a global reference to the singleton object, it calls the `getUniqueInstance` method of the singleton object. The singleton class has a static attribute called `uniqueInstance`, which holds the unique instance of the class. When `getUniqueInstance` is called, the unique instance is returned. If a unique instance doesn't exist, `getUniqueInstance` creates and returns a unique instance.

Notice that the constructor of the singleton is private. This ensures that the unique instance of the singleton can be created only through the static `getUniqueInstance` method.

PROS AND CONS

This pattern provides you with a way to ensure that only one instance of the class will be created, without having to create a number of global variables.

It is also easy to create a similar pattern, where you allow some small number of instances to be created. For example, you may have a class that can be instantiated only twice. It is easy to modify the singleton pattern to accommodate this.

Some difficulties may result from keeping track of the singleton objects once they're created and making sure that the appropriate clients can access them.

PARTICIPANT DETAILS

The singleton pattern takes only two parameters:

- `Singleton`
- `Client`

The `singleton` is the class that may be instantiated only once. It contains a private attribute, `uniqueInstance`, that holds the single instance of the class. It has a static method called `getUniqueInstance` that can be used to return the value of `uniqueInstance` to the clients. Its constructor is private so that the singleton can be instantiated only through `getUniqueInstance`.

The `client` is any class that uses the `singleton` object. It has a method called `getSingleton`, which calls the `getUniqueInstance` method of the singleton:

```
protected void getSingleton()
    {
        /*Begin Template Expansion*/

        // TO DO: This is just an example how to use Singleton pattern.
        You can customize the operation based on your application needs.

        Singleton theSingleton = Singleton.getUniqueInstance();

        /*End Template Expansion*/
    }
```

Structural Patterns

The second category of GOF patterns includes the *structural patterns*. These are patterns that describe how objects or classes are composed to form larger structures. Some of the patterns use inheritance to build structures of classes. Others use composition to build structures of objects.

There are seven structural GOF patterns: adapter, bridge, composite, decorator, façade, flyweight, and proxy. The following are the definitions for each of them:

Adapter Allows a client to use the interface of a class, even if the interface is not what the client expects. The pattern creates a new interface for an adaptee that is in the format the client expects.

Bridge Separates the implementation of a class from its abstraction, so that the abstraction and implementation can vary independently.

Composite Builds a tree of simple and composite objects, and allows clients to work with both simple and composite objects in the same manner.

Decorator Allows you to dynamically add functionality to objects without subclassing.

Façade Constructs an interface for a subsystem. Clients can use the interface to request functionality from the subsystem without needing to know about the subsystem's inner workings.

Flyweight Uses the factory pattern to build and share large numbers of small objects.

Proxy Creates a surrogate object in the place of another object. Frequently used to substitute a small, simple object in place of a large, complex one until the complex object is actually needed. Helpful when there is a difference between requesting an instance of an object and actually using it.

In the following sections, we examine each of these items in more detail. We look at the general strategy of each pattern, examine the pattern participants, discuss the pros and cons, look at some sample code, and discuss how to implement the pattern in XDE.

Adapter

The adapter pattern is used to convert the interface of a class into a different interface, one that clients expect. This pattern is sometimes also referred to as a *wrapper*. It lets a client use an adaptee class, even if the adaptee's interface isn't what the client is expecting.

Pattern Strategy

Sometimes, you receive a class that you want to use in your design, but the interface for that class doesn't meet the requirements for your project. You may not be able to change the interface, so you can use the adapter pattern instead. The adapter pattern creates a "middleman" between your client class and the class you want to use (the *adaptee*). The client class can call methods of the *adapter*, whose interface is exactly what the client expects. The adapter then takes that request and sends the appropriate message(s) to the adaptee. The result of all this is that the client can send a request to the adaptee and receive a response, even if the adaptee's interface isn't what the client is expecting. Figure 10.6 shows the classes that participate in this pattern.

FIGURE 10.6

Adapter pattern class diagram

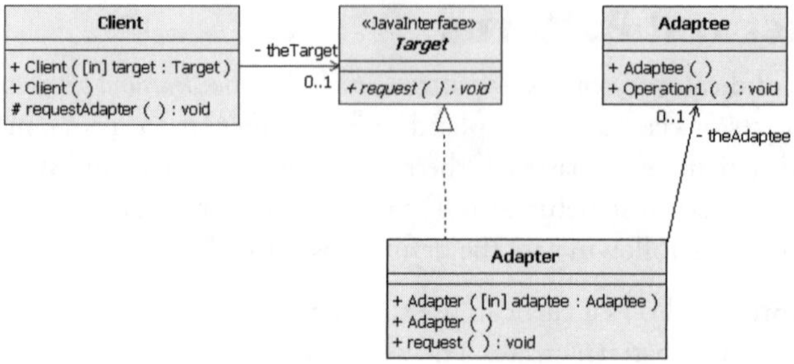

In this class diagram, the adaptee is the class that the client needs to use. The client sends a request to the target interface, which is in the format that the client expects. The adapter, which realizes the target interface, then takes that request and sends messages to the adaptee to process the request.

PROS AND CONS

This solution does add a little complexity to your design, but it allows you to reuse existing classes without having to make modifications to them or to their interfaces. It gives you the flexibility of using these existing classes just as you would use any other class in your design. You also have the option of creating an adapter that can work with several adaptees.

This pattern does assume that you're not planning to modify the adaptee's behavior at all. If you do need to modify this behavior, you may need to subclass the adaptee and modify the adapter to use the subclass.

PARTICIPANT DETAILS

The adapter pattern has five parameters:

- `Target`
- `Adaptee`
- `Adapter`
- `Client`
- `Specific request`

The `client` class is the class that needs the functionality provided by the adaptee. It has an attribute, `theTarget`, which is the target interface that the client expects. It begins the process by using its own `requestAdapter` method, which sends a request to the target interface for processing. Note that the client does not need to know which adaptees it needs; all it has to do is send the request to the target interface. XDE creates this code for you:

```
public class Client
{
    /** @modelguid {12E9D5F4-03E5-4BCC-B8E2-F6B2753DA675} */
    private Target theTarget;
```

```
    /**
    This is the overloaded constructor for Client class.
     * @modelguid {022106AB-A0A0-4DA8-83CF-D8919074B8C9}
    */
    public Client(Target target)
    {
        /*Begin Template Expansion*/
        theTarget = target;
        /*End Template Expansion*/
    }

    /**
    This is the default constructor of the Client class.
     * @modelguid {C391DF5C-76F2-4DB9-9262-64C262D88D2C}
    */
    public Client()
    {
    }

    /**
    This operation gives an example how to use the Adapter pattern.  The client
    requests a call to the Target.
     * @modelguid {0ECEBACF-C89C-4D63-BF18-6105D6CCA6A4}
    */
    protected void requestAdapter()
    {
        /*Begin Template Expansion*/

        // TO DO: You can customize the operation based on your application needs;

        theTarget.request();

        /*End Template Expansion*/
    }

}
```

The target class is the interface that the client expects. It has an abstract method called request, which is implemented in the adapter class.

The adapter class is responsible for taking the client's request and translating it into one or more requests that the adaptee will understand. The adapter has one attribute, called `theAdaptee`, which references the adaptee class needed to process the client's request. By default, there is only one attribute, but an adapter can reference as many adaptees as are needed to process the client's request. When the adapter receives a request through the `request` method, it calls the appropriate method(s) of the adaptee, as you can see here. This is the `request` method of the adapter class:

```
public void request()
    {
```

```
        /*Begin Template Expansion*/

        // TO DO: You can customize the operation based on your application needs.
        // The specificRequest operation signature must match the
        specificRequest operation you selected from your model.

          theAdaptee.Operation1();

        /*End Template Expansion*/
    }
```

The adaptee is the class that actually provides the functionality the client needs. Frequently, this is a pre-existing class with an interface that has already been developed and can't be changed. Using this pattern, you don't have to change the adaptee at all. In the class diagram example shown previously in Figure 10.6, the adaptee had one method, called `Operation1`. This is the fifth parameter in the pattern, the specific request parameter. When you are working through the wizard in XDE, you can enter one or more operations for the adaptee.

Bridge

The bridge pattern is used to decouple the interface of a class and its implementation, so that the abstraction and the implementation can vary independently.

PATTERN STRATEGY

The classes in the bridge pattern are shown in Figure 10.7.

FIGURE 10.7

Bridge pattern class diagram

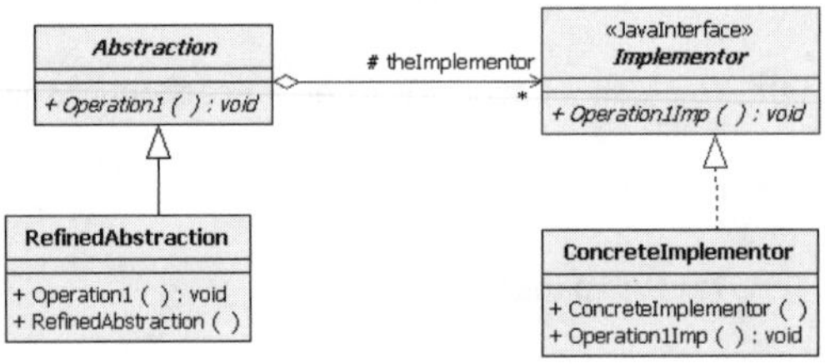

The *abstraction* is an interface for the objects being implemented. It has a reference to the object that implements the implementor interface. Clients of this pattern send requests to the RefinedAbstraction class, which is inherited from the abstraction class. The `RefinedAbstraction` class uses its relationship to the concrete implementor to carry out the request. With this pattern, clients can use concrete implementers of the implementor interface without having to know which concrete implementor is being used.

PROS AND CONS

By decoupling the abstraction and the implementation of an object, clients can use the functionality without having to know anything about implementation issues. You have the flexibility to change the implementation without impacting the client at all. Another benefit is the ability to define or remove a relationship between the abstraction and implementation at runtime.

PARTICIPANT DETAILS

The bridge pattern takes five parameters:

- `Abstraction`
- `Refined abstraction`
- `Implementor`
- `Concrete implementor`
- `Operation`

The RefinedAbstraction class is the interface that clients deal with. RefinedAbstraction is inherited from the abstraction class, which provides an interface for the objects being implemented. Through its relationship to a concrete implementor, the refined abstraction carries out the client's request, as shown in Figure 10.8.

FIGURE 10.8
Bridge pattern Sequence diagram

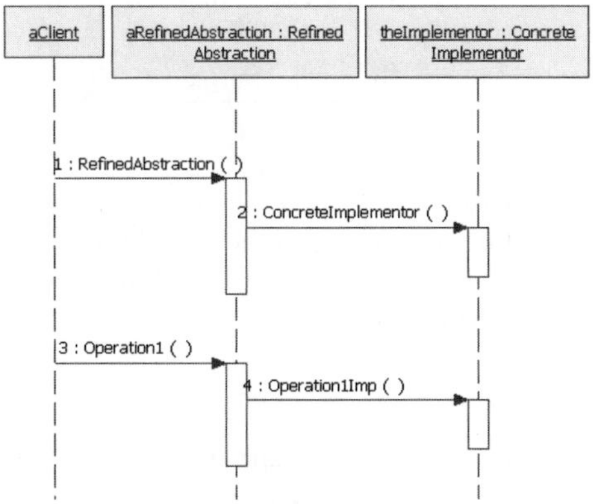

The abstraction class is the interface that the refined abstraction is inherited from. It maintains the relationship to the object that implements the implementor interface.

The `implementor` defines the interface for the specific implementation classes. It does not have to be consistent with the abstraction interface, and in fact it is frequently different. Note that in our example discussed earlier, the abstraction interface defines a method called `Operation1`, while the implementor interface defines a method called `Operation1Imp`.

The concrete `implementor` is the class that actually implements the functionality needed by the client. It implements the methods defined in the implementor interface.

Composite

The composite pattern groups a number of objects together into a whole-part hierarchy. Using the composite pattern, a client can treat objects and composites (a collection of objects) uniformly. In other words, the client does not have to be concerned about whether it is dealing with a composite or a single object.

PATTERN STRATEGY

The pattern begins when a client sends a request to the component interface. Figure 10.9 shows the structure of the composite pattern.

FIGURE 10.9
Composite pattern class diagram

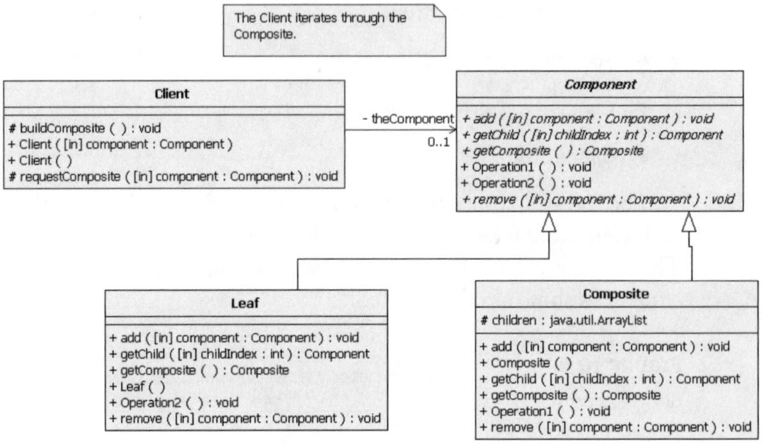

As you can see in this structure, the client interacts with the abstract component class. It therefore doesn't care whether it is dealing with a single object (leaf) or a composite. If it is dealing with a leaf, the leaf object just handles the request directly. If it is dealing with a composite, the leaves and composites within that composite handle the request.

PROS AND CONS

This pattern gives you the flexibility to create and use single objects or complex hierarchies without affecting client code.

One thing to remember is that if the client calls the `add`, `remove`, `getChild`, or `getComposite` methods on a leaf, an exception is raised. Be sure you've coded to handle the exception.

PARTICIPANT DETAILS

The composite pattern takes six parameters:

- `Component`
- `Leaf`
- `Composite`
- `Client`
- `Operation`
- `Operation 2`

The client class is the class that requests some functionality. In the example shown earlier in Figure 10.9, the client may want to request the functionality in Operation2, which is implemented by a leaf, or the functionality in Operation1, which is implemented by a composite. Using this pattern, the client doesn't have to worry about whether a leaf or a composite ultimately handles the request; it simply sends the request to the component interface.

The component parameter is the interface for the leaves and composites in the structure. It contains method signatures for the methods provided by the leaves and composites in the structure. In the earlier example, it contains method signatures for Operation1 and Operation2. It also has abstract methods for adding an element to a composite, removing an element from a composite, getting the elements in a composite, and getting the complete composite. These methods are implemented in the composite class, but in the leaf class they are implemented with an exception.

The leaf is a class whose objects in the structure do not have children. That is, the leaf objects are not composites. Their main purpose is in implementing some of the functionality from the component interface. In our example, the leaf implements Operation2. Because the leaf realizes the component interface, it does have code for the add, remove, getChild, and getComposite methods, although these methods are somewhat meaningless for a leaf. The code generated for a leaf class is shown here:

```
public class Leaf extends Component
{
    /** @modelguid {54DB8CC8-BDFC-4DB8-A236-40B55715206F}*/
    public void add(Component component) throws java.util.NoSuchElementException
    {
        /*Begin Template Expansion*/

        // TO DO: You can customize the operation based on your application needs.

        throw new java.util.NoSuchElementException("No children");

        /*End Template Expansion*/
    }

    /** @modelguid {4EF3990C-D814-4E72-88AB-D0F26F5AF197}*/
    public Component getChild(int childIndex)
    throws java.util.NoSuchElementException
    {
        /*Begin Template Expansion*/

        // TO DO: You can customize the operation based on your application needs.

        throw new java.util.NoSuchElementException("No children");

        /*End Template Expansion*/
    }
```

```
    /** @modelguid {2687C3C3-5B0B-4735-8A32-07C3B8F0CE5A}*/
    public void remove(Component component)
    throws java.util.NoSuchElementException
    {
        /*Begin Template Expansion*/

        // TO DO: You can customize the operation based on your application needs.

        throw new java.util.NoSuchElementException("No children");

        /*End Template Expansion*/
    }

    /**
    This is the default constructor of the Leaf class.
     * @modelguid {2668CA30-D335-46D5-98D9-BEC0A3BB4DBD}*/
    public Leaf()
    {
    }

    /** @modelguid {7D57F254-E71A-4E53-89FE-60859A732F5A}*/
    public Composite getComposite()
    {
        /*Begin Template Expansion*/
        return null;
        /*End Template Expansion*/
    }

    /**
    This is the overloaded operation2 from the Component class.  operation2 can
    be implemented based on your application.
     * @modelguid {F31573EF-A9E9-42F8-8E49-7A407C7E4CC8}*/
    public void Operation2()
    {
    }

}
```

The composite class is a collection of leaves and other composites. When it receives a request, it can process it either directly or with the help of the leaves and composites that are its children. It has an attribute called children, which is an array of the leaves and composites it contains. It implements the add, remove, getChild, and getComponent methods from the component interface, as shown here:

```
public class Composite extends Component
{
    /**
    This is the collection of elements in Composite structure
     * @modelguid {2172253E-60D7-4873-89B4-9C77CBE32AFE}
```

```
*/
protected java.util.ArrayList children;

/**
This operation adds a child  (leaf or composite)  to the collection of
children.
 * @modelguid {36ACA057-CEA4-4DBC-A5E2-FA51C8AB4D58}
*/
public void add(Component component) throws java.util.NoSuchElementException
{
    /*Begin Template Expansion*/

    // TO DO: You can customize the operation based on your application needs.

    children.add(component);


    /*End Template Expansion*/
}

/**
This operation gets a child at a certain index.
 * @modelguid {2AC091F0-CD9D-4C8C-8B2D-A95A530BE0DF}
*/
public Component getChild(int childIndex)
throws java.util.NoSuchElementException
{
    /*Begin Template Expansion*/
    // TO DO: You can customize the operation based on your application needs.

    if (childIndex < children.size())
       return (Component) children.get(childIndex);
    else
       return null;

    /*End Template Expansion*/
}

/**
This operation removes a component (leaf or composite) from the collection
of children.
 * @modelguid {3D0EA6D3-474A-43A4-89C0-B4A91600093C}
*/
public void remove(Component component)
throws java.util.NoSuchElementException
{
    /*Begin Template Expansion*/
```

```
        // TO DO: You can customize the operation based on your application needs.

        children.remove(component);

        /*End Template Expansion*/
    }

    /**
    This is the default constructor for the Component class.
     * @modelguid {83FDEF74-D94E-4F5A-B384-04399F588994}
    */
    public Composite()
    {
        /*Begin Template Expansion*/

        // TO DO: You can customize the constructor based
        on your application needs.

        children = new java.util.ArrayList();


        /*End Template Expansion*/
    }

    /**
    This operation returns an instance of the current Composite.
     * @modelguid {09139123-8935-40DB-A68A-FEBB64421917}
    */
    public Composite getComposite()
    {
        /*Begin Template Expansion*/
        return this;
        /*End Template Expansion*/
    }

    /**
    This is the implementation of Component specific operation.
     * @modelguid {2FCCE1AE-9B26-4EDD-9811-451AA8074771}
    */
    public void Operation1()
    {
        /*Begin Template Expansion*/

        // TO DO: You can customize the operation based on your application needs.

        for (int i = 0; i < children.size(); i++) {
           // Update your code to match the Operation signature.
```

```
            // ((Component) children.elementAt(i)).Operation1();
        }

        /*End Template Expansion*/
    }

}
```

The final two parameters in this pattern are the `operation` and `operation 2` parameters. The `operation` parameter is a single operation or a list of operations that are implemented by the composite class. The `operation 2` parameter is a single operation or a list of operations that are implemented by the leaf class.

Decorator

The decorator pattern is used to dynamically add responsibilities to an object. Although you can usually use subclasses to add responsibilities, there are times when the inheritance structure is unnecessarily complex and difficult to maintain. The decorator pattern can be a good alternative.

PATTERN STRATEGY

The classes in the decorator pattern are shown in Figure 10.10.

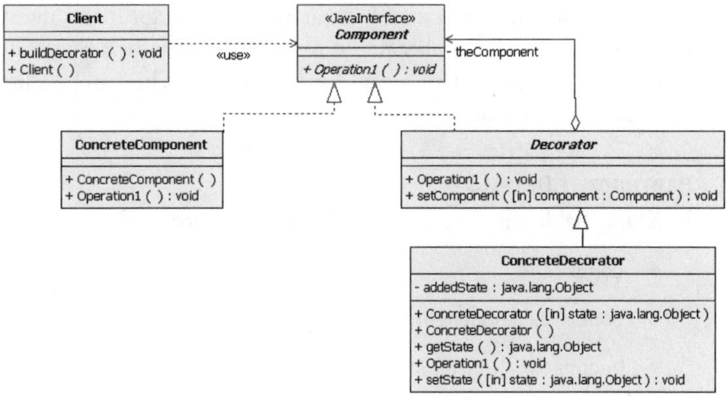

FIGURE 10.10
Decorator pattern class diagram

The concrete component is the class that provides some basic functionality. It is "decorated" with additional responsibilities provided by the decorators.

The process begins when you build the decorator pattern. The client first instantiates the concrete component and the concrete decorators that supplement the concrete component's behavior. The client then calls the `setComponent` method of the decorator so that the decorator knows which concrete component it is decorating. Once the decorator pattern has been built, the client calls the decorator's methods rather than the concrete component's. The decorator may perform some additional behavior, then call the concrete component's method, then perform some more behavior. Using this pattern, you can add behavior either before or after the concrete component's method is run. This process is shown in the sequence diagram in Figure 10.11.

FIGURE 10.11
Decorator pattern sequence diagram

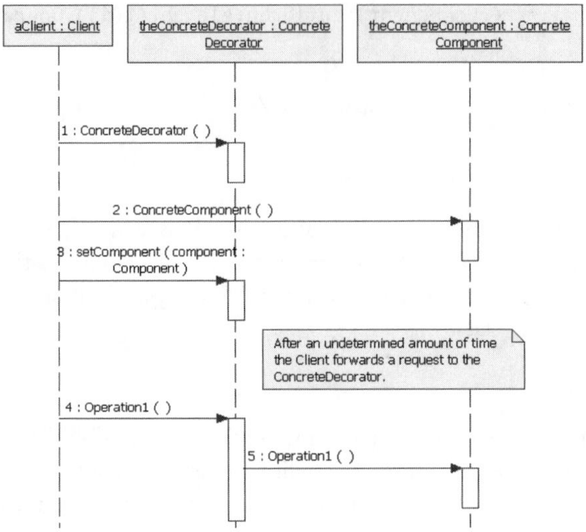

PROS AND CONS

This pattern can be used to add responsibilities dynamically, without having to build a large and complex inheritance structure. It separates the behavior into a number of small objects, each of which is easy to maintain because it is small. This can be a downfall, though. You may end up with too many small classes that are all somewhat alike. This can be a little harder to maintain without good documentation.

PARTICIPANT DETAILS

In XDE, the decorator pattern has six participants:

- `Component`
- `Concrete component`
- `Decorator`
- `Concrete decorator`
- `Client`
- `Operation`

The `component` defines the interface for both the concrete component and the decorators. It declares the method(s) provided in the `operation` parameter, while the concrete component and concrete decorator implement these methods.

The `concrete component` is the class whose behavior is supplemented by the decorators, but it has no knowledge of the decorators. It implements the methods in the `operation` parameter. In our example, it implements `Operation1`:

```
public class ConcreteComponent implements Component
```

```
{
    /**
    This is the default constructor for ConcreteComponent class.
     * @modelguid {96855F42-0038-4AA4-8786-728BDFC58F28}
    */
    public ConcreteComponent()
    {
    }

    /**
     *
     * @modelguid {685792D9-4940-4FE1-9FAD-CC6B60C465AE}
     */
    public void Operation1()
    {
    }

}
```

The `concrete decorator` is a class that supplements the concrete component's behavior. It implements the decorator interface and may have some additional methods to add more functionality. The `client` calls a method of the concrete decorator (in our example, `Operation1`). The concrete decorator may then:

- Run some additional functionality, then call `Operation1` in the concrete component.
- Run some additional functionality, then call `Operation1` in the concrete component, then run some more additional functionality.
- Call another decorator to run some functionality, then take one of the previous two approaches.

In this pattern, a decorator can use additional decorators to add even more functionality to the concrete component. The relationship between these decorators is shown in the aggregation between the decorator interface and the component interface on the class diagram from Figure 10.10, shown previously.

Façade

The façade pattern is used to create an interface for a subsystem, rather than for a single class. It helps minimize the complexity of a system by encapsulating logic into a subsystem. Client classes work with the façade, so they do not need to know the details of how the subsystem functionality is carried out.

PATTERN STRATEGY

Just as an interface can be created for a class, it can be created for a subsystem. The subsystem interface defines all of the high-level responsibilities of the subsystem. When a client needs some functionality from a subsystem, it sends the request to the façade, which then sends it to the class(es) within the subsystem that actually carry out the functionality. Figure 10.12 shows the classes in the façade pattern.

FIGURE 10.12
Façade pattern class diagram

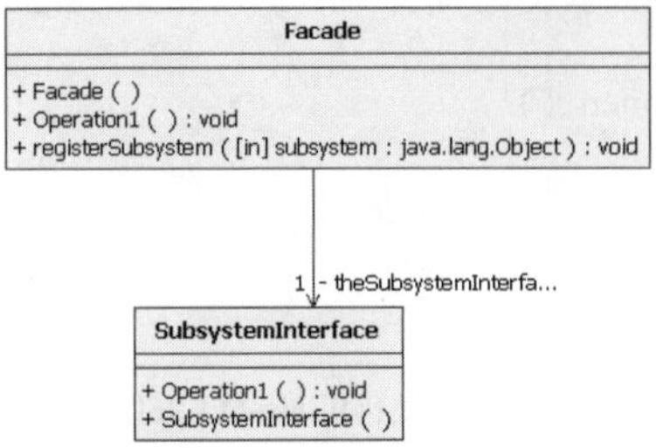

The façade is responsible for keeping track of the classes within the subsystem and knowing which classes are needed to implement which operations. Each class within the subsystem extends the subsystem interface class shown in Figure 10.12. When a client creates a façade, the façade registers the classes within the subsystem. Then, when the client sends a request, the façade passes the request on to the class(es) within the subsystem. This process is shown in Figure 10.13.

FIGURE 10.13
Façade pattern sequence diagram

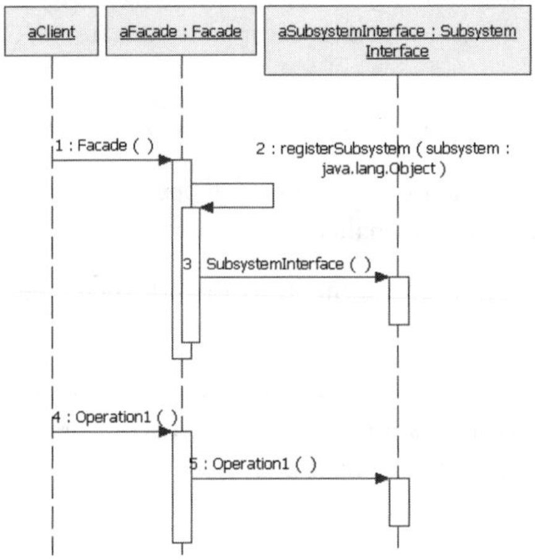

PROS AND CONS

This pattern helps in a number of ways. First, it helps simplify the high-level design by allowing you to create subsystems that only need to communicate with each other through their interfaces. Just as importantly, it increases the flexibility of your system. If you want to replace one subsystem with another, this is easy to do, as long as the two subsystems implement the same interface. Finally, it promotes weak coupling between the clients and the subsystem classes, minimizing the impact of changes to the system. You can, for example, completely change the way the subsystem behavior is implemented, but if you don't change the interface, the rest of the system won't be impacted.

The pattern itself is very beneficial, but be sure no clients are "sidestepping" the pattern by directly sending messages to classes within the subsystem.

PARTICIPANT DETAILS

The façade pattern has three participants:

- `Façade`
- `Subsystem interface`
- `Operation`

The `façade` defines the functionality that the subsystem as a whole provides, but it does not implement that functionality. When a client sends a request, it sends it to the façade. The façade then communicates with the classes inside the subsystem to process the request. As an example, if the client requests `Operation1`, the façade passes the request along to a class that actually implements the functionality. The following is the code for `Operation1` in the façade class:

```
public void Operation1()
    {
        /*Begin Template Expansion*/

        // TO DO:  Invoke the appropriate method on the SubSystemInterface.
        // The operation signature must match the one you choose for "operation"
        template parameter.

        theSubsystemInterface.Operation1();

        /*End Template Expansion*/
    }
```

The `subsystem interface` is a generic term for the classes within the subsystem. These subsystem classes are the classes that actually implement the subsystem's functionality.

The final parameter is the `operation` parameter, which is a list of operations that are defined in the façade and implemented by the subsystem.

Flyweight

The flyweight pattern is used to share objects, where each object does not maintain its own state, but instead stores it externally. If you need to have a large number of small objects, this pattern can frequently be helpful. An example from *Design Patterns* looks at a font. Each character in the font is represented as a single instance of a character class. However, the positions of the characters on the screen are kept externally. Therefore, there needs to be only one instance of the class for each character, rather than one instance of the class for each instance of each character on the screen.

PATTERN STRATEGY

The pattern divides the data in a class into the *intrinsic* data and the *extrinsic*. Intrinsic data is the data that remains with the class and is stored in the instantiated objects. In the font example, intrinsic data has to do with the size and shape of each character. This is data that does not change from instance to instance. Extrinsic data is the data that is stored outside the objects. In the font example, the extrinsic data is the location of the character on the screen.

The concrete flyweight is the small class whose extrinsic data is stored. It typically has a number of instances, such as those that are part of the font example that we just discussed. It can be either *shared*, meaning that a number of clients can use it, or *unshared*, in which case only a single client uses it. In this pattern, both shared and unshared flyweights are created by a flyweight factory, which uses the factory method to create concrete flyweights. The client class uses the flyweights that are created, and it also stores the extrinsic data of the flyweights. Figure 10.14 shows the classes that participate in this pattern.

FIGURE 10.14

Flyweight pattern class diagram

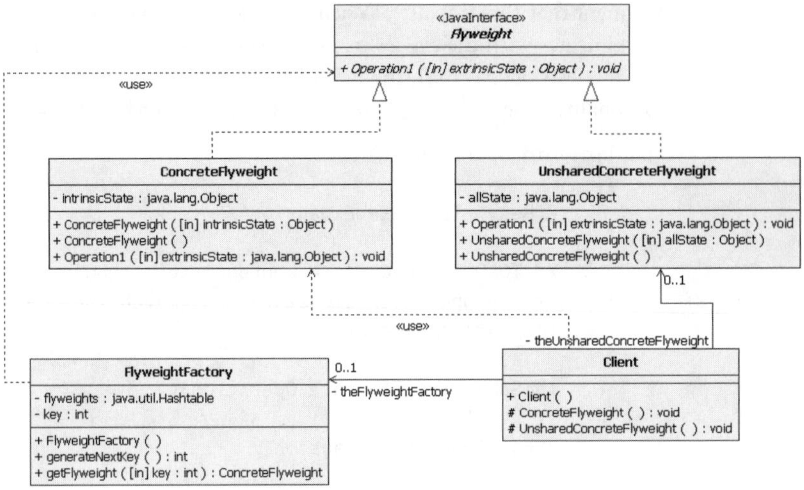

PROS AND CONS

The flyweight pattern can help make a system more efficient, because you do not need to create and keep track of as many small objects as you otherwise would. It does, to a certain extent, couple the client and the flyweight. Because the client maintains state information about the flyweight, the principles of encapsulation are not entirely followed by this pattern.

PARTICIPANT DETAILS

The flyweight pattern has six participants:

- `Flyweight`
- `Concrete flyweight`
- `Unshared concrete flyweight`
- `Flyweight factory`
- `Client`
- `Operation`

The `client` is the class that needs to use the flyweight, and it is also the class that stores the extrinsic behavior related to the flyweight. It has an attribute called `UnsharedConcreteFlyweight`, which is used to hold any unshared flyweights for this client. It also has methods it can use to request the creation of a shared concrete flyweight or an unshared concrete flyweight. XDE generates this code for you:

```
public class Client
{
    /** @modelguid {25787793-E6F3-49F3-B763-FDAD25BBE08A} */
    private UnsharedConcreteFlyweight theUnsharedConcreteFlyweight;

    /** @modelguid {673C21B9-6B46-4129-81EB-58A96936C005} */
    private FlyweightFactory theFlyweightFactory;

    /** @modelguid {4C49B1D6-E1C3-4F77-AA25-46064DADC5BB} */
    public Client()
    {
    }

    /**
    This operation gives an example how to manipulate ConcreteFlywights.
     * @modelguid {70AC8C20-F45C-47AE-B6E7-7A68919F0424}
    */
    protected void ConcreteFlyweight()
    {
        /*Begin Template Expansion*/

        // TO DO: This is an example how to use Flyweight pattern.
        You can customize the operation based on your application needs.

        int key = theFlyweightFactory.generateNextKey();
        java.lang.Object extrinsicState = new java.lang.Object();
        ConcreteFlyweight anConcreteFlyweight =
theFlyweightFactory.getFlyweight(key);
        anConcreteFlyweight.Operation1(extrinsicState);


        /*End Template Expansion*/
    }

    /**
    This operation gives an example how to manipulate
    UnsharedConcreteFlyweights.
     * @modelguid {06A8B13F-B7F2-4B59-8958-116269B28F40}
    */
    protected void UnsharedConcreteFlyweight()
    {
```

```
            /*Begin Template Expansion*/

            // TO DO: This is an example how to use Flyweight pattern.
            You can customize the operation based on your application needs.

            java.lang.Object extrinsicState = new java.lang.Object();
            UnsharedConcreteFlyweight anUnsharedConcreteFlyweight
            = new UnsharedConcreteFlyweight();
            anUnsharedConcreteFlyweight.Operation1(extrinsicState);

            /*End Template Expansion*/
        }

    }
```

Notice that in the preceding code, the client passes the extrinsic state information to the flyweight when a method call is made. This keeps the flyweight from having to maintain that extrinsic information itself.

Both the `ConcreteFlyweight` and `UnsharedConcreteFlyweight` classes implement the operations in the flyweight interface. Each has an attribute (`instrinsicState` in the `ConcreteFlyweight` class and `allState` in the `UnsharedConcreteFlyweight` class) that maintains the object's intrinsic data.

The `flyweight` parameter is an interface implemented by the `ConcreteFlyweight` and `Unshared-ConcreteFlyweight` classes.

The `flyweight factory` is a class that generates concrete flyweights, either shared or unshared, for use by the clients.

Finally, the `operation` parameter includes the operation(s) that are in the flyweight interface and are implemented by either the concrete flyweight or the unshared concrete flyweight. In the example shown earlier in Figure 10.9, the operation parameter included `Operation1`.

Proxy

The proxy pattern can be used when you need to use a placeholder for another object. This pattern is typically used when you need a small placeholder for a large, complex object that takes some time to build. A placeholder can be helpful when there's a difference between requesting an instance of an object and actually using it. You can use the proxy when the object is requested and load the actual object only when it's needed.

PATTERN STRATEGY

In this pattern, a client needs to use a *subject*, but when the client needs to know the subject is there and when the client actually requests some functionality for the subject may be different.

We are assuming that the subject takes a significant amount of time to load, or for some other reason you don't want to load the subject until you actually need it. The pattern involves an interface called subject that is implemented by both the real subject and the *proxy* (or placeholder). Because both the real subject and the proxy share the same interface, the client can send messages to the proxy when it needs a reference to the real subject, and it can send messages to the real subject when it needs to carry out some functionality. Figure 10.15 is the class diagram for the proxy pattern.

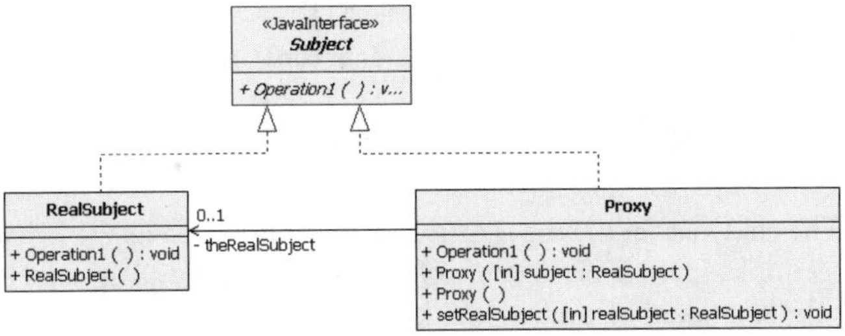

FIGURE 10.15
Proxy pattern class diagram

PROS AND CONS

Using the proxy is an easy way to reference an object without actually having to construct or retrieve it. This pattern can help save time and improve efficiency because the system does not need to load an object until the object is really needed. This can be especially helpful in distributed systems.

The only downside is the small amount of complexity that is added. Rather than maintain one class and its interface, you have to build and maintain three classes.

PARTICIPANT DETAILS

In XDE, the proxy pattern takes four parameters:

- `Subject`
- `Real subject`
- `Proxy`
- `Request`

The `subject` is an interface that defines all of the behavior that the real subject implements. Both the proxy class and the real subject class implement the subject interface.

The `proxy` class maintains a reference to the real subject. When the client makes a request, the proxy sends the request to the real subject. In the class diagram shown earlier in Figure 10.15, the client may request `Operation1`. In this example, the proxy class calls the `Operation1` method of the real subject. XDE provides this code for you, which is contained in the proxy class:

```
/**
This is any custom operation from the model.  It can implement any logic
required by your application.
 * @modelguid {07586CA2-D38E-42FE-AD4A-FCBF2C002FD7}
*/
public void Operation1()
{
    /*Begin Template Expansion*/

    // TO DO: You can customize the operation based on your application needs.
    // This operation invokes the method of the element being proxied.
```

```
        if (theRealSubject != null)
           (theRealSubject).Operation1();

        /*End Template Expansion*/
    }
```

The `real subject` is the class that actually implements the behavior of the subject interface (in our example, it implements `Operation1`). It is typically a large and complex object that takes some significant amount of time to build.

The final parameter, the `request` parameter, is simply the operation or operations that are defined in the subject interface and implemented in the real subject. In the previous example, the request is `Operation1`.

Behavioral Patterns

The final group of GOF patterns includes the *behavioral patterns*. These are the patterns that are concerned with algorithms and assigning responsibilities to objects. While structural and creational patterns focus on objects or classes, behavioral patterns also focus on the relationships between them.

There are 11 behavioral patterns. Their definitions are as follows:

Chain of responsibility Allows you to pass a request along a chain of objects until it is received by an object that can handle the request. If none of the objects in the chain can handle the request, the request is dropped. Decouples the sender of a request to the receiver because the sender does not know which object will handle the request.

Command Creates a separate object for a request, so that you can treat a request like any other object. Supports logging and queuing of requests, as well as an undo feature.

Interpreter Defines a mechanism for storing and processing the rules of a grammar. Used to parse a statement and interpret it.

Iterator Iterates sequentially through a collection of objects, optionally performing some functionality on each member of the collection. Protects the client from needing to know about the inner workings of the aggregate.

Mediator Creates an object that understands how a set of other objects interact. Encapsulates this control logic into a mediator object, to prevent other objects from having to refer to each other explicitly.

Memento Stores the state of an object into a separate memento object. The memento can be used later to restore the state of the object.

Observer Allows one or more objects to observe a subject object. When the subject's state is changed, the pattern notifies the observer objects of the change.

State Makes an object appear as if its class has changed by changing the behavior of the object when its state has changed.

Strategy Allows you to define and encapsulate different algorithms to solve the same problem (for example, different formats to save a file). The pattern allows the algorithms to change without affecting the clients.

Template method Creates a template object that holds the structure of an algorithm but does not actually implement the steps of the algorithm. The algorithm's steps are implemented in subclasses, allowing the implementation of the algorithm to change without affecting clients or changing the algorithm's overall structure.

Visitor Encapsulates a new method in a visitor object, and allows the visitor to perform the operation on the data in one or more other objects.

In this section, we will take a detailed look at each of these behavioral patterns, including their purpose, pros and cons, parameters, and implementation in XDE.

Chain of Responsibility

The chain of responsibility pattern is used to send a request along a chain of objects, until one of the receiving objects handles the request. It helps decouple the sender of a request from the receiver.

An example of this lies in an online help system. When the user selects a field and presses F1, help typically appears for that particular field. If there is no help available for the field, the system displays help for the screen. If there is no help available for the screen, the system might display some generic help. If that isn't available either, the request may be lost.

In this example, the request for help may first go to an object we'll call `FieldHelp`. If `FieldHelp` is unable to find help for the field that was selected, it passes the request along to another object we'll call `ScreenHelp`. If `ScreenHelp` can't handle the request, it passes it along to a `GenericHelp` object. If `GenericHelp` can't handle it either, the request is lost.

One thing to note here is that the chain of responsibility pattern does not guarantee that a request will be handled. It simply guarantees that the request will be passed through a chain of objects that might be able to handle it.

PATTERN STRATEGY

The pattern consists of two key classes: the *client* class sends a request along the chain, and the *handler* accepts a request and either handles it or passes it along to the next handler in the chain (the successor of the handler). Figure 10.16 is the class diagram for the pattern.

FIGURE 10.16

Chain of responsibility pattern class diagram

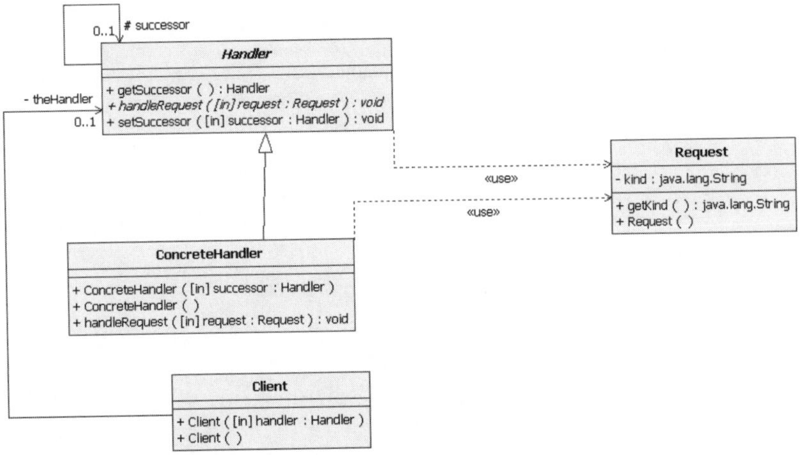

As you can see, XDE creates four classes to implement the pattern. The handler holds the functionality for getting or setting a successor and for determining whether to handle a request or pass it along. Each concrete handler inherits this functionality from the handler. The request class is simply a class that holds the request that is passed along the chain. The client class starts the whole request process by passing a request to the first concrete handler in the chain. Figures 10.17 and 10.18 show how the chain is constructed. In Figure 10.17, the handlers have been created but haven't been linked into a chain. The `setSuccessor` method is used to create the chain in this case. In Figure 10.18, the handlers are created and the chain is formed all at the same time.

FIGURE 10.17
Creating a chain of responsibility

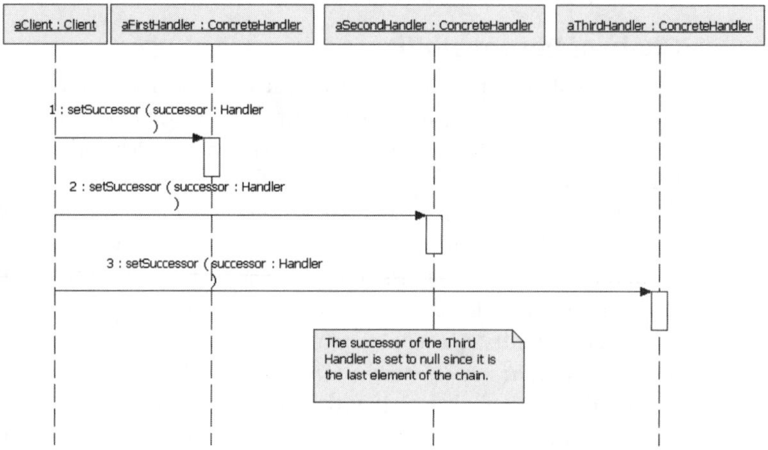

FIGURE 10.18
Creating handlers and a chain of responsibility

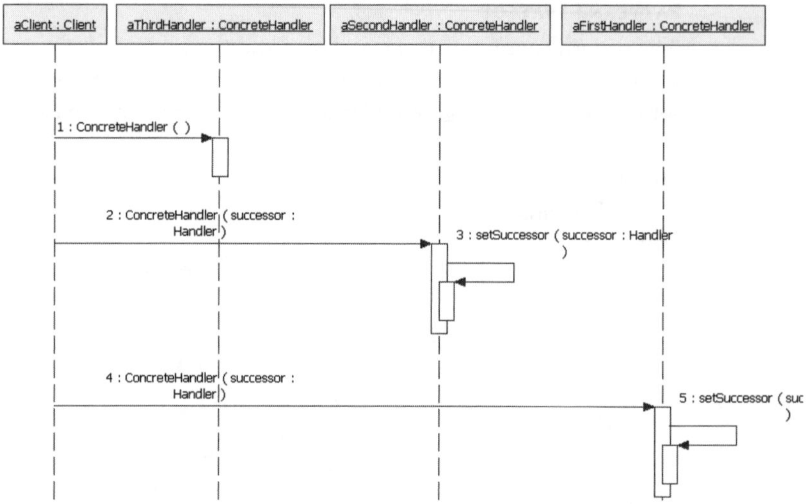

When a request needs to be handled, the client sends the request to the first handler on the chain. It either handles the request or passes it along. Figure 10.19 shows how a request is passed through the chain. If none of the objects in the chain can handle the request, the request is lost.

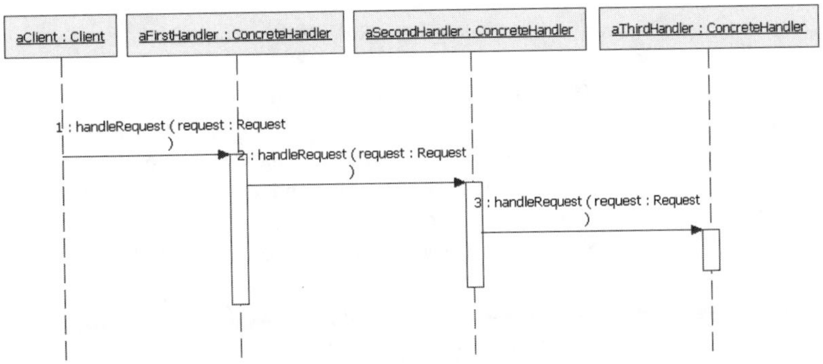

FIGURE 10.19
Passing a request through a chain of responsibility

PROS AND CONS

Using this pattern helps prevent a client from having to know which objects can handle its request. The client only needs to pass the request to the beginning of the chain, so it doesn't need to have logic related to which handler can respond to which request. This helps simplify the client's design. This pattern also usually results in creating a number of small handlers that are easier to maintain than one large class that can handle all requests.

Keep in mind as you are using this pattern that there is no guarantee that a request will be handled at all. You may need to write some specialized code for this case so that the user isn't left wondering what happened.

PARTICIPANT DETAILS

The chain of responsibility pattern takes four parameters in XDE:

- `Handler`
- `Concrete handler`
- `Request`
- `Client`

The `handler` class is a generic class from which each concrete handler is inherited. It has a `getSuccessor` and a `setSuccessor` method to get and set the next handler in the chain. It also contains an abstract `handleRequest` method, which is implemented in the concrete handlers.

The `concrete handler` is a class that receives a request and then either responds to the request or passes it along to another concrete handler. In our earlier example, the FieldHelp, ScreenHelp, and GenericHelp classes were all concrete handlers. They inherit the ability to get and set their successor, and to handle a request. Either it can receive its successor as part of the constructor when it is created, or the successor can be set later using the `setSuccessor` method the concrete handler inherits from the handler.

The concrete handler implements the `handleRequest` method it inherits from the handler. XDE provides some code for this method, as follows:

```
public void handleRequest(Request request)
    {
        /*Begin Template Expansion*/

        // TO DO: This operation handles the request.
        If the request can be handed it does so;otherwise it forwards
        the request to its successor.
        You can customize the operation based on your application needs.

        if ( request.getKind().equals("test")) {
           // Handle event.
        }
        else {
           this.successor.handleRequest(request);
        }

        /*End Template Expansion*/
    }
```

When you use this pattern, customize the `handleRequest` method as needed. In each concrete handler, code this method to identify the type(s) of requests the concrete handler can manage, and add the code to handle those requests.

The `request` class is used to hold the actual request that is passed along the chain. It has a string attribute called `kind`, which is used to hold the type of request. You can use the `getKind` method, as we saw in the preceding code, to determine what type of request is being passed through the chain. XDE provides some default code for the request class, but it is meant to be customized. Specifically, customize the constructor and the `getKind` operation. The following is the code generated for the request class:

```
public class Request
{
    /** @modelguid {51E58059-1893-4528-8CFD-99937B344A2D} */
    private java.lang.String kind;

    /** @modelguid {2F1DA4FE-0D0C-4912-AEBA-ADEC17B6B210} */
    public Request()
    {
        /*Begin Template Expansion*/

        // TO DO: This is just an example.
        You can customize the operation based on your application needs.

        this.kind = "test";
```

```
        /*End Template Expansion*/
    }

    /** @modelguid {9885DEEE-4E96-4867-886B-C388FCB12FA8} */
    public java.lang.String getKind()
    {
        /*Begin Template Expansion*/

        // TO DO: This is just an example.
        You can customize the application based on your application needs.

        return this.kind;

        /*End Template Expansion*/
    }

}
```

In the constructor, set the value of the `kind` attribute to the type of request you are creating.

The final class in the pattern is the `client` class, which is responsible for creating a request and passing it to the first concrete handler in the chain. It can either receive the first handler as a parameter to its constructor, or create the handler itself. XDE generates the following code for the client:

```
public class Client
{
    /** @modelguid {A44AE1EC-396C-4913-9F7A-F154719B525B} */
    private Handler theHandler;

    /** @modelguid {BAA89827-3264-4FB7-9697-767B4CEB5884} */
    public Client(Handler handler)
    {
        /*Begin Template Expansion*/

        // TO DO: You can customize the initialization of the attribute.
        // The call to the Handler can be done based on your application
        needs in a custom defined operation.

        this.theHandler = handler;

        /*End Template Expansion*/
    }

    /** @modelguid {6D81FE96-2C7B-4DBC-AA9F-206B3C86A100} */
    public Client()
    {
    }
}
```

Command

The command pattern is used to encapsulate a method call or request as a separate object. Using this pattern, the request object can be stored and sent around like any other object. This pattern is used for the following reasons:

To parameterize clients with different requests You may want to create a command without having to know who receives the command or what specific method needs to run to execute the command. This pattern lets you pass the command's receiver as a parameter.

To queue or log requests You may want to collect a number of requests and then execute them in a specific order or at a specific time. This pattern lets you encapsulate each request as a separate object. You can then execute them at any time and in any order you want, queue them, or log them. Logging can be especially useful if the system encounters a problem and you need to reconstruct the commands that were executed.

To support undoable operations One of the most useful features of this pattern is the ability to support undoable operations. The pattern includes saving the state of an object before a command is run. If the command is undoable, you can return the object to its previous state.

PATTERN STRATEGY

Fundamentally, this pattern consists of a *client,* who creates a *command,* along with the state and the *receiver* of the command. A command is simply the encapsulation of a method call. The client sends the command, state, and receiver to an *invoker.* The invoker holds on to the command for a while and then executes it, resulting in calls to the receiver. The classes in this pattern are shown in Figure 10.20.

The pattern begins when the client executes its `invoke` method. This results in both an invoker and a command being created with the command's state and receiver. The client passes the command, state, and receiver to the invoker object. The state is included to support undoable operations. If the

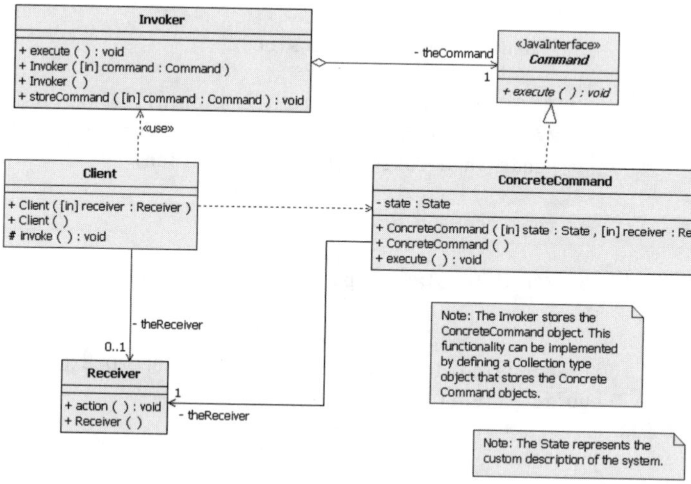

FIGURE 10.20
Command pattern class diagram

command is undoable, the concrete command stores state information for undoing the command. At some point in time, the invoker executes the command, calling an action on the receiver. This process is shown in the sequence diagram in Figure 10.21.

FIGURE 10.21
Command pattern sequence diagram

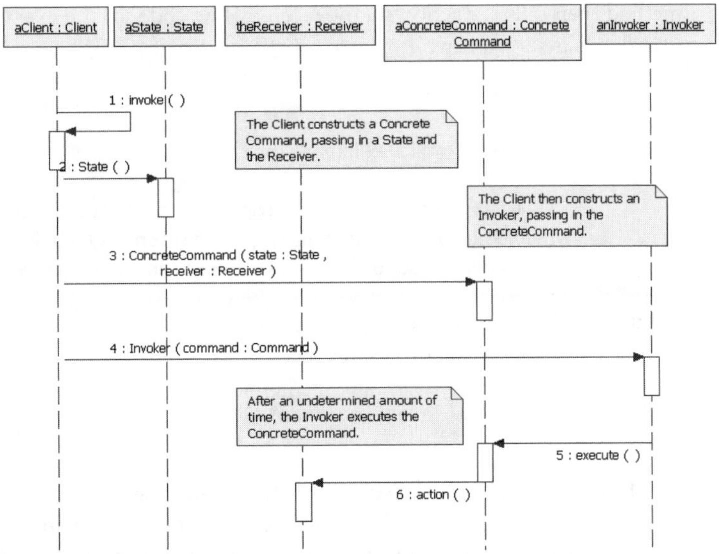

PROS AND CONS

As we mentioned earlier, the command pattern can be used to queue requests, log requests, parameterize requests, and provide undo functionality. By encapsulating the command, you can extend it, modify it, parameterize it, or save it. In short, this pattern gives you the ability to treat a command like any other object. The only real downside is the small amount of added complexity involved in creating the invoker, command, concrete command, and state classes.

PARTICIPANT DETAILS

In XDE, the command pattern takes six parameters:

- `Invoker`
- `Command`
- `Concrete command`
- `Receiver`
- `State`
- `Client`

The concrete command class stores a method call for later use. The method call consists of two items: the receiver of the command request, and the action that the receiver should carry out. However, the concrete command class does not know when the action should be called. This responsibility is left to the invoker. At some point, the invoker calls the concrete command's execute method. This method then calls the action on the receiver. The code for the execute method of the concrete command class is shown here:

```
public void execute()
    {
        /*Begin Template Expansion*/

        // TO DO: The operation implements "execute" by
        invoking the corresponding operations(s) on Receiver.
        // You can customize this operation based on your application needs.

        this.state.set();
        this.theReceiver.action();

        /*End Template Expansion*/
    }
```

The concrete command also stores a state object associated with a command. This is used to store the state of an object before the command runs. If the command is undoable, the state object is used to restore the system to its previous state. If the command is undoable, the client passes the state in to the concrete command's constructor, as shown here:

```
public ConcreteCommand(State state, Receiver receiver)
    {
        /*Begin Template Expansion*/

        // TO DO: You can customize the constructor based
        on your application needs.

        this.state = state;
        this.theReceiver = receiver;

        /*End Template Expansion*/
    }
```

The command class is simply an interface to the concrete command classes. It defines one abstract method called execute, which is implemented in the concrete command.

The state parameter, as mentioned earlier, is used to store the state of an object. If the command is undoable, the information in the state can be used to restore that object to its original state.

The receiver is the class that ultimately carries out the command. When the invoker tells the concrete command to execute the command, the concrete command calls an action method on the receiver. If this pattern had not been used, the client simply calls the action on the receiver directly. This pattern gives you the option of queuing requests, logging them, or parameterizing them.

The `invoker` is responsible for knowing when the command should be carried out. It stores the concrete command object and executes it at the appropriate time.

Finally, the `client` is the class that starts the whole process. In the `invoke` method, it creates the invoker and the concrete command, and specifies the receiver of the command. The `invoke` method of the client class is shown here:

```
protected void invoke()
    {
        /*Begin Template Expansion*/

        // TO DO: This is an example how to use the Command pattern.
        You can customize the operation based on your application need.

        State aState = new State();
        ConcreteCommand aConcreteCommand = new ConcreteCommand(aState,
theReceiver);
        Invoker anInvoker = new Invoker();
        anInvoker.storeCommand(aConcreteCommand);

        /*End Template Expansion*/
    }
```

Interpreter

The interpreter pattern is used to define a "language" that can be interpreted by your system. Using macros is an example of this. A macro allows us to record the steps in a process in a way that is easy to understand. When the macro is run, it is translated into instructions the system can understand—setting a font, changing the page layout, and so on. Another example of this pattern is in a report generator. These types of programs typically give the user an interface in business language. Once the user has entered their criteria, these criteria are translated into SQL that the system can use to retrieve and display the appropriate data. As a final example, consider a compiler. A compiler allows a programmer to write code in a format that makes sense to a human, and then it translates that code into a format that makes sense to the operating system.

Pattern Strategy

In this pattern, the *client* first instantiates a *context,* which is used to hold the expression or statement that the system is translating. The context also keeps track of how much of the statement has been translated.

The statement itself is represented as a tree of nonterminal expressions and terminal expressions. A nonterminal expression is made up of a series of subexpressions, while a terminal expression is directly translated. The subexpressions in a nonterminal expression may be either terminal expressions or more nonterminal expressions, which are themselves made up of terminal or nonterminal expressions. The client uses the `interpret` method in the terminal and nonterminal expressions to translate the statement. Figure 10.22 shows the classes in the interpreter pattern. Figure 10.23 is a sequence diagram that shows how a statement is translated.

FIGURE 10.22

Interpreter pattern class diagram

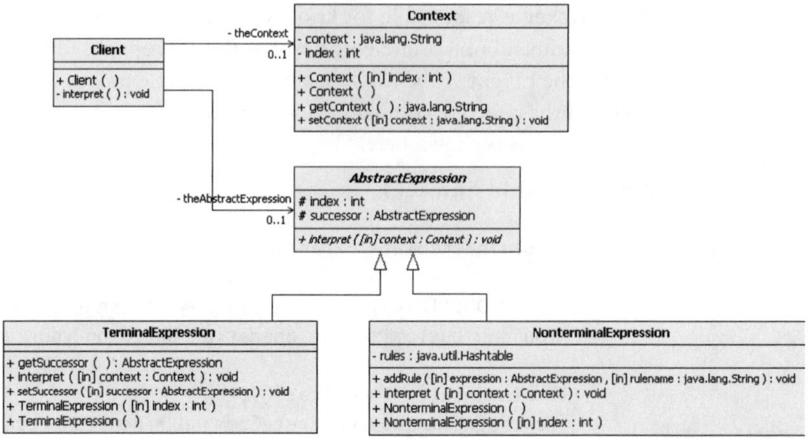

FIGURE 10.23

Interpreting a statement

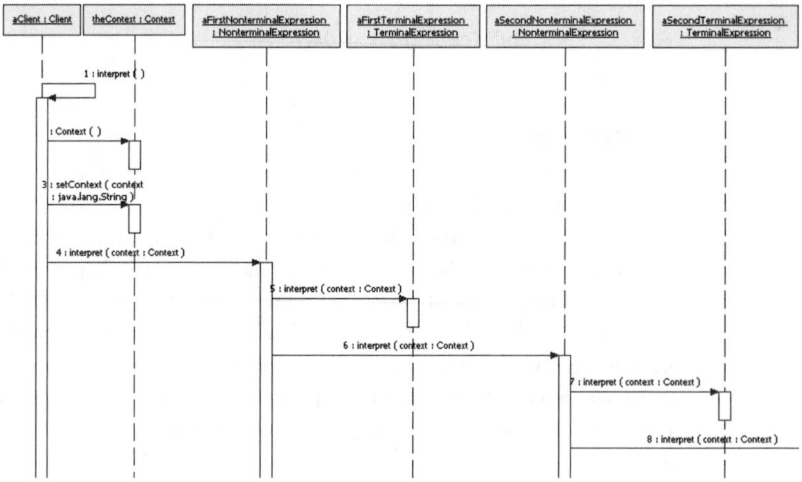

PROS AND CONS

This pattern can help make your system much more user-friendly. It gives you the flexibility to prompt for information in a way that the user understands and then translate it so that you can use it in your system.

The major disadvantage is the time and effort you need to invest to actually implement this pattern. You must define a language, program the methods you need to parse and translate the statements in the language, and program all of the error handling that the system needs.

PARTICIPANT DETAILS

There are five participants in the interpreter pattern:

- `Abstract expression`
- `Terminal expression`
- `Nonterminal expression`
- `Context`
- `Client`

The `context` is the class that holds the initial expression to be translated, and it also keeps track of how much of the expression has been translated. It has an integer attribute called `index`, which holds the current position in the expression to be translated. It also has a string attribute called `context`, which is the original expression that will be translated.

The `terminal expression` and `nonterminal expression` parameters are the classes that translate the pieces of the overall expression. A terminal expression interprets the terminal symbols in the grammar. It may have successors, which are other terminal or nonterminal expressions that make up a nonterminal expression. When the `interpret` method is called on a terminal expression, it parses the expression and calls successors, if there are any. The following is the `interpret` method in the terminal expression class:

```
public void interpret(Context context)
    {
        /*Begin Template Expansion*/

        // TO DO: This is an example how to implement
        "interpret" operation.  You can customize the
        operation based on your application needs.

        java.lang.String myContext = context.getContext();

        // TO DO: Add your code here for parsing the
        context.  Check the result of parsing and decide if
        abort or continue interpreting the context.

        boolean bParseResult = true;
        if (bParseResult) {
           super.successor.interpret(context);
        } else {
           // Handle error and exit process.
        }

        /*End Template Expansion*/
    }
```

A nonterminal expression is an expression made up of terminal expressions and/or other nonterminal expressions. It is responsible for keeping track of the rules in the grammar, and it stores those rules in the `rules` attribute. It interprets a context by parsing it into its elements, and interpreting each of these in turn. The following is the `interpret` method of the nonterminal expression class:

```
public void interpret(Context context)
    {
        /*Begin Template Expansion*/

        // TO DO: This is just an example how to implement
        "interpret" operation. You can customize the
        operation based on your application needs.

        java.util.Enumeration anEnumeration = rules.elements();
        while ( anEnumeration.hasMoreElements()) {
           AbstractExpression anAbstractExpression =
           (AbstractExpression) anEnumeration.nextElement();
           anAbstractExpression.interpret(context);
        }

        /*End Template Expansion*/
    }
```

The `abstract expression` parameter is an interface for both the terminal expression and the nonterminal expression classes. It defines an abstract `interpret` method, which is implemented in the terminal and nonterminal expression classes.

Finally, the `client` is the class responsible for building the tree of terminal and nonterminal expressions for the context statement. The following is the XDE code generated for the constructor of the client:

```
public Client()
    {
        /*Begin Template Expansion*/

        // TO DO: This is an example how the Interpreter
        pattern can be used. You can customize the
        operation based on these
        // guidelines. Handle the initialization of types
        of AbstractExpression (TerminalExpression and
        NonterminalExpression) as required by your
        application.  The "tree" of expressions
        // can be done using the setSuccessor() method.

        theContext = new Context();
        theAbstractExpression = new TerminalExpression();
        theAbstractExpression.interpret(this.theContext);

        /*End Template Expansion*/
    }
```

Iterator

You use the iterator pattern to walk through, or iterate through, a collection of objects. For example, you may want to iterate through all of the entries in an online order, multiplying their quantities and prices to come up with the total cost of the order. In general, iterators are used to

- Define different methods of iteration (beginning to end, in alphabetical order, traversing a parse tree, and so on).
- Define conditional operations on a collection (for example, give a 10 percent discount to only the line items in an order that have a quantity greater than 5).
- Separate the iteration functionality from the other functionality of the aggregate to keep the aggregate from becoming too complex.
- Easily reuse iterator functionality.
- Easily change the iteration method on an aggregate.

PATTERN STRATEGY

The pattern has three primary concepts: the *iterator,* the *aggregate,* and the *object.* The object could be any class in the system. In our order example, we use the lineitem class as the object. The aggregate is simply a collection of objects. This could be a list, an array, or any other type of collection supported by your programming language. Again returning to the order example, an order is a collection of line items, so order is our aggregate. Finally, the iterator is a class that traverses the aggregate, performing some functionality on each object. The pattern defines interfaces for the aggregate and iterator, so the class diagram for the iterator pattern looks like Figure 10.24.

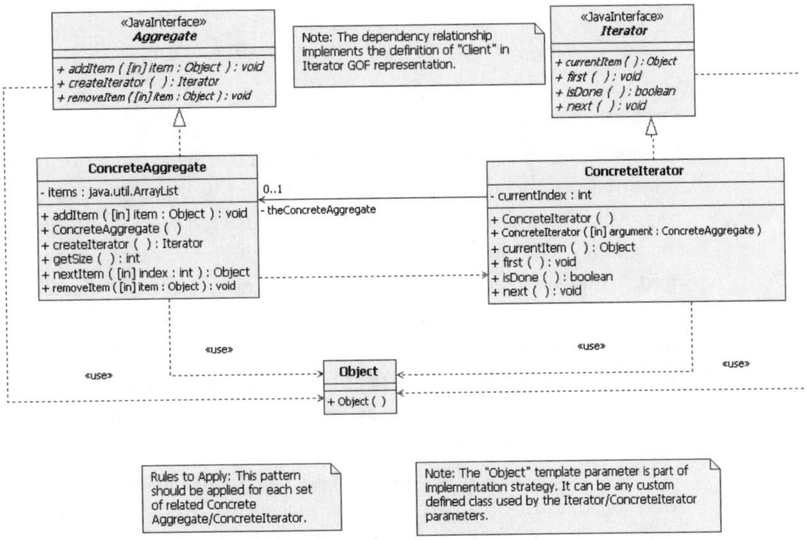

FIGURE 10.24

Iterator pattern class diagram

To iterate through the aggregate, the client first creates a concrete aggregate, which creates a concrete iterator. The concrete iterator has methods such as `first`, `next`, `isDone`, and `CurrentItem`, to keep track of its place in the aggregate, and to move through the objects in the aggregate. The sequence diagram in Figure 10.25 shows the iterator pattern.

NOTE *There are several variations to the iterator pattern. The approach described here is that taken by XDE. See the book* Design Patterns *cited at the beginning of this chapter for variations to this pattern.*

FIGURE 10.25

Iterator pattern sequence diagram

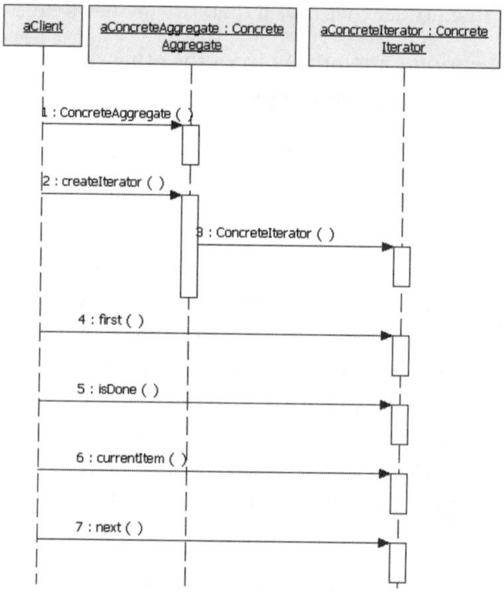

PROS AND CONS

By separating the aggregate's behavior from the behavior related to traversing the aggregate, you can simplify both the aggregate and the iterator. The aggregate can focus on implementing its other responsibilities, and it doesn't have to be cluttered with methods it needs to view, edit, or retrieve a single entry from within the aggregate. The iterator, on the other hand, can focus only on the logic it needs to traverse the aggregate, and it does not need to be cluttered with other functionality.

Another benefit of creating an iterator is that you can reuse it. A single iterator can be used for multiple aggregates, eliminating the need to reprogram this logic in multiple places. You can also create several varieties of iterator: front-to-back iteration, back-to-front, every fourth element, or any other means of traversal you may need. Once you've defined each of these, you can apply them to as many aggregates as necessary.

One thing to consider when you are using this pattern is that the concrete aggregate creates the concrete iterator. That isn't a problem when you're coding the concrete aggregate, but if the concrete aggregate is part of a reuse library and can't be changed, you may run into a problem. Also, if the aggregate encapsulates objects related through an inheritance hierarchy, you may need to use downcasting to access members of the aggregate.

Participant Details

The iterator pattern takes five parameters:

- `Iterator`
- `Concrete iterator`
- `Aggregate`
- `Concrete aggregate`
- `Object`

The `concrete aggregate` is the list or collection that is being iterated upon. It has an attribute called `items`, which is the collection of objects in the aggregate. Note that it has methods for adding and removing items from itself, but all the logic for moving through the aggregate has been placed in the concrete iterator. The concrete aggregate is responsible for creating the concrete iterator that is used to traverse the aggregate.

The `aggregate` interface defines the public interface for the concrete aggregate. It includes definitions for the `addItem`, `removeItem`, and `createIterator` methods that are implemented in the concrete aggregate.

The `concrete iterator` is responsible for moving through the aggregate. It has methods for traversing the aggregate, as shown here:

```
public class ConcreteIterator implements Iterator
{
    /** @modelguid {2F85DC5D-CCEE-442D-BF57-39D2B85ECB2B} */
    private int currentIndex;

    /** @modelguid {21FF8F22-531A-4875-BA55-2EA589CEF42E} */
    private ConcreteAggregate theConcreteAggregate;

    /**
    This operation retrieves the item at current position.
     * @modelguid {85EA65C7-A0E0-41EE-8CD8-0699A8CCE00B}
    */
    public void first()
    {
        /*Begin Template Expansion*/

        // TO DO: You can customize the code by
        implementing your own way to go to the "first"
        element in the collection.

        this.currentIndex  = 0;

        /*End Template Expansion*/
    }
```

```
/**
The operation returns the next element in collection (if it exists).
 * @modelguid {71BD7457-F534-4959-9039-C8E7694D97E2}
*/
public void next()
{
    /*Begin Template Expansion*/

    // TO DO:You can customize the code by implementing
    your own way to go to  the "next" element in the collection.

    this.currentIndex++;

    /*End Template Expansion*/
}

/**
This operation returns false if are still elements in the collection to
iterate through, otherwise true is returned.
 * @modelguid {4592221A-2131-45BB-84CA-8EF4D89DBF8C}
*/
public boolean isDone()
{
    /*Begin Template Expansion*/

    // TO DO: You can customize the operation based on your application needs.

    boolean bIsDone = false;
    if ( currentIndex == theConcreteAggregate.getSize() ) {
       bIsDone = true;
    }

    return bIsDone;

    /*End Template Expansion*/
}

/**
This operation retrieves the item at current position.
 * @modelguid {3C2B6888-ECC3-4B4D-954E-8218D349BF53}
*/
public Object currentItem()
{
    /*Begin Template Expansion*/

    // TO DO:You can customize the code by implementing
    your own way to iterate through the collection.
```

```
            return theConcreteAggregate.nextItem(currentIndex);

            /*End Template Expansion*/
        }

        /** @modelguid {B8F1BB55-CF1B-45BB-BD28-91298C9DD282} */
        public ConcreteIterator()
        {
            /*Begin Template Expansion*/

            // TO DO: You can customize the constructor based
            on your application needs.

            currentIndex = 0;

            /*End Template Expansion*/
        }

        /** @modelguid {B04651D3-7EBA-4DB7-829F-20882EE77C02} */
        public ConcreteIterator(ConcreteAggregate argument)
        {
            /*Begin Template Expansion*/

            // TO DO: You can customize the constructor based
            on your application needs.

            theConcreteAggregate = argument;
            currentIndex = 0;

            /*End Template Expansion*/
        }

    }
```

The `iterator` interface defines the public interface of the concrete iterator. In this pattern, the `iterator` interface defines the `first`, `next`, `currentItem`, and `isDone` methods.

Finally, the `object` parameter is the object that makes up the aggregate.

Mediator

The mediator pattern allows for looser coupling between objects by encapsulating the interactions between the objects. The mediator is most helpful when complex and changing relationships exist between a set of objects. Rather than needing to maintain this complex web of relationships, you can have the objects "talk" to each other through the mediator. The mediator encapsulates the relationship logic, and it passes appropriate requests to the appropriate classes. By using this pattern, each class does not need to know about the methods of each of the other classes.

PATTERN STRATEGY

The mediator pattern has two primary components: the *mediator,* which acts as the go-between for other classes, and the *colleague,* which is one of the classes that communicates through the mediator. Figure 10.26 is a class diagram for the mediator pattern.

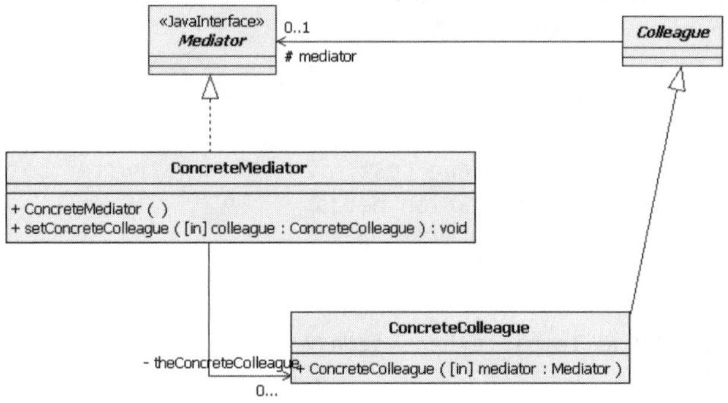

FIGURE 10.26
Mediator pattern class diagram

When a concrete colleague is instantiated, it receives a reference to the mediator it will be using. The `setConcreteColleague` method in the concrete mediator lets the concrete mediator know about a new colleague. Now, when the colleague needs to send a message, it can send it to the mediator rather than directly to another class. The mediator determines which class(es) need to be involved in carrying out the responsibility and sends the appropriate messages.

NOTE *If you are familiar with the use of a control object, you've seen a mediator. The control acts as a mediator between the boundary and entity objects.*

PROS AND CONS

Encapsulating the relationship logic (which can get very complex) into its own object helps simplify the model and prevent the classes from becoming too tightly coupled.

The main problem with this pattern is in the mediator class itself. Because the relationship logic can be very complex, the mediator may be difficult to understand, code, and maintain.

PARTICIPANT DETAILS

The mediator pattern takes four parameters in XDE:

- `Mediator`
- `Concrete mediator`
- `Colleague`
- `Concrete colleague`

The `mediator` defines an interface for communicating with the colleague objects. By default in XDE, it does not contain any methods, but you can add operations to the interface for each of the public methods of the concrete mediator.

The concrete mediator implements any methods defined in the mediator interface. It has an attribute, theConcreteColleague, which holds the concrete colleague object. The value of theConcreteColleague is set through the setConcreteColleague method. XDE also adds a constructor method for the concrete mediator. The code generated for the concrete mediator looks like this:

```
public class ConcreteMediator implements Mediator
{
    /** @modelguid {150704B0-CF31-4678-8F5B-27D1A7D17EEB} */
    private ConcreteColleague theConcreteColleague;

    /**
    This operation creates and returns a ConcreteMediator objects.
     * @modelguid {52C5B28E-142E-4A4D-A4D8-CD21D979756C}
    */
    public ConcreteMediator()
    {
    }

    /**
    This operation stores an ConcreteColleague object.
     * @modelguid {ED3496A6-9818-4C65-B82E-67A771CD3720}
    */
    public void setConcreteColleague(ConcreteColleague colleague)
    {
        /*Begin Template Expansion*/

        // TO DO: You can customize the constructor based
        on your application needs.

        theConcreteColleague = colleague;

        /*End Template Expansion*/
    }

}
```

The colleague class is a parent for the concrete colleague. It has one attribute, mediator, which holds a reference to the mediator object that the concrete colleague will use.

When instantiated, the concrete colleague is an object that communicates with other objects using the concrete mediator. When the concrete colleague is instantiated, it receives a reference to the mediator it will be using; it can then send messages to the mediator. The following is the code generated for the concrete colleague:

```
public class ConcreteColleague extends Colleague
{
    /**
    This operation creates a ConcreteColleague object, storing the Mediator
    object.  The created ConcreteColleague object is returned.
```

```
         * @modelguid {B1315B46-590C-4DDC-A39A-503457A27373}
        */
        public ConcreteColleague(Mediator mediator)
        {
            /*Begin Template Expansion*/

            // TO DO: You can customize the operation based on your application needs.

            this.mediator = mediator;

            /*End Template Expansion*/
        }

    }
```

Memento

The memento pattern takes a snapshot of an object's state so that the object can be returned to that state at a later point in time. A good example of this arises while you are implementing an Undo feature. If a user selects the Undo option, the system may need to return an object to its previous state.

Pattern Strategy

The memento pattern involves three primary classes. The originator class is the class whose state is stored. The originator can create a memento, where the memento is the class that stores the originator's state. The caretaker class requests the memento from the originator and keeps track of the memento. If the originator needs to go back to a previous state, the caretaker passes the memento back to the originator. Figure 10.27 shows the class diagram for the memento pattern.

FIGURE 10.27
Memento pattern class diagram

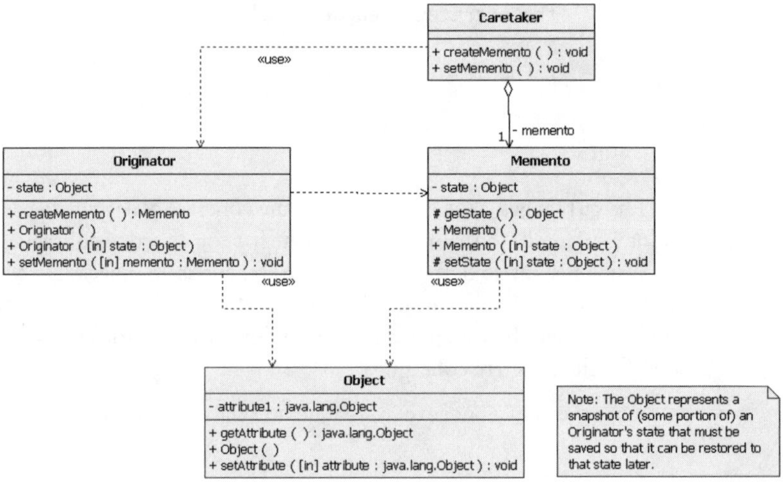

PROS AND CONS

You can use this pattern to save state information without having to encapsulate it in the originator. This allows the developer of the originator to focus on the originator's primary responsibilities, not the details of storing state information. It also helps simplify the design of the originator for the same reason—the designer doesn't put all of the state details in the originator.

One concern with this pattern is the overhead involved in storing and retrieving the state information. For the most part, this isn't a problem; storing the originator's state may be as simple as storing the values of an attribute or two. If, however, the state information is a little more complex, there is some overhead associated with storing and retrieving it.

PARTICIPANT DETAILS

In XDE, the memento takes four parameters:

- `Memento`
- `Caretaker`
- `Originator`
- `Object`

The `memento` class stores the state of the originator class. It contains an attribute called `state`, which is an object used to hold the originator's state. When it is instantiated, it can receive a state as a parameter, which is then placed in the `state` attribute. Later, the originator uses the `getState` method to retrieve the state. The memento class also has a `setState` method, which the originator or caretaker can use at any time to record the state of the originator. XDE generates standard get and set code for the `setState` and `getState` methods. `getState` simply returns the value of the state attribute, while `setState` updates the value of the state attribute.

The `caretaker` class is responsible for keeping track of the memento object. Its `createMemento` method creates a new originator and memento. The `setMemento` method creates a new originator and sets its state to the state stored in the memento. The code generated by XDE for these methods is shown here:

```
public void createMemento()
    {
        /*Begin Template Expansion*/

        // TO DO: You can customize the operation based on
        your application needs. The Caretaker requests a
        memento from the Originator.

        Originator anOriginator = new Originator();
        this.memento = anOriginator.createMemento();

        /*End Template Expansion*/
    }
```

```
public void setMemento()
    {
        /*Begin Template Expansion*/

        // TO DO: You can customize the operation based on
        your application needs. The Caretaker passes back
        the memento  to the Originator. /n
        Originator anOriginator = new Originator();
        anOriginator.setMemento(memento);

        /*End Template Expansion*/
    }

}
```

The `originator` object is the object whose state is stored. The originator class has an attribute called `state`. This attribute is an object that holds the current state of the originator. The `createMemento` method creates a new memento that can then be used to hold the originator's state. The `setMemento` method passes an existing memento back to the originator so that the originator can use it to return to a previous state. As with other methods in this pattern, XDE codes the `createMemento` and `setMemento` methods. The code for these two methods is shown here:

```
public Memento createMemento()
    {
        /*Begin Template Expansion*/

        // TO DO: You can customize the operation based on your application needs.

        return new Memento();

        /*End Template Expansion*/
    }

public void setMemento(Memento memento)
    {
        /*Begin Template Expansion*/

        // TO DO: You can customize the operation based on your application needs.

        this.state = memento.getState();

        /*End Template Expansion*/
    }
```

The `object` class is used to hold the state of the originator. Its attribute, `attribute1`, is an object that can be used to store the state. Frequently, you need to store a few attributes rather than just one to hold state information for the originator. If this is the case, simply add the new attributes to the object class.

Observer

You can use the observer pattern to notify one or more objects that another object has changed. For example, say you are working on an Internet-based ordering system. If customer 1 is in the middle of placing an order for yellow widgets, and in the meantime, customer 2 purchases the last yellow widget, you need to notify customer 1's order that yellow widgets are no longer available.

As another example, you may have a situation where data updated on one open screen needs to be automatically updated on another open screen. Any time you have objects that need to know about a state change in another object, use the observer pattern.

PATTERN STRATEGY

The pattern is made up of two key concepts. A *subject* is an object that, when changed, needs to notify other objects that it has been changed. An *observer* is an object that needs to know when the subject has changed. Once the observer is notified that the subject changed, it can act accordingly.

Figure 10.28 is a class diagram showing the observer participants.

FIGURE 10.28

Observer pattern class diagram

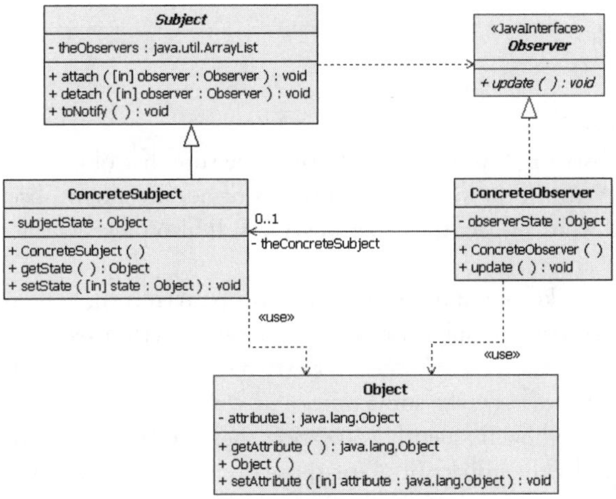

As you can see in the figure, the concrete subject class is inherited from a generic subject class. The generic subject class allows you to add and remove observers, and let observers know when the subject has changed. The concrete subject has methods that check or change the state of the concrete subject.

The pattern is implemented when an observer "subscribes" to the subject. When the subject is changed, it notifies all of its observers. Figure 10.29 shows a generic sequence diagram describing the pattern.

In this generic example, the object `aFirstConcreteObserver` makes a change to the subject using the `setState` method. The subject then calls its own `toNotify` method, which looks for all of the observers. The subject notifies each of the observers by calling the observer's `update` method. The observer then checks the state of the subject through the `getState` method and does whatever it needs to do to respond to the subject's change.

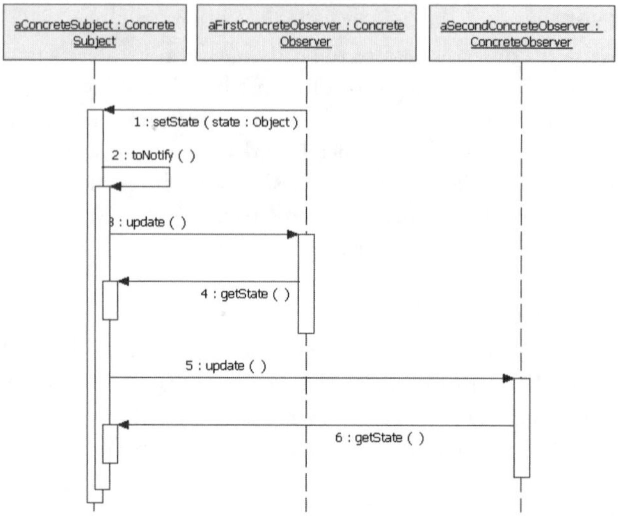

FIGURE 10.29
Observer pattern sequence diagram

PROS AND CONS

Using the observer pattern is a great way to be sure that objects are appropriately notified about significant events in the system. The process of adding a new observer dynamically is quite straightforward and won't impact the other observers. It also prevents the subject from having to know who its observers are.

One thing to keep in mind when using this pattern is the time you need to update all of the observing objects if the subject changes; this can directly affect the efficiency of your system. You may be able to update a single observer extremely quickly, but if there are 1,000 observers of a single subject, the update may take some time.

Consider also how frequently you expect these updates to occur. If the subject changes very frequently, consider the impact of all of those updates on the system.

PARTICIPANT DETAILS

There are five parameters in XDE for this pattern:

- `Subject`
- `Concrete subject`
- `Observer`
- `Concrete observer`
- `Object`

The `subject` parameter is the parent for the concrete subject class in the pattern. It has an attribute, `theObservers`, which is an array used to hold references to the subject's observers. A client can call the attach and detach methods to add or remove observers from the subject. A client can call the toNotify method to notify the concrete subject's observers that the concrete subject has changed.

XDE supplies code for the subject's methods, as follows:

```
public abstract class Subject
{
    /**
    This attribute stores a reference to an Observer.
     * @modelguid {4A2EE377-0A2A-4D3D-9710-0EDCB75384BE}
    */
    private java.util.ArrayList theObservers;

    /**
    This operation attaches an Observer object to the Subject object.
     * @modelguid {C28F9574-4088-4067-BAC8-232AD0C9041E}
    */
    public void attach(Observer observer)
    {
        /*Begin Template Expansion*/

        // TO DO: You can customize the operation based on your application needs.

        theObservers.add(observer);

        /*End Template Expansion*/
    }

    /**
    This operation removes an Observer object to the Subject object.
     * @modelguid {94A3F2A8-8135-43EE-955F-9C398D4B5C10}
    */
    public void detach(Observer observer)
    {
        /*Begin Template Expansion*/

        // TO DO: You can customize the operation based on your application needs.

        theObservers.remove(observer);

        /*End Template Expansion*/
    }

    /**
    This operation notifies the Subject object that a change has been observed.
     * @modelguid {E982750C-65A3-4D4C-8E55-1C8FC01618C2}
    */
    public void toNotify()
    {
```

```
        /*Begin Template Expansion*/

        // TO DO: All observers are notified whenever the
        subject undergoes a change in its state. You can customize
        // the operation based on your application needs.

        for (int i=1; i <= theObservers.size(); i++) {
           ((Observer) theObservers.get(i)).update();
        }

        /*End Template Expansion*/
    }

}
```

The concrete subject parameter is the class that is being observed for changes. It inherits the attributes and operations of the subject class and contains some additional attributes and operations. The subjectState attribute holds the state of the concrete subject. The getState and setState methods are used to retrieve and update the state of the concrete subject, respectively. XDE adds a constructor for the concrete subject. As with the subject class, XDE provides code for these methods, as shown here:

```
public class ConcreteSubject extends Subject
{
    /**
    The attribute is the state of the ConcreteSubject.
     * @modelguid {55ECDF12-0C14-433D-BECF-61CA1993C2BE}
    */
    private Object subjectState;

    /**
    This operation creates and returns a ConcreteSubject object.
     * @modelguid {7254EA04-22D0-480C-B8CA-7DD0FBD226A3}
    */
    public ConcreteSubject()
    {
        /*Begin Template Expansion*/

        // TO DO: You can customize the operation based on your application needs.
        // Add your custom code to invoke Subject::toNotify()
        in order to kick off the Observers.

        /*End Template Expansion*/
    }

    /**
    This operation returns the state of the ConcreteSubject object.
     * @modelguid {334B61FB-8DE3-4A02-974D-33B99EC2F124}
    */
```

```
    public Object getState()
    {
        /*Begin Template Expansion*/

        // TO DO: You can customize the operation based on your application needs.

        return this.subjectState;

        /*End Template Expansion*/
    }

    /**
    This operation sets the state of the ConcreteSubject object.
     * @modelguid {D0C7B395-F9C1-4C67-84B1-3553DB6B8F9E}
    */
    public void setState(Object state)
    {
        /*Begin Template Expansion*/

        // TO DO: You can customize the operation based on your application needs.

        subjectState = state;

        /*End Template Expansion*/
    }

}
```

The `observer` class is the interface created for the concrete observer. It contains only one operation, called `update`, which, when implemented, notifies the observer that the subject has changed. Because this is an interface class, XDE does not provide any code, other than the method name, in the generated source code files.

The `concrete observer` implements the observer interface; it is also the class that is notified when the subject changes. It has one attribute, `observerState`, which is used to hold the state of the concrete observer object. The `update` method gets the state of the concrete subject and sets the concrete observer's state to the same state. You can customize this method as needed to have the observer respond appropriately to the subject's change. XDE also adds a constructor method for the concrete observer. Here is the code that is generated for the concrete observer:

```
public class ConcreteObserver implements Observer
{
    /**
    This attribute represents the state of the ConcreteObserver.
     * @modelguid {4C931491-E8B0-4384-A5AF-CAADF4EF2FCA}
    */
    private Object observerState;

    /** @modelguid {4756AAC7-3F69-4FB5-A076-433EB782F059} */
```

```
    private ConcreteSubject theConcreteSubject;

    /**
    This operation creates and returns a ConcreteObserver.
     * @modelguid {CD20E5C3-1ED0-4B47-9A11-B1A7C4086570}
    */
    public ConcreteObserver()
    {
    }

    /**
    This operation updates the ConcreteObserver's state to be consistent with
    the ConcreteSubject's state.
     * @modelguid {A1CDFEE7-DFF3-4E1F-A2C4-A90D4FE1BBA3}
    */
    public void update()
    {
        /*Begin Template Expansion*/

        // TO DO: You can customize the operation based on
        your application needs. Each observer will query the subject
        // to synchronize its state with the subject's state.

        observerState = theConcreteSubject.getState();

        /*End Template Expansion*/
    }

}
```

Finally, you can use the `object` class to hold the state of another object. In this pattern, it is being used to hold the state of the concrete subject and concrete observer. By default, it contains an attribute called `attribute1`, which holds the state value. You can customize this class as needed, but here is the default code that is generated:

```
public class Object
{
    /** @modelguid {AF0712B1-7DD0-44FE-833F-383A98594474} */
    private java.lang.Object attribute1;

    /** @modelguid {F752E2B0-F7D3-42D8-BA11-FF22F65DA6C4} */
    public java.lang.Object getAttribute()
    {
        /*Begin Template Expansion*/

        // TO DO: You can customize the operation based on your application needs.

        return attribute1;
```

```
        /*End Template Expansion*/
    }

    /** @modelguid {FCF2730C-CE6F-4E27-A0FC-0A3B4762A6A9} */
    public void setAttribute(java.lang.Object attribute)
    {
        /*Begin Template Expansion*/

        // TO DO: You can customize the operation based on your application needs.

        this.attribute1 = attribute;

        /*End Template Expansion*/
    }

    /** @modelguid {D47591AB-9D78-4F7E-A3E5-5EBA983105B7} */
    public Object()
    {
    }

}
```

State

You can use this pattern to make an object appear as if its class has changed. You can also use it to change the behavior of an object when the state of the object changes. An example provided in *Design Patterns* is that of a TCP connection. The connection object can be in one of several different states: Established, Listening, or Closed. The connection object behaves differently, depending upon which state it is in. You can use the state pattern to simplify this process.

PATTERN STRATEGY

The pattern consists of three primary concepts: a *context*, a *state*, and a *concrete state*. A concrete state is a class that implements the behavior associated with a specific state. In the TCP connection example we mentioned earlier, we had three concrete states, one for Established, one for Listening, and one for Closed. The state is the interface to the concrete states such as these. The context is the objects whose state may change; it provides the interface to clients of the pattern.

The classes in this pattern are shown in Figure 10.30.

FIGURE 10.30

State pattern class diagram

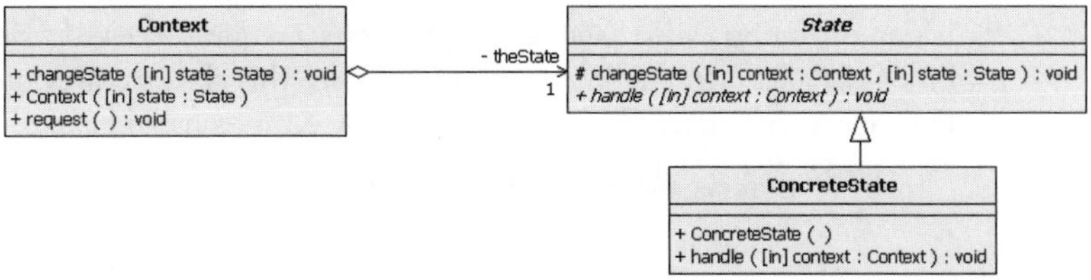

The context maintains a relationship with a concrete state object representing the context's current state. When the context receives a request from a client, it passes the request along to the concrete state object. If the state of the context changes, it replaces its reference to the current concrete state object with a new concrete state object. In the TCP example, when a connection is closed, the context (connection) replaces an instance of Established with an instance of Closed.

PROS AND CONS

Because the pattern encapsulates state behavior into concrete state classes, you should find that it becomes very easy to add a new state. All you need to do is create a new concrete state class. This pattern also helps keep the design and code of the context from becoming too complex because all of the state behavior has been moved to other classes. Specifically, it eliminates the need for such statements as those in the following pseudocode:

```
If the object is in this state
   Do this
Else if the object is in this other state
   Do something else
Else …
```

A few of these statements in the context are reasonable, but if numerous states exist, this type of code can quickly get overwhelming. The state pattern helps simplify the code by removing the need for these statements.

This pattern also makes the state transitions explicit. Without this pattern, you can use the values of one or more attributes to track the current state of an object, but you aren't explicitly tracking state; you're simply changing the values of some attributes. This pattern makes the state transitions explicit by instantiating or destroying specific state objects.

This pattern does require you to build and maintain more classes, but the concrete state classes tend to be small.

PARTICIPANT DETAILS

In XDE, this pattern has three participants:

- `State`
- `Concrete state`
- `Context`

The `concrete state` implements the behavior associated with the context in a specific state. It has an operation called `handle` that processes a request received from a context. XDE provides a little bit of default code, but you need to customize this class to carry out the behavior of the context in the appropriate state. The code generated by XDE is listed here:

```
public class ConcreteState extends State
{
    /**
    This operation handles a request from a Context object.
```

```
         * @modelguid {54346A88-17C6-4EA1-8A2B-0EF1014A24D0}
        */
        public void handle(Context context)
        {
            /*Begin Template Expansion*/

            // TO DO: You can customize the operation based on your application needs.
            // Be sure you provide the specific state class in this call.

            super.changeState(context, this);

            /*End Template Expansion*/
        }

        /**
        This operation creates a ConcreteState object, storing the state.  The
        created ConcreteState object is returned.
         * @modelguid {333F3D92-5873-47E1-A4A6-B294EE6F32CE}
        */
        public ConcreteState()
        {
        }

    }
```

The `state` interface provides a definition of the `handle` method implemented by the concrete state, and it also includes a `changeState` method to change the state of the context.

The `context` parameter defines the class whose state is changed using this pattern. The client works directly with the context; there is no need for the client to know that the state or concrete state classes exist. The context maintains an attribute called `theState`, which is a reference to the current concrete state object. When the client sends a request by calling the context's `request` method, the context passes the request along to the concrete state object in the `theState` attribute. The context's `request` method is shown here:

```
public void request()
    {
        /*Begin Template Expansion*/

        // TO DO: You can customize the operation based on
        your application needs. The request defines the
        interface of interest to clients.

        this.theState.handle(this);

        /*End Template Expansion*/
    }
```

Strategy

The strategy pattern is used to define a family of algorithms, encapsulate each one, and make them interchangeable. Using this pattern, you can let the algorithm vary independently from the clients that use it.

A frequently-used example of this pattern is the Save As functionality in many applications. Saving information in a text file is different from saving it into a spreadsheet, which is different from saving it in a graphics format. But you don't want to have to create complex conditional statements along the lines of this: "If the user selects a text file, save the information this way. If the user selects a spreadsheet, save the information this other way." The strategy pattern helps eliminate complex conditional statements used to select algorithms.

A few more examples of the strategy pattern include the following:

- Using different algorithms to break a string of text into multiple lines
- Plotting data in different formats, such as line charts or bar charts
- Using different algorithms for calculations, such as tax calculations
- Translating text into different languages
- Using different file compression methods to compress a file

PATTERN STRATEGY

The strategy pattern includes three classes. A *concrete strategy* provides the functionality for a specific algorithm. For example, you may have a concrete strategy for saving files in a text format and another concrete strategy for saving files in a spreadsheet format. All concrete strategies implement the same interface, called *strategy*. The third class is the *context*, which maintains a reference to the concrete strategy and provides an interface for clients of the pattern. Figure 10.31 shows the classes that participate in the strategy pattern.

Frequently, the client starts the process by instantiating a concrete strategy and passing it to the context. Alternatively, the context could create its own concrete strategy. Once the concrete strategy has been instantiated, the client works only with the context. The client begins by sending a request to the context. The context then sends the request to the appropriate concrete strategy. The context can send all of the information needed for the algorithm to the concrete strategy or it can simply send a reference to itself. If the context sends a reference, the concrete strategy object can call the context as needed to get information.

FIGURE 10.31
Strategy pattern class diagram

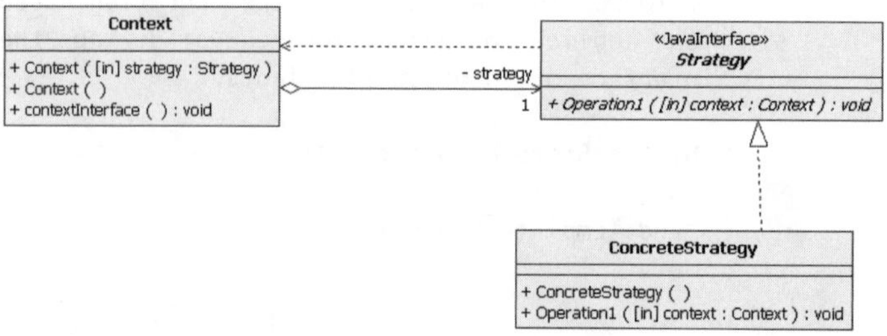

Typically, the client will not interact with the concrete strategy once the concrete strategy is implemented. The strategy pattern in XDE includes a sequence diagram that shows a slightly different approach. This approach is shown in Figure 10.32.

FIGURE 10.32

Strategy pattern sequence diagram

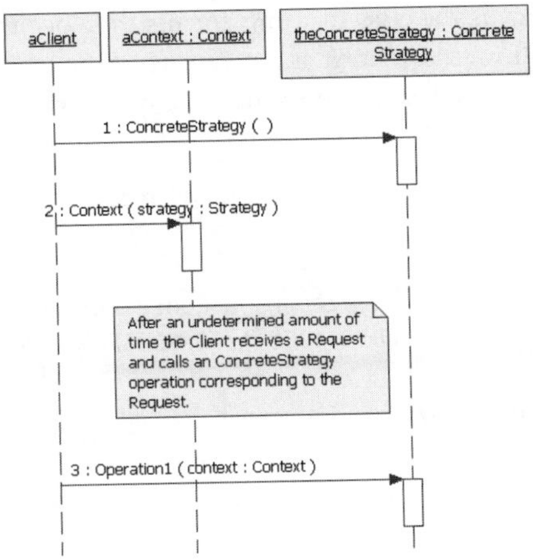

PROS AND CONS

You can use this pattern to organize families of algorithms and then use the appropriate one without having to put complex `IF` or `CASE` statements in your code. You can organize the algorithms into an inheritance structure to take advantage of any commonality among them. By separating out the algorithms, the pattern also makes each algorithm easier to understand and maintain.

The strategy pattern also gives you the option of dynamically deciding which algorithm should be implemented. This increases the flexibility of your application, especially at run-time. If the algorithms are fairly generic, you can also reuse them in future applications.

A disadvantage of using this pattern is that the client needs to understand the different concrete strategies to decide which one to instantiate and pass to the context. This pattern also increases the number of classes you need to build and maintain, and it may increase the number of objects instantiated at any one time.

PARTICIPANT DETAILS

The strategy pattern takes four parameters:

- `Strategy`
- `Concrete strategy`
- `Context`
- `Algorithm interface`

The `algorithm interface` parameter is a specific algorithm you create. In the example we discussed in the introduction to this "Strategy" section, the algorithm interface defines saving data to a text format or a spreadsheet format. In the diagram shown earlier in Figure 10.31, the algorithm interface is the `Operation1` method.

The `concrete strategy` is the class that implements the algorithm interface. It can either receive the information it needs from the context as a parameter, or it can receive a reference to the context itself. In XDE, the default code has the concrete strategy receiving a reference to the context, as shown here:

```
public class ConcreteStrategy implements Strategy
{
    /**
    This operation creates and returns a ConcreteStrategy object.
     * @modelguid {8F68C1F2-CD58-4BE8-A373-9D6BF0F4E28F}
    */
    public ConcreteStrategy()
    {
    }

    /**
    This operation implements the an algorithm interface.
     * @modelguid {8ECA985A-2D13-4DE7-A0A6-0B9C40C369A1}
    */
    public void Operation1(Context context)
    {
    }

}
```

Once it receives the reference to the context, the concrete strategy can call the context as needed to get information.

The `strategy` defines the interface for the concrete strategy classes. The `context` class maintains a relationship to the concrete strategy. The `client` interacts directly with the context to request some functionality.

Template

The template pattern lets you define the structure of an algorithm in a class but defer part of the implementation of the algorithm into subclasses. In other words, the parent class holds part of the algorithm's implementation while one or more subclasses implement the rest.

Pattern Strategy

Essentially what this pattern does is break down a complex algorithm into a series of smaller operations. The pieces of the algorithm that don't change are implemented in the operations of the parent class, while the pieces of the algorithm that are variable are overridden in the subclasses.

Operations for pieces of the algorithm that are implemented in the parent class are referred to as concrete operations. These are not intended to be overridden in the subclasses. The other portions of the algorithm can be implemented in one of two ways: the parent class can provide some default behavior, which can then be overridden in the subclasses if necessary; or the parent may have only an abstract operation, which must then be overridden in the subclasses. Figure 10.33 shows the participants in the template pattern.

FIGURE 10.33

Template pattern class diagram

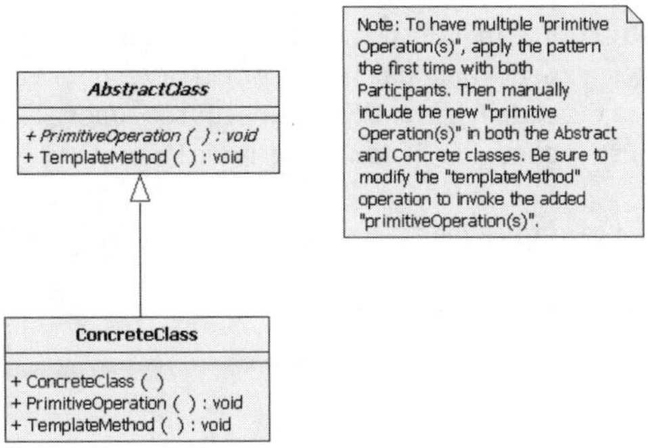
AbstractClass
+ PrimitiveOperation ( ) : void
+ TemplateMethod ( ) : void
ConcreteClass
+ ConcreteClass ( )
+ PrimitiveOperation ( ) : void
+ TemplateMethod ( ) : void
Note: To have multiple "primitive Operation(s)", apply the pattern the first time with both Participants. Then manually include the new "primitive Operation(s)" in both the Abstract and Concrete classes. Be sure to modify the "templateMethod" operation to invoke the added "primitiveOperation(s)".

PROS AND CONS

This pattern breaks a complex algorithm down into simpler ones. Because breaking down a complex algorithm can make it easier to understand and maintain, using this pattern can help you design, build, and maintain your system more easily. It also allows you to reuse code; you can reuse all or a portion of the algorithm's classes in another, similar algorithm.

PARTICIPANT DETAILS

The template pattern takes four parameters:

- `Abstract class`
- `Concrete class`
- `Primitive operation`
- `Template method`

The `abstract class` defines the structure for the algorithm. It may implement portions of the algorithm functionality, or it may leave the implementation entirely to its subclasses. It contains the `template` method, which is the complex algorithm being implemented using the template pattern. The complex algorithm is broken down into one or more template methods, which are defined in the abstract class and implemented in the subclasses. The following is an example of the code for an abstract class:

```
public abstract class AbstractClass
{
    /**
    This operation defines a skeleton of an algorithm using the abstract
    primitive operations for steps in the algorithm.
```

```
        * @modelguid {93E24183-A299-41C9-9E13-D08F71E2B02D}
        */
        public void TemplateMethod()
        {
            /*Begin Template Expansion*/

            // TO DO: You can customize the operation based on your application needs.
            // Add your code and call the primitive operations.
            The primitive operation is your custom operation
            defined/selected  in/from  the model.

            // this.PrimitiveOperation();

            /*End Template Expansion*/
        }

        /**
        This abstract operation must be implemented by a ConcreteClass to be used
        in implementing a step of a algorithm.
         * @modelguid {2F9DE990-FB3B-4F24-B66A-611CC7718F54}
        */
        public abstract void PrimitiveOperation();

    }
```

The concrete class is one of the subclasses of the abstract class. It implements one or more of the primitive operations that make up the complex algorithm. The following is the XDE-generated code for a concrete class:

```
public class ConcreteClass extends AbstractClass
{
    /**
    This operation creates and returns a ConcreteClass object.
     * @modelguid {4896595A-9A1D-4B60-8CB5-00DC7A68F9C3}
    */
    public ConcreteClass()
    {
    }

    /**
    This operation implements a primitive operation to perform a step in the
    algorithm defined in the AbstractClass.
     * @modelguid {F416C651-086C-4994-B174-0F1B88987C6A}
    */
    public void PrimitiveOperation()
    {
    }

    /**
```

```
        This operation calls one or more primitiveOperations.
         * @modelguid {AAF3C167-EE40-43E3-81D7-F1B5926803E3}
        */
        public void TemplateMethod()
        {
        }

    }
```

Visitor

The visitor pattern is used to define a new operation without dramatically changing the classes of the elements on which it operates. In other words, the visitor pattern encapsulates a new method into its own class. The visitor class has methods that act on data held in other classes. This pattern lets you add a new method without having to change any existing classes, other than adding an `accept` method to the existing classes. This pattern is useful if one or more of the following are true:

- You need new functionality that acts on data in existing classes, but you don't have the option of changing the existing classes dramatically.
- You want to perform an operation on the data contained in a number of objects that have different interfaces.
- You have a number of small operations you'd like to add, but you don't want to change your existing classes.

PATTERN STRATEGY

The *visitor* visits the objects in the object structure that have given the visitor permission to visit. Each object in the object structure is an instance of a *concrete element*. The concrete elements all implement the *element* interface, which has one method definition called `accept`. Because the concrete elements all implement the `accept` method, the visitor can be accepted by all concrete elements and can potentially visit all of them. In other words, the concrete elements have all given the visitor permission to drop by.

As an analogy, think of the object structure as a street. The concrete elements are all of the houses along the street. The people in the houses all have a front door, which is analogous to the `accept` operation. We're assuming that by deciding to have a front door, the people in the houses have agreed to have visitors.

The classes in the visitor pattern are shown in Figure 10.34.

The visitor includes operations that act on the data in the concrete elements. In our analogy, this means that the visitor knows how to come in and rearrange all of your furniture or eat all the food in your refrigerator. Note that this isn't a traditional object-oriented approach. We're allowing one object to access and manipulate the data contained in another. There are, however, situations in which this is acceptable.

The process begins when the object structure tells a concrete element that it should accept a visitor. The concrete element calls the `visitConcreteElement` operation of the visitor, letting the visitor know that it can visit. A parameter to the `visistConcreteElement` operation is a reference to the concrete element, so that the visitor can operate on the concrete element. The process is shown in Figure 10.35.

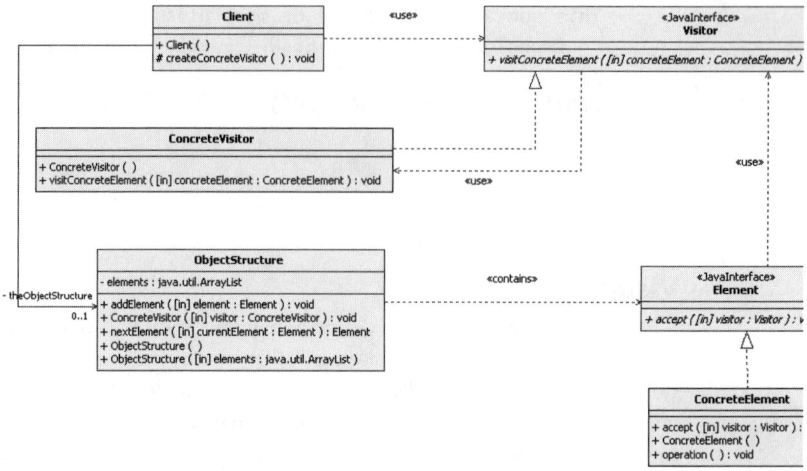

FIGURE 10.34
Visitor pattern class diagram

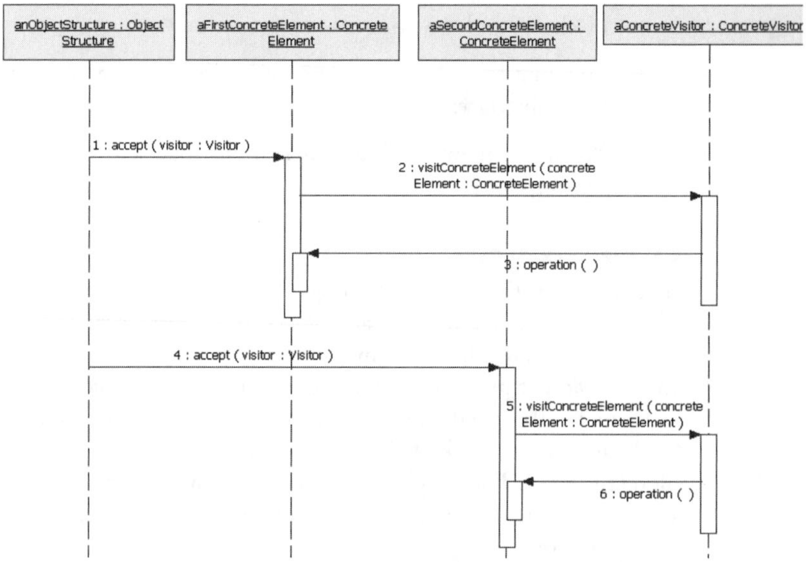

FIGURE 10.35
Visitor pattern sequence diagram

PROS AND CONS

Using this pattern is a good way to add functionality without having to make major modifications to any existing classes. It lets you encapsulate small, related operations into a single class rather than spreading them across multiple classes. At the same time, it lets you put unrelated operations in their appropriate classes. It provides an easy way to add new operations; all you need to do is create a new visitor or add a new method to an existing visitor. It can visit any class, so the elements do not have to be related to accept a visitor.

You must add the `accept` method to every element that the visitor may visit, or you must inherit all of the elements from a common ancestor with an `accept` method.

PARTICIPANT DETAILS

The visitor pattern has six participants:

- Visitor
- Concrete visitor
- Element
- Concrete element
- Object structure
- Client

The concrete element is the class that holds data the visitor will be manipulating. It implements an accept method, which the object structure calls to tell the concrete element to tell the visitor that it can visit. The concrete element also has other operations, such as Operation1 in Figure 10.34, shown earlier. The element interface defines the accept operation for the concrete element classes.

The object structure is a container that holds the concrete element instances. It has an attribute called elements, which is a collection of concrete elements and operations for adding and removing elements from itself. It also has a ConcreteVisitor method, which the client uses to let the object structure know which visitor to use. When the ConcreteVisitor method is invoked, the object structure tells all of its elements to accept the visitor. The following is the code for the ConcreteVisitor method of the object structure:

```
public void ConcreteVisitor(ConcreteVisitor visitor)
    {
        /*Begin Template Expansion*/

        // TO DO: You can customize the operation based on your application needs.

        for (int i=1; i <= elements.size(); i++) {
           ((Element) this.elements.get(i)).accept(visitor); [AU: purple]
        }

        /*End Template Expansion*/
    }
```

The concrete visitor is the class that accesses the elements in the object structure. It has a method called visitConcreteElement, which is used to inform the concrete visitor that it may visit a concrete element. This method takes a reference to the concrete element as a parameter. Once it has been given permission to access a concrete element, the concrete visitor can use the public interface of the concrete element. The visitor interface defines the visitConcreteElement method of the concrete visitor.

Finally, the client is responsible for instantiating the visitor and the object structure (although it could instead receive a reference to one or both). Once it has an instance of the visitor and the object structure, the client passes the visitor reference to the object structure. The object structure can then call the accept method of its concrete elements.

Exercise: Considering Patterns

Now that you have learned about the various patterns available, it's time to determine if any should be used in our Timekeeping application. Think about the different patterns discussed in this chapter and select six patterns that *could* be applied to this application. Applying some of the patterns may involve fleshing out some details about the timekeeping system. To get the creative juices flowing, the adapter pattern could be applied to the paycode class if the paycodes are retrieved from a legacy system. One strategy you could use to retrieve the paycodes would be to go directly to a database table and get them. A more elegant solution would use the adapter pattern to adapt the interface of the paycode class to the interface for paycodes in the legacy system.

To give you a hint in selecting the six patterns, we came up with specific situations for applying the following patterns:

- Abstract Factory
- Adapter
- Builder
- Command
- Façade
- Factory Method
- Iterator
- Mediator
- Memento
- Observer
- Singleton
- State
- Strategy

Once you have identified at least six potential patterns to implement, use the steps in Chapter 9 to actually implement one of those patterns. We implemented the patterns earlier in the accompanying model.

Summary

In this chapter, we examined the 23 patterns in the Gang-of-Four library provided with XDE. You can use any or all of these patterns in your application by right-clicking an element on a diagram or in the Model Explorer and selecting Apply Favorite Pattern.

There are three types of GOF patterns. Creational patterns deal with the creation of classes and objects. Structural patterns are concerned with how classes or objects might be grouped together to form larger structures. Behavioral patterns are concerned with how responsibilities are allocated among objects and how objects and classes are related.

For each pattern, we discussed why the pattern would be used, how the pattern works, any advantages and disadvantages of the pattern, the parameters of the pattern, and the code generated for the pattern. For more information about the structure of these patterns, please refer to *Design Patterns*, cited at the beginning of this chapter.

In Chapter 12, "Creating Your Own Patterns," we go through the process of adding a new pattern in XDE. First, however, it is important that we discuss the concept of Reusable Asset Specifications. These are discussed next in Chapter 11, "Introduction to Reusable Asset Specifications."

Chapter 11

Introduction to Reusable Asset Specifications

RATIONAL SOFTWARE RECENTLY DEVELOPED a specification to make the reuse of project artifacts and other assets easier and more standardized. This specification is known as a *Reusable Asset Specification* (RAS). In XDE, the RAS can be used to package assets together and then to reuse these assets in other XDE models. In this chapter, we examine the structure and content of reusable asset specifications and discuss how to create and use them in XDE.

Featured in this chapter:

- Defining an asset
- Working with assets
- Assets in XDE
- Creating a reusable asset specification
- Documenting a reusable asset specification
- Importing a reusable asset specification

What Is an Asset?

As an industry, information technology has been working with the idea of *reuse* for some time now. We started off by very haphazardly grabbing code from one system and reusing it in another. Then we got a little more organized and started developing more formal ways of tracking and reusing existing code.

What we haven't done yet is expand this idea to analysis, design, testing, or other areas of the systems development life cycle. Some industries have; in fact there are some organizations that have accomplished a great deal with reuse. The information technology industry, however, is just starting to put these ideas into practical use.

Reusable asset specifications (which we will refer to as "assets" for the remainder of this chapter) are pieces of design, code, testing, analysis, and so on, that combine to form a solution that can be understood and reused. Simply put, an asset is a collection of artifacts. More specifically, it is a collection of artifacts that allows the asset to be both understood and applied. The artifacts in the asset could be any one of the following:

- Requirements artifacts, such as software requirement specifications, supplementary specifications, or requirements management plans
- Design artifacts, such as UML diagrams, Rose or XDE models, or database design models
- Development artifacts, such as source code, libraries, or executable files
- Testing artifacts, such as test cases, test scripts, or a test plan
- Configuration management artifacts, such as a configuration management plan
- Deployment artifacts, such as deployment scripts or a deployment plan
- Standards or guidelines
- Management artifacts, such as cost or schedule estimates or risk management plans
- Any other document or artifact that can be used to understand and apply the asset

By itself, a collection of artifacts doesn't tell you much. You also need to know the problem that the collection of artifacts is trying to solve and how you can apply the collection to your projects. So, the RAS also contains information related to the problem and to the application of the asset.

Working with Assets

In this section, we look at the activities involved in setting up and using assets. There are four fundamental processes involved in working with assets:

- Identifying new assets that can be reused
- Packaging new assets into Reusable Asset Specifications
- Maintaining existing assets
- Using assets in projects

All of these are explained in detail in the following sections.

Identifying New Assets

Traditionally, developers were the ones to look for reusable pieces of code and to keep libraries of the pieces of code they found. In the RAS world, however, we can reuse just about anything, from requirements to code.

Therefore, there's a little shift in our thinking. The entire team should be responsible for looking for artifacts that can be packaged and reused. One strategy is for the team to review all of the artifacts at the end of a project, specifically for the purpose of finding artifacts that might be reused. Another approach is to ask the team to identify potentially reusable artifacts as the project goes along.

Here are a few questions to consider when you are looking at an artifact or group of artifacts and deciding whether it can be reused:

- Is this artifact or group of artifacts fairly generic, or is it very specific to a particular system or problem domain? The more generic it is, the easier it may be to apply to future systems.
- If the artifact or group of artifacts isn't very generic, is there a way to modify it to make it more generic for future application?
- Does this artifact or group of artifacts represent a new or improved way to solve a specific problem?
- Can you say specifically what problem the artifact or group of artifacts is trying to solve?
- Could the artifact or group of artifacts be reused alone?
- If the artifact or group of artifacts cannot be reused alone, what other artifacts would need to be reused also?
- Is the artifact or group of artifacts a reasonable size? It may be difficult, for example, to reuse a group of 300 artifacts.

These are just a few sample questions. You may find it helpful to develop a more comprehensive list for your organization. Once you have the list, be sure everyone on the team understands how to identify artifacts that might be reused.

After the team identifies an artifact or group of artifacts for potential reuse, they should take the time to conduct a thorough quality assurance check on the artifact. After all, it can do more harm than good to reuse an artifact that is flawed.

Packaging New Assets into Reusable Asset Specifications

Once the team identifies a new asset, they should properly package it for reuse. A RAS has four parts:

- Overview
- Classification
- Solution
- Usage

Together, these parts give you a complete picture of the asset, the problem it is solving, and how it can be applied.

NOTE *Please note that the RAS is currently evolving and that the final specification may differ from what is presented here.*

The logical structure of an asset is shown in Figure 11.1.

FIGURE 11.1
RAS logical structure

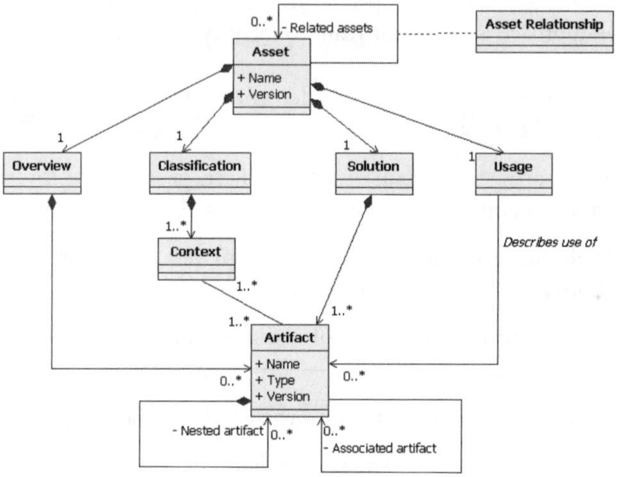

As shown in Figure 11.1, an asset contains one overview section, one classification section, one solution section, and one usage section, and may be related to zero or more other assets. The classification section defines the context(s) in which the asset may be applied. Each of the four sections (overview, classification, solution, and usage) is related to zero or more of the artifacts in the asset. Each of the artifacts in the asset may be related to other assets contained within that asset, or to other assets associated with that asset.

COMPLETING THE OVERVIEW SECTION

The overview section defines why the asset was created in the first place. It includes the following information:

Asset overview An abstract of the asset, the problem it solves, and the solution it provides.

Intent and motivation A description of the motivating factors and the intended use of the asset.

Problem description A description of the problem for which the asset provides a solution.

Applicability A description of the intended targets to which the asset may be applied.

Related assets An overview of any assets that may be related to this asset.

Standards Any standards that the asset may submit to or be compliant with.

Support A description of any support issues that the asset may have.

The intent of this section is to help the reader understand what the asset is and how it can be applied.

Completing the Classification Section

The classification section includes classification schemas and descriptors for the structure of the asset. The classification section also describes the context(s) in which the asset may be applied. We first discuss descriptors and then return to the subject of contexts.

Descriptors

A classification is made up of one or more descriptor groups, each of which contains one or more descriptor name-value pairs. This structure of a classification is shown in Figure 11.2.

FIGURE 11.2
Classification structure

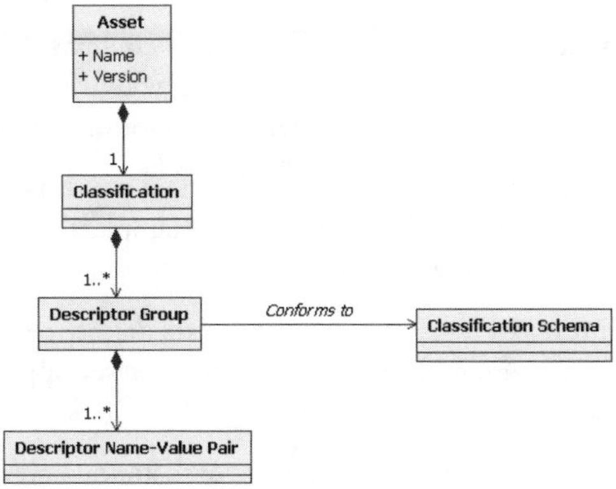

A *descriptor* is a piece of information used to classify an asset. Some examples of descriptors include the following:

- Type of asset
- Author of the asset
- Creation/modification date of the asset
- Technologies used by the asset
- Version of the asset
- Problem solved by the asset
- Asset ID

Any piece of information you want to collect about an asset can be included as a descriptor. In the classification section, you list the desired descriptors, along with their values, as *descriptor name-value pairs.*

A *descriptor group* is a collection or grouping of these descriptors. As shown previously in Figure 11.2, a descriptor group can contain one or more descriptor name-value pairs. The classification section can contain one or more descriptor groups. The descriptor groups help you organize the descriptors into meaningful sections.

The final piece of Figure 11.2 is the *classification schema*, a standard set of descriptors to use in an asset. If you are using a classification schema, the set of descriptors and descriptor groups you use is dictated by the schema.

Contexts

A context is a perspective of the asset. There are several different types of contexts in a RAS:

Artifact context Any given artifact may have multiple contexts associated with it. These contexts could be any of the other contexts in this list.

Asset deployment context The asset deployment contexts define the deployment environments within which the asset may be reused. For example, you may list the specific operating systems that the asset requires or the hardware requirements for deploying software using the asset.

Asset development context The asset development contexts define the development environments within which the asset may be reused. For example, these assets may list the programming language(s) supported by the asset.

Asset domain context The asset domain contexts define the domain(s) in which the asset may be applied. You may, for example, have an asset that can be applied in the banking industry but is not suitable for the manufacturing industry.

Asset root context The root context is the asset's logical entry point. This could be a filesystem location, as in this example:

> Asset artifacts and documentation are located in `F:\ACMEAsset`.

Or a model location, as in this example:

> Asset artifacts and documentation are located in the XDE model `ACMEAssetLibrary.mdx`.

Every asset has one and only one root context.

Asset reuse scope context The asset reuse scope context describes the scope of intended reuse. For example, an asset may have a scope of reuse of "project level," "team level," "department level," or "product line level."

Asset text context The asset text contexts define the testing configurations that should be used to validate the asset.

These different contexts help the team understand how the asset may be applied. In other words, they define the business, technological, and other requirements for applying the asset. The structure of these contexts is shown in Figure 11.3.

As you can see in the figure, a classification includes one or more contexts. A root context must be provided, but the other types of contexts are optional.

FIGURE 11.3

Context structure

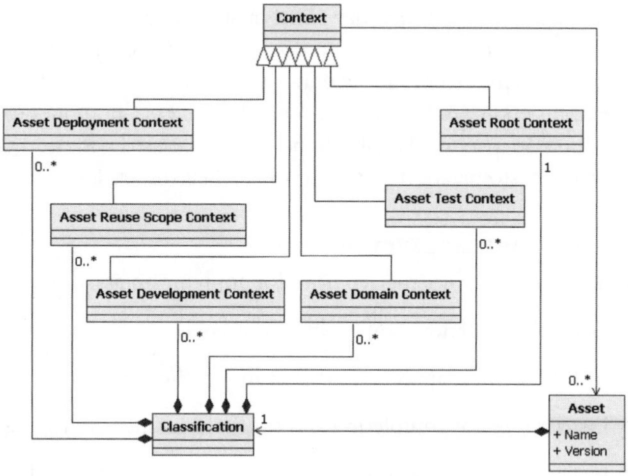

COMPLETING THE SOLUTION SECTION

The solution section is the collection of artifacts that constitute the solution. This section is the core of the asset; it contains the analysis, design, code, test, or other artifacts that make up the asset. Figure 11.4 shows the structure of the solution section.

The solution contains one or more artifacts, each of which may be related to other artifacts. An artifact must also be related to at least one context, the root context, and it may also be related to other contexts, suggesting that the artifact is applicable only in a certain context, or that the artifact structure or content varies in different contexts.

FIGURE 11.4

Solution structure

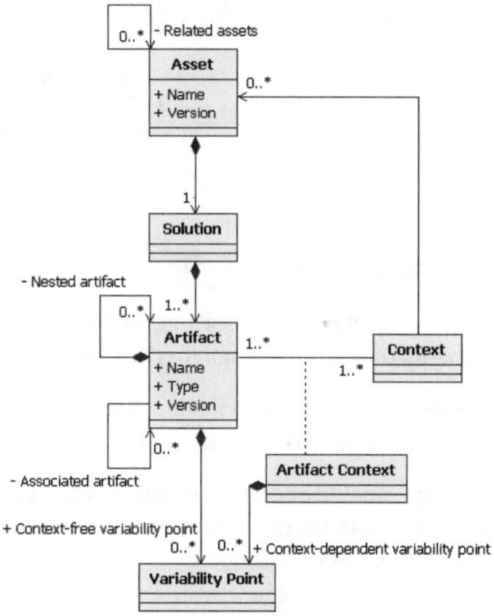

An artifact may have *variability points* associated with it. A variability point defines a location within the artifact that may be customized. For example, you may have an artifact that is formatted differently when the asset is applied in a .NET or a Java context.

A variability point may be context-free. In this case, it applies to the artifact regardless of the context. A context-dependent variability point is associated with both an artifact and a context and suggests that the customization can occur only when the artifact is used in a particular context.

COMPLETING THE USAGE SECTION

The usage section defines the activities for applying an asset. In particular, this section provides

- General instructions for applying the asset
- Instructions for applying the asset in specific contexts
- Instructions for completing and using the artifacts in the asset
- Instructions for customizing the artifacts (using the variability points) in general or in specific contexts

The structure of the usage section is shown in Figure 11.5.

FIGURE 11.5

Usage structure

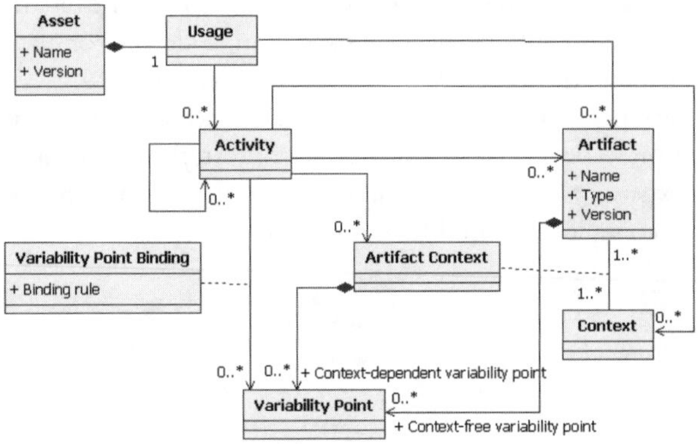

REUSABLE ASSET SPECIFICATION PROFILES

The sections we've just described (overview, classification, solution, and usage) are the core components of a RAS. These are required elements that any extension to the specification must include.

However, the RAS specification is intended to be extended. Some specific extensions being considered are specifications for a design pattern, a framework, or a component. These extensions are referred to as profiles.

These profiles, once developed, may include additional specification components. Please refer to Rational Software's website, `www.Rational.com`, for updated information on the profiles. Rational also provides information that helps you create your own profiles.

The usage section contains one or more activities. An *activity* is a step or process that must occur to apply the asset. The activities may be specific to a context, or they may apply to the asset regardless of the context. In addition, an activity can apply either to specific artifacts or to specific artifacts in a specific context.

PHYSICAL STRUCTURE OF AN ASSET

Once the team logically develops the asset, they can put the needed information into physical files. A RAS is represented by an XML file, which contains the following:

- Overview documents
- Descriptors
- Activities
- Variability point bindings
- Solution artifacts (models, code, tests, and so on)

The XML file can point to directories that contain the physical files that the sections of the XML file reference. Figure 11.6 shows an example.

FIGURE 11.6

Physical structure of an asset

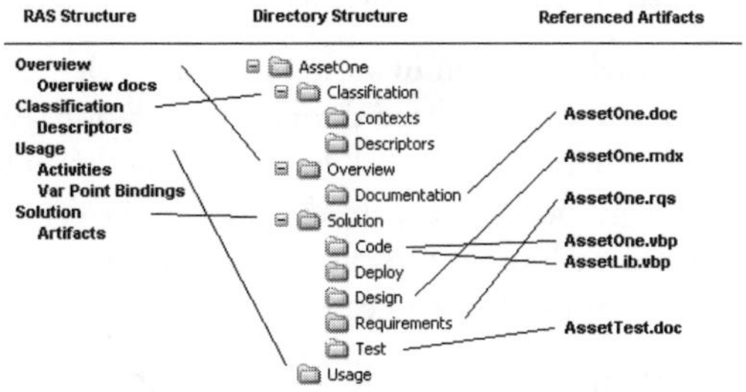

Maintaining Existing Assets

As we discussed in Chapter 9, "Using Patterns," someone needs to maintain the library of available assets. Many organizations have a role called *object librarian*. This individual or group is responsible for organizing, storing, and maintaining the reusable assets.

Organizing the assets can be a simple or a complex effort, depending upon the number of assets you have and how you expect to retrieve them. In the simplest form of organization, you can maintain a list of the assets and store all of them in one place. Another strategy is to organize the asset by one of the contexts. For example, you could use the technological contexts to group the assets into Visual Basic, C++, C#, Java, and other collections, based on the programming language of the asset.

For a more elaborate organizational structure, you would take two or more of the contexts into account. For example, you may want to group assets by domain and then by development context, or by reuse scope context and then by development context. No matter how you decide to organize the assets, be sure that the organizational structure is applied consistently.

Storing the assets is a matter of moving the files to a central directory or repository. Using XDE, you can create libraries of patterns that can be used in the XDE models for future projects.

Maintaining the assets is a lot like maintaining a system. When an asset needs to change, first ask why the change needs to take place. It could be, for example, that a change has taken place in the asset's business domain and the asset needs to be adjusted accordingly.

Once you've defined what needs to change, the changes should be analyzed, designed, implemented, tested, and released. For larger changes in particular, you may want to consider doing this in an iterative manner.

Using Assets in Projects

Developing reusable assets is only half the story; without applying those assets to future projects, you haven't gained much.

When you begin a new project, one thing to consider is how much you might be able to reuse from past projects. At the beginning of the project, you may not know yet how much can be reused, but at the very least you may be able to get a rough idea. As the project goes along, more requirements are elicited, and the architecture is developed, you may be able to identify new opportunities for reuse. The following are a few suggestions for where you can look for reuse opportunities:

At the beginning of the project You may not have many of the requirements yet, but chances are that you know enough about the project to identify some initial reuse candidates. Focus on the business domain context and look for assets in that domain. If you know what development environment or deployment environment you have, you can also look for assets with those environments.

At the beginning of each iteration in an iterative lifecycle At the beginning of an iteration, look at the work that will be completed during that iteration. As you progress through the project, the requirements and architecture will become more thoroughly defined. With this knowledge, look for assets that might be applicable to the work in the current iteration. Performing this exercise at the beginning of each project iteration can help you be sure you keep reuse in mind and take advantage of reuse as much as you can.

During each iteration in an iterative lifecycle While you may set up a more formal review or discussion to look for reuse opportunities at the beginning of each iteration, the team should always be looking for these types of opportunities informally. As team members do their work, they may encounter a common problem that can be solved with a reusable asset. A developer may, for example, run across a problem such as security monitoring that has already been solved with a security component.

It's important, therefore, that all the team members know where they can find reusable assets if they need them. The object librarian should let everyone know what assets are available and how they can be accessed.

During each phase of a waterfall lifecycle At the beginning of the project, look for assets in the problem domain of your current project. As you gather the requirements, continue to look at the asset domain contexts to find assets in the current problem domain. Look at the asset reuse scope context to find assets applicable to the requirements group. During design and development, also look at the asset development context to find assets that apply to the current development environment, and look at the asset deployment context to find assets that apply to the environment you will be deploying into. During testing, look at the asset text context to find assets that apply to the testing environment. Finally, when you are preparing for deployment, look at the asset deployment context.

Assets in XDE

Now that we have introduced the concept of an asset and described its components, we turn to asset development and use in XDE. In XDE, a RAS is a model containing code templates, patterns, or both. This means that while you would generally convert a pattern into a RAS, you can convert it to a model instead.

For a pattern to be converted into a RAS, the following must be true:

- The package or model owning the pattern must have the stereotype <<Asset>>.
- The pattern must be linked to an XML documentation file with a RAS format.
- The pattern must have a root context.

Using the Add Pattern Asset option to create a pattern creates a pattern that can be converted into a RAS. We discuss pattern creation in Chapter 12, "Creating Your Own Patterns."

Reusable Asset Specifications are created using XDE's export option. Once they have been created, they can be imported into other XDE models. In the following sections, we discuss how to create and import a RAS.

Creating a Reusable Asset Specification

As we just mentioned, a model does not need to have any patterns in it to package it as a RAS. Creating a RAS enables you to package the patterns and artifacts of an asset. You can then import this package into another XDE model or give it to someone else on your team to use.

To export a RAS asset:

1. Choose File ➢ Export, which brings up the Export dialog box:

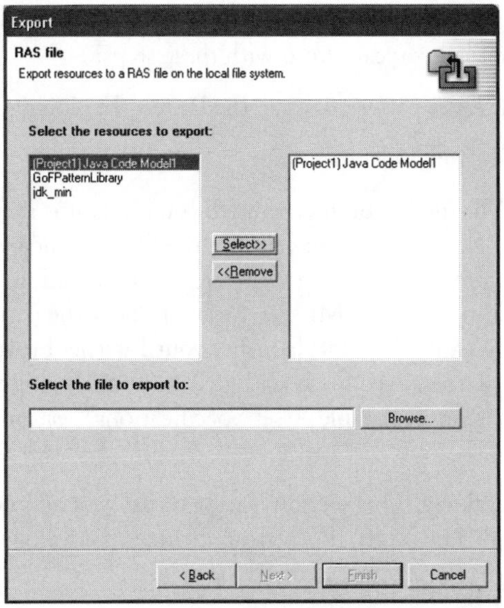

2. Select a RAS file, and then click Next, which brings up a listing of the package assets in the current model.
3. Select the asset to export and click Select. The selected asset is moved to the right-hand box.
4. Repeat step 3 for any other resources you'd like to add to the asset.
5. Select a location and enter a filename for the new RAS.
6. Click Finish to complete the process.

Once you've completed this process, XDE will have generated a file with a `.ras` extension. This file is a Zip archive, containing the asset and the following associated XML schema:

- `RASAsset.xsd`, which is an XML schema file.
- `Rasset.xml`, which is the primary XML document for the asset.
- A number of additional XML files, one for each of the artifacts associated with the asset. These files are named `resource1.xml`, `resource2.xml`, and so on.

Documenting a Reusable Asset Specification

Each RAS has an associated XML file that the asset developer can use to document the asset. The asset may also optionally have an associated HTML file, which can be used as user documentation. The XML file serves as a template for the HTML file. You need to edit the HTML file to add information related to the asset, such as the author, version, and so on.

When you create a pattern (see Chapter 12), XDE can automatically create the XML and HTML files for you. Check to be sure the Add Documentation property is enabled when you create the pattern; we'll return to this in Chapter 12.

If you didn't have XDE create the XML and HTML files for you, or if you'd like to manually regenerate these files, you can do so with these steps:

1. Right-click the pattern asset in the Pattern Explorer.
2. Select Generate Documentation.

After the XML file has been generated, you can edit it if you want to change the structure. Once you've made any changes, you can generate the HTML file by right-clicking the pattern asset again in the Pattern Explorer and selecting Generate Documentation.

To view the generated HTML file, locate it under the pattern asset in the Model Explorer and double-click it. As a result, XDE launches your Internet browser and loads the file.

The format of the XML file is set by XDE. It conforms to the RAS we discussed in the "Packaging New Assets into Reusable Asset Specifications" section earlier in this chapter. The layout is as follows:

Overview section This section is used to list general information about the asset. In the XML format provided by XDE, this section includes the following:

- Asset version
- Asset creation date

- Asset name
- Profile ID
- Profile name
- Profile version

Classification section This section is used to record additional attributes about the asset. The classification section generated by XDE includes the following:

- Author
- Packager
- Keyword
- Problem solved
- Benefit
- Liability
- Known uses
- Template parameter descriptions

Solution section This section is used to list the artifacts that are included in this asset. In the HTML file, this section will include links to the artifacts.

Usage section This section is used to describe how the asset can be applied. In the HTML file, you add text that describes how the asset can be used.

Related asset section This section is used to list any other assets that are related to the current asset. In the HTML file, you can add links to documentation for related assets, or you can describe the related assets directly in the HTML file.

Once you've made any changes to the XML file and generated the HTML file, edit the following information in the HTML file:

- In the overview section, add the asset version and asset name.
- In the classification section, add values for all of the descriptors.
- In the solution section, add links to the artifacts in the asset.
- In the usage section, describe how the asset can be applied.
- In the related asset section, list and describe any other assets that are related to this one.

Importing a Reusable Asset Specification

You can import a RAS into an XDE model. This functionality gives you the ability to share reusable assets with the other members of your team. To import an existing RAS asset, follow these steps:

1. Choose File ➢ Import.

2. From the list of import options, select RAS. Click Next to continue, which takes you to the Import RAS dialog box:

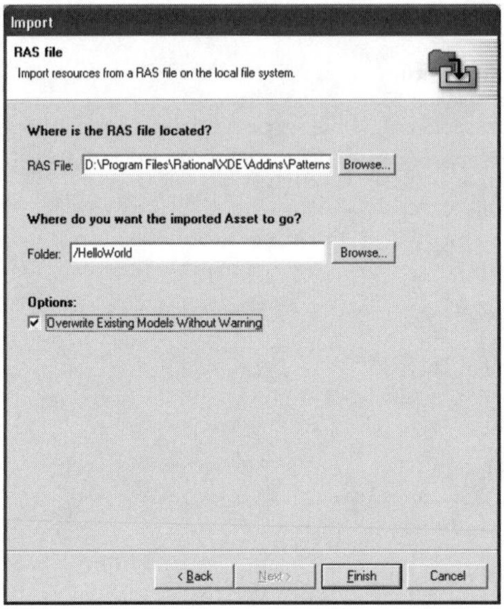

3. Locate the RAS file to import.
4. Select the project and folder into which the RAS should be imported.
5. Select the Overwrite Existing Models Without Warning check box if you want to replace an existing model with the same name as the RAS you are importing.
6. Click Finish to complete the process.

NOTE *The Reusable Asset Specification is used to package patterns. The file structure is XML and the file can be created from the pattern in XDE. For this reason, there is no exercise for Chapter 11. The exercise in Chapter 12 gives you experience in creating your own pattern. Once you have created one, we show you how to save a Reusable Asset Specification for that pattern.*

Summary

In this chapter, we examined the structure of a RAS. This specification was developed by Rational for the purpose of allowing team members to share reusable patterns and artifacts.

An asset that has been placed in the RAS format contains four primary items: an overview section, a classification section, a solution section, and a usage section.

The overview of the asset provides general information about the asset, such as its name and purpose.

The classification section provides more detailed information about the asset. These details are included in the form of descriptors, where each descriptor is a piece of information about the asset.

Examples of descriptors include the author of the asset, the version of the asset, or the asset ID. The classification section also includes contexts, where the contexts describe the business, technological, or other environments in which the asset can be used.

The solution section groups the artifacts that are contained in the asset. The HTML documentation for the asset includes links to each of the artifacts in the solution section.

Finally, the usage section describes how to use the asset. It lists the specific activities that need to occur to apply the asset, and it describes how the activities might vary in different contexts.

XDE provides support for the RAS by allowing you to export a file in RAS format. When you do, XDE automatically creates an XML file for the asset in RAS format. XDE can also generate an HTML file using the XML file as a template. The HTML file can then serve as user documentation for the asset.

In the next chapter, we discuss how to create your own patterns using XDE. Once you've created a pattern, you can export it into a RAS file so that it can be used in other models and by other team members.

Chapter 12

Creating Your Own Patterns

WE INTRODUCED YOU TO the power of patterns in Rational XDE in the preceding three chapters. Patterns can help you keep applications consistent and reduce the amount of time you need to build or test an application. Because they are proven and tested, the patterns can also increase the quality of an application. Now, we show you how you can extend this functionality even more by creating your own patterns.

The first step is to identify patterns, as described in Chapter 10, "Gang-of-Four Patterns." In brief, the team should always keep an eye out for new patterns. You can identify new patterns a number of ways:

- Look for classes, interfaces, or other model elements that you've used to solve a particular problem. Try to identify groups of elements that can be used to solve similar problems in the future.
- Look for common problems, such as database connectivity, error handling, or communication between systems. Define and optimize a solution for these types of problems and turn the solution into a pattern.
- Look for standards that your organization should be following. Build patterns to implement or enforce these standards.
- Look for pre-existing patterns, such as the Gang-of-Four (GOF) patterns, that you can add to your pattern repository.

As you identify new patterns, be sure they are thoroughly designed and tested before adding them to a pattern repository, and be sure that someone has taken responsibility for organizing and maintaining the patterns in the repository. Now you are ready to create your own patterns.

Featured in this chapter:

- Creating a pattern
- Pattern libraries
- Binding a pattern
- Expanding a pattern
- Creating pattern stereotypes
- Turning a pattern into a Reusable Asset Specification

Creating a Pattern

In XDE, patterns are modeled as parameterized collaborations. In other words, they consist of a collection of classes and other elements that interact with one another (a collaboration). They are considered parameterized collaborations because the pattern user identifies the specific classes and other elements that participate in the pattern.

Patterns can include any number of modeling elements, including the following:

- Use cases
- Actors
- Classes
- Interfaces
- Attributes
- Operations
- Relationships
- Components
- Use case diagrams
- Class diagrams
- Sequence diagrams
- Component diagrams

Patterns can be as simple as a class or two, or as complex as a collection of classes and their relationships. The patterns are organized using pattern libraries and can be applied to multiple XDE models. You can define a pattern using the Pattern Explorer or the Model Explorer, and then you can add details to the new pattern.

The process of fully defining a pattern has five steps:

1. Create the pattern.
2. Add pattern elements.
3. Add template parameters.
4. Set pattern properties.
5. Document the pattern.

NOTE *In this section, we won't discuss creating patterns through the use of stereotypes. See the section, "Creating Pattern Stereotypes," later in this chapter for information related to pattern stereotypes.*

Creating the Pattern

The first step is, of course, to create the pattern itself. When you first create a pattern, it holds little more than the pattern name and location. In the subsequent steps, you add all of the details to the pattern.

You can store a pattern in a package of a model or as a model itself. If the pattern is stored in a package, it is called *package-based*; otherwise it is *model-based*.

To create a pattern, follow these steps:

1. Start the Pattern Creation wizard using one of the following methods:
   - Right-click a package or model in the Model Explorer and choose Add UML ➢ Pattern Asset.

- In the Pattern Explorer, click the Add Pattern Asset button.
- In the Pattern Explorer, right-click a pattern library and select Add Pattern Asset.

You will see the Add Pattern Asset dialog box, shown here:

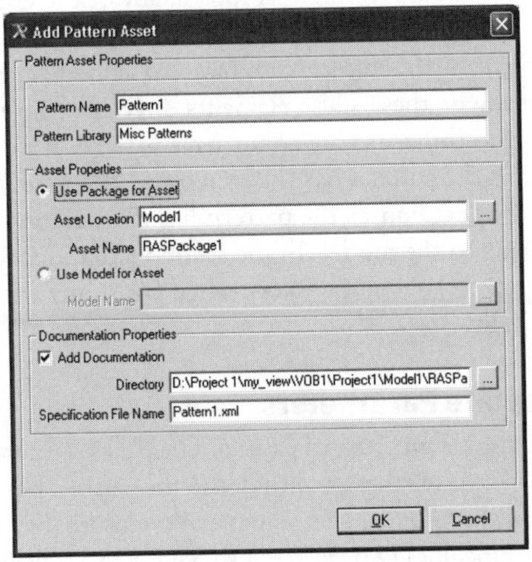

2. Enter the name of the pattern and the library that will hold the pattern. To use an existing library, just type the library name. To create a new library, type the new library name. When you click OK, XDE opens the existing library or creates the new library for you.
3. In the Asset Properties section of the dialog box, select one of the following options:

   Use Package For Asset This option creates the pattern in a model that's currently open; the pattern it creates is package-based (located in a package rather than as its own model). Enter the model that should contain the pattern in the Asset Location field, and enter the name of a package to hold the asset in the Asset Name field. You can also select a package inside a model for the Asset Location field. In this case, the new package specified in the Asset Name field is created inside the package in the Asset Location field. The new package has the stereotype <<Asset>>.

   Use Model For Asset This option creates the pattern in a new or existing model. The new or existing model is given a stereotype of <<Asset>>. Enter the directory and filename for the XML documentation file.

NOTE *The package or model that holds the pattern is known as the pattern's* root context.

4. If you want to create documentation for the pattern, select the Add Documentation check box. Note that if you want to convert the pattern to a Reusable Asset Specification in the future, you must have generated documentation.

Now that you have created a pattern, you should add the pattern elements, including the classes, interfaces, attributes, operations, diagrams, and other pattern elements.

Adding Pattern Elements

Some of the elements in the pattern are parameters that the user provides values for; we'll get to those in just a minute. There are other elements, however, that you may want to include in the pattern without needing the user's input.

For example, in the Pattern Explorer look at any of the GOF patterns that come with XDE. Each pattern has a class diagram called <pattern> Participants that shows all of the classes and relationships in the pattern. Some of the patterns also have sequence diagrams that show how to use the pattern.

You can add any of these static elements directly using the Model Explorer. When you create a pattern, one of two things is true about your pattern. If you made the pattern model-based, the model that houses the pattern has the stereotype <<Asset>>. If you made the pattern package-based, the package that houses the pattern has the stereotype <<Asset>>. In the first situation, add static elements to the model. In the second situation, add the static elements to the package with the <<Asset>> stereotype. Now, when you apply the pattern, these static elements are added automatically.

Adding Template Parameters

Now let's turn to the parameters in a pattern. The parameters are the specific classes, operations, interfaces, or other modeling elements that are included in the pattern. Let's look at an example to illustrate this.

You would use the GOF Singleton pattern to ensure that a class is instantiated no more than once. The pattern includes two classes: a singleton and a client. The singleton is the class that may only be instantiated once, and the client is a class that uses the singleton. There are two parameters for this pattern: the singleton and the client. When you apply the pattern, you supply the names of the specific classes that will be the singleton and the client.

In this example, both of the template parameters were classes, but you can define other types of parameters as well. Some of the available parameter types are shown in Figure 12.1.

ADDING A PARAMETER

To add a template parameter, do one of the following:

- Right-click the pattern in the Pattern Explorer and select Add Template Parameter.
- Right-click the pattern in the Model Explorer and choose Add UML ➢ Template Parameter.

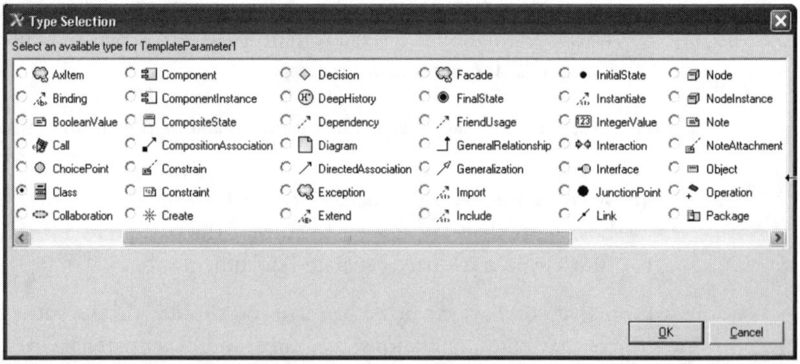

FIGURE 12.1
Template parameter types

XDE creates a template parameter of type class and assigns it the name `TemplateParameter1`. Note that the new template parameter appears in both the Pattern Explorer and the Model Explorer, regardless of where you created it.

SETTING PARAMETER BASIC PROPERTIES

By default, a new parameter will be a class named `TemplateParameter1`. Naturally, you need to modify the parameter types and names as you build your patterns. The parameter name, type, and other information are controlled by the parameter properties. There are five basic properties for each parameter.

Name The Name property is simply the name of the parameter. Each parameter should have a unique name.

Multiplicity The Multiplicity property specifies how many instances of the parameter the user must provide. For example, you may have a parameter that accepts two or more classes.

Type Name The Type Name is a name you choose to refer to the type of the parameter. For example, you may have a parameter that is a class. Its Type property will be set to class, but you can set the Type Name property to Client to show that the parameter plays a client role in the pattern. You can choose whatever name you'd like for this field. The name you chose appears in the Pattern Explorer; in this example, we've given the `Parameter1` parameter a type name of Client, as shown here:

Type The Type property is the UML type of the parameter. This property may be set to Class, Interface, Association, Operation, or any of the other UML types supported by XDE:

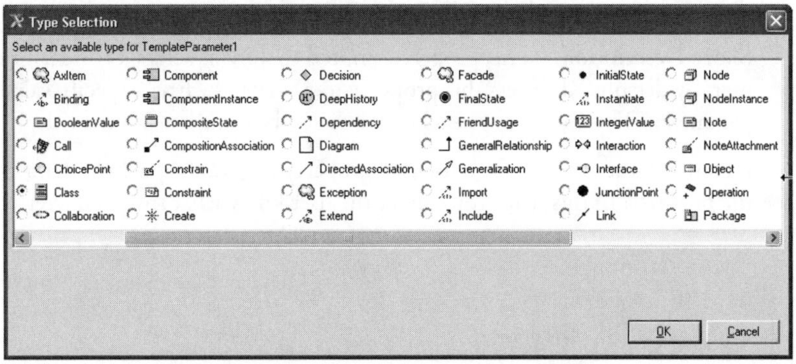

External Documentation URL This property is the URL of a page that provides documentation for the parameter. The property is optional, but useful for the pattern user. When a user is applying the pattern, they have the ability to view the document you specified in the External Documentation URL property.

NOTE *If you don't see the Pattern Properties window, choose Show View ➢ Pattern Properties if you are using XDE for Java, or choose View ➢ Other Windows ➢ Pattern Properties if you are using XDE for .NET.*

SETTING PARAMETER ADVANCED PROPERTIES

The basic parameter properties let you set the name and type of the parameter, but there's a lot more information you can provide to customize the pattern wizard for the parameter. For example, you can set the description of the parameter that appears as the user is running the Apply Pattern wizard. The advanced properties are divided into six sections, as shown here:

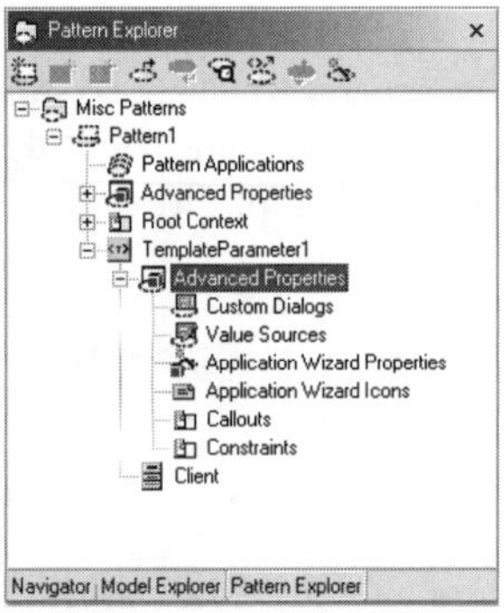

Custom Dialogs

When a user of the pattern runs the pattern wizard, they see a different dialog box for each parameter. You can use the Custom Dialogs area of the parameter properties to control what the user sees in the dialog box for the parameter. There are four pattern properties in the Custom Dialogs area:

Title The Title property controls the title of the Apply Pattern wizard dialog box. By default, the title is the name of the parameter.

Short Description This property, limited to 45 characters, provides brief instructions for the user. By default, XDE sets this property to a phrase such as "Specify values for the `Parameter1` parameter." This prompt appears in the dialog box underneath the title.

Detailed Description You use this property to give the pattern user a detailed description of the property. In this field, you can let the user know what the parameter is intended to do, how it is used in the pattern, and what its default value is. For example, the GOF Prototype pattern has a parameter called `Prototype`. Its detailed description is as follows:

The Prototype declares an interface for cloning itself. The Prototype parameter requires a value of type Class. The default value = Prototype.

Enter any information that helps the pattern user understand what the parameter is for and how to provide an appropriate value for the parameter.

Argument Selection Prompt Use this property to let the user know the type and number of values expected for the parameter. For example, you may set this property to Selected Classes to let the user know that the wizard is expecting multiple classes for this parameter.

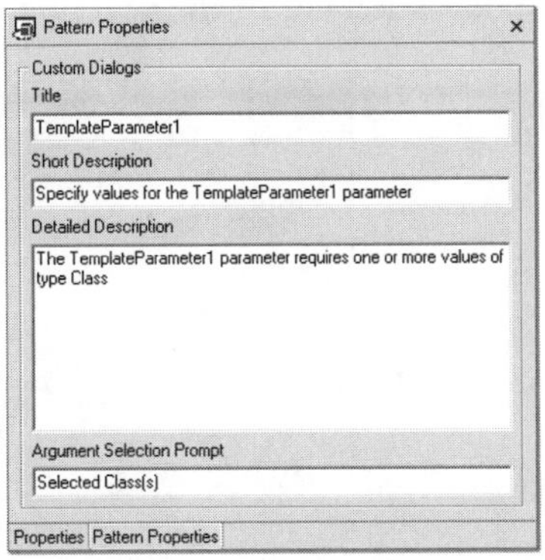

Each of these properties controls a portion of the dialog box the user sees for the parameter. The placement of the properties on the screen is shown in Figure 12.2.

FIGURE 12.2

Custom dialog parameter properties

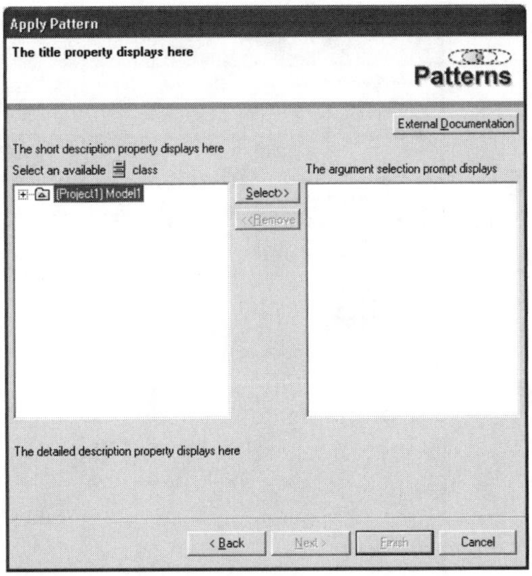

Value Sources

Value sources allow you to specify where the values for a parameter should come from. There are three basic options:

User The user selects the values individually (for example, the user selects three classes in the model as parameter values).

Collection The values come from a collection (for example, all classes that have an association relationship to the Class1 class).

Generated The values are generated from a string that the user enters.

All of the value source options are a combination of one or more of these three basic options. To select a value source option, select one of the items in the list box in the Value Sources area:

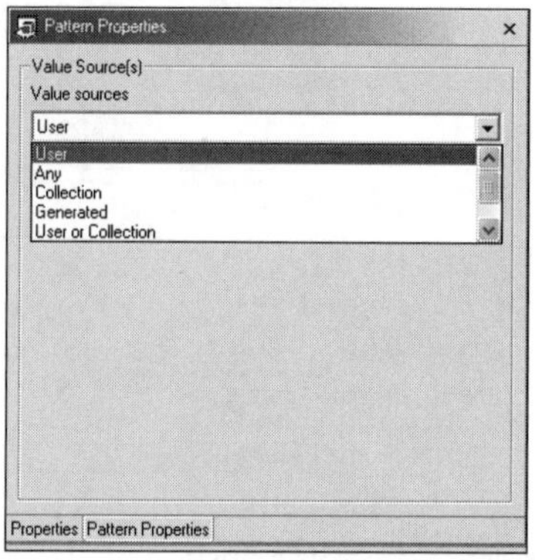

If you select User or another option containing User, the wizard allows the user to select one or more items from a tree view of the model such as the one shown here:

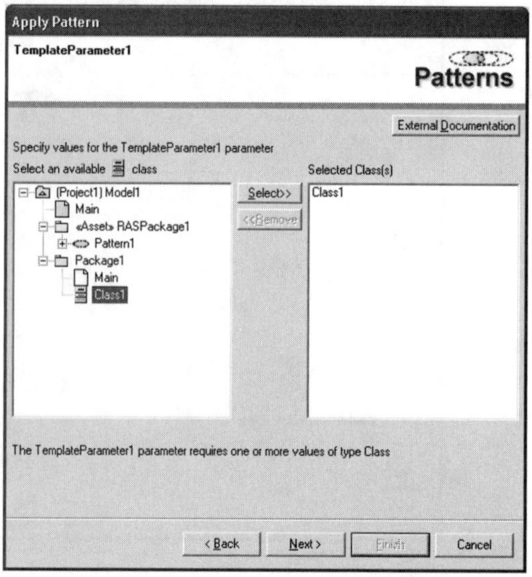

If you select Collection, or another option containing Collection, the user is prompted for a collection owner and collection name. The *collection owner* is the element that defines the collection. For example, in the collection "all classes with a dependency relationship to Class1," the Class1 class is the collection owner. The *collection name* defines which elements are contained in the collection. In the preceding example, "all classes with a dependency relationship to Class1" is the collection name.

The collection owner may be an existing class, package, or other element in the model, or it may be a parameter to the pattern. If the collection owner is an existing element, the user selects the Context radio button and selects the collection owner by using the ellipsis (...) button next to the Collection Owner field. When you select the ellipsis button, you will see the Collection Owner dialog box, as shown here:

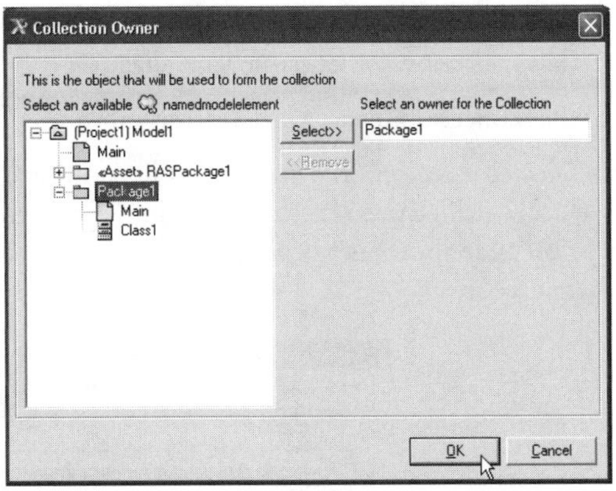

If the collection owner is a template parameter, the user selects the Argument radio button and then selects the collection owner using the drop-down list box:

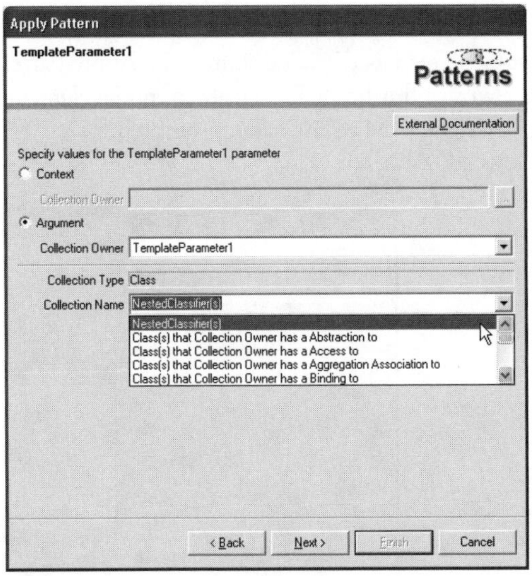

Once they have selected a collection owner, the user chooses a collection name from the drop-down list box on the lower portion of the screen. The collection name defines the elements that will be included in the collection. Some examples of collection names are as follows:

- Nested classifiers
- Class(es) that collection owner has an abstraction to
- Class(es) that collection owner has an aggregation association to
- Class(es) that collection owner has a composition association to
- Class(es) that collection owner has a directed association to
- Class(es) that collection owner has a dependency to
- Class(es) that collection owner has a generalization to
- Class(es) that collection owner has a realization to

Once they've selected a collection owner and collection type, the user can click the Expand Collection button to see which elements are included in the collection.

The final type of value source is a generated value. You can set the value source in the attribute's Value Sources property area:

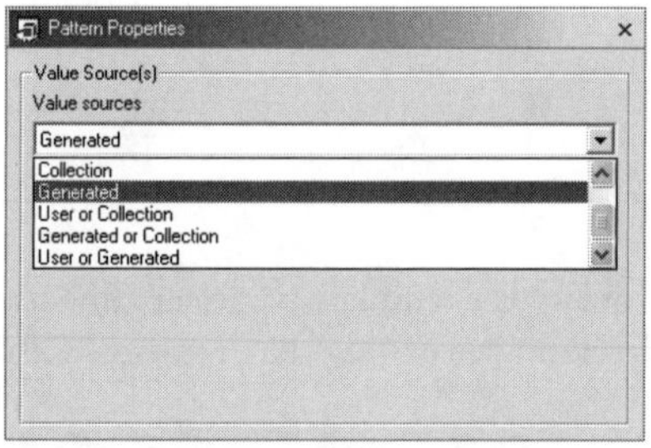

If you select Generated as the value source, the Apply Pattern wizard prompts the user for a string value. When the wizard finishes, XDE creates a model element using the value the user types in. For example, if the user enters **MyClass** when prompted for a class parameter, XDE generates a class called MyClass, as shown here:

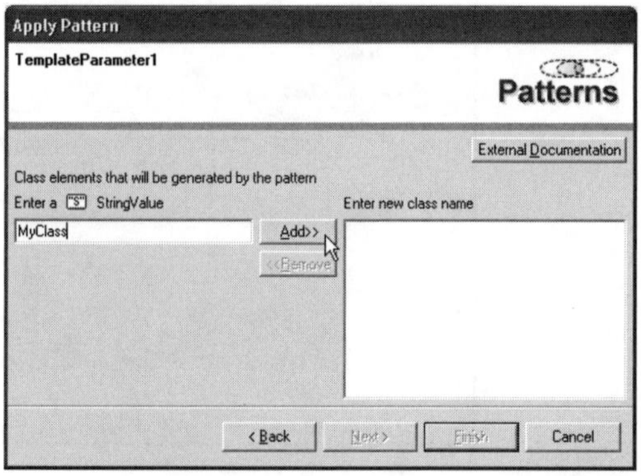

Application Wizard Properties

You can use these properties to set the order in which the template parameters appear in the Apply Pattern wizard, or whether a template parameter should appear at all in the wizard. The application wizard properties are shown here and are then described briefly:

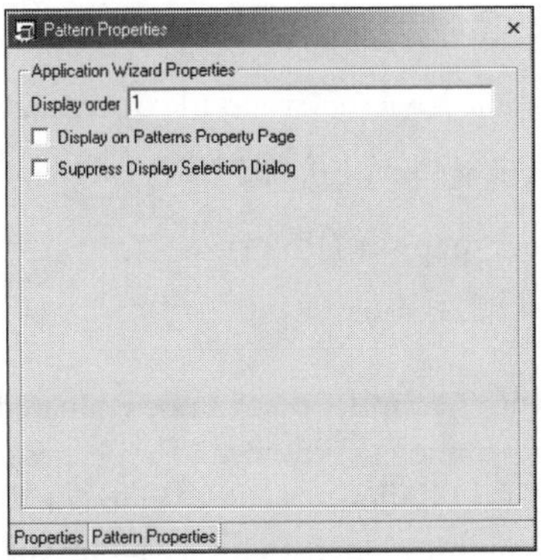

Display Order This property sets the order in which the template parameters are displayed. Assign each parameter an integer value in this field. Those with the lowest values display first.

Display On Patterns Property Page This check box gives you the option of combining more than one parameter in a single dialog box. If you select this option, the parameter appears on a page in the wizard called the property page, and the user can select or enter the parameter's values directly on that page, as shown here:

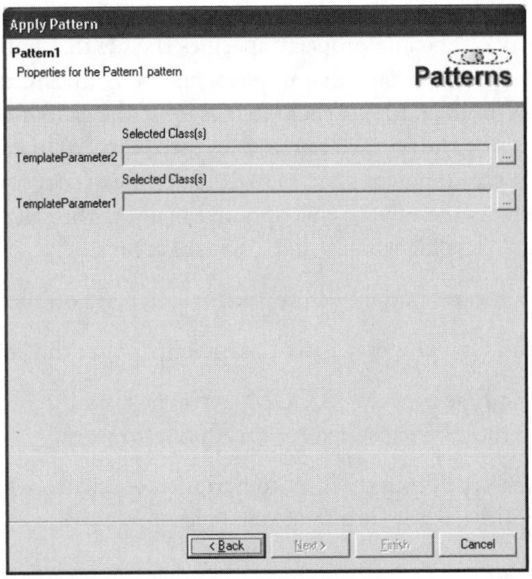

Suppress Display Selection Dialog This check box gives you the option of skipping the parameter completely when the user runs the wizard.

Application Wizard Icons

This property sets the icon that appears in the upper-right corner of the dialog box when the user is prompted for the parameter. You can select an icon in any of the following formats:

- Windows bitmap (BMP)
- Windows icon (ICO)
- Joint Photographic Experts Group file interchange format (JPG or JPEG)
- Graphics interchange format (GIF)
- Portable network graphics (PNG)

Callouts

A *callout* is a component or scriptlet that can be evaluated as a part of the wizard. To add a callout to a parameter, open the parameter's Advanced Properties in the Pattern Explorer. Right-click the Callouts node and choose Add Callouts ➢ On Argument Value. Note that you can add only one callout per parameter. There are five properties for a callout: the type, file, user data, failure description, and whether the callout is enabled.

Type property The Type property specifies the callout's language. The options are as follows:

- Java
- COM
- Scriptlet
- JavaScript

File property The File property specifies the file that holds the callout. If the type of callout is Java, the file must be a class that implements the IPatternCalloutUser interface in `com.rational.rose.ea.sdk.bridge.IpatternCalloutUser`. If the callout is in the current class path, you can reference it using the syntax `com.company.project.callout`. If the callout is in a JAR file, reference it using the complete path, as in `C:\Jar1.JAR (com.company.project.callout)`. Be sure to include the parentheses with this option. Finally, if the callout is a class file, reference it using the directory and class filename, as in `C:\Class1.class`.

The value you enter in the File property will depend on the value you selected in the Type field:

- If the Type property is set to JavaScript, enter the Java filename in the File field.
- If the Type property is COM, enter the class ID or programmatic ID in the File field. The class must be registered for this option to work.
- If the Type property is set to Scriptlet, you will see another field, called Code. Enter the scriptlet directly into the Code field.

User Data property This property allows you to send a sting value to the callout. Enter the string directly in the User Data field.

Failure Description property In this property, add a message that should be displayed to the Apply Pattern wizard user if the callout returns a value of false.

Enabled Select this check box to enable the evaluation of this callout when the Apply Pattern wizard is run. XDE runs the callout as soon as the user provides a value for the parameter.

Constraints

By using a *constraint*, you can check the parameter value entered by the user to make sure it is correct before the Apply Pattern wizard finishes. In the constraints area, you can enter one or more expressions that must be true before the parameter value is accepted, and you can enter a message to display to the user if they have entered an unacceptable value.

To add a constraint to a parameter, right-click the parameter in the Pattern Explorer and choose Add Constraint ➢ On Argument Value. When you select the new constraint in the Pattern Explorer, you see the constraint properties, as shown here:

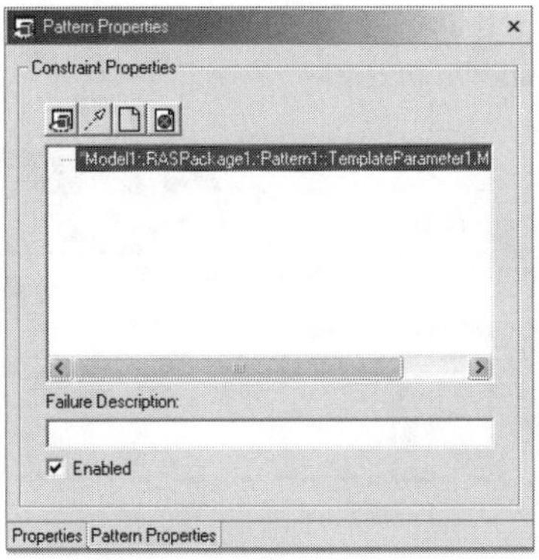

As you add constraints to the parameter, they appear in the Constraint Properties window. There are two types of constraints: property expressions and relationship expressions. *Property expressions* evaluate the value of a specific property of a specific model element; *relationship expressions* test for the presence or absence of a specific relationship. You can also enter *failure descriptions*, which are messages that display to the user if a property expression or relationship expression evaluates to false. Property expressions, relationship expressions, and failure descriptions are described below:

Property expressions To add a property expression, click the Build A Property Expression button: . In the Build Property Expression dialog box, enter the model element or parameter you want to evaluate and the specific property you want to examine. For example, you could look at the name of the `TemplateParameter1` parameter by selecting `Template1` in the Element drop-down list and `Name` in the Property drop-down list. Select an operator from the Operator drop-down list, and enter a value in the Value field, as shown here:

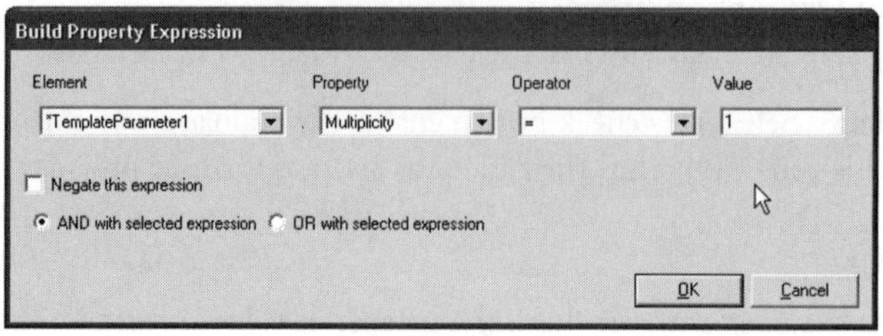

You can use the AND With Selected Expression and the OR With Selected Expression radio buttons to combine property and relationship expressions into more complex evaluations.

Relationship expressions To add a relationship expression, click the Build A Relationship expression button: . In the Element drop-down lists, select the two model elements or template parameters that should have a relationship. In the Relationship drop-down list, select the type of relationship the Apply Pattern wizard should check for. The Build Relationship Expression dialog box is shown here:

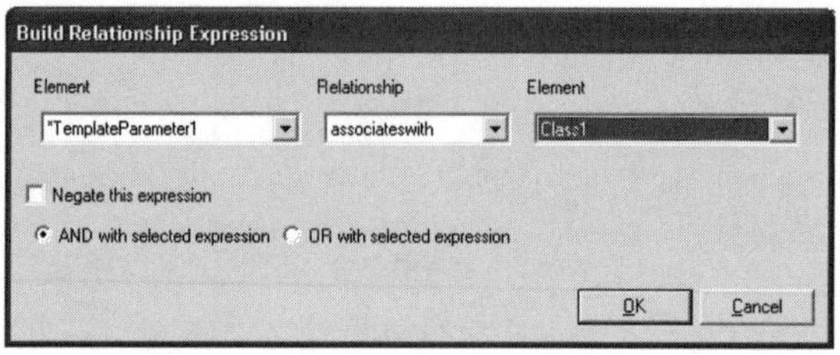

Failure Description The Failure Description property allows you to enter a message that should display to the user if one or more of the constraints evaluates to false. If a constraint is false, the Apply Pattern wizard won't continue until the problem has been resolved. Enter the message in the Failure Description field:

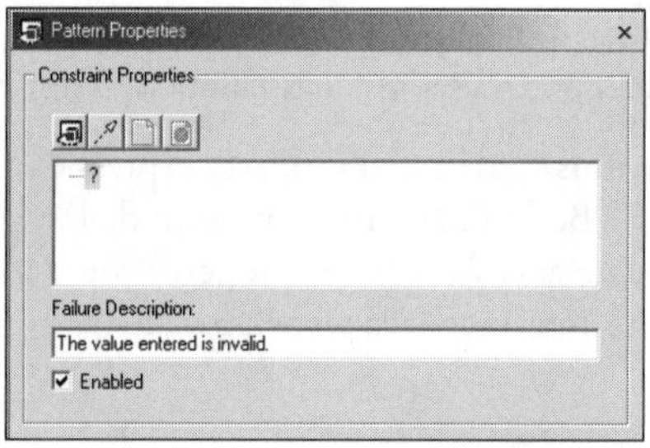

Setting Pattern Properties

Once you've added all of the parameters for the pattern and set the parameters' properties, the next step is to set the properties of the pattern itself. Like parameter properties, there are basic pattern properties and advanced pattern properties. Let's start with the basic properties.

SETTING BASIC PATTERN PROPERTIES

The basic pattern properties let you control things such as the pattern name, library name, and documentation URL. There are eight basic properties, as shown in the Pattern Properties window:

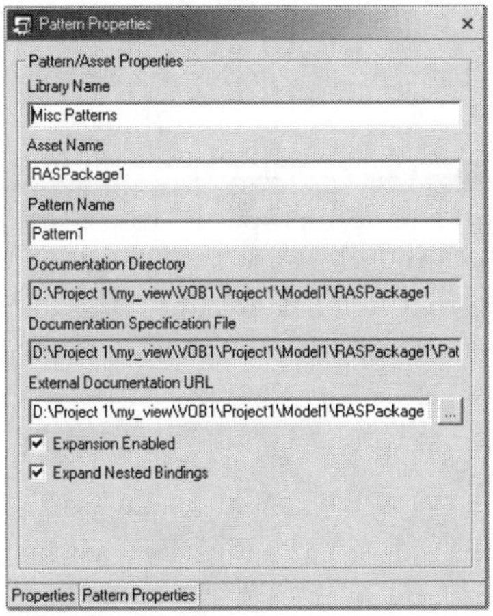

Library Name The Library Name property displays the name of the pattern library that the pattern is currently in. See the section "Pattern Libraries" later in this chapter for more information about pattern libraries. The default value for this property is Misc Patterns.

If you change the value in the Library Name property, the pattern is moved from one library to another. If you enter a new name into this property, XDE creates a new pattern library and moves the pattern into it.

Asset Name The Asset Name property is the name of a Reusable Asset Specification (RAS) package that contains the pattern. See the section "Turning a Pattern into a Reusable Asset Specification" later in this chapter for more information.

Pattern Name This property is the name of the pattern itself. You can give a pattern any name you'd like, but the pattern name should be unique within a pattern library.

Documentation Directory This property points to the physical directory that holds any documentation associated with this pattern. When you export the pattern as a RAS, only the files in this location maintain their relative path for import. This property cannot be modified.

Documentation Specification File This property contains the name of the RAS-compliant XML file for the pattern. The XML file is a template for the HTML documentation file that can be generated automatically for the pattern. This property cannot be modified.

External Documentation This property contains the URL of a page that provides documentation for the pattern. When a pattern user runs the Apply Pattern wizard, they have the option of viewing the file you enter in this property.

Expansion Enabled This property allows the pattern to be expanded. See the section "Expanding a Pattern" later in this chapter for more information.

Expand Nested Bindings This property allows any nested patterns to be expanded. See the section "Expanding a Pattern" later in this chapter for more information.

SETTING ADVANCED PATTERN PROPERTIES

You can use the advanced pattern properties to configure the Apply Pattern wizard for the pattern you are defining. These properties include items such as the pattern's default binding and expansion locations, wizard icons to use, and constraints. The advanced properties are divided into eight sections, as shown here:

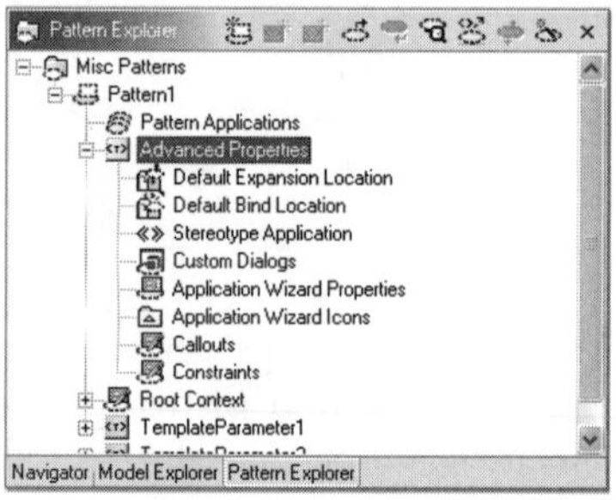

We now describe these properties in more detail.

Default Expansion Location

The expansion location is the package into which the pattern is applied. In other words, any new classes or other model elements that the pattern creates are created inside the expansion location. There are three expansion location properties: the Expansion Location Specified By, the Expansion Location Modifier, and the Path to Append To Specified Expansion Location.

Expansion Location Specified By This property sets the default expansion location. When the user runs the Apply Pattern wizard, they have the option of selecting a different location.

You can set the location in one of three ways:

By context Using this option, you specify exactly where the pattern should be expanded. Generally, you select a package, but if the pattern's root context is not a package, select a model element that is the same type as the root context.

By template parameter Using this option, use one of the pattern's parameters to determine where the pattern should be expanded. In the drop-down list, select one of the pattern's template parameters.

By callout When you use this option, a callout determines where the pattern should be expanded. If you select this option, XDE automatically adds a callout to the pattern under the Default Expansion Location node on the Advanced Properties tree. You need to set the Type, File, User Data, Failure Description, and Enabled fields on the new callout. See "Callouts" later in this section for information on setting these fields.

Expansion Location Modifier This property helps refine the location of the pattern's expansion. For example, you may have selected a package by context in the Expansion Location Specified By property, but now you want to specify that the pattern will actually be expanded into that package's owner. You can do this by selecting OwnerOf in the Expansion Location Modifier property. The possible values are as follows:

Element This is the default setting. When you use this option, the value you provided in the Expansion Location Specified By property becomes the expansion location.

ModelOf When you use this option, the pattern expands into the model containing the element in the Expansion Location Specified By property.

OwnerOf When you use this option, the pattern expands into the owner of the element in the Expansion Location Specified By property. If, for example, the Expansion Location Specified By property is set to `Package1`, which is contained inside `Package2`, the pattern will expand into `Package2`.

PackageOf When you use this option, the pattern expands into the package containing the element you defined in the Expansion Location Specified By property.

Path To Append To Specified Expansion Location If you'd like, you can add a directory path to the expansion location using this property. The path is a list of packages where each package owns the next and the package names are separated by two colons. For example, if your expansion location is `Package4`, which is contained in `Package3`, which is contained in `Package2`, which is contained in `Package1`, you would list `Package4` as the expansion location. The value of the Path To Append To Specified Expansion Location property would be `Package1::Package2::Package3`.

Default Bind Location

When a pattern is applied, it is first bound and then expanded. Binding a pattern is the process of supplying values for all of the pattern's parameters. When the Apply Pattern wizard runs, it places a record of the binding in the model to which the pattern was applied.

The binding appears as a collaboration in the model. Underneath this collaboration, XDE lists all of the pattern's parameters, as well as the values that you supplied for each of the parameters.

The Default Bind Location properties control where this binding will be placed. There are three properties in this area: Binding Location Specified By, Auto Generate Bound Collaboration Name, and Bound Collaboration Name.

Binding Location Specified By This property is very similar to the Expansion Location Specified By property we just examined. The Binding Location Specified By property sets the default binding location. When the user runs the Apply Pattern wizard, they can select a different location if they want. There are two ways to set the default binding location:

By context Using this option, you select a package or other model element that holds the pattern binding. While you will generally choose a package, you can choose a different type if the pattern's root context is not a package.

By template parameter When you use this option, you use the value in a template parameter to dictate the location of the pattern binding.

Auto Generate Bound Collaboration Name If this check box is selected, XDE automatically generates a name for the pattern binding. By default, this name is the pattern name, followed by `_Binding` and then a number to ensure that the binding name is unique. For example, if we bind the GOF Decorator pattern twice, the default binding names will be `Decorator_Binding1` and `Decorator_Binding2`.

Clear this check box if you'd rather provide your own pattern binding name.

Bound Collaboration Name If the Auto Generate Bound Collaboration Name check box is not selected, you can enter a value in this property. The value you enter here becomes the name of the binding collaboration in the model when you apply the pattern.

Stereotype Application

Some patterns are applied as soon as you set an element's stereotype to a particular value. Choose Tools ➢ Patterns ➢ Update Pattern Stereotypes to associate a stereotype with a pattern. See "Creating Pattern Stereotypes" later in this chapter for more information.

Once a pattern has been associated with a stereotype, XDE can automatically bind the pattern, automatically bind and expand the pattern, or wait for the user to manually bind and expand the pattern. The Stereotype Application property controls which of the three options occurs. Set this property to one of the following:

Bind only When you use this option, the pattern is bound immediately (but not expanded) when the user assigns the stereotype to the element.

Bind and expand When you use this option, XDE will automatically both bind and expand the pattern when the user assigns the stereotype to the element.

Off When you use this option, the pattern will not be bound or expanded when the element is assigned the stereotype.

Custom Dialogs

Just as you can set the description and prompts for a template parameter, you can set the description and prompts the user sees for the pattern itself. There are three properties in this area: the title of the dialog box, a short description of the pattern, and a detailed description of the pattern. When you create a pattern, XDE creates default values for each of these three properties, but you can change the values if you want. The values you enter in these fields appear on the wizard dialog box, as shown here:

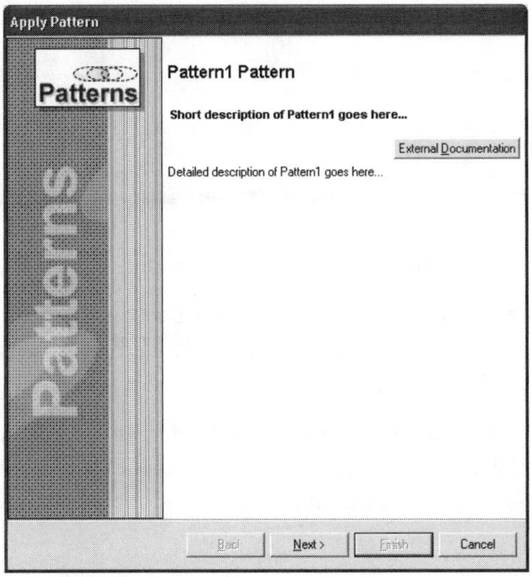

Title Use the Title property to set the pattern title used in the Apply Pattern wizard dialog box. You don't have to use the pattern name here.

Short Description You can use this property to give a short, 45-character description of the pattern and its application.

Detailed Description You can use this property to give the user detailed information about the pattern and how it should be applied.

Application Wizard Properties

You can use these properties to configure the overall structure of the Apply Pattern wizard. Specifically, they allow you to change the wizard's title and control whether or not the binding and expansion dialogs should be displayed. The properties are shown next.

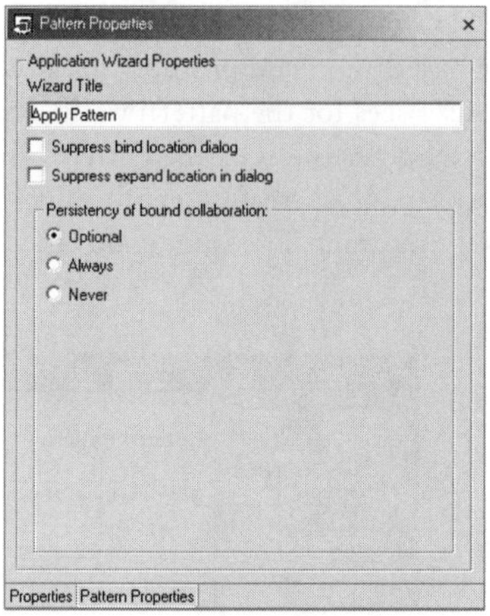

We now describe these properties in more detail.

Wizard Title This property sets the text that displays in the title bar of the Apply Pattern wizard dialog boxes. When you create a pattern, XDE sets the value of this property to "Apply Pattern."

Suppress Bind Location Dialog If you select this check box, the wizard skips the dialog box that allows the user to select the pattern's bind location. Because the user is not able to select a bind location, the wizard uses the default bind location you defined in the Default Bind Location properties.

NOTE *You must set up a default bind location in order for this property to function correctly. If there is no default bind location, the Bind Location dialog box appears in the wizard regardless of the Suppress Bind Location Dialog check box.*

Suppress Expand Location In Dialog If you select this check box, the wizard skips the dialog box that allows the user to select the pattern's expansion location. Like the Suppress Bind Location Dialog property, this property relies on default values. If you select the check box, the wizard uses the default expansion location you set up in the Default Expansion Location properties.

NOTE *You must set up a default expansion location for this property to function correctly. If there is no default expansion location, the Expansion Location dialog box appears in the wizard regardless of the Suppress Expand Location in Dialog check box.*

Persistency Of Bound Collaboration When you bind a pattern, XDE records the fact that the pattern was bound, and it also records the values supplied to the pattern parameters. All of these items are recorded in a pattern binding, which is a collaboration in the XDE model.

When a pattern user is running the Apply Pattern wizard, they may have the option of saving the binding as a collaboration in the model. You can use the Persistency Of Bound Collaboration property to control whether or not the user can save the binding. The options are as follows:

Optional This is the default setting. When you use this option, the pattern user sees a check box titled Persist This Bound Collaboration when they run the wizard. If they select the check box, the binding is saved in the model.

Always When you use this option, the user does not see the Persist The Bound Collaboration check box. Instead, XDE always save the binding in the binding location specified by the user.

Never When you use this option, the user does not see the Persist The Bound Collaboration check box. XDE does not save the binding and does not prompt for a binding location.

Application Wizard Icons

You can use these properties to determine which icons will be displayed in the Apply Wizard dialog boxes. You can list an icon in any of the following formats:

- Windows bitmap (BMP)
- Windows icon (ICO)
- Joint Photographic Experts Group file interchange format (JPG or JPEG)
- Graphics interchange format (GIF)
- Portable network graphics (PNG)

There are a number of application wizard icon properties you can set. Each of these will control the icon for a different part of the Apply Pattern wizard.

Intro icon This is the icon that displays in the Pattern Introduction window of the wizard. The default icon looks like this:

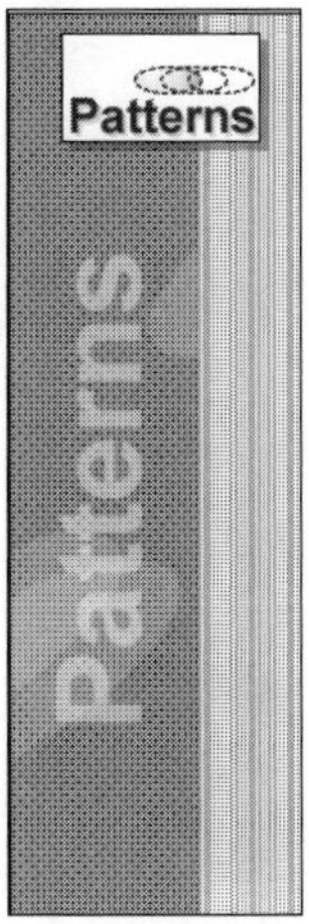

Properties icon This is the icon that displays on the Pattern Properties window of the wizard. The default icon looks like this:

Expand icon This is the icon that displays on the Pattern Expansion Location window of the wizard. The default icon looks like this:

Bind icon This is the icon that displays on the Pattern Bind window of the wizard. The default icon looks like this:

Summary icon This is the icon that displays on the Pattern Summary window of the wizard. The default icon looks like this:

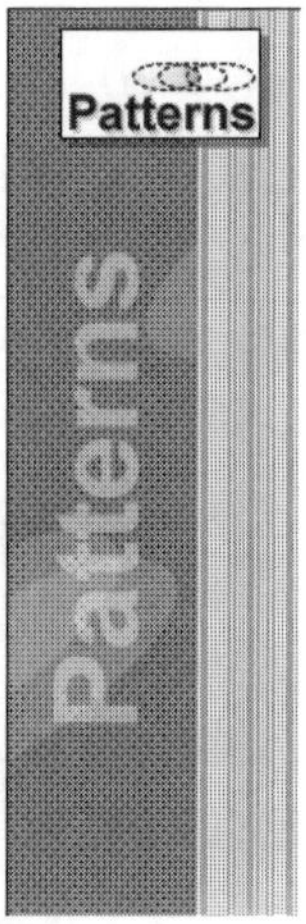

Callouts

We've discussed callouts as they apply to parameters. Now, let's look at them as they apply to patterns.

A callout is a component or scriptlet that can be evaluated as a part of the wizard. If the callout returns an error, the wizard won't continue until the error has been resolved. You can only add a callout to a parameter when it is given a value, but you can add a callout to a pattern at other times. Specifically, you can create a callout to run at any of the following events:

- OnBind
- PreApply
- PostMapping
- OnScriptlet
- OnMatch
- OnMerge
- PreExpand
- PostExpand
- PostApply
- ErrorHandler

To add a callout to a pattern, right-click the Callouts node under the pattern's Advanced Properties section in the Pattern Explorer and select Add Callouts, and then select the type of callout to create (OnBind, PreApply, and so on). There are five properties for a callout: the Type, File, User Data, Failure Description, and whether the callout is enabled.

Type property The Type property specifies the callout's language. The options are as follows:

- Java
- COM
- Scriptlet
- JavaScript

File property The File property specifies the file that holds the callout. If the type of callout is Java, the file must be a class that implements the IPatternCalloutUser interface in `com.rational.rose.ea.sdk.bridge.IpatternCalloutUser`. If the callout is in the current class path, you can reference it using the syntax `com.company.project.callout`. If the callout is in a JAR file, reference it using the complete path, as in `C:\Jar1.JAR (com.company.project.callout)`. Be sure to include the parentheses with this option. Finally, if the callout is a class file, reference it using the directory and class file name, as in `C:\Class1.class`.

The value you enter in the File field will depend on the type you selected in the Type property:

- If the Type property is set to JavaScript, enter the Java filename in the File field.
- If the Type property is COM, enter the class ID or programmatic ID in the File field. The class must be registered for this option to work.
- If the Type property is set to Scriptlet, you see another field, called Code. Enter the scriptlet directly into the Code field.

User Data property This property allows you to send a string value to the callout. Enter the string directly in the User Data field.

Failure Description property This property lets you add a message that should be displayed to the pattern wizard user if the callout returns a value of false.

Enabled Select this check box to enable the evaluation of this callout when the Apply Pattern wizard is run.

Constraints

You can use constraints to perform tests against the elements in a pattern before the pattern is bound and expanded. For example, if you want to be sure that the value provided for two parameters of the pattern are classes with an aggregation relationship, you can perform this type of test.

In the constraints area, you can enter one or more expressions that must be true before the pattern is bound and expanded, and you can enter a message to display to the user if a constraint is not met.

To add a constraint to a pattern, right-click the Constraints node under the Advanced Properties section of the pattern in the Pattern Explorer. Select Add Constraint and then the type of constraint to add. The options are as follows:

- OnBind
- PreApply
- PostMapping
- PreExpand
- PostExpand
- PostApply

When you select the new constraint in the Pattern Explorer, you see the constraint properties:

As you add constraints to the pattern, they appear in the Constraints Properties window. There are two types of constraints: property expressions and relationship expressions. Property expressions evaluate the value of a specific property of a specific model element, while a relationship expression tests for the presence or absence of a specific relationship.

Property expressions To add a property expression, click the Build A Property Expression button: . In the Build Property Expression dialog box, enter the model element or parameter you wish to evaluate and the specific property you wish to examine. For example, you could look at the name of the `TemplateParameter1` parameter by selecting `Template1` in the Element drop-down list and `Name` in the Property drop-down list. Select an operator from the Operator drop-down list, and enter a value in the Value field:

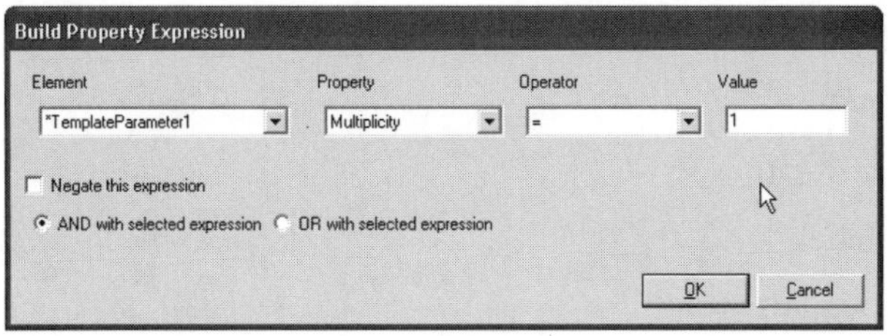

You can use the AND With Selected Expression and the OR With Selected Expression radio buttons to combine property and relationship expressions into more complex evaluations.

Relationship expressions To add a relationship expression, click the Build A Relationship Expression button: . In the Element drop-down lists, select the two model elements or template parameters that should have a relationship. In the Relationship drop-down list, select the type of relationship to check for. The Build Relationship Expression dialog box is shown here:

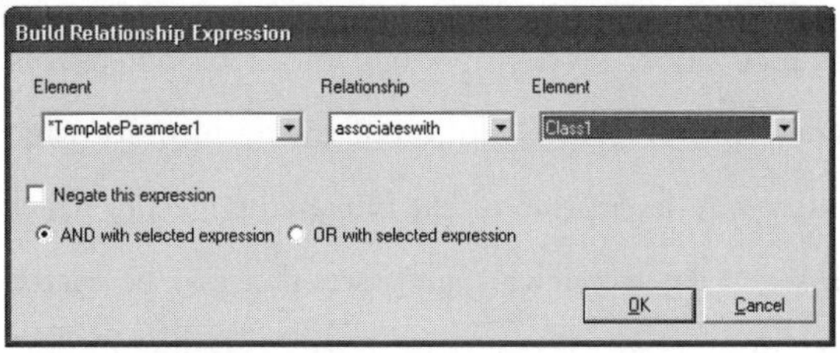

Failure Description The Failure Description property allows you to enter a message that should display to the user if one or more of the constraints evaluates to false. If a constraint is false, the Apply Pattern wizard won't continue until the problem has been resolved.

Documenting the Pattern

When XDE creates a pattern, it automatically sets it up in the Reusable Asset Specification format. Part of this specification is an XML file that you can use to document the pattern. The XML file is a template that XDE uses to generate HTML documentation for your pattern.

To generate documentation for a pattern, right-click the pattern in the Pattern Explorer and select Generate Documentation. XDE creates both the XML file and the corresponding HTML file that you can use to document the pattern. Once you've generated the HTML file, simply edit it as necessary.

NOTE *In the Patterns section of the XDE preferences is a check box titled Generate RAS Documentation For New Assets. If this check box is selected, the XML and HTML files have been automatically created.*

In the remainder of this section, we briefly discuss the structure of the generated XML file. A complete discussion of the structure of the XML file is available in Chapter 11, "Introduction to Reusable Asset Specifications."

The RAS document has four components:

- Overview
- Classification
- Solution
- Usage

We discuss each of these in this section. After you have created a pattern, edit the HTML file to include the author, version, and other information about the pattern.

Overview Section

The overview section includes some general information about the pattern, such as the pattern name, the problem it is solving, and any standards that the pattern follows. The overview section contains the following:

Asset overview An abstract of the pattern, the problem it solves, and the solution it provides

Intent and motivation A description of the motivating factors and the intended use of the pattern

Problem description A description of the problem for which the pattern provides a solution

Applicability A description of the intended targets to which the pattern may be applied

Related assets An overview of any assets that may be related to this asset

Standards Any standards that the pattern may submit to or be compliant with

Support A description of any support issues that the pattern may have

Classification Section

You can use the classification section to record some more detailed information about the pattern, such as the pattern author, creation date, or version. Each of these pieces of information is known as a descriptor, and you can track as many different descriptors as you need for the pattern.

The classification section also defines the different contexts in which the pattern can be used. Here are some example questions this section may answer:

- In what business domains can the pattern be used?
- What programming languages can be used to apply the pattern?
- Into what environment can the pattern be deployed?
- Can the pattern be reused on the team level, project level, product line level, or department level?

SOLUTION SECTION

The solution section is the part of the documentation that links to the pattern artifacts themselves. In the HTML file, this section contains links to each of the pattern artifacts.

The solution section also defines each artifact's variability points. A variability point describes how the artifact is applied differently in different contexts. For example, you may have an artifact that is mandatory in one type of project and optional in another.

USAGE SECTION

The usage section describes in detail how the pattern is applied in different contexts. It includes the following elements:

- General instructions for applying the asset
- Instructions for applying the asset in specific contexts
- Instructions for completing and using the artifacts in the asset
- Instructions for customizing the artifacts (using the variability points) in general or in specific contexts

Pattern Libraries

A pattern library is a collection of patterns in XDE. The Gang-of-Four patterns, for example, constitute a library. You can create as many different libraries as you want to organize your patterns.

Despite the name, pattern libraries do not physically hold patterns. The patterns themselves may be located in numerous XDE models. The library is simply a way to look at patterns as if they were all stored in one place.

There are two different ways to open a library:

Using the tools menu Choose Tools ➢ Patterns ➢ Open Library, and then the library you want to open, as shown here:

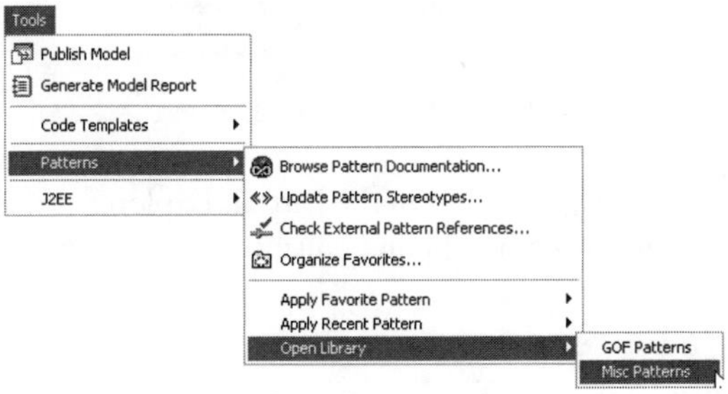

Using the Pattern Explorer Select the Open button from the toolbar. In the Pattern Selection dialog box, select the library to open.

With the second option, if you want to open a single pattern rather than the whole library, select the pattern in the Pattern Selection dialog box. This is especially useful if you need only one or two patterns in a large library because opening an entire library can take a little time.

To delete a pattern, right-click it in the Pattern Explorer, and select the Delete option. You can choose Edit ➢ Undo to immediately recover a pattern you accidentally deleted.

Binding and Expanding a Pattern

There are two sides of pattern application: binding the pattern and expanding the pattern. Binding a pattern is the process of providing values for all of the pattern's parameters, so that the pattern can be applied. Expanding the pattern is the process of actually applying the pattern to the modeling elements and other parameters provided.

Binding a Pattern

When you run the Apply Pattern wizard, the pattern is both bound and expanded. However, XDE gives you the option of binding the pattern without expanding it. This gives you the freedom to test a pattern, change the parameters until you feel they are correct, and then expand the pattern. Any changes you make to the bound collaboration do not affect the original pattern definition. When you are happy with the bound collaboration, you can expand the pattern.

A pattern binding is modeled as a collaboration. If you bind but do not expand a pattern, the binding appears underneath the Pattern Applications node of the pattern in the Pattern Explorer. Within the binding, you see the pattern parameters, binding location, and expansion location, as shown here:

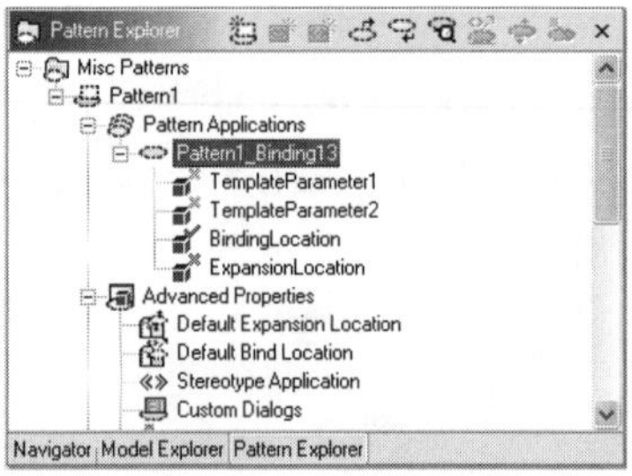

To bind a pattern, right-click it in the Pattern Explorer and select Bind. XDE prompts you for a binding location and creates the bound collaboration in that location.

Expanding a Pattern

When you expand a pattern, XDE uses the parameter values provided in the bound collaboration to apply the pattern to a model.

To expand a bound collaboration, right-click it in the Pattern Explorer and select Expand. Be sure to provide an expansion location, either in the original pattern or in the bound collaboration, so that XDE knows where to expand the pattern.

Creating Pattern Stereotypes

Some patterns can be automatically applied to a model element as soon as that element receives a particular stereotype. Choose Tools ➢ Patterns ➢ Update Pattern Stereotypes to view and edit the stereotypes associated with patterns. XDE launches a wizard that lets you add a stereotype, edit a stereotype, make the stereotype available to other models, or remove a stereotype. In this section, we look at each of these options.

Creating a New Pattern-Applying Stereotype

The first option is to create a new stereotype that automatically applies a pattern to a model element. For example, if you have a pattern that will add error-handling methods to a class, you may want to create a stereotype called <<ErrorHandler>>. As soon as you assign this stereotype to a class, the pattern is applied and the class gets the error-handling methods.

Using this option, you can create a new stereotype for a pre-existing pattern, or you can associate an existing stereotype with a pre-existing pattern.

To create a new pattern-applying stereotype, follow these steps:

1. Start the Patterns Stereotype wizard by choosing Tools ➢ Patterns ➢ Update Pattern Stereotypes.
2. Click Next on the introductory screen.
3. Select Create A New Pattern-Applying Stereotype.

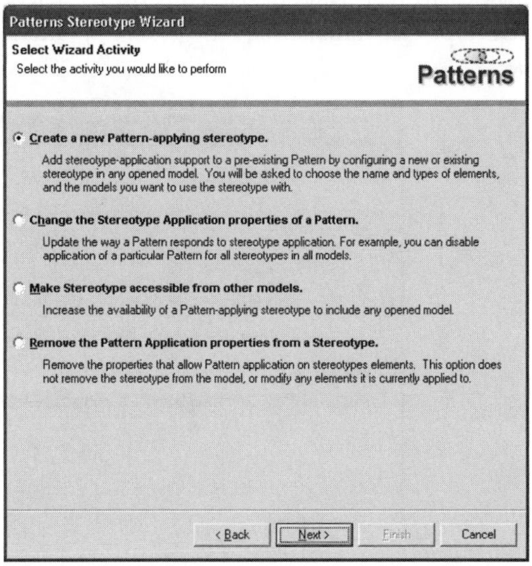

4. Select the pattern you want to use. This pattern is automatically applied to any element that has the associated stereotype. Be sure to select the collaboration, not the pattern's package. Click Next to continue.

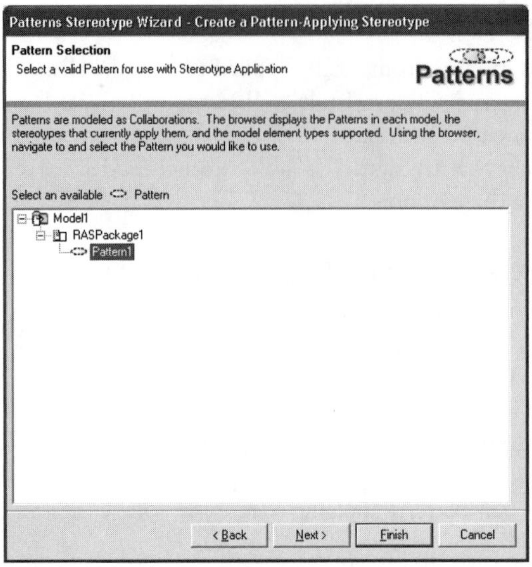

5. The wizard examines the pattern's parameters to determine whether the pattern is a good candidate for a stereotype association. The parameters should have a default value assigned for the pattern to be a good candidate.

6. Enter a new stereotype name, or select an existing stereotype from the drop-down list. This is the stereotype that automatically triggers the application of the pattern. Click Next to continue.

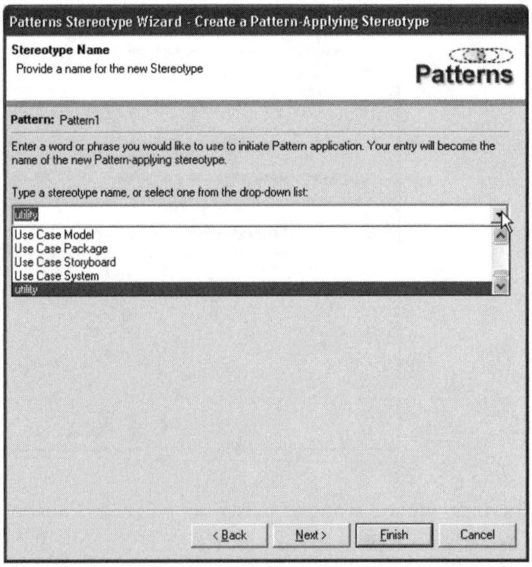

7. Select the model element(s) that can have the pattern applied to them. The wizard creates a stereotype for each of the model elements you select here. When you are finished selecting, click Next to continue.

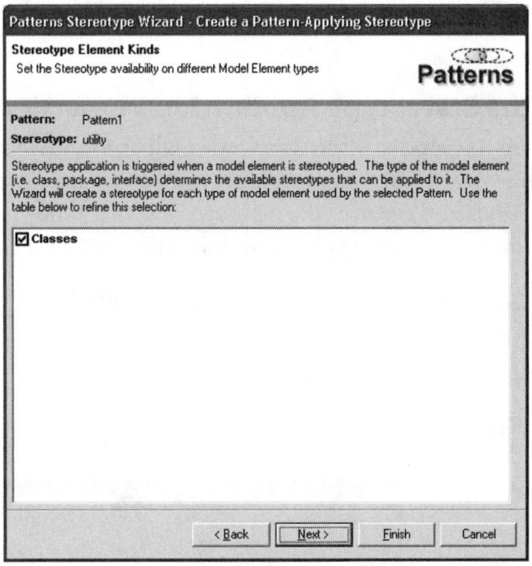

8. Select the model(s) that has access to the stereotype. Select a model and click Add to give that model access to the stereotype. When you are finished adding models, click Next to continue.

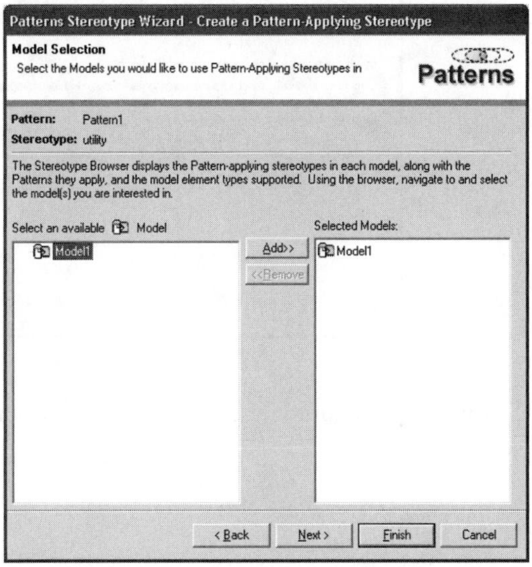

9. You see a summary screen. Click Back to make any changes or click Finish to complete the process.

Now, when you go into a model that you selected in step 8, you can see that the new stereotype is available. If you assign the stereotype to a model element, XDE automatically applies the pattern to it.

Changing the Stereotype Application Properties of a Pattern

Running this option produces the same end result as modifying the pattern's Stereotype Application properties. This wizard determines whether assigning a stereotype automatically binds the pattern, automatically binds and expands the pattern, or neither binds nor expands the pattern.

To change the Stereotype Application properties, follow these steps:

1. Start the Patterns Stereotype wizard by choosing Tools ➢ Patterns ➢ Update Pattern Stereotypes.
2. Click Next on the introductory screen.
3. Select Change The Stereotype Application Properties Of A Pattern. Click Next to continue.

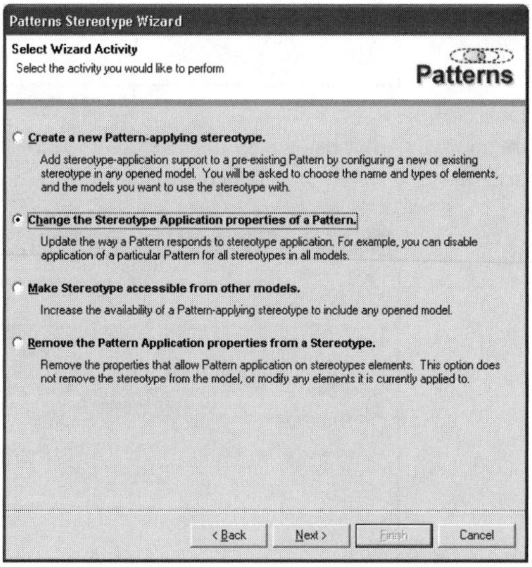

4. Select the pattern you want to modify. Select the collaboration, not the pattern's package. Click Next to continue.

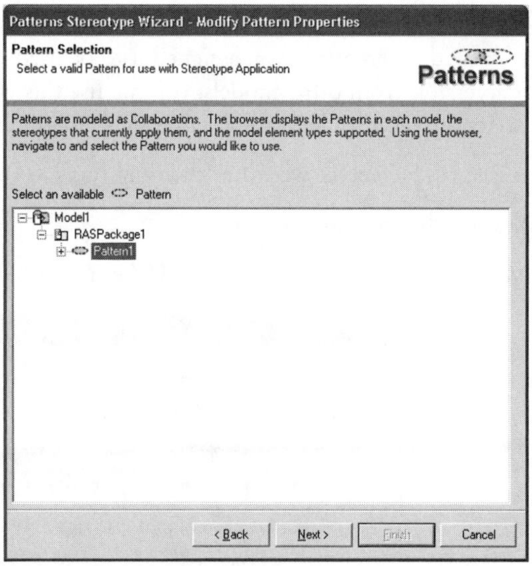

5. Select the Enable Pattern Application Via Stereotype check box if you want the pattern to be applied automatically to model elements with the stereotype.
6. If you selected the Enable Pattern Application Via Stereotype check box, select one of the following:

   Create a Binding and then Expand the Pattern. This option binds and expands the pattern.

   Only create a Binding for this Pattern. This option binds but does not expand the pattern.

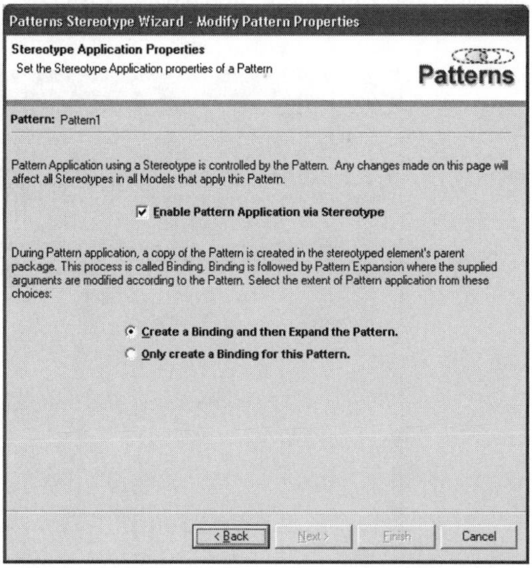

7. Click Finish to complete the wizard.

Making a Stereotype Accessible from Other Models

When you first created a stereotype, you assigned it to be used in one or more models. If you need to now make it accessible from other models, you can use this wizard.

To make a stereotype accessible from other models, follow these steps:

1. Start the Patterns Stereotype wizard by choosing Tools ➢ Patterns ➢ Update Pattern Stereotypes.
2. Click Next on the introductory screen.
3. Select Make Stereotype Accessible From Other Models and click Next to continue.

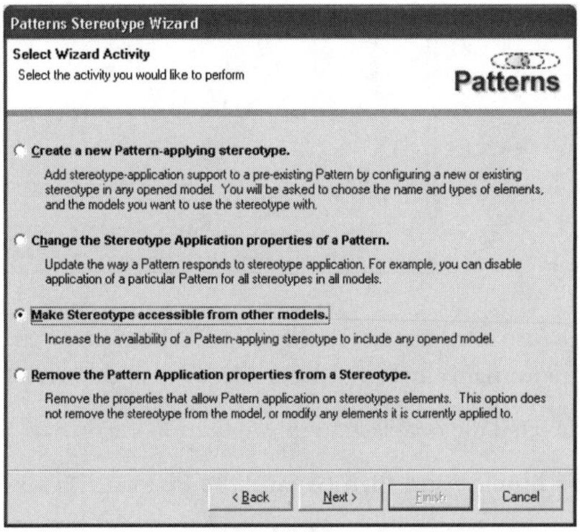

4. Select the pattern(s) you want to modify, and click Add to add them to the Selected Stereotypes list. When you are finished adding, click Next to continue.

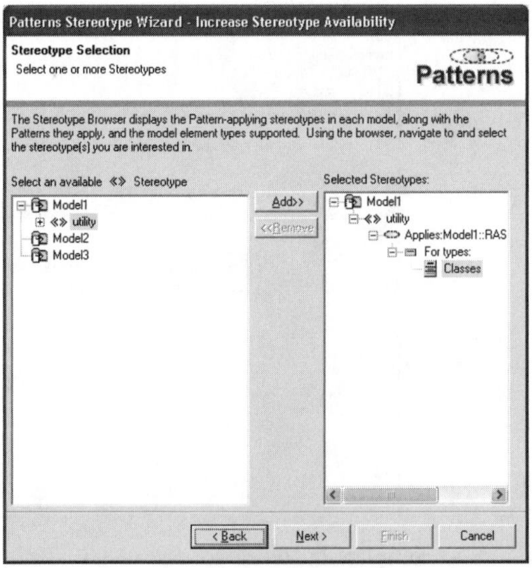

5. Select the model(s) that should have access to the stereotype, and click Add to add them to the Selected Models list. When you are finished adding, click Next to continue.

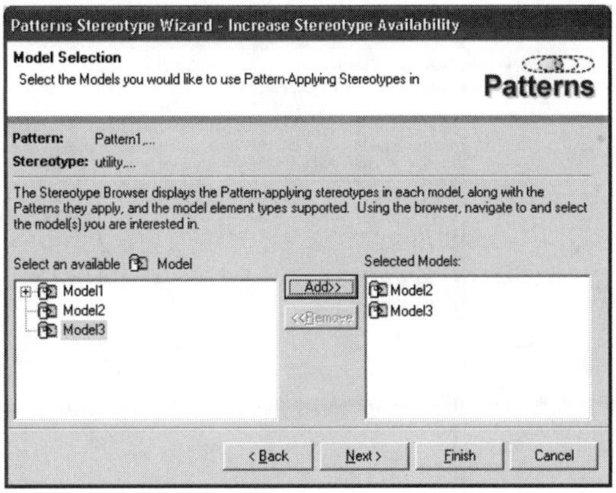

6. Click Finish to complete the wizard.

The selected models can now use the stereotype.

Removing the Pattern Application Properties from a Stereotype

This option removes the ability to apply a pattern using a stereotype. To remove the pattern application properties from a stereotype, follow these steps:

1. Start the Patterns Stereotype wizard by choosing Tools ➢ Patterns ➢ Update Pattern Stereotypes.
2. Click Next on the introductory screen.
3. Select Remove The Pattern Application Properties From A Stereotype and click Next to continue.

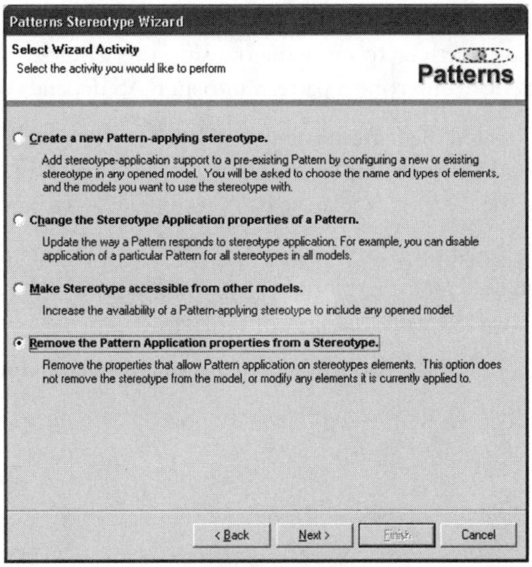

4. Select the stereotype(s) to remove. Click Add to add a stereotype to the Selected Stereotypes list. When you have finished adding, click Next to continue.

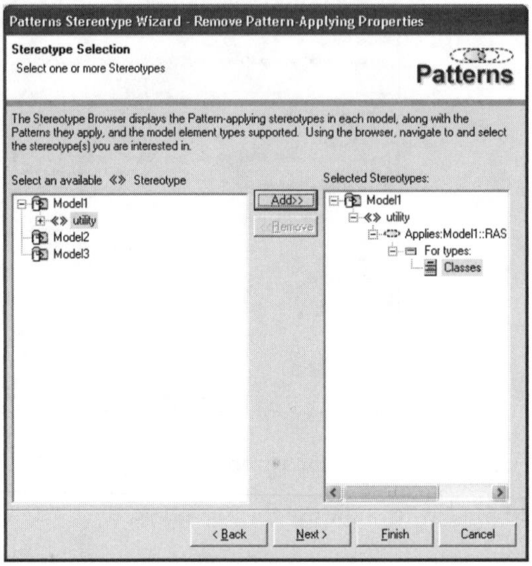

5. Click Finish to complete the wizard.

The pattern application properties have been removed from the stereotype but the stereotype itself won't be deleted. Existing model elements that used the stereotype will not be changed.

Turning a Pattern into a Reusable Asset Specification

The good news is, while "turning a pattern into a Reusable Asset Specification" may sound like a long and laborious process, XDE makes it quite simple. When you create a pattern, XDE can automatically set up everything to make the transition very quick.

The process for converting a pattern into an RAS depends on how the pattern was created.

- If you created the pattern using Add UML ➢ Asset in the Model Explorer, or Add Pattern Asset in the Pattern Explorer, and you selected the Add Documentation check box when you created the pattern, export the RAS using File ➢ Export.
- If you created the pattern using Add UML ➢ Asset in the Model Explorer, or Add Pattern Asset in the Pattern Explorer, but you did not select the Add Documentation check box when you created the pattern, follow these steps:
  1. Right-click the pattern in the Pattern Explorer and select Generate Documentation.
  2. Export the RAS using File ➢ Export.

- If you created the pattern as a collaboration in the Model Explorer, and the property Treat-NewCollaborationsAsPatterns was set to True, take these steps:
  1. Right-click the collaboration in the Model Explorer and choose Select in the Pattern Explorer.
  2. Right-click the collaboration in the Pattern Explorer and select Convert To Asset.
  3. Export the RAS using File ➢ Export.
- If you created the pattern as a collaboration in the Model Explorer, and the property Treat-NewCollaborationsAsPatterns was set to False, these are the steps to take:
  1. Right-click the collaboration in the Model Explorer and choose Select in the Pattern Explorer.
  2. Right-click the collaboration in the Pattern Explorer and select Convert To Asset.
  3. Export the RAS using File ➢ Export.

Exercise: Creating a Pattern

In this exercise, we create a new pattern and save it in a model. We implement a pattern called NullObject, which is defined in *Pattern Languages of Program Design 3* by Robert C. Martin (Addison-Wesley, 1998).

The NullObject pattern is used to ensure that a supplier always exists in a specific relationship. There are times when a client may have an optional relationship to a supplier or when the relationship may be temporal. Without the NullObject pattern, you may find yourself coding an `IF` statement to check the presence or absence of a supplier. For example, "Does this company have any employees?" or "Does this employee have any timecards?" If you use the NullObject pattern, the company *always* has an employee, even if it is just a null "placeholder" employee. An employee *always* has a timecard, even if it is just another placeholder.

Because you know the relationship always exists, you can simplify your code. You don't have to check for the presence of the relationship before you call a method.

The NullObject pattern has four elements:

- A client
- An ancestor class, which is the parent of both the null object and real object
- A null object, which is a child of the ancestor class
- A real object, which is a child of the ancestor class

Creating the Pattern

The first step is to create the NullObject pattern itself. Before you do this, however, you need to create a model that holds the new pattern. To create a model and the pattern, follow these steps:

1. Create a new project, and name it **MyPatterns**.

2. Add a new, blank model to the project and name it **MyPatternModel**.
3. Open the Model Explorer. You should see the new model:

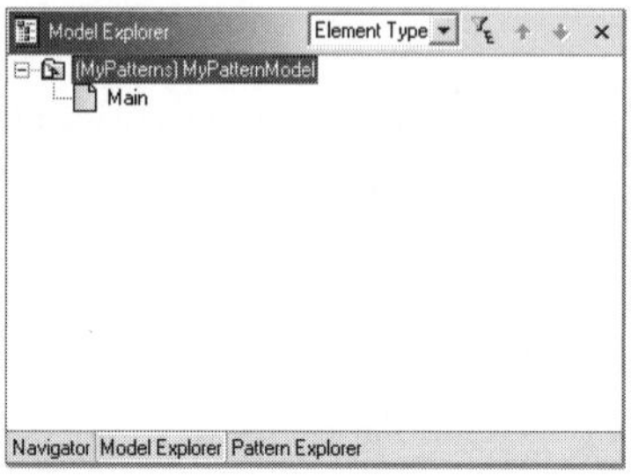

4. Right-click MyPatternModel in the Model Explorer, and choose Add UML ➢ Pattern Asset.
5. Set the Pattern Name field to **NullObject**.
6. Keep the pattern library as **Misc Patterns**, which is the default.
7. Under Asset Properties, be sure the Use Package For Asset radio button is selected.
8. Be sure the Asset Location is set to MyPatternModel.
9. Set the Asset Name field to **NullObject**.
10. Be sure the Add Documentation check box is selected and that a directory is in the Directory field. The Specification File Name should be `NullObject.xml`. At this point, the screen should look like this:

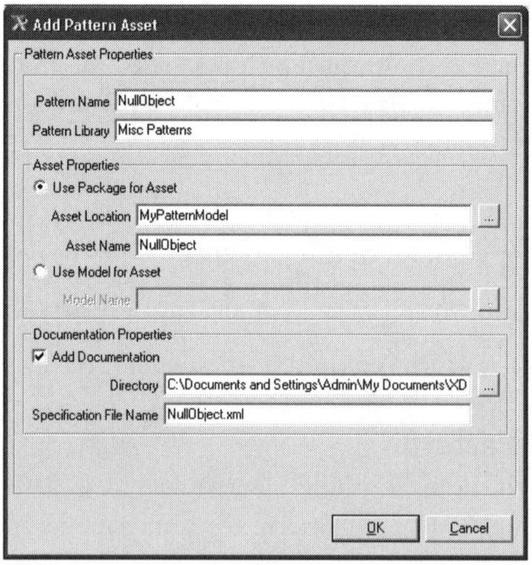

11. Click OK. XDE creates a package in the Model Explorer called **NullObject**, with a stereotype of <<Asset>>:

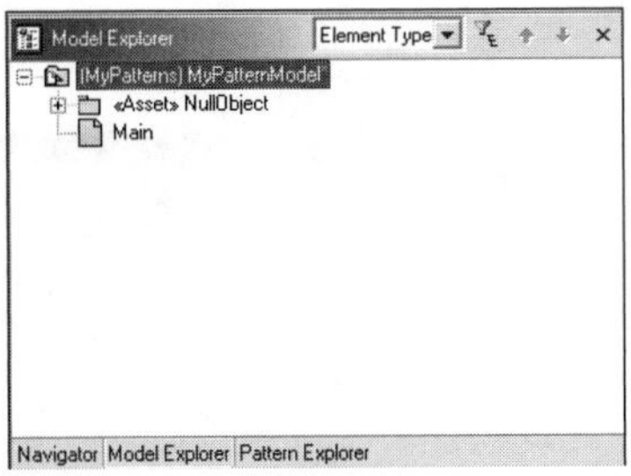

12. Right-click the NullObject package in the Model Explorer and choose Select in Pattern Explorer. The Pattern Explorer opens, and you see the new pattern, as shown here:

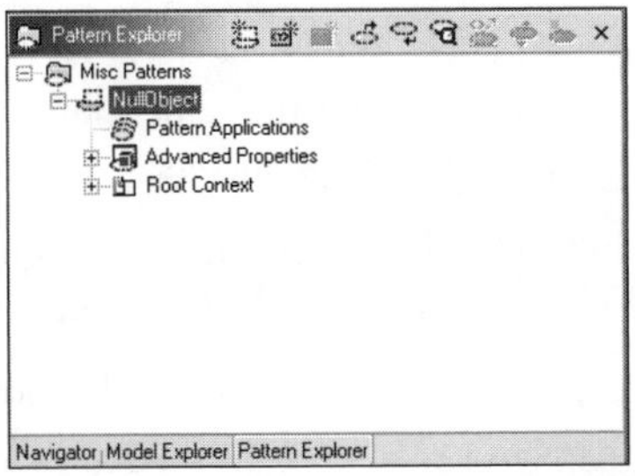

Adding Parameters

Next, you add parameters for the client, ancestor class, null object, and real object. You also add default values for each of these. To create and configure the parameters, follow these steps:

1. In the Pattern Explorer, right-click the Null Object pattern and select Add Template Parameter. XDE adds a new parameter called `TemplateParameter1`.
2. Select the new parameter. In the Pattern Properties window, change the parameter's name to **`Client`**. Set the Multiplicity property to 1. Set the Type Name to Client.
3. Repeat steps 1 and 2 to add three additional parameters. Name these parameters **`AncestorClass`**, **`NullObject`**, and **`RealObject`**. Set the Multiplicity property to 1 for all three of these parameters. Set the Type Name to **AncestorClass**, **NullObject**, and **RealObject**, respectively.
4. Next, set the value source for the parameters. To do so, first expand the Advanced Properties node under the Client parameter.
5. Select the Value Sources node.

6. Using the drop-down list, change the Value Sources property to User Or Generated. This gives the user the option of entering a new name for the client class or selecting an existing class.

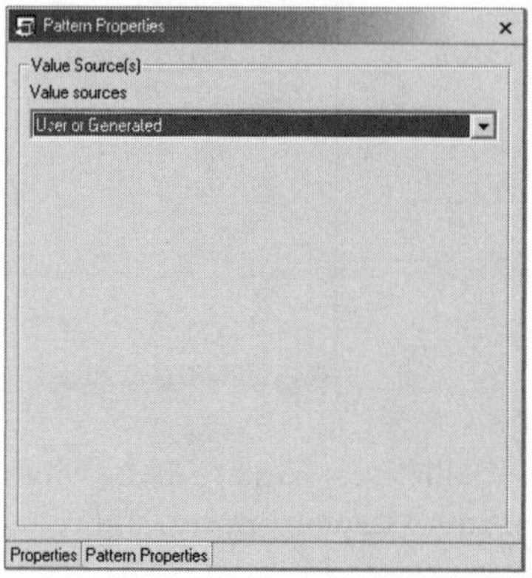

7. Repeat steps 4 through 6 to set the value source to User Or Generated for the `AncestorClass`, `NullObject`, and `RealObject` parameters.
8. Now, add default values for the parameters. Right-click the Client property and select Add Argument. XDE creates a node called Default Argument.
9. Right-click the Default Argument node and choose Edit Argument Values ➢ Generated Values.
10. On the Generated Values screen, type **Client** as the default value, and click Add. Click OK to finish the default value definition.

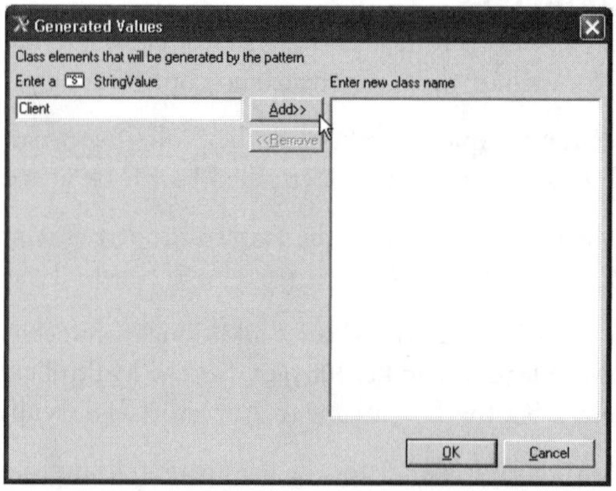

11. Repeat steps 8 through 10 to add a default value of **AncestorClass** to the `AncestorClass` parameter, a default value of **NullObject** to the `NullObject` parameter, and a default value of **RealObject** to the `RealObject` parameter.

Finally, you will add one more argument, called `DoOperation`. This is the operation that the client requests of the null object or real object. It is declared in the ancestor class and inherited by the null object and the real object. To add the argument, follow these steps:

1. Create a new parameter, named **`DoOperation`**, under the NullObject pattern.
2. Set the parameter's Type property to Operation and the Type Name property to **DoOperation**. Set the Multiplicity to 1.
3. Set the value source of the `DoOperation` parameter to User.
4. In the Model Explorer, add a new operation to the AncestorClass class in the NullObject collaboration. Name the new operation **<%=DoOperation%>**. When the pattern is expanded, the operation name is replaced with the name in the `DoOperation` parameter, as shown next.

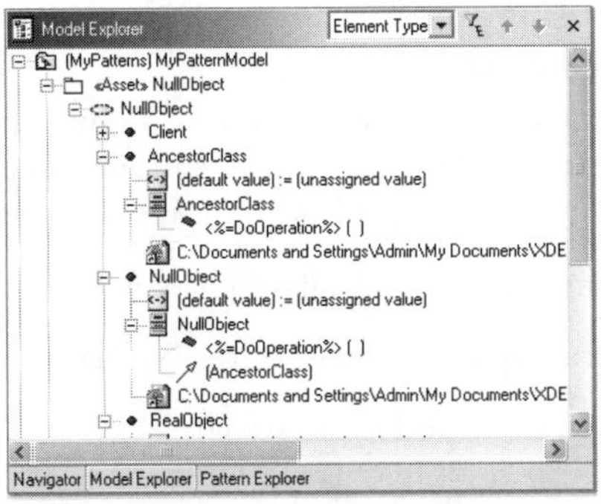

5. Set the IsAbstract property of the `DoOperation` operation in the AncestorClass class to True.
6. Repeat steps 1 through 5 to add the operation `<%=DoOperation%>` to the NullObject class and the RealObject class. Do not make these operations abstract.

Adding a Class Diagram

Now that you have parameters defined, you can create the relationships between them using a class diagram that becomes part of the pattern. When you apply the pattern later, this diagram is created. To create the class diagram, take these steps:

1. In the Model Explorer, right-click the NullObject collaboration in the NullObject asset package and choose Add Diagram ➢ Class. Name the new diagram **NullObject Participants**.
2. In the Model Explorer, expand the Client parameter node. You see a Client class underneath it.
3. Drag the Client class onto the new diagram.
4. Repeat steps 2 and 3 to add the AncestorClass, NullObject, and RealObject classes to the diagram.
5. Create a generalization relationship from the NullObject class to the AncestorClass class.

6. Create a generalization relationship from the RealObject class to the AncestorClass class.

7. Create a directed association from the Client class to the AncestorClass class. Your diagram should now look like this:

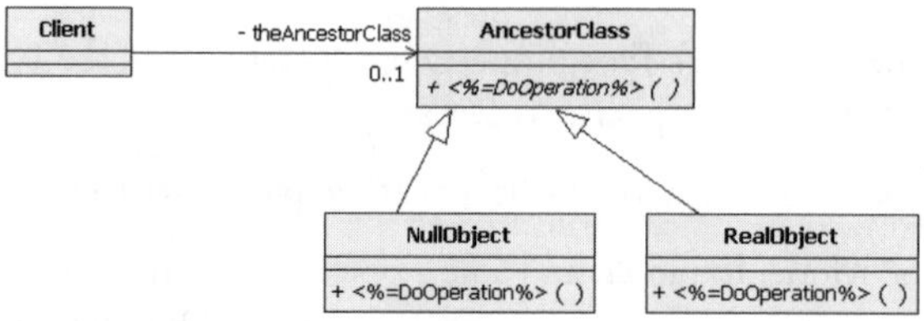

8. In the Model Explorer, right-click the MyPatternModel model and select Save MyPattern-Model.mdx.

Applying the Pattern

The pattern has been built, so now it is time to apply it to the timekeeping system. In the timekeeping example, we'll use a null object to be sure an employee always has a relationship to at least one timecard. Follow these steps to apply it to the timekeeping project:

1. Open the timekeeping model if you have not already done so.

2. In the Pattern Explorer, right-click the NullObject pattern and select Apply Pattern.

3. Click Next on the introductory screen.

4. For the `Client` parameter, select the Selected Element radio button. Navigate through the model and select the Employee class.

5. For the `AncestorClass` parameter, select the Generated Value radio button. Keep the default value of AncestorClass.

6. For the `NullObject` parameter, select the Generated Value radio button. Keep the default value of NullObject.

7. For the `RealObject` parameter, select the Selected Element radio button. Navigate through the model and select the Timecard class.

8. For the `DoOperation` parameter, select the Selected Element radio button. Navigate through the model and select the Save operation.

9. Select the Analysis Elements package in the timecard model as the expansion and binding location.

10. Click Finish to complete the wizard.

Summary

In this chapter, we explored the process of creating your own patterns. The GOF patterns that come with XDE are powerful, proven patterns, but there may be times when you'll want to create your own.

To create a pattern, you can choose Add UML ➢ Asset in the Model Explorer, or the Add Pattern Asset command in the Pattern Explorer. If you select the Add Documentation check box while you're creating the pattern, you can convert it easily into a Reusable Asset Specification later.

Once a pattern has been created, you can add both static elements and parameters to it. A static element is an item, such as a diagram, that will be created when the pattern is applied. A parameter is an item that the user must provide a value for before an element can be created.

The next step is to set the parameter properties and the pattern properties. These properties control how the pattern is applied, and how the Apply Pattern wizard looks and behaves for the pattern.

You can generate documentation for the pattern by right-clicking it and selecting Generate Documentation. XDE will create an RAS-compliant XML file and HTML file that you can use to document the pattern.

You can use pattern libraries to organize your patterns. The libraries don't actually hold the patterns; they remain in the models. However, the libraries can act as virtual pattern repositories.

Applying the pattern occurs in two steps, which can be performed at once or individually. Binding the pattern involves providing values for the parameters. Expanding the pattern will actually apply it to a model, using the values from the pattern binding.

Some patterns can automatically be applied when you assign a particular stereotype to a model element. This feature is controlled using Tools ➢ Patterns ➢ Update Pattern Stereotypes.

By creating your own patterns, you can help to be sure that common problems are solved consistently. This, in turn, can increase the reliability and quality of your applications.

Appendix

Getting Started with the UML

The UML is made up of a number of different types of diagrams. Each gives the reader a slightly different perspective of the system's design. Some are high-level and are intended to give you an understanding of the functionality in the system. Others are very detailed and include the specific classes and components that will be built to implement the system. Still others are mid-way between these two levels: they provide design details but from a higher-level perspective.

The set of diagrams gives you a complete picture of the system design. Different members of the team create different types of diagrams, and each is used by a different set of people. While building the system, the developers refer to the diagrams to understand what classes and components need to be built. Later, when a team is maintaining the system, they can refer to the diagrams to understand the system structure, analyze the impact of a potential change, and document any design changes that were made.

The UML is constantly being refined to incorporate new ideas and technologies. For example, it can now be used to model an XML Document Type Definition (DTD). As the object-oriented world changes, the UML can change along with it. At the same time, though, it is a standard, and modifications to it are centrally managed. The UML is controlled by the Object Management Group, which has members from large and small companies around the world.

Rational Software has developed a systems development lifecycle titled the Rational Unified Process (RUP). RUP complements the UML by providing specific process steps, roles, responsibilities, guidelines, workflows, and templates that can be used to develop software. Although RUP complements the UML, you may use the UML without using RUP.

The UML includes many different diagram types. Business use case diagrams are used to model the organization. Business workflow (activity) diagrams are used to show the processes within the organization. While business use case diagrams show the functions of the organization, use case diagrams show the functionality to be provided by the system and the people and entities that interact with the system. Activity diagrams show the flow of logic through a use case. Sequence and collaboration diagrams show the objects that are needed to implement the functionality of a use case, and include the messages between the objects. Statechart diagrams are used to model dynamic behavior, and are frequently used in real-time systems. Component diagrams show the components that will be created for the system and the relationships between them. Finally, deployment diagrams are used to show the network structure and where the system will be deployed on the network.

Building a Business Use Case Diagram

A business use case diagram is a mechanism for modeling the work done by the organization itself. The diagram contains *business use cases,* which are functions performed by the organization; *business actors,* which are entities outside the organization that interact with it; and *business workers,* which are roles within the organization.

The business use case diagram allows someone to understand what the organization does and who interacts with it. It is supplemented by activity diagrams, which detail the workflows within the organization.

A business process team or a business analysis team typically creates the diagram. It is nontechnical and can be used by any member of the organization to better understand the organization.

By default, XDE doesn't have the business modeling icons and stereotypes, but you can add them. The first step is to create a business use case diagram.

To create a new business use case diagram, follow these steps:

1. Right-click a package or model.
2. Choose Add Diagram ➢ Use Case.

Here is an example of a business use case diagram:

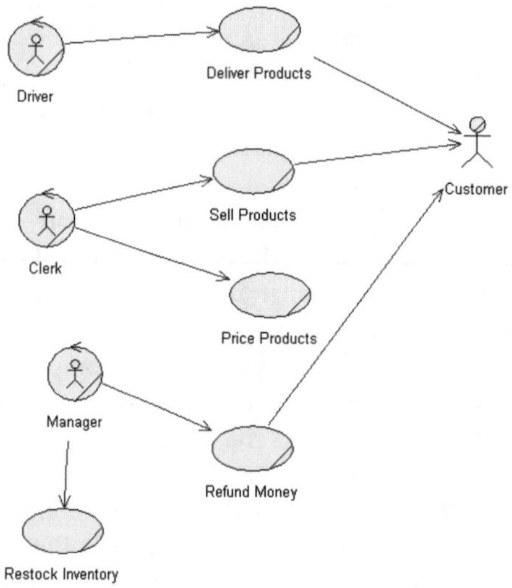

Once you have a business use case diagram, you can add business use cases to it. A *business use case* is a process within an organization that provides a result of value to a business actor.

Follow these steps to add business use cases to your diagram:

1. Determine the business use cases.
2. Select the Use Case Toolbox button.
3. Click in the business use case diagram to add the use case.

4. Name the business use case.
5. In the Properties window, find the UML Stereotype property. Click the ellipsis button. You will see the Properties window:

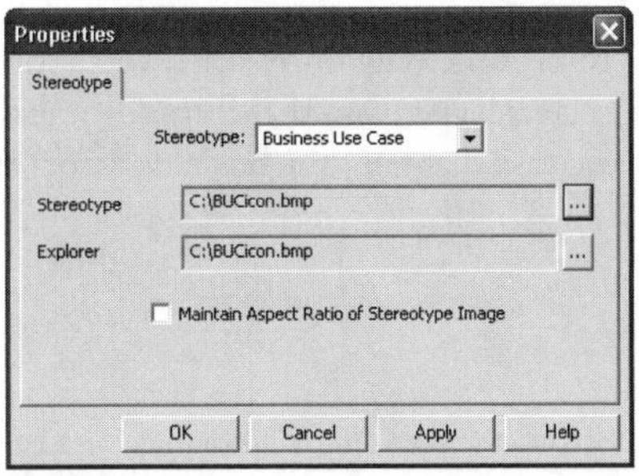

6. In the Stereotype drop-down list field, type **Business Use Case.**
7. In the Stereotype icon field, click the ellipsis button. Navigate to the file `BUCicon.bmp`. After you've selected `BUCicon.bmp`, XDE automatically sets both the stereotype icon and the Explorer window icon to the business use case.
8. Step 7 needs to be done only once; when you add more business use cases, you can select the Business Use Case stereotype from the drop-down list.

The next step is to add business actors to the diagram. A *business actor* is an individual, group, company, or other entity outside of the organization that directly interacts with the organization.

Follow these steps to add business actors to your diagram:

1. Determine the business actors.
2. Select the Actor toolbox button.
3. Click in the business use case diagram to add the business actor.
4. Name the business actor.
5. In the Properties window, find the UML Stereotype property. Click the ellipsis button. You will see the Properties window:

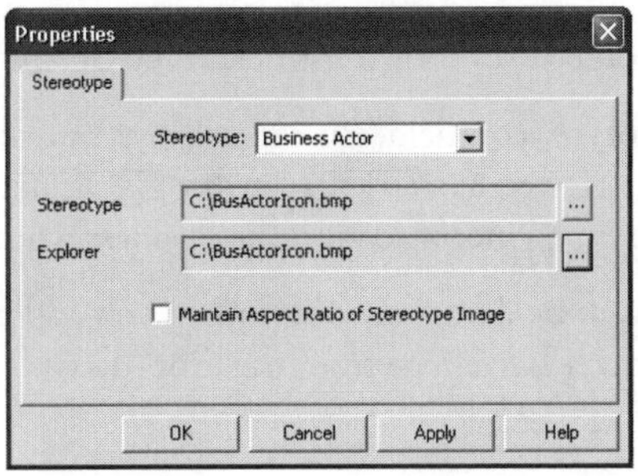

6. In the Stereotype drop-down list field, type **Business Actor.**
7. In the Stereotype icon field, click the ellipsis button. Navigate to the file `BusActorIcon.bmp`. After you've selected `BusActorIcon.bmp`, XDE automatically sets both the stereotype icon and the Explorer window icon to the business actor.
8. Step 7 needs to be done only once; when you add more business actors, you can select the Business Actor stereotype from the drop-down list.

On the business use case diagram, the business actors are drawn with the following symbol:

You can also add business workers to a business use case diagram. A *business worker* is a role within the organization.

Use these steps to add business workers to the diagram:

1. Determine the business workers.
2. Select the Class toolbox button.
3. Click in the business use case diagram to add the business worker.
4. Name the business worker.
5. In the Properties window, find the UML Stereotype property. Click the ellipsis button. You will see the Properties window:

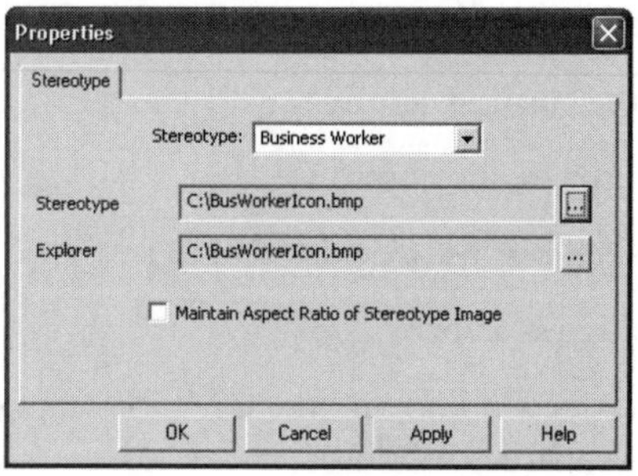

6. In the Stereotype drop-down list field, type **Business Worker.**
7. In the Stereotype icon field, click the ellipsis button. Navigate to the file `BusWorkerIcon.bmp`. After you've selected `BusWorkerIcon.bmp`, XDE automatically sets both the stereotype icon and the Explorer window icon to the business worker.
8. Step 7 needs to be done only once; when you add more business workers, you can select the Business Worker stereotype from the drop-down list.

You use the following symbol to display a business worker on a business use case diagram:

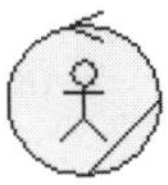

A *communicates relationship* between a business actor and a business use case shows how a business actor or business worker interacts with the organization.

Follow these steps to add relationships between the business actors and business use cases:

1. Select the Directed Association toolbox button.
2. Click the business actor first and then click the business use case to draw an association from the business actor to the business use case. Click the business use case first and then click the business actor to draw an association from the business use case to the business actor.

A communicates relationship is drawn as an arrow, as shown here:

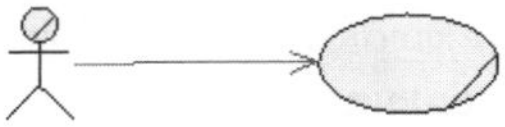

An *organization unit* is used to group together business modeling elements such as business actors and business use cases. These units can help organize the model and show how the company itself is organized.

Follow these steps to group the business actors, business workers, and business use cases into organization units.

1. Select the Package toolbox button.
2. Click inside a business use case diagram to place the organization unit.
3. In the Properties window, find the UML Stereotype property. Click the ellipsis button. You will see the Properties window:

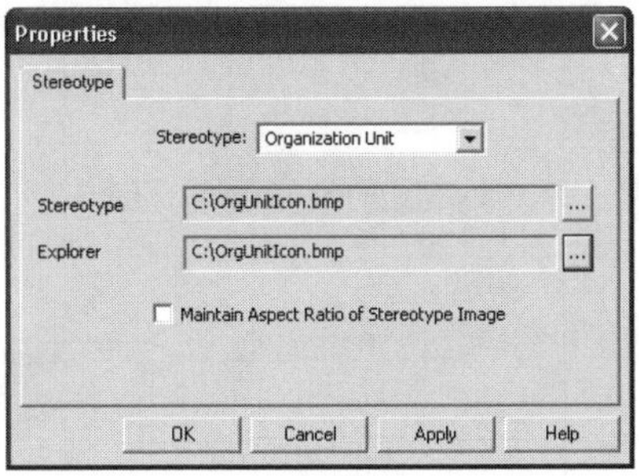

4. In the Stereotype drop-down list field, type **Organization Unit**.
5. In the Stereotype icon field, click the ellipsis button. Navigate to the file `OrgUnitIcon.bmp`. After you've selected `OrgUnitIcon.bmp`, XDE automatically sets both the stereotype icon and the Explorer window icon to the organization unit.

6. Step 5 needs to be done only once; when you add more organization units, you can select the Organization Unit stereotype from the drop-down list.

On a business use case diagram, you use the following symbol for an organization unit:

Building a Workflow (Activity) Diagram

Activity diagrams are commonly used in two situations. In business modeling, they can be used to document the workflow of a process within the organization. In systems modeling, they can be used to document the flow of logic through a use case.

An activity diagram that focuses on workflow shows you the people or groups within the workflow, the steps in the process, decision points in the process, areas where steps in the process can occur in parallel, objects affected by the workflow, states of the objects, and transitions between steps in the process. The UML contains notation for all of these items.

To create a new activity diagram, take these steps:

1. Right-click a use case, class, or package in the Explorer.
2. Choose Add Diagram ➢ Activity.

In XDE, an activity diagram is created inside an Activity Graph. When you add a new activity diagram, XDE automatically adds the Activity Graph for you. Here is an example of an activity diagram:

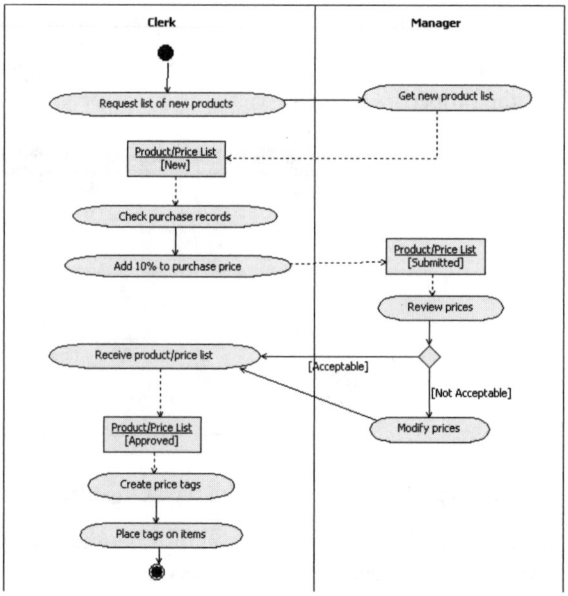

A *swimlane* is a vertical section of the diagram that contains all of the workflow steps that a particular person or group performs. You divide the diagram into many swimlanes, one for each person or group in the process.

To partition your diagram into swimlanes for each actor or worker's responsibilities, follow these steps:

1. Determine the participants in the workflow.
2. Select the Swimlane toolbox button.
3. Click in the diagram to add the swimlane.
4. Name the swimlane with the name of the role or group in the workflow.

By default, each swimlane can be moved around on the diagram independently of the others. If you want, you can merge the swimlanes, which lines them up horizontally, as shown here:

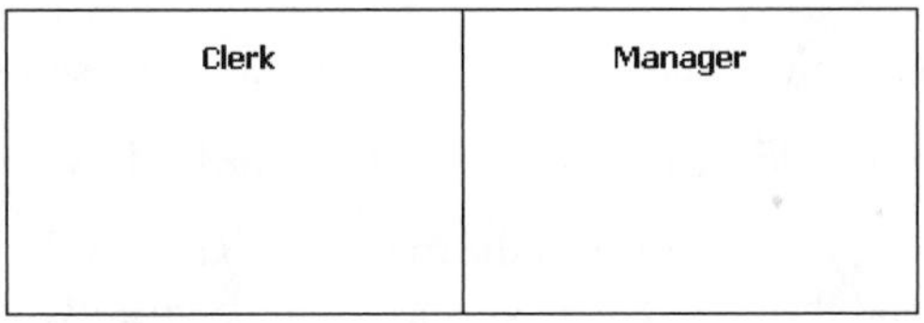

To merge the swimlanes, select the swimlanes to merge, then right-click and select Swimlane ➢ Merge Swimlanes. To detach them later, right-click any of the merged swimlanes and select Swimlane ➢ Detach Swimlane(s).

An *activity* is a step in the workflow. It can contain *actions*, which are steps within the activity. The activity is placed in the swimlane of the individual or group that performs the activity.

To add detailed activities to the activity diagram:

1. Select the Activity toolbox button.
2. Click in the diagram to add the activity.
3. Name the activity.

An activity is drawn as a rounded rectangle, as shown here:

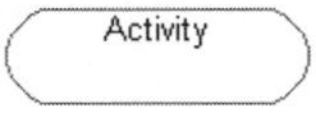

Now that you have activities on your diagram, the next step is to add the transitions between them. A *transition* shows how the process moves from one step (activity) to the next. There are several details you can add to the transition, including events, guard conditions, send targets, and send events.

An *event* triggers the movement from one activity to another and it can have *arguments*. Typically, an event corresponds to an operation of a class, and the event arguments correspond to the operation's arguments.

A *guard condition* controls when the transition can or cannot occur; the guard condition must be true in order for the transition to occur. Not every transition needs a guard condition, but if two or more transitions leave an activity or decision point, they should have either different events or mutually exclusive guard conditions. A guard condition is drawn along the transition arrow, and is enclosed in square brackets.

An *action* occurs while the process is transitioning from one activity to another; the action is typically a quick process that occurs as part of the transition itself. The action is drawn along the transition arrow, and is preceded by a slash.

The *send target* suggests that, as part of the transition, a message is sent to some object. The send target is the object receiving the message. The *send event* is a message sent to another object. It may also have arguments. On an activity diagram, the send target is drawn along the transition arrow, and is preceded by a ^.

Follow these steps to set the sequence of the activities:

1. Select the Transition toolbox button.
2. Click one activity, then click another to draw a transition from the first activity to the second.
3. (Optional) Add a guard condition using the UML Guard Condition property.
4. (Optional) Add an event to the transition. Right-click the transition and choose Add ➢ UML, and then Call Event, Change Event, Signal Event, or Time Event.
5. If you added a change event, set the change condition using the Change property of the event. Note that you may need to select the event in the Explorer window to see the event properties.
6. If you added a time event, set the trigger time using the When property of the event. Note that you may need to select the event in the Explorer window to see the event properties.

On an activity diagram, the event, guard condition, action, send target, and send event are all drawn along the transition line, as shown here:

A *decision point* in the workflow indicates when the workflow can take two or more different paths. Transition arrows leading from the decision to activities show the different paths that the workflow can follow. Guard conditions on the transitions indicate under which conditions each path will be followed. Guard conditions must be mutually exclusive.

Follow these steps to add decision points to the logic:

1. Select the Decision toolbox button.
2. Click in the diagram to place the decision.
3. Draw transitions from the decision to the activities that may occur after the decision.
4. Place guard conditions on each transition arrow. The guard conditions control which path is taken after the decision.

On an activity diagram, a decision point is drawn as a diamond:

An *object* is an entity affected by the workflow. An *object flow state* is a way of modeling the object and its current state. It can serve as input into a process step, in which case a dashed object flow arrow is drawn from the object to the process step. Or it can be affected by a process step, in which case an object flow arrow is drawn from the step to the object.

To add object flow states to the workflow:

1. Select the ObjectFlow State toolbox button.
2. Click inside the diagram to place the object flow state.
3. Drag and drop a class from the Model Explorer onto the ObjectFlow State.
4. Drag and drop a state from the Explorer onto the ObjectFlow State. States may have been created on a statechart diagram; if not, you need to create the state before performing this step.
5. Select the Transition relationship icon from the UML Class toolbox.
6. Create a transition between the activity and the object flow state. The transition should go from the activity to the object flow state if the activity changes the state of the object, and from the object flow state to the activity if the activity uses the object as an input.

On an activity diagram, an object is drawn as a box:

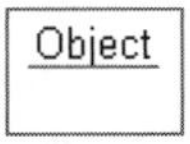

A *synchronization* indicates that two or more steps in the workflow may be completed in parallel. A *synchronization bar* is used to show where two or more activities may occur simultaneously. These can be very effective in analyzing the efficiency of a workflow; examining the amount of parallel activity can help optimize a workflow.

Follow these steps to add synchronizations to the workflow:

1. Select the Synchronization toolbox button.
2. Click in the diagram to place the synchronization bar.
3. Draw a transition arrow from an activity to the synchronization bar, indicating that the parallel processing begins after that activity.
4. Draw transition arrows from the synchronization bar to the activities that can occur in parallel.
5. Create another synchronization bar to indicate the end of the parallel processing.
6. Draw transition arrows from the synchronous activities to the final synchronization bar to indicate that the parallel processing stops once all of those activities are complete.

A synchronization point is drawn as a straight line:

Building a Use Case Diagram

A use case diagram is a graphical representation of the high-level system scope. It includes *use cases,* which are pieces of functionality the system provides, and *actors,* who are the users of the system. Looking at a use case diagram, you should be able to easily tell what the system does and who interacts with it.

You can create one or more use case diagrams for a single system. If you create more than one, each shows a subset of the actors and/or use cases in the system. You can also group the use cases and actors into packages to help organize the model.

The use case diagram can be helpful in communicating with the end users of the system. It is designed to be straightforward and nontechnical so that everyone on the team can come to a common understanding of the system scope. It is usually created by the technical team, but in conjunction with an end user representative.

To create a new use case diagram:

1. Right-click a package or model.
2. Choose Add Diagram ➢ Use Case.

Here is an example of a use case diagram:

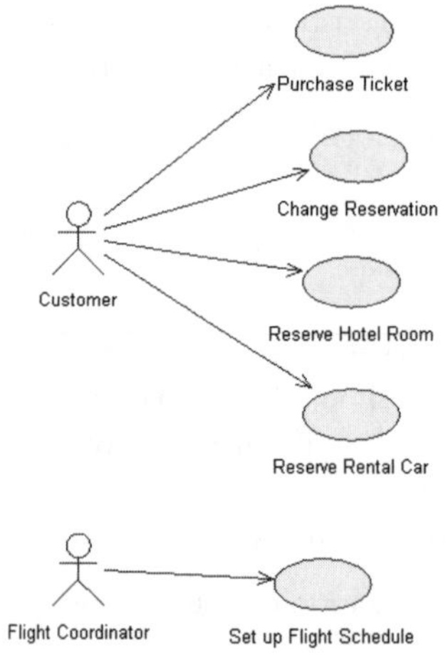

An *actor* is a person, system, piece of hardware, or other thing that interacts with your system. Follow these steps to add actors to the diagram:

1. Determine the actors for your system.
2. Select the Actor toolbox button.
3. Click in the use case diagram to add the actor.
4. Name the actor.

On a use case diagram, an actor is drawn using the following symbol:

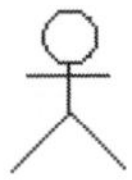

A *use case* is a piece of functionality the system provides. It is usually named in the format <*verb*><*noun*>, such as "Deposit Check" or "Withdraw Cash." Use cases are high-level and implementation-independent.

Follow these steps to add use cases to the diagram:

1. Select the Use Case toolbox button.
2. Click in the use case diagram to add the use case.
3. Give the use case a name.

A use case is drawn as an oval, as shown here:

A *communicates relationship* between an actor and a use case indicates that the actor initiates the use case. An actor may initiate one or more use cases.

To add relationships between the actors and use cases:

1. Select the Directed Association toolbox button.
2. Click the actor first and then click the use case to add an association from the actor to the use case. Click the use case first and then click the actor to add an association from the use case to the actor.

On a use case diagram, a communicates relationship is drawn as an arrow between an actor and a use case, as shown here:

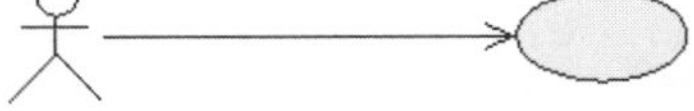

An *includes relationship* suggests that one use case must include another. In other words, running one use case means that the other must be run as well. One use case may be included by one or more other use cases.

To add includes relationships between appropriate use cases, follow these steps:

1. Select the Include toolbox button.
2. Click the base use case first, and then click the included use case.

An includes relationship is drawn as a dependency with a stereotype of <<include>>, as shown here:

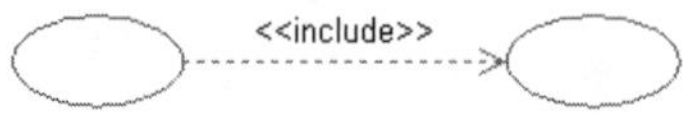

An *extend relationship* is used when one use case optionally extends the functionality provided by another. In other words, if one use case runs, an extending use case may or may not run.

To add extend relationships between appropriate use cases:

1. Select the Extend toolbox button.
2. Click the base use case first, and then click the extending use case.

An extend relationship is drawn as a dependency with a stereotype of <<extend>>, as shown here:

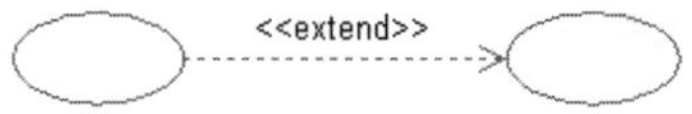

A *package* is a UML mechanism used to group items together. Grouping can help organize the model and can also help in managing any changes in the model elements. You may nest one package inside another to further organize the model.

Follow these steps to group the use cases, actors, and other elements into packages:

1. Right-click a package or model and choose Add UML ➢ Package.
2. Name the new package.
3. In the Explorer window, drag and drop use cases, actors, use case diagrams, or other modeling elements into the new package.

In the UML, a package is drawn using the following symbol:

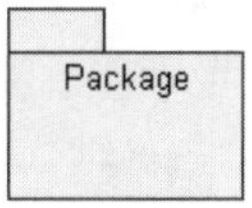

A *generalization relationship* between two use cases indicates that one use case (the child) inherits all of the functionality provided by the other use case (the parent).

To add generalization relationships between appropriate use cases:

1. Select the Generalization toolbox button.
2. Click first on the child use case and then on the parent use case.

A generalization relationship is drawn as an arrow from the child to the parent, as shown below:

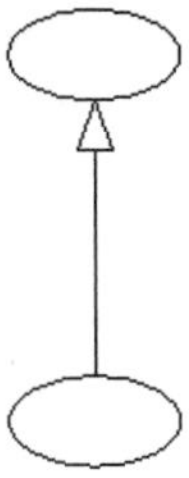

A generalization relationship between actors indicates that one actor (the child) inherits the characteristics of another actor (the parent). The child actor may initiate all of the use cases that the parent can initiate.

To add generalization relationships between appropriate actors:

1. Select the Generalization toolbox button.
2. Click the child actor first and then click the parent actor.

The generalization relationship is drawn as an arrow from the child actor to the parent actor, as shown here:

Building an Interaction Diagram

An *interaction diagram* is a graphical representation of how the objects and actors in a system interact with one another to achieve the desired goal of the system. There are two types of interaction diagrams: *sequence diagrams* and *collaboration diagrams*. Sequence diagrams illustrate the interactions of objects along a timeline. Collaboration diagrams show the interactions, but without the timeline. These two diagrams display the same information, just in different ways.

You can create multiple interaction diagrams for each use case in a system. More than one is typically created to illustrate the interaction, given different scenarios.

Sequence diagrams are usually created to show the flow of functionality and control throughout the objects in the system. Collaboration diagrams are typically used to illustrate which objects communicate with other objects. Sequence diagrams answer questions about how the system works. Collaboration diagrams answer questions about the soundness of the structure of the system.

At this time, XDE does not support collaboration diagrams. However, you can add sequence diagrams to your model. In XDE, a sequence diagram is created in an *interaction instance*, which is contained within a *collaboration instance*. A collaboration instance is sometimes referred to as a *use-case realization*, and a relationship can exist between the collaboration instance and the use case it realizes. We show this as a realizes relationship:

Here is an example of the structure of collaboration instances in XDE:

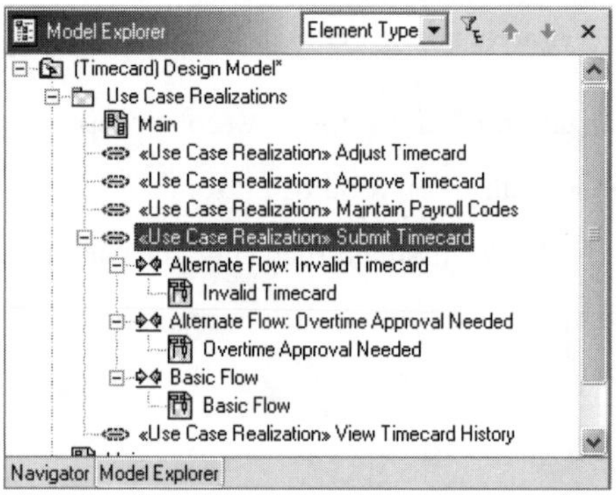

In this example, the collaboration instance is the use-case realization Submit Timecard. The use-case realizations for the other use cases are also collaboration instances. For the Submit Timecard use case, the interaction instances are Alternate Flow: Invalid Timecard, Alternate Flow: Overtime Approval Needed, and Basic Flow. The actual sequence diagrams are Invalid Timecard, Overtime Approval Needed, and Basic Flow.

To create a new Sequence diagram if a collaboration instance does not yet exist (for example, to create the first sequence diagram for a use case), follow these steps:

1. Right-click a use case or package.
2. Select Add Diagram ➢ Sequence: Instance.
3. Type the name of the new sequence diagram.
4. If a collaboration instance and an interaction instance do not already exist, XDE automatically creates them for you. You can rename the collaboration instance (usually with the name of the use case) and interaction instance (usually with the name of the basic or alternate flow) if you want.

To create a new sequence diagram if the collaboration instance already exists (for example, to create a new sequence diagram for a use case that already has some sequence diagrams), follow these steps:

1. Right-click the existing collaboration instance in the Explorer and choose Add UML ➢ Interaction Instance.
2. Name the new interaction instance (usually with the name of the basic or alternate flow).
3. Right-click the new interaction instance and choose Add Diagram ➢ Sequence: Instance.
4. Name the new sequence diagram.

Once you have created the sequence diagram, you next need to determine which actors and objects to place on it. One method is to drag all actors involved in the use case to the sequence diagram, then walk through the functionality, adding objects to facilitate that functionality as needed.

Here is an example of a sequence diagram:

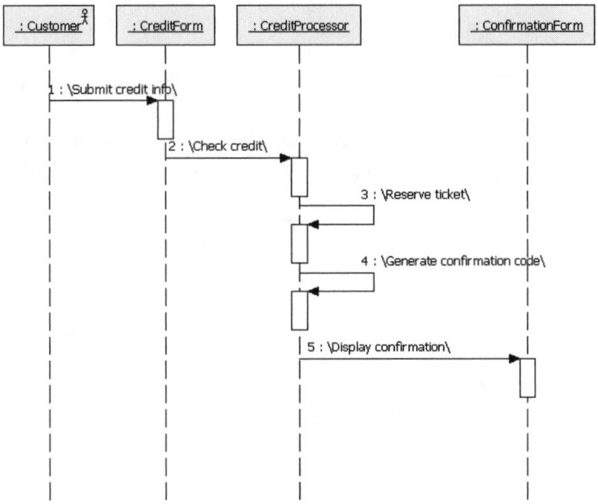

To add actors and objects to the sequence diagram, follow these steps:

1. Select any actors involved in the use case and drag them into the new sequence diagram.
2. Select the Lifeline toolbox button.
3. Click in the sequence diagram to add an object.
4. Name the object.
5. Add additional objects as needed.

We've just added objects to the diagram, but we may want to map those objects to classes. To do so, drag the appropriate class from the Explorer window onto the object.

You can also directly add an object mapped to a class by dragging a class from the Explorer window onto the sequence diagram. XDE adds a new object and maps it to the class.

At this point, the objects and actors are on the sequence diagram, but interaction diagrams would be fairly useless without showing the interactions. Messages are used to accomplish this. A message is simply some form of communication between one object or actor and another. Messages are drawn between the lifelines of actors or objects on a sequence diagram, as shown here:

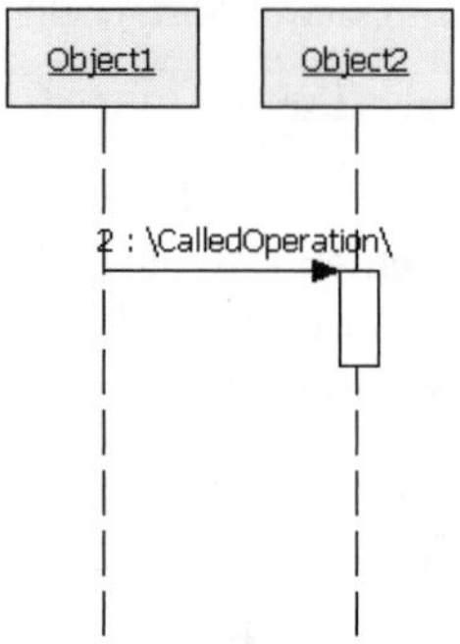

Messages can also be *reflexive*, meaning that the object communicates some information to itself.

On a sequence diagram, actors are drawn using the actor symbol, while objects are drawn with boxes:

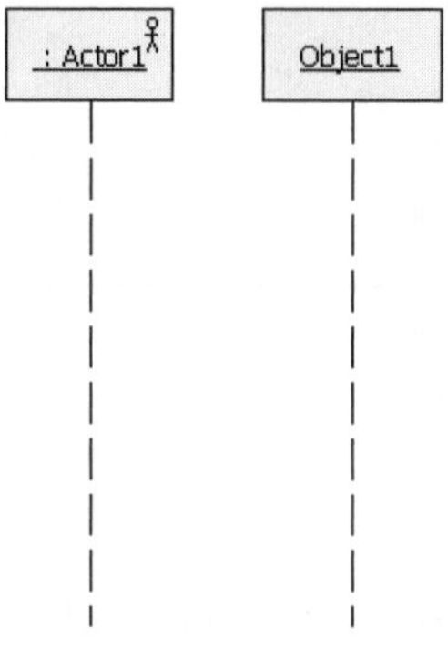

Follow these steps to add messages to the diagram:

1. Select the Message toolbox button.
2. Click the lifeline of the actor or object that initiates the message.
3. Click the lifeline of the actor or object that receives the message.
4. If you are building an analysis-level (implementation-independent) diagram, name the message.
5. If you are building a design-level (implementation-dependent) diagram, select the text above the message. When you do, you see a drop-down list of the receiving object's operations. Select the appropriate operation.

Building a Class Diagram

A class diagram is used to show a subset of the classes, interfaces, packages of classes, and relationships in the system. A typical system has many different class diagrams.

In XDE, different icons are used to represent different kinds of classes on a class diagram. For example, XDE contains icons for interfaces, client pages, session Enterprise JavaBeans (EJB), COM objects, and many other types of classes. XDE also contains icons that distinguish analysis classes from design classes. An *analysis class* is an implementation-independent view of the system, intended to be an initial sketch of the system design. *Design classes* are implementation-specific and correlate to the classes that are eventually created in the source code.

XDE can generate code that includes the class name, attribute types, default values, operation signatures, and class relationships. Developers use the class diagrams to see the system structure and to know what operations to create for a given class.

Follow these steps to create a new class diagram:

1. Right-click a package or model.
2. Choose Add Diagram ➢ Class.

Here is an example of a class diagram:

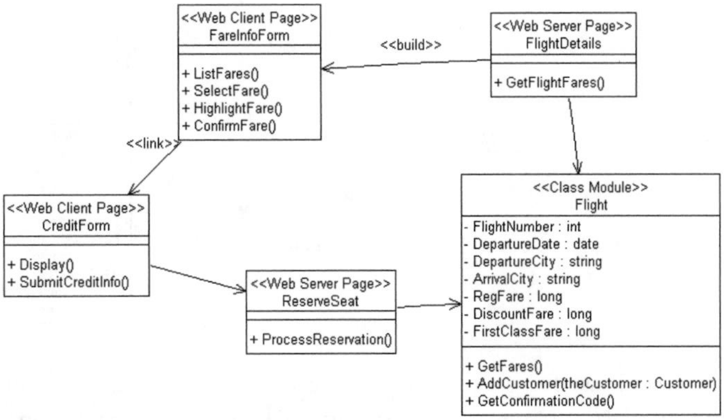

An *analysis class* is an implementation-independent class. The analysis classes are used to document some of the concepts within the system and to create a conceptual view of the system design.

Take these steps to add analysis classes to the model:

1. Select the Class option from the UML Class toolbox.
2. Click in the class diagram to add the class.
3. Name the class.
4. Click the ellipsis button in the UML Stereotype property and set the stereotype to Boundary, Entity, or Control.

The following icons are used to represent boundary, entity, and control classes, respectively:

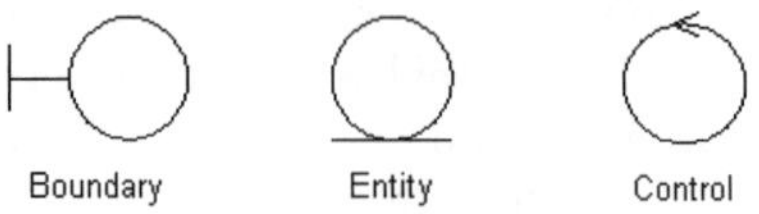

A design class is an implementation-specific class within the model. It corresponds to a class in the source code.

To add design classes to the model:

1. Select the Class option from the toolbox.
2. Click in the diagram to add the class.
3. Name the class.

On a class diagram, design classes are drawn as boxes, as shown here:

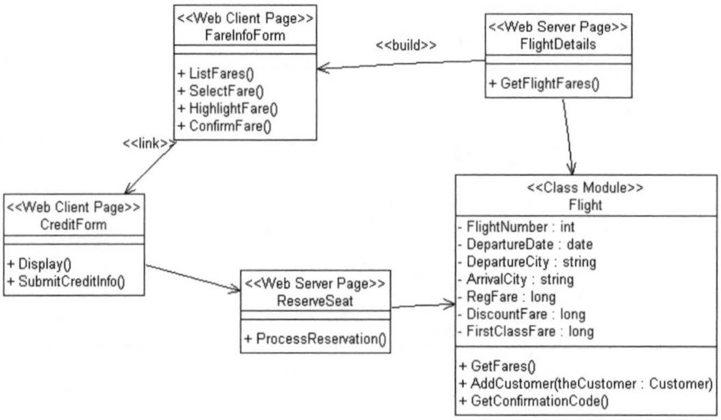

An *interface* is used to expose the public operations of a class without exposing the implementation. An interface contains method signatures, but no implementation.

To add interface classes, follow these steps:

1. Select the Interface button from the toolbox.
2. Click in the diagram to add the interface.
3. Name the interface.

On a class diagram, an interface is drawn as a circle. There is an association relationship between the interface and the class(es) that realize it.

An *attribute* is a piece of information associated with a class. All objects in a given class share the same attributes, but each object may have its own attribute values.

Follow these steps to add attributes to the classes:

1. Right-click a class on the diagram.
2. In analysis, choose Add UML ➢ Attribute.
3. In design with Java, choose Add Java ➢ Field.
4. In design with .NET, choose Add C-Sharp ➢ Property or Add Visual Basic ➢ Property.
5. Type the attribute name, followed by a colon, and then the attribute's data type (for example, **Address:String**).
6. (Optional) Enter a default value for the attribute, by following the data type with an equals sign and then the default value (for example, **Address:String = 123 Main St.**).
7. Select the new attribute in the Explorer window.
8. Set the UML Visibility property (public, private, protected).

An attribute is drawn in the second compartment of a class, as shown here:

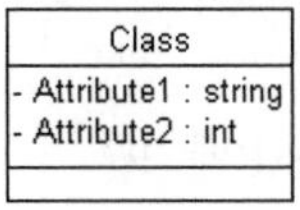

An *operation* is a method within the class. In XDE, you can define the operation name, parameters, visibility, return type, and parameter data types. Certain operations, such as `Get()` and `Set()` methods for attributes, can be automatically generated by XDE.

Follow these steps to add operations to the classes:

1. Right-click a class on the diagram.
2. In analysis, choose Add UML ➢ Operation.
3. In Java, choose Add Java ➢ Method.
4. In .NET, choose Add UML ➢ Operation.
5. Enter the operation signature, including parameters and a return type. Use the format *OpName(Parm1:Parm1DataType, Parm2:Parm2DataType):ReturnType* (for example, **AddNumbers(X:Int, Y:Int): Long**).
6. Select the new operation in the Explorer window.
7. Set the UML Visibility property (public, private, protected).

An operation is drawn in the lower compartment of a class, as shown here:

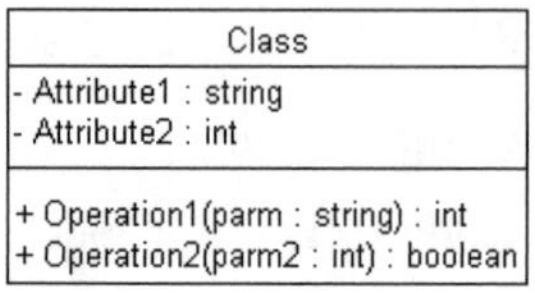

Web Modeling

Thanks to the recent work of people such as Jim Conallen, the UML is now being used more and more frequently to model web applications. Rose includes a number of class stereotypes for web modeling, such as client pages, server pages, and HTML forms.

These web classes are placed on a class diagram and, like traditional classes, can include attributes, operations, and relationships. Using class diagrams, you can view the web classes and their interrelationships, and you can also see how the web classes interact with the other classes in the system.

A *server page* contains logic that runs on the server, and uses server resources such as database connections, security services, or file services. When you add a new server page, XDE automatically adds a client page and a build relationship between the client and server pages.

To add server pages to the model, take these steps:

1. Right-click a virtual directory model in the Explorer window.
2. Choose Add Java ➢ Server Page.

Or you can select the Server Page option from the Web toolbox, and click inside a diagram to add the new server page.

A server page is drawn using the following symbol:

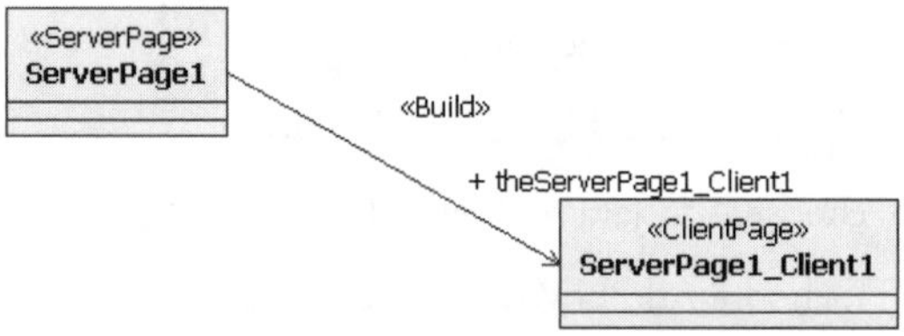

A *client page* contains logic that runs on the client machine.

Here is how you can add client pages to the model:

1. Right-click a virtual directory model in the Explorer window.
2. Choose Add Java ➢ Client Page.

Or, you can select the Client Page option from the Web toolbox and click inside a diagram to add the new client page. A client page is drawn using the following symbol:

An *HTML form* represents a simple HTML page and the fields contained within that page. Follow these steps to add HTML forms to the model:

1. Select the HTML Form option from the Web toolbox and click inside a class diagram. XDE displays the Add Form dialog box.
2. Select the form's owner. The owner may be either a server page or a client page.
3. (Optional) Select the server page to which this new form will submit its information. Click OK to finish.

An HTML form is drawn using the following symbol:

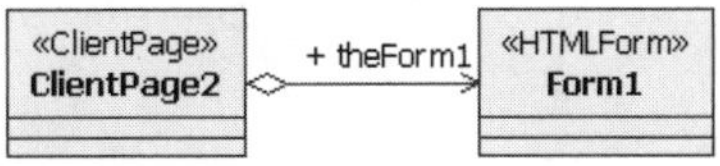

Adding Class Relationships

There are many different types of relationships between classes. An *association relationship* indicates that one class needs to communicate with another. Associations may be unidirectional or bidirectional. An *aggregation relationship* suggests a whole/part relationship between two classes. A *generalization relationship* indicates a parent/child inheritance relationship between two classes. Finally, a *dependency relationship* is a weaker form of association, suggesting that a change to one class may affect another.

Association names can be added to a relationship to clarify the relationship's purpose. Role names can also be used that show what role each class plays in the relationship. Multiplicity settings show how many instances of one object are related to a single instance of the other object.

Relationships are drawn on class diagrams as arrows between the two related classes. Different types of arrows are used to indicate different types of relationships.

An association relationship is a semantic connection between classes. It indicates that one class needs to communicate with another (for example, one class needs to send a message to the other). Directed associations suggest that the messages can be sent in only one direction, while associations suggest that messages can be sent in both directions (in other words, each class can call a method of the other).

Follow these steps to add association relationships between the classes:

1. Select the Directed Association or the Association toolbox button.

2. Click one class and then the other. For a directed association, click the client first and then click the supplier.

Here is an example of a directed association:

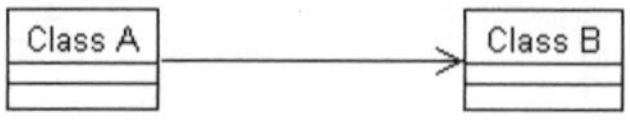

An aggregation relationship is used to denote a whole/part relationship between classes. In this situation, one class logically contains another. Association and aggregation relationships are created identically during code generation.

To add aggregation relationships, follow these steps:

1. Select the Aggregation Association toolbox button.
2. Click the "whole" class first and then click the "part" class.

An aggregation relationship is drawn as an association with a diamond next to the "whole" class:

A composition relationship is like an aggregation relationship, but in a composition the lifetimes of the objects are linked. The "part" cannot exist without the "whole," and when the "whole" is created or destroyed, the "part" is also created or destroyed.

Take these steps to add composition relationships:

1. Select the Composition Association toolbox button.
2. Click the "whole" class first and then click the "part" class.

A composition relationship is drawn as an aggregation with a filled diamond, as shown here:

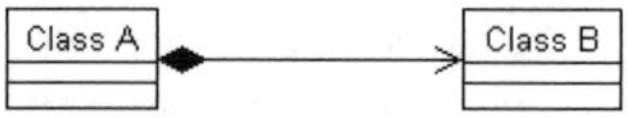

A generalization relationship is used to show an inheritance relationship between two classes. The child class inherits all attributes, operations, and relationships of the parent.

To add generalization relationships, follow these steps:

1. Select the Generalization toolbox button.
2. Click the child class first and then click the parent class.

A generalization relationship is drawn as an arrow from the child class to the parent class, as shown here:

A dependency relationship is a weaker form of an association relationship. Although one class still needs to communicate with the other, neither class is responsible for instantiating, destroying, or otherwise managing the other. When XDE generates code for an association relationship, it creates a reference to one class inside the other through a new attribute. With a dependency relationship, no attributes are created to support the relationship. Dependency relationships must be unidirectional.

To add dependency relationships:

1. Select the Dependency toolbox button.
2. Click first on one class and then on the other.

A dependency relationship is drawn as a dashed arrow:

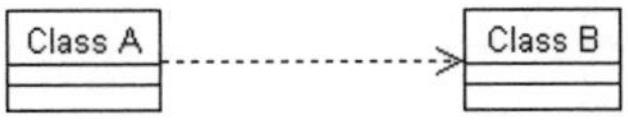

Multiplicity shows how many instances of one class are related to a single instance of another class. Multiplicity indicators are placed at both ends of a relationship to show the number of instances in both directions. Multiplicity is not included on a generalization relationship.

Follow these steps to add multiplicity to the relationships:

1. Select the relationship on a diagram.
2. Modify the End1Multiplicity and the End2Multiplicity properties.

The multiplicity indicators are drawn at both ends of a relationship, as shown here:

Role names indicate what role a class plays in a relationship. For example, in the relationship between Person and Company, a Person could play the role of Employee. Role names are used in the code-generation process; when an attribute is created to support a relationship, the attribute is named with the role name.

To add role names to the relationships, take these steps:

1. Select the relationship on a diagram.
2. Modify the End1Name and End2Name properties.

Role names are drawn on both sides of the relationship, as shown here:

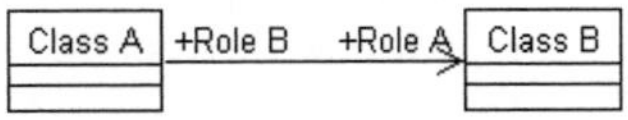

Building a Statechart Diagram

A statechart diagram is used to show the dynamic behavior of an object. It shows the various states in which an object can exist, what state an object is in when it is created, what state an object is in when it is destroyed, how an object moves from one state to another, and what an object does when it is in various states. All of this information helps a developer get a complete picture of how a particular object should behave.

Using XDE, you can create one or more statechart diagrams for a class, and include all of the information listed earlier. Statechart diagrams do not need to be created for every class in a model. Classes with significant dynamic behavior, complex behavior, or behavior that is not well understood among the development team are good candidates for statechart diagrams.

Follow these steps to create a statechart diagram:

1. Right-click a package, class, or operation.
2. Choose Add Diagram ➢ Statechart.
3. Name the new diagram.

Here is an example of a statechart diagram:

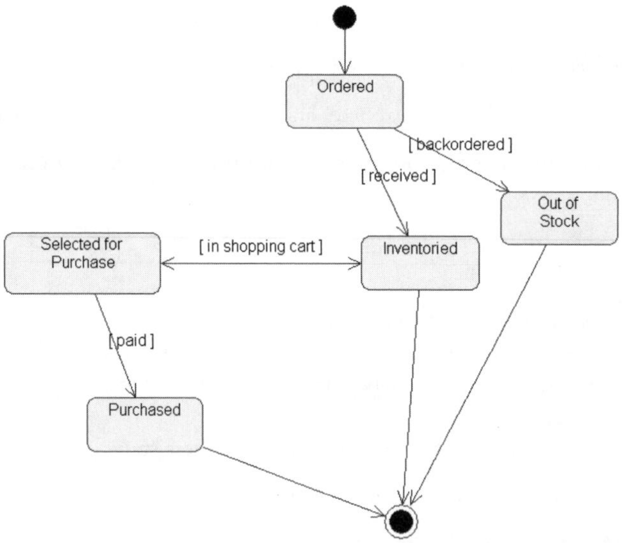

A *state* is a condition in which an object can exist. For example, an invoice can be New, Paid, Delinquent, or Canceled. Each of these represents a different state.

To add states to the diagram, follow these steps:

1. Select the State button from the toolbox.
2. Click in the diagram to add the state.
3. Name the state.

A state is drawn as a rounded rectangle:

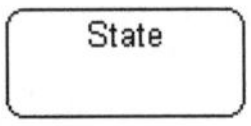

An *initial state* shows the state an object is in when it is first instantiated. A statechart diagram has one, and only one, initial state. An initial state is shown as a black dot on the diagram. A *final state* shows what state an object is in right before it is removed from memory. A statechart diagram may have zero, one, or more final states. A final state is shown as a bull's-eye on the diagram.

To add initial and final states, follow these steps:

1. Select the Initial State or Final State button from the toolbox.
2. Click in the diagram to place the initial state or final state.

The following are the symbols used for the initial and final states:

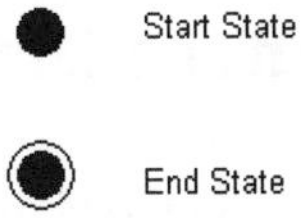

An *activity* is some bit of processing that occurs while the object is in a particular state. Activities can occur upon entry into the state, while exiting the state, while in the state, or upon a particular event.

Follow these steps to add activities to the states:

1. Right-click the state.
2. To add a do action, choose Add UML ➢ Do Action.
3. To add an entry action, choose Add UML ➢ Entry Action.
4. To add an exit action, choose Add UML ➢ Exit Action.

The activities are shown inside the states:

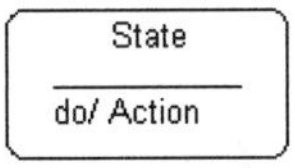

A *transition* indicates how an object can move from one state to another. It may include an *event,* which triggers the transition, or a guard condition. An event may also be sent to another object during the transition. A *guard condition,* which is enclosed in square brackets, controls when the transition may or may not occur. An *action* on the transition is a small piece of processing that occurs during the transition itself. The format for these items on a transition line is as follows:

```
Event(Arguments) [Guard] /Action ^SendEventTarget.SendEvent(Arguments)
```

To add transitions between the states:

1. Select the State Transition button from the toolbox.
2. Click the state where the transition begins.
3. Click the state where the transition ends.
4. Select the new transition.
5. Edit the guard condition and other transition properties as needed.

The events, guard conditions, and actions are all drawn along the association arrow, as shown here:

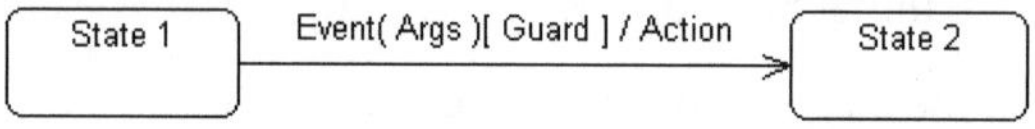

Building a Component Diagram

A component diagram is used to model the physical components in your system: source code files, executable files, DLL files, ActiveX objects, and so on. Using a component diagram, the team can specify what components exist and what their relationships are to each other.

This exercise is especially helpful in optimizing the design and planning for deployment. By mapping each component to its appropriate architectural layer (database, business logic, presentation, and so on), the team can see the interaction between the layers themselves. The team can analyze and optimize the communication between the layers before coding is complete.

XDE supports a number of different component stereotypes, such as <<executable>>, <<EJB-JAR>>, <<file>>, <<library>>, and <<EJBDescriptor>>.

To create a new component diagram, follow these steps:

1. Right-click a package in the Explorer window.
2. Choose Add Diagram ➢ Component.
3. Name the new diagram.

Here is an example of a component diagram:

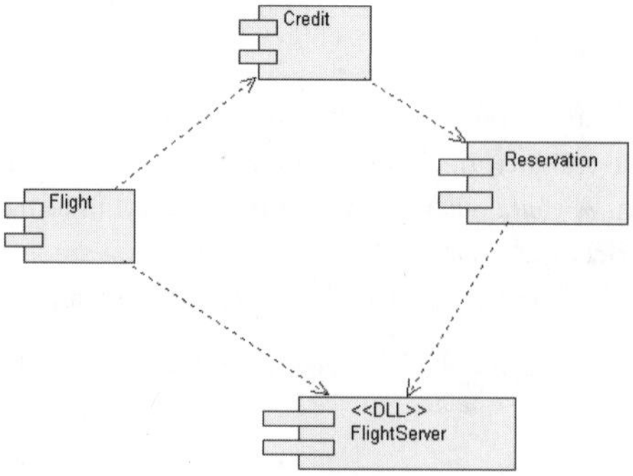

A *component* is one of the physical files that make up a system. Source code components realize many of the various classes contained within the model. When you reverse engineer an application, XDE automatically creates the components for you.

Follow these steps to add components to the model:

1. Select the Component button from the toolbox.
2. Click in the diagram to add the component.
3. Name the component.
4. Edit the component's Stereotype and other properties as necessary.
5. Select the Reside button from the toolbox.
6. Click a class that resides in the component.
7. Click the component. XDE creates a reside relationship between the class and the component.
8. Repeat steps 5 through 7 for any additional classes that reside in the component.

A component is drawn using the following symbol:

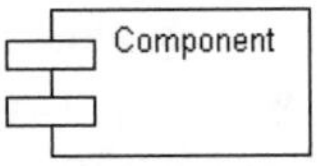

Building a Deployment Diagram

Deployment diagrams illustrate the physical distribution of a system. These diagrams show the processors, connections, processes, and other types of hardware involved in the system.

Here is an example of a deployment diagram:

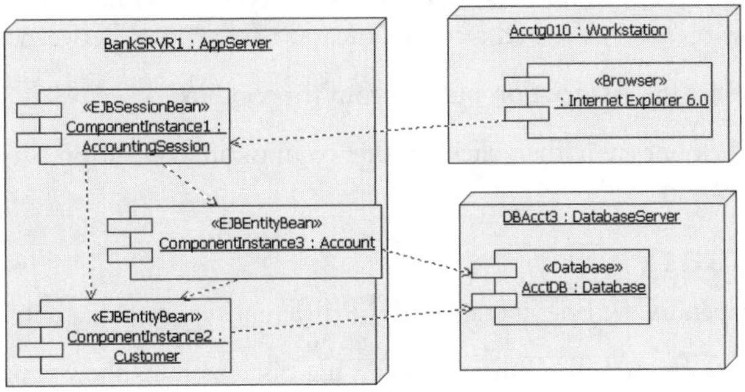

Follow these steps to create a deployment diagram:

1. Right-click a package or model in the Explorer window.
2. Choose Add Diagram ➢ Deployment.

Nodes are servers, workstations, and other items on a network. One type of node is a processor. *Processors* are machines on the network with processing power, including servers and workstations. They do not include printers and other such devices. Processors run processes (executable code).

A node is drawn using the following symbol:

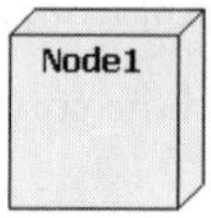

Follow these steps to add a node to the Deployment diagram:

1. Select the Node button in the toolbox.
2. Click in the diagram to place the new node.
3. Name the new node.

In addition to nodes, you can add fax machines, desktop machines, printers, routers, and other types of hardware to your deployment diagram. In XDE, you can add Internet clouds, communication links, desktops, Ethernets, fax machines, FDDI interfaces, network hubs, laptop computers, mainframes, mini computers, modems, plotters, printers, radio towers, network routers, satellites, satellite dishes, scanners, and tower computers.

Follow these steps to add other items to the deployment diagram:

1. Select the appropriate item from the toolbox.
2. Click in the diagram to place the new item.
3. Name the new item.

Communication associations are used to connect the nodes on the diagram. Each association represents a physical connection between nodes. If you want, you can create stereotypes such as <<LAN>> or <<Internet>> to show what type of connection exists.

Follow these steps to add a communication association between items:

1. Select the Association button from the toolbox.
2. Click one item, then click another to draw an association between them.

Summary

In this appendix, we briefly examined the different types of diagrams that you can create in the UML.

Business use case diagrams Business use case diagrams show you what functions an organization performs, and who interacts with the organization. The pieces of a business use case diagram include:

- Business use cases, which represent functionality provided by the organization
- Business actors, which are people, companies, or other entities that are external to the organization, but interact with the organization

- Business workers, which are roles within the organization
- Organization units, which are divisions, teams, or other groups within the organization

Activity diagrams You can use activity diagrams to model the workflow through a business process, or the logic flow through a piece of the system. An activity diagram contains:

- Activities, which are steps in the workflow or process
- Swimlanes, which are used to show who is responsible for performing the activities
- Transitions, which show the flow from one activity to another
- Decision points, which show choices in the flow of logic
- Objects, which are entities used by or changed by the workflow
- Synchronizations, which are used to show two or more activities occurring in parallel

Use case diagrams Use case diagrams show you the functionality provided by a system, and who or what interacts with the system. A use case diagram includes:

- Use cases, which are pieces of functionality the system provides
- Actors, which are entities external to the system, but interact with the system (for example, users of the system)
- Communicates relationships, showing which actors communicate with which use cases
- Include relationships, which show that one use case includes the functionality provided by another
- Extend relationships, which show that one use case optionally extends the functionality provided by another
- Packages, which are used to group actors and/or use cases together
- Generalization relationships, which are used to show that one use case inherits behavior from another

Sequence diagrams A sequence diagram is used to show the objects, actors, and messages needed to carry out the functionality in a flow of events. A sequence diagram is arranged in time order, and contains

- Objects participating in the flow of events
- Actors participating in the flow of events
- Messages, which are stimuli sent between actors and objects

Collaboration diagrams A collaboration diagram, like a sequence diagram, is used to show the objects, actors, and messages needed to carry out the functionality in a flow of events. While a sequence diagram is organized by time, a collaboration diagram is organized around the objects. Collaboration diagrams are not supported by XDE at this time.

Class diagrams Class diagrams show a subset of the classes, interfaces, packages, and subsystems within the design. A class diagram contains:

- Analysis classes, which are implementation-independent classes
- Design classes, which are implementation-specific classes
- Interfaces, which define the public interface of a class without exposing the implementation
- Attributes, which are pieces of information held by a class
- Operations, which define behaviors provided by a class
- Associations, which are relationships between classes
- Aggregations, which are "whole/part" relationships between classes
- Compositions, which are aggregations in which the lifetimes of the objects are linked
- Generalizations, which are inheritance relationships between classes
- Dependencies, which show that one class depends upon another

Statechart diagrams You use a statechart diagram to model the states in which an object can exist, and how the object transitions from one state to another. A statechart diagram includes:

- States, which are conditions in which an object can exist
- An initial state, which shows what state an object is in when it is instantiated
- Final states, which show what state an object is in when it is destroyed
- Activities, which represent processing that occurs when an object is in a particular state
- Transitions, which show how an object transitions from one state to another

Component diagrams You use a component diagram to show the physical components in the system. A component diagram includes:

- Components, which are the physical files that make up the system
- Dependencies between the components

Deployment diagrams You use a deployment diagram to show the physical environment in which the system will be deployed. A deployment diagram includes:

- Nodes, which are servers, workstations, and other items in the deployment environment
- Links between the nodes
- Lists of processes running on each processor

Index

Note to the Reader: Page numbers in **bold** indicate the principal discussion of a topic or the definition of a term. Page numbers in *italic* indicate illustrations.

Numbers

A

D

H

I

J

K

L

M

R

S

U

V

W

X

TRANSCEND TECHNIQUE

Learn the Essentials of Programming C# Web Services

Visual C#. NET Programming is a comprehensive introduction to all key aspects of C#, Microsoft's newest programming language. C# is based on C++ but adds a number of features that make it the ideal language for programming Web applications on the Windows platform.

- Features information on language essentials, working with files and directories, building a Windows interface, working with XML, and building Web Services.
- From the beginning, this book emphasizes creating Web Services. By the end of the book, you will be able to build a complex Web Service.

Author ***Harold Davis*** *is recognized as a top teacher of programming topics, and brings a unique creative dimension to his writing.*

Visual C# .NET Programming
By Harold Davis • 0-7821-4046-7 • $39.99
Available August 2002

SYBEX®
www.sybex.com

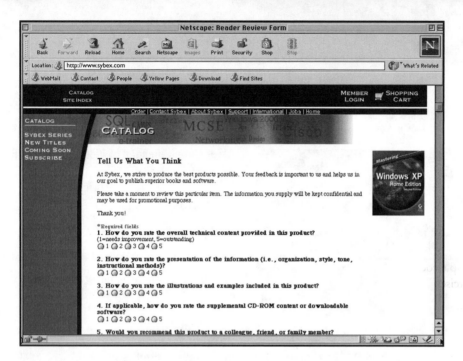